Senescence and Aging in Plants

Anthony H. C. Huang, Richard N. Trelease, and Thomas S. Moore, Jr. *PLANT PEROXISOMES, 1983.*

Roland Douce *MITOCHONDRIA IN HIGHER PLANTS: STRUCTURE, FUNCTION, AND BIOGENESIS, 1985.*

L. D. Noodén and A. C. Leopold (editors) *SENESCENCE AND AGING IN PLANTS, 1988.*

Senescence and Aging in Plants

Edited by

L. D. Noodén
Biology Department
University of Michigan
Ann Arbor, Michigan

and

A. C. Leopold
Boyce Thompson Institute for Plant Research
Cornell University
Ithaca, New York

ACADEMIC PRESS INC.
Harcourt Brace Jovanovich, Publishers
San Diego   New York   Berkeley   Boston
London   Sydney   Tokyo   Toronto

ACADEMIC PRESS, INC.
1250 Sixth Avenue
San Diego, California 92101

United Kingdom Edition published by
ACADEMIC PRESS INC. (LONDON) LTD.
24-28 Oval Road, London NW1 7DX

Library of Congress Cataloging-in-Publication Data

Senescence and aging in plants / edited by L.D. Noodén, A.C. Leopold.

    p. cm.
    Includes bibliographies and index.
    ISBN 0-12-520920-7   (alk. paper)
    1. Plants—Aging.   I. Noodén, L. D. II. Leopold, A. Carl (Aldo
Carl), (Date).
    QK762.5.S45   1988
    581.3'72—dc19   87-33652
                                           CIP

PRINTED IN THE UNITED STATES OF AMERICA
88 89 90 91   9 8 7 6 5 4 3 2 1

Contents

3 Photosynthesis
Shimon Gepstein

4 Respiration in Senescing Plant Organs:
Its Nature, Regulation, and Physiological Significance
Theophanes Solomos

5   Nucleic Acid and Protein Synthesis

Colin J. Brady

6   The Interplay between Proteolysis and Amino Acid Metabolism during Senescence and Nitrogen Reallocation

Mark B. Peoples and Michael J. Dalling

7 Water Economy of Fruits and Fruiting Plants: Case Studies of Grain Legumes

J. S. Pate

8 Ethylene and Plant Senescence

Autar K. Mattoo and Nehemia Aharoni

9 Cytokinins and Senescence

Johannes Van Staden, Elizabeth L. Cook, and L. D. Noodén

10 Abscisic Acid, Auxin, and Other Regulators of Senescence

L. D. Noodén

11 Calcium and Senescence

B. W. Poovaiah

14 Seed Aging: The Genome and Its Expression

E. H. Roberts

15 Postlude and Prospects

L. D. Noodén

Contributors

Numbers in parentheses indicate the pages on which the authors' contributions begin.

NEHEMIA AHARONI (241), Department of Fruit and Vegetable Storage, Agricultural Research Organization, The Volcani Center, Bet Dagan, 50-250, Israel

COLIN J. BRADY (147), CSIRO, School of Biological Sciences, Macquarie University, North Ryde, New South Wales, 2109 Australia

ELIZABETH L. COOK (281), UN/CSIR, Research Unit for Plant Growth and Development, Department of Botany, University of Natal, Pietermaritzburg, Republic of South Africa

MICHAEL J. DALLING (181), Calgene Pacific, Ivanhoe, Victoria, 3079, Australia

SHIMON GEPSTEIN (85), Department of Biology, Technion-Israel Institute of Technology, Haifa, Israel

P. RICHARD HETHERINGTON (441), Department of Crop Science, University of Guelph, Guelph, Ontario, Canada NlG 2W1

EDWARD J. KENDALL (441), Department of Crop Science, University of Guelph, Guelph, Ontario, Canada N1G 2W1

AUTAR K. MATTOO (241), Plant Hormone Laboratory, USDA/ARS, Beltsville Agricultural Research Center, Beltsville, Maryland 20705

BRYAN D. MCKERSIE (441), Department of Crop Science, University of Guelph, Guelph, Ontario, Canada N1G 2W1

L. D. NOODÉN (1, 281, 329, 391, 499), Biology Department, University of Michigan, Ann Arbor, Michigan 48109

J. S. PATE (219), Botany Department, University of Western Australia, Nedlands, 6009 Australia

MARK B. PEOPLES (181), CSIRO, Division of Plant Industry, Canberra, Australia

B. W. POOVAIAH (369), Department of Horticulture, Washington State University, Pullman, Washington 99164

E. H. ROBERTS (465), Department of Agriculture, University of Reading, Reading, England RG6 2AT

TISSA SENARATNA (441), Department of Crop Science, University of Guelph, Guelph, Ontario, Canada N1G 2W1

THEOPHANES SOLOMOS (111), Department of Horticulture, University of Maryland, College Park, Maryland 20742

KENNETH V. THIMANN (Foreword), Thimann Laboratories, University of California, Santa Cruz, California 95064

J. E. THOMPSON (51), Department of Horticultural Science, University of Guelph, Guelph, Ontario, Canada N1G 2W1

JOHANNES VAN STADEN (281), UN/CSIR, Research Unit for Plant Growth and Development, Department of Botany, University of Natal, Pietermaritzburg, Republic of South Africa

MARK A. WALKER (441), Department of Crop Science, University of Guelph, Guelph, Ontario, Canada N1G 2W1

Foreword

Aging, senescence, maturation—all are terms with slightly different meanings, as the editors of this volume have emphasized—but all bear on the same general group of phenomena. These in general occur at the end of a period of growth and development, and they may include: (1) preparation for the subsequent changes, especially preparation for the breakdown of cells or tissues; (2) the breakdown process itself; and (3) in some cases, what we can regard (if we think in terms of purposiveness) as preparation for another period of growth and development. Senescence in whole plants is partly a summation of the changes in individual organs and partly has an integral quality of its own. The senescence processes in leaves and in flowers are basically very similar—perhaps the importance of ethylene as a factor in the changes is more clear-cut in flowers than in leaves—but the process of senescence in fruits, at least in soft fruits, is clearly different in that the intermediate stage when some breakdown has begun but the tissues are not yet *dying* is greatly prolonged. This is the *mature* period of edible fruits and represents a holding phase, something like the pupation phase of insects, which interrupts two phases of active development. In the past we have not sufficiently recognized the overall similarities between maturation and senescence and this one important difference, with the unfortunate result that the work on fruits and flowers has been largely done by those interested in horticulture, while that on leaves and on whole plants has been centered in schools of physiology. About 25 years ago, perhaps influenced by Leopold's article in *Science*,[1] these groups began to come together and the general field of plant senescence was born.

If we consider the varied ways in which plants show senescence processes we can see how this syndrome enters into so many aspects of physiology. In what seems the most straightforward case, namely the behavior of annuals and biennials, senescence follows flowering and the setting of seeds. Molisch's original idea that this kind of senescence was due to the migration of major amounts of organic constituents out of

[1] *Science* **134**,1727–1732 (1961).

the leaves and into the fruits, i.e.; senescence by starvation, was long ago discredited, mainly because of the efforts of one of the editors of this book. Unfortunately, no complete explanation has as yet taken its place, although many aspects of the process have been clarified, partly by our other editor.

At the other extreme from herbaceous plants are the flowering trees, which may set fruit in abundance, as in commercial fruit trees, yet the only sign of senescence they show is the usual autumnal shedding of leaves, and this takes place whether or not fruits have been set, as witness those apple varieties that fruit only in alternate years. A third type is represented by the herbaceous perennials, whose shoots senesce and die down but whose roots stay alive. Some of these plants, e.g., petunias and chrysanthemums, can be brought through a mild winter intact, thus showing that the usual autumnal senescence is not an essential step in their development.

The fourth group, and the most curious of all, are the bulbs, in which *both* shoots and roots senesce after flowering and growth (whether they flower in the spring or autumn), while only the bulb itself—a few fleshy leaves, with some dry scales, and a central apex bearing the primordia of the next season's flowers—remains alive. Here the nonessentiality of senescence seems at its most localized form. Certainly materials do migrate (as in Molisch's model) from shoots and roots into the bulb, but whether that is a cause of senescence or a result of it remains unknown. Indeed, the particular type of senescence that bulbs (along with corms and tubers) present seems not to have aroused much curiosity as yet.

This kind of comparative thinking raises the central question of what acts as the trigger for the senescence process. Indeed, this is really the focus, even if not stated, of most senescence research. One can well imagine that, once started, the process has to run its course; when hydrolytic enzymes have been produced they continue to act on the proteins and other polymeric substrates until the resulting breakdown has gone so far as to become irreversible. In its early stages, at least in leaves, senescence must be fully reversible, for protein breakdown begins within 6 hours of darkness, so that it must begin every night and revert every morning. The senescence of the cotyledons of some seedlings can be reversed, up to a point, by decapitating the shoot, but this is far from being a general phenomenon. In some species the senescence is very slow to start; isolated stems of many succulents remain viable for months, and, for instance, in Woolhouse's experiments with ivy leaves (*Hedera helix*), 40 days of continuous darkness barely begins it. Indeed, detached Hoya leaves in our laboratory have survived 3 months in total darkness with only partial loss of chlorophyll.

Since loss of chlorophyll is such a prominent feature, it was natural to believe at first that senescence must begin in the chloroplast, but in fact isolated chloroplasts seem to have little protease, and they remain green much longer than when they stay in the leaf. They can even carry on a trace of photosynthesis after 3 days, although most photosynthesis workers do not keep them for more than an hour or so. These facts point clearly to the initiation of senescence being localized in the cytoplasm, or in some organelle therein.

A complication in ascribing an integral place in senescence to the loss of chlorophyll is that the loss of chlorophyll may take place without the other breakdown processes, but this is in most cases "photobleaching," and can be reversed by strong reducing agents; it does not occur in nitrogen even in bright light. It can be imitated in some leaves by chelating agents, which delay senescence in darkness, but in light cause simple loss of chlorophyll. The misleadingly[2] named "nonsenescing" mutant of *Festuca pratensis* shows the opposite effect, for its leaves stay green in late autumn while much of its protein is being normally hydrolyzed. However, it now develops that one critical component of the proteins, namely the light-harvesting chlorophyll *a/b* protein, does not break down in the mutant.

What seems to stand out as an important generalization is the inhibition or delay of senescence by cycloheximide, for this evidently implicates the synthesis of one or more proteins as a determining step. Cycloheximide delays or inhibits the breakdown of at least four enzyme systems of nitrogen metabolism. It is notable that overall synthesis of protein, as demonstrated by the incorporation of ^{14}C-amino acids, continues during senescence in spite of the predominance of protein breakdown. Among the proteins being synthesized are several proteases, of which the activity clearly increases during senescence.

Sabater and his group in Madrid have developed the view that senescence in darkness is accompanied by the formation of one group of proteins, while kinetin, in delaying senescence, leads to the formation of different proteins; light, which also delays senescence, forms still a third group of proteins. Three of these proteins might of course be the three known leaf proteases, which might support their idea that (some of) the newly formed proteins play a role in the further stages of senescence. Our own data seem to show that some newly formed proteins differ from those initially present in their sensitivity to proteolysis.

Other workers have paid more attention to the increase in proteases, or perhaps increase in sensitivity to existing proteases, as a basis for the

---

[2]If the definition of senescence includes general proteolysis, then this mutant does senesce, though somehow it stabilizes its chlorophyll.

extensive protein breakdown that occurs. Our knowledge of the proteases, or endopeptidases, of leaves has expanded considerably, especially in the laboratories of Dalling and of Huffaker. But in addition to these purely hydrolytic enzymes, there has recently been discovered in animal tissue a new type of protease, one that is activated by, and dependent on, a supply of ATP. It hydrolyzes the protein substrate and the ATP at the same time. Such ATP-dependent enzymes, if indeed they are present in plants, would impart new significance to the sharp rise in ATP content that occurs in leaves in parallel with the rise in respiratory rate during senescence.

But in order to explain the very rapid proteolysis, is it enough for the level of proteases to increase (in oat leaves the increase is only about 3-fold), or could it be that the contact between these enzymes and their substrates is somehow facilitated? In that connection we have recently found, in comparing the course of senescence in light and darkness, that the increase in proteases that occurs when detached leaves senesce in darkness, occurs also when they are in light; it even takes place at almost the same rate, in the first few days after excision. Yet little or no protein breakdown takes place in light in that period. This could mean that the light enables resynthesis to keep pace with protein breakdown. But more probably it may mean that in light the proteases are not able to reach their substrates, either in the cytoplasm or in the chloroplasts. In other words, the proteolysis typical of senescence may only take place after the permeability of one or more membranes has increased enough to allow enzymes, or their protein substrates, to pass through. Thus, the sought-after triggering action of senescence may be a change in permeability of the tonoplast, and later perhaps of the chloroplast envelope. In green tissue, therefore, where light delays senescence, this would mean that the action of light is to sustain the membrane structure. Perhaps some small molecule that is a photoproduct has to diffuse to the membrane continuously to prevent its structure from opening up. The ability of the straight chain aliphatic alcohols to delay proteolysis suggests that they act to close up the membrane in a parallel way. Yet these same alcohols have the opposite effect on the plasmalemma, for they cause rapid leakage of ions and small molecules into the ambient fluid. The orientation of the straight chain in the membrane seems to be critical, for the isomeric branched-chain alcohols have far smaller effects, almost zero in some cases. Perhaps the straight chains allow these molecules to be intercalated between the long straight-chain lipids that constitute a large part of the membrane.

What then is the role of detachment? Could the small wound caused by the severance send an agent through the tissue to modify the membranes at a distance? Detachment does not itself initiate senescence, for many detached leaves can survive when supplied with nutrients in tissue culture and ultimately give rise to callus and even to shoots. Detachment does accelerate senescence, but this may only be because cytokinins are no longer available (since they are mainly formed in roots), and if sterile detached leaves or derooted whole seedlings are supplied with cytokinins, they do senesce more slowly. The corollary of that, in turn, is that cytokinin substitutes for at least some of the functions of light. Since leaves can be cultured in nutrient media in total darkness, provided cytokinins and other hormones are supplied, the substitution for light can be complete. But to judge by the relative rates of senescence of attached and detached leaves, detachment only somewhat accelerates the process and is not an initiating factor.

Consideration of the role of detachment naturally leads us to consider the senescence of detached flowers, and the considerable amount of work that has been done on this aspect by horticulturists. From the viewpoint of simple aging the flower is a complex structure, since the calyx is typically older than the corolla, while the stamens and/or pistil may be younger. But from the horiticultural viewpoint, it is the senescence of the corolla that has been the main focus of attention. Changes in petal color are usually relatively minor and in good part due to small changes in pH, either toward acidity (e.g., blue petals turning reddish) or to weak alkalinity (e.g., red petals turning bluish). The relative stability of the anthocyanin in leaves is attested to by the brilliant autumn colors, especially in the northeastern United States, in leaves that have lost most of their chlorophyll but kept the more recently formed anthocyanin. In flowers there is also some overall fading, which is believed to be mostly oxidative, and can often be imitated by treating with hydrogen peroxide. More interesting are the tissue changes. Halevy points out that there are two main types: petals that absciss directly and those that wilt first. A fruit orchard in the late spring exemplifies the former, while many popular vase flowers such as roses, violets, and carnations typify the latter.

In most cases pollination initiates senescence of the petals but stimulates growth of the ovary. Although this could be thought of as a logical sequence to ensure propagation, such a view is perhaps an oversimplification, for, at least in *Petunia*, foreign pollen, which will not fertilize, can start the senescence. Here the small amount of auxin provided by the pollen is probably the active agent.

In parallel with leaves, flowers go through a late stage of increasing respiration, usually a 250–300% rise. Since fruits have long been known to undergo this "climacteric," I suggest that this is one of the few real generalities of the senescence process. Whether, as in leaves, this is a tightly coupled respiration, giving rise to a proportional increase in ATP, remains to be determined.

In leaves the closure of stomata usually initiates senescence, but many flower petals do not possess stomata, so that we cannot apply a parallelism here. A better parallel is seen in the action of ethylene. In leaves, applied ethylene, either as Ethephon or as ACC, will usually accelerate senescence, and this is true in oft-studied flowers like *Ipomoea* or the carnation. The flowers of some composites, however, including the chrysanthemum, do not respond to ethylene. Sometimes pollination induces increased sensitivity to ethylene, so that the flowers, e.g., cyclamen, which have been completely unresponsive until pollinated, suddenly have their senescence brought about by endogenous or applied ethylene.

Another comparison between leaves and flowers can be made in regard to the response to metabolizable sugars. Green leaves show only a modest delay in senescence when fed sucrose or glucose, and to substitute fully for white light requires sugar concentrations around 100 mM, which might be expected from the normal high concentration of carbohydrates in active leaves. Flowers, on the other hand, are highly responsive to sugar, and numerous market preparations for delaying flower senescence are based mainly on sucrose.

The typical wilting of flowers presumably results from an increase in membrane "leakiness," so that turgor is not maintained. This provides another possible similarity with the leaf, and perhaps it is an important one, for it suggests that a change in membrane structure may be a general feature of the initiation of senescence. In fruits too a change in permeability may be a major factor. For ripening, which is at least a first phase of senescence, is characterized by such hydrolytic processes as the softening of cell walls, loosening of the middle lamella, and conversion of starch to sugar. The production of ethylene that signals the climacteric of the fruit must surely mean that methionine has been liberated, indicating the onset of proteolysis. Also, the climacteric rise in respiration, in apples, pears, mangoes, and figs at least, is around 250–300%, exactly the magnitude of the respiratory rise in senescing leaves. Both leaves and fruits produce ethylene at this time and, as noted above, their metabolic changes can be accelerated by exogenous ethylene. Ethylene may or may not be the major controlling factor in leaf senescence, but of course it is in most climacteric fruits. Thus the use of the terms "ripening" for fruits and "senescence" for leaves and flowers tends to draw attention away from the many similarities.

Taking most of the above facts into consideration, and with some modest amount of speculation, especially in ascribing cause and effect relationships, we can tentatively suggest the following sequence of events:

1. Attack by the vacuolar protease(s) on one or more membrane protein(s) located in the tonoplast membrane; this may be accompanied by active synthesis of additional proteases;

2. Resultant weakening of the semipermeability of the tonoplast, allowing the proteases to escape and to attack the much more abundant protein substrates of the cytosol;
3. Some increases in total protease and in lipolytic enzymes may follow;
4. (For leaves) subsequent hydrolytic attack on the proteins of the chloroplast, both of the envelope and the thylakoids;
5. Resultant liberation of sugars and amino acids, including methionine;
6. Production of ethylene;
7. Increase in respiratory rate, due mainly to the liberation of respirable substrates, such as amino acids;
8. Transport of soluble hydrolytic products out of senescing tissue or organs;
9. (For flowers) abscission or wilting;
10. Various secondary changes.

The events are arranged essentially in temporal order.

How the closure of stomata results in the initiation of step 1 remains quite unknown at present. It is reasonable to suppose, however, that the influences of light and cytokinin in preventing the onset of the whole syndrome are exerted by continually resynthesizing and replacing the membrane proteins, so that the loss of semipermeability is greatly retarded. If this is true, then light and cytokinin act directly on step 1.

Even though this proposed sequence goes somewhat beyond the facts, it seems highly desirable to have a basic framework of concepts within which the events are ordered. No doubt the several factors play roles of differing importance in different plants. Our mutual colleague, Paul Waggoner, quotes Francis Bacon as saying, back in 1620, that ''the human understanding is prone to suppose the existence of more order and regularity in the world than it finds.'' So my generalization may need broadening as more plants come to be studied.

In the senescence of a whole plant we have to superimpose this syndrome, acting in the separate organs, upon the transport system of the plant. While mature leaves produce very little auxin, they do form ethylene, whereas roots and root-tips instead form cytokinin and supply it to the shoot. Since the senescence of detached leaves, and also of some flowers, is so greatly delayed by cytokinin, there is reason to think that, *first*, the shorter days and lower autumn temperatures decrease the flow of nutrients to the roots; *second*, that the roots respond by decreasing their output of cytokinins; and then *third*, this lowered supply of cytokinin causes (or allows) senescence of the leaves. The role of ethylene in this case may be mainly to activate the abscission layer, as in fruits. In Noodén's work with the soybean, it is clear that growing fruits (pods) promote senescence of the nearby leaves. This effect has been thought by some to be due to the role of fruits acting as a *sink*, diverting cytokinins from the leaves. While the decrease in cytokinin titer may play a part, the evidence does not favor its being the primary cause of foliar senescence. Indeed, there is reason to regard fruits as a possible *source* of a senescence-promoting hormone such as abscisic acid or methyl jasmonate or some other compound of similar action. In any case, the relationship between fruiting and senescence is still somehow a very intimate one, since (as we noted at the outset) leaf senescence does very often follow closely after fruit maturation, but then on the other hand, we have to consider why evergreen trees such as the orange and lemon retain their dark green leaves all through the fruiting period and beyond. Perhaps evergreen trees have an extra source of cytokinin in or near the leaves, keeping them in a sort of mature but nonsenescent state.

The role of ethylene was mentioned above, but if it is to be considered as a senescence hormone we face some curiously contradictory pieces of evidence. Many researches show, in a number of different leaves and flowers, that exogenously applied ethylene promotes senescence, and silver salts are being used to inhibit or delay senescence of some flowers on a commercial scale. Yet cytokinin, fusicoccin, indole-acetic acid, and those same silver salts, all of which delay senescence of leaves (in the dark), actually promote the production of ethylene—in some cases by as much as 500%. This and other contradictions are perhaps more marked in fruits and flowers than in leaves, so that while the remarkable researches of Yang and Lürssen and their collaborators have given us the chemical pathway leading to ethylene, the whole story of the physiological role of ethylene in senescence has still to be told.

One of the fascinations of working on senescence is the broad approach that it gives to understanding different aspects of plant behavior. The three steps proposed above for the senescence of leaves on the whole plant are only one example. It may not be wholly true, and some may consider it fanciful, but the fact that we can put it forward shows the extent to which our understanding of the forces controlling plant development has progressed. Another example is more specialized. Not long ago I was wondering why some orchids, when placed in too sunny a spot, developed tip-burn. Then I realized that in the sun the transpiration probably becomes too rapid for the limited water supply from the roots, especially as orchids are generally bedded in bark rather than in moist soil. The water deficiency would be greatest at the end of the line, i.e., at the leaf tip, and as a result the stomata there will close preferentially. But we know that when stomata close senescence sets in; the tip-burn is thus a local senescence. Nitrogen deficiency of cereal plants has a similar effect, and in this case we have shown directly that stomata are closed in increasing frequency from the first to the fourth leaf (the plants only form five leaves in full nitrogen deficiency) and consequently the leaves senesce. Incidentally, although the relationship between stomatal closure and the acceleration of senescence seems very general in land plants, what are we to think of the situation in aquatic plants, whose leaves are fully submerged? This is, of course, only one of the many unsolved questions that have come into focus as the work on plant senescence has burgeoned.

This book, which presents such a broad variety of researches on senescence in widely differing plant material, will certainly bring to light a large number of such unsolved problems. As a result we can hope that it will bring new workers into the field, with fresh approaches and ideas.

Kenneth V. Thimann
Thimann Laboratories
University of California
Santa Cruz, California

Preface

The keen observations of plant senescence described in Molisch's classic book (1929, transl. 1938) represent remarkable insight into the phenomenon in plants. During the following two decades, further advance was hindered by the limited knowledge of biochemistry and physiology at that time. Since then, considerable progress has been made in analyzing senescence as an array of biochemical processes involved in normal developmental as well as in postharvest physiology. It has also become evident that different types of degenerative processes occur, some being more active (senescence), others more passive (aging). Progress in understanding plant aging has been slower than in the more dramatic senescence events, hence the contemporary emphasis on senescence.

At the time when the first Gordon Conference on plant senescence was organized by Jacob Biale and James E. Baker in 1976, plant senescence was only beginning to establish an identity as a field, and physiological-biochemical studies of senescence were mainly oriented around the senescence of organs, e.g., leaves, flowers, and fruit, rather than processes. That conference, however, brought together investigators from diverse fields and began a dialog that has stimulated the emergence of a fairly cohesive field. The next Gordon Conferences (1980, 1984) organized by James E. Baker, Larry D. Noodén, and John E. Thompson were oriented toward primary senescence as well as aging processes. The book edited by Kenneth V. Thimann (1980) provides a cornerstone summary of senescence in the major plant organs.

This book aims, as its primary purpose, to provide summaries of the most important and tractable of these processes. This means, however, that many lesser topics that do not fall within one of these major areas will receive little coverage. At this time, it seems more important to pull together the major areas that should contribute to the evolution of this subject than to try to cover all research relevant to senescence and aging. We have also included short coverages of some nontraditional topics such as calcium metabolism and the water economy (flux) of plants and especially of their fruits. These are very active areas of investigation, yielding information that seems likely to be important in this field. We had hoped to include a chapter on the evolution and ecology of senescence, but this did not materialize.

It should be noted that several helpful collections of research papers or short summary articles (cited where appropriate in this book) have appeared over the past decade; a recent book by Leshem, Halevy, and Frenkel (1986) also shifts toward a process orientation. It has a particular emphasis on membranes and the role of free radicals.

This new organization aims to clarify the distinction between different kinds of degenerative processes, particularly between senescence versus aging. An important question underlying this new organization is, what are the precise biochemical natures of senescence and aging? What is central to senescence or aging, and what is peripheral? We know that many of the manifestations of senescence in different tissues differ, but are the central processes the same? Is senescence one process or many? And now, as plant aging begins to be investigated, is aging one process or many?

We hope that this collection of reviews by specialists in their fields will provide a useful and stimulating update of the present state of knowledge concerning the processes involved in plant senescence and aging. As a research area, this is a sector showing rapidly expanding knowledge and understanding. There is much yet to be learned, however, and we hope that this book will facilitate such progress.

L. D. Noodén
A. Carl Leopold

Molisch, H. (1938). "The Longevity of Plants" (Transl. by E. H. Fulling). Science Press, Lancaster, PA.
Thimann, K. V. (Ed.) (1980). "Senescence in Plants." CRC Press, Boca Raton, FL.
Leshem, Y. Y., Halevy, A. H., and Frenkel, C. (1986). "Processes and Control of Plant Senescence." Elsevier Science Publ., New York.

1

The Phenomena of
Senescence and Aging

L. D. Noodén
Biology Department
University of Michigan
Ann Arbor, Michigan

SENESCENCE AND AGING IN PLANTS

I. EMERGENCE OF SENESCENCE AS A CONCEPT

Senescence has meant many things in the past, but the concept is now being focused. The idea that death might be actively induced by endogenous factors that are a natural part of an organism's development has been gaining support slowly. Medawar (1957), for example, distinguishes between natural and accidental death, the former being due in part to internal factors that make the organism more vulnerable. There, senescence is related to certain internal changes that increase the probability of death with increasing chronological age (Comfort, 1956, 1964; Medawar, 1957). Still, these representations place emphasis on external factors, e.g., disease, as the final cause of death, rather than allowing death to be a mainly endogenous process. Medawar and Comfort drew their concepts from animal gerontology, whereas Molisch (1938) and his predecessors clearly recognized many cases where degeneration of plant organisms or their parts were clearly under endogenous controls.

That there are differences in the causes of death among species was made evident from studies of the survivor patterns for cohorts of organisms. Pearl and Miner (1935) described several possible types of survivor curves. For example, in Fig. 1.1, curve A is characteristic of a population in which death is predominantly caused by disaster, predation, or other random external selection forces. The constant rate of removal results in a survivor curve that

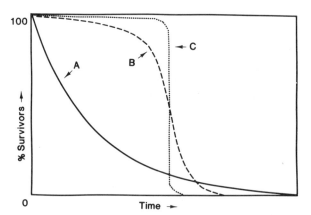

Fig. 1.1. Survival curves for three groups of organisms. (A) Survival curve at a constant rate of mortality (50% per unit of time). (B) Survival curve of a population that exhibits increased susceptibility to death with age. (C) Survival curve for a population with abrupt termination of all members by natural processes, senescence. Note that these figures do not include infant or seedling mortality. [Redrawn from Pearl and Miner (1935).]

drops exponentially, gradually approaching zero. Curve B is characteristic of some organisms in which survival remains very high until maturation of the organism and will be discussed in Section II,A. Another type of survivor pattern has the abrupt termination of all members of a population as shown in curve C. Natural examples of this type were first recognized by botanists, because of its common occurrence in the annual or biennial (monocarpic) plants; however, some species of salmon and certain invertebrates also show a similar pattern. Such an abrupt, synchronous degeneration leading to death is characteristic of endogenous control, senescence.

The extensive literature summarized by Comfort (1956, 1964) and Medawar (1957) was concerned primarily, though not exclusively, with animals. Studies on plants progressed relatively independently, and that is reflected in the earlier reviews of plant senescence (Molisch, 1938; Crocker, 1939; Leopold, 1961; Wangermann, 1965). The endogenous nature of senescence is more striking in plants, and, for this reason, it has been possible to formulate a more direct definition of senescence at an early stage (Leopold, 1961). In these terms, the process of senescence can be represented as endogenously controlled deteriorative changes, which are natural causes of death in cells, tissues, organs, or organisms (Leopold, 1975; Noodén and Leopold, 1978). Thus, senescence is a natural developmental process, which may even be thought of as terminal differentiation, and it may be completely endogenous. A similar, though perhaps reluctant, concept of senescence is emerging in reference to animals (Finch and Schneider, 1985).

II. CONCEPTS

A. Senescence versus Aging

Whereas senescence represents endogenously controlled degenerative processes leading to death, aging encompasses a wide array of passive or nonregulated, degenerative processes driven primarily by exogenous factors (Leopold, 1975). This passive degeneration termed *"aging"* is a consequence of lesions ("wear and tear") that accumulate over time (Leopold, 1975; Noodén and Leopold, 1978). Aging does not in itself necessarily cause death but may decrease resistance to stress and otherwise increase the probability of death. Because the biochemical nature of senescence and aging is not known precisely, it is premature to attempt to define these processes more exactly or to draw a fine line between them. The withering of petals following pollination and the postreproductive death of monocarpic plants seem to be cases of senescence. The loss of viability in stored seeds, on the other hand, is a clear case of aging (Noodén and Leopold, 1978; see also Chapters 13 and 14). The reader is forewarned that the term *aging* has had an even wider range of uses in biology than senescence, and the restrictive definition advocated here is relatively recent. Either senescence or aging could render an organism more vulnerable to disasters and thereby contribute to mortality, even if they are not the ultimate cause of death. This increase in vulnerability could begin early in the life of an organism, but one would suspect that natural selection would shift it to later stages, most likely postreproductive, for established individuals. The late decline seen in the survivor curve B in Fig. 1.1 could be the result of senescence or aging or even a combination of both.

B. The Basic Units of Senescence

It seems useful to consider where senescence occurs, both in terms of living versus nonliving things and levels of organization. Inanimate objects such as glass tumblers may deteriorate, and they may have a characteristic longevity (Kendig and Hutton, 1979). Indeed, they may become more susceptible to total breakage with age, but such phenomena are not senescence in the sense used here. Likewise, molecules clearly differ in their stability and that is inherent in their structure, though it is also influenced by environmental factors, e.g., temperature and solvent. While the longevity of molecules may have an endogenous basis, it does not seem appropriate to call this senescence. The rationale applied to molecules can be extended to organelles. Thus, changes in both organelles and molecules occur as part of either aging or the senescence processes in cells and organisms. Populations and communities may decline in their vigor and productivity (Leopold, 1975, 1980), but that seems to be a different phenomenon from senescence. Thus, senescence appears to be a cellular process, and it seems to apply to tissues, organs, and organisms. In fact, senescence may be related to multicellularity and the attendant cell specializations that limit the renewal of these cells (Pearl, 1928; Comfort, 1956).

C. Death and Death Processes

In order to understand the senescence and aging processes better, it would be helpful to clarify the endpoint by discriminating between the living and dead states. The indicators of morbidity have been of great interest for some time, even before much was known about the chemistry of living material. Some of the earlier ideas on death marker events, such as electrical death spasm, border on the mystical (see, e.g., Bose, 1907, 1927). Molisch (1938) has summarized the earlier work on key indicators of life. They include plasmolytic responsiveness, electrical induction of protoplast contraction, silver reduction, and exclusion of certain dyes.

Recently, exclusion of nonpermeating dyes such as Evan's blue has been used to measure survival of cultured cells (Gaff and Okong'o-Ogola, 1971; Holden *et al.*, 1973; Pech and Romani, 1979; Gahan, 1982; Bowen, 1984). Rapid dye penetration would reflect a major increase in the permeability of the cell membrane. Reciprocally, these changes would also allow solute leakage, which is also a characteristic of late senescing cells (Section II,D and Chapter 2). These changes may, however, occur gradually and may not provide a distinctive threshold or final step for determination of death.

The cytological aspects of cell death have been investigated fairly extensively, particularly for animal cells (Barlow, 1982; Gahan, 1982; Kahl, 1982, 1983; Bowen, 1984; Davies and Sigee, 1984; Lockshin and Zakeri-Milovanovic, 1984). Reflecting some diversity in these processes, cell death or, perhaps better, the processes leading up to cell death have been grouped into three categories (Davies and Sigee, 1984): (1) programmed cell death; (2) necrosis; and (3) chronic degeneration. Programmed cell death represents senescence as defined in Section I. Necrosis is due to massive trauma such as acute chilling injury, wounding, and some reactions to microbial pathogens. It is a consequence of acute external stress, and it seems distinct from aging. Chronic degeneration is visualized as an accumulation of sublethal damage with time, and this may be identified with aging (Section II,A). Aging and necrosis may differ in more than just their rates and in the intensity of the exogenous stimuli that drive them. The gradual degeneration of cultured plant cells might be cited as an example of chronic degeneration (Cocking, 1984); however, this may differ in its biochemical mechanism from the loss of seed viability which exemplifies aging.

Environmental factors may tilt the balance between "wear and tear" and repair toward accumulation of lesions. It is also possible, however, that low levels of environmental stress such as chilling could trigger senescence (Section IV,F).

The main characteristic of cell death, whether from senescence, acute stress, or aging, seems to be the loss of the cell's ability to maintain homeostasis. Given the essential role of the membranes in maintaining the cell and preventing the loss of the cell contents to the environment, the loss of the integrity of the plasma membrane seems likely to be a key, though late, event. This loss could arise through an exogenous trauma, through internally programmed changes, or through just plain "wear and tear" over a long period. Translating this into thermodynamic terms, the cell is alive as long as it can maintain its entropy below that of its environment; this requires not only integrity of its membranes, but a constant input of energy. Once the "costs" of self-maintenance, i.e., basal metabolic rate (Penning de Vries, 1975), can no longer be paid, the cell dies.

Measures of cellular reducing capacity through the use of redox dyes such as Janus green B or triphenyltetrazolium chloride have long been used as tests of cell and seed viability (Woodstock, 1973; Gahan, 1982; Priestley, 1986). While these tests clearly have practical value, it does not always follow that all enzyme activities cease when cells die. The breakdown of internal compartmentation and dispersal of toxins, hydrolases, and other degradative enzymes (Matile, 1975; Marty *et al.*, 1980; Huang *et al.*, 1983; Robinson, 1985) may also mark late events in dying cells (Matile, 1975; Gahan, 1981), although probably not death per se.

Some interesting observations on photon emissions may reflect both metabolic deterioration and loss of compartmentation in dying cells. For example, dying cells in wounded root tissue show chemiluminescence, apparently due to release of peroxidase (Salin and Bridges, 1981). Low-level chemiluminescence can result from oxy-radicals and singlet oxygen formed during lipoperoxidation (Boveris *et al.*, 1984). Lipoperoxidation may well be an important factor in changing membrane properties, thereby altering their effectiveness as barriers (Chapter 2). Wounded cells undergo fatty acid oxidation, but this change seems to follow rather than precede membrane disaggregation and depolarization (Kahl, 1982, 1983). Ultraweak photon emissions may also result from conformational changes or alteration of the weak interactions between molecules in living cells. DNA may be the most important source of such emissions (Rattemeyer *et al.*, 1981). These photon emissions may eventually provide an important index of the breakdown in internal compartmentation.

D. The Senescence Syndrome: An Outline

Which of the changes associated with senescence are central (or primary) and which are peripheral (or secondary)? Collectively, the central and peripheral changes form a syndrome of physiological changes associated with senescence. In this book and elsewhere, the term *senescence* is used loosely to refer to the senescence syndrome. To what extent are the different patterns of senescence (Section IV) the same at the biochemical level? While the senescence-related changes in different tissues in plants do show diversity, there are underlying similarities, especially at the ultrastructural level (Butler and Simon, 1971; Halevy and Mayak, 1979; Gahan, 1981, 1982), suggesting that the processes of senescence are analogous. Still, there may also be differences in the involvement of chloroplast degeneration (Chapter 15). In any case, senescence is not a chaotic breakdown in order within the affected cells, but an orderly loss of normal functions (Brady, 1973; Noodén and Leopold, 1978; Thomas and Stoddart, 1980). Moreover, senescence appears to be an active rather than a passive process.

Ultrastructural studies provide a valuable overview of cell senescence, even if they do not always yield biochemical precision. In cells with chloroplasts, some of the earliest senescence-related changes are visible in these organelles (Shaw and Manocha, 1965; Butler and Simon, 1971). The early changes in the chloroplasts include swelling of the thylakoids and appearance of lipid droplets and plastoglobuli (Fig. 1.2C). These plastoglobuli are more dynamic than they seem in electron micrographs, for they change composition as senescence progresses (Tevini and Steinmuller, 1985). Also an early event, ribosomes may be lost from the cytoplasm and from the stroma of the chloroplasts (Chapter 5). As senescence advances to its end point, plasmalemma integrity is lost (Fig. 1.2G), and this is consistent with the idea that death is a loss of homeostasis. Relatively late changes also occur in the mitochondrial and vacuolar membranes (Fig. 1.2E). One of the most curious ultrastructural changes is an autophagic process in which organelles become enveloped in vacuole-like structures sometimes leaving whorls of membranes (Figs. 1.2E and 1.3). These may develop from vacuoles, ER, or leucoplasts (Villiers, 1967, 1971, 1972; Matile and Winkenbach, 1971; Baker, 1975; Matile, 1975; Hurkman and Kennedy, 1976; Nagl, 1977; Marty, 1978; Wittenbach *et al.*, 1982). These "vacuolar" breakdown processes seem to offer an alternative to the more gradual processes outside and should not be dismissed (Woolhouse, 1987).

Senescing cells may also show some differences in their ultrastructural changes. The breakdown of the nucleus is a late event in most senescing cells, but it may occur relatively early in xylem cell differentiation (Lai and Srivastava, 1976; Gahan, 1982). Dictyosomes usually disappear fairly early in senescence, but they persist in senescing pollen tubes (Larson, 1965). There are other differences in the senescence syndrome among different types of cells (Butler and Simon, 1971; Baker, 1975; Gahan, 1982), particularly with regards to chloroplasts that may or may not be present (Chapter 15). These variations may, however, reflect differences in the peripheral rather than the central changes. For the time being, it seems best to look for commonality in the biochemistry of senescence in these different cells; at the very least, this will provide a framework for comparisons.

What features might be central to the senescence process? The internal programming of senescence implies that it is under genetic control, presumably by the nucleus (Chapters 5 and 15). Thus, one might expect the process to begin with changes in gene expression, perhaps relatively small quantitatively. Such changes could be quite different from the more massive nuclear changes that occur late in most senescing cells. In fact, RNA and protein synthesis are often altered early in the senescence process (Chapter 5). A shutoff of certain RNA and protein synthesis may be important, but the selective activation of the synthesis of certain mRNAs and proteins seems more likely to be the initiation of the active processes leading to senescence (Chapter 15). Because of the importance of nucleic acid and

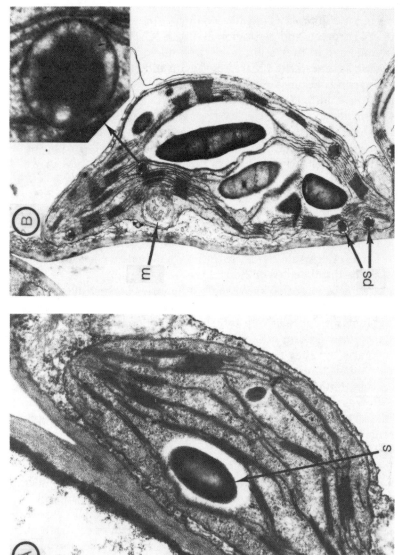

Fig. 1.2 A, B

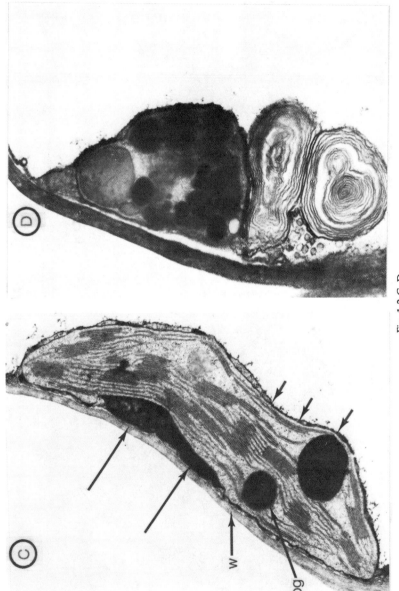

Fig. 1.2 C, D

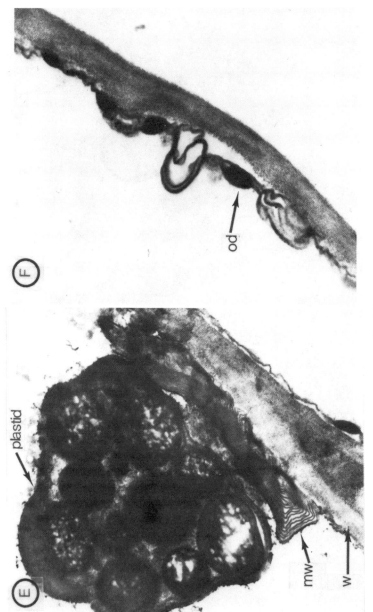

Fig. 1.2 E, F

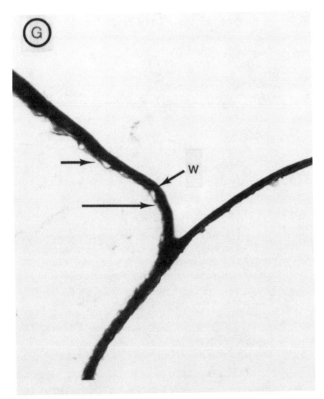

Fig. 1.2. Ultrastructural changes in senescing tobacco leaves. Progressive senescence of attached leaves. (A) Chloroplasts of partially expanded leaves have elliptical profiles. The lamellar system is not fully elaborated and small starch grains (s) are present in the stroma. (B) In fully expanded leaves, the chloroplast profile is distended by large starch grains (s). Cytoplasmic pockets in chloroplasts, though infrequent, may contain mitochondria (m). Plastosomes (ps) are common in chloroplasts at this stage of development. The inset shows detail of a plastosome. (C) Chloroplasts of yellow–green leaves contain large plastoglobuli (pg). Osmiophilic deposits occur in the cytoplasm adjacent to the plastid surface (short arrows), with massive deposits (long arrows) between the cell wall (w) and the plastid envelope. (D) Plastids of senescent, yellow tissue contain numerous plastoglobuli (darkly stained bodies). Cytoplasmic membrane whorls are common in cells at this stage of breakdown. (E) Degradative changes in senescent, yellow tissue now include loss of the tonoplast and breakdown of the plastoglobuli. Between the plastid (the membrane-enclosed body occupying most of this figure) and the membrane whorl (mw) is a remnant of the cytoplasm. (F) All that remains of senescent cells when plastids are completely degraded is an irregular membrane (which appears to include the plasma membrane plus other membrane remnants) along the cell wall (w). Sometimes these remnant membranes appear single, sometimes double, and sometimes whorled. Osmiophilic deposits (od) seem to be associated with this membrane. (G) Cells of fully senescent tissue are devoid of contents except for a membrane (long arrows) along the cell wall (w), probably residual plasma membrane. [Reprinted with permission from Hurkman and Kennedy (1976).]

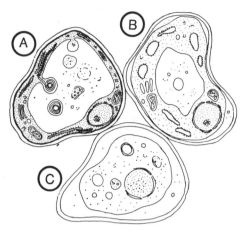

Fig. 1.3. Subcellular changes in mesophyll cells of the senescing *Ipomoea* corolla. (A) Autophagic activity of the vacuole; invaginations of the tonoplast result in the sequestration of cytoplasmic material into the "lysosomal" compartment. (B) Shrinkage of the vacuole, dilution of the cytoplasm, and inflation of cytoplasmic membrane systems. (C) Massive autolysis coincides with the breakdown of the tonoplast. [Reprinted with permission from Oxford University Press (Matile and Winkenbach, 1971).]

protein metabolism in senescence, separate chapters (5 and 6) in this volume deal with these topics. Nucleic acid, particularly RNA, and protein breakdown are components of the senescence syndrome, and these catabolic processes are coordinated with changes in synthesis. A strong case has been made for involvement of changes in the cell membranes, especially during the late stages of senescence (Chapter 2). More subtle, yet important, earlier changes may involve the permeability characteristics of the membranes.

Between the initiation and completion of the senescence process, numerous changes occur. Some no doubt simply reflect a shutdown of the cells' specialized functions and are therefore peripheral in terms of that cell's senescence. Others could be more closely related to central process of senescence. The breakdown of proteins and RNAs seems important, but it is unclear how this fits into the central senescence process. Mitochondrial function continues until quite late, and that may be related to a continued need for energy by the active processes in senescence (Chapter 4; see also Noodén and Leopold, 1978; Thimann, 1980b; Thomas and Stoddart, 1980; Gahan, 1982; Noodén and Thompson, 1985) as well as to maintain homeostasis and possibly to process and transport the metabolites which are released in senescing tissues. While inhibition of ATP production may cause necrosis, it inhibits rather than promotes senescence (Chapter 15) and this may reflect the active nature of senescence.

In cells with chloroplasts, these organelles begin to degenerate relatively early. Their loss may have fatal consequences as in monocarpic senescence (Chapter 12) but not in all cells (Chapter 15). A causative role for chloroplast deterioration in senescence is not general, for many types of cells that lack chloroplasts experience cell senescence (Chapter 15).

A striking feature of senescence, whether cellular or organismal, is that it is a correlative phenomenon (Section III,C). As with many other correlative controls, senescence is generally considered to be controlled by hormones (Wareing, 1977; Goodwin *et al.*, 1978; Leopold and Noodén, 1984). Both senescence-promoting and -retarding hormones exist; ethylene (Chapter 8) and cytokinin (Chapter 9) may be the most important representatives of these opposing classes. While cytokinin functions in a wide range of tissues, it is not a universal retardant of senescence. Other hormones, particularly auxin and gibberellins, may have significant regulatory roles in certain tissues (Chapter 10). Clearly, there are differences in the hormonal controls among tissues and among different species. Ethylene is frequently a senescence promoter, but it may not be the primary senescence promoter in many tissues (Noodén and Leopold, 1978; Noodén, 1980). While abscisic acid was once considered to have a major senescence-promoting function, that role needs clarification (Chapter 10). To illustrate the extremes in tissue differences, auxin seems to function not only as a senescence retardant in some leaf tissues (Chapter 10) but also as a promoter of xylem differentiation (Jacobs, 1979; Shininger, 1979), which is also a senescence event. These differences in hormonal regulation do not, however, exclude a commonality in the primary senescence processes in different tissues. Hormonal controls are a central issue in senescence studies, because they represent a key aspect of regulation and they provide a convenient "handle" by which to work out the components of senescence.

Biochemical and physiological studies on senescence ultimately need to be related to the larger picture in the intact plant. Effecting this relationship may be a particularly acute problem from studies employing detached parts (Section III,D). Detachment of plant organs may provide great experimental convenience but may create artifacts by eliminating correlative factors (Noodén, 1984). Nonetheless, it seems inappropriate to discard all results obtained from studies on detached organs (Woolhouse, 1987). A more constructive approach is warranted, for much can be learned from these observations (Noodén, 1980).

The term senescence has sometimes been restricted to those processes that follow the point of no return (Wang and Woolhouse, 1982). Yet the changes that occur before the point of no return do not seem less important than those that take place after (Noodén and Leopold, 1978) and they may well be the transforming processes that drive the senescence syndrome. Moreover, the point of no return occurs very late, at least in leaves. Recovery is still possible even after all visible chlorophyll has been lost from tobacco leaves (Mothes and Baudisch, 1958) or after 85% of the protein is gone from bean leaves (Krul, 1974). Indeed, there are numerous reports of reversal of senescence at fairly late stages (Butler and Simon, 1971; Noodén and Leopold, 1978; Thomas and Stoddart, 1980). Thus, senescence need not be irreversible, though its end point, death, may be.

While it can be said that all developmental events lead to senescence, where does senescence actually start? The uncertainty about the central biochemistry of senescence clouds the answer to that question. A reasonable possibility would be that it may begin with synthesis of new messenger RNAs (see above). Beyond this, one could point to a great range of enzymes that contribute to the decline of important functions, either by virtue of their own decrease or through their degradative actions.

III. EXPERIMENTAL ANALYSIS OF SENESCENCE

A. Why Study Senescence?

Senescence is a pervasive developmental process operating at many stages and many levels during the life cycle of an organism. It has an important function in cell differentiation, not only in the most obvious example of xylem differentiation, but also in other cases such as the development of leaf lobing patterns and the breakdown of specialized cells in the embryo and the female gametophyte. Its function at the organ level is illustrated by senescence of leaves, flower parts, and fruits. Perhaps, the most remarkable senescence is the postreproductive senescence of the whole organism (monocarpic senescence).

Much can be learned about the biochemistry of normal processes from studies of the disassembly of their components, for example, the orderly breakdown of the chloroplast. Furthermore, the senescence syndrome may share many of the enzymes involved in the normal turnover of cell components. Because senescence must involve a loss of self-maintenance, senescence studies should help us to learn how cells maintain themselves under nonsenescing conditions.

Viewing senescence at a higher level, studies on whole plant senescence should shed important perspectives on the regulation and physiological interdependence of activities in the different organs of the whole plant. The perspective offered through senescence will be helpful in understanding the whole plant, especially the way in which the organism focuses its resources at particular sites or mobilizing centers. Monocarpic senescence and the reclamation of resources from the assimilatory organs probably increases reproductive success (Harper, 1977; Willson, 1983). It can be also seen that organ and whole organism senescence have important adaptive functions, helping the organism to cope with a changing environment.

Lastly, there are many economic incentives for trying to understand senescence. Microbes and insects contribute to post-harvest losses of quality in vegetables and fruits, but senescence exacts a very high toll (Wills *et al.*, 1981; Burton, 1982). The keeping quality of flowers, vegetables, and fruits is a function of the progress of senescence (Halevy and Mayak, 1979, 1981; Wills *et al.*, 1981; Burton, 1982). Senescence of the lower leaves in potted flower plants decreases their value, and seedlings may senesce during shipment as they are subjected to insufficient illumination and other adversities. In monocarpic crop plants, the loss of assimilatory capacity as senescence progresses contributes to limitation of yield (Noodén, 1980, 1984).

B. Measures of Senescence

Quantitative measures of senescence are essential for progress in understanding this developmental event. Ideally, these measures would employ the central components of senescence, but given the uncertainty over what is central to senescence (Section II,D and Chapter 15), that is difficult at this time. The problem has been discussed elsewhere (Noodén, 1985) in a preliminary way for monocarpic senescence in soybean, but that may be a more specialized issue. For the time being, it seems necessary and sufficient to employ prominent components of the senescence syndrome as measures. In Chapter 10, it can be seen that chlorophyll loss has been used much more than any other parameter, particularly in studies of leaf senescence. Some studies employ the lowering of protein levels, and a few use declining photosynthesis as additional or alternative parameters. As a technical matter, two common procedures in senescence studies are bound to cause problems: the extraction of chlorophyll with acetone may lead to its degradation (Okatan *et al.*, 1981), and the Lowery procedure for protein determination is subject to extensive interference (Peterson, 1979). Determination of protein as nitrogen in digests (Derman *et al.*, 1978) or through dye binding to washed protein on paper disks (Van den Broek *et al.*, 1973) can avoid many problems. Given the centrality of chlorophyll in photosynthesis and the fact that ribulose bisphosphate carboxylase is the major leaf protein (Lyttleton and Ts'o, 1958; Peterson *et al.*, 1973; Telek and Graham, 1983), chlorophyll and total soluble protein are not fundamentally different measures. Both reflect changes in chloroplasts that may or may not be central to senescence (Chapter 15). The reports of "stay-green" mutants of soybean (Bernard and Weiss, 1973; Kahanak *et al.*, 1978) and meadow fescue grass (Thomas and Stoddart, 1975) have raised questions about the use of chlorophyll as an index of senescence. The leaves of the stay-green soybeans abscise at about the same time as normal plants (Kahanak *et al.*, 1978), and those of the meadow fescue undergo many of the changes characteristic of the normal leaves (Thomas and Stoddart, 1980). Thus, only part of the senescence syndrome is altered by these mutations. Measures of total extractable chlorophyll would not show the striking differences in chlorophyll loss patterns that occur in cytokinin- and auxin-treated leaves (Engelbrecht and Conrad, 1961; see also Chapter 10). Nonetheless, visible or extractable chlorophyll provide useful measures of the senescence syndrome.

Photosynthetic rate is influenced by sink "demand," which may complicate its use as a measure of senescence, especially in whole plants and in monocarpic plants that have been defruited to alter senescence (Noodén, 1980; see also Chapter 12). Thus, chlorophyll and photosynthetic enzymes provide more of a measure of photosynthetic capacity than the rate per se.

Leakiness of the cell membranes may be a good parameter (Halevy and Mayak, 1979), but the increases in leakage rates occur relatively late in the senescence process. Likewise, water loss, i.e., wilting, represents a very late stage. Leaf abscission may be a good supplementary measure for the attached leaves of species that shed their leaves. Thus, it appears that no single measure is perfect, but any prominent component of the senescence syndrome for a particular tissue can be employed, especially if checked against other parameters. Convenience of use should be an important consideration and nondestructive procedures that allow the same organs to be followed through time seem preferable.

We will argue in Section III,D that the study of senescence in intact plants (attached parts) is particularly important. Detachment not only removes the organ from the normal influence of correlative controls (Section III,C), but may prevent the normal exodus of nutrients that may be released during the senescence process, thereby causing their accumulation. Studies of the senescence of organisms or attached tissues should, however, consider the influence of remote parts of the plant on senescence. For example, treatments altering pod development could secondarily affect monocarpic senescence in soybean (Noodén, 1980, 1985).

C. Correlative Controls

The various parts of a plant influence each other in ways that serve to achieve a coordination of their developmental processes (Sachs, 1882; Sutcliffe, 1976; Moorby, 1977; Wareing, 1977; Goodwin *et al.*, 1978; Barlow and Carr, 1984). The oldest, and so far most successful, approach to analyzing these correlative controls has been surgical, e.g., excision of one structure to permit analysis of its effects on another. These excision effects did not escape notice of careful observers in the past (see reviews in Molisch, 1938; Paech, 1940; Leopold, 1961; Wangermann, 1965). Given the importance of integration of senescence into the activities and life cycle of the whole plant (Barlow, 1982; see also Section IV) and the potential of correlative controls to provide insights into regulation of senescence, it seems important to summarize the main patterns of these controls.

Perhaps, the earliest and most extensive literature on correlative controls centers around flowers. In particular, it was observed that the petals of many flowers were capable of persisting for a long time but quickly faded after pollination, sometimes within an hour (Kerner von Marilaun, 1894; Fitting, 1911; Molisch, 1938; Arditti, 1979; Gori, 1983). Not only the petals, but stamens and other peripheral flower parts, may senesce after pollination. In orchids, petunia, carnation, foxglove, and other flowers, pollination causes the female structure to produce an influence, probably ethylene or a precursor, that is transmitted to the petals and other parts, where it induces senescence (Akamine, 1963; Burg and Dijkman, 1967; Nichols, 1977; Gilissen, 1977; Gori, 1983; Stead, 1985; Hoekstra and Weges, 1986).

It should be noted that the senescence of some flowers, especially the short-lived flowers, is controlled by factors other than pollination (Gori, 1983; Stead, 1985); for example, iris flowers may senesce after a short period independent of pollination (Bancher, 1938), and morning glory flowers open and roll up within a day, possibly regulated by an endogenous clock (Sweeney, 1969; Winkenbach and Matile, 1970; Kende and Baumgartner, 1974).

While pollination may promote senescence of the petals, it also may prevent senescence of the ovary and the flower stalk (peduncle or pedicel) (Fitting, 1911; Molisch, 1938). The presence of the flower is required to maintain the pedicel and peduncle (Steinitz *et al.*, 1981; Lyons and Widmer, 1983, 1984).

Numerous reports indicate that the growing shoot apex may cause senescence of the cotyledons or the older leaves below. Shoot apex or seedling plumule removal rejuvenates the senescing leaves or cotyledons below (Petrie *et al.*, 1939; Paech, 1940; Mothes and Baudisch, 1958; Leopold, 1961; Newman *et al.*, 1973; Krul, 1974; Raafat and Herwig, 1975; Postius *et al.*, 1976; Choudhury and Mahatra, 1977; Van Onckelen *et al.*, 1981; Schneiter and Miller, 1981; Neumann and Stein, 1986). Decapitation can turn the senescence syndrome around, even after it has progressed quite far, e.g., regreening of yellow leaves in tobacco (Mothes and Baudisch, 1958) and resynthesis of protein after an 85% loss in bean leaves (Krul, 1974). Conversely, removal of the roots may promote senescence, particularly in leaves (Molisch, 1938; Wangermann, 1965; Noodén, 1985). As a further example of complications, in a bean seedling cutting with two opposite leaves, application of cytokinin to one leaf promotes senescence in the other (Leopold and Kawase, 1964).

Abscission may be a senescence process (Section IV,C), and the development of senescent cells in the abscission zone of leaf petioles may be under control of the blade (Scott and Leopold, 1966; Kozlowski, 1973; Jacobs, 1979; Addicott, 1982).

Nowhere is the correlative control of leaf senescence more apparent than in monocarpic senescence. In many monocarpic plants including pea, bean, soybean, sunflower, sweet mignonette, petunias, and other plants, removal of the flowers or fruits prevents this rapid senescence and prolongs the life of the plants, indefinitely in some species (Molisch, 1938; see also Chapter 12). Of course, nothing lives forever. It should be noted though that deflowering or defruiting may not prevent the physiological decline in all species where it prevents death and may actually promote leaf senescence in some species. In addition, older fruit may cause senescence and abortion of young fruit (Van Steveninck, 1957; Noodén, 1980, 1984), apparently as a part of a natural thinning process.

A parallel case of a "mobilizing" center regulating senescence events elsewhere may be seen in germinating seeds, where the embryo axis may cause a breakdown of the stored nutrients and senescence of the storage tissues, cotyledons, or endosperm (Brown and Morris, 1890; Young et al., 1960; Laidman, 1982; Murray, 1984; Bewley and Black, 1985).

The effects of removal either of the shoot apex or the reproductive structures establish that leaves may be induced to senesce by other parts. Not surprisingly, the longevity of leaves and even leaf-like cotyledons can be extended if they are disconnected from other parts such as growing shoots or fruit, particularly if these excised parts can be rooted (Molisch, 1938; Chibnall, 1939; Mothes, 1959). Likewise, detachment of leaves from pod-bearing soybeans delays and greatly changes their senescence pattern (Neumann et al., 1983). Within a leaf, however, the petiole may promote blade senescence, i.e., petiole removal extends the life of excised betel and hibiscus leaves (Mishra and Gaur, 1972, 1977; Misra and Biswal, 1973).

Even shoot apices themselves may senesce under correlative influences. For example, black locust shoot apices senesce and abscise in response to an influence from the leaves (Wareing and Roberts, 1956). In decapitated pea seedlings, one of the two opposite axillary buds at the cotyledonary node tends to become dominant and induce senescence of the other, and this can be averted by removing the dominant bud (Sachs, 1966; Lovell, 1977). Grafting cotton, sunflower, or pea shoot apices from plants with declining growth rates onto younger plants restores shoot growth but not indefinitely

(Mason, 1922; Habermann, 1964; Ecklund and Moore, 1969). In pea plants, a graft-transmissible substance, apparently a gibberellin, from the pea roots delays apex senescence (Proebsting *et al.*, 1977; Sponsel, 1985).

Correlative controls also operate in senescence at the cell level (Barlow and Carr, 1984); the prime case here is xylem differentiation (Jacobs, 1979; Shininger, 1979). Auxin derived from young leaf blades induces and orients the development of xylem reconnecting severed vascular bundles (Fig. 1.4) (Jacobs, 1952, 1959). Death of some cells in the corn stalk seems to be promoted by the ear (Pappelis and Katsanos, 1969).

Thus, numerous examples of correlative controls of senescence in cells, organs, and whole organisms can be identified. Hormones generally seem to play a central role in mediating correlative controls (Wareing, 1977; Goodwin *et al.*, 1978; Leopold and Noodén, 1984); however, with the possible exception of xylem differentiation, pollination-induced petal senescence and root retardation of leaf senescence, the role of hormones as mediators of these controls is relatively unknown. Because of the central role of hormones as chemical messengers, great expectations are held by plant physiologists for primary mediation of correlative functions by hormones. However, even the identification of these correlative interactions seems an important step toward elucidation of the hormonal controls (Section III,E) and ultimately the regulation of senescence.

D. Attached versus Detached Structures

A reductionist approach requires that senescence be studied in the simplest possible system, for example, a detached leaf; however, the correlative nature of many senescence events imposes some limitations on the reliabil-

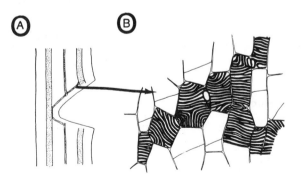

Fig. 1.4. (A) Left, regeneration of connection between severed vascular bundles in stem of *Coleus*. (B) Right, differentiation of parenchyma cells into reticulate xylem cells in the development of this strand. [Reprinted with permission from Sinnott and Bloch (1954).]

ity of experimentation with detached structures. It has been recognized for some time that excised parts display some very substantial differences in their senescence compared with their intact counterparts (see, e.g., Molisch, 1938; Lewington et al., 1967; Simon, 1967). Given the importance of correlative controls in senescence (Section III,C), it is not surprising that detachment produces some big changes. Excision may delay (Section III,C) or accelerate leaf senescence; generally darkness in combination with detachment promotes senescence (Wangermann, 1965; Simon, 1967; Biswal and Biswal, 1984). Attached and detached leaves also may differ in their responses to abscisic acid and cytokinin (Engelbrecht, 1964; Müller and Leopold, 1966; El-Antably et al., 1967; Noodén and Leopold, 1978; see also Chapters 9 and 10). Excised and intact parts may also show significant differences in their ultrastructural changes (Butler and Simon, 1971; Mittelheuser and Van Steveninck, 1971; Hurkman, 1979).

Redistribution of nutrients, especially nitrogen, is a prominent feature in the senescence of most intact parts, particularly leaves, but also flower parts (Williams, 1955; Halevy and Mayak, 1979; Noodén, 1980, and Chapter 12). Although excised parts, e.g., leaves, are still capable of basipetal transport of the released nutrients such as amino acids, phosphate, and sugars (Michael, 1936; Leonard, 1939; Müller and Leopold, 1966; Simon, 1967), blockage of the exodus of these materials by excision would surely alter the metabolism of the leaf blades (Lazan et al., 1983). In intact soybean leaves, blockage of redistribution by depodding causes the amino acids that have accumulated in the blades to be converted to other proteins, apparently including seed storage protein (Franceschi et al., 1983).

Excised parts are certainly useful in the study of the metabolic aspects and hormonal controls of senescence, and the fact that excision alters their metabolism doesn't require that studies on senescence-related metabolism in excised parts should be discarded. It is, however, necessary to relate these data to the events in intact organs. Particular caution is needed in the interpretation of senescence-related changes induced by darkness or heat-shock, whether applied to attached or detached parts.

E. Hormonal Controls

How do we determine whether or not a particular hormone governs the senescence of a tissue? The PESIGS rules representing parallel variation, excision, substitution, isolation, generality, and specificity (Jacobs, 1959, 1979) are based on Koch's postulates, and they provide a simplified rationale. Unfortunately, the hormonal controls of senescence haven't been analyzed comprehensively in any one system. The rule concerning generality may not always apply to senescence controls (see Chapters 10 and 12) and recognizing that at an early stage will avoid conflict (Noodén and Leopold, 1978; Noodén and Lindoo, 1978; see also Chapter 10). Another important complication is the likelihood that any major step in development, such as senescence, is under control of more than one hormone and therefore application of Koch's postulates might be difficult (Leopold and Noodén, 1984).

Much of the data available on hormonal controls compares the variation between the amount of the hormone available and the relative activity of the senescence process. Kinetic studies or comparisons of the time courses, hormone levels versus quantitative senescence parameters, are also helpful. The hormone changes may occur well before or together with senescence. Although a hormone change following the start of senescence would suggest the hormone does not initiate senescence, this could still be important in sustaining or completing the process. One substantial problem with the data correlating hormone levels with senescence is the heavy reliance on bioassays to determine hormone quantities. This is a particular problem for abscisic acid and the other hormones covered in Chapter 10, but also for many studies on the cytokinins (Chapter 9). The difficulties include not only potential interference from impurities, but problems in correcting for losses during purification. In addition, many of the bioassays used to make inferences about senescence regulators are not senescence assays (e.g., coleoptile growth is a dominant assay for senescence-inducing substances, Chapter 10). The reliance on bioassays and relatively impure samples is a reflection of earlier times when the methods were still being worked out and the studies on changes in hormone levels were just beginning. Nonetheless, these data can at least point the way to new studies with more precise methods.

Experimental manipulations that produce parallel variation between a hormone and senescence seem a stronger test. One example is bean seedling shoot removal, which reverses both the senescence of the cotyledons and the increase in endogenous abscisic acid (Van Onckelen *et al.*, 1981). This is certainly an area where knowing the correlative controls can aid in designing experimental probes.

The bulk of the studies on hormonal controls of senescence involve exogenous hormone applications, cynically termed "spray and pray." The size of the literature describing these studies is attributable to the potential economic benefits from modifying senescence through hormone treatments. Both the usefulness and the limitations in studying hormonal controls through exogenous hormone applications are discussed elsewhere (McGlasson *et al.*, 1978; Leopold and Noodén, 1984).

Another manipulation in the study of senescence is excision of either the affected part (hormone target tissue) or the hormone source. Then, the hormones to be studied are substituted for the source to determine their effects on the target. As pointed out by Jacobs (1979), this procedure may be complicated by the possibility that excision deprives the target of more than just the hormone under study. Nonetheless, excision and substitution, together with studies that compare the variation of hormone levels and senescence processes, can provide powerful methods for analyzing the hormonal controls of a process. Unfortunately, these manipulations are seldom employed in the study of senescence or even of hormonal controls in general. This deficiency seems to stem mainly from an insufficient understanding of the correlative controls, which are essential for good experimental design.

Hormones are the best candidates for controlling senescence, certainly for the mediation of correlative controls. They do, however, need broader experimental probing beyond the effects of simple hormone applications and parallel variation, which constitute the bulk of the contemporary data. A better understanding of the hormonal controls seems essential for further analysis of the metabolic aspects of senescence and the problem of which metabolic components are central to senescence (Section II,D).

IV. PATTERNS OF SENESCENCE

A. Overview

The fact that degeneration leading to death of plant parts is a natural developmental process was recognized long ago (Molisch, 1938), and, more recently, senescence has been implicated as a pervasive process with many developmental and adaptive functions (Leopold, 1961). Senescence occurs at any of several levels, from individual cells to tissues to organs to whole organisms (Leopold, 1961; Gahan, 1981, 1982; Noodén and Thompson, 1985). The cellular patterns of senescence are very diverse, and these have been reviewed in some detail as steps in a plant's life cycle (Barlow, 1982). A whole book (Thimann, 1980a) has summarized the senescence of particular organs. Here, these senescence patterns are named or categorized on the basis of the level (e.g., cellular) at which they act rather than on the biochemistry of the senescence processes, which are mostly unknown.

In addition to surveying the senescence patterns and their functions, this section will examine some degenerative processes that may not be senescence. Flowering plants will be emphasized; however, numerous examples occur in the gymnosperms, lower vascular plants, bryophytes, and fungi, but relatively few are known among the algae.

B. Cellular Patterns

Individual cells or small numbers of cells may be selectively targeted to senesce alongside others that do not. For example, the insect-trapping hairs inside *Aristolochia* flowers (Fig. 1.5) senesce after fertilization and release the pollen-laden insects (Sachs, 1882; Molisch, 1938). The early degeneration of hair cells on the stigma surface seems to provide nutrition for early growth of pollen (Jensen and Fisher, 1969; Herrero and Dickinson, 1979). Root hairs degenerate after a short time, while the surrounding epidermal cells continue to live (Molisch, 1938; Cormack, 1949). Other surface hairs may also be short lived (Burkhard, 1912, cited in Molisch, 1938; Fahn, 1967, 1982). Following discharge of the sperm nuclei, the pollen tube may also die (Schulz and Jensen, 1968; Barlow, 1982), or it may degenerate at an earlier stage as part of an incompatibility response (Heslop-Harrison, 1978a,b).

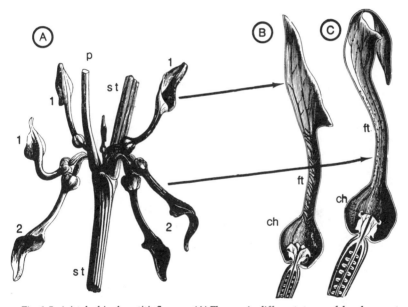

Fig. 1.5. *Aristolochia clematitis* flowers: (A) Flowers in different stages of development on a stem segment (st) with part of a petiole (p). (1) Young flowers not yet fertilized. Note the upright positioning. (2) fertilized flowers with the pedicels bent downwards. (B), (C). Longitudinal sections of flowers before pollination (B) and after (C). Note that insects enter through the top of the flower in (B), crawl down through the floral tube (ft), and become trapped in the swollen chamber (ch) of the tube due to the downward pointing hairs inside the floral tube. Following pollination, the hairs within the floral tube (ft) in (B) have senesced, releasing the insect in (C). [From Sachs (1882).]

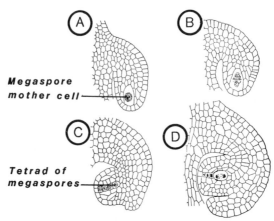

Megaspore mother cell

Tetrad of megaspores

Fig. 1.6. Megasporogenesis and early development of the embryo sac of *Anemone patens*. (A) Young ovule with megaspore mother cell. (B) Completion of first meiotic division. (C) Linear tetrad of megaspores. (D) Three of the megaspores disintegrate, while one enlarges and begins mitotic divisions to form the embryo sac. [Reprinted with permission from Haupt (1953).]

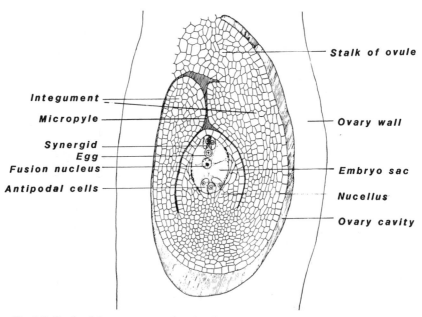

Stalk of ovule

Integument

Micropyle

Synergid
Egg
Fusion nucleus

Antipodal cells

Ovary wall

Embryo sac

Nucellus

Ovary cavity

Fig. 1.7. Ovule of *Anemone patens* showing the mature embryo sac, ovary wall, nucellus, ovary cavity, stalk of ovule, integument, micropyle, embryo sac, synergid, egg, fusion nucleus (will produce the endosperm), and antipodal cells. [Reprinted with permission from Haupt (1953).]

Usually, three out of the four cells produced by meiosis during female gametophyte formation degenerate (Fig. 1.6), and usually the surviving cell (megaspore) is that farthest from the micropylar end (Maheshwari, 1950; Johansen, 1950). In the embryo sac (female gametophyte, Fig. 1.7), the synergids may senesce at an early stage after pollination but before the pollen tube penetrates the embryo sac, and the antipodals may follow at a later stage when the endosperm multiplies (Nutman, 1939; Schulz and Jensen, 1968; Mogensen, 1978; Tilton, 1981). The suspensor cells (Fig. 1.8), which seem to function in pushing the embryo into the endosperm tissue and possibly also in supplying hormones, degenerate as the embryo grows

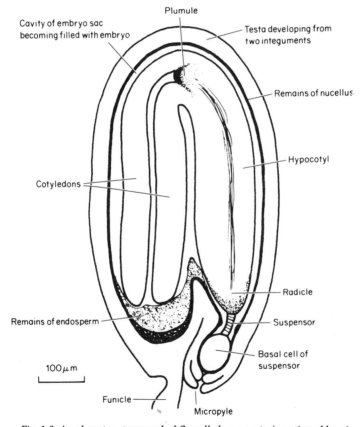

Fig. 1.8. An almost mature seed of *Capsella bursa-pastoris* sectioned longitudinally to show the orientation of the embryo. Note the disintegrated endosperm and nucellus. The suspensor cells usually senesce at or before this stage. [Reprinted with permission from Bell and Woodcock (1983).]

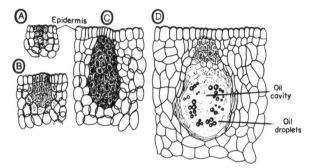

Fig. 1.9. Lysigenous development of an essential oil cavity in
the peel of a citrus fruit. Sections (A–D) are at right angles to the
surface of the peel at progressive stages of development. Sections
(E) and (F) are parallel to the surface of the peel. [Reprinted with
permission from Pergamon (Fahn, 1967; adapted from Martinet,
1871).]

(Nagl, 1976; Barlow, 1982). Both gametogenesis and embryo development
involve orderly sequences of cellular senescence.

Some secretory structures and ducts are produced through lysigeny or
disintegration of the cells (see, e.g., Fig. 1.9) or cell walls, but many of these
cells, e.g., articulated laticifers, often are not dead when they reach their
functional maturity (Esau, 1965; Fahn, 1967, 1982; Cutter, 1978). Often,
fibers and sclereids are dead at maturity, though sometimes the protoplasts
within these cells survive a long time (Esau, 1965; Fahn, 1967, 1982; Cutter,
1978). While senescence and death clearly occur in some of these specialized cells, the cells continue to live in many cases, and the loss of some
subcellular components prepares the cells for a new function rather than
death.

Parts of the hyphae of endotrophic mycorrhizae [particular vesicular-ar-
buscular mycorrhizae, but also orchidaceous (Fig. 1.10) and ericaceous my-
corrhizae] may senesce and thereby release nutrients to the host plant (Harley and Smith, 1983; Hudson, 1986). Other examples of senescence in fungi
are discussed by Munkres (1985).

The functions of cellular senescence are diverse. In some cases, the
changes serve to clear away the protoplast; in others, the protoplast breakdown products may be needed to nurture the neighboring cells.

C. Tissues

In numerous and diverse circumstances, larger groupings of cells (tissues)
may degenerate and die. The cells surrounding the microsporocytes or
pollen (tapetum, Fig. 1.11), embryo sac (nucellus) or embryo (endosperm

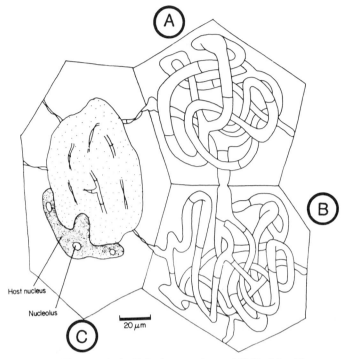

Fig. 1.10. Three cortical cells in the root of an orchid *(Dactylorchis purpurella)*, which has been infected by an endomycorrhizal fungus. Two of these cells (A and B) contain intact hyphal coils and one (C) contains hyphal coils undergoing lysis. Note the involvement of the host cell nucleus in (A). The fungal material appears to be absorbed by the host cell. This appears to be a mechanism for transferring nutrients to the host. [Reprinted with permission from Hudson (1986).]

and nucellus, Fig. 8) may disintegrate. Here, the constituents of the dying cells are thought to be redistributed to the sporogenous tissue or the embryo. The nucellar layer next to the growing embryo may break down, but this does not seem to be due to crushing by the embryo (Nutman, 1939; Tilton and Lersten, 1981; Barlow, 1982). Likewise, areas of the endosperm may break down as the embryo grows (Nutman, 1939; Esau, 1965; Laidman, 1982). In some species, apomixis (production of an embryo without fertilization) is associated with the death of certain cells, megaspore mother cells and some nucellar cells, leaving other nucellar cells to become an embryo (Haberlandt, 1922; Gustafsson, 1947). The layer of cells (tapetum) that surrounds the microsporocyte cells disintegrates (Fig. 11), and their constituents may become important components of the pollen grains' outer surfaces (Hesse, 1980; Barlow, 1982; Blackmore and Ferguson, 1986). These

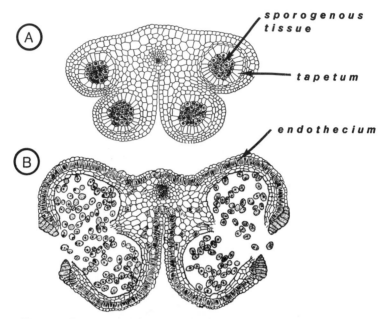

sporogenous
tissue

tapetum

endothecium

Fig. 1.11. Cross section of lily *(Lilium)* anthers. (A) Young anther, with four microsporangia containing sporogenous tissue. Note the conspicuous tapetum surrounding the sporogenous tissue. (B) Mature anther with two pollen sacs containing pollen grains. The tapetum surrounding the sporogenous tissue has broken down, while the endothecium has developed bands of thickening. [Reprinted with permission from Haupt (1953).]

cases may represent mainly nurturing functions, but it is not clear why the surrounding cells must be sacrificed as opposed to simply transferring nutrients from elsewhere within the plant.

The senescence of groups of cells in particular locations within developing leaves of guar (Sparks and Postlethwaite, 1967), monstera (Melville and Wrigley, 1969), and certain palms (Kaplan, 1983) helps to shape these leaves. Thus, localized cell death may play a role in leaf morphogenesis, even if it is not as prominent as in animal limb development (Hinchcliffe, 1981; Lockshin, 1981). In addition to the hairs of *Aristolochia* flowers cited above (Section IV,B), parts of flowers may senesce, releasing trapped pollinators or otherwise altering the configuration that limits the movement of pollinators or effecting self-pollination (Kerner von Marilaun, 1894; Gori, 1983).

Root cortex cells may die through a lysigenous process that produces aerenchyma (McPherson, 1939; Esau, 1965; Drew *et al.*, 1981). Likewise, pith cells in spruce buds (Lewis and Dowding, 1924; Cecich, 1981) and mesophyll cells in mangrove or Iceland tea leaves may form air spaces by processes that are at least partially lysigenous (Sifton, 1940; DeChalain and Berjak, 1979; Drennan and Berjak, 1982). A network of water-holding cells is formed in *Sphagnum* leaves (Fig. 1.12), apparently through lysigeny.

While many of the cases described above may represent senescence as we have defined it (Section I,A), there are numerous situations in which mechanical processes such as physical detachment from the plant, and thereby separation from the nutrient supply, could play a prominent role. Sometimes tearing, rhexigeny, causes cell death; for example, aerenchyma may be produced by such a tearing process (Esau, 1965). Extension of emerging lateral roots induces death in the overlying cortical cells (Esau, 1965), but these cells overlying the emerging lateral root may undergo considerable degeneration in advance of being crushed (Bonnett, 1969). Some cells are sloughed off from root caps or from the root surface and die as a natural part of root growth through the soil (Jost, 1907; Esau, 1965; Barlow, 1982). Although deprivation of nutrients could play a role in the death of these cells, they show some deterioration before their shedding (Juniper *et al.*,

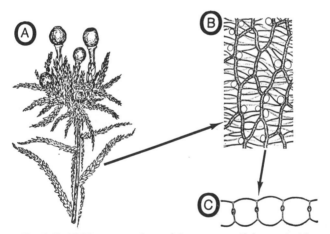

Fig. 1.12. (A) The gametophyte of the peat moss *(Sphagnum)* with a group of the sporophytes on stalks growing out of the top. Note the small leaves on the gametophyte. (B) Surface view of part of a *Sphagnum* leaf. The thin, shaded cells are the living cells containing chlorophyll; the areas enclosing these living cells are the large dead cells. Note the conspicuous transverse thickenings on the walls of these cells and the pores opening into them. (C) Section of leaf cut across the view shown on the left; note the small living cells between the large, dead cells. The dead cells probably hold or store water, and the pores may facilitate its entry. [From Brown (1935).]

1977; Henry and Deacon, 1981; Gahan, 1982). Furthermore, deterioration still occurs in aerial roots where the cells do not get peeled off (Blackman and Yeung, 1981). Thus, senescence may be an important factor in the death of these cells, as degeneration may precede the mechanical event. A somewhat analogous process occurs in the outer bark or rhytidome (Esau, 1965; Borger, 1973). The cork cells of the bark (phellem) are dead at maturity; senescence and/or mechanical and nutritional influences may be important here.

Tissues involved in abscission or dehiscence present a more difficult problem. Specialized layers of cells, abscission zones, may be differentiated in a wide variety of locations, e.g., in various parts of petioles; at the base of petals, stamens, and other flower parts; in the stalks bearing fruits; in roots; in branches; and even in the main stem (Esau, 1965; Fahn, 1967; Kozlowski, 1973; Addicott, 1982). The cells in these layers undergo varying degrees of preparation, especially softening of the cell walls, but they may not die until the cells are actually torn apart mechanically or they are exposed to drying as a consequence of fracture of nearby cells. These preparatory changes do have some of the characteristics of senescence (Scott and Leopold, 1966; Addicott, 1982). Indeed, the tissues that facilitate dehiscence, for example, the opening of stamens to release pollen or the opening of fruits to release their seeds, are likely to be dead at maturity (Esau, 1965; Fahn, 1967; Stanley and Kirby, 1973; Addicott, 1982). Dehiscence tissues therefore present less of a question; they do senesce. Extending the problem a step further, certain parts, e.g., petals or even leaves, may be quite fresh looking and certainly alive at the time of shedding, only to shrivel and die soon after shedding (Section IV,G).

The degeneration of cells to form xylem tracheids or vessels, which are empty tubes, devoid of protoplasm (Esau, 1965; Fahn, 1967, 1982; Cutter, 1978), also seems to be a clear case of senescence, and some effort has been made to describe the ultrastructural changes (Butler and Simon, 1971; Gahan, 1982; Woolhouse, 1984).

The transition from sapwood to heartwood is accompanied by death of the transverse ray cells and the longitudinally oriented parenchyma, but the most important changes seem to be due to deposition of toxic materials in the walls of and development of embolisms in the main conducting elements of the xylem, which are already dead (Stewart, 1966; Kozlowski, 1971). Since in most species about 90% (varies from 60–95%) of the cells in sapwood are already dead tubes and the loss of conducting function is apparently related to the conducting elements filling with air and materials being deposited in their walls, this transition should probably not be viewed primarily as a senescence process.

Phloem differentiation has been considered to be senescence (Woolhouse, 1984). A prominent feature of phloem sieve tube differentiation is the breakdown, or at least pycnosis, of the nucleus (Esau, 1965; Kozlowski, 1971; Evert, 1977); however, these cells continue to live and function for some time after the nucleus has been lost or has become nonfunctional. Indeed, the phloem sieve tubes of some species may be among the longest lived cells known, apparently in excess of 100 years (Lamont, 1980). Given the importance of the nucleus in directing senescence (Chapter 5), the loss of the nuclear function may be precisely what allows these cells to live so long. Thus, sieve tube differentiation does not seem to be senescence.

D. Organs

Senescence is as pervasive in organs as it is in tissues; however, the ultimate functions are more limited. Usually, senescence paves the way for removal of an unneeded or diseased organ. Senescence may be induced in almost any organ, most notably leaves (Leopold, 1961; Simon, 1967; Thimann, 1980b), but also in roots (Head, 1973), root nodules (Sutton, 1983), flower parts (Halevy and Mayak, 1979, 1981; Mayak and Halevy, 1980), branches and shoots (Millington and Chaney, 1973), unfertilized ovaries, and developing fruits (Simons, 1973; Sweet, 1973; Stephenson, 1981). The complete lysis of the cap in inky cap mushrooms (Iten, 1969) provides a striking example among fungi. There is a huge and diverse literature on this subject, which would be both burdensome and inappropriate for detailed review here. It seems relevant, however, to cover a few special aspects.

Even a single organ may follow different patterns of senescence. Leaves are a prime example, where a range of patterns exist (Leopold, 1961). Leaves may senesce as part of progressive senescence, the older leaves senescing as new leaves are produced, or all the leaves may senesce together (more or less). This may be part of the monocarpic life cycle (Section IV,E). All leaves may senesce synchronously on a seasonal basis, e.g., in autumn in woody plants or when the shoots senesce in certain herbaceous perennials. During terminal bud development in *Populus*, the blade may abort or senesce, leaving the stipules to develop into bud scales (Goffinet and Larson, 1981, 1982). Leaves may also senesce when diseased or when subjected to environmental stress (Section IV,F). The correlative and environmental controls of these different foliar senescence patterns seem to be different, but the fundamental metabolic aspects need not differ. Comparing leaves, flower parts, and fruit tissues, there are great differences in the hormonal controls (Chapter 10), except that cytokinin may play a fairly prominent and pervasive (even if not exclusive) role as an antisenescence hormone (Chapter 9).

The entire aerial portion — shoot, leaves, and all — senesce in many terrestrial plants, and thereby the plant retreats to an underground root or stem system, which carries the organism through an unfavorable season (Leopold, 1961). This pattern is top senescence and should not be confused with whole plant senescence. Some aquatic plants sometimes undergo a reverse phenomenon, bottom senescence, leaving the terminal buds to overwinter (Sculthorpe, 1967; Weber and Noodén, 1974).

Fruit ripening, which usually involves color changes and often flavor as well as textural changes, can and should be distinguished from fruit senescence, which is the actual degeneration leading to the death of the tissues around the seeds (Biale, 1964; Hulme, 1971; Baker, 1975). Unfortunately, fruit ripening and senescence may be difficult to separate. Indeed, some aspects of ripening are probably prerequisite to or even provide the initial stages of senescence. Sorting out metabolic changes and hormonal controls of fruit senescence as opposed to ripening is therefore difficult if not impossible. Many of the symptoms, e.g., color change, sweetening, etc., used to describe fruit maturation may be more closely linked to ripening than senescence. Then, what really represents senescence of the fruit? At this point, only the development of leakiness in the cell membranes seems to be a clear component of senescence.

The cells within an individual organ may senesce at different times. The different parts of a leaf, for example, may senesce at different rates (Simon, 1967; Moore and Lovell, 1970; Wood et al., 1986). Soybean leaf yellowing begins over the main veins (vein yellowing) and then continues in the intervenal regions progressing toward the main veins (Benner and Noodén, 1984). Grass leaves may senesce from the apex toward the base. Moreover, the xylem cells, surface hairs, sclereids, etc. differentiate (senesce) within a leaf before the senescence of the blade as a whole (Esau, 1965; Fahn, 1967, 1982; Cutter, 1978). During the major phase of blade senescence, the tissues around the vascular bundle seem to senesce later (Shaw and Manocha, 1965; Butler and Simon, 1971; Peoples et al., 1980), and there is reason to believe the sieve tubes remain functional until very late, even after yellowing in leaves (Matile and Winkenbach, 1971; Benner and Noodén, 1984). In addition, the stomatal guard cells persist far beyond the other leaf cells, perhaps dying only after the surrounding cells have collapsed (Hagen, 1918; Molisch, 1938; Kenda et al., 1953; Heath and Mansfield, 1969; Peoples et al., 1980; Zeiger and Schwartz, 1982). This peculiar longevity of the guard cells may be a result of their lack of a symplastic connection with their surrounding cells (Gunning and Robards, 1976; Gunning and Overall, 1983).

E. Organisms

With the possible exception of plant clones (Chapter 12), whole organisms have well-defined life spans; eventually, they degenerate and die, some slowly, some abruptly. In plants (or at least native, adapted plants), death is often induced by internally programmed changes and may even be a part of preparation for an adverse season. Thus, one might expect some correlation between whole plant senescence and the life cycle patterns described as annual, biennial, and perennial. Cutting across these patterns is another set of descriptions designated monocarpy and polycarpy for species showing single and repeated reproductive phases, respectively (Hildebrand, 1882; Molisch, 1938). A duplicative set of terms, semelpary and iteropary, was coined later (see Noodén, 1980).

During the nineteenth century and the early part of this century, considerable effort was made to catalog plants according to their life cycle patterns (Hildebrand, 1882; Weber, 1919; Molisch, 1938; Wangermann, 1965; Harper, 1977; Willson, 1983). Annual and biennial plants tend to be monocarpic, while the perennials tend to be polycarpic. Nonetheless, there are some remarkable examples of monocarpic perennials, e.g., the century plant, *Agave americana* (Weber, 1919), corypha palm (Janzen, 1976), several bamboo species (Arber, 1934; Evans, 1972; Janzen, 1976), and others, including some large, highly branched trees such as *Cerberiopsis candelabrum* (Veillon, 1971) and *Tachigalia versicolor* (Foster, 1977). Because a relatively high proportion of a monocarpic plant's assimilatory capacity is committed to making reproductive structures and they often develop dramatically (Harper, 1977; Willson, 1983), both in terms of size and speed, this reproductive pattern is sometimes termed "big bang" (Schaffer and Schaffer, 1977). Not all monocarpic species senesce abruptly; some species of bamboo degenerate over a period of a year (Arber, 1934). Many monocarpic plants have vegetative phases of a variable duration (Molisch, 1938; Wangermann, 1965; Harper, 1977; Inouye and Taylor, 1980; Young, 1984), and some may or may not span a winter, depending on when the seeds germinate (Wangermann, 1965; see also Chapter 12). A few species such as house leek may be monocarpic or polycarpic depending on conditions (Klebs, 1905; Crocker, 1939).

The validity of the monocarpic–polycarpic concepts has been questioned by Woolhouse (1982), mainly because of the occurrence of intermediate forms and some variability in the time of senescence (and reproductive development) relative to the seasons. The existence of intermediate cases does not invalidate the categories of polycarpy and monocarpy, which seem useful nevertheless. The term monocarpic senescence refers to the degeneration followed by death at the end of the reproductive phase. This term may encompass several different physiological mechanisms (Noodén and Lindoo, 1978, and Chapter 12). Whether or not polycarpic plants also undergo whole plant senescence is not clear (Chapter 12). This pattern of whole plant senescence might tentatively be termed polycarpic senescence for the purpose of discussion. How the physiology of top senescence, which

L. D. Noodén

occurs at the end of each reproductive phase (Leopold, 1961), relates to monocarpic senescence is not known.

Among monocarpic plants, there are many different patterns in the relation of the time course of leaf senescence to root senescence or to fruit development (Chapter 12). Indeed, different environmental conditions may cause some difference, even within a species. For many species, particularly soybean, progressive senescence of the lower leaves may halt after vegetative growth ceases, and then all of the leaves, young and old, senesce at about the same time as the fruit matures (Singh and Lal, 1935; Kumura and Naniwa, 1965; Lindoo and Noodén, 1977; see also Chapter 12). In accordance with the general concept of senescence (Section I), chronological age of the leaves is not a major factor. In some species, e. g., certain varieties of rice (Mondal and Choudhuri, 1984), the leaves undergo a sequential pattern, older leaves first. By contrast, in the air plant *(Bryophyllum daigremontianum)*, the upper, younger leaves senesce first (Resende, 1964). Interestingly, some varieties of rice show a nonsequential or simultaneous pattern (Mondal and Choudhuri, 1984). It appears that the simultaneous pattern in many cultivars may be a product of selection and breeding to optimize seed yields by sharpening the vegetative reproductive transition (Denholm, 1975; Noodén, 1980). This reproductive strategy and the evolution of monocarpy may be favored by "low adult survival, early senescence, increased time between reproductive episodes, high population growth rate or high juvenile survival" (Young, 1984).

Monocarpy is polyphyletic in its origin, having evolved independently in numerous and diverse groups (Noodén and Lindoo, 1978; Noodén, 1980). Even species in the same genus, for example, palms of the genus *Arenga* (Evans, 1972) or giant lobelias (Young, 1984), may be monocarpic or polycarpic. The controls of monocarpic senescence may differ among the monocarpic plants, even some fairly closely related groups, e.g., pea, soybean, and common bean. It appears likely, then, that evolution has produced the same end through different means. At present, however, there is no compelling reason to believe top senescence is related to monocarpic senescence, either as an evolutionary precursor or in terms of physiology, but this possibility should be kept in mind.

F. Relationship between Stress and Senescence

Stress of various types is able to induce or accelerate many changes that resemble the senescence syndrome (Section II,D). This subject is now represented by a very large specialized literature, and a thorough treatment, a difficult task, will not be attempted here. The relationship between stress and senescence has been summarized in a very general way by Brady

(1973). It does seem important to make a distinction between chronic (long-term, low intensity) and acute (short-term, high-intensity) stress. Acute stresses such as severe chilling, heat, drought, and some rapid responses to pathogens, possibly including the hypersensitive responses cause death (necrosis) over a fairly brief period. Both degrees of stress break down the cells' homeostatic ability (Davies and Sigee, 1984; Gahan, 1984; see also Section II,C) and interfere with self-maintenance not only by inducing lesions but by inhibiting repair and possibly also raising the "cost" of repair (Penning de Vries, 1975).

While extreme drought simply overwhelms and quickly kills a plant or organ, chronic, sublethal drought does seem to accelerate senescence. Water stress affects many processes in the same direction as normal senescence (e.g., photosynthesis, respiration, protein synthesis, RNA synthesis, chlorophyll, and protein levels), and it may also increase leaf shedding as well as alter hormone levels (Naylor, 1972; Brady, 1973; Boyer, 1976; Kozlowski, 1976; Wright, 1978; Paleg and Aspinall, 1981). Conversely, flooding of the roots can also produce senescence symptoms in whole plants (Wright, 1978; Kozlowski, 1984).

Of all the stressful environmental factors, mineral deficiency is probably best known for its ability to induce senescence-like responses, particularly leaf yellowing, but the leaf yellowing patterns differ quite a lot depending on which element is deficient (Sprague, 1964; Butler and Simon, 1971; Marschner, 1986). The longstanding idea that developing fruits induce monocarpic senescence by creating a deficiency in minerals, especially nitrogen, in the leaves is discussed in Chapter 12.

A host of other environmental stresses may, on occasion, trigger senescence-like changes. These include heat and cold (Levitt, 1980a,b; Turner and Kramer, 1980; Li and Sakai, 1982). Salinity may also cause changes resembling senescence; in particular, high salt levels around the roots may cause leaf yellowing (Waisel, 1972; Wright, 1978; Levitt, 1980b). Light deprivation, especially in combination with excision, induces senescence (Simon, 1967; Biswal and Biswal, 1984), but this may not have much bearing on natural senescence, except possibly for shading of lower leaves. Air pollutants may also cause changes resembling senescence, especially in leaves (Treshow, 1970; Butler and Simon, 1971; Halbwachs, 1984; Soikkeli and Karenlampi, 1984; Taylor, 1984). Of all the stress phenomena, disease presents the most diverse responses in affected plants. These responses range from fairly rapid, as with the hypersensitive reaction and some acute toxic reactions, to relatively prolonged responses (Butler and Simon, 1971; Farkas, 1978). Included among these changes is chlorophyll loss, which is induced by a number of toxins produced by pathogens (Cooper, 1981; Pegg, 1981; Staples and Toenniessen, 1981). Toxin-induced necrosis probably differs from senscence, except that in both cases, a critical and perhaps final step is membrane damage that completes the breakdown in homeostasis (Cooper, 1981; Pegg, 1981).

A real difficulty arises in distinguishing stress effects resulting in senescence (programed degeneration) and those producing chronic degeneration or aging (Section II,C). In fact, it seems unproductive to attempt to make this distinction here. It should be noted that in some instances chronic, low-intensity stress prolongs the life of an organism, though it may have the opposite effect on certain parts (Chapter 12). Ultimately, acute stress, chronic stress (where it is fatal), and senescence all seem to involve a breakdown of membrane function and presumably homeostatic ability (Thompson, 1984; see also Sections II,C and D).

G. Nonsenescence Processes

Not all forms of deterioration are senescence (Sections II,A and B), and, of course, senescence is not the only cause of death (Section II,C). We have already made a distinction between the deterioration involved in aging and senescence (Section II,A). Some special cases of death resulting from rhexigeny, compression, and abscission, or other means of separating cells from their source of nutritional support or moisture, are considered in Sections IV,C and IV,D. These are primarily exogenous influences, and, like stress (Section IV,F), they may drive death processes, but they are not in themselves senescence. Where it has been studied carefully, the cells involved degenerate in preparation for the mechanical event, so they probably would soon die anyhow.

Partial or even massive breakdown of certain cell components may simply be part of a continuing cell differentiation, rather than a decline leading directly to death. Phloem sieve tube differentiation and fruit ripening also do not seem to be senescence processes, even though they may have degenerative components (Sections IV,B and D); mostly, these processes simply represent continued development for a specialized function rather than death. Likewise, the cotyledons may serve a storage function in the seeds, and then after massive breakdown of their stored materials, they may become photosynthetic organs bearing some resemblance to leaves in many (epigeous) species, thereby supplying some additional needs of the young seedlings (Fahn, 1967; Kozlowski, 1971; Murray, 1984; see also Chapter 15).

Another pattern of considerable experimental interest, the degeneration and death of cultured cells, especially protoplasts, has been summarized by Cocking (1984). This phenomenon is often referred to as senescence, and the symptoms suggest a deterioration of the plasma membrane. Thus, membrane protectants such as Ca^{2+}-alginate and polyamines (Cocking, 1984; see also Chapter 2) can help to remedy this problem. Without detracting from the importance and the intrinsic interest of this phenomenon, it seems to be more of an artificial than a natural process, and it comes closer to being chronic degeneration (Davies and Sigee, 1984; see also Section II,C) than senescence.

Not every form of metabolic decline or decrease in vigor represents senescence. The process of aging exemplified by the loss of viability in stored seeds discussed in Section II,A and Chapters 12 and 13; this is primarily an exogenously driven process. Downward metabolic adjustments are often made as a part of a seasonal or even daily adjustment. For example, photosynthetic capacity in single cells (e.g., algae) or in the leaves of many species may undergo a daily cycle of increase and decrease, which seems to be regulated by an endogenous clock (Sweeney, 1969; Bünning, 1973). Similarly, numerous observations indicate that assimilatory rate and capacity are influenced by the consumption of assimilate by sinks (sink "demand"), and a decrease in the activity or removal of the sinks may cause a decline in the activity of these assimilatory organs (Noodén, 1980, and Chapter 12). The latter phenomenon seems akin to the metabolic stepdown, which has been studied extensively in microbes (Ingraham *et al.*, 1983). These changes are not senescence, but rather part of an ongoing series of metabolic adjustments through which cells, organs, and organisms enhance their survival by adapting to changing conditions. Likewise, the normal turnover of molecules and organelles within cells cannot be considered senescence. Under special circumstances, e.g., a combination of certain chemical treatments such as EDTA plus illumination, chlorophyll may break down through processes that do not seem to be senescence (Thiman *et al.*, 1982; Satler and Thimann, 1983).

Finally, it should be noted that the term *aging* is also applied to changes occurring in excised, washed tissues (Van Steveninck, 1975) and a "senescence factor" has been described for the fungus *Podospora* (Esser and Tudzynski, 1980). These interesting phenomena do not qualify as aging or senescence by the criteria outlined here (Section I,A; see also Noodén and Thompson, 1985). Likewise, the juvenile and adult phases in leaf and shoot development often discussed in terms of plant aging (Crocker, 1939; Robbins, 1957; Doorenbos, 1965; Borchert, 1976) seem to be neither aging nor senescence.

ACKNOWLEDGMENT

The helpful suggestions of Carl Leopold are gratefully acknowledged.

REFERENCES

Addicott, F. T. (1982). "Abscission." Univ. of California Press, Berkeley.

Akamine, E. K. (1963). Ethylene production in fading *Vanda* orchid blossoms. *Science* **140,** 1217–1218.

Arber, A. (1934). "The Gramineae. A Study of Cereal, Bamboo and Grass." Cambridge Univ. Press, Cambridge, England.

Arditti, J. (1979). Aspects of the physiology of orchids. *Adv. Bot. Res.* **7,** 421–655.

Baker, J. E. (1975). Morphological changes during maturation and senescence. *In* "Postharvest Physiology Handling and Transportation of Tropical and Subtropical Fruits and Vegetables" (E. B. Pastastico, ed.), pp. 128–147. Avi, Westport, Connecticut.

Bancher, E. (1938). Zellphysiologische Untersuchung uber den Abbluhvorgang bei *Iris* und *Gladiolus. Oesterr. Bot. Z.* **87,** 221–244.

Barlow, P. W. (1982). Cell death — An integral part of plant development. *In* "Growth Regulators in Plant Senescence" (M. B. Jackson, B. Grant, and I. A. Mackenzie, eds.), Monogr. No. 8, pp. 27–45. Br. Plant Growth Regul. Group, Wantage, England.

Barlow, P. W., and Carr, D. J., eds. (1984). "Positional Controls in Plant Development." Cambridge Univ. Press, London and New York.

Bell, P. R., and Woodcock, C. L. F. (1983). "The Diversity of Green Plants." Arnold, London.

Benner, J. L., and Noodén L. D. (1984). Translocation of photosynthate from soybean leaves to the pods during senescence. *Biochem. Physiol. Pflanz.* **179,** 269–275.

Bernard, R. L., and Weiss, M. G. (1973). Qualitative genetics. *In* "Soybeans: Improvement, Production and Uses." pp. 117–154. Am. Soc. Agron., Madison, Wisconsin.

Bewley, J. D., and Black, M. (1985). "Seeds Physiology of Development and Germination." Plenum, New York.

Biale, J. B. (1964). Growth maturation and senescence in fruits. *Science* **146,** 880–888.

Biswal, U. C., and Biswal, B. (1984). Photocontrol of leaf senescence. *Photochem. Photobiol.* **39,** 875–879.

Blackman, S. J., and Yeung, E. C. (1981). Aerial root cap structure of an orchid, *Epidendrum. Can. J. Bot.* **59,** 1702–1708.

Blackmore, B., and Ferguson, I. K., eds. (1986). "Pollen and Spores. Form and Function." Academic Press, London.

Bonnett, M. T., Jr. (1969). Cortical cell death during lateral root formation. *J. Cell Biol.* **40,** 144–159.

Borchert, R. (1976). The concept of juvenility in woody plants. *Acta Hortic.* **56,** 21–36.

Borger, G. A. (1973). Development and shedding of bark. *In* "Shedding of Plant Parts" (T. T. Kozlowski, ed.), pp. 205–236. Academic Press, New York.

Bose, J. C. (1907). "Comparative Electro-physiology." Longmans, Green, and Co., London.

Bose, J. C. (1927). "Plant Autographs and Their Relations." Longmans, Green, London.

Boveris, A., Puntarulo, S. A., Roy, A. H., and Sanchez, R. A. (1984). Spontaneous chemiluminescence of soybean embryonic axes during imbibition. *Plant Physiol.* **76,** 447–451.

Bowen, I. D. (1981). Techniques for demonstrating cell death. *In* "Cell Death in Biology and Pathology" (I. D. Bowen and R. A. Lockshin, eds.), pp. 379–444. Chapman & Hall, London.

Bowen, I. D. (1984). Laboratory techniques for demonstrating cell death. *In* "Cell Ageing and Cell Death" pp. 5–40. Cambridge Univ. Press, London and New York.

Bowen, I. D., and Lockshin, R. A. (1981). Introduction. *In* "Cell Death in Biology and Pathology" (I. D. Bowen and R. A. Lockshin, eds.), pp. 1–7. Chapman & Hall, London.

Boyer, J. S. (1976). Water deficits and photosynthesis. *In* "Water Deficits and Plant Growth" (T. T. Kozlowski, ed.), Vol. 4, pp. 153–190. Academic Press, New York.

Brady, C. J. (1973). Changes accompanying growth and senescence and effect of physiological stress. *In* "Chemistry and Biochemistry of Herbage" (G. W. Butler and R. W. Bailey, eds.), Vol. 2, pp. 317–351. Academic Press, London.

Brown, H. T., and Morris, G. H. (1890). Researches on the germination of some of the Gramineae. *J. Chem. Soc.* **57**, 458–528.

Brown, W. H. (1935). "The Plant Kingdom." Ginn, Boston, Massachusetts.

Bünning, E. (1973). "The Physiological Clock; Circadian Rhythms and Biological Chronometry," 3rd Ed. Springer-Verlag, Berlin and New York.

Burg, S. P., and Dijkman, M. J. (1967). Ethylene and auxin participation in pollen induced fading of *Vanda* orchid blossoms. *Plant Physiol.* **42**, 1648–1650.

Burton, W. G. (1982). "Post-harvest Physiology of Food Crops." Longman, New York.

Butler, R. D. (1967). The fine structure of senescing cotyledons of cucumber. *J. Exp. Bot.* **18**, 535–543.

Butler, R. D., and Simon, E. W. (1971). Ultrastructural aspects of senescence in plants. *Adv. Gerontol. Res.* **3**, 73–129.

Cecich, R. A. (1981). Cavity formation in winter buds of *Pinus banksiana*. *Am. J. Bot.* **68**, 786–789.

Chibnall, A. C. (1939). "Protein Metabolism in the Plant." Yale Univ. Press, New Haven, Connecticut.

Choudhury, N. K., and Mahatra, P. K. (1977). Senescence of *Cucurbita maxima* cotyledons and the effect of gibberellic acid and potassium nitrate on the excised cotyledons. *J. Indian Bot. Soc.* **56**, 275–277.

Cocking, E. C. (1984). Aspects of degeneration and death in cultured plant cells. *In* "Cell Ageing and Cell Death" (I. Davies and D. C. Sigee, eds.), pp. 203–209. Cambridge Univ. Press, London and New York.

Comfort, A. (1956). "The Biology of Senescence." Routledge & Kegan Paul, London.

Comfort, A. (1964). "The Biology of Senescence." Rinehart, New York.

Cooper, R. M. (1981). Pathogen-induced changes in host ultrastructure. *In* "Plant Disease Control" (R. C. Staples and G. H. Toenniessen, eds.), pp. 105–142. Wiley, New York.

Cormack, R. G. (1949). The development of root hairs in angiosperms. *Bot. Rev.* **15**, 583–612.

Crocker, W. (1939). Ageing in plants. *In* "Problems of Ageing" (E. V. Cowdry, ed.), 1st Ed., pp. 1–31. Williams & Wilkins, Baltimore, Maryland.

Cutter, E. G. (1978). "Plant Anatomy. Part I: Cells and Tissues," 2nd Ed. Addison-Wesley, Reading, Massachusetts.

Davies, I., and Sigee, D. C. (1984). Cell ageing and cell death: perspectives. *In* "Cell Ageing and Cell Death" (I. Davies and D. C. Sigee, eds.), pp. 347–350. Cambridge Univ. Press, London and New York.

DeChalain, T. M. B., and Berjak, P. (1979). Cell death as a functional event in the development of the leaf intercellular spaces in *Avicennia marina* (Forsskål) Viorh. *New Phytol.* **83**, 147–155.

Denholm, J. V. (1975). Necessary condition for maximum yield in a senescing two-phase plant. *J. Theor. Biol.* **52**, 251–254.

Derman, B. D., Rupp, D. C., and Noodén, L. D. (1978). Mineral distribution in relation to fruit development and monocarpic senescence in Anoka soybeans. *Am. J. Bot.* **65**, 205–213.

Doorenbos, J. (1965). Juvenile and adult phases in woody plants. *Encycl. Plant Physiol.* **15**(1), 1222–1233.

Drennan, P. M., and Berjak, P. (1982). Degeneration of the salt glands accompanying foliar maturation in *Avicennia marina* (Forsskål) Vierh. *New Phytol.* **90**, 165–176.

Drew, M. C., Jackson, M. B., Giffard, S. C., and Campbell, R. C. (1981). Inhibition by silver ions of gas space (aerenchyma) formation in the adventitious roots of *Zea mays* L. subjected to exogenous ethylene or to oxygen deficiency. *Planta* **153**, 217–224.

Ecklund, P. R., and Moore, T. C. (1969). RNA and protein metabolism in senescent shoot apices of 'Alaska' peas. Am. J. Bot. **56**, 327–334.

El-Antably, H. M. M., Wareing, P. F., and Hillman, J. (1967). Some physiological responses to D, L abscisin (Dormin). Planta **73**, 74–90.

Engelbrecht, L. (1964). Über Kinetinwirkungen bei intakten Blättern von Nicotiana rustica. Flora **154**, 57–69.

Engelbrecht, L., and Conrad, K. (1961). Vergleichende Untersuchengen zur Wirkung von Kinetin und Auxin. Ber. Dtsch. Bot. Ges. **74**, 42–46.

Esau, K. (1965). "Plant Anatomy," 2nd Ed. Wiley, New York.

Esau, K., Cheadle, V. I., and Gill, R. H. (1966). Cytology of differentiating tracheary elements II. Structures associated with cell surfaces. Am. J. Bot. **53**, 765–771.

Esser, K., and Böckelmann, B. (1985). Fungi. In "Interdisciplinary Topics in Gerontology" (H. P. Von Hahn, ed.), Vol. 21, pp. 231–246. Karger, Basel.

Esser, K., and Tudzynski, P. (1980). Senescence in fungi. In "Senescence in Plants" (K. V. Thimann, ed.), pp. 67–83. CRC Press, Boca Raton, Florida.

Evans, G. C. (1972). "The Quantitative Analysis of Plant Growth." Blackwell, Oxford.

Evert, R. F. (1977). Phloem structure and histochemistry. Annu. Rev. Plant Physiol. **28**, 199–222.

Fahn, A. (1967). "Plant Anatomy." Pergamon, Oxford.

Fahn, A. (1982). "Plant Anatomy," 3rd Ed. Pergamon, Oxford.

Farkas, G. L. (1978). Senescence and plant disease. In "Plant Disease: An Advanced Treatise" (J. G. Horsfall and E. B. Cowling, eds.), Vol. 3, pp. 391–412. Academic Press, New York.

Finch, C. E., and Schneider, E. L., eds. (1985). "Handbook of the Biology of Aging," 2nd Ed. Van Nostrand-Reinhold, New York.

Fitting, H. (1911). Untersuchungen über die vorzeitige Entblätterung von Blüten. Jahrb. Wiss. Bot. **49**, 187–263.

Foster, R. B. (1977). Tachigalia versicolor is a suicidal tree. Nature (London) **268**, 624–626.

Franceschi, V. R., Wittenbach, V. A., and Giaquinta, R. T. (1983). Paraveinal mesophyll of soybean leaves in relation to assimilate transfer and compartmentation. III. Immunohisto-chemical localization of specific glycopeptides in the vacuole after depodding. Plant Physiol. **72**, 586–589.

Gaff, D., and Okong'o-Ogola, O. (1971). The use of non-permeating pigments for testing the survival of cells. J. Exp. Bot. **22**, 756–758.

Gahan, P. B. (1981). Cell senescence and death in plants. In "Cell Death in Biology and Pathology" (I. D. Bowen and R. A. Lockshin, eds.), pp. 145–163. Chapman & Hall, London.

Gahan, P. B. (1982). Cytochemical and ultrastructural changes in cell senescence and death. In "Growth Regulators in Plant Senescence" (M. B. Jackson, B. Grout, and I. A. Mackenzie, eds.), Monogr. No. 8, pp. 47–55. Br. Plant Growth Regul. Group, Wantage, England.

Gahan, P. B. (1984). Reversible and irreversible damage in plant cells of different ages. In "Cell Ageing and Cell Death" (I. Davies and D. C. Sigee, eds.), pp. 155–169. Cambridge Univ. Press, London and New York.

Gilissen, L. J. W. (1977). Style-controlled wilting of the flower. Planta **133**, 275–280.

Goffinet, M. C., and Larson, P. R. (1981). Structural changes in Populus deltoides terminal buds and in the vascular transition zone of the stems during dormancy induction. Am. J. Bot. **68**, 118–129.

Goffinet, M. C., and Larson, P. R. (1982). Lamina abortion in terminal bud-scale leaves of Populus deltoides during dormancy induction. Bot. Gaz. **143**, 331–340.

Goodwin, P. B., Gollnow, B. I., and Letham, D. S. (1978). Phytohormones and growth correlations. In "Phytohormones and Related Compounds—A Comprehensive Treatise," (D. S.

Letham, P. B. Goodwin, and T. J. V. Higgins, eds.), Vol. 2, pp. 215–249. Elsevier/North-Holland, Amsterdam.

Gori, D. F. (1983). Post-pollination phenomena and adaptive floral changes. *In* "Handbook of Experimental Pollination Biology" (C. E. Jones and R. J. Little, eds.), pp. 31–45. Van Nostrand-Reinhold, New York.

Gunning, B. E. S., and Overall, R. (1983). Plasmodesmata and cell-to-cell transport in plants. BioScience **33,** 260–265.

Gunning, B. E. S., and Robards, A. W., eds. (1976). "Intercellular Communication in Plants: Studies on Plasmodesmata." Springer-Verlag, Berlin and New York.

Gustafsson, A. (1947). Apomixis in higher plants. Part II. The causal aspect of apomixis. Lunds Univ. Årsskr., N. F., Avd. 2 **43(2),** 71–178.

Haberlandt, G. (1922). Über, Zellteilungshormone und ihre Beziehungen zur Wundheilung, Befruchtung, Parthenogenesis und Adventiveembryonie. *Biol. Zentralbl.* **42,** 145–172.

Habermann, H. M. (1964). Grafting as an experimental approach to the problem of physiological aging in *Helianthus annuus* L. *Int. Hortic. Congr., 16th* **4,** 243–251.

Hagen, F. (1918). Zur Physiologie des Spaltöffnungsapparates. *Beitr. Allg. Bot.* **1,** 260–291.

Halbwachs, G. (1984). Organismal responses of higher plants to atmospheric pollutants: Sulphur dioxide and fluoride. *In* "Air Pollution and Plant Life" (M. Treshow, ed.), pp. 175–214. Wiley, Chichester, England.

Halevy, A. H., and Mayak, S. (1979). Senescence and postharvest physiology of cut flowers — Part 1. *Hortic. Rev.* **1,** 204–236.

Halevy, A. H., and Mayak, S. (1981). Senescence and postharvest physiology of cut flowers — Part 2. *Hortic. Rev.* **3,** 59–143.

Harley, J. L., and Smith, S. E. (1983). "Mycorrhizal Symbiosis." Academic Press, London.

Harper, J. L. (1977). "Population Biology of Plants." Academic Press, London.

Haupt, A. W. (1953). "Plant Morphology." McGraw-Hill, New York.

Head, G. C. (1973). Shedding of roots. *In* "Shedding of Plant Parts" (T. T. Kozlowski, ed.), pp. 237–293. Academic Press, New York.

Heath, O. V. S., and Mansfield, T. A. (1969). The movements of stomata. *In* "The Physiology of Plant Growth and Development" (M. B. Wilkins, ed.), pp. 301–332. McGraw-Hill, New York.

Henry, C. M., and Deacon, J. W. (1981). Natural (non-pathogenic) death of the cortex of wheat and barley seminal roots, as evidenced by nuclear staining with acridine orange. *Plant Soil* **60,** 255–274.

Herrero, M., and Dickinson, H. G. (1979). Pollen-pistil incompatibility in *Petunia hybrida:* changes in the pistil following compatible and incompatible intraspecific crosses. *J. Cell Sci.* **36,** 1–18.

Heslop-Harrison, J. (1978a). "Cellular Recognition Systems in Plants." Univ. Park Press, Baltimore, Maryland.

Heslop-Harrison, J. (1978b). Recognition and response in the pollen-stigma interaction. *Symp. Soc. Exp. Biol.* **32,** 121–138.

Hesse, M. (1980). Zur Frage der Anheftung des Pollens an blütenbesuchende Insekten mittels Pollenkitt und Viscinfäden. *Plant Syst. Evol.* **133,** 135–148.

Hildebrand, F. (1882). Die Lebensdauer und Vegetationsweise der Pflanzen, ihre Ursachen und ihre Entwicklung. *Bot. Jarhb.* **2,** 51–135.

Hinchcliffe, J. R. (1981). Cell death in embryogenesis. *In* "Cell Death in Biology and Pathology" (I. D. Bowen and R. A. Lockshin, eds.), pp. 35–78. Chapman & Hall, London.

Hoekstra, F. A., and Weges, R. (1986). Lack of control by early pistillate ethylene of the accelerated wilting of *Petunia hybrida* flowers. *Plant Physiol.* **80,** 403–408.

Holden, H. T., Lichter, W., and Sigel, M. M. (1973). Quantitative methods for measuring cell growth and death. In "Tissue Culture: Methods and Applications" (P. F. Kruse, Jr. and M. K. Patterson, Jr., eds.), pp. 408–412. Academic Press, New York.

Huang, A. H. C., Trelease, R. N., and Moore, T. S., Jr. (1983). "Plant Peroxisomes." Academic Press, New York.

Hudson, H. J. (1986). "Fungal Biology." Arnold, London.

Hulme, A. C., ed. (1971). "The Biochemistry of Fruits and Their Products," Vol. 2. Academic Press, London.

Hurkman, W. J. (1979). Ultrastructural changes of chloroplasts in attached and detached, aging primary wheat leaves. *Am. J. Bot.* **66**, 64–70.

Hurkman, W. J., and Kennedy, G. S. (1976). Ultrastructural changes of chloroplasts in aging tobacco leaves. *Proc. Indiana Acad. Sci.* **85**, 89–95.

Ingraham, J. L., Maaløe, O., and Neidhardt, F. C. (1983). "Growth of the Bacterial Cell." Sinauer, Sunderland, Massachusetts.

Inouye, D. W., and Taylor, O. R., Jr. (1980). Variation in generation time in *Frasera speciosa* (Gentianaceae), a long-lived perennial monocarp. *Oecologia* **47**, 171–174.

Iten, W. (1969). Zur Funktion hydrolytischer Enzyme bei der Autolyse von *Coprinus. Ber. Schweiz. Bot. Ges.* **79**, 175–198.

Jacobs, W. P. (1952). The role of auxin in differentiation of xylem around a wound. *Am. J. Bot.* **39**, 301–309.

Jacobs, W. P. (1959). What substance normally controls a given biological process? I. Formulation of some roles. *Dev. Biol.* **1**, 527–533.

Jacobs, W. P. (1979). "Plant Hormones and Plant Development." Cambridge Univ. Press, London and New York.

Janzen, D. H. (1976). Why bamboos wait so long to flower. *Annu. Rev. Ecol. Syst.* **7**, 347–391.

Jensen, W. A., and Fisher, D. B. (1969). Cotton embryogenesis: The tissues of the stigma and style and their relation to the pollen tube. *Planta* **84**, 97–121.

Johansen, D. A. (1950). "Plant Embryology." Chronica Botanica, Waltham, Massachusetts.

Jost, L. (1907). "Lectures in Plant Physiology." Clarendon Press, Oxford.

Juniper, B. E., Gilchrist, A. J., and Robins, A. J. (1977). Some features of secretory systems in plants. *Histochem. J.* **9**, 659–680.

Kahanak, G. M., Okatan, Y., Rupp, D. C., and Noodén, L. D. (1978). Hormonal and genetic alternation of monocarpic senescence in soybeans. *Plant Physiol.* **61**, Suppl., 26.

Kahl, G. (1982). Molecular biology of wound healing: the conditioning phenomenon. In "Molecular Biology of Plant Tumors" (G. Kahl and J. S. Schell, eds.), pp. 211–267. Academic Press, New York.

Kahl, G. (1983). Wound repair and tumor induction in higher plants. In "The New Frontiers in Plant Biochemistry" (T. Akazawa, T. Asahi, and H. Imasaki, eds.), pp. 193–216. Jpn. Sci. Soc., Tokyo.

Kaplan, D. R. (1983). The development of palm leaves. *Sci. Am.* **249**, 98–105.

Kenda, G., Thaler, I., and Weber, F. (1953). Schliesszellen-Chloroplaster vergilben nicht. *Protoplasma* **42**, 246–249.

Kende, H., and Baumgartner, B. (1974). Regulation of aging in flowers of *Ipomoea tricolor* by ethylene. *Planta* **116**, 279–289.

Kendig, F., and Hutton, R. (1979). "Life Spans, or How Long Things Last." Holt, New York.

Kerner von Marilaun, A. (1894). "The Natural History of Plants" (F. W. Oliver, transl.). Blackie, Glasgow.

Klebs, G. (1905). Über Variationen der Blüten. *Jahrb. Wiss. Bot.* **42**, 155–320.

Klebs, G. (1910). Alterations in the development and forms of plants as a result of environment. *Proc. R. Soc. London, Ser. B* **82**, 547–558.

Kozlowski, T. T. (1971). "Growth and Development of Trees." Academic Press, New York.

Kozlowski, T. T., ed. (1973). "Shedding of Plant Parts." Academic Press, New York.

Kozlowski, T. T. (1976). Water supply and leaf shedding. In "Water Deficits and Plant Growth" (T. T. Kozlowski, ed.), Vol. 4, pp. 191–231. Academic Press, New York.

Kozlowski, T. T. ed. (1984). "Flooding and Plant Growth." Academic Press, Orlando, Florida.

Krizek, D. T., McIlrath, W. J., and Vergara, B. S. (1966). Photoperiodic induction of senescence in *Xanthium* plants. *Science* 151, 95–96.

Krul, W. R. (1974). Nucleic acid and protein metabolism in senescing and regenerating soybean cotyledons. *Plant Physiol.* 54, 36–40.

Kumura, A., and Naniwa, I. (1965). Studies on dry matter production of soybean plant. I. Ontogenic changes in photosynthetic and respiratory capacity of soybean plant and its parts. *Proc. Crop Sci. Soc. Jpn.* 33, 467–471.

Lai, V., and Srivastava, L. M. (1976). Nuclear changes during differentiation of xylem vessel elements. *Cytobiologie* 12, 220–243.

Laidman, D. L. (1982). Control mechanisms in the mobilisation of stored nutrients in germinating cereals. In "The Physiology and Biochemistry of Seed Development, Dormancy and Germination" (A. A. Khan, ed.), pp. 371–405. Elsevier, Amsterdam.

Lamont, B. B. (1980). Tissue longevity of the aborescent monocotyledon *Kingia australis* (Xanthorrhoeaceae). *Am. J. Bot.* 67, 1262–1264.

Larson, D. A. (1965). Fine structural changes in the cytoplasm of germinating pollen. *Am. J. Bot.* 52, 139–154.

Lazan, H. B., Barlow, E. W. R., and Brady, C. J. (1983). The significance of vascular connection in regulating senescence of the detached flag leaf of wheat. *J. Exp. Bot.* 34, 726–736.

Leonard, E. R. (1962). Inter-relations of vegetative and reproductive growth with special reference to indeterminate plants. *Bot. Rev.* 28, 353–410.

Leonard, O. A. (1939). Translocation of carbohydrates in the sugar beet. *Plant Physiol.* 14, 55–74.

Leopold, A. C. (1961). Senescence in plant development. *Science* 134, 1727–1732.

Leopold, A. C. (1975). Aging, senescence and turnover in plants. *BioScience* 25, 659–662.

Leopold, A. C. (1980). Aging and senescence in plant development. In "Senescence in Plants" (K. V. Thimann, ed.), pp. 1.–12. CRC Press, Boca Raton, Florida.

Leopold, A. C., and Kawase, M. (1964). Benzyladenine effects on bean leaf growth and senescence. *Am. J. Bot.* 51, 294–298.

Leopold, A. C., and Noodén, L. D. (1984). Hormonal regulatory systems in plants. In "Encyclopedia of Plant Physiology, N.S. Vol. 10: Hormonal Regulation of Development II" (T. K. Scott, ed.), pp. 4–22. Springer-Verlag, Berlin and New York.

Levitt, J. (1980a). "Responses of Plants to Environmental Stresses. Vol. 1: Chilling, Freezing, and High Temperature Stresses." Academic Press, New York.

Levitt, J. (1980b). "Response of Plants to Environmental Stresses. Vol. 2: Water, Radiation, Salt, and Other Stresses." Academic Press, New York.

Lewington, R. J., Talbot, M., and Simon, E. W. (1967). The yellowing of attached and detached cucumber cotyledons. *J. Exp. Bot.* 18, 526–534.

Lewis, F. J., and Dowding, E. S. (1924). The anatomy of the buds of Coniferae. *Ann. Bot.* 38, 217–228.

Li, P. H., and Sakai, A. (1982). "Plant Cold Hardiness and Freezing Stress." Academic Press, Orlando, Florida.

Lindoo, S. J., and Noodén, L. D. (1977). Studies on the behavior of the senescence signal in Anoka soybeans. *Plant Physiol.* 59, 1136–1140.

Livne, A., and Vaadia, Y. (1972). Water deficits and hormone relations. In "Water Deficits and Plant Growth" (T. T. Kozlowski, ed.), Vol. 3, pp. 255–275. Academic Press, New York.

Lockshin, R. A. (1981). Cell death in metamorphosis. *In* "Cell Death in Biology and Pathology" (I. D. Bowen and R. A. Lockshin, eds.), pp. 79–121. Chapman & Hall, London.

Lockshin, R. A., and Zakeri-Milovanovic, Z. (1984). Nucleic acids in cell death. *In* "Cell Ageing and Cell Death" (I. Davies and D. C. Sigee, eds.), pp. 243–268. Cambridge Univ. Press, London and New York.

Lovell, P. H. (1977). Correlative influences in seedling growth. *In* "The Physiology of the Garden Pea" (J. F. Sutcliffe and J. S. Pate, eds.), pp. 265–290. Academic Press, London.

Lyons, R. E., and Widmer, R. E. (1983). Effects of gibberellic acid and naphthalene-acetic acid on petiole senescence and subtended peduncle growth of *Cyclamen persicum* Mill. *Ann. Bot.* **52**, 885–890.

Lyons, R. E., and Widmer, R. E. (1984). A gibberellin-auxin synergism associated with peduncle elongation and senescence in *Cyclamen persicum* Mill. 'Swan Lake'. *Bot. Gaz.* **145**, 170–175.

Lyttleton, J. W., and Ts'o, P. O. P. (1958). The localization of fraction I protein of green leaves in the chloroplasts. *Arch. Biochem. Biophys.* **73**, 120–126.

McGlasson, W. B., Wade, N. L., and Adato, I. (1978). Phytohormones and fruit ripening. *In* "Phytohormones and Related Compounds — A Comprehensive Treatise" (D. S. Letham, P. B. Goodwin, and T. J. V. Higgins, eds.), Vol. 2, pp. 447–493. Elsevier/North-Holland, Amsterdam (1978).

McPherson, D. C. (1939). Cortical air spaces in the roots of *Zea mays* L. *New Phytol.* **38**, 190–202.

Maheshwari, P. (1950). "An Introduction to the Embryology of Angiosperms." McGraw-Hill, New York.

Mandahar, C. L., and Garg, I. D. (1975). Effect of ear removal on sugars and chlorophylls of barely leaves. *Photosynthetica* **9**, 407–409.

Marschner, H. (1986). "Mineral Nutrition in Higher Plants." Academic Press, London.

Marty, F. (1978). Cytochemical studies on GERL, provacuoles, and vacuoles in root meristematic cells of Euphorbia. *Proc. Natl. Acad. Sci. USA* **75**, 852–856.

Marty, F., Branton, D., and Leigh, R. A. (1980). Plant vacuoles. *In* "The Biochemistry of Plants. Vol. 1: The Plant Cell" (N. E. Tolbert, ed.), pp. 625–658. Academic Press, New York.

Mason, T. G. (1922). Growth and abscission in sea island cotton. *Ann. Bot.* **36**, 454–484.

Matile, P. (1975). "The Lytic Compartment of Plant Cells." Springer-Verlag, Berlin and New York.

Matile, P., and Winkenbach, F. (1971). Function of lysosomes and lysosomal enzymes in senescing corolla of the morning glory *(Ipomoea purpurea). J. Exp. Bot.* **122**, 759–771.

Mayak, S., and Halevy, A. H. (1980). Flower senescence. *In* "Senescence in Plants" (K. V. Thimann, ed.), pp. 131–156. CRC Press, Boca Raton, Florida.

Medawar, P. B. (1957). "The Uniqueness of the Individual." Methuen, London.

Melville, R., and Wrigley, F. A. (1969). Fenestration in the leaves of *Monstera* and its bearing on the morphogenesis and colour patterns of leaves. *J. Linn. Soc. Bot.* **62**, 1–16.

Michael, G. (1936). Uber die Beziehungen zwischen Chlorophyll und Eiweissabbau im vergilbenden Laubblätt von *Tropaeolum. Z. Bot.* **29**, 385–425.

Millington, W. F., and Chaney, W. R. (1973). Shedding of shoots and branches. *In* "Shedding of Plant Parts" (T. T. Kozlowski, ed.), pp. 149–204. Academic Press, New York.

Mishra, S. D., and Gaur, B. K. (1972). Control of senescence in betel leaves by depetiolation. *Exp. Gerontol.* **7**, 31–35.

Mishra, S. D., and Gaur, B. K. (1977). Role of petiole in protein metabolism of senescing betel *(Piper betle* L.) leaves. *Plant Physiol.* **59**, 961–964.

Misra, G., and Biswal, U. C. (1973). Factors concerned in leaf senescence. I. Effects of age, chemicals, petiole and photoperiod on senescence in detached leaves of *Hibiscus Rosa-sinensis* L. *Bot. Gaz.* **134,** 5–11.

Mittelheuser, C. J., and Van Steveninck, R. F. M. (1971). The ultrastructure of wheat leaves I. Changes due to natural senescence and the effects of kinetin and ABA on detached leaves incubated in the dark. *Protoplasma* **73,** 239–252.

Mogensen, H. L. (1978). Pollen tube-synergid interactions in *Proboscidea louisianica* (Martineaceae). *Am. J. Bot.* **65,** 953–964.

Molisch, H. (1938). "The Longevity of Plants" (H. Fullington, transl.). Science Press, Lancaster, Pennsylvania.

Mondal, W. A., and Choudhuri, M. A. (1984). Sequential and non-sequential pattern of monocarpic senescence in two rice cultivars. *Physiol. Plant.* **61,** 287–292.

Moorby, J. (1977). Integration and regulation of translocation within the whole plant. *Symp. Soc. Exp. Biol.* **31,** 425–454.

Moore, K., and Lovell, P. (1970). Chlorophyll content and the pattern of yellowing in senescent leaves. *Ann. Bot.* **34,** 1097–1100.

Moore, R. (1984). A model for graft compatibility-incompatibility in higher plants. *Am. J. Bot.* **71,** 752–758.

Moore, R. (1986). Graft incompatibility between pear and quince: The influence of metabolites of *Cydonia oblonga* on suspension cultures of *Pyrus communis. Am. J. Bot.* **73,** 1–4.

Morriset, C. (1968). Observations ultrastructurales sur les espaces intracellulaires dans les meristemes radienlaires de germinations de tomate (*Lycopersicon esculentum* L. Solanée). *C. R. Hebd. Seances Acad. Sci., Ser. D* **267,** 845–848.

Mothes, K. (1959). Bermerkungen über isolierten Blättern. *Colloq. Ges. Physiol. Chem.* **10,** 72–81.

Mothes, K., and Baudisch, W. (1958). Untersuchungen über die Reversibilität der Ausbleichung grüner Blätter. *Flora* **146,** 521–531.

Müller, K., and Leopold, A. C. (1966). Correlative aging and transport of ^{32}p in corn leaves under the influence of kinetin. *Planta* **68,** 167–185.

Munkres, K. D. (1985). Aging of fungi. *Rev. Biol. Res. Aging* **2,** 29–43.

Murray, D. R., ed. (1984). "Seed Physiology." Academic Press, Orlando, Florida.

Nagl, W. (1976). Ultrastructure of lysis of embryo-suspensors. *Ber. Dtsch. Bot Ges.* **89,** 301–311.

Nagl, W. (1977). "Plastolysomes" — Plastids involved in the autolysis of the embryo-suspensor in *Phaseolus. Z. Pflanzenphysiol.* **85,** 45–51.

Naylor, A. W. (1972). Water deficits and nitrogen metabolism. *In* "Water Deficits and Plant Growth." (T. T. Kozlowski, ed.), Vol. 3, pp. 241–254. Academic Press, New York.

Neumann, P. M., and Stein, Z. (1986). Ion supply capacity of roots in relation to rejuvenation of primary leaves *in vivo. Physiol. Plant.* **67,** 97–101.

Neumann, P. M., Tucker, A. T., and Noodén, L. D. (1983). Characterization of leaf senescence and pod development in soybean explants. *Plant Physiol.* **72,** 182–185.

Newman, D. W., Rowell, B. W., and Byrd, K. (1973). Lipid transformations in greening and senescing leaf tissue. *Plant Physiol.* **51,** 229–233.

Nichols, R. (1977). A descriptive model of the senescence of the carnation (*Dianthus caryophyllus*) inflorescence. *Acta Hortic.* **71,** 227–232.

Noodén, L. D. (1980). Senescence in the whole plant. *In* "Senescence in Plants" (K. V. Thimann, ed.), pp. 219–258. CRC Press, Boca Raton, Florida.

Noodén, L. D. (1984). Integration of soybean pod development and monocarpic senescence. *Physiol. Plant.* **62,** 273–284.

Noodén, L. D. (1985). Regulation of soybean senescence. *In* "World Soybean Research Conf. III Proceedings" (R. Shibles, ed.), pp. 891–900. Westview Press, Boulder, Colorado.

Noodén, L. D., and Leopold, A. C. (1978). Phytohormones and the endogenous regulation of senescence and abscission. In "Phytohormones and Related Compounds: A Comprehensive Treatise" (D. S. Letham, P. B. Goodwin, and T. J. V. Higgins, eds.), Vol. 2, pp. 329–369. Elsevier/North-Holland, Amsterdam.

Noodén, L. D., and Lindoo, S. J. (1978). Monocarpic senescence. What's New Plant Physiol. 9, 25–28.

Noodén, L. D., and Thompson, J. W. (1985). Aging and senescence in plants. In "Handbook of the Biology of Aging" (C. E. Finch and E. L. Schneider, eds.), 2nd Ed., pp. 105–127. Van Nostrand-Reinhold, New York.

Nutman, P. S. (1939). Studies in vernalisation of cereals. VI. The anatomical and cytological evidence for the formation of growth-promoting substances in the developing grain of rye. Ann. Bot. 3, 731–757.

Okatan, Y., Kahanak, G. M., and Noodén, L. D. (1981). Characterization and kinetics of soybean maturation and monocarpic senescence. Physiol. Plant. 52, 330–338.

Paech, K. (1940). Ursache und Verlauf des Alterns bei Pflanzen. I. Z. Altersforsch. 2, 182–305.

Paech, K., and Eberhardt, F. (1956). Altern und Zelltod. In "Handbuch der Pflanzenphysiologie" (W. Ruhland, ed.), Vol. 2, pp. 908–936. Springer-Verlag, Berlin and New York.

Paleg, L. G., and Aspinall, D. (1981). "Physiology and Biochemistry of Drought Resistance in Plants." Academic Press, New York.

Pappelis, A. J., and Katsanos, R. A. (1969). Ear removal and cell death rate in corn Stalk Tissue. Phytopathology 59, 129–131.

Pearl, R. (1928). "The Rate of Living." Knopf, New York.

Pearl, R., and Miner, J. R. (1935). Experimental studies in the duration of life. XIV. The comparative mortality of certain lower organisms. Q. Rev. Biol. 10, 60–79.

Pech, J. C., and Romani, R. J. (1979). Senescence of pear Pyrus communis fruit cells cultured in a continuously renewed auxin-deprived medium. Plant Physiol. 63, 814–817.

Pegg, G. F. (1981). The role of nonspecific toxins and hormone changes in disease severity. In "Plant Disease Control" (R. C. Staples and G. H. Toenniessen, eds.), pp. 13–31. Wiley, New York.

Penning de Vries, F. W. T. (1975). The cost of maintenance processes in plant cells. Ann. Bot. 39, 77–92.

Peoples, M. B., Beilharz, V. C., Waters, S. P., Simpson, R. J., and Dalling, M. J. (1980). Nitrogen redistribution during grain growth in wheat (Triticum aestivum L.). II. Chloroplast senescence and the degradation of ribulose-1,5-bisphosphate carboxylase. Planta 149, 241–251.

Peterson, G. L. (1979). Review of the Folin phenol protein quantitation method of Lowry, Rosebrough, Farr and Randall. Anal. Biochem. 100, 201–220.

Peterson, L. W., Kleinkopf, G. E., and Huffaker, R. C. (1973). Evidence for lack of turnover of ribulose-1, 5-diphosphate carboxylase in barley leaves. Plant Physiol. 51, 1042–1045.

Petrie, A. H. K., Watson, R., and Ward, E. D. (1939). Physiological ontogeny in the tobacco plant, I. Aust. J. Exp. Biol. Med. Sci. 17, 93–122.

Postius, C., Klemme, B., and Jacobi, G. (1976). Dark starvation and plant metabolism. V. Comparative studies on the alteration of enzyme activities during dark starvation and senescence. Z. Pflanzenphysiol. 78, 122–132.

Priestly, D. A. (1986). "Seed Aging." Comstock, Ithaca, New York.

Proebsting, W. M., Davies, P. J., and Marx, G. A. (1977). Evidence for graft-transmissible substance which delays apical senescence in Pisum sativum L. Planta 135, 93–94.

Raafat, A., and Herwig, K. (1975). Some physiological aspects of retardation of leaf senescence by 6-benzylaminopurine or disbudding in intact plants. Agrochimica 19, 507–521.

Rattemeyer, M., Popp, F. A., and Nagl, W. (1981). Evidence of photon emission from DNA in living systems. Naturwissenschaften 68, 572–573.

Resende, F. (1964). Senescence induced by flowering. *Port. Acta Biol., Ser. A* **8**, 248–266.

Robbins, W. J. (1957). Physiological aspects of aging in plants. *Am. J. Bot.* **44**, 289–294.

Robinson, D. G. (1985). "Plant Membranes." Wiley, New York.

Sachs, J. (1882). "Text-book of Botany" (S. H. Vines, transl.). Clarendon Press, Oxford.

Sachs, T. (1966). Senescence in inhibited shoots of peas and apical dominance. *Ann. Bot.* **30**, 447–456.

Salin, M. L., and Bridges, S. M. (1981). Chemiluminescence in wounded root tissue. Evidence for peroxidase involvement. *Plant Physiol.* **67**, 43–46.

Sasaki, S., and Kozlowski, T. T. (1969). Utilization of seed reserves and currently produced photosynthesis by embryonic tissues of pine seedlings. *Ann. Bot.* **33**, 473–482.

Satler, S. O., and Thimann, K. V. (1983). Metabolism of oat leaves during senescence VII. The interaction of carbon dioxide and other atmospheric gases with light in controlling chlorophyll loss and senescence. *Plant Physiol.* **71**, 67–70.

Schaffer, W. M., and Schaffer, M. V. (1977). The adaptive significance of variations in reproductive habit in the Agavaceae. *In* "Evolutionary Ecology" (B. Stonehouse and C. Perrins, eds.), pp. 261–276. Univ. Park Press, Baltimore, Maryland.

Schneiter, A. A., and Miller, J. F. (1981). Description of sunflower growth stages. *Crop Sci.* **21**, 901–903.

Schulz, R., and Jensen, W. A. (1968). *Capsella* embryogenesis: the synergids before and after fertilization. *Am. J. Bot.* **55**, 541–552.

Schumacher, W. (1932). Über Eiweissumsetzungen in Blütenblattern. *Jahrb. Wiss. Bot.* **75**, 581–608.

Schumacher, W., and Matthael, H. (1955). Über den Zusammenhang zwischen Streckungswachstum und Eiweiss-synthese. *Planta* **45**, 213–216.

Scott, P. C., and Leopold, A. C. (1966). Abscission as a mobilization phenomenon. *Plant Physiol.* **41**, 826–830.

Sculthorpe, C. D. (1967). "The Biology of Aquatic Vascular Plants." Arnold, London.

Shaw, M., and Manocha, M. S. (1965). Fine structure in detached, senescing wheat leaves. *Can. J. Bot.* **43**, 747–755.

Shininger, T. L. (1979). The control of vascular development. *Annu. Rev. Plant Physiol.* **30**, 313–337.

Sifton, H. B. (1981). Lysigenous air spaces in the leaf of Labrador tea, *Ladum groenlandicum* Oeder. *New Phytol.* **39**, 75–79.

Simon, E. W. (1967). Types of leaf senescence. *Symp. Soc. Exp. Biol.* **21**, 215–230.

Simons, R. K. (1973). Anatomical changes in abscission of reproductive structures. *In* "Shedding of Plant Parts" (T. T. Kozlowski, ed.), pp. 383–434. Academic Press, New York.

Singh, B. N., and Lal, K. N. (1935). Investigations of the effect of age on assimilation of leaves. *Ann. Bot.* **49**, 291–307.

Sinnott, E. W., and Bloch, R. (1945). The cytoplasmic basis of intercellular patterns in vascular differentiation. *Am. J. Bot.* **32**, 151–156.

Smith, D. L. (1981). Cotyledons of the Leguminosae. *In* "Advances in Legume Systematics," Part 2 (R. M. Polhill and P. H. Ravin, eds.), pp. 927–940. Royal Botanic Gardens, Kew, England.

Soikkeli, S., and Karenlampi, L. (1984). Cellular and ultrastructure effects. *In* "Air Pollution and Plant Life" (M. Treshow, ed.), pp. 159–174. Wiley, Chichester, England.

Sparks, P. D., and Postlethwaite, S. N. (1967). Comparative morphogenesis of the dimorphic leaves of *Cyamopsis tetragonoloba*. *Am. J. Bot.* **54**, 281–285.

Sponsel, V. M. (1985). Gibberellins in *Pisum sativum* — their nature, distribution and involvement in growth and development of the plant. *Physiol. Plant.* **65**, 533–538.

Sprague, H. B., ed. (1964). "Hunger Signs in Crops," 3rd Ed. McKay, New York.

Stanley, R. G., and Kirby, E. G. (1973). Shedding of pollen and seeds. In "Shedding of Plant Parts" (T. T. Kozlowski, ed.), pp. 295–340. Academic Press, New York.

Staples, R. C., and Toenniessen, G. H., eds. (1981). "Plant Disease Control." Wiley, New York.

Stead, A. D. (1985). The relationship between pollination, ethylene production and flower senescence. In "Ethylene and Plant Development" (J. A. Roberts and G. A. Tucker, eds.), pp. 71–81. Butterworth, London.

Steinitz, B., Cohen, A., and Leshem, B. (1981). Factors controlling the retardation of chlorophyll degradation during senescence of detached statice *Limonium sinuatum* flower stalks. Z. *Pflanzenphysiol.* 100, 343–350.

Stephenson, A. G. (1981). Flower and fruit abortion: proximate causes and ultimate functions. *Annu. Rev. Ecol. Syst.* 12, 253–279.

Stewart, C. M. (1966). Excretion and heartwood formation in living trees. *Science* 153, 1068–1074.

Sutcliffe, J. F. (1976). Regulation in the whole plant. *Encycl. Plant Physiol.* 11B, 394–417.

Sutton, W. D. (1983). Nodule development and senescence. In "Nitrogen Fixation. Vol. 3: Legumes" (W. J. Broughton, ed.), pp. 114–212. Oxford Univ. Press (Clarendon), London and New York.

Sweeney, B. N. (1969). "Rhythmic Phenomena in Plants." Academic Press, New York.

Sweet, G. B. (1973). Shedding of reproductive structures in forest trees. In "Shedding of Plant Parts" (T. T. Kozlowski, ed.), pp. 341–382. Academic Press, New York.

Taylor, O. C. (1984). Organismal responses of higher plants to atmospheric pollutants: Photochemical and other. In "Air Pollution and Plant Life" (M. Treshow, ed.), pp. 215–238. Wiley, Chichester, England.

Telek, L., and Graham, H. D. (1983). "Leaf Protein Concentrates." Avi, Westport, Connecticut.

Tevini, M., and Steinmuller, D. (1985). Composition and function of plastoglobuli. 1. Lipid composition of leaves and plastoglobuli during beech leaf senescence. *Planta* 163, 91–96.

Thimann, K. V., ed. (1980a). "Senescence in Plants." CRC Press, Boca Raton, Florida.

Thimann, K. V. (1980b). The senescence of leaves. In "Senescence in Plants" (K. V. Thimann, ed.), pp. 85–115. CRC Press, Boca Raton, Florida.

Thimann, K. V., Satler, S. O., and Trippi V. (1982). Further extension of the syndrome of leaf senescence. In "Plant Growth Substances 1982" (P. F. Wareing, ed.), pp. 539–548. Academic Press, London.

Thomas, H., and Stoddart, J. L. (1975). Separation of chlorophyll degradation from other senescence processes in leaves of a mutant genotype of meadow fescue (*Festuca pratensis* L.). *Plant Physiol.* 56, 438–441.

Thomas, H., and Stoddart, J. L. (1980). Leaf senescence. *Annu. Rev. Plant Physiol.* 31, 83–111.

Thompson, J. E. (1984). Physical changes in the membranes of senescing and environmentally stressed plant tissues. In "Physiology of Membrane Fluidity" (M. Shinitzky, ed.), Vol. 2, pp. 85–108. CRC Press, Boca Raton, Florida.

Tilton, V. R. (1981). Ovule development in *Ornithogalum caudatum* (Liliaceae) with a review of selected papers on Angiosperm reproduction. IV. Egg apparatus structure and function. *New Phytol.* 88, 505–531.

Tilton, V. R., and Lersten, N. R. (1981). Ovule development in *Ornithogalum caudatum* (Liliaceae) with a review of selected papers on angiosperm reproduction. III. Nucellus and megagametophyte. *New Phytol.* 88, 477–504.

Treshow, M. (1970). "Environment and Plant Response." McGraw-Hill, New York.

Turner, N. C., and Kramer, D. J., eds. (1980). "Adaptation of Plants to Water and High Temperature." Wiley (Interscience), New York.

Van den Broek, H. W. J., Noodén, L. D., Sevall, J. S., and Bonner, J. (1973). Isolation, purification, and fractionation of nonhistone chromosomal proteins. *Biochemistry* 12, 229–236.

Van Onckelen, H. A., Horemans, S., and deGreef, J. A. (1981). Functional aspects of abscisic acid metabolism in cotyledons of *Phaseolus vulgaris* L. seedlings. *Plant Cell Physiol.* **22**, 507–515.

Van Steveninck, R. F. M. (1957). Factors affecting the abscission of reproductive organs in yellow lupin (*Lupinus luteus* L.) I. The effect of different patterns of flower removal. *J. Exp. Bot.* **8**, 373–381.

Van Steveninck, R. F. M. (1975). The "washing" or "aging" phenomenon in plant tissues storage tissue slices. *Annu. Rev. Plant Physiol.* **26**, 237–258.

Veillon, J. M. (1971). Une Apocynacée monocarpique de Nouvelle-Calédonie *Cerberiopsis candelabrum* Vieill. *Adansonia* **11**, 625–639.

Villiers, T. A. (1967). Cytolysomes in long-dormant plant embryo cells. *Nature (London)* **214**, 1356–1357.

Villiers, T. A. (1971). Lysomal activities of the vacuole in damaged and recovering plant cells. *Nature (London), New Biol.* **233**, 57–58.

Villiers, T. A. (1972). Cytological studies in dormancy II. Pathological ageing changes during prolonged dormancy and recovery upon dormancy release. *New Phytol.* **71**, 145–152.

Waisel, Y. (1972). "Biology of Halophytes." Academic Press, London.

Wang, T. L., and Woolhouse, H. W. (1982). Hormonal aspects of senescence in plant development. *In* "Growth Regulators in Plant Senescence" (M. B. Jackson, B. Grout, and I. A. Mackenzie, eds.), Monogr. No. 8, pp. 5–25. Br. Plant Growth Regul. Group, Wantage, England.

Wangermann, E. (1965). Longevity and aging in plants and plant organs. *In* "Handbuch der Pflanzenphysiologie," Vol. 15/2, pp. 1037–1057. Springer-Verlag, Berlin and New York.

Wareing, P. F. (1977). Growth substances and integration in the whole plant. *Symp. Soc. Exp. Biol.* **31**, 337–365.

Wareing, P. F., and Roberts, D. M. (1956). Photoperiodic control of cambial activity in *Robinia pseudacacia* L. *New Phytol.* **55**, 356–367.

Weber, F. (1919). Der natürliche Tod der Pflanzen. *Naturwiss. Wochenschr.* **18**, 447–457.

Weber, J. A., and Noodén, L. D. (1974). Turion formation and germination in *Myriophyllum verticillatum:* Phenology and its interpretation. *Mich. Bot.* **13**, 151–158.

Williams, R. F. (1955). Redistribution of mineral elements during development. *Annu. Rev. Plant Physiol.* **6**, 25–42.

Wills, R. H. H., Lee, T. H., Graham, D., McGlasson, W. B., and Hall, E. G. (1981). "Postharvest." Avi, Westport, Connecticut.

Willson, M. F. (1983). "Plant Reproductive Ecology." Wiley, New York.

Winkenbach, F., and Matile, P. (1970). Evidence for *de novo* synthesis of an invertase inhibitor protein in senescing petals of *Ipomoea. Z. Pflanzenphysiol.* **63**, 292–295.

Wittenbach, V. A., Lin, W., and Hebert, R. R. (1982). Vacuolar localization of proteases and degradation of chloroplasts in mesophyll protoplasts from senescing primary wheat leaves. *Plant Physiol.* **69**, 98–102.

Wood, L. J., Murray, B. J., Okatan, Y., and Noodén, L. D. (1986). Effect of petiole phloem disruption on starch and mineral distribution in senescing soybean leaves. *Am. J. Bot.* **73**, 1377–1383.

Woodstock, L. W. (1973). Physiological and biochemical tests for seed vigor. *Seed Sci. Technol.* **1**, 127–157.

Woolhouse, H. W. (1982). Hormonal control of senescence allied to reproduction in plants. *In* "Strategies of Plant Reproduction" (W. J. Mundt, ed.), BARC Symp. No. 6, pp. 201–233. Littlefield-Adams, Totowa, New Jersey.

Woolhouse, H. W. (1984). Senescence in plant cells. *In* "Cell Ageing and Cell Death" (I. Davies and D. C. Sigee, eds.), pp. 123–153. Cambridge Univ. Press, London and New York.

Woolhouse, H. W. (1987). Regulation of senescence in the chloroplast. *In* "Plant Senescence: Its Biochemistry and Physiology" (W. W. Thomson, E. A. Nothnagel, and R. C. Huffaker, eds.), pp. 132–145. Am. Soc. Plant Physiol., Rockville, Maryland.

Wright, S. T. C. (1978). Phytohormones and stress phenomena. *In* "Phytohormones and Related Compounds" (D. S. Letham, P. B. Goodwin, and T. J. V. Higgins, eds.), Vol. 2, pp. 495–536. North-Holland/Elsevier, Amsterdam.

Wyllie, A. H. (1981). Cell death: a new classification separating apoptosis from necrosis. *In* "Cell Death in Biology and Pathology" (I. D. Bowen and R. A. Lockshin, eds.), pp. 9–34. Chapman & Hall, London.

Young, S. L., Huang, R. C., Vanecko, S., Marks, J. D., and Varner, J. E. (1960). Conditions affecting enzyme synthesis in cotyledons of germinating seeds. *Plant Physiol.* 35, 288–292.

Young, T. P. (1984). The comparative demography of semelparous *Lobelia telekii* and iteroparous *Lobelia keniensis* on Mount Kenya. *J. Ecol.* 72, 637–650.

Zeiger, E., and Schwartz, A. (1982). Longevity of guard cell chloroplasts in falling leaves: Implication for stomatal function and cellular aging. *Science* 218, 680–682.

The Molecular Basis for Membrane Deterioration during Senescence

J. E. Thompson
Department of Horticultural Science
University of Guelph
Guelph, Ontario, Canada

SENESCENCE AND AGING IN PLANTS

I. INTRODUCTION

Cellular membranes are selective, dynamic barriers that play an essential role in regulating biochemical and physiological events. During senescence, there is a progressive loss of membrane integrity. This is perhaps most clearly evident from ultrastructural studies showing progressive deteriorative changes in organelles and membranes, and from permeability studies indicating increased leakage of solutes. However, there is also increasing evidence for subtle changes in the molecular organization of senescing membranes that result in an orderly and progressive loss of function and structural integrity.

Senescence is an active process initiated by some combination of internal and environmental triggers, and membrane deterioration is an early and fundamental feature of this process. For example, in senescing carnation flowers, changes in permeability reflecting membrane deterioration are initiated before the climacteric rise in ethylene production (Eze *et al.*, 1986). It is also becoming clear that the molecular mechanisms underlying senescence are different for the various types of membranes in the cell. In particular, membranes such as the plasma membrane, endoplasmic reticulum, and vacuolar membranes, which collectively comprise a microsomal fraction, appear to senesce by a different mechanism than do the highly specialized energy-transducing thylakoid membranes of the chloroplast (McRae and Thompson, 1985).

The objective in this review is to formulate a conceptual framework for membrane deterioration that is consistent with experimental data and that delineates the sequence of molecular events that culminate in loss of membrane integrity. The presentation of material is organized around apparent differences in this sequence between microsomal and plasma membranes, which are representative of the more typical lipoprotein membranes found in cells and the more highly specialized energy-transducing membranes such as those found in the chloroplast.

II. SENESCENCE OF MICROSOMAL AND PLASMA MEMBRANES

As senescence progresses, the various types of membranes in cells lose those specialized properties upon which procedures for their isolation are often based. This means that isolation of, for example, purified plasma membrane in various stages of senescence-related deterioration is difficult, because the isolation procedures are designed to exclude membranes that have an altered buoyant density or an altered surface charge (Yoshida *et al.*,

1983; Gruber *et al.*, 1984). In addition, senescing plasma membranes lose their specialized functional properties, in particular, marker enzyme characteristics, which are usually the basis for assessing the purity of the isolated membrane preparation (Yoshida *et al.*, 1983; Gruber *et al.*, 1984). Notwithstanding these difficulties, some insights into membrane senescence have been gleaned from studies using partially purified plasma membrane (Lees and Thompson, 1980; Borochov *et al.*, 1982), and this will become easier and more feasible as improved techniques for isolating purified plasmalemma become available.

The problem of isolating purified types of membrane in various stages of deterioration can, to some extent, be circumvented by working with isolated microsomal membranes. A microsomal fraction is heterogeneous, comprising small vesicles of membrane derived primarily from the plasma membrane, endoplasmic reticulum, and tonoplast. The advantage of working with a microsomal fraction is that membranes in various stages of deterioration can be isolated. The disadvantage is that senescence-related changes in membrane properties discerned from studies with microsomes cannot be ascribed to a particular type of membrane. However, this difficulty can be overcome by further fractionating microsomes on continuous gradients and comparing the distributions throughout the gradient of the particular property of interest and of enzymes known to serve as markers for the various types of membranes in a microsomal fraction. For example, it is in this manner that the ability of inositol triphosphate (IP_3) to release Ca^{2+} from microsomal membranes has been attributed to an association of IP_3 with endoplasmic reticulum membranes (O'Rourke *et al.*, 1985).

A. Increased Production of Free Radicals

Various studies demonstrating that fruit ripening and the vase life of flowers can be modulated by radical scavengers (Baker *et al.*, 1977, 1978; Wang and Baker, 1979) suggest that free radicals are involved in senescence. Membranes could be expected to be highly prone to free radical attack inasmuch as unsaturated fatty acids are major components of most membrane lipid bilayers. The consequences of free radical attack on membranes are numerous and include the induction of lipid peroxidation (Kellogg and Fridovich, 1975), lysis (Goldstein and Weissmann, 1977), and fatty acid deesterification (Niehaus, 1978).

Direct electron spin resonance measurements of frozen tissue have provided evidence for increasing levels of free radicals in pea foliage with advancing senescence (Leshem *et al.*, 1981). However, the free radicals being formed were not identified. More recently, a combination of spin-trapping techniques and the use of specific detectors of free radicals has provided additional evidence for increased production of free radicals during senescence and has allowed identification of the radical species being formed.

Of particular interest is the finding that microsomal membranes from the petals of senescing carnation flowers and from senescing bean cotyledons produce increased levels of superoxide radical (O_2^-) with advancing senescence (Mayak et al., 1983; Lynch and Thompson, 1984). This has been documented by using 1,2-dihydroxybenzene-3,5-disulfonic acid (Tiron), which reacts with O_2^- to form the Tiron semiquinone, a more stable free radical species that is detectable by electron spin resonance (ESR). The amplitude of the Tiron ESR spectrum reflects the steady-state level of O_2^-, and through experiments in which the initial rate of Tiron semiquinone formation is monitored, it can be established that changes in the steady-state levels of superoxide with age reflect increased production of the free radical (McRae and Thompson, 1983). In addition, the Tiron ESR spectrum reflecting O_2^- levels is sensitive to superoxide dismutase (McRae et al., 1982; Mayak et al., 1983), an enzyme that specifically scavenges the superoxide radical, thus confirming that the radical species being detected by Tiron is O_2^-. Levels of O_2^- produced by microsomal membranes rise during senescence by > 2-fold for membranes from the petals of senescing carnation flowers (Mayak et al., 1983) and by $\cong 10$-fold for smooth microsomal membranes isolated from senescing bean cotyledons (Lynch and Thompson, 1984). Additionally, this increased production of O_2^- during natural aging can be simulated by in vitro aging of isolated microsomal membranes from young tissue in buffer (Mayak et al., 1983).

The formation of O_2^- by senescing microsomal membranes has been attributed to a membrane-associated lipoxygenase. This contention is supported by the observations that there is a strong temporal correlation during senescence between changes in microsomal lipoxygenase activity and changes in O_2^- production by the membranes (Fig. 2.1), that the formation of O_2^- is sensitive to changes in the availability of substrate for lipoxygenase, and that O_2^- formation and lipoxygenase activity are affected in a parallel fashion by specific inhibitors of lipoxygenase (Lynch and Thompson, 1984). Thus it would appear that O_2^- is formed as an intermediate during the conversion of polyunsaturated fatty acids to their conjugated hydroperoxydiene derivatives.

Baker et al. (1985) have reported that specific inhibitors of lipoxygenase significantly delay the senescence of cut carnation flowers. There are both cytosolic and membranous forms of lipoxygenase in senescing tissue (Lynch and Thompson, 1984; Lynch et al., 1985), and with advancing age more of the enzyme becomes associated with membranes. In this sense, lipoxygenase can be classified as an ambiquitous enzyme (Hopewell et al., 1985),

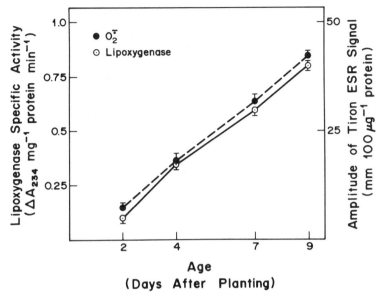

Fig. 2.1. Parallel changes in lipoxygenase activity and superoxide (O_2^-) production for microsomal membranes from senescing bean *(Phaseolus vulgaris)* cotyledons. [From Lynch and Thompson (1984).]

although it has yet to be demonstrated that the membranous and cytosolic activities are attributable to the same gene product. In the event they are, it will be of importance to determine what factors affect partitioning of the enzyme between the cytosolic and membranous compartments in senescing tissue.

B. Changes in the Molecular Organization of Lipid Bilayers

1. Bulk Lipid Fluidity

It is now well documented for a variety of senescing tissues, including leaves, cotyledons, flowers, and fruit, that the plasma membrane and microsomal membranes sustain a decrease in bulk lipid fluidity with advancing age. The evidence for this has come mainly from experiments in which changes in lipid fluidity have been inferred from measurements of the rotational motion of lipid-soluble paramagnetic and fluorescent probes partitioned into protoplasts, isolated membranes or liposomes prepared from the total lipid extracts of membranes (Borochov *et al.*, 1976, 1978; McKersie *et al.*, 1978; Thompson *et al.*, 1982; Legge *et al.*, 1982b; Ben-Arie *et al.*, 1982; Paliyath *et al.*, 1984; Fobel *et al.*, 1987). In senescing tissues that show a climacteric-like rise in ethylene production, the decrease in membrane fluidity occurs abruptly and coincident with or just prior to the rise in ethylene production (Thompson *et al.,* 1982). The functions of membrane proteins are known to be sensitive to lipid fluidity (Quinn and Williams, 1978), and thus a change in bulk lipid fluidity of the magnitude sustained by plasma and microsomal membranes during senescence is likely to have a deleterious impact on the functions of membrane-associated enzymes and receptors.

Of particular interest is the finding that during senescence there is a strong temporal correlation between changes in bulk lipid fluidity of microsomal membranes and changes in O_2^- production (Fig. 2.2). These observations indicate that there is a relationship during senescence between free radical production and membrane rigidification. This contention is further supported by the finding that during *in vitro* aging of microsomal membranes there is a decrease in bulk lipid fluidity that can be correlated with the enzymatic production of O_2^- by the membranes (Mayak *et al.,* 1983). Heat denaturation of the membranes or addition of *n*-propyl gallate, a nonspe-

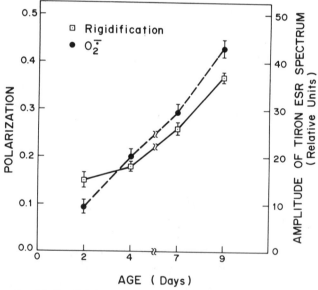

Fig. 2.2. Parallel changes in bulk lipid fluidity (rigidification) and superoxide (O_2^-) production for microsomal membranes from senescing bean *(Phaseolus vulgaris)* cotyledons. [Fluidity was measured as described by Thompson *et al.* (1982). The data for O_2^- production are from Lynch and Thompson (1984).]

cific scavenger of free radicals, prevents the formation of O_2^- as well as the change in membrane fluidity (Mayak *et al.*, 1983). Moreover, the addition of xanthine/xanthine oxidase, which generate O_2^-, accentuates the decrease in membrane fluidity (Mayak *et al.*, 1983). Thus it is apparent that O_2^- or highly reactive derivatives of O_2^- induce membrane rigidification.

2. Lipid Composition and Peroxidation

By far the most conspicuous change in the lipid composition of senescing plasma and microsomal membranes is a dramatic decline in membrane phospholipid, which becomes manifest as an increased membrane sterol:phospholipid ratio. This has been demonstrated for senescing flowers of *Ipomoea* (Beutelmann and Kende, 1977), rose flowers (Borochov *et al.*, 1978), bean cotyledons (McKersie *et al.*, 1978), bean leaves (Chia *et al.*, 1981), and carnation flowers (Thompson *et al.*, 1982). These observations imply a role for lipases in membrane deterioration. Measurements of phospholipase activity during the course of senescence in *Tradescantia* suggest that there is no increase in the activity of this group of enzymes (Suttle and Kende, 1980), but increased phospholipase activity has been reported for senescing rose petals (Borochov *et al.*, 1982). Of perhaps greater significance, though, is the likelihood that the susceptibility of the bilayer to attack by lipases increases with advancing senescence, for this would result in enhanced lipase activity without the need for synthesis of additional new enzyme. Perturbed phospholipid bilayers are known to be a more effective substrate for phospholipases (Goormaghtigh *et al.*, 1981), and there is increasing evidence that with advancing senescence the lipid bilayers of plasma and microsomal membranes become progressively perturbed and destabilized (see Section II,C). Thus as the membrane senesces, it becomes more prone to attack by lipases, such that deesterification can be envisaged as occurring in an essentially autocatalytic fashion. There is also evidence that O_2^- facilitates chemical deesterification of fatty acids from phospholipids (Niehaus, 1978), and thus enhanced production of this radical species through membrane-associated lipoxygenase with advancing senescence may also contribute to phospholipid breakdown.

The rise in sterol:phospholipid ratio of senescing microsomal and plasma membranes is undoubtedly one of the major factors contributing to the rise in bulk lipid microviscosity, for enhanced levels of sterols relative to phospholipid are known to reduce bilayer fluidity (Shinitzky, 1984). It is also conceivable that membranous lipoxygenase contributes to the decrease in bulk lipid fluidity by causing a selective depletion of unsaturated fatty acids from the membrane and an ensuing increase in the saturated:unsaturated fatty acid ratio. For some senescing membranes, there is very little change in the saturated:unsaturated fatty acid ratio (McKersie *et al.*, 1978), but for others, including microsomal membranes from senescing carnation flowers, there is a significant decline in the level of unsaturation that can be attributed to membranous lipoxygenase (Fobel, 1986).

There are several lines of evidence indicating that free radical-induced lipid peroxidation contributes to deterioration during senescence. Indeed, this is to be expected in light of the finding that senescing membranes contain lipoxygenase (Lynch and Thompson, 1984; Lynch et al., 1985). Increased levels of H_2O_2 and lipid hydroperoxides have been measured in ripening fruit, and inhibition of H_2O_2 formation has been shown to delay fruit ripening (Frenkel, 1978). Fluorescent products of lipid peroxidation have been reported in pear and banana pulp, and the levels of these pigments appear to increase with natural or ethylene-induced ripening (Maguire and Haard, 1975). Senescing leaves also accumulate fluorescent pigments (Wilhelm and Wilhelnova, 1981), and Dhindsa et al. (1981) have reported a correlation between lipid peroxidation and increased membrane permeability in senescing leaf tissue.

Recent data have indicated that fluorescent products of lipid peroxidation accumulate in senescing microsomal membranes (Fig. 2.3). The fluorescence emission and excitation maxima of these fluorescent products are very similar to those of the lipofucsins known to accumulate in certain animal tissues during aging and after induction of lipid peroxidation reactions (Tappel, 1975). There is good evidence that these fluorescent products are a family of compounds with a characteristic Schiff base structure ($-N=C-C=C-N$) that is formed by the reaction of peroxidized lipids with compounds containing free amino groups (Tappel, 1975). Hydroperoxides also accumulate in senescing microsomal membranes, particularly during the early stages of senescence (Lynch et al., 1985). This accumulation of peroxidized lipids can be expected to contribute to destabilization of the bilayer in senescing membranes and is consistent with the finding that lipoxygenase is associated with senescing membranes. It is also of interest that lipoxygenase catalyzes the first step in the conversion of linolenic acid to jasmonic acid (Vick and Zimmerman, 1983), a compound that actively promotes senescence (Ueda and Kato, 1980).

In senescing cotyledons of *Phaseolus vulgaris*, levels of glutathione and superoxide dismutase activity decline on a fresh weight basis as the cotyledons age, rendering the tissue more susceptible to oxidative damage (Pauls and Thompson, 1984). Indeed, apart from an increase in peroxidase, which would scavenge H_2O_2 only if appropriate cosubstrates were available, the defense mechanisms for coping with activated oxygen species (O_2^-, H_2O_2, OH·) are less effective in older cotyledon tissue (Pauls and Thompson, 1984). In some tissues, there is also an increase in lipoxygenase activity with advancing senescence (Grossman and Leshem, 1978; Leshem et al., 1981;

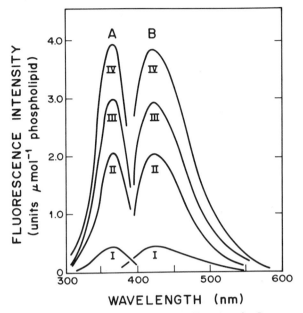

Fig. 2.3. Excitation (A) and emission (B) spectra for fluorescent peroxidation pigments in microsomal membranes from senescing bean *(Phaseolus vulgaris)* cotyledons. I, II, III, and IV identify spectra for membranes from 2-day-old, 4-day-old, 7-day-old, and 9-day-old cotyledon tissue, respectively. [From Pauls and Thompson (1984).]

Pauls and Thompson, 1984), an observation that is consistent with a role for reactive oxygen species and lipid peroxidation in senescence.

In other tissues, however, changes during senescence in activities of enzymes that could be expected to produce peroxides and malondialdehyde seem at first glance to be inconsistent with the view that oxygen-free radicals are involved in senescence. Indeed, in soybean cotyledons and detached wheat and rye leaves, total lipoxygenase activity declines with advancing senescence (Kar and Feierabend, 1984; Peterman and Siedow, 1985). Similarly, whereas microsomal lipoxygenase activity in bean *(Phaseolus vulgaris)* cotyledons rises progressively with advancing senescence (Lynch and Thompson, 1984), microsomal lipoxygenase activity in senescing carnation petals does not increase until the later stages of senescence (Lynch *et al.,* 1985). There is, however, an accumulation of lipid hydroperoxides in carnation microsomal membranes during the early stages of senescence (Lynch *et al.,* 1985). This may well be an important observation, for it suggests that it is more the availability of substrate for the enzyme than changes in the actual level of activity in the membranes or in the tissue that determines when peroxidative reactions will be initiated. Thus lipoxygenase in the membrane or in the cytosol will remain essentially latent until substrate in the form of free fatty acid is released. In addition, since there is evidence for both cytosolic and membranous forms of lipoxygenase in senescing tissue (Lynch and Thompson, 1984), it is conceivable that the degree of partitioning of the enzyme between the cytosol and membranous compartments is an important factor in initiating peroxidative damage, particularly if the fatty acid substrates for the enzyme are of membrane origin. In any case, it can be argued that a role for lipoxygenase in senescence, whereby it initiates the accumulation of peroxidized lipids in membranes and thus contributes to ensuing membrane dysfunction, need not be predicated upon measurable increases in total activity of the enzyme with advancing age.

3. Phase Changes

Other experiments, in which membranes isolated from senescing plant tissue have been examined by wide-angle X-ray diffraction, have provided evidence for major changes in membrane lipid phase properties with advancing senescence. Specifically, increasing proportions of gel phase lipid appear in the membrane bilayers as senescence intensifies. This has been demonstrated for microsomal membranes from senescing cotyledons (McKersie et al., 1976; McKersie and Thompson, 1977, 1979), senescing rose flowers (Legge et al., 1982b), and senescing pea foliage (Leshem et al., 1984), and for partially purified plasma membrane from senescing cotyledons (Lees and Thompson, 1980). Diffraction patterns recorded at room temperature from young membrane feature a broad diffuse X-ray reflection centered at a Bragg spacing of 4.6 Å (Fig. 2.4A) that derives from the fatty acid side chains of the phospholipids and indicates that the lipid is exclusively in the liquid–crystalline phase. By comparison, in diffraction patterns recorded at room temperature for senescent membranes, two sharp reflections, in addition to the broad diffuse reflection, can be seen, one which is quite intense at a Bragg spacing of 4.2 Å and another fainter reflection at a Bragg spacing of 3.75 Å (Fig. 2.4B). These sharp reflections derive from lipid in the gel phase and become more intense as senescence progresses and the proportion of gel phase lipid increases. Thus senescent membranes contain a mixture of liquid–crystalline and gel phase lipid domains, and these coexisting domains render the membrane leaky and contribute to the loss of intracellular compartmentation that is a characteristic feature of senescence (Barber and Thompson, 1980).

The actual formation of gel phase lipid in membranes during senescence is perhaps more clearly apparent from measurements of the lipid phase

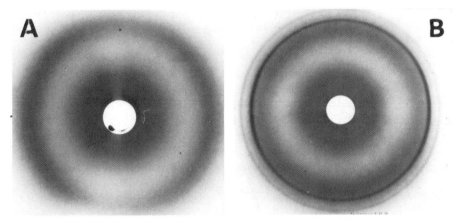

Fig. 2.4. Wide-angle, X-ray diffraction patterns recorded at room temperature for smooth microsomal membranes isolated from senescing bean *(Phaseolus vulgaris)* cotyledons. (A) Young cotyledons. (B) Senescent cotyledons. The diffuse outermost X-ray reflection in A centered at a Bragg spacing of 4.6 Å derives from lipid in the liquid-crystalline phase. The sharp reflections in B at Bragg spacings of 4.2 and 3.75 Å derive from lipid in the gel phase. [From McKersie *et al.* (1976).]

transition temperature. The transition temperature is defined operationally as the highest temperature at which gel phase lipid can be detected, and it is clear from Fig. 2.5 that the transition temperature rises progressively with advancing senescence. This has been demonstrated for microsomal membranes and plasma membrane from a variety of tissues (McKersie and Thompson, 1977, 1979; Lees and Thompson, 1980; Legge *et al.*, 1982b) and reflects the presence of higher melting lipids in the gel phase domains as senescence progresses.

It is to be noted that the changes during senescence in bulk lipid fluidity of microsomal and plasma membranes detectable by fluorescence depolarization and electron spin resonance after labeling the membranes with fluorescent or paramagnetic probes is not attributable to the presence of gel phase lipid. This is apparent, for example, from the finding that Arrhenius plots of the motion parameter, τ_c (rotational correlation time), which is measured by electron spin resonance and is related to lipid fluidity, feature no discontinuities or changes in slope that could be construed as reflecting liquid–crystalline to gel phase transitions (McKersie *et al.*, 1978; Legge *et al.*, 1982b). Yet, corresponding X-ray diffraction data clearly indicate that there are liquid–crystalline to gel phase transitions in these membranes at temperatures within the range examined by electron spin resonance (McKersie *et al.*, 1978; Legge *et al.*, 1982b). One possible interpretation of these observations is that the particular spin labels used in these studies partitioned

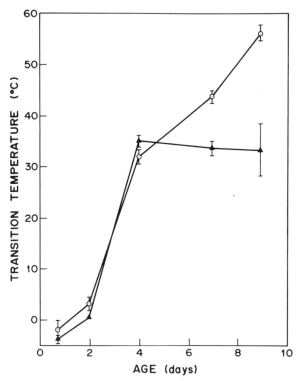

Fig. 2.5. Changes during senescence in the lipid phase transition temperature for smooth microsomes (O) and rough microsomes (▲) from cotyledons of bean *(Phaseolus vulgaris).* [From McKersie and Thompson (1977).]

exclusively into liquid–crystalline lipid domains and did not probe lipid in the gel phase domains. If this were so, the decline in bulk lipid fluidity during senescence detectable by electron spin resonance (or fluorescence depolarization) would pertain exclusively to residual liquid–crystalline lipid domains and would be independent of the presence of gel phase lipid. However, this interpretation must be tempered in light of a recent report that some spin labels partition preferentially into gel phase lipid (Raison and Orr, 1986).

Indirect evidence for the formation of gel phase lipid in senescing membranes has also been obtained by freeze-fracture electron microscopy of senescing cowpea cotyledons (Platt-Aloia and Thomson, 1985). This technique has an advantage over X-ray diffraction of microsomal membranes in that the membranes sustaining the lateral phase separation of lipids can be identified. In young tissue, the membranes featured evenly dispersed intramembranous particles. However, once senescence had begun, small areas or domains could be discerned in the plasmalemma that were free of intramembranous particles and corresponded to regions of gel phase lipid from which protein had been displaced into adjacent liquid – crystalline regions. These particle-free areas increased in both size and number as senescence progressed.

The reactive molecular species responsible for the lateral phase separation of lipids in senescing microsomal membranes have been identified, in part, by examining the phase properties of liposomes prepared from total lipid extracts of the membranes and from purified phospholipid (McKersie and Thompson, 1979; Barber and Thompson, 1983; Thompson *et al.*, 1983). Changes in transition temperature as measured by X-ray diffraction have been reported for smooth microsomes from senescing bean cotyledons, for liposomes prepared from the total lipid extracts of these membranes, and for liposomes prepared from purified phospholipid (McKersie and Thompson, 1979). The transition temperature profiles for the membranes and the total lipid extracts are closely similar, indicating that the membrane proteins have little effect on the phase properties of the lipid. However, the transition temperature for purified phospholipid does not change substantively with advancing senescence, indicating that components of the neutral lipid fraction are responsible for the gel phase domains in senescing membranes. This, in fact, was confirmed by experiments in which neutral lipids isolated from senescent microsomal membranes from bean cotyledons were reconstituted into liposomes of pure phospholipid (McKersie and Thompson, 1979; Barber and Thompson, 1983). Moreover, when the components of this neutral lipid fraction from senescent membranes were separated by Iatroscan chromatography (Barber and Thompson, 1983; Thompson *et al.*, 1983) or thin-layer chromatography (Barber, 1984), and the separated components reconstituted into liposomes of pure phospholipid, two of the separated subfractions proved able to induce the formation of gel phase lipid (Barber, 1984). One of these subfractions cochromatographs with alkanes and the other with long-chain alcohols (Barber, 1984). However, capillary gas – liquid chromatography of the separated subfractions has revealed that each comprises a multitude of distinguishable components (Barber, 1984), and thus the precise identity of the reactive gel phase-forming molecular species remains unknown.

Inasmuch as neutral lipids are the causative agents for the formation of gel phase lipid, there are two additional questions that have to be answered. First, is the neutral lipid simply a cytosolic contaminant entrapped within the vesicles of isolated membranes? This question was addressed by isolating microsomal membranes from young bean cotyledon tissue, which contain no gel phase lipid at room temperature, in cytosol from senescent cotyledon tissue, which should contain the putative contaminant. The transition temperature of microsomes isolated in senescent cytosol proved not to be significantly different from that for membranes isolated in normal buffer (McKersie, 1978). This observation supports the contention that the gel phase lipid is not attributable to a cytosolic contaminant.

The second question is whether the neutral lipid is a contaminant that has partitioned into the membranes during isolation. This is a more difficult question to answer, but the data illustrated in Fig. 2.5 argue that this is not the case. Changes in transition temperature with age for smooth microsomal membranes from senescing bean cotyledons and for rough microsomal membranes isolated from the same tissue are illustrated in Fig. 2.5. It is clear that the patterns of change in transition temperature with age are distinctly different for the two types of membrane. If the gel phase were due to one or more contaminants that had partitoned into the membranes, one would expect the contaminants to be in both types of membrane and the pattern of change in transition temperature with age also to be the same for both types of membranes. The fact that this is not the case indicates that the gel phase is not due to a contaminant.

Of particular interest is the finding that gel phase lipid can be induced in membranes and in lipsomes of pure phospholipid by treatment with ozone, a source of free radicals (Pauls and Thompson, 1980, 1981; Thompson et al., 1983). This is an important observation in the context of evaluating the question of contaminants, because it indicates that the reactive neutral lipids able to form gel phase lipid can be formed right in the membrane. It also supports the notion that the reactive gel phase forming components are products of free radical mediated peroxidation of phospholipids. Indeed, neutral lipid fractions have been isolated from ozone-treated membranes and ozone-treated liposomes of pure phospholipids, which are able to induce the formation of gel phase lipid when reconstituted into liposomes of pure phosphatidylcholine and which, when separated by Iatroscan chromatography, have the same gel phase-forming components found in the neutral lipid fraction isolated from senescent membranes (Pauls and Thompson, 1981; Thompson et al., 1983). It seems likely, therefore, that these gel phase-forming components are products of lipid peroxidation and that during senescence they may be formed through the peroxidative pathway involving lipoxygenase that is thought to be operative in these membranes.

4. Nonbilayer Lipid

There are various structural configurations that membrane lipids can assume, and these are distinguishable by ^{31}P nuclear magnetic resonance (NMR) of liposomes (Cullis and de Kruijff, 1978; Verkleij, 1984). This technique has been used to discern the accumulation in senescing membranes of molecular species able to induce the formation of inverted micelles in liposomes (Barber, 1984; Thompson *et al.*, 1987). For liposomes prepared from total lipid extracts of young membranes, lamellar ^{31}P-NMR spectra were obtained, but for liposomes prepared from total lipid extracts of senescent membranes, the ^{31}P-NMR spectra featured a strong isotropic peak suggesting the presence of inverted micelles in the older membranes. Similar spectra reflecting the presence of inverted micelles were observed when a neutral lipid extract from senescent membranes was reconstituted into liposomes of pure phosphatidylcholine. Freeze fracture electron microscopy of the reconstituted liposomes containing neutral lipids from senescent membranes confirmed the presence of inverted micelles (Barber, 1984; Thompson *et al.*, 1987).

There is evidence for the induction of nonbilayer lipid configurations following peroxidation. Indeed, many of the products of peroxidation are not cylindrically shaped because they have bulky side groups (e.g., hydroperoxy-, cyclic peroxide, and epoxide groups) and, thus, could promote conversion to nonbilayer configurations. Lipid peroxidation has been shown to increase the rate of transbilayer lipid migration (Barsukov *et al.*, 1980; Shaw and Thompson, 1981). Moreover, trace amounts of hydroperoxide derivatives of fatty acids act as fusogens (Gast *et al.*, 1982), and oxidized di- and trienoic fatty acids serve as Ca^{2+} ionophores in model bilayers (Serhan *et al.*, 1981). All of these phenomena have been associated with the formation of inverted micelles (Verkleij *et al.*, 1979; Gerritsen *et al.*, 1980). Thus it is highly conceivable that lipid peroxidation occurring during natural senescence, and possibly spearheaded by membranous lipoxygenase, promotes the formation of nonbilayer lipid configurations in senescing membranes.

C. A Tentative Model for Senescence of Microsomal Membranes

A model, which is intended to serve as a framework for interpreting experimental data for senescing microsomal membranes (and to a lesser extent plasma membranes), is illustrated in Fig. 2.6. Parts of this model are still speculative. The focal point of the model is bilayer destabilization. There are three manifestations of this destabilization, i.e., rigidification of bulk membrane lipid, the formation of gel phase lipid, and the formation of nonbilayer lipid configurations, specifically inverted micelles. It is proposed that this destabilization leads, in turn, to membrane leakiness, advanced proteolytic activity, and a generalized loss of membrane function. Turning to events upstream in the model, bilayer destabilization is thought to be induced by a sequence of enzymatic reactions that bring about deesterification, resulting in the release of free fatty acids and, through lipoxygenase,

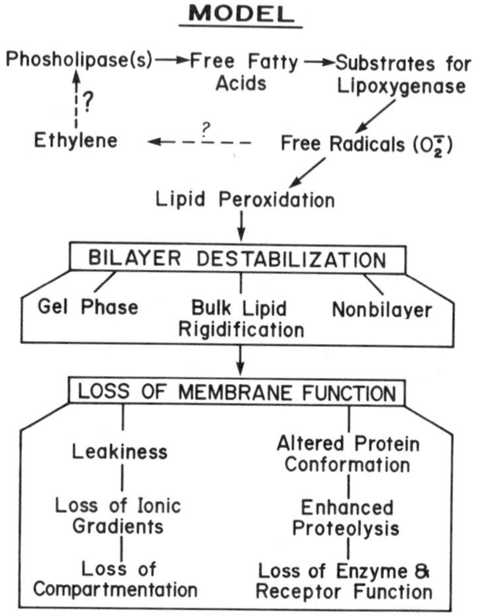

MODEL

Phosholipase(s) —→ Free Fatty —→ Substrates for
Acids   Lipoxygenase

Ethylene ←— — —?— — Free Radicals (O_2^-)

Lipid Peroxidation

| BILAYER DESTABILIZATION |

Gel Phase   Bulk Lipid   Nonbilayer
Rigidification

| LOSS OF MEMBRANE FUNCTION |

Leakiness   Altered Protein
Conformation

Loss of Ionic   Enhanced
Gradients   Proteolysis

Loss of   Loss of Enzyme &
Compartmentation   Receptor Function

Fig. 2.6. Proposed sequence of events leading to loss of microsomal membrane integrity during senescence.

the initiation of lipid peroxidation. This sequence of reactions explains the loss of membrane fatty acids that accompany senescence (McKersie *et al.*, 1978; Chia *et al.*, 1981), the increased production of O_2^- (Mayak *et al.*, 1983), and membrane rigidification attributable to free radical-mediated lipid peroxidation (Pauls and Thompson, 1980).

1. Permeability

Leakage of pigments, sugars, and electrolytes has been observed during senescence (Hanson and Kende, 1975; Suttle and Kende, 1978), and these observations support the contention that membrane deterioration leading to loss of intracellular compartmentation is an inherent feature of senescence. Prior to senescence, cellular membranes exhibit selective permeability, a property that is largely attributable to the relatively impermeable nature of the bimolecular lipid layer. It is not unreasonable, therefore, to assume that any molecular disorder in this lipid bilayer incurred during senescence could result in membrane leakiness. Many peroxidized lipids are bulky and will perturb the bilayer, tending to make it more permeable. Nonbilayer lipids are known to have ionophoretic activity (Serhan *et al.*,

1981). Increased permeability to ions in the presence of coexisting domains of liquid – crystalline and gel phase lipid has been noted previously in studies with liposomes (Papahadjopoulos *et al.*, 1975; Van Dijck *et al.*, 1975; Barber and Thompson, 1980) and is thought to reflect discontinuities in the bilayer at the boundary regions between discrete lipid domains. Thus, it seems reasonable to propose that progressive destabilization of the bilayer contributes in a major way to membrane leakiness in senescing tissues.

2. Loss of Specialized Membrane Functions

The physical state of membrane lipid bilayers profoundly influences the activity of membrane-associated enzymes and receptors (Quinn and Williams, 1978). This dependence has largely been attributed to changes in membrane fluidity (Shinitzky, 1984). The lipid environment is thought to impinge on enzyme and receptor function by influencing the conformation of membrane proteins or by imposing restrictions on the motion of membrane proteins. It has also been suggested that vertical displacement of membrane proteins may occur in response to fluidity changes (Borochov and Shinitzky, 1976; Shinitzky and Rivnay, 1977), and this would substantially alter ligand – receptor interactions.

It is likely, therefore, that the progressive destabilization of membrane bilayers accompanying senescence contributes to loss of membrane protein function. There is evidence for a senescence-related decline in enzyme activities associated with microsomal and plasma membranes (Lai *et al.*, 1971; Lai and Thompson, 1972; Thompson, 1974; McKersie and Thompson, 1975). There is also evidence for decreased ethylene-binding capability with advancing senescence (Goren *et al.*, 1984; Brown *et al.*, 1986). The receptor protein for ethylene is lipophilic and thought to be associated with microsomal membranes (Sisler, 1980; Dodds and Hall, 1980; Evans *et al.*, 1982). From Scatchard analyses of ethylene binding by petals of senescing carnation flowers, it has been estimated that the number of ethylene binding sites per cell decreases by about 50% with advancing senescence (Brown *et al.*, 1986). It is also apparent from the Scatchard analyses that the affinity of binding sites for ethylene decreases with advancing senescence of the flowers. The decline in number of binding sites can be essentially accounted for by the extensive breakdown in membranes that accompanies senescence. However, the decreased affinity for ethylene in the older tissue suggests that the binding sites become altered with advancing senescence, possibly as a result of conformational changes induced by the decrease in bulk lipid fluidity of the membranes.

Protein degradation is an important feature of the dismantling of membranes, and there is a growing conviction that selective degradation of membrane proteins during senescence is more likely to be achieved through membrane-associated proteases than by the bulk proteases presumed to be in the vacuole (Woolhouse, 1984). The presumed trigger for degradation is a conformational change in the protein that allows it to be recognized by a protease. The model illustrated in Fig. 2.6 proposes that destabilization of the bilayer in senescing membranes induces conformational changes in membrane-associated proteins that render them more prone to proteolytic attack. It is also conceivable that free radicals produced through membrane-associated lipoxygenase act directly on proteins, altering their conformation and causing them to be recognized by specific proteases. This contention is given credence by the fact that free radical-treated proteins are known to be more prone to proteolytic attack (Gardner, 1979).

3. Ethylene Biosynthesis

Microsomal membranes from plant tissues have been found to be capable of catalyzing the conversion of 1-aminocyclopropane-1-carboxylic acid (ACC) to ethylene (Mayak *et al.*, 1981; McRae *et al.*, 1982; Mattoo *et al.*, 1982), although there is some question as to whether this system is the native ethylene-forming enzyme. In particular, the microsomal system has been reported to exhibit a higher K_m for ACC than the native ethylene-forming enzyme (15 mM as compared to 60 μM) (Mayak *et al.*, 1981; McKeon and Yang, 1984) and does not show substrate stereospecificity (Hoffman *et al.*, 1982; McKeon and Yang, 1984; Venis, 1984). These observations have been interpreted as indicating that the ethylene-forming activity of microsomal membranes is either unrelated to the native enzyme converting ACC to ethylene *in situ* or reflects some alteration to the native enzyme incurred during homogenization and fractionation of the tissue. Indeed, the only *in vitro* system for converting ACC to ethylene that is biochemically similar to the *in situ* conversion is intact vacuoles (Guy and Kende, 1984). The conversion of ACC to ethylene is, nonetheless, heat denaturable and has physiological pH and temperature optima (Mayak *et al.*, 1981). Moreover, a recent report indicates that for microsomal membranes from senescing carnation flowers, a physiological K_m for ACC is discernable when a finer concentration gradient of ACC is deployed in measurements of the conversion of ACC to ethylene (Adam *et al.*, 1985).

Several lines of evidence indicate that the conversion of ACC to ethylene by microsomal membranes is facilitated by hydroperoxides generated through membrane-associated lipoxygenase (Legge and Thompson, 1983; Bousquet and Thimann, 1984; Lynch *et al.*, 1985). For example, the ability of microsomal membranes from senescing carnation flowers to convert ACC to ethylene correlates closely with levels of hydroperoxides formed by lipoxygenase in the same membranes. In addition, specific inhibitors of lipoxygenase curtail the formation of lipid hydroperoxides and the production of ethylene from ACC to much the same extent, whereas treatment of microsomes with exogenous phospholipase A_2, which generates fatty acid substrates for lipoxygenase, enhances the production of hydroperoxides as well as the conversion of ACC to ethylene (Lynch *et al.*, 1985). Depletion of lipid hydroperoxides by the addition of glutathione and glutathione peroxidase almost completely inhibits the formation of ethylene from ACC by microsomal membranes and also reduces the formation, to a corresponding degree, of an ACC-dependent radical species produced by the microsomal system and detectable by electron spin resonance (Legge and Thompson, 1983).

Given the propensity of lipid hydroperoxides produced by membranous lipoxygenase to promote the conversion of ACC to ethylene, if one further proposes that ethylene facilitates the sequence of reactions liberating fatty acid substrate for lipoxygenase (Fig. 2.6), it becomes clear how ethylene could be formed autocatalytically. There is at least indirect evidence to support the contention that ethylene may facilitate the peroxidative pathway leading to bilayer destabilization. This comes from experiments in which it has been demonstrated that treatment of young carnation flowers with exogenous ethylene accelerates the decrease in microsomal membrane fluidity that accompanies normal aging (Thompson *et al.*, 1982). It must be noted, however, that these results do not distinguish between a direct or an indirect effect of ethylene on the peroxidative pathway leading to membrane rigidification. Moreover, inasmuch as it does not faithfully reflect the characteristics of ACC-to-ethylene conversion *in situ*, this microsomal system must still be regarded as a model system for studying the formation of ethylene from ACC.

III. THYLAKOID MEMBRANE SENESCENCE

There is growing evidence that the molecular mechanisms underlying senescence of thylakoid membranes are quite different from those leading to deterioration and dismantling of microsomal and plasma membranes in senescing tissue. Deteriorative changes in chloroplast structure are normally apparent soon after leaf expansion has been completed. However, the energy-transducing thylakoid membranes show symptoms of deterioration long before the envelope. In fact, it is quite common for the envelope membranes to remain morphologically intact well into the later stages of leaf senescence (Harris and Arnott, 1973).

A. Free Radical Production

Electron spin resonance studies have demonstrated that thylakoid membranes also produce superoxide radical (O_2^-) during senescence (Fig. 2.7), but by a different mechanism and with markedly different effects than is the case for microsomal membranes (McRae and Thompson, 1983, 1985). Production of O_2^- by thylakoids is sensitive to superoxide dismutase and appears to be mediated through a photochemical reaction involving chlorophyll (McRae and Thompson, 1983), whereas O_2^- produced by senescing microsomal membranes is formed through lipoxygenase (Lynch and Thompson, 1984). For primary leaves of *Phaseolus vulgaris*, the formation of O_2^- by illuminated thylakoids has been shown to increase by about 4-fold during the early stages of senescence and to decline again as senescence intensifies (McRae and Thompson, 1983). A similar pattern of O_2^- production was noted during aging of isolated chloroplasts in buffer (McRae and Thompson, 1983).

This propensity of chloroplasts to produce increased levels of O_2^- with advancing senescence is not counterbalanced by an augmented scavenging capability. For example, in primary leaves of *Phaseolus vulgaris*, the specific activity of superoxide dismutase remains constant with advancing senescence, and total activity in leaf homogenates actually declines (McRae and Thompson, 1983). Inasmuch as O_2^- can react with H_2O_2 to form the very reactive $OH^.$, it is also important to learn whether H_2O_2 is scavenged in

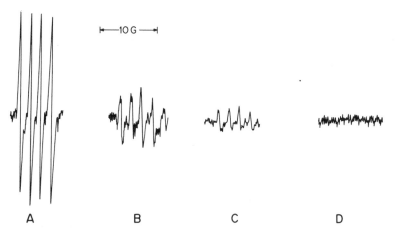

Fig. 2.7. Tiron electron spin resonance spectra reflecting superoxide production by illuminated thylakoid membranes from primary leaves of bean *(Phaseolus vulgaris)*. (A) Membranes plus 10 m*M* Tiron. (B) Membranes plus 100 units/ml superoxide dismutase plus 10 m*M* Tiron. (C) 10 m*M* Tiron alone. (D) Membranes plus 10 m*M* Tiron in the absence of oxygen. [From McRae and Thompson (1983).]

senescing leaf tissue. For primary leaves of *Phaseolus vulgaris,* peroxidase tends to increase in leaf homogenates with advancing senescence, but only low and essentially constant activities of both catalase and perodxidase are detectable in chloroplasts during senescence (McRae and Thompson, 1983). Presumably these latter activities are largely attributable to contaminating cytosol in the chloroplast fraction.

B. Loss of Thylakoid Membrane Integrity

1. Photosynthesis

Loss of photosynthetic competence during senescence is attributable, at least in part, to impairment of photosynthetic electron transport in the thylakoid membranes. Electron transport through photosystems I and II decreases in, for example, senescing bean leaves; however, of particular interest is the finding that the rate of noncyclic electron transport declines to a greater degree than the activities of either of the photosystems (Jenkins and Woolhouse, 1981b). This has prompted the proposal (Jenkins and Woolhouse, 1981b) that it is largely an impairment of electron flow between the two photosystems that limits the availability of photosynthetic reducing power with advancing senescence. Jenkins and Woolhouse (1981a,b) have also demonstrated that there is no change in phosphorylation control of electron transport as bean leaves senesce. There are reports of a decline in the functional concentration of the cytochrome f-b_6 complex with advancing leaf senescence (Ben-David *et al.,* 1983; Holloway *et al.,* 1983), and Holloway *et al.* (1983) have deduced from measurements of partial photochemical reactions and concentrations of electron carriers that in senescing barley leaves the rate-limiting step is the transfer of electrons from plastohydroquinone to the cytochrome b-f_6 complex. This could, therefore, account for the rate-limiting nature of intersystem electron transfer in the senescing chloroplast. However, Holloway *et al.* (1983) also note that the temporal correlation between loss of electron transport activity and the decline in cytochrome f is nonlinear and suggest that factors in addition to the limiting concentration of the cytochrome b-f_6 complex render this partial reaction rate limiting.

2. Thylakoid Membrane Fluidity

The reactions of photosynthetic electron transport are thought to be dependent upon the fluidity of the thylakoid membranes, inasmuch as the ability of electron carriers to interact is determined by their relative translational mobilities (Ford and Barber, 1980, 1983; Yamamoto *et al.,* 1981). Indeed, Yamamoto *et al.* (1981) were able to induce a decline in the electron

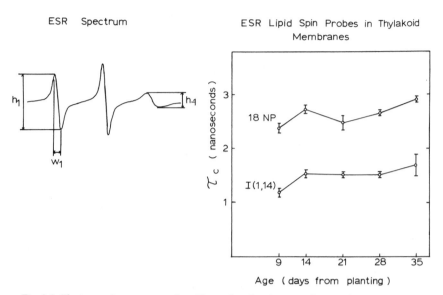

Fig. 2.8. Electron spin resonance data illustrating the absence of a significant change during senescence in τ_c (rotational correlation time) for thylakoid membranes isolated from the primary leaves of *Phaseolus vulgaris* and labeled with 3-(octadecylaminomethyl)-2,2,5,5-tetramethyl-1-pyrrolidinyl-oxyl (18NP) or 16-doxylstearic acid [I(1,14)]. $\tau_c = 6.5 \times 10^{-10}w_1[(h_1/h_{-1})^{1/2} - 1]$ [From McRae *et al.* (1982).]

transport activity of pea thylakoids by decreasing lipid fluidity. If there were a decrease in thylakoid membrane fluidity during senescence, this would be an attractive additional explanation for the rate-limiting nature of intersystem electron transport in the senescing leaf.

Unlike plasma and microsomal membranes (Section II,B,1), thylakoid membranes do not, however, sustain a decrease in bulk lipid fluidity with advancing age. This has been demonstrated by using a variety of paramagnetic and fluorescent lipid-soluble probes to measure both rotational motion and lateral diffusion (Figs. 2.8 and 2.9). The contention that there are no changes in fluidity is supported by the finding that the fatty acid composition of the thylakoid membranes remains essentially unaltered with advancing senescence. In particular, linolenic acid, which is highly unsaturated and would tend to maintain the membrane in a fluid state, remains characteristically high during senescence. Thus the rate-limiting nature of intersystem electron transport in the senescing leaf does not appear to reflect a change in thylakoid membrane fluidity. Small amounts of gel phase lipid are detectable in senescent chloroplast membranes, but only at a very late stage, long after photosynthetic function has been lost, when the chlo-

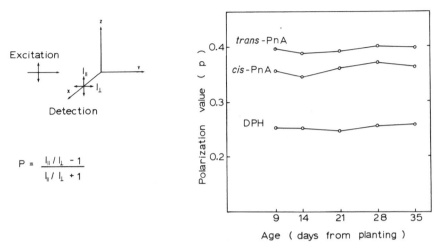

Fig. 2.9. Fluorescence depolarization data illustrating the absence of a significant change in polarization during senescence for thylakoid membranes isolated from the primary leaves of *Phaseolus vulgaris* and labeled with *trans*-parinaric acid (*trans*-PnA), *cis*-parinaric acid (*cis*-PnA), or diphenylhexatriene (DPH). [From McRae *et al.* (1982).]

roplasts are clearly moribund and in an advanced stage of deterioration (McKersie and Thompson, 1978; McRae and Thompson, 1985). By this stage as well, there has been considerable breakdown of lipid (McKersie and Thompson, 1978; Chia *et al.*, 1981), but these lipid changes do not appear to be major contributors to the loss of photosynthetic electron transport capability. Accordingly, at least in the initial stages, the mechanism of thylakoid membrane deterioration during senescence appears to differ from that operative in plasma and microsomal membranes for which large decreases in lipid fluidity with advancing senescence are well documented.

3. Protein and Chlorophyll Breakdown

Degradation of protein and chlorophyll is a paramount feature of chloroplast senescence, and some informative insights into the mechanisms underlying this degradation have been obtained from studies with a nonyellowing mutant of *Festuca pratensis* described by Thomas and Stoddart (1975). Normally, chlorophyll and protein are degraded in a coordinated manner, but in this nonyellowing mutant, the linkage between chlorophyll degradation and proteolysis is disrupted. Stromal components, photoreduction capability, and the morphological integrity of granal stacks all decline in a normal fashion during senescence of the mutant, but the thylakoid membranes persist, albeit unstacked, and retain structural proteins (Thomas, 1977).

This peculiar inability of the mutant to dismantle its thylakoid membranes is not attributable to alterations in bulk proteases (Thomas, 1982a, 1983). Indeed, the hydrophobic membrane proteins, in particular, remain disproportionately high during senescence of the mutant as compared with the normal yellowing genotype (Thomas, 1982b). This supports the notion advanced by Woolhouse (1984) that bulk proteases are not the agents of selective thylakoid protein degradation during senescence.

There is evidence that chlorophyll can regulate the degradation of protein in the chlorophyll–protein complexes of the thylakoid membrane. One of the best illustrations of this is the finding that the apoprotein of the light-harvesting complex is rapidly turned over in mutants of *Hordeum vulgare* lacking chlorophyll *b* (Bennett, 1983). Thus, breakdown of chlorophyll may be a necessary prerequisite for degradation of associated protein. Two distinguishable chlorophyll-bleaching mechanisms have been identified, one involving peroxidation and requiring a substituted phenol and H_2O_2 (Martinoia *et al.*, 1982) and the other showing a dependence upon linolenic acid (Lüthy *et al.*, 1984). Recent evidence indicates that the initial step in chlorophyll degradation involves a hydroxylation reaction at C-10 yielding chlorophyll *a*-1 (Maunders *et al.*, 1983). The precise manner in which chlorophyll degradation promotes proteolysis is not understood, although a change in the molecular structure of chlorophyll is likely to induce a conformational change in associated protein, which may in turn render the protein susceptible to proteolytic attack. It is of interest to note that the lesion in the nonyellowing mutant of *Festuca pratensis* does not appear to be a deficiency in linolenic acid-dependent chlorophyll bleaching activity (Thomas *et al.*, 1985).

It can be convincingly argued (Woolhouse, 1984) that degradation of thylakoid proteins during senescence is likely to be mediated by membrane-associated proteases involved in normal protein turnover. What remains unclear is the nature of the trigger that allows proteolysis to prevail in the senescing chloroplast. Woolhouse (1984) proposed that degradation ensues, in part, because of decreased synthesis of thylakoid proteins in the senescing leaf. Preliminary studies with primary leaves of *Phaseolus vulgaris* have indicated that, whereas synthesis of the 32 kDa herbicide-binding protein of photosystem II remains strong throughout senescence, synthesis of other thylakoid proteins, including the α and β subunits of ATPase and the apoprotein of the light-harvesting complex, declines (Roberts *et al.*, 1987). However, it is also conceivable that proteins in the senescing thylakoid membrane sustain free radical-mediated changes in conformation that render them more prone to proteolytic degradation, particularly since there is evidence for an increased load of reactive oxygen species in senescing chloroplasts (McRae and Thompson, 1983). Proteins altered in this manner would then be recognized by an appropriate proteolytic enzyme in the thylakoid membrane. It is conceivable, therefore, that as photosynthesis declines during senescence, there is an enhanced production of free radicals through a photochemical reaction involving chlorophyll and enhanced proteolytic activity attributable to free radical-mediated changes in the molecular structure and organization of proteins.

IV. MITOCHONDRIAL MEMBRANES

Little is known about the mechanisms underlying deterioration of the energy-transducing membranes of mitochondria during senescence, apart from the observation that the structural and functional integrity of mitochondria persists to the very late stages of senescence (Romani, 1978; Eisenberg and Staby, 1985; see also Chapters 1 and 4). In leaves, for example, whereas photosynthetic activity progressively declines throughout senescence (Jenkins and Woolhouse, 1981a,b; see also Chapter 3), respiratory activity remains strong (Macnicol, 1973). Many senescing systems exhibit cyanide-resistant respiration with advancing age (Henry and Nyns, 1975; Solomos, 1977; Romani, 1984), but the physiological significance of this pathway and the molecular mechanisms by which it is acquired have not been elucidated. Changes in the protein composition of mitochondrial membranes has been noted in pea cotyledons with advancing age (Nakayama *et al.*, 1978), and succinate dehydrogenase is more labile and less tenaciously associated with the inner membrane in mitochondria from senescent pea cotyledons, a finding that has been ascribed to a conformational change in the protein (Nakayama and Asahi, 1981). Such molecular events suggest that dismantling of the mitochondrial membranes may also entail selective proteolytic activity, possibly triggered by conformational changes in the membrane proteins, although no clear insights into how this is achieved are available yet for mitochondria.

V. MODULATION OF MEMBRANE SENESCENCE

Loss of membrane integrity is initiated during the early stages of senescence, and there are growing indications that if this can be prevented the entire process of senescence is slowed. For example, Baker *et al.* (1985) have reported that specific inhibitors of lipoxygenase, which could be expected to block membrane deterioration by preventing the formation of O_2^- and the initiation of lipid peroxidation, significantly delay senescence of cut carnation flowers.

Apart from conventional controlled atmosphere storage of fruits and vegetables, perhaps the best documented procedure for delaying senescence is treatment with Ca^{2+} (Poovaiah and Leopold, 1973; Lieberman and Wang, 1982; Ferguson, 1984). The efficacy of this procedure has been ascribed, at least in part, to an ability of Ca^{2+} to maintain membrane integrity. In particular, Ca^{2+} is thought to associate with the outside surface of the plasma membrane and, by acting as a divalent ligand, stabilize the plasmalemma. This is evident from experiments indicating that exogenous Ca^{2+} preserves membrane integrity (Lieberman and Wang, 1980) and selectively rigidifies the membrane surface (Legge *et al.*, 1982a).

Thus, the senescence-delaying capability of exogenous Ca^{2+} can be largely ascribed to an extracellular effect whereby the cation stabilizes cell walls and the external surface of the plasmalemma. However, there are also indications that release of compartmentalized endogenous Ca^{2+} during the early stages of senescence may activate lipases and thereby initiate membrane deterioration (Ferguson, 1984; Leshem *et al.*, 1984). Indeed, Ferguson (1984) argues that disruption of Ca^{2+} homeostasis, an ensuing rise in cytosolic Ca^{2+}, and activation of Ca^{2+}-requiring enzymes are likely to be characteristic features of senescence. This would certainly be consistent with a decline in membrane selective permeability. As well, there is evidence that triggering mechanisms for Ca^{2+}-release, analogous to the mechanism involving hormonally mediated turnover of phosphorylated phosphatidyl inositol, now well characteized in animal systems, may also be operative in plants. In particular, inositol triphosphate has been shown to be capable of releasing Ca^{2+} from plant microsomal membranes (Drøbak and Ferguson, 1985). This raises the interesting possibility that ethylene may facilitate senescence by releasing endogenous compartmentalized Ca^{2+} through, for example, inositol triphosphate.

Exogenous polyamines have also been shown to delay senescence. Indeed, there are various manifestations of this including reduced leakage, amelioration of lipid peroxidation, and inhibition of ethylene production (Naik and Srivastava, 1978; Kitada *et al.*, 1979; Altman, 1982; Ben-Arie *et al.*, 1982). Recent biophysical measurements of lipid fluidity have indicated that these effects can be attributed to an ability of polyamines, which would be polycationic at physiological pH, to selectively rigidify the surface of membranes (Roberts *et al.*, 1986).

VI. CONCLUSIONS

There appear to be distinguishable mechanisms of senescence for microsomal membranes, which are representative of the more typical lipoprotein membranes, including the plasma membrane, endoplasmic reticulum, and the tonoplast, and the highly specialized energy-transducing thylakoid membranes of the chloroplast. Specifically, microsomal membranes and thylakoid membranes both produce increased levels of free radicals with advancing senescence, but the mechanisms by which these free radicals are produced and their effects on the molecular organization of the membranes are distinctly different. In addition, there are marked changes in lipid fluidity and phase properties of senescing microsomal membranes that are not seen in senescing thylakoid membranes.

In the case of microsomal membranes, the enhanced free radical titer initiates lipid peroxidation and destabilization of the membrane bilayer. There are indications that this, in turn, leads to leakage, enhanced proteolytic activity, and a generalized loss of membrane function. Thus, senescence of microsomal membranes appears to be lipid driven.

By contrast, although there is a dramatic decline in photosynthetic electron transport capability in senescencing thylakoid membranes, this is not accompanied by pronounced changes in the molecular organization of the lipid bilayer, despite augmented production of O_2^-. Rather, chlorophyll breaks down, and there is evidence for differential changes during senescence in the rates at which thylakoid membrane proteins are synthesized.

REFERENCES

Adam, Z., Itzhaki, H., Borochov, A., and Mayak, S. (1985). Substrate stimulation of an enzyme converting 1-aminocyclopropane-1-carboxylic acid to ethylene. *Plant Sci.* 42, 89–93.

Altman, A. (1982). Retardation of radish leaf senescence by polyamines. *Physiol. Plant.* 54, 189–193.

Baker, J. E., Wang, C. Y., Lieberman, M., and Hardenburg, R. (1977). Delay of senescence in carnations by a rhizobitoxine analog and sodium benzoate. *HortScience* 12, 38–39.

Baker, J. E. Lieberman, M., and Anderson, J. D. (1978). Inhibition of ethylene production in fruit slices by a rhizobitoxine analog and free radical scavengers. *Plant Physiol.* 61, 886–888.

Baker, J. E., Wang, C. Y., and Terlizzi, D. E. (1985). Delay of senescence in carnations by pyrazon, phenidone analogs and Tiron. *HortScience* 20, 121–122.

Barber, R. F. (1984). Senescence-related changes in the molecular organization of membrane lipid bilayers. Ph.D. Thesis, Univ. of Waterloo, Waterloo, Ontario, Canada.

Barber, R. F., and Thompson, J. E. (1980). Senescence-dependent increase in permeability of liposomes prepared from cotyledon membranes. *J. Exp. Bot.* 31, 1305–1313.

Barber, R. F., and Thompson, J. E. (1983). Neutral lipids rigidify unsaturated acyl chains in senescing membranes. *J. Exp. Bot.* 34, 268–276.

Barsukov, L. I., Victorov, A. V., Vasilenko, I. A., Eustigneeva, R. P., and Bergelson, L. D. (1980). Investigation of the inside–outside distribution, intermembrane exchange and transbilayer movement of phospholipids in sonicated vesicles by shift reagent NMR. *Biochim. Biophys. Acta* 598, 153–168.

Ben-Arie, R., Lurie, S., and Mattoo, A. K. (1982). Temperature-dependent inhibitory effects of calcium and spermine on ethylene biosynthesis in apple discs correlates with changes in microsomal membrane microviscosity. *Plant Sci. Lett.* 24, 239–247.

Ben-David, H., Nelson, N., and Gepstein, S. (1983). Differential changes in the amount of protein complexes in the chloroplast membrane during senescence of oat and bean leaves. *Plant Physiol.* **73,** 507–510.

Bennett, J. (1983). Regulation of photosynthesis by reversible phosphorylation of the light-harvesting chlorophyll a/b protein. *Biochem. J.* **212,** 1–13.

Beutelmann, P., and Kende, H. (1977). Membrane lipids in senescing flower tissue of *Ipomoea tricolor. Plant Physiol.* **59,** 888–893.

Borochov, A., Halevy, A. H., and Shinitzky, M. (1976). Increase in microviscosity with aging in protoplast plasmalemma of rose petals. *Nature (London)* **263,** 158–159.

Borochov, A., Halevy, A. H., Borochov, H., and Shinitzky, M. (1978). Microviscosity of plasmalemmas in rose petals as affected by age and environmental factors. *Plant Physiol.* **61,** 812–815.

Borochov, A., Halevy, A. H., and Shinitzky, M. (1982). Senescence and the fluidity of rose petal membranes. Relationship to phospholipid metabolism. *Plant Physiol.* **69,** 296–299.

Borochov, H., and Shinitzky, M. (1976). Vertical displacement of membrane proteins mediated by changes in microviscosity. *Proc. Natl. Acad. Sci. USA* **73,** 4526–4530.

Bousquet, J. F., and Thimann, K. V. (1984). Lipid peroxidation forms ethylene from 1-aminocyclopropane-1-carboxylic acid and may operate in leaf senescence. *Proc. Natl. Acad. Sci. U.S.A.* **81,** 1724–1727.

Brown, J. H., Legge, R. L., Sisler, E. C., Baker, J. E., and Thompson, J. E. (1986). Ethylene binding to senescing carnation petals. *J. Exp. Bot.* **37,** 526–534.

Chia, L. S., Thompson, J. E., and Dumbroff, E. B. (1981). Simulation of the effects of leaf senescence on membranes by treatment with paraquat. *Plant Physiol.* **67,** 415–420.

Cullis, P. R., and de Kruijff, B. (1978). Polymorphic phase behaviour of lipid mixtures as detected by ^{31}P NMR. Evidence that cholesterol may destabilize bilayer structure in membrane systems containing phosphatidylethanolamine. *Biochim. Biophys. Acta* **507,** 207–218.

Dhindsa, R. J., Dhindsa, P. P., and Thorpe, T. A. (1981). Leaf senescence: correlated with increased levels of membrane permeability and lipid peroxidation and decreased levels of superoxide dismutase and catalase. *J. Exp. Bot.* **32,** 93–101.

Dodds, J. H., and Hall, M. A. (1980). Plant hormone receptors. *Sci. Prog. (Oxford)* **66,** 513–535.

Drøbak, B. H., and Ferguson, I. B. (1985). Release of Ca^{2+} from plant hypocotyl microsomes by inositol-1,4,5-triphosphate. *Biochem. Biophys. Res. Commun.* **130,** 1241–1246.

Eisenberg, B. A., and Staby, G. L. (1985). Mitochondrial changes in harvested carnation flowers (*Dianthus caryophyllus* L.) during senescence. *Plant Cell Physiol.* **26,** 829–837.

Evans, D. E., Bengochea, T., Cairns, A. J., Dodds, J. H., and Hall, M. A. (1982). Studies on ethylene binding by cell-free preparations from cotyledons of *Phaseolus vulgaris* L.: Subcellular location. *Plant Cell and Environ.* **5,** 101–107.

Eze, J. M. O., Mayak, S., Thompson, J. E., and Dumbroff, E. B. (1986). Senescence in cut carnation flowers: temporal and physiological relationships among water status, ethylene, abscisic acid and membrane permeability. *Physiol. Plant.* **68,** 323–328.

Ferguson, I. B. (1984). Calcium in plant senescence and fruit ripening. *Plant Cell Environ.* **7,** 477–489.

Fobel, M. (1986). Evidence for the involvement of lipoxygenase in membrane deterioration during senescence of carnation flowers. M.S. thesis, Univ. of Waterloo, Waterloo, Ontario, Canada.

Fobel, M., Lynch, D. V., and Thompson, J. E. (1987). Membrane deterioration in senescing carnation flowers. Co-ordinated effects of phospholipid degradation and the action of membranous lipoxygenase. *Plant Physiol.* **85,** 204–211.

Ford, R. C., and Barber, J. (1980). The use of diphenylhexatriene to monitor the fluidity of the thylakoid membrane. *Photobiochem. Photobiophys.* **1,** 263–270.

Ford, R. C., and Barber, J. (1983). Incorporation of sterol into chloroplast thylakoid membranes and its effect on fluidity and function. *Planta* 158, 35–41.

Frenkel, C. (1978). Role of hydroperoxides in the onset of the senescence process in plant tissues. *In* "Postharvest Biology and Biotechnology" (H. O. Hultin and M. Milner, eds.), pp. 443–448. Food Nutr. Press, Westport, Connecticut.

Gardner, H. W. (1979). Lipid hydroperoxide reactivity with proteins and amino acids: a review. *J. Agric. Food Chem.* 27, 220–229.

Gast, K., Zirwer, D., Ladhoff, A.-M., Schreiber, J., Koelsch, R., Kretschmer, K., and Lasch, J. (1982). Auto-oxidation-induced fusion of lipid vesicles. *Biochim. Biophys. Acta* 686, 99–109.

Gerritsen, W. J., de Kruijff, B., Verkleij, A. J., de Gier, J., and van Deenen, L. L. M. (1980). Ca^{2+}-induced isotropic motion and phosphatidylcholine flip-flop in phosphatidylcholine-cardiolipin bilayers. *Biochim. Biophys. Acta* 598, 554–560.

Goldstein, I. M., and Weissmann, G. (1977). Effects of generation of superoxide anion on permeability of liposomes. *Biochem. Biophys. Res. Commun.* 70, 452–458.

Goormaghtigh, E., Van Campenhoud, M., and Ruysschaert, J. M. (1981). Lipid phase separation mediates binding of pancreatic phospholipase A2 to its substrate. *Biochem. Biophys. Res. Commun.* 101, 1410–1418.

Goren, R., Mattoo, A. K., and Anderson, J. D. (1984). Ethylene binding during leaf development and senescence and its inhibition by silver nitrate. *J. Plant Physiol.* 117, 243–248.

Grossman, S., and Leshem, Y. Y. (1978). Lowering endogenous lipoxygenase activity in *Pisum sativum* foliage by cytokinin as related to senescence. *Physiol. Plant.* 43, 359–362.

Gruber, M. Y., Cheng, K.-H., Lepock, J. R., and Thompson, J. E. (1984). Improved yield of plasma membrane from mammalian cells through modifications of the two-phase polymer isolation procedure. *Anal. Biochem.* 138, 112–118.

Guy, M., and Kende, H. (1984). Conversion of 1-aminocyclopropane-1-carboxylic acid to ethylene by isolated vacuoles of *Pisum sativum* L. *Planta* 160, 281–287.

Hanson, A. D., and Kende, H. (1975). Ethylene-enhanced ion and sucrose efflux in morning glory flower tissue. *Plant Physiol.* 55, 663–669.

Harris, J. B., and Arnott, H. J. (1973). Effects of senescence on chloroplasts of the tobacco leaf. *Tissue Cell* 5, 527–544.

Henry, M. F., and Nyns, E. J. (1975). Cyanide-insensitive respiration. An alternative mitochondrial pathway. *Subcell. Biochem.* 4, 1–65.

Hoffman, N. E., Yang, S. F., Ichihara, A., and Sakamura, S. (1982). Stereospecific conversion of 1-aminocyclopropane-1-carboxylic acid to ethylene by plant tissues. Conversion of stereoisomers of 1-amino-2-ethylcyclopropane-1-carboxylic acid to 1-butene. *Plant Physiol.* 70, 195–199.

Holloway, P. J., Maclean, D. J., and Scott, K. J. (1983). Rate-limiting steps of electron transport in chloroplasts during ontogeny and senescence of barley. *Plant Physiol.* 72, 795–801.

Hopewell, R., Martin-Sanz, P., Martin, A., Saxton, J., and Brindley, D. N. (1985). Regulation of the translocation of phosphatidate phosphohydrolase between the cytosol and the endoplasmic reticulum of rat liver. *Biochem J.* 232, 485–491.

Jenkins, G. I., and Woolhouse, H. W. (1981a). Photosynthetic electron transport during senescence of the primary leaves of *Phaseolus vulgaris* L. I. Non-cyclic electron transport. *J. Exp. Bot.* 32, 467–478.

Jenkins, G. I., and Woolhouse, H. W. (1981b). Photosynthetic electron transport during senescence of the primary leaves of *Phaseolus vulgaris* L. II. The reactivity of photosystems one and two and a note on the site of reduction of ferricyanide. *J. Exp. Bot.* 32, 989–997.

Kar, M., and Feierabend, J. (1984). Metabolism of activated oxygen in detached wheat and rye leaves and its relevance to the initiation of senescence. *Planta* 160, 385–391.

Kellogg, E. W., and Fridovich, I. (1975). Superoxide, hydrogen peroxide and singlet oxygen in lipid peroxidation by the xanthine oxidase system. *J. Biol. Chem.* **250**, 8812–8817.

Kitada, M., Igarashi, K., Hirose, S., and Kitagawa, H. (1979). Inhibition by polyamines of lipid peroxide formation in rat liver microsomes. *Biochem. Biophys. Res. Commun.* **87**, 399–394.

Lai, Y. F., and Thompson, J. E. (1972). Effects of germination on Na$^+$-K$^+$-stimulated adenosine-5′-triphosphatase and ATP-dependent ion transport of isolated membranes from cotyledons. *Plant Physiol.* **50**, 452–457.

Lai, Y. F., Thompson, J. E., and Barrell, R. W. (1971). Changes in 5′-nucleotidase and glucose-6-phosphatase of *Phaseolus vulgaris*. *Phytochemistry* **10**, 41–49.

Lees, G. L., and Thompson, J. E. (1980). Lipid composition and molecular organization in plasma membrane-enriched fractions from senescing cotyledons. *Physiol. Plant.* **49**, 215–221.

Legge, R. L., and Thompson, J. E. (1983). Involvement of hydroperoxides and an ACC-derived free radical in the formation of ethylene. *Phytochemistry* **22**, 2161–2166.

Legge, R. L., Thompson, J. E., Baker, J. E., and Lieberman, M. (1982a). The effect of calcium on the fluidity and phase properties of microsomal membranes isolated from postclimacteric Golden Delicious apples. *Plant Cell Physiol.* **23**, 161–169.

Legge, R. L., Thompson, J. E., Murr, D. P., and Tsujita, M. J. (1982b). Sequential changes in lipid fluidity and phase properties of microsomal membranes from senescing rose petals. *J. Exp. Bot.* **33**, 303–312.

Leshem, Y. Y., Liftmann, Y., Grossman, S., and Frimer, A. A. (1981). Free radicals and pea foliage senescence: increase of lipoxygenase and ESR signals and cytokinin-induced changes. *In* "Oxygen and Oxy-radicals in Chemistry and Biology" (E. L. Powers and M. A. J. Rodgers, eds.), pp. 676–678. Academic Press, New York.

Leshem, Y. Y., Sridhara, S., and Thompson, J. E. (1984). Involvement of calcium and calmodulin in membrane deterioration during senescence of pea foliage. *Plant Physiol.* **75**, 329–335.

Lieberman, M., and Wang, S. Y. (1980). Preservation of the ethylene-forming system in deteriorating (senescent) postclimacteric apple tissue slices by calcium and magnesium. *Plant Physiol.* **65**(6), Suppl., 215.

Lieberman, M., and Wang, S. Y. (1982). Influence on calcium and magnesium on ethylene production by apple tissue slices. *Plant Physiol.* **69**, 1150–1155.

Lüthy, B., Martinoia, E., Matile, P., and Thomas, H. (1984). Thylakoid-associated 'chlorophyll oxidase': distinction from lipoxygenase. *Z. Pflanzenphysiol.* **113**, 423–434.

Lynch, D. V., and Thompson, J. E. (1984). Lipoxygenase-mediated production of superoxide anion in senescing plant tissue. *FEBS Lett.* **173**, 251–254.

Lynch, D. V., Sridhara, S., and Thompson, J. E. (1985). Lipoxygenase-generated hydroperoxides account for the nonphysiological features of ethylene formation from 1-aminocyclopropane-1-carboxylic acid by microsomal membranes of carnations. *Planta* **164**, 121–125.

McKeon, T. A., and Yang, S. F. (1984). A comparison of the conversion of 1-amino-2-ethylcyclopropane-1-carboxylic acid stereoisomers to 1-butene by pea epicotyls and by a cell free system. *Planta* **160**, 84–87.

McKersie, B. D. (1978). Fluidity and phase properties of membranes from senescing plant tissues. Ph.D. Thesis, Univ. of Waterloo, Waterloo, Ontario, Canada.

McKersie, B. D., and Thompson, J. E. (1975). Cytoplasmic membrane senescence in bean cotyledons. *Phytochemistry* **14**, 1485–1491.

McKersie, B. D., and Thompson, J. E. (1977). Lipid crystallization in senescent membranes from cotyledons. *Plant Physiol.* **59**, 803–807.

McKersie, B. D., and Thompson, J. E. (1978). Phase behaviour of chloroplast and microsomal membranes during leaf senescence. *Plant Physiol.* **61**, 639–643.

McKersie, B. D., and Thompson, J. E. (1979). Phase properties of senescing plant membranes. Role of neutral lipids. *Biochim. Biophys. Acta* **550**, 48–58.

McKersie, B. D., Thompson, J. E., and Brandon, J. K. (1976). X-ray diffraction evidence for decreased lipid fluidity in senescent membranes from cotyledons. *Can. J. Bot.* **54**, 49–55.

McKersie, B. D., Lepock, J. R., Kruuv, J., and Thompson, J. E. (1978). The effects of cotyledon senescence on the composition and physical properties of membrane lipids. *Biochim. Biophys. Acta* **508**, 197–212.

Macnicol, P. K. (1973). Metabolic regulation in the senescing tobacco leaf. II. Changes in glycolytic metabolite levels in the detached leaf. *Plant Physiol.* **51**, 798–801.

McRae, D. G., and Thompson, J. E. (1983). Senescence-dependent changes in superoxide anion production by illuminated chloroplasts from bean leaves. *Planta* **158**, 185–193.

McRae, D. G., and Thompson, J. E. (1985). Senescence-related changes in photosynthetic electron transport are not due to alterations in thylakoid fluidity. *Biochim. Biophys. Acta* **810**, 200–208.

McRae, D. G., Baker, J. E., and Thompson, J. E. (1982). Evidence for involvement of the superoxide radical in the conversion of 1-aminocyclopropane-1-carboxylic acid to ethylene by pea microsomal membranes. *Plant Cell Physiol.* **23**, 375–383.

Maguire, Y. P., and Haard, N. F. (1975). Fluorescent product accumulation in ripening fruit. *Nature (London)* **258**, 599–600.

Martinoia, E., Dalling, M. J., and Matile, P. (1982). Catabolism of chlorophyll: demonstration of chloroplast-localized peroxidative and oxidative activities. *Z. Pflanzenphysiol.* **107**, 269–279.

Mattoo, A. K., Achilea, O., Fuchs, Y., and Chalutz, E. (1982). Membrane association and some characteristics of the ethylene forming enzyme from etiolated pea seedlings. *Biochem. Biophys. Res. Commun.* **105**, 271–278.

Maunders, M. J., Brown, S. B., and Woolhouse, H. W. (1983). The appearance of chlorophyll derivatives in senescing tissue. *Phytochemistry* **22**, 2443–2446.

Mayak, S., Legge, R. L., and Thompson, J. E. (1981). Ethylene formation from 1-aminocyclo-propane-1-carboxylic acid by microsomal membranes from senescing carnation flowers. *Planta* **153**, 49–55.

Mayak, S., Legge, R. L., and Thompson, J. E. (1983). Superoxide radical production by micro-somal membranes from senescing carnation flowers: an effect on membrane fluidity. *Phytochemistry* **22**, 1375–1380.

Naik, B. I., and Srivastava, S. K. (1978). Effect of polyamines on tissue permeability. *Phytochemistry* **17**, 1885–1887.

Nakayama, N., and Asahi, T. (1981). Changes in properties of succinate dehydrogenase during senescence of pea cotyledons. *Plant Cell Physiol.* **22**, 79–89.

Nakayama, N., Iwatsuki, N., and Asahi, T. (1978). Degenerative changes in properties of the mitochondrial inner membrane in pea cotyledons during germination. *Plant Cell Physiol.* **19**, 51–60.

Niehaus, W. G. (1978). A proposed role of superoxide anion as a biological nucleophile in the deesterification of phospholipids. *Bioorg. Chem.* **7**, 77–84.

O'Rourke, F. A., Halenda, S. P., Zavoico, G. B., and Feinstein, M. B. (1985). Inositol triphosphate releases Ca^{2+} from a Ca^{2+}-transporting membrane vesicle fraction derived from human platelets. *J. Biol. Chem.* **260**, 956–962.

Paliyath, G., Poovaiah, B. W., Manske, G. R., and Magnuson, J. A. (1984). Membrane fluidity in senescing apples: effects of temperature and calcium. *Plant Cell Physiol.* **25**, 1083–1087.

Papahadjopoulos, D., Moscarello, M., Eylar, E. H., and Isac, T. (1975). Effects of proteins on thermotrophic phase transitions of phospholipid membranes. *Biochim. Biophys. Acta* **401**, 317–335.

Pauls, K. P., and Thompson, J. E. (1980). *In vitro* simulation of senescence-related membrane damage by ozone-induced lipid peroxidation. *Nature (London)* **283**, 504–506.

Pauls, K. P., and Thompson, J. E. (1981). Effects of *in vitro* treatment with ozone on the physical and chemical properties of membranes. *Physiol. Plant.* **53**, 255–262.

Pauls, K. P., and Thompson, J. E. (1984). Evidence for the accumulation of peroxidized lipids in membranes of senescing cotyledons. *Plant Physiol.* **75**, 1152–1157.

Peterman, T. K., and Siedow, J. N. (1985). Behavior of lipoxygenase during establishment, senescence and rejuvenation of soybean cotyledons. *Plant Physiol.* **78**, 690–695.

Platt-Aloia, K. A., and Thomson, W. W. (1985). Freeze-fracture evidence of gel-phase lipid in membranes of senescing cowpea cotyledons. *Planta* **163**, 360–369.

Poovaiah, B. W., and Leopold, A. C. (1973). Deferral of leaf senescence with calcium. *Plant Physiol.* **52**, 236–239.

Quinn, P. J., and Williams, W. P. (1978). Plant lipids and their role in membrane function. *Prog. Biophys. Mol. Biol.* **24**, 109–173.

Raison, J. K., and Orr, G. R. (1986). Phase transitions in thylakoid polar lipids of chilling-sensitive plants. *Plant Physiol.* **80**, 638–645.

Roberts, D. R., Dumbroff, E. B., and Thompson, J. E. (1986). Exogenous polyamines alter membrane fluidity in bean leaves—a basis for potential misinterpretation of their true physiological role. *Planta* **167**, 395–401.

Roberts, D. R., Thompson, J. E., Dumbroff, E. B., Gepstein, S., and Mattoo, A. K. (1987). Differential changes in the synthesis and steady state levels of thylakoid proteins during bean leaf senescence. *Plant Mol. Biol.* **9**, 343–353.

Romani, R. J. (1978). Metabolic integrity and postharvest homeostasis—a brief review. *J. Food Biochem.* **2**, 221–228.

Romani, R. J. (1984). Respiration, ethylene, senescence and homeostasis in an integrated view of postharvest life. *Can. J. Bot.* **62**, 2950–2955.

Serhan, C., Anderson, P., Goodman, E., Dunham, P., and Weissman, G. (1981). Phosphatidate and oxidized fatty acids are calcium ionophores. Studies employing arsenazo III in liposomes. *J. Biol. Chem.* **256**, 2736–2741.

Shaw, J. M., and Thompson, T. E. (1981). Effect of phospholipid oxidation products on transbilayer movement of phospholipids in single lamellar vesicles. *Biochemistry* **21**, 920–927.

Shinitzky, M. (1984). Membrane fluidity and cellular functions. *In* "Physiology of Membrane Fluidity" (M. Shinitzky, ed.), Vol. 1, pp. 1–52. CRC Press, Boca Raton, Florida.

Shinitzky, M., and Rivnay, B. (1977). Degree of exposure of membrane proteins determined by fluorescence quenching. *Biochemistry* **16**, 982–986.

Sisler, E. C. (1980). Partial purification of an ethylene-binding component from plant tissue. *Plant Physiol.* **66**, 404–406.

Solomos, T. (1977). Cyanide-resistant respiration in higher plants. *Annu. Rev. Plant Physiol.* **28**, 279–297.

Suttle, J. C., and Kende, H. (1978). Ethylene and senescence in petals of *Tradescantia*. *Plant Physiol.* **62**, 267–271.

Suttle, J. C., and Kende, H. (1980). Ethylene action and loss of membrane integrity during petal senescence in *Tradescantia*. *Plant Physiol.* **65**, 1067–1072.

Tappel, A. L. (1975). Lipid peroxidation and fluorescent molecular damage to membranes. *In* "Pathobiology of Cell Membranes" (B. F. Trump ;and A. Arstila, eds.), Vol. 1, pp. 145–170. Academic Press, New York.

Thomas, H. (1977). Ultrastructure, polypeptide composition and photochemical activity of chloroplasts during foliar senescence of a non-yellowing mutant genotype of *Festuco pratensis*. *Planta* **137**, 53–60.

Thomas, H. (1982a). Leaf senescence in a non-yellowing mutant of *Festuca pratensis*. II. Proteolytic degradation of thylakoid and stroma polypeptides. *Planta* **154**, 219–223.

Thomas, H. (1982b). Leaf senescence in a non-yellowing mutant of *Festuca pratensis*. I. Chloroplast membrane polypeptides. *Planta* **154**, 212–218.

Thomas, H. (1983). Proteolysis in senescing leaves. *Br. Plant Growth Regul. Group Monogr.* No. 9, 45–59.

Thomas, H., and Stoddart, J. L. (1975). Separation of chlorophyll degradation from other senescence processes in leaves of a mutant genotype of meadow fescue *(Festuca pratensis)*. *Plant Physiol.* **56**, 438–441.

Thomas, H., Lüthy, B., and Matile, P. (1985). Leaf senescence in a non-yellowing mutant of *Festuca pratensis. Planta* **164**, 400–405.

Thompson, J. E. (1974). The behaviour of cytoplasmic membranes in *Phaseolus vulgaris* cotyledons during germination. *Can. J. Bot.* **52**, 534–541.

Thompson, J. E., Mayak, S., Shinitzky, M., and Halevy, A. H. (1982). Acceleration of membrane senescence in cut carnation flowers by treatment with ethylene. *Plant Physiol.* **69**, 859–863.

Thompson, J. E., Pauls, K. P., Chia, L. S., and Sridhara, S. (1983). Free radical-mediated changes in the organization of membrane lipid bilayers; a simulation of the effects of senescence. *In* "Biosynthesis and Function of Plant Lipids" (W. W. Thomson, J. B. Mudd, and M. Gibbs, eds.), Monogr. Ser., pp. 173–194. Am. Soc. Plant Physiol., Bethesda, Maryland.

Thompson, J. E., Legge, R. L., and Barber, R. F. (1987). The role of free radicals in senescence and wounding. *New Phytol.* **105**, 317–344.

Ueda, K., and Kato, J. (1980). Isolation and identification of a senescence-promoting substance from wormwood *(Artemisia absinthium* L.). *Plant Physiol.* **66**, 246–249.

Van Dijck, F. W. M., Ververgaert, P. H. J. T., Verkleij, A. J., Van Deenen, L. L. M., and De Gier, J. (1975). Influence of Ca^{2+} and Mg^{2+} on the thermotropic behavior and permeability properties of liposomes prepared from dimyristoyl phosphatidylglycerol and mixtures of dimyristoyl phosphatidylglycerol and dimyristoylphosphatidylcholine. *Biochim. Biophys. Acta* **406**, 465–478.

Venis, M. A. (1984). Cell-free ethylene-forming systems lack stereochemical fidelity. *Planta* **162**, 85–88.

Verkleij, A. J. (1984). Lipidic intramembranous particles. *Biochim. Biophys. Acta* **779**, 43–63.

Verkleij, A. J., Mombers, C., Gerritsen, W. J., Leunissen-Bijvelt, J., and Cullis, P. R. (1979). Fusion of phospholipid vesicles in association with the appearance of lipidic particles as visualized by freeze-fracturing. *Biochim. Biophys. Acta* **555**, 358–361.

Vick, B. A., and Zimmerman, D. C. (1983). The biosynthesis of jasmonic acid: a physiological role for plant lipoxygenase. *Biochem. Biophys. Res. Commun.* **111**, 470–477.

Wang, C. Y., and Baker, J. E. (1979). Vase life of cut flowers treated with rhizobitoxine analogs, sodium benzoate and isopentyl adenosine. *HortScience* **14**, 59–60.

Wilhelm, J., and Wilhelnova, J. N. (1981). Accumulation of lipofuscin-like pigments in chloroplasts from senescent leaves of *Phaseolus vulgaris. Photosynthetica* **15**, 55–60.

Woolhouse, H. W. (1984). The biochemistry and regulation of senescence in chloroplasts. *Can. J. Bot.* **62**, 2934–2942.

Yamamoto, Y., Ford, R. C., and Barber, J. (1981). Relationship between thylakoid membrane fluidity and the functioning of pea chloroplasts. Effect of cholesterol hemisuccinate. *Plant Physiol.* **67**, 1069–1072.

Yoshida, S., Uemura, M., Niki, T., Sakai, A., and Gusta, L. V. (1983). Partition of membrane particles in aqueous two-polymer phase system and its practical use for purification of plasma membranes from plants. *Plant Physiol.* **72**, 105–114.

Photosynthesis

Shimon Gepstein
Department of Biology
Technion-Israel Institute of Technology
Haifa 32000, Israel

I. INTRODUCTION

The interrelations between the process of photosynthesis and foliar senescence can be discussed from different levels, the whole plant or at the organismic, cellular, or molecular. At present, the study of photosynthesis in senescing organs is undergoing a transition; the classic methods are being replaced or compared with the new ones of detection. Two decades of intensive research have established a gross characterization of changes occurring during senescence. The new methodology emerges at a time when many classic methods are no longer showing much progress and we are still far from understanding the mechanisms underlying the regulation of chloroplast senescence. The application of the new approaches using molecular biological techniques which have already proved to be useful in providing information on the photosynthetic machinery in general, will obviously help in studying those events associated with the regulation of chloroplast senescence. Indeed, several "firsts" in this field have already been reported, including immunological studies indicating changes in specific chloroplast proteins during senescence, and gene expression studies suggesting sites of control for synthesis of specific proteins.

Photosynthesis is a complex multistep process that takes place in special organelles, the chloroplasts. Thus, when reviewing the process of photosynthesis in relation to leaf senescence one must consider many aspects that are associated with these interrelationships. In short, this chapter touches on many aspects, some of them exclusively associated with chloroplasts and photosynthesis in senescing leaves. However, other aspects of significance in senescing cells in general will also be considered briefly; these include lipid metabolism, protein synthesis, protein degradation, and nucleic acids. The literature relating to those aspects is covered in greater depth in the relevant chapters in this volume.

II. SENESCENCE OF CHLOROPLASTS

A. Urastructural Changes in Chloroplasts during Senescence

The earliest and most striking anatomical changes associated with leaf senescence occur in chloroplasts (Butler and Simon, 1970; Thimann, 1980; Woolhouse, 1984). These organelles undergo ordered sequential changes of their photosynthetic capability from maturity through the process of senescence. Initially, stroma thylakoids vesiculate and thereafter lose their integrity. Coincident with thylakoid disintegration, a gradual increase in the volume and, in some plants, also in the number of plastoglobuli (osmiophilic granules) occurs (Dodge, 1970; Hudak, 1981; Greening et al., 1982; Wittenbach et al., 1982). This close correlation led to the suggestion that plastoglobuli accumulate lipids of adjacent thylakoids (Lichtenhaler, 1968). Subsequent to loss of integrity of stroma thylakoids, the grana thylakoids swell and then undergo gradual disintegration (Barton, 1966; Huber and Neumann, 1976; Thomas, 1977; Greening et al., 1982). Since photosystem II (PSII) is localized mainly in the grana and PSI is distributed both in the grana and stroma lamellae (Anderson, 1981), the earlier loss of stroma lamellae explains why PSI declines faster than PSII (Bricker and Neuman, 1982). Electron microscopic study of the nonyellowing mutant of *Festuca* (Thomas, 1977) suggested that only the stroma matrix was destroyed while the thylakoid membranes retained their integrity, in contrast to the normal genotype, which lost both the stroma and thylakoid systems (Fig. 3.1). Generally, the chloroplast envelope retains its integrity until very late when the internal membranes are already completely broken. Woolhouse (1984) suggested that maintenance of the envelope integrity might have an advantage in many species where the process of regreening resulting from herbivore grazing occurs. During regreening resulting from partial defoliation new thylakoids are initiated from the inner membrane of the chloroplast envelope even at advanced stages of senescence. In addition, the chloroplast envelope has a major role in the process of export of materials, which is characteristic of leaf senescence when a controlled unloading of chloroplast contents takes place (Sexton and Woolhouse, 1984). The mitochondria, in contrast to the chloroplasts, retain their function and are able to supply energy for vein loading, protein synthesis, and other energy-requiring senescence processes (Chapter 1).

B. Autonomous Degradation of Chloroplasts

Two models have been proposed to explain the loss of the photosynthetic apparatus during senescence. The first, which has been supported by Lampa *et al.* (1980), Wittenbach *et al.* (1982), and Camp *et al.* (1982), is that the chloroplast number per mesophyll cell declines during senescence. According to this hypothesis, similar to lysosomes in animal cells, the vacuoles play a central role during leaf senescence, possibly by the uptake of the whole chloroplast and other organelles (Matile, 1978; Chapter 1). This view is supported by the observation of marked reductions in chloroplast number per cell during senescence which is correlated with the loss of chlorophyll (Chl) and ribulose-biphosphate carboxylase (RuBPCase) and other characteristic symptoms of leaf senescence. The alternative hypothesis is that autonomous and sequential degradation *in situ* of the individual chloroplast constiuents occurs during senescence. Several lines of evidence are in accord with this hypothesis. The first comes from ultrastructural studies that show a differential and sequential change of constiuents within the chloroplast. The chloroplast envelope is degraded well after the disintegration of the internal thylakoids (Harris and Arnott, 1973). Additionally, there is now convincing evidence that chloroplasts contain several hydrolytic enzymes such as proteases (Waters *et al.*, 1982). Chl-degrading enzymes (Martinoia *et al.*, 1982), galactolipase (Dalgarn *et al.*, 1979), and other enzymes which

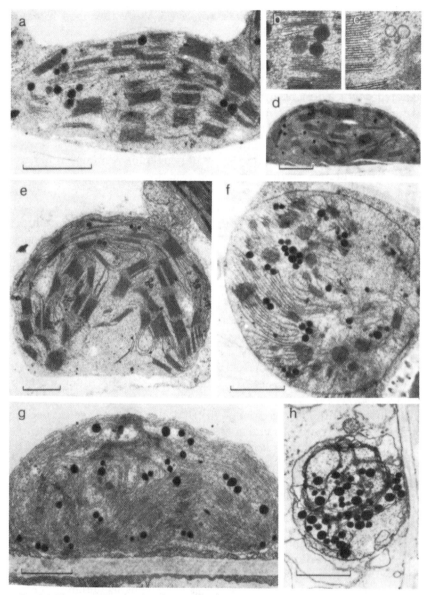

Fig. 3.1. Electron micrographs of mesophyll chloroplasts from *Festuca pratensis* at different times after the initiation of senescence. (a) Normal plastid, day 0. (b) Plastoglobuli in normal plastid, day 0. (c) Plastoglobuli in mutant, day 0. (d) Normal plastid, day 3. (e) Mutant plastid, day 3. (f) Rapidly senescing, normal plastid, day 3. (g) Mutant plastid, day 6. (h) Normal plastid, day 6. Horizontal bar = 1 μm. [From Thomas (1977).]

are possibly able to carry out the degradation within the organelle. The observation that Chl a/b ratios markedly changed during senescence is in favor of an autonomous and differential change within the chloroplast rather than loss of the whole organelle (Jenkins and Woolhouse, 1981a,b). However, direct evidence come from the studies of Martinoia *et al.* (1982) and Wardley *et al.* (1984) who followed the changes in the chloroplast number per cell of barley and wheat leaves during senescence. Both demonstrated that the chloroplast number remains essentially constant until the final stages of senescence when more than 80% of Chl and RuBPCase are lost. Wardley *et al.* (1984) explained the discrepancy between their results and those of others as due to the methodology used for estimating the number of chloroplasts within the cells. The studies carried out with isolated protoplasts prepared from young and senescing leaves have proved to be less reliable. The yield of released intact chloroplasts from senescing leaves is markedly less when compared to young leaves, and this may explain the false observation of the reduction in chloroplast number per cell during leaf senescence.

Although there is increasing evidence that chloroplasts contain the required hydrolytic enzymes and that they are probably autonomous in respect to their own degradation, the possibility of some involvement of vacuolar hydrolytic enzymes in the chloroplast degradation process cannot be excluded.

III. CHLOROPHYLL DEGRADATION

Disappearance of Chl is one of the most prominent phenomena of senescence, and eventually the rate of Chl degradation is usually considered to be a reliable criterion of leaf senescence and a measure of the age-related deterioration of the photosynthetic capacity (Thimann, 1978, 1980; Thomas and Stoddart, 1980). However, it is now known that there are some exceptions that show poor correlation or no correlation at all between Chl breakdown and the other characteristic symptoms of senescence (Thomas and Stoddart, 1980). An extreme example of a mutant of *Festuca pratensis* that does not exhibit any loss of Chl until its death has been reported by Thomas and Stoddart (1975). These results may imply that degradation of Chl is not the primary cause of the age-related decline in photosynthetic capacity. It has been speculated that the reduced Chl breakdown in the mutant is due to altered lipid metabolism in the thylakoids which reduces the accessibility of Chl and other membrane constiuents to the degradative systems (Thomas 1982c; Harwood *et al.*, 1982). However, we should keep in mind that apart from a few exceptions, leaf senescence is closely associated with Chl degradation.

The biochemical pathway of Chl metabolism has not yet been established. Although some Chl degradation in leaves results from photooxidation, there is some evidence to suggest the involvement, alternatively, of at least three enzymes in the initial steps of Chl degradation. One is chlorophyllase (chlorophyll-chlorophyllido hydrolase) which catalyzes the hydrolysis of the phytyl ester group (Kuroki *et al.*, 1981; Purvis and Barmore, 1981). Chlorophyllase was found to be a component of thylokoid membranes in citrus leaves and fruits (Amir-Shapira *et al.*, 1986). Normally until maturity, no Chl breakdown occurs, probably due to structural separation of the enzyme from its substrate. However, with the onset of senescence, thylakoid disruption may allow the enzymes access to the Chl (Amir-Shapira *et al.*, 1986, 1987). During *in vitro* incubation of chloroplast fragments of citrus leaf, chlorophyllide release coincided with Chl degradation (Fig. 3.2). Detergents, when introduced into the incubation media caused increased Chl degradation (Amir-Shapira *et al.*, 1986, 1987). Good correlation between chlorophyllase activity and Chl degradation has been demonstrated in maturing citrus fruits, and exposure of the fruit to ethylene at concentrations known to induce Chl breakdown brought about a significant increase in chlorophyllase activity (Hirschfeld and Goldschmidth, 1983;

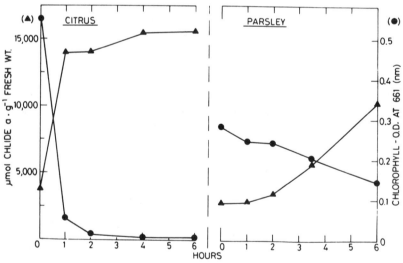

Fig. 3.2. Kinetics of *in vitro* degradation of chlorophyll and release of chlorophyllide during autodigestion of citrus and parsley chloroplast fragments. [From D. Amir-Shapira, E. E. Goldschmidt, and A. Altman (unpublished observations).]

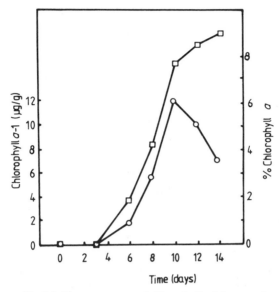

Fig. 3.3. The appearance of chlorophyll *a*-1 in senescing leaf tissue of *Phaseolus vulgaris*. Chlorophyll *a*-1 levels following excision (at day 0) are expressed in g/g leaf tissue (O) and as a percentage of the total chlorophyll *a*-type pigments (□). Chlorophyll *a* declined from 156 μg/g tissue at day 0 to 80.2 μg/g tissue at day 14. [From Maunders *et al.* (1983).]

Amir-Shapira *et al.*, 1987). Although chlorophyllase may be active in the initiation of Chl breakdown, there is some evidence indicating that no relationship exists between leaf age and chlorophyllase activity in a number of species. In *Raphanus* leaves, the activity of the enzyme even declined during senescence (Phillips *et al.*, 1969), and in some cases increased chlorophyllase was found to be associated with Chl synthesis rather than its degradation (Shimizu and Tamaki, 1963). Another second possible pathway of Chl degradation involves activity of Chl oxidase at the initial step (Maunders *et al.*, 1983; Schoch *et al.*, 1984). In detached bean leaves where senescence was induced by continuous darkness, Chl *a*-1 (the first product of a hydroxylation reaction) accumulated for several days and thereafter decreased. It has been proposed that the initial step of Chl breakdown is a hydroxylation process similar to that involved in the catabolism of heme in animal tissue (Brown and Troxler, 1983). The intermediate Chl *a*-1 probably undergoes further catabolism, and this may explain the decline in *a*-1 level following the increase in its amount at the onset of senescence in bean leaves (Fig. 3.3). Chl *a*-1 was identified by chromatographic procedures as the main and the initial product of chlorophyll oxidase (Schoch *et al.*, 1984).

Oxidation of Chl by chlorophyll oxidase was dependent on free fatty acids such as linoleic acid. This oxidase, however, differs from lipoxygenase in that it also may be activated upon addition of oleic and stearic acid. On the basis of these results it has been proposed by Luthy *et al.* (1984) that Chl breakdown by chlorophyll oxidase is initiated by hydrolysis of glyco- and phospholipids in thylakoids, which release free fatty acids that activate chlorophyll oxidase.

The third possible degradative pathway of which Chl bleaching *in vitro* has been reported to involve peroxidase (Kato and Shimizu, 1985).

In spite of the efforts described above, the fate of Chl *in vivo* is obscure and eventually needs considerable further study. However, since disappearance of Chl is easy to measure, many studies, dealing with Chl loss *in vivo* have been published. The Chl a/b ratio was followed during leaf senescence and consistently was shown to decline with advanced senescence (Jenkins and Woolhouse, 1981a; Bricker and Newman, 1982). In attached sycamore leaves, light preferentially enhanced Chl loss in addition to the age-related changes so that during a period of 14 days, the Chl a/b ratio dropped from a value of about 3.0 to 1.5 in the dark and to about 0.5 for leaves exposed to light. Other metabolic parameters (soluble proteins, RNA, amino nitrogen) were not significantly affected by light. Thus, Maunders and Brown (1983) concluded that during normal seasonal senescence of sycamore leaves, Chl might be degraded photochemically rather than by the metabolic reactions described above.

IV. CHANGES IN LIPIDS DURING CHLOROPLAST SENESCENCE

The striking ultrastructural changes of thylakoids and the concomitant rise in the size and number of plastoglobuli during senescence (Section 2A) suggest that fundamental changes occur in the chloroplast membranes during senescence. The lipids in other membranes show both quantitative as well as qualitative changes with the advance of senescence (Mazliak, 1983; Borochov and Faiman-Weinberg, 1984; Thompson, 1984; Chapter 2). X-ray diffraction studies carried out with various plant tissues have shown that during senescence membrane lipids undergo phase transition from a liquid–crystalline to a gel phase resulting in: (1) formation of domains of gel phase lipid in the membranes and (2) decreased fluidity of the liquid–crystalline lipid domains (McKersie *et al.*, 1976; Thompson, 1984). These age-related changes associated with membrane rigidification could certainly lead to membranal leakiness and loss of permeability, which are well-known characteristic features of senescing tissues (Barber and Thompson, 1980; Mazliak, 1983; Borochov and Faiman-Weinberg, 1984; Thompson, 1984; Chapter 2). Moreover, the formation of gel phase lipid has been found to cause dislocation and, in turn, may alter the whole pattern of protein organization. These changes may account for the deterioration in the function of several membranal proteins and of membrane-associated enzymes (Thompson, 1984).

Free radicals that accumulate in aging tissues and are known to have deleterious effects on membranes, may initiate lipid peroxidation and in turn induce membrane rigidification (Pauls and Thompson, 1980; Thompson, 1981; Mazliak, 1983; Borochov and Faiman-Weinberg, 1984).

A large decrease in the noncyclic photosynthetic electron transport was observed during bean leaf senescence (Jenkins and Woolhouse, 1981a). It seemed logical to attribute this decline to the changes in the thylakoid lipid fluidity. However, recent study has shown that unlike the plasmalemma and microsomal membranes, chloroplast membranes exhibit no significant changes in fluidity with advancing senescence (McRae *et al.*, 1985).

The drastic changes that occur in the molecular organization of membranes as leaf senescence intensifies are characteristic of all cellular membranes, including thylakoids (McKersie and Thompson, 1978). However, there is also preferential loss of lipids associated exclusively with the chloroplast thylakoid membrane. The galactolipids monogalactosyl diacylglycerol and digalactosyl diacylglycerol decrease before other nonchloroplast lipid constituents (Dalgarn *et al.*, 1979). The enzyme galactolipase has been purified from bean chloroplast (Anderson *et al.*, 1974); however, its physiological role in the process of chloroplast degeneration during senescence is not clear (Burns *et al.*, 1977). Studies of the nonyellowing mutant of *Festuca* support the notion that lipid metabolism plays a significant role in the regulation of leaf senescence (Hardwood *et al.*, 1982). Hydrolysis of acyl lipids, mainly the galactolipids of the thylakoids, was impaired in the nonyellowing mutant in contrast to the normal genotype. Moreover, the loss of acyl lipid in the normal genotype was associated with a concomitant accumulation of neutral lipids, which are 60–80% of linoleic acid. Linoleic acid was found to be an effective activator of thylakoid proteolysis and of the enzyme chlorophyll-oxidase; both are characteristic features of leaf senescence (Thomas, 1982c).

V. CHANGES IN STROMAL ENZYMES DURING LEAF SENESCENCE

Age-related deterioration in the photosynthetic capacity has usually been investigated by measuring partial reactions of photosynthesis and enzymes activities *in vitro*. For practical reasons, many investigators focused their study on RuBPCase, the key enzyme of the photosynthetic carbon reduction cycle which constitutes 50% or more of total soluble leaf protein (Lyttleton and Tso', 1958). It has been demonstrated that loss of photosynthetic activity is usually accompanied by a concomitant decrease in the activity of RuBPCase (Batt and Woolhouse, 1975; Hall *et al.*, 1978; Peoples and Dalling, 1978; Wittenbach, 1979; Friedrich and Huffaker, 1980; Camp *et al.*, 1984; Woolhouse, 1984). However, the onset of the decline in RuBPCase activity did not seem to be closely associated with the decrease in photosynthesis activity in several species (Wittenbach *et al.*, 1980; Secor *et al.*, 1983). The decline in RuBPCase activity may be attributed to either loss of enzyme protein or changes in enzyme activation during senescence of leaves. Using an immunological approach, Hall *et al.* (1978), suggested that the decrease in RuBPCase activity was due to a decline in the catalytic activity rather than a loss of RuBPCase protein. By contrast, Camp *et al.* (1984) demonstrated that total activity of RuBPCase declined continuously with age, while the percentage of activated RuBPCase remained essentially constant throughout the senescence of wheat leaves. Their results suggest that the loss of this protein is the main cause in the decline of RuBPCase activity. It is pertinent to ask whether the reduction in RuBPCase activity can account for the decline in photosynthesis during senescence. Camp *et al.* (1984) explored this problem and showed that even in cases where a deterioration in RuBP-Case activity was observed, the level that remained was more than sufficient to support normal rates of photosynthesis. They demonstrated that even in very late stages of wheat leaf senescence when more than 50% of the RuBPCase activity is lost, its activity was three times that required for the measured level of photosynthesis. Batt and Woolhouse (1975) studied changes of several regulatory enzymes of the Calvin cycle during leaf development in *Perilla* and found that they could be classified into two groups: (1) those enzymes that reach maximum activity at the completion of leaf expansion and thereafter began to decline (RuBPCase, phosphoribulokinase, and NADPH-dependent glyceraldehyde-3-phosphate dehydrogenase) and (2) enzymes that maintain their activities at maximum until late stages in leaf senescence (phosphoglycero-kinase, fructose-1-6-bisphosphatase, ribose-5-phosphate isomerase, and NADH-linked glyceraldehyde-3-phosphate dehydrogenase). It was hypothesized that the different pattern of change of these two categories of enzymes stemmed from their sites of synthesis. The first group are synthesized on 70 S chloroplast ribosomes and decline at a relatively early stage of leaf senescence, whereas the second group are synthesized on 80 S cytoplasmic ribosomes and maintain their activity until later stages. Camp *et al.* (1984) observed that chloroplastic fructose-1,6-bisphosphatase decline at earlier stages of senescence in contrast to the finding of Batt and Woolhouse (1975) who classified them with enzymes that decline only at late stages of senescence. The discrepancy could be explained by the fact that Batt and Woolhouse (1975) did not distinguish between the cytoplasmic and the chloroplasmic enzyme, whereas Camp *et al.* (1984) measured only the chloroplastic enzyme. In general, it seems that enzymes that are encoded in chloroplasts and synthesized on 70 S ribosomes within the organelle are lost earlier, whereas the second group of enzymes that are encoded in the nucleus and synthesized on 80 S ribosome decline at later stages of senescence (Sexton and Woolhouse, 1984). RuBPCase presents a particularly interesting problem because it is composed of two subunits, the large subunit (MW, 55,000) is encoded in the chloroplast and synthesized within the organelle, and the small subunit (MW, 14,000) is synthesized on 80 S cytoplasmic ribosomes.

Brady (1981) and Spiers and Brady (1981) found similar rates of synthesis of both subunits. Further measurements of the amounts of translatable mRNA of both subunits during senescence indicated that there was a simultaneous decline in the amounts of the messages. These results suggested that slowing down of RuBPCase synthesis was the critical factor explaining the earlier decline of this protein. However, in many species the turnover of RuBPCase is very low (Peterson *et al.*, 1973) and essentially, cessation of synthesis alone would not explain the decrease in the amount of RuBPCase. Therefore, an increase in proteolysis during senescence must accompany the decline in synthesis to account for the apparent loss of the protein.

VI. CHANGES IN THE COMPONENTS OF THE CHLOROPLAST THYLAKOID MEMBRANES DURING FOLIAR SENESCENCE

The light harvesting and energy-transducing functions of the chloroplast are now believed to be associated with 5 main protein complexes in the inner membranes of the chloroplasts (Fig. 3.5). Three of these complexes are involved in electron transport: photosystem II (PSII), photosystem I (PSI), and the cyt b_6/f complex which is located between the two photosystems. These three complexes are linked by mobile electron carriers: plastoquinone, plastocyanin, and ferredoxin. The fourth complex is associated with ATP synthesis and consists of a membrane sector (CF_0) and peripheral coupling factor (CF_1) (Anderson and Anderson, 1982), the fifth complex comprising the protein–Chl light harvesting complex. Changes in these complexes during senescence are of particular significance and would obviously influence the whole process of photosynthesis.

The experimental approach most frequently used to study changes in the "light reactions" during senescence was measurements of *in vitro* partial reactions of this process such as the Hill reaction (Sestak, 1977; Holloway *et al.*, 1983), noncyclic electron transport (Biswall and Mohanty, 1976; Jenkins and Woolhouse, 1981a; Holloway *et al.*, 1983) activities of PSI and PSII (Jenkins and Woolhouse, 1981b) and the activity of coupling factor CF_0-CF_1 (Jenkins and Woolhouse, 1981a, 1984). Jenkins and Woolhouse (1981a) demonstrated a marked decline in the rates of noncyclic electron transport by about 80% with the progression of bean leaf senescence. Similar values were also obtained in other various plants (Bricker and Newmann, 1982; Holloway *et al.*, 1983). Since photosynthetic transport produces ATP and NADPH, both required for enzymic reactions of the photosynthetic carbon reduction cycle (Calvin cycle), a decline in this process would inevitably reduce the rate of CO_2 fixation.

The rate of photophosphorylation that is coupled to electron transport was measured (Jenkins and Woolhouse, 1981a) and the P/2e ratio which expresses the coupling efficiency was about 1.3 and essentially remained constant throughout the senescence of *Phaseolus vulgaris* leaves. These results indicated that chloroplasts retained their coupling factor during senescence. The deterioration of the electron transport might result from a loss or inactivation of a membrane component of the electron transport chain. Attempts have been made by several investigators to identify the site of the impairment of electron transport, which is believed to occur during senescence. Activities of PSI and of PSII were measured in chloroplasts isolated from various ages of *Phaseolus vulgaris* leaves by using artificial electron donors or acceptors and known electron transport inhibitors and were found to decline by about 25 and 33%, respectively (Jenkins and Woolhouse, 1981b). This decline could not account for the sharp decrease of 80% observed in the rates of electron flow. Thus, it was suggested that impairment of electron transport occurred between the two photosystems. Further study by the same group (Jenkins *et al.*, 1981) employing measurements of kinetics of chlorophyll fluorescence measurements *in vivo*, support the same notion, namely that the impairment of electron flow may lie between the two photosystems. However, they could not identify precisely the site or the component that is responsible for this impairment. Holloway *et al.* (1983) found that prior to leaf maturation the rate-limiting step was located before the oxidation site of plastohydroquinone; however, in senescing leaves the decline in noncyclic electron flow appeared to be limited to the concentration of both cytochromes f and b_6. They also concluded that neither P-700 of the reaction center of PSI nor plastocyanin (a mobile carrier that transfers electrons from cyt b_6/f complex to PSI) constitutes the limitation of electron flow during senescence.

Although the conclusions of various studies regarding the impairment of the electron flow during senescence (Jenkins and Woolhouse, 1981a; Holloway *et al.*, 1983) are in agreement, one can find various reasons to challenge their validity. For example, it could be argued that "old" chloroplasts are more fragile than their young counterparts and an essential factor is lost during isolation, or that intrinsic proteases are liberated upon homogenization and may cause an *in vitro* degradation of proteins that does not reflect the *in vivo* situation (Shurts-Swirski and Gepstein, 1985). Moreover, *in vitro* measurements of electron transport using artificial electron donors or acceptors might be subjected to age-related artifacts of electron transfer from and to the artificial agents.

Using an immunological approach, Ben-David *et al.* (1983) could overcome several artifacts. First, the *in vitro* protein degradation was inhibited soon after the leaves were harvested by incubation with TCA and by the use of protease inhibitors. Second, since the crude leaf extract was used, any loss of the thylakoid component during the homogenization process could be detected in this assay. These authors have attempted to correlate the loss of electron transport activity with the loss of specific thylakoid components.

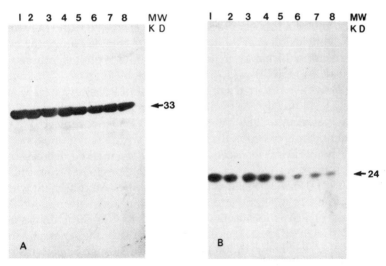

Fig. 3.4. Differential changes in the amounts of representative subunits of PSI and PSII during oat leaf senescence. Samples of leaf homogenates of various ages were electrophoresed on SDS–PAGE (12.5%), electrotransferred to nitrocellulose paper, incubated with either the 33 kDa subunit of PSII (A) or with the 24 kDa subunit of PSI (B) and detected with peroxidase-conjugated protein A. Leaf homogenates (5 mg, fresh weight) of various ages (10, 14, 17, 19, 26, 28, 29, and 31 days) were loaded on lanes 1–8, respectively. [From A. Livne and S. Gepstein (unpublished observations).]

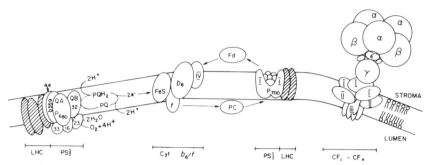

Fig. 3.5. Scheme drawing of the probable organization of the main components of the thylakoid membranes.

Antibodies against individual subunits of the main photosynthetic protein complexes were used to follow changes in the amounts occurring during senescence. No significant change was found in the amount of the PSI reaction center and the coupling factor (CF_1) during senescence of oat and bean leaves. However, a sharp decline in the amounts of the different components of cyt b_6/f complex was detected. These results agree with the previous studies of electron transport and of photophosphorylation activities (Jenkins and Woolhouse, 1981a; Holloway *et al.*, 1983) and they further support the conclusion that the loss of cyt b_6/f complex limits the rate of electron transport which may, in turn, limit the rate of photosynthesis in the senescing leaf. Though PSI and PSII are more stable than cyt b_6/f, a number of investigators have reported a preferential loss of PSI electron transport as compared to PSII during foliar senescence (Jenkins and Woolhouse, 1981a; Bricker and Newmann, 1982). Various lines of evidence indicated that the average number of chlorophylls associated with each photosystem remained constant during senescence. Yet, there is a marked decrease in the 734 nm 77 K fluorescence emission spectrum that originates from PSI (Jenkins *et al.*, 1981). Preferential loss of these activities are consistent with the decrease in the Chl a/b ratio and with the early loss of stroma thylakoids (where most of PSI is located), as evidenced by ultrastructured studies. Preferential loss of PSI protein as compared to PSII during senescence of oat leaves was observed using antibodies raised against specific proteins in the two photosystems (Fig. 3.4).

Recent study (Roberts *et al.*, 1987) examined the turnover of thylakoid proteins during senescence of bean leaves, in order to determine whether the differential depletion of proteins reflect selective changes in the role of synthesis or degradation of specific proteins. Indeed, differential changes in the role of synthesis were found in pulse-labeling experiments. Formation of cyt f and b_6, α and β subunits of ATPase, PSI, and LHCP declines during senescence, whereas synthesis of the 32-KDa herbicide binding protein continues throughout senescence. The deterioration of the synthesis of proteins from both cytoplasmic or chloroplastic compartments contributes to the decline in photosynthetic electron transport in senescing bean leaves (Roberts *et al.*, 1987).

VII. CHLOROPLAST PROTEIN DEGRADATION

Net loss of both thylakoid and stromal proteins during senescence is the result of the balance between two opposing processes — synthesis and degradation (Chapter 5). The absolute amount of a polypeptide in a state of turnover can be reduced by decreasing its rate of synthesis, increasing the rate of degradation, or both (Huffaker and Peterson, 1974). Regarding decreased synthesis, it should be emphasized that although there are some reports indicating reduced protein synthesis with age on the one hand (Callow and Woolhouse, 1973; Callow *et al.*, 1972) there are also reports of an increase in the amount of specific protein (Bricker and Newmann, 1980; Garcia *et al.*, 1983) on the other. Thus, there is not enough information available to provide us with a coherent picture regarding protein synthesis and its regulation during chloroplast senescence. Regarding increased degradation the data available indicate a sharp rise in proteolytic activity during senescence. However, it should be noted that a rise in proteolytic activity as measured *in vitro* may not necessarily represent protein degradation *in vivo*. For example, Thomas (1982b) showed that the proteases of the nonyellowing mutant of *Festuca*, rose during senescence much like the normal genotype. These results argue against protease lesion in this mutant and suggest that the accessibility of proteins to proteases is the main factor (Thomas, 1982a,b). It has been speculated that a change in the thylakoid lipids might cause protein dislocation which in turn exposed it to proteolytic attack (Thomas, 1982c; Harwood *et al.*, 1982). In addition, in many cases the amounts of proteases present in leaf tissue prior to the onset of senescence have been found to be more than sufficient to account for the breakdown of proteins during senescence (Waters *et al.*, 1982).

The present concept of the modes of protease regulation during senescence can be classified into three groups: (1) *de novo* synthesis of proteases; (2) activation; and (3) compartmentation. The observation that inhibitors of protein synthesis such as cycloheximide inhibit foliar senescence and proteolytic activity argues for *de novo* enzyme synthesis (Peterson and Huffaker, 1975; Martin and Thimann, 1972; Thomas, 1976; Huffaker and Miller, 1978). Protease activation by pH changes has also been suggested (Peoples and Dalling, 1978). However, there are examples in which protein degradation is not accompanied by an apparent increase in proteolytic activity (Van Loon *et al.*, 1978). Several reviews have appeared in recent years (Frith and Dalling, 1980; Ryan and Walter-Simmons, 1981) as well as many papers describing and classifying the proteolytic enzymes associated with foliar senescence of various plants (Dalling *et al.*, 1976; Peoples and Dalling, 1978; Wittenbach, 1978, 1979; Huffaker and Miller, 1978; Miller and Huffaker, 1982; Ragster and Chrispeels, 1979; Martin and Thimann, 1972; Shurtz-Swirski and Gepstein, 1985; Chapter 6). Still, no enzyme has been purified to homogenity, and their role and mode of regulation are still not fully understood. One must regretfully conclude that the problem of chloroplast degradation still awaits clarification.

Until recently, it was believed that acid proteases that are located in vacuoles are responsible for the marked increase in breakdown of cellular proteins during senescence (Boller and Kende, 1979; Matile, 1978; Heck *et al.*, 1981; Wittenbach *et al.*, 1982; Waters *et al.*, 1982). In fact, Camp *et al.* (1982) and Wittenbach *et al.* (1982) used these results to interpret their observation of reduction in the number of chloroplasts per cell during senescence as a consequence of lysosomal-like digestion of the whole organelle by the vacuole. Recent studies are not in line with this notion (Section II,B) and it seems that chloroplasts undergo a sequence of structural and functional changes which suggests progressive degradation within the chloroplast rather than changes in number, although Choe and Thimann (1977) found functional and structural stability of isolated chloroplasts compared with the marked degradation of chloroplasts in leaf segments. There is increasing evidence to suggest the presence of proteases within the chloroplasts (Peoples and Dalling, 1978; Ragster and Chrispeels, 1981; Thomas and Huffaker, 1981; Dalling *et al.*, 1983).

Besides the ultrastructural and biochemical changes observed within the chloroplast, there is also compelling evidence that peptide hydrolases are present in the chloroplast of barley leaves which are apparently free of vacuole contamination (Dalling *et al.*, 1983; Hamp and DeFillipes, 1980), one with an acidic pH optimum (4.5) and another enzyme which is activated by SDS with neutral pH optimum.

The methods used for studying leaf and chloroplast proteases usually employ an animal protein substrate such as hemoglobin, gelatin, casein, etc., or in a few cases the RuBPCase. However, if there is a substrate specificity, as in several bacterial and animal systems (Holzer and Heinrich, 1980), we should not be able to detect these proteases unless we use the endogenous natural substrates. To circumvent this problem an immunological approach has been attempted to study leaf proteases by following degradation of specific endogenous chloroplast polypeptides both in *in vitro* and *in vivo* (Shurtz-Swirski and Gepstein, 1985). Indeed, it has been found that upon autodigestion of isolated chloroplasts, several polypeptides of PSII (44–47 and 33 kDa) were extremely stable as compared to other polypeptides such as subunits of RuBPCase, cyt b_6/f complex, PSI and the coupling factor of ATPase (R. Shurtz-Swirski and S. Gepstein, unpublished observations). Of course, these results cannot discriminate between the two interpretations, substrate specificity of the proteases, or compartmentation and accessibility of the protein to the hydrolytic enzymes. There are reports of chloroplastic proteases that are associated with chloroplast development (Hamp and DeFillipes, 1980) and with processing of polypeptide precursors of chloroplast proteins. An example is the 32-kDa protein associated with PSII that is synthesized on 80 S ribosomes as a 33-kDa protein in the cytoplasm and is processed to its final 32-kDa form (Hoffman-Falk *et al.*, 1982). The processing of this polypeptide and some other polypeptides that originate in the cytoplasm requires the presence of proteases within the chloroplast itself. The 32-kDa polypeptide of PSII is of particular interest since it is turned over very rapidly in contrast to most of the other chloroplast proteins (Mattoo *et al.*, 1981). Woolhouse (1984) has presented a hypothesis to explain the 32-kDa polypeptide rapid turnover which may have general implications for understanding chloroplast proteolysis. This polypeptide is exposed at the outer surface of the thylakoid and may be subjected to free radial attack under conditions of high light intensity and low CO_2 concentration. Thus, it may render this polypeptide inactive and will induce fast degradation. Recently, Kyle *et al.* (1984) have demonstrated a correlation between photoinhibition of electron transport and the rapid turnover of a 32-kDa polypeptide. This protein (also designated Q_B) functions as the secondary electron acceptor on the reducing side of PSII. Under high light intensities O_2 may react with Q_B^{-2} and would result in the production of oxygen radical within the Q_B protein. The 32-kDa Q_B protein was found to disappear under these conditions and *de novo* synthesis of this protein replaces the damaged protein. These results support the hypothesis concerning the involvement of a free radical attack in the initiation of the degradation of the 32-kDa protein (Chapter 6). From other bacterial and animal systems it is known that free radical attack may result in activation and modification of the protein, which, in turn, becomes susceptible to proteolytic attack (Fucci *et al.*, 1983; Chapter 6).

Thus, besides activation of chloroplast protease as a means of *in situ* control, changes or activation of a substrate by free radical attack or by other factors may also be considered as a possible mode of regulation of chloroplast degradation.

Shimon Gepstein

VIII. LEAF CONDUCTANCE AND CO_2 ASSIMILATION IN SENESCING LEAVES

Stomata are the main entryways for CO_2 from the atmosphere to the mesophyll cells, where CO_2 assimilation takes place. Thus, it is pertinent to discuss the interrelation between photosynthesis and stomatal aperture during foliar senescence. There is accumulating evidence that leaf diffusion conductance decreases with the progress of senescence. Insufficient CO_2 supply as a result of reduction in leaf conductance may account for the decreased rates of assimilation, especially when leaves are exposed to high irradiation or stress.

Thimann and Satler (1979) observed that stomatal apertures varied in parallel with the rate of oat leaf aging. Agents which caused stomatal closure in light also often promoted Chl loss and vice versa; treatments that resulted in stomatal opening in the dark delayed the onset of chlorophyll degradation (Thimann, 1980). Based on these results, they suggested that stomatal aperture controls the rate of leaf senescence. However, these results, which correlated stomatal conductance and senescence, may also be consistent with the possibility of concomitant decrease in stomatal conductance and in chlorophyll loss or reduced photosynthesis.

Although guard cells retain some of their physiological functions until very late stages of senescence (Zeiger and Schwartz, 1982), leaf conductance has been found to be reduced with leaf age (Friedrich and Huffaker, 1980; Setter *et al.*, 1980 ; Wittenbach, 1983).

Several mechanisms have been advanced to explain the effects of leaf age on its conductance: (1) a decrease in the ability of guard cells to accumulate K^+, possibly due to age-related deterioration of the proton pumping that is required for this process (Gepstein, 1982; Gepstein *et al.*, 1983); (2) changes in hormonal balance (Setter *et al.*, 1980b); and (3) a gradual decline in photosynthesis which results from increased CO_2 concentration within the substomatal cavity and this in turn might induce stomatal closure (Setter *et al.*, 1980a; Wittenbach, 1983). Whatever the reason for reduction of leaf conductance, the important question is whether the age-related decline in photosynthesis is induced by stomatal closure. Several studies have been carried out to measure the rates of CO_2 exchange and H_2O diffusion simultaneously (Davis and McCree, 1978; Wittenbach, 1983; Schulze and Hall, 1982). Good correlation was found between these two processes and between the accelerated decline of RuBPCase and stomatal closure (Wittenbach, 1983).

A concomitant decrease in transpiration and photosynthesis was interpreted to mean that the decline in photosynthesis was induced by stomatal closure (Setter *et al.*, 1980b; Wittenbach, 1983). However, if conductance is more preferentially reduced compared with CO_2 assimilation, then a decrease in internal CO_2 concentration should be expected. When measurements of internal CO_2 were made, no significant changes were found throughout senescence of bean leaves (Davis and McCree, 1978).

These results may fit very well with the optimal stomatal variation concept hypothesized by Cowan and Farquhar (1977) and has been designated as the optimal stomatal variation concept. According to this hypothesis stomatal conductance varies as a result of environmental or internal factors to match the photosynthetic capacity of the leaf. For a wide spectrum of C_3 and C_4 plants photosynthetic capacity was linearly correlated with leaf conductance. According to this hypothesis, conditions that result in reduction of photosynthetic capacity may also result in reduction of leaf conductance. If, under varying conditions, assimilation and conductance change linearly, then the intercellular CO_2 concentration should remain constant. However, if these two parameters are not proportionally correlated, e.g., if conductance is affected preferentially, then CO_2 concentration decreases. The relation between leaf conductance and maximum CO_2 assimilation during senescence was studied. Similarly to other short- and long-term effects, linear correlation was observed, and the internal CO_2 concentration remained unchanged throughout leaf senescence (Schulze and Hall, 1982). Thus, the general approach of optimal stomatal function that is applicable to many plant processes may provide a useful conceptual base for explaining the observed decline of conductance and of photosynthetic capacity during leaf senescence.

IX. CONCLUSIONS

This review highlights the great number of unanswered questions concerning chloroplast senescence and the biochemical control of this developmental stage. It is clear that chloroplast senescence shares some general features that are characteristic of senescence, including changes in the structure, composition, and function of membranes, alterations of protein synthesis, and degradation and behavior of nucleic acids. In addition, specific aspects associated exclusively with the photosynthetic machinery have been reviewed and the conclusions point to the following events occurring during chloroplast senescence:

1. Changes in the molecular organization of the thylakoids.
2. Differential and sequential changes in the main protein complexes of the thylakoid. The cyt b_6/f complex is lost preferentially and may limit the rate of electron transport.

3. Changes in the activities of key enzymes in the Calvin cycle.

4. Changes in the rates of protein synthesis and/or degradation of certain chloroplast proteins.

It is anticipated that with new tools of molecular biology that have already been proven to provide useful information on the photosynthetic apparatus, it will be possible to gain insight into the mechanisms that are involved in the triggering and regulation of chloroplast senescence.

REFERENCES

Amir-Shapira, D., Goldschmidt, E. E., and Altman, A. (1986). Analysis of chlorophyll in aquaeous and detergent suspensions of chloroplast fragments. *Plant Sci.* **23,** 201–206.

Amir-Shapira, D., Goldschmidt, E. E., and Altman, A. (1987). Chlorophyll catabolism in senescing plant tissues: *In vivo* breakdown intermediates suggest different degradative pathways for *Citrus* fruit and parsely leaves. *Proc. Natl. Acad. Sci. U.S.A.* **84,** 1901–1905.

Anderson, J. M. (1981). Consequences of spatial separation of photosystem 1 and 2 in thylakoid membranes of higher plant chloroplasts. *Febs Lett.* **124,** 1–10.

Anderson, J. M., and Anderson, B. (1982). The architecture of photosynthetic membranes: lateral and transverse organization. *TIBS* **7,** 288–292.

Anderson, M. M., McCarthy, R. E., and Zimmer, E. A. (1974). The role of galactolipids in spinach chloroplast lamellar membranes. I Partial purification of a bean leaf galactolipid lipase and its action on subchloroplast particles. *Plant Physiol.* **53,** 699–704.

Barber, R. F., and Thompson, J. E. (1980). Senescence-dependent increase in the permeability of liposomes prepared from bean cotyledons microsomes. *J. Exp. Bot.* **31,** 1305–1310.

Barton, R. (1966). Fine structure of mesophyll cells in senescing leaves of *Phaseolus*. *Planta* **71,** 314–325.

Batt, T., and Woolhouse, H. W. (1975). Changing activities during senescence and sites of synthesis of photosynthetic enzymes in leaves of the Labiate *Perilla frutescens* (L.). *J. Exp. Bot.* **26,** 569–579.

Ben-David, H., Nelson, N., and Gepstein, S. (1983). Differential changes in the amount of protein complexes in the chloroplast membrane during senescence of oat and bean leaves. *Plant Physiol.* **73,** 507–510.

Biswall, M. C., and Mohanty, P. (1976). Aging-induced changes in photosynthetic electron transport of detached barley leaves. *Plant Cell Physiol.* **17,** 323–331.

Boller, T., and Kende, H. (1979). Hydrolytic enzymes in the central vacuole of plant cells. *Plant Physiol.* **63,** 1123–1132.

Borochov, A., and Faiman-Weinberg, R. (1984). Biochemical and biophysical changes in plant protoplasmic membranes during senescence. *What's New Plant Physiol.* **15,** 1–4.

Brady, C. J. (1981). A coordinated decline in the synthesis of subunits of ribulose biphosphate carboxylase in ageing wheat leaves. I. Analysis of isolated protein, subunits and ribosomes. *Aust. J. Plant Physiol.* **8,** 591–603.

Bricker, T. M., and Newman, D. W. (1980). Quantitative changes in the chloroplast thylakoid polypeptide complement during senescence. *Z. Pflanzenphysiol.* **98,** 339–346.

Bricker, T. M., and Newman, D. W. (1982). Changes in the chlorophyll-proteins and electron transport activities of soybean (Glycine max L., Wayne) cotyledon chloroplasts during senescence. *Photosynthetica* **16,** 239–244.

Brown, S. B., and Troxler, R. F. (1983). Haem catabolism. *In* "Bilirubin Metabolism" (L.P.M. Heinwegh and S. B. Brown, eds.), Vol. 2, pp. 1–39. CRC Press, Boca Raton, Florida.

Burns, D. D., Galliard, T., and Harwood, J. L. (1977). Catabolism of sulphlipid by an enzyme from the leaves of *Phaseolus multiflorus. Biochem. Soc. Trans.* **5**, 1302–1304.

Butler, R. D., and Simon, E. W. (1970). Ultrastructural aspects of senescence in plants. *Adv. Gerontol. Res.* **3**, 73–129.

Callow, J. A., Callow, M. E., and Woolhouse, H. W. (1972). *In vitro* protein synthesis, ribosomal RNA synthesis and polyribosomes in senescing leaves of *Perilla. Cell Differ.* **1**, 79–90.

Callow, M. E., and Woolhouse, H. W. (1973). Changes in nucleic acid metabolism in regreening leaves of *Perilla. J. Exp. Bot.* **24**, 285–294.

Camp, P. J., Huber, S. C., Burk, J. J., and Moreland, D. E. (1982). Biochemical changes that occur during senescence of wheat leaves. I. Basis for the reduction of photosynthesis. *Plant Physiol.* **70**, 1641–1646.

Camp, P. J., Huber, S. C., and Moreland, D. E. (1984). Changes in enzymes of sucrose metabolism and the activation of certain chloroplast enzymes during wheat leaf senescence. *J. Exp. Bot.* **35**, 659–668.

Choe, H. T., and Thimann, K. V. (1977). The retention of photosynthetic activity by senescing chloroplasts of oat leaves. *Planta* **135**, 101–107.

Cowan, I. R., and Farquhar, G. D. (1977). Stomatal function in relation to leaf metabolism and environment. *In* "Integration of Activity in the Higher Plant" (D. H. Jenning, ed.), pp. 471–505. Cambridge Univ. Press, London and New York.

Dalgarn, D., Miller, P., Bricker, T., Speer, N., Jaworski, J. G., and Newmann, D. W. (1979). Galactosyl transferase activity of chloroplast envelopes from senescent soybean cotyledons. *Plant Sci. Lett.* **14**, 1–6.

Dalling, M. J., Boland, G., and Wilson, J. H. (1976). Relation between acid proteinase activity and redistribution of nitrogen during grain development in wheat. *Aust. J. Plant Physiol.* (Suppl.) **61**, S-145.

Dalling, M. J., Tang, A. B., and Huffaker, R. C. (1983). Evidence for the existence of peptide hydrolase activity associated with chloroplasts isolated from barley mesophyll protoplasts. *Z. Pflanzenphysiol.* **111**, 311–318.

Davis, S. D., and McCree, K. J. (1978). Photosynthetic rate and diffusion conductance as a function of age in leaves of bean plants. *Crop Sci.* **18**, 280–282.

Dodge, Y. D. (1970). Changes in chloroplast fine structure during the autumnal senescence of *Betula* leaves. *Ann. Bot.* **34**, 817–824.

Friedrich, J. W., and Huffaker, R. C. (1980). Photosynthesis, leaf resistances, and ribulose-1,5-bisphosphate carboxylase degradation in senescing barley leaves. *Plant Physiol.* **65**, 1103–1107.

Frith, G. J., and Dalling, M. J. (1980). The role of peptide hydrolases in leaf senescence. *In* " Senescence in Plants" (K. V. Thimann, ed.), pp. 117–130. CRC Press, Boca Raton, Florida.

Fucci, H., Oliver, C. N., Coon, M. J., and Stadtman, E. R. (1983). Inactivation of key metabolic enzymes by mixed function oxidation reaction. Possible implication in protein turnover and ageing. *Proc. Natl. Acad. Sci. U.S.A.* **80**, 1521–1525.

Garcia, S., Martin, M., and Sabater, B. (1983). Protein synthesis by chloroplasts during the senescence of barley leaves. *Physiol. Plant.* **57**, 260–266.

Gepstein, S. (1982). Light-induced H^+ secretion and the relation to senescence of oat leaves. *Plant Physiol.* **70**, 1120–1124.

Gepstein, S., Jacobs, M., and Taiz, L. (1983). Inhibition of stomatal opening in Vicia faba epidermal tissue by vanadate and abscisic acid. *Plant Sci. Lett.* **28**, 67–73.

Greening, M. T., Butterfield, F. J., and Harris, N. (1982). Chloroplast ultrastructure during senescence and regreening of flax cotyledons. *New Phytol.* **92**, 279–285.

Hall, N. P., Keys, A. J., and Merret, M. J. (1978). Ribulose-1,5-diphosphate carboxylase protein during flag leaf senescence. *J. Exp. Bot.* **29**, 31–37.

Hamp, R., and DeFillipes, L.F. (1980). Plastid protease activity and prolamellar body transformation during greening. *Plant Physiol.* **65**, 663–668.

Harris, J. B., and Arnott, H. J. (1973). Effects of senescence on chloroplasts of the tobacco leaf. *Tissue Cell* **5**, 527–544.

Harwood, J. L., Jones, A. V. H. M., and Thomas, H. (1982). Leaf senescence in a nonyellowing mutant of *Festuca pratensis. Planta* **156**, 152–157.

Heck, V., Martinoia, E., and Matile, P. (1981). Subcellular localization of acid proteinase in barley mesophyll protoplasts. *Planta* **151**, 198–200.

Hirschfeld, K. R., and Goldschmidt, E. E. (1983). Chlorophyllase activity in chlorophyll-free citrus chromoplasts. *Plant Cell Rep.* **2**, 117–118.

Hoffman-Falk, H., Mattoo, A. K., Marder, J. B., Edelman, M., and Ellis, R. J. (1982). General occurrence and structural similarity of the rapidly synthesized 32,000-dalton protein of the chloroplast membrane. *J. Biol. Chem.* **257**, 4583–4587.

Holloway, P. J., Maclean, D. J., and Scott, K. J. (1983). Rate-limiting steps of electron transport in chloroplasts during ontogeny and senescence of barley. *Plant Physiol.* **72**, 795–801.

Holzer, H., and Heinrich, P. C. (1980). Control of proteolysis. *Annu. Rev. Biochem.* **49**, 63–91.

Huber, D. J., and Newman, D. W. (1976). Relation between lipid changes and plastid ultra-structural changes in senescing and regreening soybean cotyledons. *J. Exp. Bot.* **27**, 490–511.

Hudak, J. (1981). Plastid senescence. I. Changes of chloroplast structure during natural senescence in cotyledons of Sinapsis alba L. *Photosynthetica* **15**, 174–178.

Huffaker, R. C., and Miller, B. L. (1978). Reutilization of ribulose bisphosphate carboxylase. *In* "Photosynthetic Carbon Assimilation" (H. W. Siegelman, ed.), pp. 139–152. Plenum, New York.

Huffaker, R. C., and Peterson, L. W. (1974). Protein turnover in plants and possible means of its regulation. *Annu. Rev. Plant Physiol.* **25**, 363–392.

Jenkins, G. I., and Woolhouse, H. W. (1981a). Photosynthetic electron transport during senescence of the primary leaves of *Phaseolus vulgaris* L. I. Non-cyclic electron transport. *J. Exp. Bot.* **32**, 467–478.

Jenkins, G. I., and Woolhouse, H. W. (1981b). Photosynthetic electron transport during senescence of the primary leaves of *Phaseolus vulgaris* L. II. The activity of photosystems one and two, and a note on the site of reduction of ferricyanide. *J. Exp. Bot.* **32**, 989–997.

Jenkins, G. I., Baker, N. R., and Woolhouse, H. W. (1981). Changes in chlorophyll content and organisation during senescence of the primary leaves of *Phaseolus vulgaris* (L.) in relation to photosynthetic electron transport. *J. Exp. Bot.* **32**, 1009–1020.

Kato, M., and Shimizu, S. (1985). Chlorophyll metabolism in higher plants VI. Involvement of peroxidase in chlorophyll degradation. *Plant Cell Physiol.* **26**, 1291–1301.

Kuroki, M., Shioi, Y., and Sasa, T. (1981). Purification and properties of soluble chlorophyllase from tea leaf sprouts. *Plant Cell Physiol.* **22**, 717–725.

Kyle, D. J., Ohad, I., and Arentzen, C. J. (1984). Membrane protein damage and repair. Selective loss of a quinone-protein function in chloroplast membranes. *Proc. Natl. Acad. Sci. U.S.A.* **81**, 4070–4074.

Lampa, G. K., Elliot, L. V., and Bendica, A. J. (1980). Changes in chloroplast number during pea leaf development. An analysis of a protoplast population. *Planta* **148**, 437–443.

Lichtenhaler, H. K. (1968). Plastoglobuli and the fine structure of plastids. *Endeavour* **27**, 144–149.

Luthy, B., Martinoia, E., Matile, P., and Thomas, H. (1984). Thylakoid-1 associated 'chlorophyll oxidase': distinction from lipoxyggenase. *Z. Pflanzenphysiol.* **113**, 423–434.

Lytteleton, J. W., and Tso, P. O. P. (1958). The localization of fraction I protein of green leaves in the chloroplasts. *Arch. Biochem. Biophys.* **73**, 120–126.

McRae, D. G., Chambers, J. A., and Thompson, J. E. (1985). Senescence related changes in photosynthetic electron transport are not due to alterations in thylakoid fluidity. *Biochim. Biophys. Acta* **810**, 200-208.

McKersie, B. D., and Thompson, J. E. (1978). Phase behaviour of chloroplast and microsomal membranes during leaf senescence. *Plant Physiol.* **61**, 639-643.

McKersie, B. D., Thompson, J. E., and Brandon, J. K. (1976). X-ray diffraction evidence for decreased lipid fluidity in senescent membranes from cotyledons. *Can. J. Bot.* **54**, 1074-1078.

Martin, C., and Thimann, K. V. (1972). The role of protein synthesis in the senescence of leaves. I. The formation of protease. *Plant Physiol.* **49**, 64-71.

Martinoia, E., Dalling, M. J., and Matile, P. (1982). Catabolism of chlorophyll: demonstration of chloroplast-localized peroxidative and oxidative activities. *Z. Pflanzenphysiol.* **107**, 269-279.

Martinoia, E., Heck, H., Dalling, M. J., and Matile, P. (1983). Changes in chloroplast number and chloroplast constituents in senescing barley leaves. *Biochem. Physiol. Pflanzen* **178**, 147-155.

Matile, P. (1978). Biochemistry and function of vacuoles. *Annu. Rev. Plant Physiol.* **29**, 193-213.

Mattoo, A. K., Pick, U., Hoffman-Falk, H., and Edelman, M. (1981). The rapidly metabolised 32K dalton polypeptide of the chloroplast in the proteinaceous shield regulating PSII electron transport and mediating diuron herbicide sensitivity. *Proc. Natl. Acad. Sci. U.S.A.* **78**, 1572-1576.

Maunders, M. J., and Brown, S. B. (1983). The effect of light on chlorophyll loss in senescing leaves of sycamore (*Acer pseudoplaternus* L.). *Planta* **158**, 309-311.

Maunders, M. J., Brown, S. B., and Woolhouse, H. W. (1983). The appearance of chlorophyll derivatives in senescing tissue. *Phytochemistry* **22**, 2443-2446.

Mazliak, P. (1983). Plant membrane lipids: changes and alterations during aging and senescence. *In* "Post-harvest Physiology and Crop Preservation" (M. Lieberman, ed.) pp. 123-140. Plenum, New York.

Miller, B. L., and Huffaker, R. C. (1982). Hydrolysis of RuBPCase endoproteinases from senescing barley leaves. *Plant Physiol.* **69**, 58-62.

Pauls, K. P., and Thompson, J. E. (1980). *In vitro* simulation of senescence related membrane damage by ozone-induced lipid peroxidation. *Nature (London)* **283**, 504-506.

Peoples, M. B., and Dalling, M. J. (1978). Degradation of ribulose-1,5 bisphosphate carboxylase by proteolytic enzymes from crude extracts of wheat leaves. *Planta* **138**, 153-160.

Peterson, L. W., and Huffaker, R.C. (1975). Loss of ribulose 1,5 diphosphate carboxylase and increase in proteolytic activity during senescence of detached primary barley leaves. *Plant Physiol.* **55**, 1009-1015.

Peterson, L. W., Kleinkopf, G. E., and Huffaker, R. C. (1973). Evidence for lack of turnover of RuDP carboxylase in barley leaves. *Plant Physiol.* **55**, 1042-1045.

Phillips, D. R., Horton, R. F., and Fletcher, R. F. (1969). Ribonuclease and chlorophyllase activities in senescing leaves. *Physiol. Plant.* **22**, 1050-1054.

Purvis, A. C., and Barmore, C. R. (1981). Involvement of ethylene in chlorophyll degradation in peel of citrus fruits. *Plant Physiol.* **69**, 854-856.

Ragster, L., and Chrispeels, M. J. (1979). Azocoll-digesting proteinases in soybean leaves. Characteristics and changes during leaf maturation and senescence. *Plant Physiol.* **64**, 857-862.

Ragster, L., and Chrispeels, M. J. (1981). Haemoglobin-digesting acid proteinases in soybean leaves. *Plant Physiol.* **67**, 110-115.

Roberts, D. R., Thompson, J. E., Dumbroff, E. B., Gepstein, S., and Mattoo, A. K. (1987). Differential changes in the synthesis and steady state levels of thylokoid proteins during bean leaf senescence. *Plant Mol. Biol.* **9**, 343-353.

Ryan, C. A., and Walker-Simmons, M. (1981). Plant proteinases. *In* "The Biochemistry of

108   *Shimon Gepstein*

Plants: A Comprehensive Treatment" (A. Marcus, ed.), pp. 321–350. Academic Press, New York.

Schoch, S., Ruoiger, W., Luthy, B., and Matile, P. (1984). 13^2-Hydroxychlorophyll *a*, the first product of the reaction of chlorophylloxidase. *J. Plant Physiol.* **115**, 85–89.

Schulze, E. D., and Hall, A. E. (1982). Stomatal responses, water loss and CO_2 assimilation rates of plants in contrasting environments. *In* "Encyclopedia of Plant Physiology" (O. L. Lange, P. S. Nobel, C. B. Osmond, and H. Ziegler, eds.), Vol. 12B, pp. 181–230. Springer-Verlag, Berlin and New York.

Secor, J., Shibles, R., and Stewart, C. R. (1983). Metabolic changes in senescing soybean leaves of similar plant ontogeny. *Crop Sci.* **23**, 106–110.

Sestak, J. (1977). Photosynthetic characteristics during ontogenesis of leaves. *Photosynthetica* **11**, 449–474.

Setter, T. L., Brun, W. A., and Brenner, M. L. (1980a). Stomatal closure and photosynthetic inhibition in soybean leaves induced by petiole girdling and pod removal. *Plant Physiol.* **65**, 884–887.

Setter, T. L., Brun, W. A., and Brenner, M. L. (1980b). Effect of obstructed translocation on leaf abscisic acid, and associated stomatal closure and photosynthesis decline. *Plant Physiol.* **65**, 1111–1115.

Sexton, R., and Woolhouse, H. W. (1984). Senescence and abscission. *In* "Advanced Plant Physiology" (M. B. Wiliins, ed.), pp. 469–497. Pitman, London.

Shimizu, S., and Tamaki, E. (1963). Chlorophyllase of tobacco plants. II. Enzymic phytylation of chlorophyllide and pheophorbide *in vitro*. *Arch. Biochem. Biophys.* **102**, 152–158.

Shurtz-Swirski, R., and Gepstein, S. (1985). Proteolysis of endogenous substrates in senescing oat leaves. I. Specific degradation of ribulose bisphosphate carboxylase. *Plant Physiol.* **78**, 121–125.

Spiers, J., and Brady, C. J. (1981). A coordinated decline in the synthesis of subunits of ribulose bisphosphate carboxylase in ageing wheat leaves. II. Abundance of messenger RNA. *Aust. J. Plant Physiol.* **8**, 608–618.

Stoddart, Y. L., and Thomas, H. (1982). Nucleic acids and proteins in plants. *In* "Encyclopedia of Plant Physiology" (D. Boulter and B. Parthier, eds.), Vol. 14A, pp. 592–636. Springer-Verlag, Berlin and New York.

Thimann, K. V. (1978). Senescence. *In* "Controlling Factors in Plant Development" (H. Shibaska, M. Funeyor, M. Katsumi, and A. Takovits, eds.), Bot. Mag. Spec. Issue, pp. 19–43. Bot. Soc. Jpn., Tokyo.

Thimann, K. V., ed. (1980). "Senescence in Plants." CRC Press, Boca Raton, Florida.

Thimann, K. V., and Satler, S.O. (1979). Relation between leaf senescence and stomatal closure: Senescence in light. *Proc. Natl. Acad. Sci. U.S.A.* **76**, 2295–2298.

Thomas, H. (1976). Delayed senescence in leaves treated with the protein synthesis inhibitor MDMP. *Plant Sci. Lett.* **6**, 369–377.

Thomas, H. (1977). Ultrastructure polypeptide composition and photochemical activity of chloroplasts during foliar senescence of a nonyellowing mutant genotype of *Festuca pratensis* huds. *Planta* **137**, 53–60.

Thomas, H. (1982a). Leaf senescence in a nonyellowing mutant of *Festuca pratensis*. I. Chloroplast membrane polypeptides. *Planta* **154**, 212–218.

Thomas, H. (1982b). Leaf senescence in a nonyellowing mutant of *Festuca pratensis*. II. Proteolytic degradation of thylakoid and stroma polypeptides. *Planta* **154**, 219–223.

Thomas, H. (1982c). Control of chloroplast demolition during leaf senescence. *In* "Plant Growth Substances" (P. F. Wareing, ed.), pp. 559–567. Academic Press, London.

Thomas, H., and Huffaker, R. C. (1981). Hydrolysis of radioactively labelled ribulose 1,5-bisphosphate carboxylase by an endopeptidase from the primary leaf of barley seedlings. *Plant Sci. Lett.* **20**, 251–262.

Thomas, H., and Stoddart, K. L. (1975). Separation of chlorophyll degradation from other senescence processes in leaves of a mutant genotype of meadow fescue (*Festuca pratensis* L.). *Plant Physiol.* **56**, 438–441.

Thomas, H., and Stoddart, J. L. (1980). Leaf senescence. *Annu. Rev. Plant Physiol.* **31**, 83–111.

Thompson, J. E. (1984). Physical changes in the membranes of senescing and environmentally stressed plant tissues. *In* "Physiology of Membrane Fluidity" (M. Shinitzky, ed.), Vol. 2, pp. 85–108. CRC Press, Boca Raton, Florida.

Van Loon, L. C., Haverkort, A.J., and Lockhurst, G. J. (1978). Changes in protease activity during leaf growth and senescence. *F.E.S.P.P.* Abstr. 280c, 544–545.

Wardley, T. M., Bhalla, P. L., and Dalling, M. J. (1984). Changes in the number and composition of chloroplasts during senescence of mesophyll cells of attached and detached primary leaves of wheat (*Triticum aestivum* L.). *Plant Physiol.* **75**, 421–424.

Waters, S. P., Noble, E. R., and Dalling, M. J. (1982). Intracellular localization of peptide hydrolases in wheat (*Triticum aestivum* L.) leaves. *Plant Physiol.* **69**, 575–579.

Wittenbach, V. A. (1978). Breakdown of ribulose bisphosphate carboxylase and change in proteolytic activity during dark-induced senescence of wheat seedling. *Plant Physiol.* **62**, 604–608.

Wittenbach, V. A. (1979). Ribulose bisphosphate carboxylase and proteolytic activity in wheat leaves from anthesis through senescence. *Plant Physiol.* **64**, 884–887.

Wittenbach, V. A. (1983). Effect of pod removal on leaf photosynthesis and soluble protein composition of field-grown soybeans. *Plant Physiol.* **73**, 121–124.

Wittenbach, V. A., Lin, W., and Herbert, R. R. (1982). Vacuolar localization of proteases and degradation of chloroplasts in mesophyll protoplasts from senescing primary wheat leaves. *Plant Physiol.* **69**, 98–102.

Woolhouse, H. W. (1984). The biochemistry and regulation of senescence in chloroplasts. *Can. J. Bot.* **62**, 2934–2942.

Zeiger, E., and Schwartz, A. (1982). Longevity of guard cell chloroplasts in falling leaves; implication for stomatal function and cellular aging. *Science* **218**, 680–682.

4

Respiration in Senescing Plant Organs: Its Nature, Regulation, and Physiological Significance

Theophanes Solomos
Department of Horticulture
University of Maryland
College Park, Maryland

Theophanes Solomos

I. INTRODUCTION

Senescence of detached plant organs is accompanied by dramatic physiological, anatomical, and biochemical changes (Biale, 1960; Rhodes, 1970, 1980a,b; Leopold, 1980; Thimann, 1980). Overtly the process is catabolic, yet anabolic reactions, too, are a prerequisite of senescence. The very fact that inhibitors of protein and nucleic acid metabolism prevent senescence bears witness to this (Frenkel *et al.*, 1968; Brady *et al.*, 1970b; McGlasson *et al.*, 1971; Martin and Thimann, 1972). Although natural senescence leads to the demise of the tissue, it nevertheless plays an important role in plant development, such as in the translocation of nutrients from senescing leaves to either developing seeds or the parent plant (Woolhouse, 1967) and in the dispersion of seeds. Thus senescence is organized disorganization and as such requires biological energy for its occurrence. In detached plant organs, respiration is the sole source of energy, since the photosynthetic capacity of fruits and cut flowers is minimal and, moreover, senescence of detached leaves proceeds faster in the dark than in the light (Thimann, 1980). In the present review, the changes in and the nature and regulation of the rate of respiration will be examined, as well as its metabolic significance with respect to senescence.

II. PATTERNS OF RESPIRATION IN DETACHED PLANT ORGANS

A. Fruit

Kidd and West (1925) first observed that the rate of respiration of detached apple fruits decreased gradually and after reaching its nadir, suddenly rose to a peak, which was followed by another decline. The authors named this sudden increase in respiratory activity the *climacteric*. Subsequent work showed that the phenomenon occurred in fruits other than apples (Biale, 1960; Rhodes, 1970, 1980a,b; Biale and Young, 1981). However, this respiratory burst is not a *sine qua non* for all ripening fruits. In citrus fruits, the rate of CO_2 output decreases gradually during storage, while that of strawberries shows no appreciable change (Haller *et al.*, 1945; Knee *et al.*, 1977; Biale and Young, 1981). Biale (1960) divided fruits into two categories, climacteric and nonclimacteric, based on whether their respiration increased or declined gradually during ripening. Biale and Young (1981) have published a comprehensive list of these two classes of fruits.

B. Leaves

The changes in respiratory activity during senescence of both attached and detached leaves have been studied extensively. Blackman (1954) carried out studies with senescing, detached laurel leaves. The respiratory drift of these leaves shows similarities with those of climacteric fruits in that the rate of respiration declines after detachment, increasing again when the color of the leaves begins to change from green to yellow (James, 1953). A climacteric-like rise in respiration has been observed during senescence of detached tobacco, oat, barley, and ivy leaves (James, 1953; Sisler and Pian, 1973; Tetley and Thimann, 1974; Malik and Thimann, 1980; Warman and Solomos, 1988). On the other hand, the rate of respiration of detached pea leaves declines gradually with senescence (Smillie, 1962). Woolhouse (1967) followed the changes in the rates of both respiration and photosynthesis in the attached leaves of *Perilla frutescens*. The data show that the sharp decline in the rate of photosynthesis is associated with a corresponding climacteric-like increase in the rate of respiration. An increase in the rate of respiration has also been observed with attached yellowing leaves of *Hedera helix* (English ivy) (Warman, 1981).

C. Flowers

The respiratory behavior of cut flowers has not been investigated as extensively as has that of fruits and detached leaves. The available data, however, exhibit both climacteric and nonclimacteric respiratory drifts in these organs. Thus, Nichols (1968) demonstrated that the respiratory drift of cut carnations is similar to that of climacteric fruits in that there is an initial sharp decline after cutting, followed by a steep rise to a peak and then a second decline (see also Maxie *et al.*, 1973). Also, sweet pea flowers show a climacteric-like respiratory drift (unpublished observation). The number of flowers having a climacteric-like drift may be quite extensive (Burg, 1973; Rogers, 1973; Halevy and Mayak, 1981). Perversely, the rate of respiration of cut roses decreases during storage (Kaltaler and Steponkis, 1976).

III. CAUSES OF THE CLIMACTERIC RISE IN RESPIRATION

It should be emphasized that respiration of detached plant organs can be stimulated by several factors, such as the addition of uncouplers of oxidative phosphorylation, chilling temperatures, wounding, addition of sugars, and irradiation (Millerd *et al.*, 1953; Eaks and Morris, 1956; Biale and Young, 1971; Dilley and Carpenter, 1975; Laties, 1978; Theologis and Laties, 1978a,b). In this presentation, the rise in respiration that is associated with, or closely followed by, the overt and biochemical changes of senescence will be scrutinized, and it will become apparent that the rise in respiration during senescence is a phenomenon quite distinct from the causes mentioned earlier in this paragraph.

The climacteric rise in respiration has been variously attributed to the decrease in organizational resistance (Blackman and Parija, 1928), enhancement of protein synthesis (Hulme, 1954), the presence of natural uncouplers of oxidative phosphorylation (Millerd *et al.*, 1953), and an attempt by the tissue to maintain metabolic homeostasis (Romani, 1984). These hypotheses will be discussed in detail later. Suffice it at present to note that the postulation of a natural uncoupler is not borne out by experimental evidence, since in most climacteric fruits, ATP increases in the course of the climacteric (Young and Biale, 1967; Rowan *et al.*, 1969; Solomos and Laties, 1976; Bennett *et al.*, 1987; Beaury *et al.*, 1987), and the rate of incorporation of ^{32}P into organic compounds is enhanced during the climacteric rise in respiration of avocados (Young and Biale, 1967) and during senescence of tobacco leaves (MacNicol *et al.*, 1973). It should also be pointed out that the net increase in protein synthesis observed in pome fruits (Hulme, 1954; Hansen, 1967) does not occur in either bananas (Wade *et al.*, 1972) or avocados (Sacher, 1967). Furthermore, the relationship between the rate of respiration and protein synthesis is not always closely linked. For instance, in most climacteric fruits, the incorporation of amino acids into proteins decreases sharply long before the climacteric peak (Richmond and Biale, 1966; Hulme *et al.*, 1968; Sacher, 1967; Baker *et al.*, 1985). In addition, apart from the requirement of protein synthesis for ripening, there is no common metabolic denominator to explain the climacteric rise in respiration that occurs in several fruits. It occurs in fruits that are widely disparate with respect to their composition, growing conditions, and physiological responses (Rhodes, 1980a,b; Biale and Young, 1981). The only common metabolic feature of climacteric fruits is their ability to both produce ethylene (C_2H_4) and to respond to exogenous application of the gas by an increase in respiration and eventual senescence. The following arguments seek to provide evidence in support of the thesis that the rise in respiration during senescence is a facet of C_2H_4 action and not of senescence as such.

In the first place, certain aspects of senescence may precede the rise in respiration, because the threshold levels of C_2H_4 for these processes are lower than that for the respiratory rise. Thus, it was shown that in melons the threshold level of C_2H_4 necessary for softening and carotenoid synthesis was 0.1 μl/liter, while that of respiration was 3 μl/liter (Pratt and Goeschl, 1968, 1969). In pears, softening and rise in respiration were induced at 0.05 μl/liter and 0.46 μl/liter C_2H_4, respectively (Wang *et al.*, 1972). In addition, certain biochemical events associated with senescence appear to show differing sensitivities to C_2H_4. For instance, McGlasson (1970) has reported that in bananas the degradation of starch requires longer exposure to C_2H_4 than does the destruction of chlorophyll. Further, the rise in respiration rate can be experimentally dissociated from certain attendant senescent events. Thus, Dostal and Leopold (1967) showed that dipping mature green tomatoes in gibberellic acid prevents the destruction of chlorophyll and synthesis of lycopene without influencing the rate of respiration. Vendrell (1969) observed that the infiltration of banana slices with 2,4-dichloro-phenoxyacetic acid (24D) induced a transient increase in C_2H_4 evolution and respiration, while delaying ripening. Quazi and Freebairn (1970) have shown that when green banana fruits are treated with C_2H_4 and then transferred to low O_2 atmospheres, they ripen without a perceptible increase in respiration, although the rate of ripening is slower than that of fruits kept in air.

Considerable effort has been expended in attempting to prove whether the rise in C_2H_4 evolution precedes or follows that of respiration (Rhodes, 1980b; Biale and Young, 1981). The results of these investigations show that in several fruits the rise in C_2H_4 production precedes (Pratt and Goeschl, 1968), coincides with (Biale and Young, 1981), or follows (Kosiyachinda and Young, 1975) that of respiration. However, it should be borne in mind that because the sensitivity of the tissue to C_2H_4 increases with maturity (Burg, 1962; Trewaras, 1982), the levels of C_2H_4 already present in the tissue may be adequate to trigger both the rise in respiration and C_2H_4 evolution. Brief exposure to C_2H_4 of early-maturity avocados induces a transient increase in respiration but not ripening (Rhodes, 1980a). Sfakiotakis and Dilley (1973) treated immature apples with propylene, a mimic of C_2H_4 (Burg and Burg, 1967), which increased the rate of respiration but failed to cause ripening.

Exogenous application of C_2H_4 enhances respiration of nonripening tomato mutants but does not induce any of the overt changes of ripening, such as softening and lycopene formation (Herner and Sink, 1973). Further, the rise in respiration requires the continuous presence of C_2H_4 and can be invoked several times in succession. A similar response to exogenous C_2H_4 has been observed with the nonclimacteric citrus fruits (Rhodes, 1980a; Biale and Young, 1981). McMurchie *et al.* (1972) treated bananas (a climacteric fruit) and oranges (a nonclimacteric fruit) with propylene. Propylene elicited a rise in respiration in both fruits, but only in the bananas did it engender production of endogenous C_2H_4. To use the authors' terminology, oranges lack the system II of C_2H_4 synthesis, which the authors consider to be associated with the induction of the autocatalytic production of C_2H_4.

C_2H_4 also enhances the rate of respiration in tissues other than fruits, such as storage roots, tubers, and bulbs, where senescence is not at issue (Reid and Pratt, 1972; Solomos and Laties, 1975, 1976). As in the case of non-ripening tomato mutants and nonclimacteric fruits, the respiratory rise in the above organs requires the continuous presence of exogenous C_2H_4. In addition, the magnitude of the respiratory peak in nonclimacteric fruits, such as oranges, is a function of the concentration of the applied C_2H_4, while that of the climacteric fruits is almost independent of the external C_2H_4 concentration as long as the latter exceeds a particular threshold value (McGlasson, 1970). The results with nonclimacteric fruits clearly indicate a relationship between a substrate, i.e., C_2H_4 in its catalytic sense, and the rate of respiration. In climacteric fruits, the application of exogenous C_2H_4 leads to the induction of C_2H_4 biosynthesis, which, in turn, because of the diffusivity barriers to gas exchange, raises the internal concentration of C_2H_4 to high levels, and these probably saturate the system (Solomos, 1987a).

The rise in respiration in tobacco and English ivy leaves is also associated with an increase in C_2H_4 evolution (Sisler and Pian, 1973; Warman and Solomos, 1988). It was shown by Nichols (1968) that the rise in respiration of cut carnations was preceded by a rise in C_2H_4 evolution. Mayak *et al.* (1977) also observed that treatment of cut carnations with propylene induces both an increase in respiration and C_2H_4 synthesis. Addition of aminovinylglycine (AVG), an inhibitor of C_2H_4 biosynthesis, to the holding

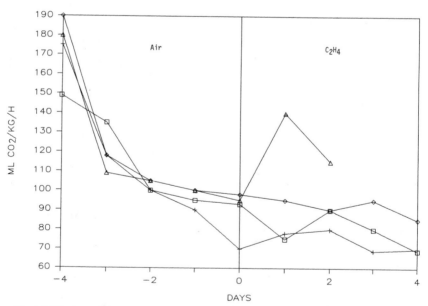

Fig. 4.1. Ethylene effect on carnations treated with STS or AVG. The flowers were kept for 4 days in either 0.5 mM STS or 1 nM AVG. Half of them were then transferred to 2 μl/liter C_2H_4. □, STS–air. +, STS–ethylene. ◇, AVG–air. △, AVG–ethylene.

solution of cut carnations prevents the rise in both C_2H_4 and CO_2 evolution, although the carnations finally wither. Application of exogenous C_2H_4 leads to a sharp increase in CO_2 evolution (Fig. 4.1). Similarly, the addition of silver ions, an inhibitor of C_2H_4 action (Beyer, 1976), abolishes the rise in respiration in cut carnations, and the application of 10 μl/liter fails to increase the respiration rate (Fig. 4.1). Thus, the inhibition of both the biosynthesis and action of C_2H_4 eliminates the rise in respiration without preventing eventual senescence. Marei and Crane (1971) have shown that the rates of CO_2 evolution run parallel with the internal concentration of C_2H_4 during the development and ripening of fig fruits. Finally, nonclimacteric fruits, such as strawberries and cherries, senesce rapidly, with no change in the rate of respiration (Knee et al., 1977; Biale and Young, 1981).

In summary, the above data indicate that the sharp rise in respiration during senescence of detached plant organs is an aspect of C_2H_4 action and not of senescence as such.

IV. MODE OF ACTION OF ETHYLENE ON PLANT RESPIRATION

C_2H_4 induces a wide spectrum of physiological responses in higher plants (Burg, 1962; Pratt and Goeschl, 1968; Abeles, 1973; Morgan, 1976; Lieberman, 1979), some of which are not linked to a rise in respiration (see later).

In theory, C_2H_4 can stimulate respiration by inducing de novo synthesis of respiratory enzymes (coarse control). Evidence with pome fruits shows that the climacteric rise in respiration is associated with an increase in the activity of malic enzyme (Dilley, 1962; Hulme et al., 1968). In the case of climacteric bananas, the activity of PFK increases about 2-fold (Salminen and Young, 1975). However, there are compelling experimental results that indicate that the respiratory potential of preclimacteric fruits and of organs whose respiration increases in response to C_2H_4 treatment may be adequate to sustain the rates of respiration observed at the climacteric peak. Thus, the rate of respiration of preclimacteric avocado and banana slices treated with uncouplers equals or even exceeds that of the climacteric peak (Millerd et al., 1953; Theologis and Laties, 1978b; Day et al., 1980). Similarly, the respiration rate of fresh potato slices is 3- to 5-fold higher than that of the tuber and can be further increased by the addition of uncouplers of oxidative phosphorylation (Laties, 1978; Day et al., 1980). Since the increase in respiration of fresh slices above that of the parent tuber is essentially instantaneous, it cannot be attributed to a sudden increase in biosynthetic activity (Day et al., 1980). Further, the respiration of fresh slices is cyanide sensitive, indicating that cytochrome oxidase is severely restricted in intact tubers. It has been calculated that the glycolytic potential of preclimacteric avocado fruits may be sufficient to handle the anticipated carbon traffic at the climacteric peak (Solomos and Laties, 1974). Salminen and Young (1975) reported that in bananas the activity of key glycolytic enzymes, apart from phosphofructo-kinase (PFK), did not change substantially in the course of the climacteric. Moreover, inhibitors of protein synthesis, while preventing ripening in pears, failed to stop the respiratory rise (Frenkel et al., 1968). It appears, therefore, that C_2H_4 enhances plant respiration by activating a pre-existing enzymatic potential. There is no solid in vitro experimental evidence to suggest direct action of C_2H_4 on isolated respiratory enzymes (but see Fuchs and Gertman, 1973, 1974). It is reasonable to assume (and, indeed, experi-mental evidence suggests) that the in vitro activation of a biochemical path-way may be affected by altering the activity of key regulatory enzymes. Such an alteration can be effected either by changes in the levels of modula-tors (Atkinson, 1977; Newsholme and Start, 1979; Turner and Turner, 1980) or by covalent modification of the enzymes under consideration (Ricard, 1980), and this, in turn, may involve the de novo synthesis of enzymes that catalyze the covalent alterations of the regulatory enzymes.

V. REGULATION OF PLANT RESPIRATION

In senescing fruits, carbohydrates are the principal source of respiratory substrates. Even in avocados, which may contain as much as 15% fat (Biale and Young, 1971), carbohydrates are the main substrates. On the one hand, fat content does not change with ripening, and avocados appear to lack the enzymes involved in the initial steps of fat mobilization (Biale and Young, 1971). On the other hand, the stable carbon isotope composition of respira-tory CO_2 resembles that of cellular carbohydrates throughout ripening (So-lomos, 1983). In the case of leaves, proteins may contribute to respiration at the later stages of senescence (James, 1953; Thimann, 1980).

The respiratory pathways of plants resemble, in general, those of other higher organisms. They include glycolysis, the pentose pathway, the TCA cycle, and the electron transport pathway (ap Rees, 1980, 1985; Day et al., 1980; Turner and Turner, 1980; Wiskich, 1980; Wiskich and Dry, 1985). The existence of a net flux through the respiratory pathway and the necessity to respond rapidly to changes in the energy demand result in the displacement from equilibrium of the overall reaction of respiration (Atkinson, 1977; Newsholme and Start, 1979). It has been observed that the mass action ratios of certain enzymatic steps of the respiratory pathway are greatly displaced from their equilibrium and that these steps are regulatory in nature (Atkinson, 1977). The attributes of regulatory enzymes are: (1) the enzymes are highly allosteric; (2) they catalyze reactions that occur at metabolic crossroads; (3) the mass action ratios of these reactions are greatly displaced from their thermodynamic equilibria constants; and (4) during a transition from one steady state to another there is an inverse relationship between the overall flux and substrates of these reactions (Chance *et al.*, 1958; Hess and Brand, 1965; Newsholme and Start, 1979). This pattern of changes indicates that the activity of the enzymes under consideration has been activated to a greater extent than has that of the immediately preceding and subsequent steps. The crossover theorem of Chance *et al.* (1958) has been used extensively in identifying regulatory reactions from the *in vivo* studies of the changes in the flux, substrates, and products of these reactions (Hess and Brand, 1965; Newsholme and Start, 1979). The possible limitations in the use of the above theorem have been pointed out by Rolleston (1972).

VI. GLYCOLYSIS

It is beyond the scope of this review to report on the kinetic properties of all the enzymes of the glycolytic pathway. In any case, they have been covered extensively by previous reviews (Turner and Turner, 1980; ap Rees, 1985). An attempt will be made here to identify the key regulatory enzymes and assess their role in the regulation of the respiratory rise during senescence of plant tissues. It should be pointed out that this evaluation is further complicated by the existence of glycolytic enzymes in different cell compartments (Dennis and Miernyk, 1982). Nevertheless, there is sufficient *in vivo* evidence to indicate that the steps of phosphofructokinase (PFK) and pyruvate kinase (PK) are pivotal in the regulation of glycolysis in plant tissues. Thus their observed mass action ratios are greatly displaced from equilibrium (Table 4.1). Though the concentration of substrates and metabolites at the site of the enzymes may be influenced by cell compartmentalization, the magnitude of the displacement from equilibrium of PFK and PK makes it unlikely to be the result of the distribution of the glycolytic intermediates in the cell compartments. Moreover, the fact that several steps of glycolysis are at or near equilibrium points to the possibility that cellular compartmentalization of the glycolytic intermediates may not be the cause of the displacement from equilibrium of PFK and PK (Table 4.1). In addition, the observed mass action ratios of the above enzymes move towards equilibrium when the glycolytic flux increases by anoxia (Barker *et al.*, 1967; Kobr and Beevers, 1971; Faiz-ur-Rahman *et al.*, 1974). Measurements of the

TABLE 4.1

Mass Action Ratios and Apparent Equilibrium
Constants for Several Glycolytic Enzymes

		Mass action ratio		
Enzyme	Peas[a]	Carrot disks[b]	*Arum maculatum* spadix[c]	Apparent equilibrium constant
Phosphoglucomutase	—	—	12.6	17.2
Glucose-phosphate isomerase	0.19	0.22	0.18	0.42
Phosphofructokinase	0.016	0.013	0.69	1.05×10^3
Triose-phosphate isomerase	—	0.23	—	0.041
Phosphoglycerate mutase	0.841	—	0.10	0.15
Enolase	0.288	—	1.87	3.70
Pyruvate kinase	6.90	9.25	11.30	11×10^3

[a] Barker *et al.* (1967).
[b] Faiz-ur-Rahman *et al.* (1974).
[c] ap Rees *et al.* (1977)

transient changes in the glycolytic intermediates in response to metabolic
perturbations of the rate of glycolysis have contributed greatly to the investigation of the *in vivo* regulation of glycolysis. In general, enhancement of
glycolysis by anoxia results in a distinct pattern of changes in the glycolytic
intermediates, i.e., crossover changes at the levels of PFK and PK (for reviews see Davies, 1978; Turner and Turner, 1980). Thus, FDP and DHAP
increase sharply with transfer to N_2 while glucose 6-phosphate (G-6-P) and
fructose 6-phosphate (F-6-P) either show no change (Barker *et al.*, 1967) or
decline (Givan, 1968; Kobr and Beevers, 1971; Faiz-ur-Rahman *et al.*, 1974).
PEP, 2-PGA, and 3-PGA also decrease precipitately with transfer to N_2
(Barker *et al.*, 1967; Barker and Kahn, 1968; Kobr and Beevers, 1971; Faiz-
ur-Rahman *et al.*, 1974). ATP, too, decreases in N_2, while AMP and ADP
increase (Barker *et al.*, 1967; Kobr and Beevers, 1971). The control of glycolysis in carrot slices treated with 50 mM KCl, which increases respiration by
110%, was attributed to a coordinated action of PFK and PK (Adams and
Rowan, 1972).

The enhancement of glycolysis by anoxia is probably due to the activation
(fine control) of the key regulatory enzymes, since the changes develop very
rapidly, making it unlikely to be due to *de novo* synthesis of new respiratory
enzymes, and since the changes in the metabolites call for an enhancement
of glycolysis (Turner and Turner, 1980; Solomos, 1983). However, in thermogenic spadices, both the coarse control (100-fold increase in PFK activity)
and fine control mechanisms are involved (ap Rees *et al.*, 1977).

Barker and Solomos (1962) found that in the course of the climacteric, crossover changes developed in bananas at the PFK and PK steps. A similar pattern of changes has been observed in several climacteric fruits as well as in senescing tobacco leaves and tissues (other than fruits), whose respiration was enhanced by exogenous C_2H_4 (Chalmers and Rowan, 1971; MacNicol, 1973; Solomos and Laties, 1974, 1976; Salminen and Young, 1975; Rychter *et al.*, 1979). It thus appears that the enhancement of respiration by C_2H_4 is attended by an increase in glycolysis and that the activation of PK and of the step of the phosphorylation of F-6-P play an important role in the regulation of glycolysis.

In vitro experiments show that plant PFK is subject to a complex regulation by several plant metabolites and ions (Table 4.2). Further, the potency of the various modulators is critically dependent on their relative concentrations with respect to each other (Turner and Turner, 1980). For instance, increasing the concentration of F-6-P diminishes the inhibitory effect of PEP on PFK (Kelly and Turner, 1969). Avocado PFK is inhibited by ATP and citrate (Lowry and Passoneau, 1964). Salminen and Young (1975) have shown that the kinetic properties of banana PFK change in the course of the climacteric respiratory rise. In particular, the enzyme from preclimacteric fruit shows negative cooperativity with respect to F-6-P, the stringency of which is diminished at the climacteric. The $S_{0.5}$ for F-6-P changes from 5.8 mM at the preclimacteric to 1.72 mM at the climacteric. The degree of inhibition by adenine nucleotides also decreases at the climacteric stage (Salminen and Young, 1975). On the basis of electrophoretic data, the authors conclude that: (1) there is no synthesis of new enzyme species in the course of the climacteric, and (2) the enzyme remains oligomeric throughout the climacteric rise. Changes in the kinetic properties of tomato PFK in the course of ripening have also been reported (Rhodes, 1980a). The activation of these two enzymes cannot be completely explained by the associated changes in their most important modulators. Thus, apart from the decrease in the levels of PEP, a negative modulator of PFK (Table 4.2), the changes in ATP and citrate call for a diminution of the glycolytic flux. ATP, which inhibits both PFK and PK, increases in most of the tissues where respiration is enhanced by C_2H_4 (Young and Biale, 1967; Rowan *et al.*, 1969; Sisler and Pian, 1973; Solomos and Laties, 1975; Warman, 1981; Bennett *et al.*, 1987). In bananas, citrate increases during ripening (Palmer, 1971). It should be borne in mind that the concentration of citrate in bananas is such (~ 15 mM) that it will severely restrict plant PFK and PK (Turner and Turner, 1980). In vacuolated plant tissues, cellular compartmentalization may alter the concentrations, especially of organic acids (Beevers *et al.*, 1966) and ions, at the site of the enzymes.

The investigation of the control of the phosphorylation of F-6-P to

Theophanes Solomos

TABLE 4.2

Modulation of Enzymes Involved in the Regulation
of Glycolysis

Enzyme	Modulators	
	Positive	Negative
PKF[a]	P_i, K^+, C^-, Mg^{2+}	PEP, 3-PGA, ATP, ADP, Gluconate-6-P, citrate
PK[a]	K^+, Mg^{2+}	ATP, Ca^{2+}, citrate
PFP[b]	F-$2,6$-P_2, Mg^{2+}	P_i
F-6-P, 2K[b,c]	P_i, F-6-P	DHAP, 3-PGA
F-2,6-P_2ase[b]		F-6-P, P_i

[a] Turner and Turner (1980).
[b] Kombrink *et al.* (1983).
[c] Cseke and Buchanan (1983).

F-1,6-P_2 is further complicated by Carnal and Black's (1979) discovery that this reaction is also catalyzed by another phosphofructokinase which, in contrast to PFK, uses inorganic pyrophosphate as a phosphate donor instead of ATP

$$P_iP_i + \text{F-6-P} \longleftrightarrow \text{F-1,6-P}_2 + P_i$$

Pyrophosphate F-6-P phosphotransferase (PFP) is widespread in plant tissues (Sabularse and Anderson, 1981a,b; Carnal and Black, 1983; Kombrink *et al.*, 1983; van Schaftingen *et al.*, 1983; Smyth *et al.*, 1984).

The properties of PFP have been studied in a number of plant tissues: mung beans (Saburlarse and Anderson, 1981a,b), spinach leaves (Cseke *et al.*, 1982), potato tubers (van Schaftingen *et al.*, 1983), and castor bean endosperm (Kombrink *et al.*, 1983). These studies have shown that: (1) P_iP_i is the exclusive phosphate donor; (2) the enzyme is localized in the cytosol; and (3) the activity of PFP is modified by several cellular metabolites and ions (Table 4.2). The most notable positive modulator of PFP is F-2,6-P_2 whose stimulatory effect is potentiated by F6P and markedly inhibited by P_i. Since F-2,6-P_2 inhibits F-1,6-P_2 phosphatase and since its levels are altered with changes in the rate of sucrose synthesis, the compound is considered a cardinal one in the allocation of photosynthates between sucrose and starch (Stitt *et al.*, 1984b; Cseke *et al.*, 1984). The levels of F-2,6-P_2 increase during gluconeogenesis of castor bean endosperms (Kruger and Beevers, 1985). It has also been shown that the content of F-2,6-P_2 increases with an enhancement of glycolysis in N_2 (Kruger and Beevers, 1985). An increase in the levels of F-2,6-P_2 has been observed in the course of the respiratory rise in carrot roots in response to C_2H_4 treatments (Stitt *et al.*, 1986) and in climacteric avocado and banana (Bennett *et al.*, 1987; Beaury *et al.*, 1987).

It has been shown that the enzymes that catalyze the synthesis of F-2,-6-P_2, F-6-P, 2 kinase (F-6-P 2K) and its breakdown, F-2,6-biphosphatase (F-2,6-P_2ase), are present in plant tissues (Cseke and Buchanan, 1983; Stitt *et al.*, 1984a; Kruger and Beevers, 1985). Further, the activity of these enzymes is subject to the regulation of cellular metabolites. In particular, F-6-P and P_i activate F-6-P 2K, while DHAP and 3-PGA inhibit it (Cseke *et al.*, 1984; Kruger and Beevers, 1985). No activator of F-2,6-P_2ase has yet been discovered. However, the enzyme is inhibited by both of its products, namely, F-6-P and P_i (Stitt *et al.*, 1984a; Kruger and Beevers, 1985). It is obvious that if PFP contributes to the enhancement of glycolysis engendered by C_2H_4, the effect of the hormone must be exerted on the enzymes involved in the regulation of the cellular levels of F-2,6-P_2.

In avocado fruits, the pattern of changes in the levels of F-6-P and DHAP alone should result in a decrease in the levels of F-2,6-P_2 during the climacteric, because F-6-P drops sharply while DHAP increases 2- to 3-fold (Solomos and Laties, 1974). However, 3-PGA decreases, and this, in conjunction with a possible rise in P_i, may be adequate to counteract the effects of the changes in F-6-P and DHAP. It should be pointed out that the amount of F-2,6-P present in preclimacteric avocados (Bennett *et al.*, 1987) and bananas (Solomos, unpublished observations; Beaury *et al.*, 1987) is adequate to saturate PFP (Sabularse and Anderson, 1981b; Kombrink *et al.*, 1983; van Schaftingen *et al.*, 1983). The degree of participation of PFP in the regulation of glycolysis has not yet been unequivocally established (ap Rees, 1985). It has been observed that in thermogenic spadices of *Arum maculatum*, the activities of PFK and PFP increase by 100-fold and 2- to 3-fold, respectively (ap Rees, 1985). The fact that adenine nucleotides are not involved in the regulation of PFP may also indicate that the function of the latter may not be closely linked to energy production.

The investigation of the role of PFP in plant respiration is further complicated by its cellular localization (cytosol). For instance, in bananas, the rise in respiration is associated with a massive breakdown of starch (Gane, 1936; Palmer, 1971). A number of experimental investigations suggest that the degradation of starch is mediated by starch phosphorylase, since sucrose is the first sugar to increase (Gane, 1936) and since the ratio of the increments in glucose and fructose during ripening is 1 : 1, indicating that sucrose is their precursor (Yang and Ho, 1958). If triose phosphates are the main forms of phosphorylated sugars translocated from the amyloplasts, as in the case of chloroplasts, then the PFP step in the cytosol will be bypassed and the plastid PFK will be the sole step regulating the levels of triose phosphates.

VII. PENTOSE PATHWAY

The enzymes of the pentose pathway have not been investigated as extensively as have those of glycolysis (Turner and Turner, 1980; ap Rees, 1985). Ashihara and Komanine (1974) have reported that of the enzymes of the pentose pathway, only the overall reaction of G-6-P dehydrogenase is displaced from equilibrium. In addition, this enzyme is shown to be under both coarse and fine controls (Turner and Turner, 1980). The latter authors consider the ratio of NADPH/NADP to be the most important factor involved in the regulation of G-6-P dehydrogenase *in vivo* in higher plants. With respect to fruits, there is no solid experimental information available concerning the changes in the activities of the pentose phosphate pathway reactions, the levels of the metabolites, or the modulators of these reactions in the course of ripening.

VIII. TRICARBOXYLIC ACID CYCLE

Mitochondria capable of linking the oxidation of Krebs cycle intermediates to phosphorylation have been isolated from fruits at various stages of ripeness (Biale and Young, 1971; Romani, 1978). Lance *et al.* (1965) state, "In the presence of cofactors, taking State 3 as the most reliable criterion, no major changes in the oxidative abilities of mitochondria from avocados during the ripening process have been found." The activity of the TCA cycle could, in principle, be controlled by (1) levels of enzymes, (2) substrate availability, (3) allosteric modulation of key regulatory enzymes, and (4) the capacity of the electron transport chain. The available experimental evidence indicates that in most tissues the levels of the enzymes of the TCA cycle are adequate to maintain the observed rates of dark respiration in intact tissue (Wiskich and Dry, 1985). It has also been pointed out earlier that a fraction of the respiratory potential is realized in preclimacteric fruits and storage organs whose respiration is enhanced by C_2H_4 (Day *et al.*, (1980).

The availability of substrate could, under certain circumstances, be a factor limiting the traffic through the cycle. Thus, Saglio and Pradet (1980) observed that when the food reserves of excised corn roots are depleted, the addition of DNP does not elicit an increase in respiration, and its ability to do so is restored by the exogenous supply of sugars. Givan and Torrey (1968) found that the addition of pyruvate enhances the rate of respiration of unstarved cells of *Acer pseudoplantanus*. Several authors have also observed that in photosynthetic tissues, there is a correlation between photosynthesis and dark respiration, which is interpreted in terms of the magnitude of levels of respiratory substrates (Azcon-Bieto and Osmond, 1983; Lambers, 1985). However, in nonphotosynthetic tissues with large food reserves, such as preclimacteric fruits, potato tubers, etc., the supply of TCA intermediates must reflect a feedback control at the early stages of carbohydrate oxidation (see below).

Several of the enzymes involved in the TCA cycle are located at metabolic control points. Wiskich (1980) has summarized the most important regulatory metabolites of the enzymes of the cycle. However, there is a paucity of *in vivo* results to indicate the operation of allosteric regulation of the enzymes in the cycle (Wiskich and Dry, 1985). The studies of the changes in the intermediates of the Krebs cycle under different respiratory regimes and during the transition from one steady state to another are limited and inconclusive. In fact, the pattern of changes that occurs in the TCA cycle intermediates during the air-to-N_2 and N_2-to-air transitions found in green peas led Wager (1961) to propose that in this tissue the TCA cycle is not a major pathway contributing to respiration. However, it should be kept in mind that measurements of the overall concentrations may not reflect the concentration present inside the mitochondria and also that the availability of cofactors may distort the interpretation of the results of the changes in the levels of the TCA intermediates. In addition, the metabolite transport system (Wiskich, 1977; Hanson, 1985), the presence of malic enzyme (Lance and Rustin, 1984; Palmer and Ward, 1985), and the action of transaminases would be expected to drastically alter the assumed cyclical utilization of the TCA cycle intermediates. In banana fruits, most of the TCA cycle intermediates increase during the climacteric rise (Palmer, 1971; Solomos, 1983). In apples, however, the content of malic acid falls during ripening due to the synthesis of malic enzyme (Dilley, 1962; Hulme *et al.*, 1968). It should be remembered that the restriction of a step of the Krebs cycle alone is not sufficient for the overall regulation of sugar oxidation, unless this constraint exerts a feedback inhibition on the initial steps of carbohydrate oxidation. In this respect, isocitrate dehydrogenase is an appropriate enzyme, since its restrictions would be expected to raise the levels of citrate, a negative modulator of both PFK and PK. Further, plant isocitrate dehydrogenase is subject to allosteric modulation. In particular, it is inhibited by NADH (Cox and Davies, 1967; Duggleby and Dennis, 1970; Wiskich, 1980).

With isolated mitochondria in the presence of TCA cycle intermediates, the availability of ADP is the predominant factor that controls the rate of oxygen uptake, unless the external ATP/ADP ratio increases to a value of 20 or higher (Day and Wiskich, 1977). *In vivo*, the cytosolic values of the ATP/ADP ratio are smaller than the above (Stitt *et al.*, 1982).

In a large number of plant tissues, including slices of preclimacteric fruits and storage organs, the addition of uncouplers of oxidative phosphorylation invariably elicits an increase in respiration (Millerd *et al.*, 1953; Beevers, 1961, 1974; Day *et al.*, 1980). These data thus indicate that oxidative phosphorylation is highly important in the regulation of respiration. This control, however, cannot be thought of as a state-4-to-state-3 transition. On the one hand, ADP is always present in intact tissues. On the other, it decreases, or at least shows marginal change, in the course of the climacteric of avocados (Young and Biale, 1967) and during the rise in respiration of *Hedera helix* leaves treated with C_2H_4 (Solomos, 1983). Hence, the control of oxidative phosphorylation in plant respiration is not exerted by the level of ADP per se, but rather by its feedback restriction on substrate level mobilization, namely glycolysis, the pentose pathway, and, possibly, on some enzymes of the Krebs cycle (Laties, 1982).

IX. ELECTRON TRANSPORT

The available experimental evidence shows that the composition of the electron transport chain in senescing fruits is similar to that of other plant tissues and that this is not altered in the course of ripening (Lance *et al.*, 1965; Moreau and Romani, 1982). Intact fruits and mitochondria isolated from them are resistant to cyanide (Moreau and Romani, 1982). It is well documented that cyanide-resistant oxidase branches from the main electron transport chain at the level of ubiquinone (Bendall and Bonner, 1971; Henry and Nyns, 1975; Storey, 1980; Laties, 1982; Siedow, 1982; Lance *et al.*, 1985). Further, the cyanide-insensitive path is not coupled to ATP formation (see preceding references). It has been observed that: (1) cyanide induces in avocado fruits the climacteric rise in respiration, C_2H_4 evolution, and, eventually, ripening; (2) the pattern of changes in the glycolytic intermediates of avocados and potato tubers treated with HCN is similar to that invoked by C_2H_4; (3) C_2H_4 enhances respiration in tissues where HCN acts similarly, while having no effect on tissues whose respiration is inhibited by HCN; and (4) C_2H_4 induces cyanide-resistant respiration in fresh potato tuber slices (Solomos and Laties, 1974, 1975; Rychter *et al.*, 1978, 1979; Day *et al.*, 1980). On the basis of these observations, it was suggested that for C_2H_4 to enhance respiration, the presence of cyanide-resistant respiration was necessary. Recently, Tucker and Laties (1984) also reported that in avocados the changes in the polysome profiles and the synthesis of new messages were identical in the C_2H_4 and cyanide-treated fruits. Two crucial questions remain to be examined experimentally: first, is the C_2H_4-enhanced respiration prevented by the inhibitors of the alternative oxidase? Second, is the alternative oxidase functioning in the absence of inhibitors of the cytochrome path?

The answer to the first question appears to be in the negative since treatment of banana slices with either SHAM, an inhibitor of the alternative oxidase (Schonbaum *et al.*, 1971), or cyanide fails to prevent the rise in respiration in response to C_2H_4 (Tucker, 1978; Solomos, 1983). Thus, the stimulation of respiration by C_2H_4 appears to be independent of the nature of the terminal oxidases. In other words, the stimulatory effects of C_2H_4 must be exerted at substrate-level mobilization, i.e., glycolysis and/or the pentose phosphate pathway.

To answer the second question, the mechanism that regulates the apportioning of electrons between the cytochrome pathway and the alternative pathways will be briefly examined. It is obvious that the existence of the nonphosphorylating alternative path calls for a strict regulation of its function, since its engagement will greatly reduce the efficiency of oxidative phosphorylation. Bahr and Bonner (1973) have shown that the engagement of the alternative oxidase is dependent neither on the redox state of the cytochromes nor on the energy state of the mitochondria, since electrons are diverted to the alternative by either cyanide or antimycin, and in both coupled and uncoupled mitochondria. The authors conclude that the apportioning of electrons between the two paths is controlled by an equilibrium mechanism. They propose that both paths share a common carrier, which is in ready equilibrium with the first component of the alternative. The standard redox potential of these two carriers differs, the common component being more positive, thus allowing the first member of the alternative oxidase to be completely oxidized, while the former is partially reduced. In other words, the flux through the cytochrome path is favored over that of the alternative. Bahr and Bonner (1973) derived an equation by which the fraction of the alternative that is engaged in the absence of inhibitors of the cytochrome path can be calculated:

$$V_T = V_{cyt} + \rho g(i), \tag{1}$$

where V_T is the total rate of oxygen uptake, $g(i)$ are the rates of oxygen uptake in the presence of different concentrations of inhibitors of the alternative oxidase of cyanide-inhibited mitochondria, and ρ is a number between 0 and 1 signifying the fraction of the alternative that is engaged. It should be pointed out that the putative first component of the alternative oxidase has not yet been unequivocally identified (Storey, 1976; Lance *et al.*, 1985). Stegink and Siedow (1986) reported evidence that suggests an engaging factor is necessary to link the alternative oxidase to the main electron transport chain. DeTroostembergh and Nyns (1978) developed a model whereby ubiquinone feeds electrons to the two paths in proportion to their capacities. According to this model, it would be expected that a portion of the alternative path would be engaged, a fact that may contradict a great deal of experimental evidence pointing to the contrary (Theologis and Laties, 1978a,b,c; Laties, 1982; Lambers, 1985; Lance $et\ al.$, 1985). Theologis and Laties (1978a) modified Eq. (1) to determine the engagement of the alternative oxidase in intact tissue respiration. This modification involves the subtraction from the total respiration, V_T, of the fraction of O_2 uptake that is resistant to the combined application of cyanide and SHAM. This procedure has been further simplified by measuring the rate of O_2 uptake in the control and in the presence of maximal concentrations of cyanide and SHAM singly, and of both combined. After subtracting the residual from the total rate of oxygen uptake, ρ is calculated as follows:

$$V_T = V_{cyt} + \rho V_{alt}. \tag{2}$$

Lance $et\ al.$ (1985) have cautioned that V_{cyt} and V_{alt} may not reflect their maximal capacities, but rather those that can be realized under experimental conditions. A further complication is introduced by the fact that in certain tissues the magnitude of the residual varies with the external oxygen concentration (Solomos, 1983). It was observed that in well-aerated banana slices, the magnitude of the residual was equal to that of the control slices (Tucker, 1978). This, in turn, will result in V_{cyt} and V_{alt} having zero capacities, which of course is not the case. It would, therefore, be advisable to calculate ρ at O_2 concentrations which, while severely restricting the "residual," have, nevertheless, no effect on the alternative oxidase.

Measurements of ρ in banana, avocado, potato, and sweet potato slices indicate that, with the possible exception of avocado slices, the alternative oxidase is not engaged ($\rho = 0$) unless the cytochrome path is saturated by the addition of uncouplers (Theologis and Laties, 1978a,b,c). Similar results have been reported with $Glycine\ max$ axes (Leopold and Mushgrave, 1980).

A survey of the respiration of intact roots and leaves of 10 plant species shows that the values of ρ varied from zero to unity (Day and Lambers, 1983; Lambers $et\ al.$, 1983). Azcon-Bieto $et\ al.$ (1983) observed that both the rate of dark respiration of wheat $(Triticum\ sativum)$ and $(Spinacia\ oleracea)$ leaves increased with increasing levels of sugars. In leaves collected at the end of the night, ρ was zero. It increased to 0.53 after the leaves had been allowed to photosynthesize for several hours. Furthermore, the addition of sucrose to slices of wheat leaves selected at the end of the night increased both the rate of O_2 uptake and ρ. The regulation of the engagement of the alternative appears to be influenced by adenylates and by the supply of reducing equivalents to the electron transport chain. Day and Lambers (1983) reported that the addition of uncouplers to intact roots of wheat and spinach enhanced the flux through both the cytochrome path and the alternative paths. This led the authors to suggest that in these roots the engagement of the alternative path was due to the restriction by adenylates of the electron flux through the cytochrome path and that the supply of TCAC intermediates was in excess of the functional capacity of the cytochrome path. On the other hand, in bean roots (*Phaseolus vulgaris*), the addition of uncouplers, while enhancing the flux through the alternative path, did not influence that through the cytochrome (Day and Lambers, 1983). This was interpreted to indicate that the capacity of the cytochrome was in itself the limiting step, thus affecting the engagement of the alternative oxidase. Collectively, the experimental evidence indicates that the alternative oxidase is engaged only if the cytochrome path is limited by oxidative phosphorylation or its capacity. This led Lambers (1982) to suggest that the alternative path acts as an energy overflow (see also Laties, 1982). The engagement of the alternative path under conditions where the flux through the electron transport chain is under the control of oxidative phosphorylation implies that the rate of substrate supply is in excess of that required by the rate of ATP production. Further, it raises a very fundamental question. If the flux of electrons through the cytochrome path is restricted by oxidative phosphorylation, site 1 should be similarly restricted. How, then, do the electrons pass through this energy-transducing step at a higher rate than in the last two? Laties (1982) proposed that the protomotive force (pmf) involves localized energy domains, with site 1 being less restricted than the other two sites. Alternatively, site 1 may be bypassed through the rotenone- and nonphosphorylating-resistant path (Palmer and Ward, 1985).

It is to be noted that engagement of the alternative oxidase has been observed mainly with tissues where the wound effect on respiration is minimal (Lambers, 1985). This renders suspect the feasibility of extrapolating the results from tissue slices to intact organs. Nevertheless, collectively the available experimental results suggest that the participation of the alternative oxidase is realized whenever the flow of available electrons through the cytochrome path is restricted by oxidative phosphorylation or by the capacity of the former. Be that as it may, it appears that substrate-level mobilization is in excess of that required for the production of ATP.

It is a well-established fact that low O_2 levels greatly delay the onset of senescence in fruits and that a gradual decrease in the external O_2 concentration causes a biphasic decrease in the rate of respiration in a number of plant tissues (James, 1953). This relationship between rate of respiration and external O_2 concentration has been attributed in turn to: (1) the existence of an "oxidase" that somehow restricts the early steps of glucose oxidation and whose affinity for O_2 is lower than that of cytochrome oxidase (Blackman, 1954); (2) the existence of two oxidases with different affinities for O_2 (Mapson and Burton, 1962); and (3) the effect of the diffusion barrier on O_2 penetration into the organs (Chevillotte, 1973). Data with sweet potato roots, apples, and avocado fruits indicate that the concentration of O_2 at which the initial decrease in respiration is perceived is not sufficiently low to limit cytochrome oxidase (Fidler *et al.*, 1973; Solomos, 1983; Tucker and Laties, 1985; Solomos, 1987b). Furthermore, a restriction of the cytochrome path would be expected to induce partial anaerobiosis, resulting, in time, in the accumulation of end products of glycolysis, a hypothesis that is not borne out by a large body of experimental evidence (Fidler *et al.*, 1973). When both CO_2 evolution and O_2 uptake are measured, the isotherm of both are parallel up to the extinction point, where the rate of O_2 uptake slows rapidly, while that of CO_2 tends to increase (Biale and Young, 1947; James, 1953). At this juncture the tissue begins to experience anaerobiosis. In the case of potato tubers and sweet potato roots, this point corresponds with an internal partial O_2 pressure of 0.5–0.7 kPa (Burton, 1982; T. Solomos, unpublished observations). Tucker and Laties (1985) have determined the isotherm of O_2 uptake in avocados at 25 kPa total pressure. Despite the 4-fold increase in the diffusivity of O_2, the shape of the isotherm at 25 kPa is still biphasic. In short, the experimental evidence indicates that the biphasic nature of the respiratory drift in response to the decrease in the external O_2 concentration is not the result of the resistance to diffusion. These authors have calculated that the apparent K_ms for O_2 of the high affinity and low affinity cytochrome oxidase were 9 μM and 74 μM, respectively. However, the authors concluded that the low affinity system is not a terminal oxidase; rather it was a regulatory protein which exerts a feedback control at the level of substrate mobilization.

If the magnitude of the actual diffusion barriers of the skin and flesh, and an estimated value of the diffusion from the intercellular spaces to the interior of the cells are all taken into consideration, together with the rate of respiration, intercellular O_2 concentration, and the assumption that the $K_m^{O_2}$ of the cytochrome oxidase is 0.05 μM (Solomos, 1988a), then the apparent $K_m^{O_2}$ of the low affinity system is about 2 μM (Table 4.3). The results of Table 4.3 further illustrate that oxygenases with relatively high $K_m^{O_2}$, such as lipoxygenase, ascorbic acid oxidase, etc., do not appreciably contribute to the respiration of the intact apple fruit. An apparent $K_m^{O_2}$ of 1.7 and 2.5 μM for the alternative oxidase has been calculated in sweet potato slices (Solomos, 1988b). Similar values had been reported previously for the alternative oxidase (Siedow, 1982). The data thus indicate that the apparent $K_m^{O_2}$ of the low affinity oxidase is similar to that of the alternative oxidase. However, that in itself, though indicative of, is insufficient to unequivocally establish, a bona fide engagement of the alternative oxidase. The investigation of the relationship between the rate of respiration and external oxygen concentration in climacteric fruits is complicated by the fact that O_2 is required for the action of C_2H_4 and nothing is certain concerning the affinity of this system

TABLE 4.3

Internal O_2 Concentration, Rate of Respiration, and Percentage of V_{max}
of Oxidases with Different $K_m^{O_2}$

Intercellular partial O_2 pressure kPa	$\mu l\ CO_2/g/hour$	Percentage of V_{max} $K_m^{O_2}$ (μM)				
		0.05	2	2.5	3	4
19.25	5.92	99.98	99.45	99.3	99.1	98.54
6.50	5.90	99.94	99.13	97.52	96.92	95.15
4.91	4.92	99.91	97.47	96.65	95.85	93.52
4.13	4.40	99.90	96.96	95.99	95.03	92.28
2.23	3.34	99.78	93.81	91.91	90.10	85.04
0.92	3.30	98.82	73.60	67.65	62.59	51.11
0.49	2.20	85.63	16.57	12.91	10.65	6.93

for O_2 (see later). Thus the observed decrease in respiration in climacteric fruits by relatively high O_2 concentrations may reflect a diminution of C_2H_4 action rather than a restriction of the terminal oxidase.

Regardless of the nature of the system with low affinity for O_2, its curtailment leads to a feedback restriction in substrate mobilization, since its curtailment does not result in the accumulation of respiratory intermediates. The nature of this feedback mechanism is not yet known. One can only speculate. It appears reasonable to assume that this "system" is somehow related to the respiratory pathways. If the alternative oxidase is engaged, and if it acts as an overflow system, its curtailment could result in the increase of oxaloacetate, which, in turn, through the activity of PEPCK, could raise the level of PEP (Lance and Rustin, 1984), a potent inhibitor of PFK (Turner and Turner, 1980). In addition, the level of NADH, and possibly NADPH, could be raised, and this may exert a feedback restriction on the pentose and glycolytic pathways (Turner and Turner, 1980). Alternatively, the presence of (an) O_2-sensing protein(s) may be invoked, and this, in turn, may restrict the early steps of glucose oxidation (Tucker and Laties, 1984).

A note of caution is in order. It has been pointed out above that low O_2 levels delay the onset of ripening and, in addition, O_2 concentrations lower than those in air decrease the rate of ripening of initiated bananas (Mapson and Robinson, 1966; Quazi and Freebairn, 1970). It is tempting to suggest that these aspects of O_2 action may be related to respiration, since hypoxia can, in certain cases, decrease the energy charge and hence the rate of plant metabolism (Atkinson, 1977; Pradet and Raymond, 1983). However, the effects of low O_2 on senescence may not be considered to be the consequence of a low adenylate energy charge. It has been demonstrated previously that the effects of low O_2 on respiration and senescence can be dissociated. O_2 concentrations between 5 and 10% have no effect on apple respiration, although they delay the onset of the climacteric (Burg and Thimann, 1959). We have observed that 8% O_2 has no effect on apple respiration but delays the onset of the rise in C_2H_4 and CO_2 evolution for several days (Solomos, unpublished observations). Burg and Burg (1967) reported that the effect of C_2H_4 on pea epicotyl segments was diminished by O_2 concentrations that did not affect respiration. Therefore, the delaying effects of relatively low O_2 concentrations on senescence must be exerted through the diminution of the activities of oxygen-utilizing enzyme(s), which have relatively low affinities for O_2 and which are involved with the induction, production, and action of C_2H_4, and/or other as yet unknown processes (Burg, 1962; Adams and Yang, 1979; Lieberman, 1979).

X. RESIDUAL

The term *residual* was coined by Theologis and Laties (1978a) to describe the portion of O_2 uptake that is resistant to the combined addition of inhibitors of both the cytochrome and alternative paths. The subtraction of the residual from the total rate of O_2 uptake implicitly assumes that it functions in the absence of inhibitors. Two questions must then be addressed experimentally. First, is the residual localized in mitochondria? Second, does it function in the absence of inhibitors of the mitochondrial terminal oxidases? Data indicating the presence of the "residual oxidase(s)" in isolated mitochondria have been reported (Lance *et al.*, 1985). However, there is compelling experimental evidence indicating that the residual is cytosolic in origin. In the first place, the magnitude of the residual in isolated mitochondria is but an insignificant fraction of the state 3 rate, while with intact tissues, the residual rate of O_2 uptake may equal that of the control tissue, depending on the external O_2 concentration (Solomos, 1983; Tucker, 1978). Work with sweet potato and avocado slices shows that the affinity for O_2 of the residual is rather small (Solomos, 1983; M. L. Tucker, personal communication). In the case of sweet potato slices, the residual is not saturated, even when the slices are kept in air-saturated solutions. Oxygen electrode traces of sweet potato and fresh potato slices are monotonic until the O_2 concentration decreases to about 15 μM (Solomos, 1983, and Solomos, unpublished observations). In cyanide-treated sweet potato slices, the rate of O_2 uptake is also of zero order until the level of O_2 begins to limit the alternative oxidase (Solomos, 1983). These observations show that in sweet potato and fresh potato slices the residual does not significantly contribute to slice respiration unless the cytochrome and the alternative paths are inhibited simultaneously. The contribution of the residual to intact fruits and storage organs must be negligible, since the rate of O_2 uptake is usually of zero order until the tension of O_2 in the intercellular spaces decreases to about 7 to 8 kPa (Table 4.3), concentrations that would be expected to severely restrict the residual "oxidase(s)." Briefly, the residual "oxidases" are cytosolic in origin and act as a compensatory system when the cytochrome and the alternative paths are inhibited at the same time. These observations raise some crucial questions. What is the pathway of glucose oxidation in the presence of both SHAM and KCN? Is the Krebs cycle partially functioning, and are the reducing equivalents then transferred to cytosolic enzymes by the mechanism proposed by Day and Wiskich (1978)? Or is glucose being oxidized exclusively by the pentose shunt? These questions will remain unanswered until detailed analytical data become available concerning the changes in the respiratory intermediates in tissues in which respiration is inhibited by the simultaneous addition of SHAM and KCN.

XI. CELLULAR ORGANIZATION

The effect of cellular organization on the regulation of respiration in plant tissues in general, and in senescing ones in particular, is very difficult to assess. Blackman and Parija (1928) speculated that the increase in the rate of respiration during the climacteric was the result of the cellular organization "decreasing" in resistance. It was visualized that during senescence the distribution of metabolites and enzymes is altered due to changes in membrane permeability, resulting in an increase in the availability of substrate to the enzymes. There is little doubt that membrane properties change in the course of senescence. However, the causal relationship between rate of respiration and enhanced membrane permeability has not been unequivocally established. Sacher (1963, 1973) observed that the apparent free space of banana fruits increases in the course of ripening and that this increase precedes the rise in respiration. Similar results were reported by Brady *et al.* (1970a,b). Hanson and Kende (1975) found an increased ion efflux from the vacuoles in the rib tissue of morning glory *(Ipomea tricolor)* flowers, which led the authors to suggest that C_2H_4 alters membrane permeability in selected cells of the tissue. Brady *et al.* (1970b), on the other hand, demonstrated that treatment of banana slices with C_2H_4 resulted in a rise in respiration prior to the increase in the leakage of amino acids. It appears that the changes in membrane permeability are probably the result of senescence, rather than the cause of it. In the first place, it is difficult to assess experimentally subtle changes in membrane permeability in bulky tissues such as fruits. Second, it has been pointed out previously that ion leakage, the method used to measure membrane permeability, may reflect changes in the ions available for leakage (Burg, 1968; Vickery and Bruinsma, 1973). In this way, the increase in the apparent free space in bananas (Sacher, 1973) and avocados (Ben Yehoshua, 1964) may overestimate the actual changes that occur *in vivo* (Burg, 1968).

It should be emphasized that changes in cellular distribution of regulatory metabolites and ions need not require drastic changes in membrane permeability. It is to be expected that their cellular distribution is under metabolic control. A case in point is the observed increase of K^+ in the cytosol of tomato fruit pericarp tissue in the course of ripening (Vickery and Bruinsma, 1973). Since K^+ is a requirement for PK, and since it is a positive modulator of PFK, its increase in the cytosol may contribute to the stimulation of respiration.

XII. PHYSIOLOGICAL SIGNIFICANCE OF THE CLIMACTERIC RISE IN PLANT SENESCENCE

It has already been pointed out that for senescence to proceed, metabolic energy is required. Teleologically, an increase in anabolic activities will be expected to decrease the level of ATP and increase that of ADP. In fact, the observed increase in the protein levels of ripening apples led Hulme (1954) to propose that the expected rise in ADP was the cause of the climacteric respiratory burst. However, enhancement of anabolic activities would require an increase in energy charge (Atkinson, 1977). The available analytical data concerning the changes in the energy charge in senescing plant tissues are scanty. In avocados, energy charge increases in the course of ripening (Young and Biale, 1967), while in C_2H_4-treated leaves, its increase is marginal (Warman, 1981). The available analytical data show that in senescing fruits and leaves, the level of ATP increases sharply during the respiratory rise (Young and Biale, 1967; Rowan *et al.* 1969; Sisler and Pian, 1973; Solomos and Laties, 1976; Malik and Thimann, 1980; Warman and Solomos, 1988; Bennett *et al.*, 1987). In senescing ivy leaves *(Hedera helix)*, the increase in ATP is associated with a net increase in the total adenylate pool. If a similar situation occurs in senescing tissues other than ivy leaves, the rise in the total adenine nucleotides calls for a diminution of respiration, since PFK is inhibited by all three of them (Turner and Turner, 1980). Therefore, C_2H_4 must introduce changes that decrease the stringency of the restraints imposed by adenylates on respiration, allowing a simultaneous enhancement of respiration and elevation of ATP and total adenylate concentration.

On the basis of the present state of knowledge regarding the nature and magnitude of the sinks of metabolic energy in senescing plant tissues, it is impossible to calculate the energy demand with any degree of precision. One can guess, however, that the turnover of ATP is rapid. Thus, at the climacteric peak of bananas, the rate of respiration is $60-70$ $\mu l/g/$hour and the level of ATP is $90-100$ nmol/g (Solomos, unpublished observations). If we assume that glucose is oxidized via the Krebs cycle and that its oxidation is tightly coupled to phosphorylation, about $18,750$ nmol of ATP are formed per hour per gram of tissue, which suggests a value of 200 for the turnover of the ATP pool. It is obvious that for respiration to proceed for any length of time, ATP must be utilized very rapidly.

The facts that: (1) protein synthesis is required for senescence to proceed (Frenkel *et al.*, 1968; McGlasson *et al.*, 1971; Martin and Thimann, 1972; Brady and Tung, 1975); (2) several messages have been observed and some characterized (Rattanapanone *et al.*, 1977; Brady *et al.*, 1982; Christoffersen and Laties, 1982; Grierson and Tucker, 1983; Grierson *et al.*, 1986); and (3) an increase in polysomes has been noted (Ku and Romani, 1970; Speirs *et al.*, 1984) in senescing fruits, and tissues, other than fruits, treated with C_2H_4 have all led to the suggestion that the climacteric respiratory burst is necessary to produce ATP adequate for sustaining these processes. However, a number of observations, discussed below, indicate that the anabolic reactions attendant upon fruit senescence may be satisfied by a respiratory increment smaller than the climacteric.

Brady and O'Connell (1976) found that treatment of banana slices with C_2H_4 for 6 hours induced a transient increase in the rate of respiration but not ripening, while a 12-hour exposure induced the typical climacteric rise in CO_2 evolution and eventual ripening. On the other hand, the amount of radioactive amino acids incorporated into protein after 24 hours was similar in both sets of slices, although their rates of respiration differed by about 2-fold. The authors calculated that the spate of enhanced protein synthesis in response to C_2H_4 was associated with an increase in the rate of protein turnover, which amounted to the replacement of $25-50\%$ of the total protein per day. It has been calculated that in bananas an even more exaggerated rate of protein turnover, together with the attendant increase in sucrose synthesis, could be sustained by a smaller rise in respiration than the climacteric (Solomos, 1983). Moreover, bananas can ripen normally although at a reduced rate, without a perceptible increase in respiration (Quazi and Freebairn, 1970). Although the synthesis of specific proteins associated with ripening may continue throughout the climacteric, the rate of amino acid incorporation into proteins, a measure of the rate of total protein synthesis, declines sharply long before the climacteric peak (for references, see Section III). In addition, a number of overt changes, such as softening and production of volatiles, occur after the climacteric peak. Tucker and Laties (1984) have demonstrated that in ripening avocados, both the increase in polysomes and poly(A)$^+$ RNA reach their maximum values in the middle of the climacteric rise and decrease sharply at the peak. Moreover, in avocado fruits, cyanide induces identical overt, physiological, biochemical, and molecular changes associated with normal ripening (Solomos and Laties, 1974; Tucker and Laties, 1984). Thus, in avocado fruits, the anabolic activities of ripening can be maintained with a greatly diminished rate of ATP production. It should also be kept in mind that nonclimacteric fruits undergo rapid changes without a concomitant respiratory increase. The question then emerges regarding the need for the observed levels of ATP: Is it an attempt by the senescing tissue to maintain the metabolic homeostasis (Romani, 1984)? Or is it due to a diminished balance between the rate of production of ATP and its utilization by the anabolic reactions attending ripening? In the case of senescing attached leaves, the demands for biological energy may be expected to exceed that of fruits, since in senescing leaves, besides the synthesis of new proteins (Thimann, 1980; Brady and Tung, 1975), the translocation of minerals and amino acids to the parent plant would be expected to increase the demand for ATP. One may further posit that the affinity of these ATP-utilizing processes may be small in order that the depletion of minerals in nonsenescing leaves is avoided. Alternatively, ATP may act as a positive modulator of these pumps. The dependence of proteolytic activities on ATP has been demonstrated in microbial and animal systems (Holtzer and Heinrich, 1980). In the absence of similar evidence with leaf proteolysis, one may speculate that high levels of ATP play a role in the extensive breakdown of leaf proteins.

XIII. SUMMARY

The foregoing has been an attempt to assess the nature, regulation, and significance of respiration in senescing plant tissues. It is transparently obvious that the answers to a host of questions are still obscure, but some glimpses of light may be discerned. The experimental evidence discussed indicates the following. (1) The climacteric rise in respiration is an aspect of C_2H_4 action and not of senescence as such. (2) This rise in respiration is mainly the result of an enhancement of respiratory pathways involved with substrate-level mobilization, namely, glycolysis and, maybe, the pentose pathway. This stimulation of glycolysis is associated with an activation of PK and phosphofructokinases. (3) The data, though indicative of the participation of the alternative oxidase in the respiration of intact fruits and storage organs, have thus far failed to substantiate it unequivocally. (4) The "residual oxidase(s)" are mainly cytosolic in origin, and their participation in intact fruit respiration is highly unlikely. (5) The climacteric respiratory burst during fruit ripening does not reflect a sudden increase in the demand for ATP by the attending anabolic activities at this stage of fruit senescence. Some speculations have been offered here concerning the role of elevated levels of ATP in leaf senescence.

REFERENCES

Abeles, F. B. (1973). "Ethylene in Plant Physiology." Academic Press, New York.
Adams, D. D., and Yang, S. F. (1979). Ethylene biosynthesis. Identification of 1-aminocyclopropane-1-carboxylic acid as an intermediate in the conversion of methionine to ethylene. *Proc. Natl. Acad. Sci. USA* **76,** 170–174.
Adams, P. B., and Rowan, K. S. (1972). Regulation of salt respiration in carrot root slices. *Plant Physiol.* **50,** 682–686.
ap Rees, T. (1980). Assessment of the contributions of metabolic pathways to plant respiration. *In* "The Biochemistry of Plants" (D. D. Davies, ed.), Vol. 2, pp. 1–30. Academic Press, New York.
ap Rees, T. (1985). The organization of glycolysis and the oxidative pentose pathway in plants. *In* "Encyclopedia of Plant Pathology. Higher Plant Cell Respiration" (R. Douce and D. A. Day, eds.), Vol. 18, pp. 391–417. Springer-Verlag, Berlin and New York.
ap Rees, T., Fuller, W. A., and Wright, B. W. (1977). Measurements of glycolytic intermediates during the onset of thermogenesis in the spadix of *Arum maculatum*. *Biochim. Biophys. Acta* **461,** 274–282.
Ashihara, H., and Komamine, A. (1974). Enzyme and metabolite profiles of the pentose phosphate pathway of *Phaseolus* mung seedlings. *Plant Sci. Lett.* **2,** 331–337.
Atkinson, D. (1977). "Cellular Energy Metabolism and its Regulation." Academic Press, New York.
Azcon-Bieto, J., and Osmond, C. B. (1983). Relationship between photosynthesis and respiration in darkened and illuminated wheat leaves. *Plant Physiol.* **71,** 574–581.
Azcon-Bieto, J., Lambers, H., and Day, D. A. (1983). The effect of photosynthesis and carbohydrate status on respiratory rates and the involvement of the alternative path in leaf respiration. *Plant Physiol.* **72,** 598–603.
Bahr, J. T., and Bonner, W. D. (1973). Cyanide insensitive respiration. II. Control of the alternative pathway. *J. Biol. Chem.* **248,** 3446–3450.
Baker, J. E., Anderson, J. D., and Hruschka, W. R. (1985). Protein synthesis in tomato fruit pericarp tissue during ripening. Characteristics of amino acid incorporation. *J. Plant Physiol.* **120,** 167–179.
Barker, J., and Khan, M. A. A. (1968). Studies in the respiratory and carbohydrate metabolism of plant tissues. XXII. The Pasteur effect in potatoes and apples. *New Phytol.* **67,** 205–212.
Barker, J., and Solomos, T. (1962). The mechanism of the climacteric rise in respiration in banana fruits. *Nature (London)* **69,** 189–191.
Barker, J., Khan, M. A. A., and Solomos, T. (1967). The mechanism of the Pasteur effect in peas. *New Phytol.* **66,** 577–596.
Beaury, R. M., Paz, N., Black, C. C., and Kays, S. J. (1987). Banana ripening: Implications of changes in internal ethylene and CO_2 concentrations, pulp fructose-2,6-biphosphate concentration and activity of some glycolytic enzymes. *Plant Physiol.* **85,** 277–282.

Beevers, H. (1961). "Respiratory Metabolism in Plants." Harper, New York.

Beevers, H. (1974). Conceptual development in metabolic control 1924–1974. *Plant Physiol.* 54, 437–442.

Beevers, H., Stiler, M. L., and Butt, V. S. (1966). Metabolism of organic acids. *In* "Plant Physiology" (F. C. Stewart, ed.), Vol. 4B. Academic Press, New York.

Bendall, D. S., and Bonner, W. D., Jr. (1971). Cyanide-insensitive respiration in plant mitochondria. *Plant Physiol.* 47, 236–245.

Bennett, A. B., Smith, G. M., and Nichols, B. (1987). Regulation of climacteric respiration in avocado fruit. *Plant Physiol.* 83, 973–976.

Ben Yehoshua, S. (1964). Respiration and ripening of discs of avocado fruit. *Physiol. Plant.* 17, 71–80.

Beyer, E. M. (1976). A potent inhibitor of ethylene action in plants. *Plant Physiol.* 58, 268–271.

Biale, J. B. (1960). Respiration of fruits. *In* "Encyclopedia of Plant Physiology," Vol. III/2, pp. 536–592. Springer-Verlag, Berlin and New York.

Biale, J. B., and Young, R. E. (1947). Critical oxygen concentrations for the respiration of lemons. *Am. J. Bot.* 34, 301–309.

Biale, J. B., and Young, R. E. (1971). The avocado pear. *In* "The Biochemistry of Fruits and Their Products" (A. C. Hulme, ed.), Vol. 2, pp. 1–63. Academic Press, New York.

Biale, J. B., and Young, R. E. (1981). Respiration and ripening in fruits—Retrospects and prospects. *In* "Recent Advances in the Biochemistry of Fruit and Vegetables" (J. Friend and M. J. C. Rhodes, eds.), pp. 1–39. Academic Press, New York.

Blackman, F. F. (1954). "Analytical Studies in Plant Respiration." Cambridge Univ. Press, London.

Blackman, F. F., and Parija, P. (1928). Analytical studies in plant respiration. I. The respiration of a population of senescent ripening apples. *Proc. R. Soc. London, Ser. B* 103, 412–445.

Brady, C. J., and O'Connell, P. B. H. (1976). On the significance of increased protein synthesis in ripening banana fruits. *Aust. J. Plant Physiol.* 3, 301–310.

Brady, C. J., and Tung, H. F. (1975). Rate of protein synthesis in senescing detached wheat leaves. *Austral. J. Plant Physiol.* 2, 163–176.

Brady, C. J., O'Connell, P. B. H., Smydzuk, J., and Wade, N. L. (1970a). Permeability, sugar accumulation and respiration rate in ripening banana fruits. *Aust. J. Biol. Sci.* 23, 1143–1153.

Brady, C. J., Palmer, J. K., O'Connell, P. B. H., and Smillie, R. M. (1970b). An increase in protein synthesis during ripening of the banana fruit. *Phytochemistry* 9, 1037–1047.

Brady, C. J., MacAlpine, G., McGlasson, W. B., and Ueda, Y. (1982). Polygalacturonase in tomato fruits and the induction of ripening. *Aust. J. Plant Physiol.* 9, 171–178.

Burg, S. P. (1962). The physiology of ethylene formation. *Annu. Rev. Plant Physiol.* 13, 265–302.

Burg, S. P. (1968). Ethylene, plant senescence and abscision. *Plant Physiol.* 43, 1503–511.

Burg, S. P. (1973). Hypobaric storage of cut flowers. *HortScience* 8, 202–205.

Burg, S. P., and Burg, E. A. (1967). Molecular requirements of the biological activity of ethylene. *Plant Physiol.* 42, 144–152.

Burg, S. P., and Thimann, K. V. (1959). The physiology of ethylene formation in apples. *Proc. Natl. Acad. Sci. U. S. A.* 45, 335–344.

Burton, W. G. (1982). "Post-harvest Physiology of Food Crops." Longman, Harlow, Essex, England.

Carnal, N. W., and Black, C. C. (1979). Pyrophosphate-dependent 6-phosphofructokinase, a new glycolytic enzyme in pineapple leaves. *Biochem. Biophys. Res. Commun.* 86, 20–26.

Carnal, N. W., and Black, C. C. (1983). Phosphofructokinase activities in photosynthetic organisms. *Plant Physiol.* 71, 150–155.

Chalmers, D. J., and Rowan, K. S. (1971). The climacteric in ripening tomato fruit. *Plant Physiol.* 48, 235–240.

Chance, R., Holmes, W., Higgins, J., and Connelly, C. M. (1958). Localization of interaction sites in multicomponent transfer systems. *Nature (London)* **182**, 1190–1193.

Chevillotte, P. (1973). Relations between the reaction of cytochrome oxidase-oxygen and oxygen uptake of cells *in vivo*. *J. Theor. Biol.* **39**, 277–295.

Christoffersen, R. E., and Laties, G. G. (1982). Ethylene regulation of gene expression in carrots. *Proc. Natl. Acad. Sci. U. S. A.* **79**, 4060–4063.

Cox, G. F., and Davies, D. D. (1967). Nicotinamide-adenine dinucleotide-specific isocitrate dehydrogenase from pea mitochondria. *Biochem. J.* **105**, 729–734.

Cseke, C., and Buchanan, B. B. (1983). An enzyme-synthesizing fructose 2,6 bisphosphate occurs in leaves and is regulated by metabolic effectors. *FEBS Lett.* **155**, 139–142.

Cseke, C., Weeden, N. F., Buchanan, B. B., and Uyeda, K. (1982). A special fructose bisphosphate function as a cytosolic regulatory metabolite in green leaves. *Proc. Natl. Acad. Sci. USA* **79**, 4322–4326.

Cseke, C., Balogh, A., Wong, J. H., Buchanan, B. B., Stitt, M., Herzog, B., and Heldt, H. W. (1984). Fructose-2.6-bisphosphate: a regulator of carbon in leaves. *Trends Biochem. Sci.* **9**, 533–535.

Davies, D. D. (1978). Control of glycolysis in plant storage tissue. *In* "Biochemistry of Wounded Plant Tissues" (G. Kahl, ed.), pp. 300–346. de Gruyter, Berlin.

Day, D. A., and Lambers, H. (1983). The regulation of glycolysis and electron transport in roots. *Physiol. Plant.* **58**, 155–160.

Day, D. A., and Wiskich, J. T. (1977). Factors limiting respiration by isolated cauliflower mitochondria. *Phytochemistry* **16**, 1499–1502.

Day, D. A., and Wiskich, J. T. (1978). Pyridine nucleotide interactions with isolated plant mitochondria. *Biochim. Biophys. Acta* **501**, 396–404.

Day, D. A., Arron, J. P., and Laties, G. G. (1980). Nature and control of respiratory pathways in plants. The interaction of cyanide-resistant respiration with cyanide-insensitive pathways. *In* "The Biochemistry of Plants" (D. D. Davies, ed.), Vol. 2, pp. 197–241. Academic Press, New York.

Dennis, D. T., and Miernyk, J. A. (1982). Compartmentation of nonphotosynthetic carbohydrate metabolism. *Annu. Rev. Plant Physiol.* **33**, 27–50.

DeTroostembergh, J. C., and Nyns, E. J. (1978). Kinetics of the respiration of cyanide-insensitive mitochondria from the yeast *Saccharomycopsis lipolytica*. *Eur. J. Biochem.* **85**, 423–432.

Dilley, D. R. (1962). Malic enzyme activity in apple fruit. *Nature (London)* **196**, 387–388.

Dilley, D. R., and Carpenter, W. J. (1975). The role of chemical adjuvants and ethylene synthesis on cut flower longevity. *Acta Hortic.* **41**, 117–132.

Dostal, H. C., and Leopold, C. A. (1967). Gibberellin delays ripening of tomatoes. *Science* **158**, 1579–1580.

Duggleby, R. G., and Dennis, D. T. (1970). Regulation of nicotinamide adenine dinucleotide-specific isocitrate dehydrogenase from a higher plant. The effect of reduced nicotinamide adenine dinucleotide and mixtures of citrate and isocitrate. *Biochem. J.* **245**, 3751–3754.

Eaks, I. L., and Morris, L. L. (1956). Respiration of cucumber fruits associated with physiological injury at chilling temperatures. *Plant Physiol.* **31**, 308–314.

Faiz-ur-Rahman, A. T. M., Trewaras, A. J., and Davies, D. D. (1974). The Pasteur effect in carrot root tissue. *Planta* **118**, 195–210.

Fidler, J. C., Wilkinson, B. G., Edney, K. L., and Sharpless, R. O. (1973). "The Biology of Apple and Pear Storage," Res. Bull. No. 3. Commonw. Bur. Hortic. Plantation Crops, East Malling, Kent, England.

Frenkel, C., Klein, I., and Dilley, D. R. (1968). Protein synthesis in relation to ripening of pome fruits. *Plant Physiol.* **43**, 1146–1153.

Fuchs, Y., and Gertman, E. (1973). Stabilization of enzyme activity by incubation in ethylene atmosphere. *Plant Cell Physiol.* **14**, 197–199.

Fuchs, Y., and Gertman, E. (1974). Studies of the effects of ethylene on yeast alcohol dehydrogenase activity. *Plant Cell Physiol.* **15,** 701–708.

Gane, R. (1936). A study of respiration of bananas. *New Phytol.* **35,** 383–402.

Givan, C. V. (1968). Short-term changes in hexose phosphates and ATP in intact cells of *Acer pseudoplantanus* L. subjected to anoxia. *Plant Physiol.* **43,** 948–952.

Givan, C. V., and Torrey, J. G. (1968). Respiratory responses to *acer pseudoplantanus* cells to pyruvate and 2,4-dinitrophenol. *Plant Physiol.* **43,** 635–640.

Grierson, D., and Tucker, G. A. (1983). Timing of ethylene and polygalacturonase synthesis in relation to the control of tomato fruit ripening. *Planta* **157,** 174–179.

Grierson, D., Maunders, M. J., Slater, A., Ray, J., Bird, C. R., Schuch, W., Holtsworth, M. J., Tucker, G. A., and Knapp, J. E. (1986). Gene expression during tomato ripening. *Philos. Trans. R. Soc. London, Ser. B* **314,** 399–410.

Halevy, A. H., and Mayak, S. (1981). Senescence and postharvest physiology of cut flowers. Part 2. *Hortic. Rev.* **3,** 59–143.

Haller, M. H., Rose, D. H., Lutz, J. M., and Harding, P. L. (1945). Respiration of citrus fruits after harvest. *J. Agric. Res.* **71,** 327–359.

Hansen, E. (1967). Ethylene-stimulated metabolism of immature pears. *Proc. Am. Soc. Hortic. Sci.* **91,** 863–867.

Hanson, A. D., and Kende, H. (1975). Ethylene-enhanced ion and sucrose efflux in morning-glory flower tissue. *Plant Physiol.* **55,** 663–669.

Hanson, J. B. (1985). Membrane transport systems of plant mitochondria. *In* "Encyclopedia of Plant Physiology. Higher Plant Cell Respiration" (R. Douce and D. A. Day, eds.), Vol. 18, pp. 248–280. Springer-Verlag, Berlin and New York.

Henry, M. F., and Nyns, E. J. (1975). Cyanide-insensitive respiration. An alternate mitochondrial pathway. *Subcell. Biochem.* **4,** 1–65.

Herner, R. C., and Sink, K. C., Jr. (1973). Ethylene production and respiratory behavior. *Plant Physiol.* **52,** 38–42.

Hess, B., and Brand, K. (1965). Enzyme and metabolite profiles. *In* "Control of Energy Metabolism" (B. Chance, R. W. Estabrook, and J. R. Williamson, eds.), pp. 111–122. Academic Press, New York.

Holtzer, H., and Heinrich, P. C. (1980). Control of proteolysis. *Annu. Rev. Biochem.* **49,** 63–91.

Hulme, A. C. (1954). The climacteric rise in respiration in relation to changes in the equilibrium between protein synthesis and breakdown. *J. Exp. Bot.* **5,** 159–172.

Hulme, A. C., Rhodes, M. J. C., Gailliard, T., and Wooltorton, L. S. C. (1968). Metabolic changes in excised fruit tissue. IV. Changes occurring in discs of apple peel during the development of the respiration climacteric. *Plant Physiol.* **43,** 1154–1161.

James, W. O. (1953). "Plant Respiration." Oxford Univ. Press, London.

Kaltaler, R. E. L., and Steponkis, P. L. (1976). Factors affecting respiration in cut roses. *J. Am. Soc. Hortic. Sci.* **101,** 352–354.

Kelly, G. J., and Turner, J. F. (1969). The regulation of pea-seed phosphofructokinase by phosphoenolpyruvate. *Biochem. J.* **115,** 481–487.

Kidd, F., and West, C. (1925). The course of respiratory activity throughout the life of an apple. *Gt. Br. Dep. Sci. Ind. Food Res. Invest. Board Rep.,* 1924 pp. 27–32.

Knee, M., Sargent, J. A., and Osborne, D. J. (1977). Cell wall metabolism in developing strawberry fruits. *J. Exp. Bot.* **28,** 377–396.

Kobr, M., and Beevers, H. (1971). Gluconeogensis in castor bean endosperms. Changes in the glycolytic intermediates. *Plant Physiol.* **47,** 48–52.

Kombrink, E., Kruger, N. J., and Beevers, H. (1983). Kinetic properties of pyrophosphate: fructose-6-phosphate phosphotransferase from germinating castor bean endosperm. *Plant Physiol.* **74,** 395–401.

Kosiyachinda, S., and Young, R. E. (1975). Ethylene production in relation to the initiation of respiratory climacteric fruit. *Plant Cell Physiol.* 16, 595–602.

Kruger, N. J., and Beevers, H. (1985). Synthesis and degradation of fructose-2.6-bisphosphate in endosperm of castor bean seedlings. *Plant Physiol.* 77, 358–364.

Ku, L. L., and Romani, R. J. (1970). The ribosomes of pear fruit. *Plant Physiol.* 45, 401–407.

Lambers, H. (1982). Cyanide-resistant respiration: a non-phosphorylating electron transport pathway as an energy overflow. *Physiol. Plant.* 55, 478–485.

Lambers, H. (1985). Respiration in intact plants and tissues: its regulation and dependence on environmental factors, metabolism and invaded organisms. *In* "Encyclopedia of Plant Physiology. Higher Plant Cell Respiration" (R. Douce and D. A. Day, eds.), Vol. 18, pp. 418–473. Springer-Verlag, Berlin and New York.

Lambers, H., Day, D. A., and Azcon-Bieto, J. (1983). Cyanide-resistant respiration in roots and leaves. Measurements with intact tissues and isolated mitochondria. *Physiol. Plant.* 58, 148–154.

Lance, C., and Rustin, P. (1984). The central role of malate in plant metabolism. *Physiol. Veg.* 22, 625–641.

Lance, C., Hobson, G. E., Young, R. E., and Biale, J. B. (1965). Metabolic processes in cytoplasmic particles of the avocado fruit. VII. Oxidative and phosphorylative activity throughout the climacteric cycle. *Plant Physiol.* 40, 1116–1123.

Lance, C., Chauveau, M., and Dizengremel, P. (1985). The cyanide-resistant pathway of plant mitochondria. *In* "Encyclopedia of Plant Physiology. Higher Plant Cell Respiration" (R. Douce and D. A. Day, eds.), Vol. 18, pp. 202–247. Springer-Verlag, Berlin and New York.

Laties, G. G. (1978). Development and control of respiratory pathways. *In* "Biochemistry of Wounded Plant Storage Tissues" (G. Kahl, ed.), pp. 421–466. de Gruyter, Berlin.

Laties, G. G. (1982). The cyanide-resistant alternative path in higher plant respiration. *Annu. Rev. Plant Physiol.* 33, 519–555.

Leopold, A. C. (1980). Aging and senescence in plant development. *In* "Senescence in Plants" (K. V. Thimann, ed.), pp. 1–12. CRC Press, Boca Raton, Florida.

Leopold, A. C., and Mushgrave, M. E. (1980). Respiratory pathway in aged soybean seeds. *Plant Physiol.* 64, 702–705.

Lieberman, M. (1979). Biosynthesis and action of ethylene. *Annu. Rev. Plant Physiol.* 30, 533–591.

Lowry, D. H., and Passoneau, J. W. (1964). A comparison of the kinetic properties of phosphofructokinase from bacterial plant and animal sources. *Naunyn-Schmiedebergs Arch. Exp. Pathol. Pharmakol.* 248, 185–194.

McGlasson, W. B. (1970). The ethylene factor. *In* "The Biochemistry of Fruits and Their Products" (A. C. Hulme, ed.), Vol. 1, pp. 475–517. Academic Press, New York.

McGlasson, W. B., Palmer, J. K., Vendrell, M., and Brady, C. J. (1971). Metabolic studies with banana fruits. II. Effect of inhibitors on respiration, ethylene production and ripening. *Aust. J. Biol. Sci.* 24, 1103–1114.

McMurchie, E. J., McGlasson, B. W., and Eaks, J. L. (1972). Treatment of fruit with propylene gives information about the biogenesis of ethylene. *Nature (London)* 237, 235–236.

MacNicol, P. K. (1973). Metabolic regulation in the senescing tobacco leaf. II. Changes in the glycolytic metabolic levels in detached tobacco leaf. *Plant Physiol.* 51, 798–801.

MacNicol, P. K., Young, R. E., and Biale, J. B. (1973). Metabolic regulation in the senescing tobacco leaf. I. Changes in the pattern of ^{32}P incorporation into leaf disc metabolites. *Plant Physiol.* 51, 793–797.

Malik, N. S. A., and Thimann, K. V. (1980). Metabolism of oat leaves during senescence. VI. Changes in ATP levels. *Plant Physiol.* 65, 855–858.

142   *Theophanes Solomos*

Mapson, L. W., and Burton, W. G. (1962). The terminal oxidases of potato tuber. *Biochem. J.* **82**, 19–25.

Mapson, L. W., and Robinson, J. E. (1966). Relations between oxygen tension, biosynthesis of ethylene, respiration and ripening changes in banana fruit. *J. Food Technol.* **1**, 215–225.

Marei, N., and Crane, J. C. (1971). Growth and respiratory response of fig (*Ficus carica* L. cv. Mission) fruits to ethylene. *Plant Physiol.* **48**, 249–254.

Martin, C., and Thimann, K. V. (1972). The role of protein synthesis in the senescence of leaves. I. Formation of protease. *Plant Physiol.* **49**, 64–71.

Maxie, E. C., Farnham, D. S., Mitchell, F. G., Sommer, N. F., Parsons, R. A., Snyder, R. G., and Rae, H. L. (1973). Temperature and ethylene effects on cut flowers of carnations (*Dianthus caryophyllus*). *J. Am. Soc. Hortic. Sci.* **98**, 568–572.

Mayak, S., Vaadia, Y., and Dilley, D. R. (1977). Regulation of senescence in carnations (*Dianthus caryophyllus*) by ethylene: Mode of action. *Plant Physiol.* **59**, 591–593.

Millerd, A., Bonner, J., and Biale, J. B. (1953). The climacteric rise in fruit respiration as controlled by phosphorylative coupling. *Plant Physiol.* **28**, 521–531.

Moreau, F., and Romani, R. (1982). Malate oxidation and cyanide-insensitive respiration in avocado mitochondria during the climacteric cycle. *Plant Physiol.* **70**, 1385–1390.

Morgan, P. W. (1976). Effects on ethylene physiology. *In* "Herbicides: Physiology, Biochemistry, Ecology" (L. J. Audus, ed.), Vol. 1, pp. 255–277. Academic Press, New York.

Newsholme, E. A., and Start, C. (1979). "Regulation in Metabolism." Wiley, New York.

Nichols, R. (1968). The response of carnations (*Dianthus carophyllus*) to ethylene. *J. Hortic. Sci.* **43**, 335–349.

Palmer, J. K. (1971). The banana. *In* "Biochemistry of Fruits and Their Products" (A. C. Hulme, ed.), Vol. 2, pp. 65–105. Academic Press, New York.

Palmer, J. M., and Ward, J. A. (1985). The oxidation of NADH by plant mitochondria. *In* "Encyclopedia of Plant Physiology. Higher Plant Cell Respiration" (R. Douce and D. A. Day, eds.), Vol. 18, pp. 173–201. Springer-Verlag, Berlin and New York.

Pradet, A., and Raymond, P. (1983). Adenine nucleotide ratios and adenylate energy charge in energy metabolism. *Annu. Rev. Plant Physiol.* **34**, 199–224.

Pratt, H. K., and Goeschl, J. D. (1968). The role of ethylene in fruit ripening. *In* "The Biochemistry and Physiology of Plant Growth Substances" (F. Wightman and G. Setterfield, eds.), pp. 1295–1302. Runge Press, Ottawa.

Pratt, H. K., and Goeschl, J. D. (1969). Physiological roles of ethylene in plants. *Annu. Rev. Plant Physiol.* **20**, 541–584.

Quazi, M. H., and Freebairn, H. T. (1970). The influence of ethylene, oxygen and carbon dioxide on ripening of bananas. *Bot. Gaz.* **131**, 5–14.

Rattanapanone, N., Grierson, D., and Stein, M. (1977). Ribonucleic acid metabolism during the development and ripening of tomato fruits. *Phytochemistry* **16**, 629–1486.

Reid, M. S., and Pratt, H. K. (1972). Effects of ethylene on potato tuber respiration. *Plant Physiol.* **49**, 252–255.

Rhodes, M. J. C. (1970). The climacteric and ripening of fruits. *In* "The Biochemistry of Fruits and Their Products" (A. C. Hulme, ed.), Vol. 1, pp. 521–533. Academic Press, New York.

Rhodes, M. J. C. (1980a). Respiration and senescence of plant organs. *In* "The Biochemistry of Plants" (D. D. Davies, ed.), Vol. 2, pp. 419–462. Academic Press, New York.

Rhodes, M. J. C. (1980b). The maturation and ripening of fruits. *In* "Senescence in Plants" (K. V. Thimann, ed.), pp. 157–205. CRC Press, Boca Raton, Florida.

Ricard, J. (1980). Enzyme flexibility as a molecular basis for metabolic control. *In* "The Biochemistry of Plants" (D. D. Davies, ed.), Vol. 2, pp. 31–80. Academic Press, New York.

Richmond, A., and Biale, J. B. (1966). Protein and nucleic acid metabolism in fruits. I. Studies of amino acid incorporation during the climacteric rise in respiration of avocado. *Plant Physiol.* **41**, 1247–1253.

Rogers, M. (1973). An historical and critical review of post harvest physiology research on cut flowers. *HortScience* **8**, 189–194.

Rolleston, F. S. (1972). A theoretical background to the use of measured concentrations of intermediates in study of the control of intermediary metabolism. *Curr. Top. Cell. Regul.* **5**, 47–75.

Romani, R. (1978). Long term maintenance of mitochondria function *in vitro* and the course of cyanide-insensitive respiration. In "Plant Mitochondria" (G. Ducet and C. Lance, eds.), pp. 3–10. Elsevier/North-Holland, Amsterdam.

Romani, R. (1984). Respiration, ethylene, senescence and homeostasis in an integrated view of postharvest life. *Can. J. Bot.* **62**, 2950–55.

Rowan, K. S., McGlasson, W. B., and Pratt, H. K. (1969). Changes in adenosine phosphates in cantaloupe fruit ripening normally and after treatment with ethylene. *J. Exp. Bot.* **20**, 145–155.

Rychter, A., Janes, H. W., and Frenkel, C. (1978). Cyanide-resistant respiration in freshly cut potato slices. *Plant Physiol.* **61**, 667–668.

Rychter, A., Janes, H. W., and Frenkel, C. (1979). Effect of ethylene and oxygen on the development of cyanide-resistant respiration in whole plant mitochondria. *Plant Physiol.* **63**, 149–151.

Sabularse, D. C., and Anderson, A. L. (1981a). Inorganic pyrophosphate: D-fructose-6-phosphate 1-phosphotransferase in mung beans and its activation by D-fructose-1.6-bisphosphate and D-glucose-1.6-bisphosphate. *Biochem. Biophys. Res. Commun.* **100**, 1423–1429.

Sabularse, D. C., and Anderson, A. L. (1981b). D-Fructose 2.6 bisphosphate: A naturally occurring activator for inorganic pyrophosphate: D-fructose-6-phosphate-phosphotransferase in plants. *Biochem. Biophys. Res. Commun.* **103**, 848–855.

Sacher, J. A. (1967). Studies of permeability RNA and protein turnover during aging of fruit and leaf tissues. *Symp. Soc. Exp. Biol.* **21**, 269–304.

Sacher, J. A. (1973). Senescence and Postharvest Physiology. *Annu. Rev. Plant Physiol.* **24**, 197–224.

Saglio, P. H., and Pradet, A. (1980). Soluble sugars, respiration, and energy charge during aging of excised maize root tips. *Plant Physiol.* **66**, 516–519.

Salminen, S. O., and Young, R. E. (1975). The control properties of phosphofructokinase in relation to the respiratory climacteric in banana fruit. *Plant Physiol.* **55**, 45–50.

Schonbaum, G. R., Bonner, W. D., Storey, B. T., and Bahr, J. T. (1971). Specific inhibition of the cyanide-insensitive respiratory pathway in plant mitochondria by hydroxamic acids. *Plant Physiol.* **47**, 124–128.

Sfakiotakis, E. M., and Dilley, D. R. (1973). Induction of autocatalytic ethylene production in apple fruits by propylene in relation to maturity and oxygen. *J. Am. Hortic. Sci.* **98**, 504–508.

Siedow, J. N. (1982). The nature of cyanide-resistant pathway in plant mitochondria. *Recent Adv. Phytochem.* **16**, 47–84.

Sisler, E., and Pian, A. (1973). Effect of ethylene and cyclic olefins on tobacco leaves. *Tob. Sci.* **17**, 68–72.

Smillie, R. M. (1962). Photosynthetic and respiratory activities of growing pea leaves. *Plant Physiol.* **37**, 716–721.

Smyth, D. A., Wu, M.-X., and Black, C. C. (1984). Phosphofructokinase and fructose-2.6-bisphosphatase activities in developing corn seedlings. *Plant Sci. Lett.* **33**, 61–70.

Solomos, T. (1983). Respiration and energy metabolism in senescing plant tissues. In "Post-

Harvest Physiology and Crop Improvement" (M. Lieberman, ed.), pp. 61–98. Plenum, New York.

Solomos, T. (1988a). Principles of gas exchange in bulky plant tissues. *HortScience* **22**, 766–771.

Solomos, T. (1987). Nature of the terminal oxidases in sweet potato slices. *In* "Plant Mitochondria: Structural, Functional, and Physiological Aspects" (A. Moore and A. B. Beechey, eds.), pp. 361–364.

Solomos, T., and Laties, G. G. (1974). Similarities between the actions of ethylene and cyanide in initiating the climacteric and ripening of avocados. *Plant Physiol.* **54**, 506–511.

Solomos, T., and Laties, G. G. (1975). The mechanism of ethylene and cyanide action in triggering the rise in respiration in potato tubers. *Plant Physiol.* **55**, 73–78.

Solomos, T., and Laties, G. G. (1976). Effects of cyanide and ethylene on the respiration of cyanide-sensitive and cyanide-resistant plant tissues. *Plant Physiol.* **58**, 47–50.

Speirs, J. Brady, C. J., Grierson, D., and Lee, E. (1984). Changes in ribosome organization and mRNA abundance in ripening tomato fruits. *Aust. J. Plant Physiol.* **11**, 225–233.

Stegink, S. S., and Siedow, J. N. (1986). Binding of butyl gallate to plant mitochondria. II. Relationship to the presence or absence of the alternative pathway. *Plant Physiol.* **80**, 196–201.

Stitt, M., Lilley, R. McC., and Heldt, H. W. (1982). Adenine nucleotide levels in the cytosol, chloroplasts and mitochondria of wheat leaf protoplasts. *Plant Physiol.* **70**, 971–77.

Stitt, M., Cseke, C., and Buchanan, B. B. (1984a). Regulation of fructose-2,6-bisphosphate concentration in spinach leaves. *Eur. J. Biochem.* **143**, 89–93.

Stitt, M., Herzog, B., and Heldt, H. W. (1984b). Regulation of photosynthetic sucrose synthesis by fructose-2,6-bisphosphate. I. Coordination of CO_2 fixation and sucrose synthesis. *Plant Physiol.* **75**, 548–53.

Stitt, M., Cseke, C., and Buchanan, B. B. (1986). Ethylene-induced increases in fructose-2,6-bisphosphate in plant storage tissue. *Plant Physiol.* **80**, 246–248.

Storey, B. T. (1976). Respiratory chain of plant mitochondria. XVIII. Point of interaction of the alternate oxidase with the respiratory chain. *Plant Physiol.* **55**, 521–525.

Storey, B. T. (1980). Electron transport and energy coupling in plant mitochondria. *In* "The Biochemistry of Plants" (D. D. Davies, ed.), Vol. 2, pp. 125–195. Academic Press, New York.

Tetley, R. M., and Thimann, K. V. (1974). The metabolism of oat leaves during senescence. I. Respiration, carbohydrate metabolism, and action of cytokinins. *Plant Physiol.* **54**, 294–303.

Theologis, A., and Laties, G. G. (1978a). Relative contribution of cytochrome-mediated and cyanide-resistant electron transport in fresh and aged potato slices. *Plant Physiol.* **62**, 232–237.

Theologis, A., and Laties, G. G. (1978b). Respiratory contribution of the alternate path during various stages of ripening in avocado and banana fruits. *Plant Physiol.* **62**, 890–896.

Theologis, A., and Laties, G. G. (1978c). Cyanide-resistant respiration in fresh and aged sweet potato slices. *Plant Physiol.* **62**, 249–255.

Thimann, K. V. (1980). The senescence of leaves. *In* "Senescence in Plants" (K. V. Thimann, ed.), pp. 85–115. CRC Press, Boca Raton, Florida.

Trewaras, A. J. (1982). The regulation of development and its relation to growth substances. *What's New Plant Physiol.* **13**, 41–43.

Tucker, M. L. (1978). The significance of cyanide-insensitive respiration in ripening and concomitant rise in respiration of banana fruit slices. M.S. Thesis, Univ. of Maryland, College Park.

Tucker, M. L., and Laties, G. G. (1984). Interrelationship of gene expression, polysome prevalence, and respiration during ripening of ethylene and/or cyanide-treated avocado fruits. *Plant Physiol.* **74**, 307–315.

Tucker, M. L., and Laties, G. G. (1985). The dual role of oxygen in avocado fruit respiration: kinetic analysis and computer modeling of diffusion-affected respiratory oxygen isotherms. *Plant Cell Environ.* **8**, 117–127.

Turner, J. F., and Turner, D. H. (1980). The regulation of glycolysis and the pentose pathway. *In* "The Biochemistry of Plants: A Comprehensive Treatise" (D. D. Davies, ed.), Vol. 2, pp. 279–316. Academic Press, New York.

van Schaftingen, E., Lederer, B., Bartrons, R., and Hers, H.-G. (1983). A kinetic study of pyrophosphate: fructose-6-phosphate phosphotransferase from potato tubers. *Eur. J. Biochem.* **129**, 191–195.

Vendrell, M. (1969). Reversion of senescence: Effects of 2.4 dichlorophenoxyacetic acid on respiration, ethylene production, and ripening of banana fruit slices. *Aust. J. Biol. Sci.* **22**, 601–610.

Vickery, R. S., and Bruinsma, J. (1973). Compartments and permeability of potassium in developing fruits of tomato *Lycopersicum esculentum* Mill. *J. Exp. Bot.* **24**, 1261–1270.

Wade, N. L., O'Connell, P. B. H., and Brady, C. J. (1972). Content of RNA and protein of the ripening banana. *Phytochemistry* **11**, 975–9.

Wager, H. G. (1961). The effect of anaerobiosis on acids of the tricarboxylic cycle in peas. *J. Exp. Bot.* **12**, 34–46.

Wang, C. Y., Mellenthin, W. M., and Hansen, E. (1972). Maturation of "Anjou" pears in relation to chemical composition and reaction to ethylene. *J. Am. Soc. Hortic. Sci.* **97**, 9–12.

Warman, T. W., and Solomos, T. (1988). Ethylene production and action during foliage senescence in *Hedera helix* L. *J. Exp. Bot.* In press.

Wiskich, J. T. (1977). Mitochondria metabolite transport. *Annu. Rev. Plant Physiol.* **28**, 45–69.

Wiskich, J. T. (1980). Control of the Krebs cycle. *In* "The Biochemistry of Plants" (D. D. Davies, ed.), Vol. 2, pp. 243–278. Academic Press, New York.

Wiskich, J. T., and Dry, J. B. (1985). The tricarboxylic acid cycle in plant mitochondria: its operation and regulation. *In* "Encyclopedia of Plant Physiology. Higher Plant Cell Respiration" (R. Douce and D. A. Day, eds.), Vol. 18, pp. 281–313. Springer-Verlag, Berlin and New York.

Woolhouse, H. W. (1967). Nature of senescence in plants. *Symp. Soc. Exp. Biol.* **21**, 179–214.

Yang, S. F., and Ho, H. K. (1958). Biochemical studies on post-ripening of banana. *J. Chin. Chem. Soc.* **5**, 71–85.

Young, R. E., and Biale, J. B. (1967). Phosphorylation in avocado fruit slices in relation to the respiratory climacteric. *Plant Physiol.* **42**, 1359–1362.

5

Nucleic Acid and Protein Synthesis

Colin J. Brady
CSIRO
School of Biological Sciences
Macquarie University
North Ryde, New South Wales, Australia

I. INTRODUCTION

As the methods available for the study of gene action have improved, a greater appreciation has been gained of the pattern of gene products that characterize particular tissues and particular stages of development. The progressive appearance and then disappearance of families of gene products through the developmental cycle of cotton seeds is an example (Duré *et al.*, 1983). The expectation from such examples is that senescence will be regulated by a set of genes acting in concert. A theme of recent reviews of the senescence of plant tissues is that tissue senescence is a carefully orchestrated phenomenon resulting in the controlled dismantling of some, but not all, cell structures (Brady, 1973; Noodén and Leopold, 1978; Thomas and Stoddart, 1980; Stoddart and Thomas, 1982; Woolhouse, 1982). The implication is that senescence results from programmed changes in gene function, and the recognition of mutations that limit the progress of senescence in quite specific ways strengthens this conclusion. The mutated genes have not been directly identified, and it remains a possibility that they have a role elsewhere through development and that the mutated products alter the normal pattern of senescence indirectly.

This chapter reviews the evidence of changing patterns of nucleic acid and protein synthesis during senescence. To do so is not to suggest that these facets of metabolism are divorced from other cell functions. As major sinks of energy in the cells, the rates and, perhaps, the products of nucleic acid and protein synthesis are intimately related to energy supply (Cocucci and Marré, 1973). Likewise, the protein synthesis system, in particular, template selection and the initiation reactions, are extremely sensitive to the ionic environment (Wyn Jones *et al.*, 1979). For this reason, and because ribosomes directly associate with internal membranes and because many of the products of protein synthesis need to be transferred through or correctly deposited within membranes, the functional state of membranes and their lipid constituents will greatly influence the patterns of protein synthesis (Chapter 2). There is then every reason to suspect that many of the changes in the accumulation patterns of proteins in senescing cells and in the patterns of synthesis reflect aspects of cell metabolism that do not involve contemporary gene activation or deactivation as the primary response.

The senescing leaf or cotyledon has been studied much more thoroughly than have other aging organs. Even so, comparatively few species have been studied in much detail. There is some information on roots and a little on stem tissues; there are studies of aging seeds relative to viability (Chapters 13 and 14) and of the ripening and senescence of fruit tissues. It is not possible to exhaustively catalogue all relevant studies here, but there is an attempt to draw examples from a number of systems and so look for a wider perspective. The most obvious reactions of senescence involve the hydrolysis of macromolecules by hydrolases of various types. The proteases and ribonucleases of senescent leaves and the various glycosidases of fruits are examples. The most complete studies of the synthesis of hydrolases, active in the selective degradation of intracellular macromolecules, is in germinating seeds and, in particular, in the much studied barley aleurone system. It is perhaps ironic that we should look to germination for an example of how senescence may be regulated, but germination includes the programmed "death," of some tissues and it is appropriate to consider it in this context.

II. NUCLEIC ACID AND PROTEIN CONTENTS

A. DNA

There are few studies of the amount of DNA in senescing tissues. Böttger and Wollgiehn (1958) found a small decrease in naturally senescing *Nicotiana rustica* leaves, and Dyer and Osborne (1971) found a larger decrease in senescing pea leaves. Udovenko and Gogoleva (1974) measured a decrease in DNA in expanded wheat leaves, and Harris *et al.*, (1982) measured decreases in nuclear DNA in tobacco and peanut leaves, especially in epidermal cells. On the other hand, Makrides and Goldthwaite (1981) observed no loss of DNA in senescing bean *(Phaseolus vulgaris)* leaves. Chang *et al.*, (1985) found that a 23% decrease in nuclear DNA occurred during the final stages of the senescence of soybean cotyledons and provided evidence that some reiterated sequences were selectively degraded. There are no gross changes in the appearance of the nucleus through senescence (Butler and Simon, 1970; Barlow, 1982). The reversal of senescence in leaves that have been almost completely depleted of chlorophyll and chlorophyll-binding proteins (Mothes and Baudisch, 1958; Wittenbach, 1977; Venkatarayappa *et al.*, 1984) indicates that the coding regions of the nuclear DNA remain largely intact.

Chloroplasts in expanded leaves contain many copies of the plastid genome. According to the species, from 5 to 800 copies of the plastid genome may be present per chloroplast, and plastid DNA may account for as much as 20% of the DNA in mesophyll leaf cells (Scott and Possingham, 1982). Surprisingly, there appears to be no published data on the fate of the plastid DNA as the thylakoid membranes dissolve and the chloroplasts dedifferentiate through senescence. It is known that the number of copies per chloroplast decreases as pea or spinach leaves approach full expansion (Lamppa *et al.*, 1980; Scott and Possingham, 1983). Loss of chloroplast DNA may contribute to the loss of leaf DNA, which has been measured in leaf pieces left in the dark for prolonged periods (Wollgiehn, 1967; Lamattina *et al.*, 1985). Since leaf senescence is largely the senescence of chloroplasts within leaf cells, and chloroplasts contribute to their maintenance by synthetic reactions involving products coded by chloroplast DNA, knowledge of the persistence and the functional state of chloroplast DNA may contribute to the understanding of leaf senescence. This is not to suggest that the key to senescence initiation lies within the chloroplast genome, for the evidence from senescence mutants and from enucleation experiments (Yoshida, 1961) clearly points towards nuclear-coded gene products being essential to the senescence reactions. The persistence of mitochondrial functions through senescence does not suggest that mitochondrial DNA is involved, and there is no information on its content in aging cells. In the fungus *Podospora*, a correlation between cell senescence and an accumulation of circular DNA molecules derived from the mitochondrial genome has been noted (Koll *et al.*, 1984).

B. RNA

Cellular RNA is present as ribosomal (rRNA), transfer (tRNA), and messenger (mRNA) components, with rRNA accounting for 85 to 90% of the total. Cytoplasmic, plastid, and mitochondrial compartments have their own populations of each component. The mitochondrial populations are proportionally small, and it is not known if they persist in mature and senescing cells. In leaf mesophyll cells, 30–40% of the ribosomes may be in the chloroplasts (Takegami, 1975; Brady and Scott, 1977; Makrides and Goldthwaite, 1981). As net protein synthesis ceases, the contents of rRNA decline to a lower level typical of the expanded, mature leaf. This is shown for *Phaseolus vulgaris* in Fig. 5.1A and for *Triticum aestivum* in Fig. 5.1B. In either case, the ratio of cytoplasmic rRNA (25S and 18S molecules) to plastid rRNA (23 S and 16 S molecules) was not greatly different in the newly expanded and senescent leaves. In *P. vulgaris*, Makrides and Goldthwaite (1981) felt that little of the plastid rRNA was present as polysomes. In *T. aestivum*, the senescent leaves contained plastid polysomes (Brady and Scott, 1977). Chloroplast rRNA is selectively lost during the senescence of *Perilla* (Callow, 1974), cucumber (Callow *et al.*, 1972), and tobacco (Takegami, 1975) leaves, and it has been suggested that many senescing leaves completely lack chloroplast ribosomes. The persistence of plastid ribosomes as chloroplasts change to chromoplasts in ripening tomato fruits is documented by Bathgate *et al.* (1985). There is very little quantitative information on the absolute content of RNA in senescing tissues; most observers have based conclusions on recovered ribosomes using a constant, and sometimes optimized, isolation procedure.

In fruits, ripening, which is a prelude to senescence, is often accompanied by a recruitment of ribosomes to polysomes. In tomato fruits, Rattanapanone *et al.* (1977) noted that the RNA content, measured as recovered ribosomes, decreased sharply during the early stages of ripening of tomato fruits

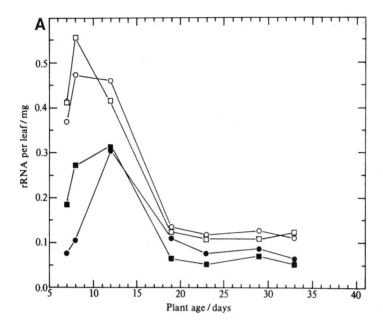

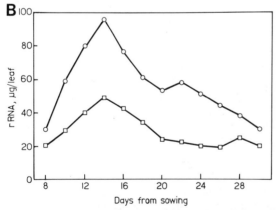

Fig. 5.1. Content of rRNAs as a function of age. (A) Cytoplasmic rRNAs (□, 25 S; O, 18 S) and plastid rRNA (■, 23 S; ●, 16 S) in attached *Phaseolus vulgaris* primary leaves (Makrides and Goldthwaite, 1981). (B) Cytoplasmic rRNA 25 S + 18 S (O) and plastid rRNA, 23 S + 16 S (□) in attached *Triticum vulgaris* cv. Falcon second leaves. [Adapted from Brady and Scott (1977).]

and then stayed more or less constant through the latter stages of ripening. Speirs *et al.* (1984) also observed a lowered recovery of rRNA in ripening as compared to mature, nonripening tomato fruits, but a higher percentage of the ribosomes were as polysomes once ripening commenced. Wade *et al.* (1972), using a chemical method involving base analyses, observed no decrease in RNA during the ripening of banana fruit.

The consistent pattern is that tissues retain a population of ribosomes through senescence. In many tissues the plastids, including fruit chromoplasts, also contain ribosomes with intact rRNA molecules.

The possibility that the availability of specific acylated tRNAs may regulate the rates of synthesis of specific proteins, and thus the performance of cells has been considered for many years. Strehler (1967) suggested that a loss of specific tRNAs or their synthetases may contribute to the aging and/or senescence of cells. There is some evidence that where multiple tRNAs for individual amino acids exist, their relative abundance changes with time (Bick *et al.*, 1970; Pillay and Cherry, 1974). Pillay and Gowda (1981) found that tRNA acylation decreased as soybean cotyledons senesced during germination. In *Spirodela polyrhiza*, Malek and Cossins (1983) found no change in tRNA acylation as fronds aged in a nitrogen-deficient medium. During ripening of tomato fruits, Mettler and Romani (1976) found changes in isoaccepting tRNAs for lysine, leucine, and methionine.

C. Protein

There are numerous studies (see Noodén and Leopold, 1978) that document the progressive loss of protein from aging leaves (Fig. 5.2; Makrides and Goldthwaite, 1981; Evans, 1983; Makino *et al.*, 1984). The loss of protein may be delayed or reduced in rate if the plants are supplied with abundant nitrogen (Evans, 1983; Makino *et al.*, 1984), if sinks for the translocated nitrogen are removed (Noodén *et al.*, 1978; Wittenbach, 1982), or, with some species, if adjacent sinks are maintained (Hall and Brady, 1977; Christensen *et al.*, 1981). Conversely, the loss may be initiated and accelerated by leaf detachment and/or by prolonged darkness.

No matter how senescence is provoked in leaves — by the natural season, by sink removal, by leaf detachment, or by darkening — the pattern of protein loss appears to be characteristic. There is a loss of a wide range of proteins, both soluble and membrane-bound, but the loss is not random, and there is a selective retention of many proteins. Unfortunately, detailed information on the contents of individual proteins is very sparse. The increasing availability of monospecific antisera for many leaf proteins should enable a more detailed picture of the disassembly of proteinaceous leaf

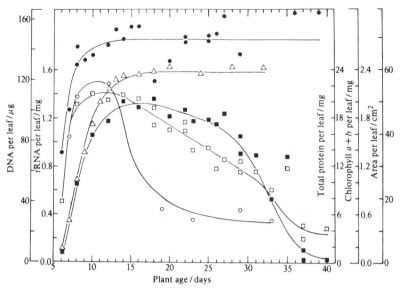

Fig. 5.2. DNA (●), rRNA (○), protein (□), chlorophyll content (■), and area (△) as a function of age in attached *Phaseolus vulgaris* primary leaves. [From Makrides and Goldthwaite (1981).]

structures to be formed. It may then be seen that the apparent common pattern of protein loss in different situations provoking senescence reflects a superficial knowledge rather than a universal response.

Because of its abundance and metabolic importance, there is more information on ribulose-bisphosphate carboxylase (RuBPCase) than on other proteins. Friedrich and Huffaker (1980) noted that 85% of the "soluble" protein lost from senescing barley leaves was RuBPCase and they suggested that this protein served as a mobile nitrogen store within the plant. Earlier, Racusen and Foote (1965), impressed by the great bulk of "fraction 1" protein in polyacrylamide gel electrophoretograms of bean leaf proteins, made a similar suggestion. Makino *et al.*, (1983) found that through 40 days of senescence of leaf 12 of rice plants, 75% of the RuBPCase protein, 63% of total "soluble" protein, and 53% of "buffer-insoluble" protein was lost. In the flag leaf of wheat, Wittenbach (1979) found that RuBPCase was about 40% of total "soluble" protein through the first 20 days postanthesis, but had fallen to 22% of "soluble" protein in the senescent leaf 27 days postanthesis. RuBPCase is a lesser component of the total "soluble" protein in senescent, as opposed to expanded, leaves, because some species of "soluble" protein, as also some membrane-associated proteins, are not degraded through senescence. Of the "soluble" proteins that are degraded, RuBPCase appears to be lost at about an average rate, as judged from the declining activities of several enzymes of the chloroplast stroma (Batt and Woolhouse, 1975; Makino *et al.*, 1983) and from the appearance of the "soluble" proteins separable by polyacrylamide gel electrophoresis (Thomas, 1982a). Although there are few quantitative figures on the loss of membrane proteins through senescence, the loss of photochemical activities (Jenkins and Woolhouse, 1981), the swelling and dissolution of thylakoid membranes seen by electron microscopy (Barton, 1966; Butler and Simon, 1970; Cohen *et al.*, 1979), and the loss of photosystem proteins revealed by gel electrophoresis (Thomas, 1982a) testify that the thylakoid polypeptides are the major components lost. In senescing oat and bean leaves, a loss of cytochromes *b*6 and *f* occurs before the photosystem proteins are lost (Ben-David *et al.*, 1983; Roberts *et al.*, 1987), and this may account for the decline in noncyclic photosynthesis (Jenkins and Woolhouse, 1981).

While a rapid decline in protein content is almost diagnostic of senescence in leaf tissues, this is not the case in the fleshy fruits, even when chlorophyll loss is part of the ripening or senescence syndrome. In avocado (Biale and Young, 1971), banana pulp (Wade *et al.*, 1972), and citrus (Lewis *et al.*, 1967), there is no change in total protein content with ripening. There may be some increase in protein during ripening of cantaloupe (Rowan *et al.*, 1969), of apple (Hulme, 1954), and of pear (Hansen, 1967; Wang and Mellenthin, 1977) fruits. In tomato fruits, there is little change in total protein through ripening, but there is an almost complete loss of the photosystem I and II and light-harvesting complex proteins (Wrench *et al.*, 1987).

Leaves and fruits are similar in their senescence patterns in that changes occur in the plastids, while the mitochondria remain unchanged (Bain and Mercer, 1964; Butler, 1967). They differ in that leaves are donor organs from which reserves are translocated to stronger sinks, while fruits continue to act as sinks, often even after ripening has been initiated. Although no intense loss of protein is seen in fruits, senescence in fruits and leaves has much in common. At the protein level, this is seen in the hydrolase enzymes that increase in leaves and fruits (Table 5.1). There is a common pattern of enzyme development in the two sets of tissues, and there is comparable evidence for flowers and other aging tissues, but there are two strong diversions. The increase in proteases commonly seen in leaves, especially during senescence in the dark, has not been observed in fruits. The wall-degrading enzymes, involved in the softening of ripening fruit, are not found to increase in aging leaves. The lists in Table 5.1 are not complete, but they are widely drawn and suggest that the pattern revealed is common. However, there is opportunity for a more complete survey of the enzyme changes involving leaves and fruits of one species. Increases in enzyme activity do

TABLE 5.1

Hydrolytic Enzymes Increasing in Senescing Fruits and Leaves

Enzyme	Fruit	Leaf
ɔtease		Tobacco (Anderson and Rowan, 1966)
		Wheat (Whittenbach, 1979)
		Oats (Martin and Thimann, 1972)
		Phaseolus vulgaris
		(De Luca D'oro and Trippi, 1982)
		Perilla
		(Kannangara and Woolhouse, 1968)
ɔonuclease	Banana (Hyodo *et al.*, 1981)	Tobacco (Balz, 1966)
	Tomato (McKeon *et al.*, 1984)	Wheat (Sodek and Wright, 1969)
	Apple (Rhodes and Wooltorton, 1967)	Oats (Udvardy *et al.*, 1969)
		Phaseolus vulgaris
		(De Luca D'oro and Trippi, 1982)
		Rhoeo (De Leo and Sacher, 1970)
vertase	Banana (Terra *et al.*, 1983)	Wheat (Roberts, 1982)
	Tomato (Iki *et al.*, 1978)	*Lolium temulentum*
	Guava (Mowlah and Itoo, 1982)	(Pollock and Lloyd, 1978)
:id phosphatase	Banana (Hyodo *et al.*, 1981)	Rice (Parida and Mishra, 1980)
	Tomato (Shirai *et al.*, 1984)	*Phaseolus vulgaris*,
	Apple (Rhodes and Wooltorton, 1967)	(Kennis and Trippi, 1982)
	Avocado (Sacher, 1973)	*Perilla* (Kannangara and Woolhouse, 1968)
1,3-Glucanase	Tomato (Hinton and Pressey, 1980)	*Rhoeo* (De Leo and Sacher, 1970)
	Peach (Hinton and Pressey, 1980)	Tobacco (Moore and Stone, 1972)
-1,4-Glucanase	Tomato (Poovaiah and Nukaya, 1979)	
(Cellulase)	Guava (Mowlah and Itoo, 1983)	
	Avocado (Awad and Young, 1979)	
	Pear (Ben-Arie *et al.*, 1979)	
	Annona muricata (Paull *et al.*, 1983)	
	Papaya (Paull and Chen, 1983)	
	Mango (Roe and Bruemmer, 1981)	
ɔlygalacturonase	Tomato (Hobson, 1964)	
	Guava (Mowlah and Itoo, 1983)	
	Avocado (Awad and Young, 1979)	
	Pear (Ben-Arie *et al.*, 1979)	
	Annona muricata (Paull *et al.*, 1983)	
	Papaya (Paull and Chen, 1983)	
	Mango (Roe and Bruemmer, 1981)	

not necessarily involve increases in enzyme protein, but there is evidence that this is involved with some of the senescence-related hydrolases (Sacher and Davies, 1974; Iki *et al.*, 1978). More complete knowledge of the changes in the hydrolase enzymes, as also of the peroxidases that increase through senescence (Frenkel, 1972), would lay a good foundation for experiments that seek common regulatory factors or gene sets involved in the senescence of leaves and fruits.

III. NUCLEIC ACID AND PROTEIN SYNTHESIS

There is an appreciable skeleton of facts concerning the changes in nucleic acids and proteins during senescence. Deficiencies exist in that the detailed observations are on few species, notably bean *(Phaseolus vulgaris)*, soybean, tobacco, and the cereal grain plants—wheat, oats, and rice; within these species, the data are incomplete and often lack quantitation. However, the methodology exists, or is developing rapidly, to allow the accumulation of more complete case histories covering individual RNA and protein species so that the present skeleton of fact should be systematically fleshed.

When one moves from asking what content of protein or RNA is present to asking what are the rates of synthesis and degradation of a protein or RNA species, one confronts methodological barriers. The rapidly developing methods of molecular biology allow the isolation and quantitation of mRNA populations and genes, but in nongrowing tissues and, particularly, in senescing tissues and in bulky organs, there is difficulty in answering questions concerning the dynamic state of proteins, rRNA, or mRNA. The problem is well illustrated in a discussion of seed germination by Marcus and Rodaway (1982) and stems from the difficulty of measuring the specific activities of radiolabeled precursors entering macromolecules, from the need to modify tissues to allow precursor uptake to proceed, and from the near impossibility of utilizing valid pulse-chase techniques. To surmount the difficulties associated with direct measurements of the synthesis and breakdown of macromolecules, inhibitors of RNA and protein synthesis have been widely used (see Section III,C).

The increasing focus of research on particular protein species, in addition to their biological activities, has given new insights into how the activity of cells may be regulated. The role of phytochrome in regulating the expression of a number of genes coding for chloroplast proteins (Tobin and Silverthorne, 1985) is an illustration that is relevant to leaf senescence. The research has identified the gene families involved and their sequences. Transformation experiments have shown that the genes contain sequences that ensure that expression is light-activated and tissue specific. Sometime through their ontogeny, the photosynthetic tissues lose the ability to respond to the signals stemming from the activation of the phytochrome system. At what level does this failure occur? Methods are available to approach this question, but, first, knowledge must be gained of the stabilities of the mRNA molecules and of the sequences of transcription and translation occurring through the normal diurnal cycles (Piechulla and Gruissem, 1987).

A. DNA Synthesis

Observations of the decay of radiolabeled DNA in mature stems (Hurst and Gahan, 1975) and roots (Sampson and Davies, 1966) suggest that some metabolism of DNA occurs through senescence. The turnover of DNA may reflect repair reactions, but there is no quantitative information on the extent of the repair reactions.

B. RNA Synthesis

In wheat (Brady *et al.*, 1971) and in *Phaseolus vulgaris* (Ness and Woolhouse, 1980a,b) externally added labeled precursors were incorporated into cytoplasmic and chloroplast rRNA in developing leaves, but only into cytoplasmic rRNA in expanded and senescing leaves. This may mean that there is turnover of cytoplasmic but not plastid ribosomes; alternatively, it may mean that when plastid ribosomes are not increasing in number, externally added molecules do not gain access to the sites of synthesis. In *Phaseolus vulgaris*, a loss of the plastid RNA polymerase activity was also noted (Ness and Woolhouse, 1980a), suggesting that regulation of this enzyme may limit RNA turnover in expanded leaves.

In the climacteric fruits, an increased incorporation of precursors into RNA, including rRNA, has been observed early in ripening in avocadoes (Richmond and Biale, 1967), apples (Hulme *et al.*, 1968, 1971), and tomatoes (De Swardt *et al.*, 1973; Rattanapanone *et al.*, 1977). While none of these observations are capable of quantitative interpretation, they probably represent a general upsurge in metabolism and turnover as part of the tissue's response to ethylene.

C. Protein Synthesis

1. Measuring Protein Synthesis

At least in leaves, senescence reflects a change in the equilibrium between the rates of synthesis and degradation of particular proteins. It is sometimes assumed that senescence results from a declining rate of protein synthesis coupled with a constant rate of protein breakdown. This thesis bears with it the assumption that the anabolic and catabolic reactions of protein turnover are completely independent of each other. This is not necessarily so, for whether or not a protein molecule is degraded may depend on whether or not it can find a particular place or conformation in a membrane or other supramolecular structure (Wheatley, 1984). As a consequence, a temporal deficiency of one macromolecule can lead to the enhanced catabolism of a range of other molecules. Hence, in studies of these aspects of senescence, the dynamic state of individual protein species needs to be assessed.

The dynamic state of proteins in cells can be approached in a number of ways. By feeding radioactive amino acids to the tissues, it can be determined which proteins are being made at a particular time and, for those made in the same cellular compartment, at what relative rates they are made. By taking care to saturate the precursor pools, which often expand in senescing tissues, and by making kinetic measurements, estimates of rates of synthesis may be attempted (Brady and Tung, 1975; Lamattina *et al.*, 1985). These may be facilitated by measuring the specific activity of the amino acyl residues attached to tRNA (Malek and Cossins, 1983). Even so, it is difficult to have confidence in the accuracy of the estimates (Marcus and Rodaway, 1982) because of the problems associated with recycling amino acids and of multiple tRNA isoforms that may be differentially used.

Davies and co-workers have attempted to overcome the recycling problem by labeling proteins with ^3H_2O. The ^3H becomes fixed in the peptide bond and is rapidly exchanged by transaminases when the free amino acids are released (Davies, 1981). There are difficulties in applying the method to bulky tissues or even to aging leaves, because it is difficult to rapidly replace the water in the cells and so apply an effective chase. Sensitive measurements require analyses over several days, and for the results to be meaningful the tissue should remain in a physiological steady state throughout this time. In senescing or ripening tissues this is generally not the case.

Protein synthesis is generally rate limited by the initiation reactions, that is, by the rate of attachment of ribosomes to the mRNAs. Consequently, except in the rare cases where elongation reactions are limited by available energy or available amino acids (Marchal *et al.*, 1983), the loading of ribosomes onto mRNA molecules to give the polysome profile can give a useful index of the relative rates of protein synthesis. Polysomes are a source of the mRNAs being translated. By completing the translation *in vitro* in the presence of labeled amino acids, radioactive products are obtained. Likewise, by translating in an *in vitro* system the total RNA or the polyadenylated RNA, after removal of proteins that may limit or regulate translation, a picture of the spectrum of translatable RNA in cells at any time may be obtained.

Newly synthesized proteins may be distinguished from pre-existing proteins by demonstrating that the density of the protein, located directly or as biological activity, increases when the opportunity is provided for its synthesis in an environment enriched in ^2H_2O or $H_2^{18}O$. While this method does distinguish newly synthesized molecules, the method must be carefully applied if a newly initiated synthesis is to be distinguished from the activation of a precursor molecule that is subject to turnover.

Finally, evidence of the role of protein synthesis in senescence, ripening, abscission, or other aging events may be sought by observing the ability of inhibitors of protein synthesis or of mRNA processing to prevent or modify the process. In all such studies, the specificity of the inhibitor, its ability to reach the appropriate sites, and the side effects that arise when virtually all protein synthesis is eliminated must be considered.

2. Rates of Protein Synthesis

Most estimates of protein synthesis in leaves, and especially in bulky tissues, have involved some modification of the tissues. For example, leaves may be detached and fruits sliced to facilitate the introduction of radioactive precursors. Undoubtedly, such handling influences the results obtained (Schuster and Davies, 1983b). The common observation is that incorporation into protein decreases as leaves age either naturally or after detachment (Martin and Thimann, 1972; Brady and Tung, 1975; Brady and Scott, 1976; Roberts *et al.*, 1987). It is also commonly observed that the content of polysomes decreases with leaf age or with the time leaves have been detached (Callow *et al.*, 1972; Brady *et al.*, 1974; Brady and Scott, 1977). Since, in this case, the effects of handling are minimal, the observations on polysomes support the conclusion from incorporation experiments that there is a decrease in protein synthesis with leaf age. However, the effect of increasing age may be small relative to the large difference in polysome content that is associated with the cessation of growth. Makrides and Goldthwaite (1981) found that the content of polysomes in the leaves of *Phaseolus vulgaris* L. fell abruptly once expansion growth was completed then dropped relatively slowly with time. Schuster and Davies (1983a) observed a very rapid fall in polysomes after growth ceased in etiolated pea epicotyl tissue, but relatively little change with time once growth had ceased. Brady and Scott (1976) recorded a sharp decrease in the polysome content of wheat leaves that coincided with the cessation of expansion growth. Because the fall occurred throughout the leaf and not only in the basal cells that had most recently completed growth, the assumed decline in protein synthesis appeared to reflect a change in the rate of protein turnover rather than the absence of net protein synthesis. In contrast, Lamattina *et al.*, (1985) found no change in the rate of protein synthesis in wheat leaves, detached and darkened, until the leaves were very senescent. Synthesis was measured as leucine incorporation, and care was taken to saturate precursor pools.

Leaves were removed from the dark in order to introduce radiolabeled leucine, and it seems likely that a response to light was involved in their experiments.

In climacteric fruits, there is an increase in protein synthesis, measured as amino acid incorporation or as polysome assembly, as ripening gets underway (Richmond and Biale, 1967; Brady *et al.*, 1970; Tucker and Laties, 1984; Speirs *et al.*, 1984). The increase in protein synthesis reflects an increase in the rates of turnover of a wide range of proteins (Brady and O'Connell, 1976; Tucker and Laties, 1984) and may be viewed as a general upsurge in metabolism as the tissues respond to the ripening stimulus. There are other examples of an increase in the rate of protein synthesis in aging cells. Atkin and Srivastava (1970) noted an increase in amino acid incorporation into protein in detached barley leaves, as did Hedley and Stoddart (1972) in *Lolium temulentum* leaves as they commenced to senesce (degreen). Bufler *et al.*, (1983) found an increase in polysomes in senescing carnation flowers. In suspension cultures of pear cells in a medium designed to maximize survival time in the absence of growth, Pech and Romani (1979) noted an increase in respiration rate and an increase in polysomes that appeared to precede cell death. They suggested that it represented an upsurge in "repair" metabolism in senescent cells.

It is difficult to conclude from this evidence that senescence per se has any decided effect on the overall rates of protein synthesis. In many experiments, responses to growth cessation or to light are confused with those due to senescence. There is so little reliable information on turnover rates in either growing or nongrowing tissues that no conclusion on changes in turnover rate during senescence can be drawn. The available evidence, scattered though it is, suggests that tissue age per se has little effect on rates of protein synthesis, but that different rates of protein turnover are established in nongrowing tissues according to the physiological state—that is, according to nutrient and hormone fluxes—and external stimuli. A change in physiological state, be it drastic as when leaves are detached or darkened, or less drastic as when more active sinks develop nearby, will result in a new metabolic rate, including an adjusted rate of protein synthesis for maintenance purposes. If the tissues cannot be maintained in the new state, a further change, which may involve an increase in protein synthesis, prior to cell death may be observed (Atkin and Srivastava, 1970; Hedley and Stoddart, 1972; Pech and Romani, 1979). An increase in protein synthesis may be related to the increase in respiration rate that is sometimes seen late in senescence (Satler and Thimann, 1983).

3. Synthesis of Ribulose-bisphosphate Carboxylase

Because of the loss of information due to averaging when measurements are made on total or total "soluble" protein in tissues, there is particular value in examining individual species of protein. Since RuBPCase is the most abundant protein in leaves, is readily soluble, is readily purified, and easily quantified by immunological techniques, it is not surprising that it has been intensively studied.

RuBPCase has two types of subunits: the large subunit ($M_r \approx 54,000$) is coded by chloroplast DNA and translated on chloroplast ribosomes; the small subunit ($M_r \approx 13,000$) is coded within the nucleus, translated on cytoplasmic ribosomes as a precursor molecule, and processed to its mature size within the chloroplast. The accumulation of the mRNAs and, presumably, the transcription of the genes is regulated by light, but the details of the regulation varies between species. (Tobin and Silverthorne, 1985). There is little information on how the population of the mRNAs for the two subunits vary with the normal diurnal cycle. The ability to respond to the light stimulus varies with tissue age (Lett *et al.*, 1980), and it would be extremely useful to know the daily cycles of transcription through development.

There are divergent views on the turnover of RuBPCase. Species appear to vary considerably in this regard, but experimental factors also influence observations. In *Perilla*, little or no incorporation of precursors into the RuBPCase protein could be measured in expanded leaves (Woolhouse, 1967) so that little or no replacement of the protein occurs. This also seems to be the case in cucumber cotyledons and expanded *Capsicum* leaves (C. J. Brady, unpublished observations) and other species (Chapter 3). Since other proteins readily incorporate amino acids in these tissues, the alternative explanation that externally added precursors fail to gain access to the sites of synthesis is not tenable. Peterson *et al.* (1973) found the turnover of the RuBPCase in barley leaves to be negligible. In this case, the leaves were etiolated before exposure to light, and it is possible that this abnormal development influenced subsequent events. In wheat (Tung and Brady, 1972; Brady and Scott, 1976), RuBPCase was found to turnover at about the average rate for all "soluble" proteins in newly expanded leaves, and this was also the case in *Zea mays* leaves (Simpson *et al.*, 1981; Davies, 1982). In rice, Makino *et al.* (1984) were able to measure the incorporation of ^{15}N into the protein in leaves in which the net content of RuBPCase protein was declining, thus illustrating that turnover persisted into early senescence (Fig. 5.3).

In wheat, the relative rates of synthesis of RuBPCase and other leaf proteins changes through the life of the leaf (Tung and Brady, 1972; Brady, 1981). The ratio of synthesis of RuBPCase to synthesis of other proteins declines as the leaves age and declines very rapidly if leaves are detached. The ratio declines at an early stage of development if alternative sinks develop, for example, in tillering as opposed to nontillering plants (C. J. Brady, unpublished observations). The decline is not associated with a loss of chloroplast ribosomes (Brady and Scott, 1977) but does correlate with

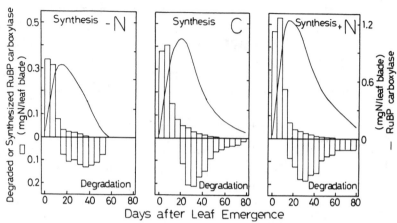

Fig. 5.3. Changes in the amounts of ribulose-bisphosphate carboxylase synthesized or degraded in leaf 12 blades on the main stem of rice from leaf emergence through senescence. Plants were grown in 1 mM NH$_4$NO$_3$ until the emergence of leaf 12, then on 0.3 mM (^{15}NH$_4$)$_2$SO$_4$ for 3 days and then on 0 ($-$N), 1 mM (C), or 2 mM ($+$N) NH$_4$NO$_3$. The synthesis and degradation of the carboxylase were calculated from the changes in ^{15}N content as described by Mae *et al.* (1983), and assuming no turnover of the carboxylase during leaf expansion. The solid curve shows changes in the content of the carboxylase. [From Makino *et al.* (1984).]

the loss of translatable mRNA for both large and small subunits (Speirs and Brady, 1981). The decline in the synthesis of RuBPCase occurs before there is a decline in the content of the protein (Brady, 1981) and may not be directly related to the induction of senescence. However, because it occurs before senescence is clearly visible, and because it is related to leaf development, and responds to many of the same signals as does senescence, it is worthy of further investigation.

4. Other Chloroplast Proteins

It has been suggested that the senescence of leaves may reflect the shutdown of expression of the chloroplast genome in expanded leaves (Ness and Woolhouse, 1980b). Since there is now a good body of information on the proteins coded by chloroplast DNA and made within the chloroplast (Whitfeld and Bottomley, 1983), there is the opportunity to explore the expression of chloroplast genes through leaf development. Silverthorne and Ellis (1980) measured the incorporation of labeled methionine into spinach leaf proteins at four stages of development. They showed that the synthesis of several proteins, including the large subunit of RuBPCase was reduced relative to total protein synthesis as the leaves aged, but the synthesis of another chloroplast-synthesized protein, the 32,000-kDa herbicide-binding polypeptide of photosystem II, was most prominent in older leaves. Labeling of the proteins *in vivo* correlated with the patterns of synthesis by isolated chloroplasts and by *in vitro* synthesis from isolated RNA. The stages of leaf development were not well characterized, but their results clearly show that the chloroplasts in expanded leaves were capable of protein synthesis.

The 32-kDa photosystem II polypeptide is recognized as undergoing rapid turnover in many plants. Its synthesis and degradation are light regulated (Mattoo *et al.*, 1984). It is rapidly synthesized in chloroplasts isolated from senescent wheat leaves (C. J. Brady, unpublished observations) and also in chloroplasts from mature tomato fruits (Bathgate *et al.*, 1985) and in senescent bean leaves (Roberts *et al.*, 1987). Its synthesis could be diagnostic of a functioning chloroplast system for protein synthesis in senescent leaves.

5. Messenger RNA Populations

In vitro translation of RNA allows the population of RNA in tissues to be examined for forms that may be specific to developmental stages. In senescing tissues, there would be particular interest in forms of RNA that appear or disappear immediately before senescence or as senescence is initiated. The products of such RNA templates would be candidates for catalysts or regulators of senescence. Moreover, from a family of products that are developmentally regulated, there is an opportunity to locate and sequence genes that are under common control. Common sequences within the genes may be used to search for regulator molecules. In such ways, hypotheses concerning "senescence genes" and "death" hormones may be evaluated. Initial efforts to apply these methods have been made in recent years.

In the second leaf of wheat, Speirs and Brady (1981) examined the population of translatable mRNAs at five stages through development. A fluorograph of the ^{35}S-labeled polypeptides translated *in vitro* by a wheat germ system primed with total RNA from the leaves is shown in Fig. 5.4. These leaves reached full expansion on day 13 (track 2) and senesced (lost protein) from day 17 through day 26. The intensely labeled product of M_r 20,000 in tracks 1 and 2 is the precursor to the small subunit of RuBPCase. On day 13, this product was 8% of the *in vitro* translation products. By day 19 it was 2% and by day 22 less than 1%. *In vivo* labeling experiments had shown that RuBPCase turned over as rapidly as the average protein in newly expanded (day 13) leaves, while after expansion the turnover of RuBPCase relative to other proteins progressively declined. Exactly the same trend is seen in the *in vitro* translates (Fig. 5.4), although here only the products translated on 80 S ribosomes, that is, the products made in the cytoplasm are seen. Using

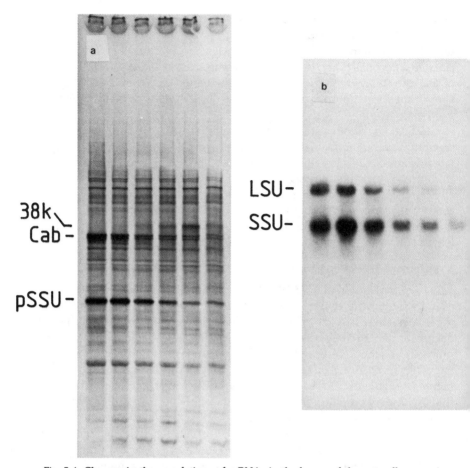

Fig. 5.4. Changes in the populations of mRNAs in the leaves of the naturally senescing second leaf of wheat. (a) Total RNA from leaves was translated *in vitro* in wheat germ translation system in the presence of L-[^{35}S]methionine. The denatured radioactive polypeptide products were separated through polyacrylamide gels and revealed by fluorography. From left to right, the RNA was from leaves 10, 13, 16, 19, 22, and 24 days after sowing; full expansion was on day 13; tracks were loaded with equal amounts of ^{35}S-labeled polypeptide. (b) Equal amounts of RNA from the same leaf series used in (a) were probed with ^{32}P-labeled DNA specific for the large subunit (upper) or the small subunit (lower) of ribulose-bisphosphate carboxylase. From left to right, the RNA was from leaves 10, 13, 16, 19, 22, and 24 days after sowing. [From J. Speirs and C. J. Brady (unpublished observations).]

an *E. coli* translation system, Speirs and Brady (1981) were able to show that the mRNA for the large subunit showed a similar trend. The selective decline in synthesis of RuBPCase in senescent leaves correlated with the amount of translatable mRNA. By hybridizing a ^{32}P-labeled DNA copy of the small subunit mRNA with the total RNA prepared from leaves of different ages, it was shown that the actual amount of small subunit mRNA also declined. A probe for the large subunit message gave a similar response. The *in vivo* observed decline in synthesis of RuBPCase was thus shown to correlate with a declining population of mRNAs for each subunit, placing the point of control at either mRNA stability or at transcription. Experiments with detached leaves indicated that similar controls operated in that the population of RuBPCase mRNAs fell within a few hours when day 11 or day 13 leaves were detached but left in the light. Such experiments emphasize that the changing pattern of synthesis of proteins through development is controlled directly in terms of the mRNA population and not indirectly via some form of translational control or by deterioration of the ribosomal system.

It is noticeable in Fig. 5.4 that certain mRNAs are much more prominent in senescing than in either growing (day 10) or newly expanded leaves (day 13). Polypeptides of 25 and 38 kDa are products of such RNAs. These may be the products of genes uniquely expressed or intensely expressed during senescence.

Watanabe and Imaseki (1982) examined the products of wheat polyadenylated-leaf RNAs translated *in vitro* by wheat germ or reticulocyte lysate systems. The leaves were cultured in continuous light, and senesced in the dark after detachment. They identified a number of products that disappeared and six products that appeared when senescence was provoked. There is a difficulty of interpretation in distinguishing which are responses to the unusual light/dark transition and which are genuinely senescence related. The lack of knowledge of normal diurnal shifts in mRNA populations was noted earlier.

Using two-dimensional separation of the products of *in vitro* translation of total RNA, Malik (1987) explored the changes in mRNA in senescing oat leaves. The changes were extensive in leaves that were excised and darkened, but much less extensive in leaves senescing naturally, or excised and kept in light. During natural senescence a number of translatable mRNAs disappeared and two new mRNA species appeared.

The coordinated control of the mRNA populations for the two subunits of RuBPCase has been noted, but not all mRNAs for chloroplast proteins change in abundance in the same way during development. The two major cytoplasmically synthesized chloroplast proteins are the small subunit of RuBPCase and the chlorophyll a/b binding protein of photosystem II. Each of these is coded by a small multigene family. Not only are they differentially expressed through leaf development, but also different genes within each family respond differently through development (Taylor and Fragoso, 1983; Lamppa *et al.*, 1985).

Colin J. Brady

During the senescence of soybean cotyledons, Skadsen and Cherry (1983) observed quantitative changes among the protein products synthesized *in vitro* from polyadenylated RNA. Products very prominent in translations of the RNA from the young tissue were much less prominent when the RNA was from senescent tissue; other products persisted, and a few were relatively most prominent in the older tissue. Significantly, no products were unique to the senescent tissue. The evidence was for selective changes in the population of mRNAs that may modify the enzymic balance

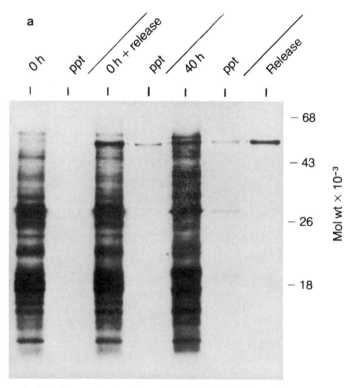

Fig. 5.5. Changes in the content of mRNA for cellulase in avocado fruit. (a) The products of *in vitro* translation of polyadenylated RNA from fruit 0 hours (track 1) and 40 hours (track 5) after ripening were initiated by exposure to ethylene. Track 7 is the *in vitro* translate of the RNA hybridizing to a cloned copy DNA, and track 3 is the *in vitro* translate of the 0 hour RNA plus the hybridized RNA. Tracks 2, 4, and 6 are the polypeptides reacting with antisera specific for cellulase. The products contain [^{35}S]methionine and they have been separated by SDS-polyacrylamide gel electrophoresis and revealed by fluorography. (b) Quantitation of the cellulase mRNA in unripe and ripe fruit in terms of the ^{32}P-labeled copy DNA bound by increasing amounts of polyadenylated RNA. The insert shows the autoradiograph of filters containing increasing amounts of RNA and hybridized to excess of a ^{32}P-labeled copy DNA probe [From Christoffersen *et al.* (1984).]

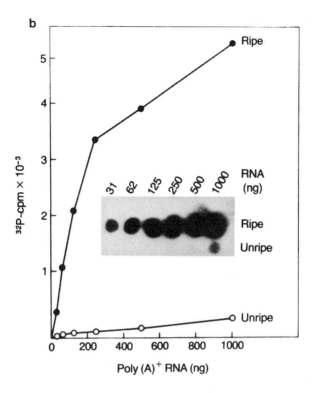

within cells. There was no evidence for the emergence of gene products that might dominate metabolism in the senescing cells.

Gene activation may be involved in altering cell metabolism in germinating seeds and in the ripening avocado fruit. The gibberellic acid-stimulated and abscisic acid-repressed transcription of the barley aleurone α-amylase genes illustrate how the techniques of molecular biology help to define the interactions between hormones and the genome. Gibberellin A_3 stimulates α-amylase production and increases the steady-state level of the α-amylase mRNA, as revealed by *in vitro* translations and by hybridization to cloned copy DNA. Nuclei from cells treated with gibberellin A_3 produce many more α-amylase transcripts than do nuclei from control or abscisic acid-treated cells. Thus, hormone treatment alters nuclear activities; the most likely effect is on gene transcription but effects on RNA stability or processing are not excluded (Jacobsen and Beach, 1985).

The dissolution of the cell wall is an integral part of the ripening of avocado fruit. A cellulase enzyme, thought to be involved in cell wall hydrolysis, accumulates during ripening. Christoffersen *et al.* (1984) showed that a small number of mRNAs increased substantially, relative to other RNAs, during ripening. One of these (Fig. 5.5a) yielded, on *in vitro* translation, a polypeptide that was selectively precipitated by cellulase-specific antisera. The increase in cellulase mRNA was quantitated by hybridization to a specific cDNA (Fig. 5.5b). The experiments relate the increase in the hydrolytic enzyme to a greater than 50-fold increase in its mRNA indicating that the control of cell wall hydrolysis involves transcriptional events initiated during ripening. Similar evidence exists in relation to endopolygalacturonase in ripening tomato fruits (DellaPenna *et al.*, 1986).

During seed germination and fruit ripening, the developmentally controlled production of hydrolase enzymes is controlled at the level of the nucleus. The age-related switching off of the synthesis of RuBPCase may be regulated at a similar level. In developing wheat embryos (Quatrano *et al.*, 1983), abscisic acid treatment reduces the abundance of the mRNA for the small subunit of RuBPCase, and in detached wheat water stress or applied abscisic acid rapidly and selectively decreases the synthesis of RuBPCase (Brady *et al.*, 1974). These are particular examples of positive and negative regulation, and serve to emphasize that senescence involves developmental events controlled by the content of mRNA. Firm evidence establishing that genes are uniquely activated during senescence is not yet available.

6. Use of Metabolic Inhibitors

Because senescence apparently represents a decline from a steady-state situation, it is necessary to understand the elements of the steady state before the initials of senescence can be appreciated. Romani (1984) has expressed this well with particular reference to ripening fruit in which the climacteric and its associated elevated rates of protein and RNA metabolism are an attempt to maintain homeostasis in the face of mounting catabolic "forces." However, this interpretation, too, refers to a period when the steady state is already disturbed, and we must ask questions of the initial disturbance. Romani's concepts focus on the point that the steady state is a dynamic position involving anabolic reactions, but of the quantitative aspects of maintenance metabolism and its regulation, pitifully little is known. It is ignorance of the factors regulating the dynamic state of macromolecules in mature, nongrowing, not senescing cells that makes it difficult to formulate a detailed thesis of the disturbances that lead to senescence.

The point can be developed further by considering the influence of inhibitors of protein synthesis on the development of senescence. At quite low concentrations, cycloheximide inhibits elongation reactions on 80 S ribosomes. It is readily taken up by cells and is an effective *in vivo* inhibitor. Cycloheximide is found to inhibit senescence — chlorophyll and protein loss — in leaf discs (Shibaoka and Thimann, 1970) and ripening in discs of fruit tissue (Frenkel *et al.*, 1968). It is easy to reach the conclusion that the inhibition of protein synthesis prevents the synthesis of enzymes that catalyze the reactions of senescence, for example, proteases to catalyze protein loss (Martin and Thimann, 1972). In the presence of cycloheximide, the additional proteases that are characteristic of the later stages of senescence are not formed, and senescence is arrested. However, consider also these points. Cycloheximide added after the induction of senescence or of ripening also inhibits further senescence (Fig. 5.6; Makovetzki and Goldschmidt, 1976; Brady *et al.*, 1970). If cycloheximide does not interfere with the catabolic enzymes, and these are the agents of senescence, why does senescence not continue once it is initiated? Again, because proteins are normally in a dynamic state, why does not the catabolic side of protein turnover continue in the presence of cycloheximide and so lead to a progressive loss of protein? Although cycloheximide has been used to measure the half-life of enzymes in plant tissues (Zucker, 1968), the method is suspect and there is clear

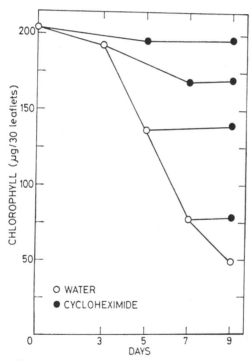

Fig. 5.6. Effects of cycloheximide added during the course of senescence of detached *Anacharis canadensis* leaflets in the dark. The leaflets were transferred to 10 µg/ml cycloheximide 0, 3, 5, or 7 days after detachment. [From Makovetzki and Goldschmidt (1976).]

evidence that cycloheximide inhibits both the anabolic and catabolic aspects of protein turnover.

Even if cycloheximide specifically inhibits protein synthesis, there are side effects that make interpretations uncertain. Protein turnover appears to be a major sink of energy in nongrowing cells (Penning de Vries, 1975; Solomos, 1983). If protein turnover is prevented by cycloheximide, ATP turnover can be expected to drop dramatically, with consequential effects on respiration rate or on the diversion of electron flow to the alternative respiratory pathway (Cocucci and Marré, 1973). Even if cycloheximide has specifically inhibited protein synthesis, the metabolic consequences are far reaching, and it is impossible to conclude that physiological consequences stem from the initial, specific inhibition. Indeed, cycloheximide inhibition of protein loss in leaf discs may point to a separate, almost opposite conclusion, along the lines that senescence depends upon the continuing dynamic state of macromolecules in the cells and cannot be due to the action of hydrolases on essentially static targets.

IV. SENESCENCE MUTANTS

The occurrence of mutations in the nuclear genome that apparently specifically interfere with the induction or progress of senescence provides one of the strongest lines of evidence that senescence is controlled by nuclear genes. The recognition of the mutations provides the opportunity for genetical analysis of the events that control the onset of senescence or of individual reactions involved. Questions such as where are the genes located, are they related to neighboring genes, when are they active, what are their sequences, and what are the gene products may all be approached directly. This is not to state that the direct analysis will be simple, but a combination of classical genetic techniques and intensive use of molecular biology can lead to the seat of the mutation and perhaps to the target molecules that regulate senescence events. The intensity of the effort required to define the detail of the mutations is such that the physiological consequences of the mutations need to be thoroughly explored and appropriate mutants selected for detailed study. Intense study of a number of mutations has been initiated.

A mutation in *Festuca pratensis* drastically reduces chlorophyll loss during senescence without altering the induction of senescence, the loss of most proteins, or the development of leaf proteases (Thomas, 1982a,b). Retention of chlorophyll in the mutant is associated with the retention of some of the hydrophobic proteins of photosystem I and the light-harvesting complex

(Thomas, 1983). Other detailed studies of the processes that may be involved in chlorophyll degradation (Thomas *et al.*, 1985) have not yet provided an explanation for the stability of the lamellae proteins in the mutant, but they have illustrated the value of mutant genotypes for the definition of control points.

A number of mutations that influence the ripening of tomato fruits have been recognized. These fall into three types — those that repress the induction of ripening, those that modify the rate at which ripening proceeds, and those in which the process is modified. Among the latter are mutations in which chlorophyll loss is slow and incomplete so that phenotypically they are comparable to the *Festuca pratensis* NY mutation. More than one mutation of each type has been recognized. These map at completely separate loci. They provide clear evidence of the nuclear controls that operate in the induction of ripening and in the regulation of its progress (Tigchelaar *et al.*, 1978). Information on the physiology of the mutants has been gathered, and the door is open to begin the search for the mutated sequences. The isolation of the mutation gene sequences will, in turn, lead to the isolation of regulator genes from the control lines, and this may provide a method of selecting the molecules that control the transcription of the genes. Perhaps, in this way, the molecular morass that lies between the presence of plant hormones, for example, ethylene in fruit tissues, and the physiological response can be explored. The number of separate mutations that have been recognized gives fair warning of the complexity of the path to be followed.

REFERENCES

Anderson, J. W., and Rowan, K. S. (1966). The effect of 6-furfurylaminopurine on senescence in tobacco leaf tissue after harvest. *Biochem. J.* **98**, 401–404.

Atkin, R. K., and Srivastava, B. I. S. (1970). Studies on protein synthesis by senescing and kinetin-treated barley leaves. *Physiol. Plant.* **23**, 304–315.

Awad, M., and Young, R. E. (1979). Postharvest variation in cellulase, polygalacturonase, and pectin methyl esterase in avocado (*Persea americana* Mill. cv. Fuerte) fruits in relation to respiration and ethylene production. *Plant Physiol.* **64**, 306–308.

Bain, J. M., and Mercer, F. V. (1964). Organization resistance and the respiratory climacteric. *Aust. J. Biol. Sci.* **17**, 78–85.

Balz, H. P. (1966). Intrazellulre Lokalisation und Funktion von hydrolytischen Enzymen bei Tabak. *Planta* **70**, 207–236.

Barlow, P. W. (1982). Cell death — An integral part of plant development. *In* "Growth Regulators in Plant Senescence" (M. B. Jackson, B. Gant, and I. A. Mackenzie, eds.), pp. 27–45. British Plant Growth Reg. Group, Wantage, England.

Barton, R. (1966). Fine structure of mesophyll cells in senescing leaves of *Phaseolus*. *Planta* **71**, 314–325.

Bathgate, B., Purdan, M. E., Grierson, D., and Goodenough, P. W. (1985). Plastid changes during the conversion of chloroplasts to chromoplasts in ripening tomatoes. *Planta* **165**, 197–204.

Batt, T., and Woolhouse, H. W. (1975). Changing sites of activity during senescence and site of synthesis of photosynthetic enzymes in leaves of the labiate *Perilla frutescens* L. Brit. *J. Exp. Bot.* **26**, 569–579.

Ben-Arie, R., Sonego, L., and Frenkel, C. (1979). Changes in pectic substances in ripening pears. *J. Am. Soc. Hortic. Sci.* **104**, 500–505.

Ben-David, H., Nelson, N., and Gepstein, S. (1983). Differential changes in the amount of protein complexes in the chloroplast membrane during senescence of oat and bean leaves. *Plant Physiol.* **73**, 507–510.

Biale, J. B., and Young, R. E. (1971). "The avocado pear." *In* "The Biochemistry of Fruits and Their Products" (A. C. Hulme, ed.), Vol. 2, pp. 65–105. Academic Press, London.

Bick, M. D., Liebke, H., Cherry, J. H., and Strehler, B. L. (1970). Changes in lencyl- and tyrosyl-tRNA of soybean cotyledons during plant growth. *Biochim. Biophys. Acta* **204**, 175–182.

Böttger, I., and Wollgiehn, R. (1958). Investigation on the relation between nucleic acid and protein metabolism in the green leaves of higher developed plants. *Flora (Jena)* **146**, 302–320.

Brady, C. J. (1973). Changes accompanying growth and senescence and effect of physiological stress. *In* "Chemistry and Biochemisty of Herbage" (G. W. Butler and R. W. Bailey, eds.), Vol. 2, pp. 317–351. Academic Press, London.

Brady, C. J. (1981). A co-ordinated decline in the synthesis of subunits of ribulose bisphosphate carboxylase in aging wheat leaves. I. Analyses of isolated protein, subunits and ribosomes. *Aust. J. Plant Physiol.* **8**, 591–602.

Brady, C. J., and O'Connell, P. B. H. (1976). On the significance of increased protein synthesis in ripening banana fruits. *Aust. J. Plant Physiol.* **3**, 301–310.

Brady, C. J., and Scott, N. S. (1976). The persistence of plastid polyribosomes and fraction 1 protein synthesis in aging wheat leaves. *In* "Colloques internationaux de centre nationale de la research scientifique No. 261. Acides nucleiques et synthese des proteines chez les végétaux" (L. Bogorad and J. H. Weil, eds.), Colloq. Int. Cent. Natl. Res. Sci., No. 261, pp. 387–393. CNRS, Paris.

Brady, C. J., and Scott, N. S. (1977). Chloroplast polyribosomes and synthesis of fraction 1 protein in the developing wheat leaf. *Aust. J. Plant Physiol.* **4**, 327–335.

Brady, C. J., and Tung, H. F. (1975). Rate of protein synthesis in senescing, detached wheat leaves. *Aust. J. Plant Physiol.* **2**, 163–176.

Brady, C. J., Palmer, J. K., O'Connell, P. B. H., and Smillie, R. M. (1970). An increase in protein synthesis during ripening of the banana fruit. *Phytochemistry* **9**, 1037–1047.

Brady, C. J., Patterson, B. D., Tung, H. F., and Smillie, R. M. (1971). Protein and RNA synthesis during ageing of chloroplasts in wheat leaves. *In* "Autonomy and Biogenesis of Mitochondria and Chloroplasts" (N. K. Boardman, A. W. Linnane, and R. M. Smillie, eds.), pp. 453–465. North Holland, Amsterdam.

Brady, C. J., Scott, N. S., and Munns, R. (1974). The interaction of water stress with the senescence pattern of leaves. *In* "Mechanisms of Regulation of Plant Growth" (R. L. Bieleski, A. R. Ferguson, and M. M. Cresswell, eds.), Bull. No. 12, pp. 403–409. Royal Soc. New Zealand, Wellington.

Bufler, G., Romani, R. J., and Reid, M. S. (1983). Polysomal populations in relation to ethylene production and the senescence of cut carnation flowers and floral parts. *Proc. Am. Soc. Hortic. Sci.* **108**, 554–557.

Butler, R. D. (1967). The fine structure of senescing cotyledons of cucumber. *J. Exp. Bot.* **18**, 535–543.

Butler, R. D., and Simon, E. W. (1970). Ultrastructural aspects of senescence in plants. *Adv. Gerontol. Res.* **3**, 73–129.

Callow, J. A. (1974). Ribosomal RNA, fraction 1 protein synthesis, and ribulose diphosphate carboxylase activity in developing and senescing leaves of cucumber. *New Phytol.* **73,** 13–20.

Callow, J. A., Callow, M. E., and Woolhouse, H. W. (1972). *In vitro* protein synthesis, RNA synthesis and polyribosomes in senescing leaves of *Perilla*. *Cell Differ.* **1,** 79–90.

Chang, D. Y., Miksche, J. P., and Dhillon, S. S. (1985). DNA changes involving repeated sequences in senescing soybean *(Glycine max)* cotyledon nuclei. *Physiol. Plant.* **64,** 409–417.

Christensen, L. E., Below, F. E., and Hageman, R. H. (1981). The effects of ear removal on senescence and metabolism of maize. *Plant Physiol.* **68,** 1180–1185.

Christoffersen, R. E., Tucker, M. L., and Laties, G. (1984). Cellulase gene expression in ripening avocado fruit: the accumulation of cellulase mRNA and protein as demonstrated by cDNA hybridization and immunodetection. *Plant Mol. Biol.* **3,** 385–392.

Cocucci, M. C., and Marré, E. (1973). The effects of cycloheximide on respiration, protein synthesis and adenosine nucleotide levels in *Rhodotorula gracilis*. *Plant Sci. Lett.* **1,** 293–301.

Cohen, A. S., Popovic, R. B., and Zalik, S. (1979). Effects of polyamines on chlorophyll and protein content, photochemical activity, and chloroplast ultrastructure of barley leaf discs during senescence. *Plant Physiol.* **64,** 717–720.

Davies, D. D. (1981). The measurement of protein turnover in plants. *Adv. Bot. Res.* **8,** 65–126.

Davies, D. D. (1982). Physiological aspects of protein turnover. *Encycl. Plant Physiol., New Ser.* **14A,** 189–228.

De Leo, P., and Sacher, J. A. (1970). Control of ribonuclease and acid phosphatase by auxin and abscisic acid during senescence of *Rhoeo* leaf sections. *Plant Physiol.* **46,** 806–811.

DellaPenna, D., Alexander, D. G., and Bennett, A. B. (1986). Molecular cloning of tomato fruit polygalacturonase: Analysis of polygalacturonase mRNA levels during ripening. *Proc. Natl. Acad. Sci. U.S.A.* **83,** 6420–6424.

De Luca D'oro, G. M., and Trippi, V. S. (1982). Changes in the protease and RNase activity during foliar senescence in *Phaseolus vulgaris* and its regulation by kinetin and cycloheximide in light and darkness. *Phyton Rev. Int. Bot. Exp.* **42,** 83–92.

De Swardt, G. H., Swanepoel, J. H., and Duvenage, A. J. (1973). Relationship between changes in ribosomal RNA and total protein synthesis and the respiration climacteric. *Z. Pflanzenphysiol.* **70,** 358–363.

Duré, L., Galav, G., Chlan, C., and Pyle, J. (1983). Developmentally regulated gene sets in cotton embryogenesis. *In* "Plant Molecular Biology" (R. B. Goldberg, ed.), UCLA Symp. Mol. Cell. Biol., N.S. Vol. 12, pp. 331–342. Alan R. Liss, New York.

Dyer, T. A., and Osborne, D. J. (1971). Leaf nucleic acids. II. Metabolism during senescence and the effect of kinetin. *J. Exp. Bot.* **22,** 552–560.

Evans, J. R. (1983). Nitrogen and photosynthesis in the flag leaf of wheat *(Triticum aestivum* L). *Plant Physiol.* **72,** 297–302.

Frenkel, C. (1972). Involvement of perixidase and indole-3-acetic acid oxidase isozymes from peas, tomato and blueberry fruit in ripening. *Plant Physiol.* **49,** 757–763.

Frenkel, C., Klein, I., and Dilley, D. R. (1968). Protein synthesis in relation to ripening of pome fruits. *Plant Physiol.* **43,** 1146–1153.

Friedrich, J. W., and Huffaker, R. C. (1980). Photosynthesis, leaf resistance and ribulose-1,5-bisphosphate carboxylase in senescing barley leaves. *Plant Physiol.* **65,** 1103–1107.

Hall, A. J., and Brady, C. J. (1977). Assimilate source-sink relationships in *Capsicum annuum* L. II. Effects of fruiting and defloration on the photosynthetic capacity and senescence of the leaves. *Aust. J. Plant Physiol.* **4,** 771–783.

Hansen, E. (1967). Ethylene-stimulated metabolism of immature "Bartlett" pears. *Proc. Am. Soc. Hortic. Sci.* **91,** 863–867.

Harris, J. B., Schaefer, V. G., Dhillon, S. S., and Miksche, J. P. (1982). Differential declines in DNA in aging leaf tissues. *Plant Cell Physiol.* **23,** 1267–1273.

Hedley, C. L., and Stoddart, J. L. (1972). Patterns of protein synthesis in *Lolium temulentum* L. I. Changes occurring during leaf development. *J. Exp. Bot.* **23,** 490–501.

Hinton, D. M., and Pressey, R. (1980). Glucanases in fruit and vegetables. *J. Am. Soc. Hortic. Sci.* **105,** 499–502.

Hobson, G. E. (1964). Polygalacturonase in normal and abnormal tomato fruit. *Biochem. J.* **92,** 324–332.

Hulme, A. C. (1954). Studies in the nitrogen metabolism of apple fruits. *J. Exp. Bot.* **5,** 159–172.

Hulme, A. C., Rhodes, M. J. C., Galliard, T., and Wooltorton, L. S. C. (1968). Metabolic changes in excised fruit tissue. IV. Changes occurring in discs of apple peel during development of the respiration climacteric. *Plant Physiol.* **43,** 1154–1161.

Hulme, A. C., Rhodes, M. J. C., and Wooltorton, L. S. C. (1971). The relationship between ethylene and the synthesis of RNA and protein in ripening apples. *Phytochemistry,* **10,** 749–756.

Hurst, P. R., and Gahan, P. B. (1975). Turnover of DNA in aging tissues of *Lycopersicon esculentum. Ann. Bot.* **39,** 71–76.

Hyodo, H., Tanaka, K., Suzuki, T., Muzukoshi, M., and Tasaki, Y. (1981). The increase in activities of acid phosphatase and RNase during ripening of banana *Musa* cultivar Giant-Cavendish fruit. *J. Jpn. Soc. Hortic. Sci.* **50,** 379–385.

Iki, K., Sekiguchi, K., Kurata, K., Tada, T., Nakagawa, H., Oguva, N., and Tukehana, H. (1978). Immunological properties of β-fructofuranosidase from ripening fruit. *Phytochemistry* **17,** 311–312.

Jacobsen, J. V., and Beach, L. R. (1985). Control of transcription of α-amylase and rRNA genes in barley aleurone protoplasts by gibberellin and abscisic acid. *Nature (London)* **316,** 275–277.

Jenkins, G. I., and Woolhouse, H. W. (1981). Photosynthetic electron transport during senescence of the primary leaves of *Phaseolus vulgaris* L. I. Non-cyclic electron transport. *J. Exp. Bot.* **32,** 467–470.

Kannangara, C. G., and Woolhouse, H. W. (1968). Changes in the enzyme activity of soluble protein fractions in the course of foliar senescence in *Perilla frutescens* (L) Britt. *New Phytol.* **67,** 533–542.

Kennis, J. D., and Trippi, V. S. (1982). Aging and abscission in *Phaseolus vulgaris:* acid phosphatase activity in relation to age and its regulation by quality of the light, sugars and cycloheximide. *Phyton. Rev. Int. Bot. Exp.* **42,** 9–16.

Koll, F., Begel, O., Keller, A. M., Vierny, C., and Belcour, L. (1984). Ethidium bromide rejuvenation of senescent cultures of *Podospora anserina:* loss of senescence-specific DNA and recovery of normal mitochondrial DNA. *Curr. Genet.* **8,** 127–134.

Lamattina, L., Lezica, R. P., and Conde, R. D. (1985). Protein metabolism in senescing wheat leaves. Determination of synthesis and degradation rates and their effects on protein loss. *Plant Physiol.* **77,** 587–590.

Lamppa, G. K., Elliot, L. V., and Bendich, A. J. (1980). Changes in chloroplast number during pea leaf development: An analysis of a protoplast population. *Planta* **148,** 437–443.

Lamppa, G. K., Morelli, G., and Chua, N.-K. (1985). Structure and developmental regulation of a wheat gene encoding the major chlorophyll a/b-binding polypeptide. *Mol. Cell Biol.* **162,** 1370–1378.

Lett, M. C., Fleck, J., Fritsch, C., Durr, A., and Hirth, L. (1980). Suitable conditions for characterization, identification, and isolation of mRNA of the small subunit of ribulose 1,5-bisphosphate carboxylase from *Nicotiana sylvestris. Planta* **148,** 211–216.

Lewis, L. N., Coggins, C. W., Jr., Labanauskas, C. K., and Dugger, W. M., Jr. (1967). Biochemical changes associated with natural and gibberellin A_3 delayed senescence in the navel orange rind. *Plant Cell Physiol.* **8,** 151–160.

McKeon, T. A., Lyman, M. L., and Prestamo, G. (1984). Production of RNase during tomato (*Lycopersicon esculentum* cv. Patio) fruit development. *Plant Physiol.* **75**, Suppl., 153.

Mae, T., Makino, A., and Ohira, K. (1983). Changes in the amounts of ribulose bisphosphate carboxylase synthesized and degraded during the life span of rice leaf (*Oryza sativa* L.). *Plant Cell Physiol.* **24**, 1079–1086.

Makino, A., Mae, T., and Ohira, K. (1983). Photosynthesis and ribulose 1,5-bisphosphate carboxylase in rice leaves. Changes in photosynthesis and enzymes involved in carbon assimilation from leaf development through senescence. *Plant Physiol.* **73**, 1002–1007.

Makino, A., Mae, T., and Ohira, K. (1984). Relation between nitrogen and ribulose-1,5-bisphosphate carboxylase in rice leaves from emergence through senescence. *Plant Cell Physiol.* **25**, 429–437.

Makovetzki, S., and Goldschmidt, E. E. (1976). A requirement for cytoplasmic protein synthesis during chloroplast senescence in the aquatic plant *Anacharis canadensis*. *Plant Cell Physiol.* **17**, 859–862.

Makrides, S. C., and Goldthwaite, J. (1981). Biochemical changes during bean leaf growth, maturity and senescence. Content of DNA, polyribosomes, ribosomal RNA, protein and chlorophyll. *J. Exp. Bot.* **32**, 725–735.

Malek, L., and Cossins, E. A. (1983). Aminoacylation of tRNA and protein turnover in nitrate and sulfate deficient *Spirodela polyrhiza*. *Plant Cell Physiol.* **24**, 1353–1359.

Malik, N. S. A. (1987). Senescence in oat leaves: Changes in translatable mRNAs. *Physiol. Plant.* **70**, 438–446.

Marchal, J., Cortay, J. C., and Cozzone, A. J. (1983). Functional aspects of bacterial polysomes during limited protein synthesis. *Biochim. Biophys. Acta* **739**, 326–333.

Marcus, A., and Rodaway, S. (1982). Nucleic acid and protein synthesis during germination. *In* "The Molecular Biology of Plant Development" (H. Smith and D. Grierson, eds.), pp. 337–361. Blackwell, Oxford.

Martin, C., and Thimann, K. V. (1972). The role of protein synthesis in the senescence of leaves. I. The formation of protease. *Plant Physiol.* **49**, 64–71.

Mattoo, A. K., Hoffman-Falk, H., Marder, J. B., and Edelman, M. (1984). Regulation of protein metabolism: coupling of photosynthetic electron transport to *in vivo* degradation of the rapidly metabolized 32 kilodalton protein of the chloroplast membrane. *Proc. Natl. Acad. Sci. U.S.A.* **81**, 1380–1384.

Mettler, I. J., and Romani, R. J. (1976). Quantitative changes in tRNA during ethylene induced ripening (aging) of tomato fruits. *Phytochemistry* **15**, 25–28.

Moore, A. E., and Stone, B. A. (1972). Effect of senescence and hormone treatment on the activity of a β-1,3-glucan hydrolase in *Nicotiana glutinosa* leaves. *Planta* **104**, 93–109.

Mothes, K., and Baudisch, W. (1958). Untersuchungen über die Reversibilität der Ausbleichung grüner Blätter. *Flora (Jena)* **146**, 521–531.

Mowlah, G., and Itoo, S. (1982). Guava (*Psidium guajava* L.) sugar components and related enzymes at stages of fruit development and ripening. *J. Jpn. Soc. Food Technol.* **29**, 472–476.

Mowlah, G., and Itoo, S. (1983). Changes in pectic components, ascorbic acid, pectic enzymes and cellulase activity in ripening and stored guava (*Psidium guajava* L.) *J. Jpn. Soc. Food Sci. Technol.* **30**, 454–461.

Ness, P. J., and Woolhouse, H. W. (1980a). RNA synthesis in *Phaseolus* chloroplasts. I. Ribonucleic acid synthesis in chloroplast preparations from *Phaseolus vulgaris* L. leaves and solubilization of the RNA polymerase. *J. Exp. Bot.* **31**, 223–233.

Ness, P. J., and Woolhouse, W. H. (1980b). RNA synthesis in *Phaseolus* chloroplasts. II. Ribonucleic acid synthesis in chloroplasts from developing and senescing leaves. *J. Exp. Bot.* **31**, 235–245.

Noodén, L. D., and Leopold, A. C. (1978). Phytohormones and the endogenous regulation of senescence and abscission. *In* "Phytohormones and Related Compounds. A Comprehensive Treatise," Vol. II. (D. S. Letham, P. B. Goodwin, and T. J. V. Higgins, eds.), pp. 329–369. Elsevier Science Publishing Co., Amsterdam.

Noodén, L. D., Rupp, D. C., and Derman, B. D. (1978). Separation of seed development from monocarpic senescence in soybeans. *Nature (London)* **271**, 354–357.

Parida, R. K., and Mishra, D. (1980). Acid phosphatase and adenosine triphosphatase activities during rice leaf development and senescence. *Photosynthetica* **14**, 431–436.

Paull, R. E., and Chen, N. J. (1983). Postharvest variation in cell wall-degrading enzymes of papaya (*Carica papaya* L.) during fruit ripening. *Plant Physiol.* **72**, 382–385.

Paull, R. E., Deputy, J., and Chen, N. J. (1983). Changes in organic acids, sugars and headspace volatiles during fruit ripening of soursop (*Annona muricata* L.). *J. Am. Soc. Hortic. Sci.* **108**, 931–934.

Pech, J. C., and Romani, R. J. (1979). Senescence of pear fruit cells cultured in a continuously renewed auxin-deprived medium. *Plant Physiol.* **64**, 814–817.

Penning de Vries, F. W. T. (1975). The cost of maintenance processes in plant cells. *Ann. Bot.* **39**, 77–92.

Peterson, L. W., Kleinkopf, G. E., and Huffaker, R. C. (1973). Evidence for lack of turnover of ribulose 1,5-diphosphate carboxylase in barley leaves. *Plant Physiol.* **51**, 1042–1045.

Piechulla, B., and Gruissem, W. (1987). Diurnal mRNA fluctuations of nuclear and plastid genes in developing tomato fruits. *EMBO J.* **6**, 3593–3599.

Pillay, D. T. N., and Cherry, J. H. (1974). Changes in leucyl, seryl and tyrosyl tRNAs in aging soybean cotyledons. *Can. J. Bot.* **52**, 2499–2504.

Pillay, D. T. N., and Gowda, S. (1981). Age-related changes in transfer RNA species and transfer RNA synthetases in germinating soybean (*Glycine max* cultivar Harcor) cotyledons. *Gerontology* **27**, 194–204.

Pollock, C. J., and Lloyd, E. J. (1978). Acid invertase activity during senescence of excised leaf tissue of *Lolium temulentum*. *Z. Pflanzenphysiol.* **90**, 79–84.

Poovaiah, B. W., and Nukaya, A. (1979). Polygalacturonase and cellulase enzymes in the normal Rutgers and mutant *rin* tomato fruits and their relationship to the respiratory climacteric. *Plant Physiol.* **64**, 534–537.

Quatrano, R. S., Ballo, B. L., Williamson, J. D., Hamblin, M. T., and Mansfield, M. (1983). ABA controlled expression of embryo-specific genes during wheat grain development. *In* "Plant Molecular Biology" (R. B. Goldberg, ed.), UCLA Symp. Mol. Cell. Biol., N.S. Vol. 12, pp. 381–389. Alan R. Liss, New York.

Racusen, D., and Foote, M. (1965). Protein synthesis in dark grown bean leaves. *Can. J. Bot.* **43**, 817–824.

Rattanapanone, N., Grierson, D., and Stein, M. (1977). Ribonucleic acid metabolism during the development and ripening of tomato fruits. *Phytochemistry* **16**, 629–633.

Rhodes, M. J. C., and Wooltorton, L. S. C. (1967). The respiratory climacteric in apple fruits. The action of hydrolytic enzymes in peel tissue during the climacteric period in fruit detached from the tree. *Phytochemistry* **6**, 1–12.

Richmond, A., and Biale, J. B. (1967). Protein and nucleic acid metabolism in fruits. II. RNA synthesis during the respiratory rise of the avocado. *Biochim. Biophys. Acta* **138**, 625–627.

Roberts, D. W. A. (1982). Changes in the forms of invertase during the development of wheat leaves growing under cold-hardening and non-hardening conditions. *Can. J. Bot.* **60**, 1–6.

Roberts, D. R., Thompson, J. E., Dumbroff, E. B., Gepstein, S., and Mattoo, A. K. (1987). Differential changes in the synthesis and steady-state levels of thylakoid proteins during bean leaf senescence. *Plant Mol. Biol.*, **9**, 343–353.

Roe, B., and Bruemmer, J. H. (1981). Changes in pectic substances and enzymes during ripening and storage of "Keitt" mangoes. *J. Food Sci.* **46**, 186–189.

Romani, R. J. (1984). Respiration, ethylene, senescence and homeostasis in an integrated view of postharvest life. *Can. J. Bot.* **62**, 2950–2955.

Rowan, K. S., McGlasson, W. B., and Pratt, H. K. (1969). Changes in adenosine pyrophosphates in cantaloupe fruit ripening normally and after treatment with ethylene. *J. Exp. Bot.* **20**, 145–155.

Sacher, J. A. (1973). Senescence and postharvest physiology. *Annu. Rev. Plant Physiol.* **24**, 197–224.

Sacher, J. A., and Davies, D. D. (1974). Demonstration of de novo synthesis of RNAse in Rhoeo leaf sections by deuterium oxide labelling. *Plant Cell Physiol.* **15**, 157–162.

Sampson, M., and Davies, D. D. (1966). Synthesis of a metabolically labile DNA in the maturing root cells of *Vicia faba*. *Exp. Cell Res.* **43**, 669–673.

Satler, S. O., and Thimann, K. V. (1983). Relation between respiration and senescence in oat leaves. *Plant Physiol.* **72**, 540–546.

Schuster, A. M., and Davies, E. (1983a). RNA and protein metabolism in pea epicotyls. I. The aging process. *Plant Physiol.* **73**, 809–816.

Schuster, A. M., and Davies, E. (1983b). RNA and protein metabolism in pea epicotyls. *Plant Physiol.* **73**, 817–821.

Scott, N. S., and Possingham, J. V. (1982). "Leaf Development." *In* "The Molecular Biology of Plant Development" (H. Smith and D. Grierson, eds.), pp. 223–255. Blackwell, Oxford.

Scott, N. S., and Possingham, J. V. (1983). Changes in chloroplast DNA levels during growth of spinach leaves. *J. Exp. Bot.* **34**, 1756–1767.

Shibaoka, H., and Thimann, K. V. (1970). Antagonism between kinetin and amino acids: experiments on the mode of action of cytokinin. *Plant Physiol.* **46**, 212–220.

Shirai, Y., Sato, T., Ogura, N., and Nakagawa, H. (1984). Effect of heat treatment on changes in acid phosphatase activity during ripening. *Agric. Biol. Chem.* **48**, 797–801.

Silverthorne, J., and Ellis, R. J. (1980). Protein synthesis in chloroplasts. VIII. Differential synthesis of chloroplast proteins during spinach leaf development. *Biochim. Biophys. Acta* **607**, 319–330.

Simpson, E., Cooke, R. J., and Davies, D. D. (1981). Measurement of protein degradation in leaves of *Zea mays* using [^{3}H] acetic anhydride and tritiated water. *Plant Physiol.* **67**, 1214–1219.

Skadsen, R. W., and Cherry, J. H. (1983). Quantitative changes in *in vitro* and *in vivo* protein synthesis in aging and rejuvenated soybean cotyledons. *Plant Physiol.* **71**, 861–868.

Sodek, L., and Wright, S. T. C. (1969). The effect of kinetin on ribonuclease, acid phosphatase, lipase and esterase levels in detached wheat leaves. *Phytochemistry* **8**, 1629–1640.

Solomos, T. (1983). Respiration and energy metabolism in senescing plant tissues. *In* "Postharvest Physiology and Crop Improvement" (M. Lieberman, ed.), pp. 61–98. Plenum, New York.

Speirs, J., and Brady, C. J. (1981). A co-ordinated decline in the synthesis of subunits of ribulosebisphosphate carboxylase in aging wheat leaves. II. Abundance of messenger RNA. *Aust. J. Plant Physiol.* **8**, 603–618.

Speirs, J., Brady, C. J., Grierson, D., and Lee, E. (1984). Changes in ribosome organization and messenger RNA abundance in ripening tomato fruits. *Aust. J. Plant Physiol.* **11**, 225–233.

Stoddart, J. L., and Thomas, H. (1982). Leaf senescence. *In* "Encyclopedia of Plant Physiology" (D. Boulter and B. Parthier, eds.), Vol. 14A, pp. 592–636. Springer-Verlag, Berlin and New York.

Strehler, B. L. (1967). The nature of cellular age changes. *Symp. Soc. Exp. Biol.* **21**, 149–177.

Takegami, T. (1975). A study on senescence in tobacco leaf discs. II. Chloroplast and cytoplasmic rRNAs. *Plant Cell Physiol.* **16**, 417–425.

Taylor, W. C., and Fragoso, L. (1983). Gene switching during maize leaf development. *In* "Plant Molecular Biology" (R. B. Goldberg, ed.), UCLA Symp. Mol. Cell. Biol., N.S. Vol. 12, pp. 381–389. Alan R. Liss, New York.

Terra, N. N., Garcia, E., and Lajolo, F. M. (1983). Starch sugar transformation during banana *Musa acuminata* ripening: the behaviour of UDP-glucose pyrophosphorylase, sucrose synthase and invertase. *J. Food Sci.* **48**, 1097–1100.

Thomas H. (1982a). Leaf senescence in a non-yellowing mutant of *Festuca pratensis*. I. Chloroplast membrane polypeptides. *Planta* **154**, 212–218.

Thomas, H. (1982b). Leaf senescence in a non-yellowing mutant of *Festuca pratensis*. II. Proteolytic degradation of thylakoid and stroma polypeptides. *Planta* **154**, 219–223.

Thomas, H. (1983). Leaf senescence in a non-yellowing mutant of *Festuca pratensis*. IV. Senescence in the light. *Photosynthetica* **17**, 506–514.

Thomas, H., and Stoddart, J. L. (1980). Leaf senescence. *Annu. Rev. Plant Physiol.* **31**, 83–111.

Thomas, H., Lüthy, B., and Matile, P. (1985). Leaf senescence in a non-yellowing mutant of *Festuca pratensis* Huds. Oxidative chlorophyll bleaching by thylakoid membranes during senescence. *Planta* **164**, 400–405.

Tigchelaar, E. C., McGlasson, W. B., and Buescher, R. W. (1978). Genetic regulation of tomato fruit ripening. *HortScience* **13**, 508–513.

Tobin, E. M., and Silverthorne, J. (1985). Light regulation of gene expression in higher plants. *Annu. Rev. Plant Physiol.* **36**, 569–593.

Tucker, M. L., and Laties, G. G. (1984). Interrelationship of gene expression, polysome prevalence, and respiration during ripening of ethylene and/or cyanide-treated avocado fruit. *Plant Physiol.* **74**, 307–315.

Tung, H. F., and Brady, C. J. (1972). Kinetin treatment and protein synthesis in detached wheat leaves. *In* "Plant Growth Substances" (D. J. Carr, ed.), pp. 589–597. Springer-Verlag, Berlin and New York.

Udovenko, G. V., and Gogoleva, L. A. (1974). Dynamics of DNA and RNA content in leaves of wheat during ontogenesis. *Fiziol. Rast. (Moscow)* **21**, 1076–1078.

Udvardy, J., Farkas, G. L., and Marré, E. (1969). On ribonuclease and other hydrolytic enzymes in excised *Avena* leaf tissues. *Plant Cell Physiol.* **10**, 375–386.

Venkatarayappa, T., Fletcher, R. A., and Thompson, J. E. (1984). Retardation and reversal of senescence in bean leaves by benzyladenine and decapitation. *Plant Cell Physiol.* **25**, 407–418.

Wade, N. L., O'Connell, P. B. H., and Brady, C. J. (1972). Content of RNA and protein of the ripening banana. *Phytochemistry* **11**, 975–979.

Wang, C. Y., and Mellenthin, W. M. (1977). Effect of aminoethoxy analog of rhizobitoxine on ripening of pears. *Plant Physiol.* **59**, 546–549.

Watanabe, A., and Imaseki, H. (1982). Changes in translatable mRNA in senescing wheat leaves. *Plant Cell Physiol.* **23**, 489–490.

Wheatley, D. N. (1984). Intracellular protein degradation: Basis of a self-regulating mechanism for the proteolysis of endogenous proteins. *J. Theor. Biol.* **107**, 127–149.

Whitfeld, P. R., and Bottomley, W. (1983). Organization and structure of chloroplast genes. *Annu. Rev. Plant Physiol.* **34**, 279–310.

Wittenbach, V. A. (1977). Induced senescence of intact wheat seedlings and its reversibility. *Plant Physiol.* **59**, 1039–1042.

Wittenbach, V. A. (1979). Ribulose bisphosphate carboxylase and proteolytic activity in wheat leaves from anthesis through senescence. *Plant Physiol.* **64**, 884–887.

Wittenbach, V. A. (1982). Effect of pod removal on leaf senescence in soybeans. *Plant Physiol.* **70,** 1544–1548.

Wollgiehn, R. (1967). Nucleic acid and protein metabolism of excised leaves. *Symp. Soc. Exp. Biol.* **21,** 231–246.

Woolhouse, H. W. (1967). The nature of senescence in plants. *Symp. Soc. Exp. Biol.* **21,** 179–214.

Woolhouse, H. W. (1982). "Leaf Senescence." *In* "The Molecular Biology of Plant Development" (H. Smith and D. Grierson, eds.), pp. 256–281. Blackwell, Oxford.

Wrench, P. M., Olive, M., Hiller, R. G., Brady, C. J., and Speirs, J. (1987). Changes in plastid proteins during ripening of tomato fruits. *J. Plant Physiol.* **129,** 89–102.

Wyn Jones, R. G., Brady, C. J., and Speirs, J. (1979). Ionic and osmotic relations in plant cells. *In* "Recent Advances in the Biochemistry of Cereals" (D. L. Laidman and R. G. Wyn Jones, eds.), pp. 63–103. Academic Press, London.

Yoshida, Y. (1961). Nuclear control of chloroplast activity in *Elodea* leaf cells. *Protoplasma* **54,** 476–492.

Zucker, M. (1968). Sequential induction of phenylalanine ammonia lyase and a lyase inactivating system in potato tuber discs. *Plant Physiol.* **43,** 365–374.

The Interplay between Proteolysis and Amino Acid Metabolism during Senescence and Nitrogen Reallocation

Mark B. Peoples
CSIRO
Division of Plant Industry
Canberra, Australia

Michael J. Dalling
Calgene Pacific
Ivanhoe, Victoria, Australia

SENESCENCE AND AGING IN PLANTS

Copyright © 1988 by Academic Press, Inc.
All rights of reproduction in any form reserved.

I. INTRODUCTION

Nitrogen is an essential element for plant growth, but despite its high abundance in the atmosphere, the availability of nitrogen is often limited. It is not surprising then that both annual and perennial plants have evolved with very effective strategies to conserve nitrogen.

The best documented and arguably the most important economically of these nitrogen conservation strategies is that associated with seed development and maturation. There are only two sources of nitrogen available for seed development—nitrogen assimilated and invested in the vegetative organs prior to anthesis and nitrogen assimilated after anthesis. The contribution of pre- and postanthesis nitrogen to the grain nitrogen yield of leguminous and nonleguminous plants has been the subject of many studies. Collectively, these investigations support the notion that even when the postanthesis nitrogen supply is high, either through high available soil-N or prolonged nitrogen fixation, a major portion of the seed nitrogen yield is derived from the reallocation of nitrogen in the vegetative organs to the seed (Dalling, 1985; Zapata *et al.*, 1987).

Nitrogen reallocation or redistribution is a complex phenomenon and consists essentially of three components: a *source* of nitrogen for reallocation, a mechanism for translocation (phloem/xylem), and a site for assimilation and storage *(sink)*. This chapter discusses the degradative and associated assimilatory aspects of nitrogen removal from the *source*. Translocation is discussed in Chapter 7.

II. QUALITATIVE AND QUANTITATIVE DESCRIPTION OF PREANTHESIS NITROGEN SOURCE

At the time of anthesis, the total N content of the plant is distributed between the different vegetative organs. These organs can therefore be considered individually as nitrogen *sources*, but they differ significantly from one another in the extent to which they contribute to the final yield of grain N (Table 6.1). The differences are a reflection of the absolute nitrogen content of the organ (function of mass and %N) and the extent of nitrogen removal from the organ. In general, the leaves, stem, and reproductive structures (e.g., pod walls, glumes) are characterized by a high efficiency of nitrogen removal (> 65%), but the roots tend not to reallocate their nitrogen content (< 30%). Dalling (1985) has suggested that these differences are a reflection of an "ordered priority system" within the plant whereby there is a need to balance organ function during senescence with any inherent tendency towards a high efficiency of N removal. The "cost" of this

TABLE 6.1

Estimates of the Relative Contribution of Nitrogen Mobilized from Vegetative and Reproductive Organs to Seed Growth in Various Plant Species

Plant species	Percent of seed N derived from various sources					References
	Roots (and nodules)	Stem and lateral axes	Leaflets	Total from vegetative parts[a]	Reproductive parts	
Broad bean (Vicia faba)	3–5	9–12	16–24	31–38	7–19	Pate and Minchin (1980); Dekhuijzen and Verkerke (1984)
Cowpea (Vigna unguiculata)	3–11	15	34–38	56–60	3–9	Pate and Minchin (1980); Peoples et al. (1983)
Groundnut (Arachis hypogaea)	0.4	9	21	30	7	Pate and Minchin (1980)
Maize (Zea mays)	10	24	19	53	1	Pan et al. (1986)
Soybean (Glycine max)	3	7–16	28–35	38–54	9–16	Pate and Minchin (1980); Buttery (1986)
Sunflower (Helianthus annuus)	12	8	26	46	13	Hocking and Steer (1983)
Wheat (Triticum aestivum L.)	6–16	23–28	29–40	63–79	12–23	Dalling et al. (1976); Simpson et al. (1983)

[a] The significance of net losses of N from vegetative or reproductive structures were assessed by comparing them with the N gained by the seed and assuming that such losses were accompanied by transfer of equivalent amounts of N to the seed. This technique should give reasonable estimates of mobilization provided that abscissed tissues have been collected and included in harvests and that there are negligible volatile losses of nitrogenous compounds.

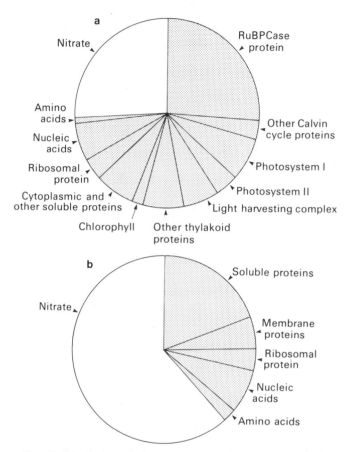

Fig. 6.1. Distribution of nitrogen among various proteins and other nitrogenous compounds in (a) mesophyll and (b) nonmesophyll cells of wheat leaves. Shaded area represents reduced N. [Adapted from data by Evans (1984) and M. J. Dalling (unpublished observations).]

compromise is reduced N removal, especially in the roots which seem to be the last organs to senesce.

Fig. 6.1 is a schematic representation of the contribution made by various N-containing compounds to the total N budget of mesophyll and nonmesophyll cells of a typical leaf; in this case, the primary leaf of a wheat seedling. We acknowledge that other examples could have been chosen; in particular, we are aware of the significant difference between C_3 and C_4 plants in the relative abundance of the chloroplast protein ribulose-1,5-bisphosphate carboxylase (RuBPCase) cf. phosphoenol pyruvate carboxylase (PEP carboxylase) and species differences in the extent of nitrate accumulation in leaves. In addition, we draw the readers' attention to the often overlooked fact that the mesophyll cells of most leaves generally only account for half the total cell population (Jellings and Leech, 1982).

From the point of view of further defining the nitrogen *source*, Fig. 6.1 serves two purposes.

First, it highlights the relative abundance of protein that accounts for 88 and 74% of the reduced N of mesophyll and nonmesophyll cells, respectively. In contrast, the total amount of nucleic acids only accounts for 8 and 19% of the reduced N of mesophyll and nonmesophyll cells, respectively. Of the proteins, RuBPCase is the most abundant, accounting for 35% of the mesophyll cell reduced N. As such, RuBPCase must therefore be considered to be the single most abundant *source* of nitrogen for reallocation.

Second, the proteins of the mesophyll cell can be divided into soluble and insoluble or membrane-bound, accounting for 62 and 38% of the total protein, respectively.

During the course of senescence, the proteins (soluble and insoluble), nucleic acids, and other N compounds are degraded and the products of degradation, exported from the organ. Protein degradation, however, plays a more important role in the plant's overall nitrogen economy than simply providing low molecular weight nitrogenous compounds for transport from senescing tissue.

It is likely that much of the nitrogen entering the plant early in its life will be passed through several age groups and types of vegetative structures, and will even be incorporated into several generations of proteins and other compounds before being finally released for reallocation to the developing seed. Several ^{15}N feeding experiments with grain and forage legumes have shown substantial release of ^{15}N from proteins, although there may be no significant decline in total organ reduced N (see, e.g., Pate and Flinn, 1973; Phillips *et al.*, 1983). Even while still increasing in total N content, root, shoot segments, or leaves may turnover 1 to 2% per day of previously assimilated ^{15}N, and later in growth this rate may rise to 2 to 3%. The contribution of nitrogen mobilization to the plant's N economy as determined from such ^{15}N studies can be up to 3-fold higher than that which would otherwise be estimated from a net nitrogen loss from senescing tissues as described in Table 6.1 (Dekhuijzen and Verkerke, 1984).

III. PROTEIN DEGRADATION

A. Generalized Concepts of Proteolysis

If proteolysis is considered a functional part of senescence, then the objective of this process, irrespective of the nature of the individual participating proteases, is to reduce the substrate protein to its constituent amino acids (Fig. 6.2). In many ways proteolysis can be most easily viewed as a

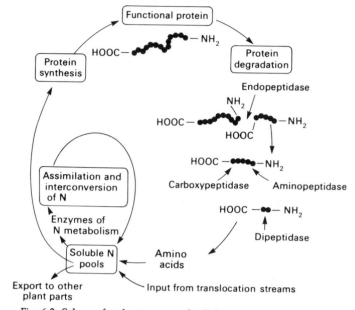

Fig. 6.2. Scheme for the turnover of cellular proteins. The amount of functional protein present is maintained by a balance of the biosynthetic and degradative processes. Some breakdown products may undergo metabolism before ultimately being reincorporated into protein or exported to other plant parts.

cascade, wherein the activities of the endopeptidases are less than those of exopeptidases and dipeptidases. This ordered sequence is necessary since as each peptide bond is hydrolyzed, the number of substrate peptides increases accordingly. Thus, if proteolysis is to continue without significant accumulation of breakdown products, the activity of those enzymes at the start of the process should be much less than those enzymes further along the cascade. Waters *et al.* (1980) present the most compelling evidence in support of this generalized concept of proteolysis.

B. Protein Turnover

The protein population of plants is in a dynamic state of flux (Fig. 6.2) where, at any one time, the absolute amount of a particular protein species is a function of the rate of synthesis and the rate of degradation (Huffaker and Peterson, 1974; Davies, 1982). This phenomenon, where some members of a protein species are being degraded while others are being synthesized, protein turnover, is of critical importance to the plant cell. The process is

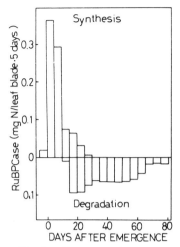

Fig. 6.3. Changes in the amounts of RuBPCase synthesized and degraded in the twelfth leaf blade of rice from leaf emergence through senescence. [From Mae *et al.* (1983).]

able to adjust the levels of key metabolic enzymes and other proteins within the cell in response to developmental changes (e.g., senescence) and the physical environment (e.g., nutrient status, stress). Furthermore, protein turnover provides the cell with an effective mechanism to achieve preferential removal of defective or aberrant proteins (Huffaker and Peterson, 1974).

In the case of the chloroplast protein RuBPCase, Mae *et al.* (1983) have demonstrated concurrent synthesis and degradation, but most importantly, they were able to show that the rate of turnover varied with leaf ontogeny (Fig. 6.3). In the young, expanding leaf, no degradation of RuBPCase could be detected. At the time of full leaf expansion, concurrent synthesis and degradation was readily detected and once senescence commenced, the rate of RuBPCase synthesis declined, but the rate of degradation stayed more or less constant. RuBPCase synthesis is discussed more extensively in Chapter 5.

C. Nature of Protein-Degrading Enzymes

Enzymes that degrade protein do so by hydrolyzing of the peptide bonds; not surprisingly, these enzymes are referred to as peptide hydrolases. The peptide hydrolases may be divided into two groups, according to the position of the peptide bond hydrolyzed (Table 6.2). If hydrolysis releases

TABLE 6.2

Classification of Protein-Degrading Enzymes[b]

Enzyme	EC number	Specific inhibitors[a]	General comments
Endopeptidases			
Serine	3.4.21	PMSF, DFP	Serine and histidine residue at active site. Diverse substrate specificity.
Cysteine	3.4.22	Diazomethanes cystatins iodoacetate	Cysteine residue at active site
Aspartic	3.4.23	DAN + Cu^{2+} pepsatin	Aspartic acid residue at active site; pH optimum below 5.0.
Metallo	3.4.24	Metal chelators	Zn is commonly the essential metal at catalytic site
Exopeptidases			
Aminopeptidases	3.4.11	Bestatin	Release N-terminal amino acid
Tripeptidases	3.4.11.4	—	Cleave N-terminal amino acid from tripeptide
Dipeptidase	3.4.13	—	Cleave dipeptide
Dipeptidyl peptidases	3.4.14	—	Release dipeptide from N terminal
Tripeptidyl peptidases	3.4.—	—	Release tripeptide from N terminal
Peptidyl dipeptidases	13.4.15	—	Release dipeptide from C terminal
Carboxypeptidases	3.4.16–18		Release C-terminal amino acid
Serine	3.4.16	DFP, PMSF	
Metallo	3.4.17	Metal chelators	
Omega peptidase	3.4.19	—	Release terminal residues from proteins and peptides with blocked terminal residues

[a] Abbreviations: DAN, diazoacetyl norleucine methyl ester; DFP, diisopropylfluorophosphate; PMSF, phenylmethylsulfonyl fluoride.
[b] Table collated from article by Barrett (1986).

peptides of more than three amino acid residues in length, the enzyme belor.gs to the subgroup endopeptidases, also called proteinases. If, on the other hand, only single amino acids, or in some instances dipeptides or tripeptides, are released on hydrolysis, that enzyme is classed as an exopeptidase, also known as peptidases.

The peptidases may be further classified according to whether they hydrolyze terminal residues from a peptide or cleave a dipeptide into its constituent amino acids. Aminopeptidases release a single amino acid from the N terminus of a peptide whereas carboxypeptidases release a single amino acid from the C terminal end (Fig. 6.2).

The proteinases can be characterized according to their active site and pH optima. The various subgroups are commonly identified by the use of specific active site inhibitors. The systematic study of proteolytic enzymes is technically demanding (Barrett, 1986) and unfortunately the majority of studies describing plant proteolytic enzymes have been so inadequate that only a small number of enzymes have been properly characterized. The limitations of these studies have been discussed by Wagner (1986) and protocols for a more meaningful characterization are outlined. In addition, the general features of those plant endo- and exopeptidases described in the literature have been collated by Mikola and Mikola (1986) and Storey (1986).

D. Generalized Concepts for the Regulation of Protein Degradation

Protein degradation is essentially a two-component system: the protein substrate and the proteolytic enzyme. Hypotheses describing the regulation of proteolysis have therefore been directed to each of these components (Huffaker and Peterson, 1974), although as will be outlined below, the intervention of a third component, an effector compound, needs to be considered.

1. Compartmentation

In principle this is a simple hypothesis and has its origins in the lysosome or vacuole hypothesis previously described for yeast and mammalian cells (Matile, 1975). The essential element of this hypothesis is that the protein substrates and the proteolytic enzyme(s) are segregated into compartments of the cell. Because the vacuole of plant cells has been shown to contain many of the classes of hydrolytic enzymes necessary for degradation of the assorted N-containing constituents of the cell (Boller and Kende, 1979), it is an obvious candidate to be one part of this model. Regulation of proteolysis is achieved by selective entry of the substrate into the vacuole (Canut *et al.*, 1986), or possibly, but less likely, secretion of the protease(s) from the vacuole. In the case of protein bodies in endosperm or cotyledon cells, the substrate proteins and the proteolytic enzymes responsible for their degradation are both located in the vacuole (Dalling and Bhalla, 1984).

Therre are several limitations to this model. The first relates to how a model, based simply on compartmentation, is able to achieve selectivity of protein degradation. To some extent this limitation may be overstated if the characteristics of the substrate and/or the intervention of an effector compound can contribute in some manner to the selectivity of degradation. The second limitation of the model relates more specifically to the role of the vacuolar compartment in chloroplast senescence. Chloroplasts which contain about 80% of the reduced-N in mesophyll cells (Fig. 6.1), are separated from the vacuolar peptide hydrolases by both the vacuole's tonoplast and the chloroplast envelope. Although there are reports of chloroplasts being engulfed in vacuoles (Wittenbach *et al.*, 1982; see also Chapter 3), this has not been widely observed (Woolhouse, 1984; Dalling and Nettleton, 1986) and there is compelling evidence that degradation of chloroplast proteins occurs within the chloroplast (Wardley *et al.*, 1984; Ferreira and Davies, 1986). Furthermore, the peptide hydrolases so far detected in the chloroplast using RuBPCase as an *in vitro* substrate are not the same as similar enzymes of the vacuole (Nettleton *et al.*, 1985; Bhalla and Dalling, 1986). The third limitation arises from studies of yeast mutants which lack the vacuolar endopeptidases (Enter and Wolf, 1984). These strains are able to grow, differentiate, and sporulate at comparable rates to wild-type strains, suggesting that vacuolar enzymes are not essential for the normal functioning of yeast cells.

2. Characteristics of the Substrate Protein

There have been several important studies with mammalian, bacterial, and yeast cell systems that have been able to establish a link, sometimes tenuous, between the susceptibility of particular proteins to degradation *in vivo* and one or more physical properties of these proteins. These studies prompted parallel studies with plant proteins; Davies (1982) has reviewed the evidence linking eight properties of proteins and their susceptibility to degradation (Table 6.3). The most comprehensive studies that relate some of these parameters with the *in vivo* susceptibility of plant proteins to degradation are those of Acton and Gupta (1979) and Cooke and Davies (1980). These studies suggest that under nonstressed conditions, large proteins, acidic proteins (low p*I*), and nonglycosylated proteins are degraded more rapidly than small, basic, or glycosylated proteins. However, more recently, the relationships between physical properties of proteins and *in vivo* susceptibility to degradation in *Lemna minor* fronds (Ferreira and Davies, 1986, 1987) and senescent barley leaves (Coates and Davies, 1983) have been found to be relatively weak. These authors suggest that such weak correlations indicate that many independent molecular properties may be contributing to the overall specificity of protein degradation.

3. Effect of ATP

Protein degradation in spinach leaves (Hammond and Preiss, 1983) and pea (Liu and Jagendorf, 1984; Malek *et al.*, 1984) and barley chloroplasts (Thayer and Huffaker, 1985) has been shown to be stimulated by ATP. This was somewhat surprising as a requirement for ATP would not be expected from a knowledge of the thermodynamics of peptide bond hydrolysis or the

TABLE 6.3
Correlation between Properties of Protein and Susceptibility to Degradation *in Vivo*[a]

Property	Hypothesis	Comments
Molecular size	Susceptibility to degradation directly related to molecular size	Early studies with *Lemna minor* supported hypothesis (Cooke and Davies, 1980; Coates and Davies, 1983), but more recent investigations have found no relationship between protein size and rate of degradation (Ferreira and Davies, 1986, 1987); across a wider range of organisms the evidence is ambivalent (Dice *et al.*, 1973; Acton and Gupta, 1979)
Isoelectric point	Acidic proteins more susceptible to degradation	Although evidence from plants and other organisms provides support for this hypothesis (Acton and Gupta, 1979; Cooke and Davies, 1980; Coates and Davies, 1983), recent studies have shown poor correlations between rate of protein degradation and protein charge (Ferreira and Davies, 1986, 1987); does not apply to membrane-bound proteins
Aberrancy	Aberrant proteins susceptible to degradation	In general evidence is contradictory. Recent studies suggest that unassembled subunits or apoprotein is rapidly degraded (Mishind *et al.*, 1985) and abnormal proteins appear to be rapidly degraded in *Acer pseudoplatanus* vacuoles (Canut *et al.*, 1986)
Amide content	Increased amide content increases susceptibility to degradation	Encouraging evidence in nonplants; no hard data for plants
Disulfide content	Reduction of –S–S– promotes degradation	No hard data
Thermodynamic	Susceptibility to inactivation directly related to susceptibility to degradation	Encouraging evidence from nonplants; no hard data from plants
Glycosylation	Glycosylation decreases susceptibility to degradation	In plants nonglycosylated proteins degraded more rapidly (Cooke and Davies, 1980); may relate to ability to be transferred across tonoplast
Hydrophobicity	Hydrophobicity increases susceptibility to degradation	No evidence reported for plants

[a] Information collated from article by Davies (1982).

mechanisms of known proteolytic enzymes. Furthermore, the necessity for ATP is apparently not related to uptake of the substrate protein into a lysosome.

In contrast to the above reports, ATP has been shown to have a stabilizing effect on glutamine synthetase (Streit and Feller, 1982a) and the large subunit of RuBPCase (Thomas, 1982). However, the precise role of ATP in these two studies was not determined.

To date there are two well-documented systems that utilize ATP during proteolysis.

a. ATP-Dependent Proteases. Waxman and Goldberg (1985) have recently reviewed the evidence in favor of this system of proteolysis. Their model is complex (Fig. 6.4), but is potentially an elegant mechanism for the modulation of proteolysis, especially when the protease and its protein substrate are in the same cellular compartment. The model has several important regulatory features. First, the peptide hydrolase (serine at catalytic site) is only active when ATP is bound to the enzyme. Second, ATP hydrolysis is essential for degradation of proteins or large polypeptides, but not for hydrolysis of small peptides. Following ATP hydrolysis, which occurs after hydrolysis of the peptide bond, the ADP remains bound to the protease and inhibits further peptide hydrolase activity. Release of the ADP occurs following binding of a new substrate protein. Third, the protease is

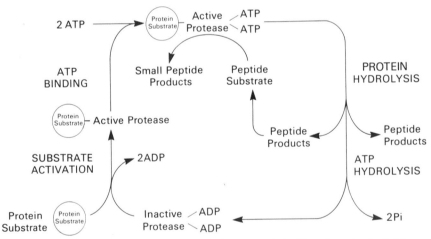

Fig. 6.4. Multistep mechanism of ATP-dependent proteolysis. The scheme is adapted from the model proposed by Waxman and Goldberg (1985) and has been modified through the inclusion of substrate activation. The scheme identifies two substrates for the protease: unfolded, but intact protein, and smaller polypeptides. While the same active site is responsible for peptide bond hydrolysis in each case, the regulation of enzymatic activity by ATP is different. Protein degradation, as opposed to polypeptide degradation, is ATP dependent.

further activated by binding of unfolded substrate proteins at a regulatory site separate to the catalytic site.

It can be seen that there are several potential sites for regulation, one by the substrate protein and the other by ATP/ADP. To date, there is no evidence for this system in plants.

b. Ubiquitin-Dependent Proteolysis. Ubiquitin is a small (76 amino acids), heat-stable, highly conserved protein that was originally isolated by Goldstein *et al.* (1975) as a material able to cause lymphocyte differentiation. Because these authors detected immunologically cross-reactive material in a diverse range of eukaryotic organisms, the term, ubiquitin, was readily adopted as the common name of the protein.

Ubiquitin was first implicated in ATP-dependent proteolysis in rabbit reticulocyte lysates, but it is now evident that a ubiquitin-dependent proteolytic pathway has several important roles in eukaryotic cell physiology and has been detected in all mammalian cell types examined (Vierstra, 1987). The operation of the ubiquitin-dependent proteolysis is outlined in Fig. 6.5.

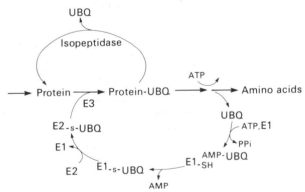

Fig. 6.5. Proposed pathway for ATP–ubiquintin-dependent protein degradation (from Vierstra, 1987). In this reaction sequence, ubiquitin (UBQ) is covalently attached to the substrate protein. Attachment of UBQ requires ATP hydrolysis and the intervention of two enzymes E1 and E3 and an intermediary protein E2. E1, UBQ-activating enzyme; causes activation of the C-terminal glycine of UBQ through the formation of an acyl-adenylate with subsequent transfer and thiol-ester linkage of the activated UBQ to E1. E2, low molecular weight carrier protein; UBQ is attached to E2 by thiol-ester linkage. E3, enzyme that causes formation of isopeptide bond between activated C-terminal glycine of UBP and E-amino group of lysine residues of the substrate protein. Endopeptidase activity directed toward the protein–UBQ complex releases peptide products and UBQ that presumably can reenter the cycle. ATP is consumed during this reaction.

By taking advantage of the highly conserved nature of those ubiquitin species already characterized, Vierstra *et al.* (1985) were able to use anti-human ubiquitin antibodies to detect free ubiquitin in green leaves, etiolated shoots, and dry seeds of *Avena sativa* L. Further analysis of the extract by SDS–PAGE and Western blotting revealed the presence of ubiquitin–protein conjugates *in vivo*. Crude plant extracts also had the capacity to degrade ubiquitin conjugates formed *in vitro* (Vierstra, 1987). Thus, there is strong circumstantial evidence for the occurrence of a ubiquitin-dependent proteolytic pathway in plants. The requirement for ATP for proteolysis helps to explain the need for respiration and the persistence of mitochondria during senescence (Chapters 1 and 4).

4. Targeting of Protein Substrates by Free Radicals

The triazine-binding or Q_B protein of chloroplasts has been shown to be selectively degraded in the light (Mattoo *et al.*, 1984). Degradation was inhibited by photosystem II inhibitors, but neither ATP nor photophosphorylation was essential. It has been suggested that the susceptibility of the Q_B protein to proteolysis is a direct consequence of its participation in electron transport (Ohad *et al.*, 1984). During photosynthesis, the Q_B protein functions as the apoprotein of bound quinone and facilitates the transfer of electrons out of photosystem II. It has been suggested that molecular oxygen and the quinone anion react with the subsequent formation of an oxygen radical within the Q_B protein during the normal course of electron transport. The oxygen radical is able to modify the Q_B protein thereby rendering it susceptible to proteolysis (Kyle *et al.*, 1984). Other proteins of the thylakoids are degraded under photoinhibitory conditions (Holloway *et al.*, 1986), and this phenomenon also seems to be associated in some manner with the generation of free radicals (A. M. Nettleton, T. M. Wardley, P. J. Holloway, and M. J. Dalling, unpublished observations; see also Chapter 3).

5. Targeting of Polypeptides by Their Failure to Assemble Either into Multiunit Proteins or To Be Incorporated into a Membrane

There is now considerable evidence that supports the view that some proteins, because of their failure to assemble into membranes or multiunit proteins, are especially susceptible to degradation (Dalling and Nettleton, 1986). The biochemical basis of this phenomenon is not understood; however, from the point of view of senescence, these observations obviously increase the importance of those reactions which lead to disassembly of multiple subunit proteins and membranes. One possibility is that hydrophobic domains that would normally be integrated into the membrane or the assembled protein contain specific recognition sites for the respective protease and when these are exposed, they lead to proteolysis.

IV. SENESCENCE, PROTEOLYSIS, AND THE METABOLISM OF NITROGEN: SOME CASE HISTORIES

The efficient nitrogen nutrition of a plant organ requires more than a complement of enzymes for the assimilation of the nitrogenous solutes imported in the translocation streams. There is a further need for the presence of mechanisms to recycle the protein amino acids released by proteolysis. The fate of individual nitrogenous solutes will be largely dependent upon the tissue's developmental phase (i.e., whether it is a net *source* or *sink*) and its requirement for particular amino compounds. An amino acid released during protein breakdown for instance may enter the cellular soluble nitrogen pool to be either reincorporated into protein or be exported to other plant parts (Fig. 6.2). It may remain in an unchanged form or be utilized to synthesize new amino acids.

The following sections describe the changes in activity of enzymes of protein degradation and nitrogen metabolism during the senescence of two selected organs: the root (including nodules of legumes) and the leaf.

A. Root and Nodule Senescence

Complete senescence of nodules and roots is of critical importance, because these organs are the source of newly assimilated nitrogen from nitrogen fixation and soil mineral nitrogen uptake and their longevity may determine the necessity to initiate nutrient mobilization in the remainder of the plant.

Mature nodules are a rich source of protein with nitrogen levels per unit dry weight many times higher than in the rest of the root (Fig. 6.6). A large proportion of this protein is of bacterial origin, the remainder being plant proteins in the uninfected cortical tissue of the nodule and in the cytosol of infected (bacteroid-containing) cells (Fig. 6.6). Leghemoglobin accounts for 30–40% of the cytosolic protein. Nodule senescence is characterized by a decrease in measureable nitrogenase activity and a reduction in soluble protein (Fig. 6.7). Soluble protein is lost initially from the cortical and the cytosolic compartments of the nodule. The bacteroids, on the other hand, may not suffer a substantial decrease in soluble protein until late in senescence (Fig. 6.7). The decline in nitrogen-fixing activity is often associated with a reduced carbohydrate supply to the nodules (Peoples *et al.*, 1983; Sutton, 1983); however, nodule degeneration can also be induced by inorganic nitrogen fertilizer, prolonged darkness, or environmental stress (Sutton, 1983), or by manipulation of the gaseous composition of the root environment (Peoples *et al.*, 1985). The onset of complete nodule senescence in annual legumes occurs during the reproductive phase, although grain legumes appear to differ in their ability to maintain nitrogen fixation

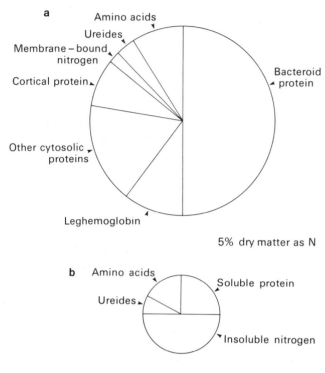

Fig. 6.6. Distribution of nitrogen among various proteins and other nitrogenous compounds in (a) soybean nodules and (b) roots. The relative areas depicted are proportional to the concentrations of nitrogen measured on a unit dry weight basis (M. B. Peoples, unpublished observations).

during fruit development (Noodén, 1980; Peoples et al., 1983; Zapata et al., 1987). With perennial and forage legumes, senescence of nodule tissue tends to be more dependent upon vegetative growth patterns or grazing and defoliation than to reproductive growth (Vance et al., 1979).

The general sequence of events accompanying root deterioration has been less well studied, yet it appears that root growth often slows early in the reproductive phase of annual plants, mineral uptake declines, and the production and transport of root hormones decreases (Noodén, 1980). A functional root contains relatively low concentrations of nitrogen, 25% of which can be identified as soluble protein (Fig. 6.6). A further 25% of root nitrogen in soybean is present as amino acids and ureides, while the remainder is represented by an "insoluble" component that is not readily released from root cellular debris by buffer extraction (Fig. 6.6). During the course of senescence, there is a gradual loss of around half of the soluble protein (Fig. 6.7), and mobilization of between 20 to 30% of total root nitrogen (Dalling *et al.*, 1976; Peoples *et al.*, 1983). Redistribution of nitrogen from roots (and nodules) contributes between 0.4 and 16% of the seeds' requirements during reproduction (Table 6.1), depending on the individual plant species.

1. Proteolysis

The occurrence of degradative enzymes is implicit in the protein turnover studies in the roots of subterranean clover (Phillips *et al.*, 1983), and in lupin and pea nodules where the half-lives of nodule proteins have been measured to be between 2 and 18 days (Coventry and Dilworth, 1976; Bisseling *et al.*, 1980).

a. Nodules. The first published study of nodule proteases was that of Vance *et al.* (1979) who observed that defoliation of alfalfa increased cytosolic acid protease activity by 400% in 7 days, coincident with a 50% decline in leghemoglobin and soluble protein. A similar relation between proteolytic activity and loss of protein has since been observed in the host cell cytosol and bacteroid fraction of alfalfa nodules during senescence induced by high nitrate (Becana *et al.*, 1985). Enzymes that degrade endogenous proteins and substrate hemoproteins (native leghemoglobin or bovine hemoglobin) at acid pH optima have also been detected in crude extracts from the host tissues of cowpea (Peoples *et al.*, 1983) and French bean nodules (Pladys and Rigaud, 1985). The same general profiles of proteolysis were found in nodules of both species during fruiting. Increased rates of proteolytic activity were detected in extracts from the nodule cortex and cytosol at flowering, just prior to the initial decline in nitrogen fixation and a decrease in soluble protein (Fig. 6.7), and the apparent preferential loss of leghemoglobin (see data in Peoples *et al.*, 1985; Pladys and Rigaud, 1985). A second rise in activity occurred during seed filling, coincident with the final rapid loss in symbiotic capacity (Fig. 6.7). Inhibitor studies with French bean suggested that this "biphasic" developmental profile may have been due to the action of different enzymes during nodule aging. Metallo and serine proteases exhibiting endopeptidase activity and aminopeptidase activity dominate degradation in functional nodules, while during seed growth protease activity sensitive to sulfhydryl group inhibitors predominated. Subsequent purification experiments confirmed that the acid hydrolases found in bean nodules at flowering were in fact distinct from the enzymes of senescent nodules. The latter could be resolved into two components by hydroxyapatite chromatography. One component accounted for the acidic

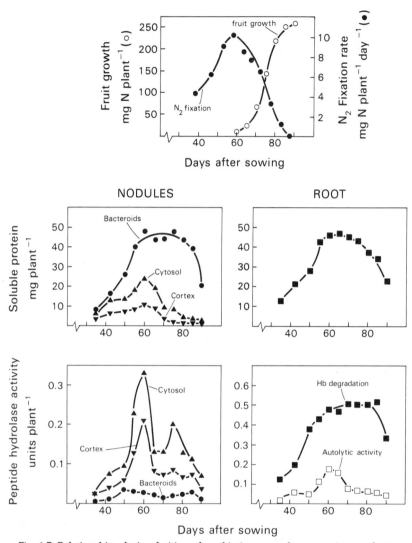

Fig. 6.7. Relationships during fruiting of symbiotic cowpea between nitrogen fixation, soluble protein levels of roots and nodules, and peptide hydrolase activities. One unit of peptide hydrolase activity is equivalent to 1 μmol of α-amino-N released/minute. Hemoglobin degrading and autolytic activity are shown for root extracts. Rates of hemoglobin degradation only are shown for nodule extracts. [Data derived from Peoples *et al.* (1983).]

degradative activity (pH optimum 3.6) during seed development, while the other, whose activity only became apparent in the oldest nodules, was most active in the alkali range (pH optimum 8.0). These two proteases purified from senescing French bean nodules were incubated *in vitro* with *Rhizobium phaseoli* bacteroids isolated from functional nodules (Pladys *et al.*, 1986). The acidic enzyme strongly depressed N_2 fixation by bacteroids (as assessed by acetylene reduction assay) whereas the alkali enzyme induced a lower O_2 requirement for optimal nitrogenase activity. Similar declines in bacteroid nitrogenase activity and optimal O_2 tensions were also observed during natural nodule aging, suggesting a role for these enzymes *in vivo*.

Since alkali enzymes appear very late in the senescence of French bean (Pladys and Rigaud, 1985) and cowpea nodules (M. B. Peoples, unpublished observations), acidic enzymes were presumably responsible for most of the host cell protein degradation; however, this does not seem to be a universal phenomenon in all species, as extensive studies of proteinases and peptidases in soybean nodules failed to detect any enzymes with acidic pH optima (Pfeiffer *et al.*, 1983).

Bacteroid-free extracts of soybean nodules possess endopeptidase, aminopeptidase, and carboxypeptidase activities. Three distinct serine endopeptidases were resolved by disc gel electrophoresis and differentiated by their preferential degradation of various protein or synthetic substrates (pH optima ranging from 7.5 to 9.8). Electrophoresis also showed four aminopeptidases that had neutral to basic pH optima and differed in their specificity towards a large number of amino acyl-β-naphthylamides. Cytosolic endopeptidase activity towards azocasein at an alkaline pH still showed developmental profiles similar to those seen in cowpea and French bean, with two peaks of activity appearing during plant ontogeny (Pfeiffer *et al.*, 1983). The first peak occurred as pod development commenced, just before the initial decrease in nitrogenase activity, while the second rise in proteolytic activity occurred between the time of full seed development and physiological maturity and was correlated with a decrease in cytosolic protein and a final decline in nitrogenase activity. Cytosolic aminopeptidases and proteolytic activity towards substrates other than azocasein, on the other hand, declined during seed filling and did not appear to be functionally significant in the process of final nodule senescence.

Bacteroid peptide hydrolases have been investigated in cowpea (Peoples *et al.*, 1983) and soybean (Pfeiffer *et al.*, 1983) nodules and were characterized by enzymes with neutral and alkaline pH optima. Surprisingly, the aminopeptidase or proteolytic activities observed were somewhat lower than the enzymes extracted from the cytosol or cortex; regardless of the high proportion of total nodule protein present in the bacteroids (Figs. 6.6 and 6.7). There was little change in the activities of these bacteroid peptide hydrolases throughout the life of cowpea or soybean nodules. Degradation appeared to occur primarily in the plant components during nodule senescence so that cytosolic and cortical proteins represented a declining proportion of total nodule protein, while bacteroid protein was retained until the advanced stages of senescence (Fig. 6.7).

No information exists with regard to the intracellular localization of any of the enzymes discussed above apart from crude separation at the tissue level (i.e., bacteroid, cytosol, cortex).

b. Roots. The most comprehensive examinations of root peptide hydrolases have been on maize (Feller *et al.*, 1978; Wallace and Shannon, 1981). Young maize roots contain aminopeptidase, carboxypeptidase, and endopeptidase activities, but detailed studies have been restricted to only two proteinase and two carboxypeptidase components (designated I and II for each) which are separable on carboxymethyl-cellulose (Wallace and Shannon, 1981). Root proteinase I has a serine group at its active site and is able to degrade casein, azocasein, and hemoglobin and inactivate nitrate reductase. Although proteinase I represents the main proteolytic component of the root, it appears to be distinct from the major proteinase fractions found in the maize shoot. It has a pH optimum of 6 when acting on root protein but exhibits maximum rates of degradation at pH 4, 5.5–8, and 9–10 on hemoglobin, casein, and azocasein, respectively. Proteinase II, on the other hand, can also degrade hemoglobin (pH optimum 4) and casein (pH optimum 5–6), but does not attack either azocasein or nitrate reductase. It also exhibits characteristics of both serine and cysteine proteinases. Increasing root age was found to be accompanied by a rise in proteinase I and carboxypeptidase I but a decline in aminopeptidase, proteinase II, and carboxypeptidase II levels. Similar peptide hydrolase activities have been detected in extracts prepared from pea primary roots (Murray *et al.*, 1979). There was a general increase in the levels of carboxypeptidase and aminopeptidase, and in the activity of enzymes capable of degrading endogenous root proteins (autodigestion), casein, and hemoglobin during pea root development. However, there appeared to be specific differences in the endopeptidase activities measured using the different protein substrates. The pH optimum of autodigestion shifted from pH 5 to pH 6–7, activity was progressively stimulated by sulfhydryl reagents in the assay mixture, and there was increased sensitivity to sulfhydryl and serine group inhibitors during root growth. The pH optima of caseolytic (pH 5.7) and hemoglobin degrading (pH 4.5) activities on the other hand, did not change over the experimental period and activities were not stimulated by addition of sulfhydryl reagents to the assay. The distribution of peptide hydrolase activities along the root indicated that the root tip was enriched in protein, carboxypeptidase, and aminopeptidase relative to the remainder of the root. Autodigestive activity was concentrated in the tip to a lesser degree and hemoglobin degrading activity not at all. In contrast, the root tip was relatively depleted in caseolytic activity. Another study with the legume cowpea followed the ability of root crude extracts to degrade endogenous root proteins or hemoglobin (both at pH 5) throughout fruit development and root senescence (Peoples *et al.*, 1983). The two assay procedures showed quite different patterns of activity during root ontogeny (Fig. 6.7). Autodigestive activity rose sharply in root extracts to a maximum at flowering coincident with peak protein levels and then fell to a low level that was maintained until pod browning and seed desiccation. Rates of hemoglobin degradation also rose prior to flowering but continued to rise slowly until late in senescence by which time around 25% of the root soluble protein had been lost.

2. Metabolism of Amino Acids and Ureides

Although the amount of nitrogen redistributed from nodules and roots is relatively small in absolute terms when compared to leaves (Table 6.1), the roots do play an integral role in the plant's N economy during senescence by cycling phloem-borne nitrogen back to the shoot in the xylem stream (Pate *et al.*, 1981; Simpson *et al.*, 1983). The nitrogen moving in the phloem sap from senescing leaves to the roots does not, however, simply pass unaltered into the xylem. The compositional differences between phloem and xylem saps indicate significant and continued metabolism of the incoming amino acids. What follows is a brief summary of the major enzymatic processes occurring in nodules and roots with speculation upon the importance of particular enzymes in the metabolism of nitrogenous solutes.

The first stable product of nitrogen fixation in the nodule following the action of the enzyme nitrogenase is ammonia which is released from the bacteroids to be assimilated into organic forms of nitrogen in the host cell via the coupled activity of the enzymes glutamine synthetase (GS) and glutamate synthase (GOGAT) (Shelp *et al.*, 1983). Despite the apparent production of glutamine as the initial product of ammonia assimilation, it is generally not the major nitrogenous solute transported from the nodule in xylem (Peoples *et al.*, 1987). Most nodulated legumes tend to export either the ureides allantoin and allantoic acid (many tropical species) or the amide asparagine (mainly temperate species) as the predominant forms of fixed nitrogen (Peoples *et al.*, 1987). Secondary reactions involving transfer of the amide- or amino-N of glutamine to other products comprise major metabolic processes within the functional nodule involving complex interactions between many enzymes in different subcellular organelles (Shelp *et al.*, 1983; Shelp and Atkins, 1984).

During periods of reduced nitrogen fixation, the soluble nitrogen content of nodules and activity of some enzymes of nitrogen metabolism do not always follow the decrease in nitrogenase. In ureide-producing species, for example, ammonium and ureide levels have been observed to decline more slowly than nitrogen fixation rates, remain relatively constant, or in some instances to accumulate in the nodule cytosol (Klucas, 1974; Luthra *et al.*,

1983; Schuller *et al.*, 1986). In pea, an amide-producer, there is a rapid drop in proportions of asparagine, homoserine, 4-amino butyrate, and ethanolamine in the nodule amino acid pool during senescence (Roponen, 1970). Of the enzymes measured in nodules (see, e.g., Klucas, 1974; Groat and Vance, 1981; Atkins *et al.*, 1984; Schuller *et al.*, 1986), loss of GOGAT activity most commonly parallels a decrease in effective nitrogen fixation. Asparagine synthetase may decline, yet levels of alanine dehydrogenase, alanine, and aspartate aminotransferases, GS, and the reductive amination function of glutamate oxidoreductase (GDH) may not change greatly. In fact, the latter two enzymes have been observed to increase in activity during senescence under some circumstances and it has been suggested that either or both enzymes could play an important role in assimilating ammonia produced following oxidative deamination of amino acids released by proteolysis (Groat and Vance, 1981). The persistence of aminotransferase activities provides the potential for interconversion of amino acids into compounds suitable for export.

In the case of enzymes of ureide synthesis, some decrease progressively during nodule senescence, while others (principally those at the end of the pathway) change very little or increase in activity. Possibly these enzymes could be responsible for the synthesis of ureides from purines released from breakdown of nucleic acids during nodule senescence.

Enzymes responsible for a wide range of biosynthetic activities concerned with nitrogen assimilation have been demonstrated in roots of many species. Nitrate and nitrite reductases are quite commonly found in roots (although species vary widely in their ability to reduce incoming nitrate in their roots; Peoples *et al.*, 1987), as are enzymes for the amination of α-keto acids to amino acids and for the synthesis of amides (Oaks and Hirel, 1985). Unfortunately there is practically no information available on changes in activity of most of these enzymes during senescence of the root. One study with the legume, pigeon pea, however, indicated that GDH activity in the root fell shortly after flowering while GS levels were maintained during pod filling (Luthra *et al.*, 1983). Root GS activity has been proposed to play a central role in the metabolism of mobilized nitrogen since glutamine remains a major component of root xylem exudate of cereals during plant senescence (Simpson and Dalling, 1981).

B. Leaf Senescence

Although the stem features prominently in the nitrogen nutrition of the shoot (Pate *et al.*, 1981) there have been few detailed investigations on the influence of shoot aging and senescence on the enzymatic metabolism and mobilization of nitrogen in the stem (see, e.g., Waters *et al.*, 1980; Atkins *et al.*, 1982; Luthra *et al.*, 1983). Senescence of the leaves, on the other hand, has been widely studied and has been the subject of a number of reviews (see, e.g., Thimann, 1980; Thomas and Stoddart, 1980; Woolhouse, 1982). Foliar senescence plays a significant role in determining the composition of many agricultural products. The accumulation or depletion of storage proteins and carbohydrates in edible plant organs such as leaves, seeds, and roots, or the economically important components of tobacco and cotton, will be affected by age-dependent changes in metabolic pathways and precursor pools in the leaf.

Depending upon the species studied, the senescence of leaves may be synchronous with either the end of the growing season or the plant's reproductive phase, or may occur as a sequential dieback of the lower (oldest) leaves throughout development. Regardless of the particular pattern followed and the initiating or controlling factors involved, the senescence of individual leaves is likely to be similar at the cellular level. The earliest physiological and biochemical changes observed in the course of foliar senescence are typically a decline in the rate of photosynthesis (see, e.g., Wittenbach *et al.*, 1980) and the progressive deterioration of chloroplast function (Woolhouse, 1984; Dalling and Nettleton, 1986; see also Chapters 1 and 3). Associated with the degeneration of the chloroplast is the loss of chlorophyll and a decrease in leaf soluble protein and total nitrogen which represents one of the most important sources of nitrogen for the developing grain during reproduction (Table 6.1).

1. Proteolysis

The net loss of protein has long been recognized as a dominant feature of foliar senescence. There has been considerable interest in the decline of chloroplast proteins, not only as a consequence of their predominant role in carbon assimilation (Chapter 3), but also because they represent the largest reserve of leaf protein nitrogen for redistribution to developing sinks (Fig. 6.1). The level of the most abundant chloroplast protein, the photosynthetic enzyme RuBPCase, has been observed to decline shortly after full leaf expansion (e.g., see Fig. 6.11), and falls more rapidly than most other proteins throughout senescence so that RuBPCase represents an ever decreasing proportion of total leaf-soluble protein (Peterson and Huffaker, 1975; Wittenbach *et al.*, 1980; Fig. 6.8). The characteristic preferential degradation of RuBPCase seen during foliar senescence has led to a number of investigations concerned with the *in vitro* characterization of proteolytic enzymes capable of hydrolyzing exogenously supplied RuBPCase as substrate. At least six peptide hydrolases have been partially purified from crude extracts of wheat leaves (Peoples *et al.*, 1979) and three enzymes have been identified in soybean (Ragster and Chrispeels, 1981b) and barley leaves (Miller

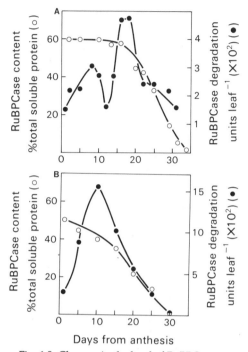

Fig. 6.8. Changes in the level of RuBPCase as a proportion of total soluble protein and the *in vitro* rates of RuBPCase degradation for (A) the flag leaf of wheat and (B) the fourth trifoliate leaf of cowpea during seed growth and development (adapted from Peoples *et al.*, 1980, 1983). One unit of *in vitro* proteolytic activity is equivalent to 1 μmol of α-amino-N released from substrate RuBPCase protein/minute. There was a gradual loss of around 50% of flag leaf chlorophyll between anthesis and day 20. In cowpea, however, leaflet chlorophyll did not decline until 10 days after anthesis, but then there was a rapid loss of almost all chlorophyll over the next 10 days.

and Huffaker, 1981) that can degrade RuBPCase at an acid pH optima. The combined *in vitro* activities of enzymes degrading RuBPCase substrate have been followed during seed development in wheat and cowpea (Fig. 6.8). The two plant species exhibited different, although related developmental profiles of proteolysis. The flag leaf of wheat exhibited two peaks of proteolytic activity against RuBPCase. The first peak occurred during the early period of protein mobilization when RuBPCase was being lost at a rate equivalent to that of other soluble proteins (see Figs. 6.8 and 6.11), but by the time about 30% of the total soluble leaf protein had been mobilized, there was a second rise in proteolytic activity and the *in vivo* loss of RuBPCase proceeded at a relatively faster rate than other proteins (Fig. 6.8). This biphasic pattern of activity was perplexing since it did not appear to be due to an activation or inactivation of preexisting enzymes (Waters *et al.*, 1980), although the separation of peptide hydrolases from flag leaves harvested during the first and the second peak of proteolytic activity did show slight increases in two of the six isolated enzymes (Peoples *et al.*, 1980). The *in vitro* degradation of RuBPCase in cowpea was characterized by a single peak of activity at the beginning of seed filling, but it resembled the second phase of proteolysis in wheat by being closely coincident with the commencement of preferential loss of leaflet RuBPCase (Fig. 6.8). Much of the *in vitro* proteolytic activity against RuBPCase has been identified as vacuolar (Wittenbach *et al.*, 1982), although there is a significant body of evidence for the existence of distinct RuBPCase degrading peptide hydrolases within the intact chloroplast (Ragster and Chrispeels, 1981a; Dalling *et al.*, 1983; Nettleton *et al.*, 1985). Highly significant correlations have been found between the mean *in vitro* rates of crude proteolytic activity at acidic pH and the corresponding rates of *in vivo* loss of RuBPCase-nitrogen (Peoples *et al.*, 1983) and total leaf nitrogen (Dalling *et al.*, 1976).

As implied above, the degradation of protein in senescing leaves is likely to depend upon the integrated action of groups of enzymes. There have been many investigations in which temporal changes in the activity of various exo- and endopeptidases have been followed throughout leaf development (see reviews in Frith and Dalling, 1980; Feller, 1986), and collectively these studies emphasize the complexity of the process. Fig. 6.9 describes the change in activity of a range of peptide hydrolases during the senescence of the flag leaf of wheat. These data illustrate the point that there is a diverse population of enzymes that are present within the leaf whose activities wax and wane at different times during the period of net protein loss. Some may be particularly involved in the turnover of functional proteins while others may come to the fore at the commencement or latter phases of protein mobilization. Nonetheless, the degradation of protein in general terms can be envisaged as a chain reaction, initiated by endopeptidases and sustained by a series of exopeptidases, each with varying substrate specificities.

The major endopeptidases of leaves are dominated by enzymes degrading protein substrates (usually of animal origin) with an acid pH optima (Frith and Dalling, 1980; Feller, 1986), although proteases with neutral and

Mark B. Peoples and Michael J. Dalling

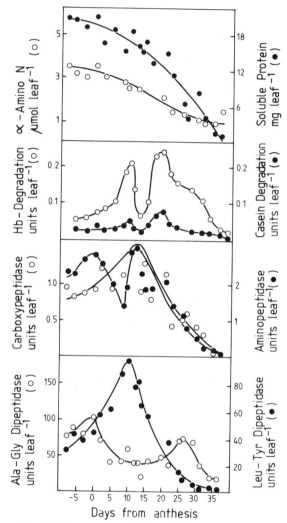

Fig. 6.9. Changes in soluble protein, α-amino-N, and activities of various endopeptidase and exopeptidase enzymes in extracts from flag leaves of wheat during reproductive development (from Waters *et al.*, 1980). One unit of peptide hydrolase activity is equivalent to 1 μmol of α-amino-N released from appropriate substrate/minute. Hemoglobin degradation was determined at pH 4.5 while casein degradation was measured at pH 7.5.

alkaline pH optima have also been detected. The role these enzymes play in leaf senescence, however, is by no means well defined. In some studies increased endopeptidase activities do not accompany nitrogen mobilization (see, e.g., Anderson and Rowan, 1965; Storey and Beevers, 1977; Feller, 1979; Ragster and Chrispeels, 1981b), while in others the initiation of protein loss is accompanied by a rise in proteolytic activity (see, e.g., Martin and Thimann, 1972; Peterson and Huffaker, 1975; Feller *et al.*, 1977).

Some studies have shown a shift during leaf senescence from proteolysis by enzymes with alkali pH optima to degradation predominantly by acidic proteases (Weckenmann and Martin, 1981), yet others have shown the reverse trend (Thomas, 1978). In the case of wheat and the legumes cowpea, lupin, and soybean (Figs. 6.8, 6.9, and 6.11; Wittenbach *et al.*, 1980), net protein loss is apparently associated with increased activity of enzymes with acid pH optimum.

Of the exopeptidases, aminopeptidases have been proposed to be involved in protein turnover or modification rather than senescence since aminopeptidase activities were found to be highest in growing or mature leaves and declined in parallel with protein (Fig. 6.9). Relatively low carboxypeptidase activities have been detected in expanding leaves, yet they also decrease in senescing leaves (Fig. 6.9). Nonetheless, carboxypeptidase activity often remained active longer than aminopeptidase activity in a number of plant species and may still possibly contribute to the rapid degradation of leaf proteins (Feller, 1986). The only exopeptidase group that did not show a significant fall in enzyme level until late senescence were the alanylglycine dipeptidases (Fig. 6.9). These enzymes reached a maximum near the termination of grain-nitrogen accumulation, during the latter stage of protein breakdown.

If we assume that those enzymes that increase during protein loss have a particular role in senescence, then in wheat flag leaves the second peak of hemoglobin- and RuBPCase-degrading activity together with activity against casein and the dipeptide alanylglycine would seem prime candidates (Figs. 6.8 and 6.9). The other peptide hydrolase activities measured would appear to be more likely associated with general protein turnover. It must be noted, however, that other factors (e.g., change in compartmentation) could increase protein degradation without an alteration of enzyme levels.

2. Metabolism of Amino Acids

Net balances of amino acids have been constructed during leaf senescence using data on the N economy of a lupin leaf, its exchanges of amino compounds through xylem input and phloem export, and net changes in its soluble and protein-bound amino acids (Atkins *et al.*, 1983). This study indicated that many amino acids were inadequately supplied via xylem, or through degradation of proteins to provide the complete amino acid complement for phloem export. As a consequence, there was a net requirement for synthesis of these compounds within the leaf to a greater (glutamate, serine, valine, isoleucine, tyrosine, phenylalanine; 80 – 100% of net deficit met by synthesis in leaf), or lesser degree (glutamine, threonine, γ-aminobutyric acid; 50 – 60% of net deficit met by synthesis in leaf), prior to loading onto the phloem. By contrast, more asparagine and aspartic acid were delivered in xylem and mobilized from protein than was required for export in phloem. Presumably, catabolism of these compounds, along with the excess glycine and lysine also released by proteolysis, would have provided the primary sources of nitrogen for synthesis of the other amino acids. In the case of wheat, however, surplus glutamine would be the principal form of nitrogen available for synthesis of required amino acids, predominantly glutamate and aspartate (Simpson and Dalling, 1981).

In the proposed scheme of metabolic conversions occurring in a senescing leaf (Fig. 6.10), glutamic acid is envisaged as playing a central role in the synthesis of amino acids to be exported in phloem sap. Glutamic acid represents a substrate that can be utilized by aspartate and alanine aminotransferases to form aspartic acid and alanine, respectively. These amino acids in turn can be substrates for a range of transaminases and other biosynthetic enzymes (denoted AT in Fig. 6.10) to produce an array of amino acids. The potential for this sequence of transformations appears to be quite high in the senescing cereal and legume leaf since glutamate, aspartate, and alanine represent between 50 and 80% of all amino acids present in the soluble N pools in these tissues (Simpson and Dalling, 1981; Atkins *et al.*, 1983). Transamination reactions could further be involved in providing the 2-oxoglutarate needed to drive the assimilation of the ammonia formed following the oxidative deamination of amino acids and the metabolism of the amides asparagine and glutamine, or as a consequence of the continued functioning of the photorespiratory N cycle during leaf senescence (Fig. 6.10; Berger *et al.*, 1985).

The amination activity of GDH (see Figs. 6.10 and 6.11) has been inferred to be important during leaf senescence in a number of different species (see, e.g., Thomas, 1978; Streit and Feller, 1982b; Luthra *et al.*, 1983). The stimulation of GDH seen during leaf senescence has been shown to be due to altered isoenzyme patterns (Simpson and Dalling, 1981) and *de novo* synthesis of GDH protein (Laurière *et al.*, 1981). This increase in GDH is commonly associated with lowered levels of GS and GOGAT, suggesting a diminished role for these enzymes during the later phases of senescence. The activities of GS and GOGAT in extracts from flag leaves of wheat, for instance (Fig. 6.11), have been found to decline in parallel with leaf protein

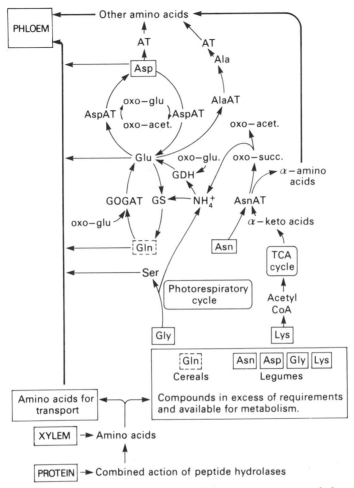

Fig. 6.10. Suggested metabolic routings for nitrogenous compounds during the senescence of cereal or legume leaves. Investigation of the amino acids released from leaf proteins during senescence and comparisons of the amino acid compositions of the xylem stream entering the leaf and of phloem sap leaving the leaf indicate that certain amino compounds are delivered in excess of their requirement for phloem export. The figure represents possible pathways for the metabolism of these surplus amino acids and the synthesis of other deficient amino compounds required for export from the leaf to other organs in phloem sap. No attempt has been made to relate biochemical processes with structural compartmentation. Information concerning the metabolism and synthesis of amino acids in senescing wheat and lupin leaves was derived from Simpson and Dalling (1981), Atkins *et al.* (1982), and Berger *et al.* (1985). Enzyme abbreviations: AlaAT, alanine aminotransferase; AspAT, aspartate aminotransferase; AsnAT, asparagine aminotransferase; GS, glutamine synthetase; GOGAT, glutamate synthase; GDH, glutamate oxidoreductase. AT denotes unspecified enzymes of amino acid biosynthesis. Other abbreviations: Asn, asparagine; Asp, aspartic acid; Ala, alanine; Gln, glutamine; Glu, glutamic acid; Gly, glycine; Lys, lysine; Ser, serine; oxo-acet., oxo-acetate; oxo-glu., oxo-glutarate; oxo-succ., oxo-succinate; TCA cycle, tricarboxylic acid cycle.

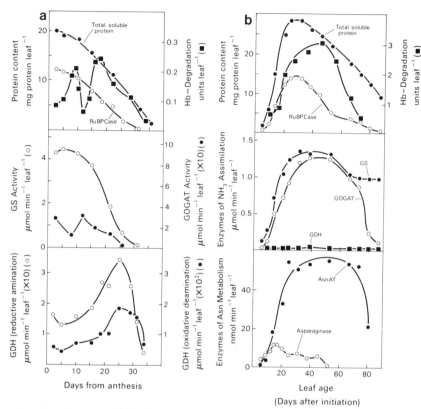

Fig. 6.11. Changes in the levels of soluble protein and RuBPCase protein, and the activities of various enzymes of nitrogen metabolism and protein degradation in (a) the flag leaf of wheat during reproductive development and (b) the top main stem leaf of lupin from emergence through senescence. The graphs for wheat were adapted from Waters *et al.* (1980), Peoples *et al.* (1980), and Simpson and Dalling (1981) and for lupin from M. B. Peoples, C. A. Atkins, J. S. Pate, and K. W. Joy (unpublished observations). Full leaf expansion of lupin occurred at around 20 days after initiation and chlorophyll commenced declining by day 40. Some 50% of the lupin leaf chlorophyll remained 85 days after initiation. One unit of peptide hydrolase activity is equivalent to 1 μmol of α-amino-N released from hemoglobin substrate at pH 4.5/minute. Enzyme abbreviations: AsnAT, asparagine aminotransferase; GS, glutamine synthetase; GOGAT, glutamate synthase; GDH, glutamate oxidoreductase.

shortly after anthesis. GDH activity, on the other hand, increased during a time of proteolysis and protein loss to peak when GS and GOGAT had all but disappeared (Fig. 6.11). Both GOGAT and the isoform of GS selectively lost with senescence are of chloroplastic origin (Streit and Feller, 1983) which would be consistent with the concept of the chloroplast as a site of early structural degeneration and protein degradation within the leaf

(Chapters 1 and 3). Almost all the GDH activity, however, is restricted to the mitochondria, and the ultrastructural integrity of the mitochondria is retained even at an advanced stage of senescence (Chapters 1 and 4). Nonetheless, the actual role GDH plays is still very much open to speculation since a study on senescing pea leaves showed that even though GS declined, its activity measured *in vitro* was sufficient to produce glutamine from all of the nitrogen released during protein hydrolysis *in vivo* (Storey and Beevers, 1978). Other investigations with senescing leaves of wheat (Berger *et al.*, 1985) and of lupin (Fig. 6.11) have indicated that GS and GOGAT contribute more to the metabolism of nitrogen than does GDH. In the case of lupin, activities of GS and GOGAT remained high during the period of rapid protein loss and intense proteolytic activity and did not fall significantly until more than 60% of the leaf's RuBPCase protein had been degraded and the leaflets commenced yellowing (60–70 days after leaflet initiation). Subsequently, GOGAT fell to only 10% of its peak activity, yet GS activity was maintained at 75% of its maximum rate (Fig. 6.11). Asparaginase declined soon after the leaf was fully expanded, yet asparagine aminotransferase activity remained fairly stable until over 70% of the total protein pool had been mobilized from the leaf (75–80 days after leaf initiation) (Fig. 6.11). Aspartate aminotransferase activity and the cytoplasmic form of alanine aminotransferase have similarly been reported to be largely retained in senescent leaves although a chloroplast-associated isoenzyme of alanine aminotransferase is inactivated as chloroplasts deteriorate (see, e.g., Thomas, 1978).

Of the other enzymes measured during leaf ontogeny, nitrate reductase (Harper and Hageman, 1972; Streit and Feller, 1982b) and the enzymes of ureide-metabolism (Thomas and Schrader, 1981; Atkins *et al.*, 1982; Luthra *et al.*, 1983) tend to be most active in young expanding leaves. These enzymes decrease rapidly after full expansion or during flowering so that the potential for nitrate assimilation and ureide catabolism can be low or declining during much of the leaf senescence.

V. CONCLUDING REMARKS

The process of senescence, whether considered from the viewpoint of an individual organ or of the whole plant, is an intriguing phenomenon. It is easy to equate such obvious things as changes in color, necrosis, or leaf fall with a series of chaotic destructive reactions under little control. The reality is, however, that senescence is a complex, tightly controlled phenomenon, and that is reflected in the metabolism of nitrogenous compounds as well as an essential element of a plant's ability to adapt to its environment.

The main value of senescence to the whole plant is that this process allows the efficient withdrawal of essential nutrients (in this chapter we have only considered nitrogen) from dispensable organs, and reallocates these nutrients to a storage site for use on some later occasion (see also Chapter 2). The logistics of such a strategy are complex, as the functional capability of an individual organ, and for that matter the whole plant, must be maintained during the period of senescence.

We have seen in this chapter that there is an important interplay between the hydrolytic and assimilative enzymes of a senescing organ. In essence, the nitrogenous compounds released during proteolysis must undergo modification prior to export from the organ (Figs. 6.2 and 6.10).

There is evidence for an ordered priority of senescence at the intracellular level (Chapters 1, 3, and 5). For example, the chloroplast, which is the major depository of nitrogen within a leaf (Fig. 6.1), undergoes degenerative changes early in leaf senescence. However, there is a persistence or even increase during senescence in the activity of enzymes necessary for assimilation of the amino acids released during chloroplast degradation (Figs. 6.10 and 6.11). The cytoplasmic form of GS persists whereas the chloroplast isoform is lost early in senescence (Streit and Feller, 1983). Similarly, the activity of GDH (a mitochondrial enzyme) actually increases in some instances late in senescence (Fig. 6.11), perhaps consistent with an increasing contribution by this enzyme to assimilation of amino acids prior to their export in the phloem.

In summary, we see that at all levels of complexity (whole plant, organ, cell type, and intracellular) there is a clearly ordered system that is directed, not only toward achieving a high degree of nutrient withdrawal from an organ, but just (or more) as importantly, effecting an efficient relocation of nutrients.

REFERENCES

Acton, G. J., and Gupta, S. (1979). A relationship between protein degradation rates *in vivo*, isoelectric points, and molecular weights obtained by using density labelling. *Biochem. J.* **184**, 367–377.

Anderson, J. W., and Rowan, K. S. (1965). Activity of peptidase in tobacco-leaf tissue in relation to senescence. *Biochem. J.* **97**, 741–746.

Atkins, C. A., Pate, J. S., Ritchie, A., and Peoples, M. B. (1982). Metabolism and translocation of allantoin in ureide-producing grain legumes. *Plant Physiol.* **70**, 476–482.

Atkins, C. A., Pate, J. S., Peoples, M. B., and Joy, K. W. (1983). Amino acid transport and metabolism in relation to the nitrogen economy of a legume leaf. *Plant Physiol.* **71**, 841–848.

Atkins, C. A., Pate, J. S., and Shelp, B. J. (1984). Effects of short-term N_2 deficiency on N metabolism in legume nodules. *Plant Physiol.* **76**, 705–710.

Barrett, A. J. (1986). The classes of proteolytic enzymes. *In* "Plant Proteolytic Enzymes" (M. J. Dalling, ed.), Vol. I, pp. 1–16. CRC Press, Boca Raton, Florida.

Becana, M., Aparicio-Tejo, P. M., and Sanchez-Diaz, M. (1985). Levels of ammonia, nitrite, and nitrate in alfalfa root nodules supplied with nitrate. *J. Plant Physiol.* 119, 359–367.

Berger, M. G., Woo, K. C., Wong, S. C., and Fock, H. P. (1985). Nitrogen metabolism in senescent flag leaves of wheat (*Triticum aestivum* L.) in the light. *Plant Physiol.* 78, 779–783.

Bhalla, P. L., and Dalling, M. J. (1986). Endopeptidase and carboxypeptidase enzymes of vacuoles prepared from mesophyll protoplasts of the primary leaf of wheat seedlings. *J. Plant Physiol.* 122, 289–302.

Bisseling, T., Van Straten, J., and Houwaard, F. (1980). Turnover of nitrogenase and leghemoglobin in root nodules of *Pisum sativum. Biochim. Biophys. Acta* 610, 360–370.

Boller, T., and Kende, H. (1979). Hydrolytic enzymes in the central vacuole of plant cells. *Plant Physiol.* 63, 1123–1132.

Buttery, B. R. (1986). Effects of soil nitrate level on nitrogen distribution and remobilization in field-grown soybeans (*Glycine max* (L.) Merr.). *Can. J. Plant Sci.* 66, 67–77.

Canut, H., Alibert, G., Carrosco, A., and Boudet, A. M. (1986). Rapid degradation of abnormal proteins in vacuoles from *Acer pseudoplatanus* L. cells. *Plant Physiol.* 81, 460–463.

Coates, J. B., and Davies, D. D. (1983). The molecular basis of the selectivity of protein degradation in stressed senescent barley (*Hordeum vulgare* cv. Proctor) leaves. *Planta* 158, 550–559.

Cooke, R. J., and Davies, D. D. (1980). General characteristics of normal and stress-enhanced protein degradation in *Lemna minor* (duckweed). *Biochem. J.* 192, 499–506.

Coventry, D. R., and Dilworth, M. J. (1976). Synthesis and turnover of leghaemoglobin in lupin root nodules. *Biochim. Biophys. Acta* 447, 1–10.

Dalling, M. J. (1985). The physiological basis of nitrogen redistribution during grain filling in cereals. *In* "Exploitation of Physiological and Genetic Variability to Enhance Crop Productivity" (J. E. Harper, L. E. Schrader, and R. W. Howell, eds.), pp. 55–71. Am. Soc. Plant Physiol., Rockville, Maryland.

Dalling, M. J., and Bhalla, P. L. (1984). Mobilization of nitrogen and phosphorus from endosperm. *In* "Seed Physiology" (D. R. Murray, ed.), Vol. 2, pp. 163–199. Academic Press, Orlando, Florida.

Dalling, M. J., and Nettleton, A. M. (1986). Chloroplast senescence and proteolytic enzymes. *In* "Plant Proteolytic Enzymes" (M. J. Dalling, ed.). Vol. 2, pp. 125–153. CRC Press, Boca Raton, Florida.

Dalling, M. J., Boland, G., and Wilson, J. H. (1976). Relation between acid proteinase activity and redistribution of nitrogen during grain development in wheat. *Aust. J. Plant Physiol.* 3, 721–730.

Dalling, M. J., Tang, A., and Huffaker, R. C. (1983). Evidence for the existence of peptide hydrolase activity associated with chloroplasts isolated from barley mesophyll protoplasts. *Z. Pflanzenphysiol.* 111, 311–318.

Davies, D. D. (1982). Physiological aspects of protein turnover. *In* "Encyclopedia of Plant Physiology. N.S. Vol. 14A: Nucleic Acids and Proteins in Plants I" (D. Boulter and B. Parthier, eds.), pp. 189–228. Springer-Verlag, Berlin and New York.

Dekhuijzen, H. M., and Verkerke, D. R. (1984). Uptake, distribution and redistribution of [15]nitrogen by *Vicia faba* under field conditions. *Field Crops Res.* 8, 93–104.

Dice, J. F., Dehlinger, P. J., and Schimke, R. T. (1973). Studies on the correlation between size and relative degradation rate of soluble proteins. *J. Biol. Chem.* 248, 4220–4228.

Enter, O., and Wolf, D. H. (1984). Vacuoles are not the sole compartments of proteolytic enzymes in yeast. *FEBS Lett.* 166, 321–325.

Evans, J. R. (1984). Photosynthesis and nitrogen partitioning in leaves of *Triticum aestivum* and related species. Ph.D. Thesis, Australian Nat. Univ., Canberra.

Feller, U. (1979). Nitrogen mobilization and proteolytic activities in germinating and maturing bush beans (*Phaseolus vulgaris* L.). *Z. Pflanzenphysiol.* 95, 413–422.

Feller, U. (1986). Proteolytic enzymes in relation to leaf senescence. In "Plant Proteolytic Enzymes" (M. J. Dalling, ed.), Vol. 2, pp. 49–68. CRC Press, Boca Raton, Florida.

Feller, U. K., Soong, T.-S. T., and Hageman, R. H. (1977). Leaf proteolytic activities and senescence during grain development of field-grown corn (*Zea mays* L.). *Plant Physiol.* **59**, 290–294.

Feller, U., Soong, T.-S. T., and Hageman, R. H. (1978). Patterns of proteolytic enzyme activities in different tissues of germinating corn (*Zea mays* L.). *Planta* **140**, 155–162.

Ferreira, R. B., and Davies, D. D. (1986). Is protein degradation correlated with either the charge or size of *Lemna* proteins? *Planta* **169**, 278–288.

Ferreira, R. B., and Davies, D. D. (1987). Protein degradation in *Lemna* with particular reference to ribulose bisphosphate carboxylase. II. The effect of nutrient starvation. *Plant Physiol.* **83**, 878–883.

Frith, G. J. T., and Dalling, M. J. (1980). The role of peptide hydrolases in leaf senescence. In "Senescence in Plants" (K. V. Thimann, ed.), pp. 117–130. CRC Press, Boca Raton, Florida.

Goldstein, G. M., Scheid, M., Hammerling, U. A., Boyse, E. A., Schlesinger, D. H., and Niall, H. D. (1975). Isolation of a polypeptide that has lymphocyte-differentiating properties and is probably represented universally in living cells. *Proc. Natl. Acad. Sci. U.S.A.* **72**, 11–15.

Groat, R. G., and Vance, C. P. (1981). Root nodule enzymes of ammonia assimilation in alfalfa (*Medicago sativa* L.). Development patterns and response to applied nitrogen. *Plant Physiol.* **67**, 1198–1203.

Hammond, J. B. W., and Preiss, J. (1983). ATP-dependent proteolytic activity from spinach leaves. *Plant Physiol.* **73**, 902–905.

Harper, J. E., and Hageman, R. H. (1972). Canopy and seasonal profiles of nitrate reductase in soybeans (*Glycine max* L. Merr.). *Plant Physiol.* **49**, 146–154.

Hocking, P. J., and Steer, B. T. (1983). Distribution of nitrogen during growth of sunflower (*Helianthus annuus* L.). *Ann. Bot.* **51**, 787–799.

Holloway, P. J., Nettleton, A. M., and Dalling, M. J. (1986). Photolability of thylakoid polypeptides during photoinhibition in vivo. *J. Plant Physiol.* **122**, 187–192.

Huffaker, R. C., and Peterson, L. W. (1974). Protein turnover in plants and possible means of its regulation. *Annu. Rev. Plant Physiol.* **25**, 363–392.

Jellings, A. J., and Leech, R. M. (1982). The importance of quantitative anatomy in the interpretation of whole leaf biochemistry in species of *Triticum, Hordeum* and *Avena. New Phytol.* **92**, 39–48.

Klucas, R. V. (1974). Studies on soybean nodule senescence. *Plant Physiol.* **54**, 612–616.

Kyle, D. J., Ohad, I., and Arntzen, C. F. (1984). Membrane protein damage and repair: Selective loss of a quinone-protein function in chloroplast membranes. *Proc. Natl. Acad. Sci. U.S.A.* **81**, 4070–4074.

Laurière, C., Weisman, N., and Daussant, J. (1981). Glutamate dehydrogenase in the first leaf of wheat. II. De novo synthesis upon dark stress and senescence. *Physiol. Plant.* **52**, 151–155.

Liu X.-Q., and Jagendorf, A. T. (1984). ATP-dependent proteolysis in pea chloroplasts. *FEBS Lett.* **166**, 248–252.

Luthra, Y. P., Sheoran, I. S., Rao, A. S., and Singh, R. (1983). Ontogenetic changes in the level of ureides and enzymes of their metabolism in various plant parts of pigeon pea (*Cajanus cajan*). *J. Exp. Bot.* **34**, 1358–1370.

Mae, T., Makino, A., and Ohira, K. (1983). Changes in the amounts of ribulose bisphosphate carboxylase synthesized and degraded during the life span of rice leaf (*Oryza sativa* L.). *Plant Cell Physiol.* **24**, 1079–1086.

Malek, L., Bogorad, L., Ayers, A. R., and Goldberg, A. L. (1984). Newly synthesized proteins are degraded by an ATP-stimulated proteolytic process in isolated pea chloroplasts. *FEBS Lett.* **166**, 253–257.

Martin, C., and Thimann, K. V. (1972). The role of protein synthesis in the senescence of leaves. I. The formation of protease. *Plant Physiol.* **49**, 64–71.

Matile, P. (1975). "The Lytic Compartment of Plant Cells." Springer-Verlag, Berlin and New York.

Mattoo, A. K., Hoffman-Falk, H., Marder, J. B., and Edelman, M. (1984). Regulation of protein metabolism: Coupling of photosynthetic electron transport to *in vivo* degradation of the rapidly metabolized 32-kilodalton protein of the chloroplast membranes. *Proc. Natl. Acad. Sci. U.S.A.* **81**, 1380–1384.

Mikola, L., and Mikola, J. (1986). Occurrence and properties of different types of peptidases in higher plants. *In* "Plant Proteolytic Enzymes" (M. J. Dalling, ed.), Vol. I., pp. 97–117. CRC Press, Boca Raton, Florida.

Miller, B. L., and Huffaker, R. C. (1981). Partial purification and characterization of endoproteinases from senescing barley leaves. *Plant Physiol.* **68**, 930–936.

Mishind, M. L., Jensen, K. H., Branagan, A. J., Plumley, F. G., and Schmidt, G. W. (1985). Roles of proteases in chloroplast biogenesis. *Curr. Top. Plant Biochem. Physiol.* **4**, 34–50.

Murray, D. R., Peoples, M. B., and Waters, S. P. (1979). Proteolysis in the axis of the germinating pea seed. I. Changes in protein degrading enzyme activities of the radicle and primary root. *Planta* **147**, 111–116.

Nettleton, A. M., Bhalla, P. L., and Dalling, M. J. (1985). Characterization of peptide hydrolase activity associated with thylakoids of the primary leaves of wheat. *J. Plant Physiol.* **119**, 35–43.

Noodén, L. D. (1980). Senescence in the whole plant. *In* "Senescence in Plants" (K. V. Thimann, ed.), pp. 219–258. CRC Press, Boca Raton, Florida.

Oaks, A., and Hirel, B. (1985). Nitrogen metabolism in roots. *Annu. Rev. Plant Physiol.* **36**, 345–366.

Ohad, I., Kyle, D. J., and Arntzen, C. J. (1984). Membrane protein damage and repair: Removal and replacement of inactivated 32-kilodalton polypeptides in chloroplast membranes. *J. Cell Biol.* **99**, 481–485.

Pan, W. L., Camberato, J. J., Jackson, W. A., and Moll, R. H. (1986). Utilization of previously accumulated and concurrently absorbed nitrogen during reproductive growth in maize. *Plant Physiol.* **82**, 247–253.

Pate, J. S., and Flinn, A. M. (1973). Carbon and nitrogen transfer from vegetative organs to ripening seeds of field pea (*Pisum arvense* L.). *J. Exp. Bot.* **24**, 1090–1099.

Pate, J. S., and Minchin, F. R. (1980). Comparative studies of carbon and nitrogen nutrition of selected grain legumes. *In* "Advances in Legume Science" (R. J. Summerfield and A. H. Bunting, eds.), pp. 105–114. Royal Botanic Gardens, Kew, England.

Pate, J. S., Atkins, C. A., Herridge, D. F., and Layzell, D. B. (1981). Synthesis, storage, and utilization of amino compounds in white lupin (*Lupinus albus* L.). *Plant Physiol.* **67**, 37–42.

Peoples, M. B., Frith, G. J. T., and Dalling, M. J. (1979). Proteolytic enzymes in green wheat leaves IV. Degradation of ribulose 1,5-bisphosphate carboxylase by acid proteinases isolated on DEAE-cellulose. *Plant Cell Physiol.* **20**, 253–258.

Peoples, M. B., Beilharz, V. C., Waters, S. P., Simpson, R. J., and Dalling, M. J. (1980). Nitrogen redistribution during grain growth in wheat (*Triticum aestivum* L.). II. Chloroplast senescence and the degradation of ribulose-1,5-bisphosphate carboxylase. *Planta* **149**, 241–251.

Peoples, M. B., Pate, J. S., and Atkins, C. A. (1983). Mobilization of nitrogen in fruiting plants of a cultivar of cowpea. *J. Exp. Bot.* **34**, 563–578.

Peoples, M. B., Pate, J. S., and Atkins, C. A. (1985). The effect of nitrogen source on transport and metabolism of nitrogen in fruiting plants of cowpea (*Vigna unguiculata* (L.) Walp.). *J. Exp. Bot.* **36**, 567–582.

Peoples, B., Sudin, M. N., and Herridge, D. F. (1987). Translocation of nitrogenous compounds in symbiotic and nitrate-fed amide-exporting legumes. *J. Exp. Bot.* **38**, 567–579.

Peterson, L. W., and Huffaker, R. C. (1975). Loss of ribulose 1,5-diphosphate carboxylase and increase in proteolytic activity during senescence of detached primary barley leaves. *Plant Physiol.* **55**, 1009–1015.

Pfeiffer, N. E., Torres, C. M., and Wagner, F. W. (1983). Proteolytic activity in soybean root nodules. Activity in host cell cytosol and bacteroids throughout physiological development and senescence. *Plant Physiol.* **71**, 797–802.

Phillips, D. A., Center, D. M., and Jones, M. B. (1983). Nitrogen turnover and assimilation during regrowth in *Trifolium subterraneum* L. and *Bromus mollis* L. *Plant Physiol.* **71**, 472–476.

Pladys, D., and Rigaud, J. (1985). Senescence in French-bean nodules: occurrence of different proteolytic activities. *Physiol. Plant.* **63**, 43–48.

Pladys, D., Trinchant, J.-C., and Rigaud, J. (1986). Proteases from French-bean nodule host-cells: *in vitro* effects on bacteroids. *Physiol. Veg.* **24**, 697–705.

Ragster, L. E., and Chrispeels, M. J. (1981a). Autodigestion in crude extracts of soybean leaves and isolated chloroplasts as a measure of proteolytic activity. *Plant Physiol.* **67**, 104–109.

Ragster, L. E., and Chrispeels, M. J. (1981b). Hemoglobin-digesting acid proteinases in soybean leaves. Characteristics and changes during leaf maturation and senescence. *Plant Physiol.* **67**, 110–114.

Roponen, I. (1970). The effect of darkness on the leghaemoglobin content and amino acid levels in the root nodules of pea plants. *Physiol. Plant.* **23**, 452–460.

Schuller, K. A., Day, D. A., Gibson, A. H., and Gresshoff, P. M. (1986). Enzymes of ammonia assimilation and ureide biosynthesis in soybean nodules: Effect of nitrate. *Plant Physiol.* **80**, 646–650.

Shelp, B. J., and Atkins, C. A. (1984). Subcellular location of enzymes of ammonia assimilation and asparagine synthesis in root nodules of *Lupinus albus* L. *Plant Sci. Lett.* **36**, 225–230.

Shelp, B. J., Atkins, C. A., Storer, P. J., and Canvin, D. T. (1983). Cellular and subcellular organization of pathways of ammonia assimilation and ureide synthesis in nodules of cowpea (*Vigna unguiculata* L. Walp.). *Arch. Biochem. Biophys.* **224**, 429–441.

Simpson, R. J., and Dalling, M. J. (1981). Nitrogen redistribution during grain growth in wheat (*Triticum aestivum* L.). III. Enzymology and transport of amino acids from senescing flag leaves. *Planta* **151**, 447–456.

Simpson, R. J., Lambers, H., and Dalling, M. J. (1983). Nitrogen redistribution during grain growth in wheat (*Triticum aestivum* L.). IV. Development of a quantitative model of the translocation of nitrogen to the grain. *Plant Physiol.* **71**, 7–14.

Storey, R. D. (1986). Plant endopeptidases. *In* "Plant Proteolytic Enzymes" (M. J. Dalling, ed.), Vol. I, pp. 119–140. CRC Press, Boca Raton, Florida.

Storey, R. D., and Beevers, L. (1977). Proteolytic activity in relationship to senescence and cotyledonary development in *Pisum sativum* L. *Planta* **137**, 37–44.

Storey, R. D., and Beevers, L. (1978). Enzymology of glutamine metabolism related to senescence and seed development in the pea (*Pisum sativum* L.). *Plant Physiol.* **61**, 494–500.

Streit, L., and Feller, U. (1982a). Inactivation of N-assimilating enzymes and proteolytic activities in wheat leaf extracts: Effect of pyridine nucleotides and of adenylates. *Experientia* **38**, 1176–1180.

Streit, L., and Feller, U. (1982b). Changing activities of nitrogen-assimilating enzymes during growth and senescence of dwarf beans (*Phaseolus vulgaris* L.). *Z. Pflanzenphysiol.* **108**, 273–281.

Streit, L., and Feller, U. (1983). Changing activities and different resistance to proteolytic activity of two forms of glutamine synthetase in wheat leaves during senescence. *Physiol. Veg.* **21**, 103–108.

Sutton, W. D. (1983). Nodule development and senescence. *In* "Nitrogen Fixation. Vol. 3: Legumes" (W. J. Broughton, ed.), pp. 144–211. Oxford Univ. Press (Clarendon), London and New York.

Thayer, S. S., and Huffaker, R. C. (1985). ATP-stimulated proteolytic activity associated with barley thylakoids. *Curr. Top. Plant Biochem. Physiol.* **4,** 223.

Thimann, K. V. (1980). The senescence of leaves. *In* "Senescence in Plants" (K. V. Thimann, ed.), pp. 85–115. CRC Press, Boca Raton, Florida.

Thomas, H. (1978). Enzymes of nitrogen mobilization in detached leaves of *Lolium temulentum* during senescence. *Planta* **142,** 161–169.

Thomas, H. (1982). Control of chloroplast demolition during leaf senescence. *In* "Plant Growth Substance" (P. F. Wareing, ed.), pp. 559–567. Academic Press, London.

Thomas, H., and Stoddart, J. L. (1980). Leaf senescence. *Annu. Rev. Plant Physiol.* **31,** 83–111.

Thomas, R. J., and Schrader, L. E. (1981). The assimilation of ureides and shoot tissues of soybeans. 1. Changes in allantoinase activity and ureide contents of leaves and fruits. *Plant Physiol.* **67,** 973–976.

Vance, C. P., Heichel, G. H., Barnes, D. K., Bryan, J. W., and Johnson, L. E. (1979). Nitrogen fixation, nodule development, and vegetative regrowth of alfalfa (*Medicago sativa* L.) following harvest. *Plant Physiol.* **64,** 1–8.

Vierstra, R. D. (1987). Ubiquitin, a key component in the degradation of plant proteins. *Physiol. Plant.* **70,** 103–106.

Vierstra, R. D., Langan, S. M., and Haas, A. L. (1985). Purification and initial characterization of ubiquitin from the higher plant, *Avena sativa. J. Biol. Chem.* **260,** 12015–12021.

Wagner, F. W. (1986). Assessment of methodology for the purification, characterization and measurement of proteases. *In* "Plant Proteolytic Enzymes" (M. J. Dalling, ed.), Vol. I, pp. 17–39. CRC Press, Boca Raton, Florida.

Wallace, W., and Shannon, J. D. (1981). Proteolytic activity and nitrate reductase inactivation in maize seedlings. *Aust. J. Plant Physiol.* **8,** 211–219.

Wardley, T. M., Bhalla, P. L., and Dalling, M. J. (1984). Changes in the number and composition of chloroplasts during senescence of mesophyll cells of attached and detached leaves of wheat (*Triticum aestivum* L.). *Plant Physiol.* **75,** 421–424.

Waters, S. P., Peoples, M. B., Simpson, R. J., and Dalling, M. J. (1980). Nitrogen redistribution during grain growth in wheat (*Triticum aestivum* L.). 1. Patterns of peptide hydrolase activity and protein breakdown in the flag leaf, glumes and stem. *Planta* **148,** 422–428.

Waxman, L., and Goldberg, A. L. (1985). ATP-dependent proteases, a novel class of regulatory enzymes in cells and organelles. *Curr. Top. Plant Biochem. Physiol.* **4,** 1–14.

Weckenmann, D., and Martin, P. (1981). Changes in the pattern of endopeptidases during senescence of bush bean leaves (*Phaseolus vulgaris* L.). *Z. Pflanzenphysiol.* **104,** 103–108.

Wittenbach, V. A., Ackerson, R. C., Giaquinta, R. T., and Hebert, R. R. (1980). Changes in photosynthesis, ribulose bisphosphate carboxylase, proteolytic activity, and ultrastructure of soybean leaves during senescence. *Crop Sci.* **20,** 225–231.

Wittenbach, V. A., Lin, W., and Hebert, R. R. (1982). Vacuolar localization of proteases and degradation of chloroplasts in mesophyll protoplasts from senescing primary wheat leaves. *Plant Physiol.* **69,** 98–102.

Woolhouse, H. W. (1982). Leaf senescence. *In* "The Molecular Biology of Plant Development" (H. Smith and D. Grierson, eds.). pp. 256–281. Blackwell, Oxford.

Woolhouse, H. W. (1984). The biochemistry and regulation of senescence in chloroplasts. *Can. J. Bot.* **62,** 2934–2942.

Zapata, F., Danso, S. K. A., Hardarson, G., and Fried, M. (1987). Nitrogen fixation and translocation in field-grown faba bean. *Agron. J.* **79,** 505–509.

Water Economy of Fruits and Fruiting Plants: Case Studies of Grain Legumes

J. S. Pate
Botany Department
University of Western Australia
Nedlands, 6009 Australia

I. INTRODUCTION

The economy of water utilization by a plant is most commonly expressed by the term water use efficiency (WUE), namely, the amount of dry matter gained by a plant per unit volume of water transpired. Measurements of this

SENESCENCE AND AGING IN PLANTS

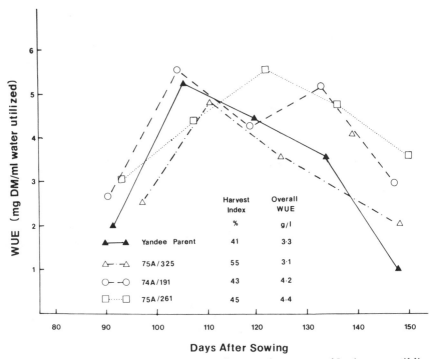

Fig. 7.1. Ontogenetic changes in water use efficiency of genotypes of *Lupinus angustifolius* showing how water use during postanthesis development shapes the overall water economy of a genotype. The data compare three reduced branching lines selected from the parent cultivar *Yandee*. (The author is greatly indebted to Dr. J. S. Gladstones for provision of seed material from his extensive breeding program on the species.)

nature may relate to the whole growth cycle of the plant and thus offer a useful index of the likely requirements of a crop plant in relation to available soil moisture and rainfall, or refer exclusively to a sequence of relatively short periods of growth and hence express seasonal or ontogenetic changes in the relationship between net carbon gain and water loss. Applying similar concepts to fruits, WUE values can be easily constructed from dry weight changes and transpiration data for either a single developing fruit or for the whole population of variously aged fruits on a plant. In the former case, useful information becomes available on the physiological behavior of the fruit per se; in the latter, the data would allow one to prescribe how the fruit load of the plant impacts upon total water usage.

Information of the above kinds is available for the postanthesis development of several of our study legumes. As a first example, data for *Lupinus angustifolius* (Fig. 7.1) illustrate the relationships between water use

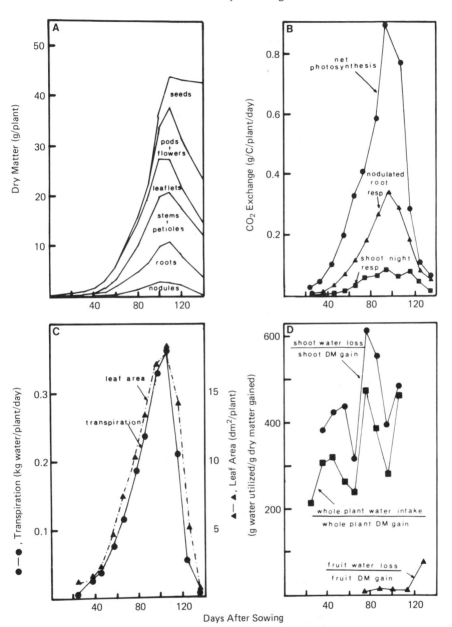

Fig. 7.2. Changes during growth of *Lupinus albus* (cv. Ultra) in (A) dry matter content of plant parts; (B) exchanges of CO_2 in photosynthesis and respiration; (C) transpiration and leaf area; and (D) water economy (transpiration ratios) of shoots, whole plants, and fruits. [Data, with modifications, from Pate *et al.* (1980).]

TABLE 7.1

Water Use Efficiency of Fruits of Various Grain Legumes

| | Water use efficiency[a] | |
| | Dry matter (mg) accumulated/water | |
Species	transpired (ml)	Reference
Pisum sativum cv. Greenfeast	36	Flinn *et al.* (1977)
Lupinus albus cv. Ultra Neutra	36	Pate *et al.* (1980)
	35	Pate *et al.* (1977)
Glycine max	50	Layzell and LaRue (1982)
Vigna unguiculata cv. Vita 3	125	Peoples *et al.*(1985)
cv. Caloona	142	J. S. Pate (unpublished observations)
cv. TVU 354	197	J. S. Pate (unpublished observations)

[a] Refers to whole maturation period of attached intact fruits under optimal temperature and light conditions for glasshouse culture of the species.

efficiency and harvest index in a parental genotype (Yandee) and a number of selections with reduced branching. Each genotype exhibits a characteristic pattern of change in water use efficiency with plant age, with two of the three reduced branching lines showing significantly higher water use efficiency than the parent genotype. Somewhat surprisingly, the line 75A 325, with the highest harvest index, does not exhibit a commensurate improvement in its water use efficiency. As a second example, data for *Lupinus albus* (Fig. 7.2) demonstrate changes with plant age and advancing season in the overall water usage (transpiration ratio) of the whole plant, plant shoot, and of its population of fruits, and the relationships of these quantities to plant dry matter gain, leaf area, CO_2 economy, and transpiration. Note the close relationship between net photosynthesis, leaf area and transpiration, increased usage of water per unit dry matter with advancing plant age, and the very much better water use efficiency of fruits than of shoot or whole plant. As a third example, the data of Table 7.1 demonstrate the substantial differences that exist in WUE between fruits of different species of grain legumes when expressed in terms of total performance over the whole maturation period of a single fruit.

II. WATER BALANCES OF DEVELOPING FRUIT AND SEEDS AND THEIR RELATIONSHIPS TO THE IMPORT OF CARBON AND NITROGEN THROUGH THE XYLEM AND PHLOEM

Expressed in simplest terms, net water exchanges between the fruit and the plant derive solely from transpiration loss of the fruit and ontogenetic changes in amounts of water held in tissues of pods and seeds. As tissue water increases rapidly in early fruit development and then declines noticeably as pods and seeds dehydrate, the transpiration rate will tend to underestimate a fruit's true water requirements in early growth, but overestimate net intake of water from the plant during later maturation. In all models of fruit functioning so far presented, we have assumed that the low resistance conducting elements of xylem and phloem offer the only significant avenues for intake of transported fluids through the fruit stalk. Then, since phloem sap bleeding spontaneously from the fruit of pea, lupin, and cowpea contains levels of dry matter, usually within the range 150–250 mg/ml, versus only 1–5 mg/ml for corresponding tracheal (xylem) sap, we may conclude that phloem is likely to supply upwards of 95% of the total dry matter requirements of the fruit. Finally, assuming that phloem import is by mass flow and that water and solutes enter as solutions at concentrations predicted from phloem sap, an assessment can be made of the extent to which this phloem stream satisfies the demands of the fruit for water.

Three sets of data exemplifying the above approach are shown in Table 7.2, the first of which, for developing fruit of *Lupinus albus* (cv. Ultra) (Pate *et al.*, 1977), shows evidence of a rate of water intake through the stalk greatly in excess of that estimated to have entered by mass flow through phloem (Table 7.2A). On balance, therefore, the lupin fruit is concluded to engage in a considerable intake of additional water through its xylem. This is not the case, however, for fruit of the small and large-fruited cultivars of cowpea shown in Table 7.2 (B and C), for each of which an oversupply of water through phloem is indicated, especially during the final stages of fruit ripening. Further extension of our budgeting approach has involved quantitatively based assessments in which the water economy of the whole fruit is related to the intake of carbon and nitrogen that it makes from the parent plant through xylem and phloem. The models generated incorporate experimentally obtained data on (1) the quantities of C and N built into fruit dry matter during specific intervals of growth; (2) the CO_2 exchanges of the fruit with its external atmosphere; (3) the C : N weight ratios and absolute concentrations of C and N in the phloem and xylem streams supplying the fruit; and (4) assessments of fruit water balance in terms of transpiration and changes in tissue water. In the first analysis, each model assumes that

TABLE 7.2

Water Balance, Dry Matter Gain, and Estimated Xylem and Phloem Exchanges of Water between Fruit and Parent Plant of Three-Grain Legumes

(A) White lupin (*Lupinus albus* cv. Nutra)

	Fruit age (weeks)					
	0-2	2-4	4-6	6-8	8-10	10-1
Transpiration loss (ml/fruit)	1.57	3.67	9.82	13.23	7.85	4.4
Change in tissue water (ml/fruit)	2.05	4.20	1.55	0.35	−1.16	−4.2
Water intake by fruit (ml)	3.62	7.87	11.37	13.58	6.69	0.2
Water intake by phloem (ml)[b]	1.13	1.69	4.87	6.92	2.98	0.2
Water intake by xylem (ml)	2.49	6.18	6.50	6.66	3.71	0.0

(B) Cowpea (*Vigna unguiculata* cv. Caloona) (small fruited)

	Fruit age (days)				
	0-6	6-9	9-12	12-15	15-18
Transpiration loss (ml/fruit)	0.904	0.801	0.900	0.884	0.845
Change in tissue water (ml/fruit)	0.609	0.678	0.046	−0.148	−0.600
Water intake by fruit (ml)	1.513	1.479	0.946	0.736	0.245
Dry matter gain (g/fruit)	0.080	0.135	0.135	0.132	0.135
Estimated phloem intake of water (ml/fruit)[b]	0.400	0.675	0.675	0.660	0.675
Estimated xylem exchange of water (+ in, − out) (ml/fruit)	+1.113	+.804	+.271	+.076	−.430

(C) Cowpea (*Vigna unguiculata* cv. TVU 354) (large fruited)

	Fruit age (days)				
	0-6	6-9	9-12	12-15	15-18
Transpiration loss (ml/fruit)	1.10	1.99	2.60	1.41	1.49
Change in tissue water (ml/fruit)	0.47	1.08	1.51	0.48	−1.03
Water intake by fruit (ml)	1.57	3.07	4.11	1.89	0.46
Dry matter gain (g/fruit)	0.087	0.150	0.370	0.510	0.580
Estimated phloem intake of water (ml/fruit)[a]	0.44	0.75	1.85	2.55	2.90
Estimated xylem exchange of water (+ in, − out) (ml/fruit)	+1.13	+2.32	+2.26	+0.66	−2.44

[a] For calculations based on C, N, and H_2 and economy of fruit, see Pate *et al.* (1977).

[b] Assumes dry gain implemented by phloem-borne assimilates entering by mass flow at 200 mg dry matter/ml (J Pate, unpublished observations).

unidirectional inputs of C and N occur to the fruit through xylem and phloem, and thereby calculates the mixtue of xylem and phloem streams that meets precisely the recorded rate of utilization of C and N by the fruit

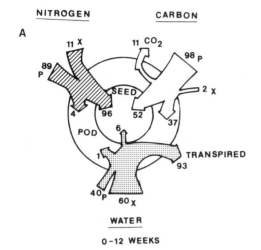

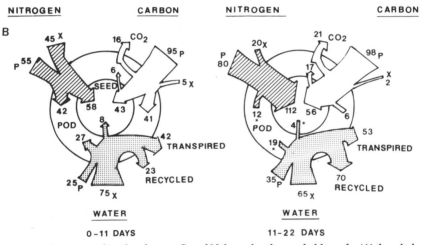

Fig. 7.3. Proportional intake of water, C, and N through xylem and phloem for (A) the whole maturation period of a white lupin fruit *(Lupinus albus)* and (B) the first and second halves of development of the cowpea fruit *(Vigna unguiculata)*. Components of a fruit's budget are expressed relative to a net intake through the fruit stalk of 100 units of H_2O, C, or N through xylem (X) or phloem (P). Exchanges of the fruit of CO_2 with its external atmosphere and transpiration loss of H_2O are indicated. The item marked "recycled water" in (B) is assumed to represent return of water to the parent plant via the xylem at times when the fruit is receiving an excess of water through phloem. *, internal mobilization.

during a set interval of growth. The amount of water carried into the fruit by this mixed xylem/phloem stream is then estimated and the value compared with the recorded consumption of water by the fruit over the same period of time.

Applied to the fruit of white lupin (Pate *et al.*, 1977), this approach has indicated that 98% of the C and 89% of the N needed by the fruit during its 12-week growth period enters through phloem, the remainder by xylem. To accomplish this, a 60:40 (v/v) mix of xylem and phloem streams is required (Fig. 7.3A), this mixture, in turn, satisfying over 95% of fruit's requirement for water. Even when white lupin fruits are examined in greater detail in terms of C, H and H_2O flow over successive 2-week intervals of growth, a good measure of agreement is still found with the hypothesis of unidirectional mass intake of water through xylem and phloem (Pate *et al.*, 1978), with no evidence, at any stage, of mass flow in phloem providing water excess to the current requirement of the fruit.

However, when a similar approach is applied to the Vita 3 cultivar of cowpea (Peoples *et al.*, 1985) gross anomalies appear in budgets based on unidirectional flow of H_2O, C and N through xylem and phloem (Fig. 7.3B), to the extent that the mixture of xylem and phloem streams that exactly meets the C and N consumption of the fruit carries into the fruit a very much greater volume of water than can ever be accounted for by tissue water changes and fruit transpiration. The conclusion is thus reached for fruits of cowpea (see also Table 7.2) that backflow of excess phloem-derived water must occur to the parent plant, presumably via the xylem. Fig. 7.3B designates this component as "recycled" water and rates it equivalent to 23% of the gross intake during the first half and 70% during the remaining period of fruit maturation. In absolute terms, it represents an average backflow to the parent plant of approximately 0.5 ml/fruit/day during the first half and 2.4/ml/fruit/day during the second half of fruit development.

Turning to the water balance of seeds, the data for the Vita 3 cowpea shown in Table 7.3 indicate that, except in the early stage of seed growth, the requirement of a seed for water is likely to be more than satisfied by input of a volume of phloem sap sufficient to provide the current dry matter gain of the seeds. The seed appears to generate its greatest surplus of water from phloem import during mid to late cotyledon filling (11–19 days, Table 7.3), when little further increase is taking place in seed volume, yet when the tissue water volume of the cotyledons of the embryo is being rapidly replaced by insoluble reserves of starch and protein. However, the greatest loss of water from the seed occurs as it dehydrates and while it is still importing through phloem (days 19–22, Table 7.3). The question then arises of how the seed voids this supposed surplus of water—whether by direct expulsion through its outer surface into the internal cavity of the fruit or by backflow to the pod through the xylem of the seed stalk.

TABLE 7.3

Water and Dry Matter Balance of Developing Seeds of Cowpea (*Vigna unguiculata* cv. Vita 3) and Estimated Excess Intake of Water through Phloem

Budget item for all seeds of a fruit[b]	Seed age (days after anthesis)					
	0-8	8-11	11-13	13-16	16-19	19-22
ange in fresh weight (g)	0.76	1.46	3.31	2.46	0.30	−4.76
rements in dry weight (g)	0.12	0.17	1.00	0.76	0.44	0.23
ange in tissue water (ml)	0.64	1.29	2.31	1.70	−0.14	−4.99
imated phloem intake of water ml)[a]	0.70	1.06	5.95	4.59	5.65	1.41
ess (+) or deficit (−) of phloem-upplied water (ml)	+0.06	−1.23	+3.64	+2.89	+2.89	+6.40

Assumes that seeds are fed by mass flow in phloem at a phloem sap concentration of 200 mg dry matter/ml, and that ls respire dry matter equivalent to 20% of their current dry matter increment. Data from Peoples *et al.* (1985).

III. DIURNAL WATER BALANCE OF FRUIT AND THE FRUITING PLANT

With the modeling procedures described above for cowpea providing conclusive, but clearly indirect, evidence of bidirectional flow of water between the fruit and plant, the question immediately arises of how such exchanges might be accomplished. One possibility is that xylem intake and backflow might take place simultaneously, with water essentially cycling through the fruit, i.e., entering through certain vascular strands of the stalk while exiting through others. This is a difficult concept to envisage in physiological terms, since different xylem pressure potentials would have to exist in closely adjacent xylem strands, and it is difficult to imagine how such gradients might be generated or maintained. The more plausible explanation, to be examined in further detail in this section, is that the fruit engages in temporal reversal of xylem flow, with periods of bulk inflow of water alternating with periods of mass outflow and that the phasing, duration, and relative magnitudes of these periods depend essentially on the current water balance of the whole fruit relative to that of the parent plant.

As a first step in testing such a hypothesis, the earlier mentioned modeling procedure for examining balances of carbon and water for the fruit has been extended to a study of night and day fluxes over specific 24-hour periods of growth (Atkins *et al.*, 1986). Daily profiles are first constructed for CO_2 exchanges and transpiration losses of the fruit, and, using mass (200 fruit) harvests of identically aged and sized fruit collected at dawn and dusk of successive days, estimates are made of day and night increments of carbon in fruit dry matter and of any changes occurring during day or night in fruit tissue water. The total carbon consumption of the fruit in these day and night periods is computed, and then, based on measured values for C content of phloem sap, estimates are obtained of the corresponding intake of water through phloem. These values for intake of phloem-borne water are finally matched against the recorded transpiration loss and tissue water change in the fruit. An assessment can thus be made of whether the fruit is currently in receipt of an excess of water, and therefore likely to be returning this water to the parent plant through the xylem, or whether the current phloem water supply is inadequate and the fruit is consequently importing through the xylem.

Table 7.4 provides data for Vita 3 cowpea fruits for two successive daily cycles in its development, following precisely the protocol outlined in the previous paragraph. In both study intervals, fruits are found to transpire more than three times faster during the day than during the night, while showing a day:night differential of at least comparable magnitude in carbon consumption and hence also in intake of phloem water. Of additional significance, however, is the fact that the fruit increases noticeably in tissue water content at night once foliar transpiration has ceased, but shrinks appreciably and loses 0.4–0.6 ml of tissue water the following day at times of high shoot transpiration and highly negative xylem water potential. Both sets of data (Table 7.4) predict that a net influx of water (0.4–0.5 ml/fruit) through xylem occurs at night, whereas a reverse xylem flow of water of even greater amount (0.7–0.9 ml/fruit) takes place from fruit to plant during daytime.

In detailed studies, partly summarized by Pate *et al.* (1985), analyses of the water relations of fruiting Vita 3 cowpea plants have been extended to a comparison of diurnal profiles of change in transpiration rate and diffusion (stomatal) resistance of fruit and vegetative parts of the plant. Leaflets and fruit stalks display a much greater day:night differential in stomatal resistance than do fruits. Reflecting this difference, leaflet and fruit stalk transpire water during daytime at rates, respectively, between 10–20 and 5–7 times faster per unit area than do fruits, whereas fruit transpiration rates per unit surface area at night are generally greater than those of either fruit stalk or leaflet.

Data on diurnal water balance of Vita 3 cowpea have finally been examined in relation to the proportional contributions made by the fruits day and night to the total water loss of the plant. As shown by Pate *et al.* (1985), plants transpire 25–134 ml per photoperiod and 2–7 ml per night over postanthesis development, during which time the plant's complement of fruits records 0.1–1.8 ml of nighttime transpiration and 0.1–6.5 ml of daytime transpiration. The proportion of the plant's water loss attributable to

TABLE 7.4

Day:Night Water and Carbon Budgets for Two Stages during the Late Development of Fruits of Cowpea (*Vigna unguiculata* (L.) cv. Vita 3)

Item of budget (mg or ml/fruit)	Days after anthesis			
	15/16[e]		17/18[f]	
	Night	Day	Night	Day
Intake of C by fruit (mg)[a]	39.0	139.1	41.2	152.3
Phloem intake of water (ml)[b]	0.46	1.65	0.49	1.8
Change in tissue water (ml)	+0.55[c]	−0.44[d]	+0.43	−0.63
Transpiration loss (ml)	0.38	1.37	0.51	1.51
Balance of water (3 + 4) (ml)	0.93	0.93	+0.94	+0.93
Net flux of water in xylem (5 − 2) (ml) (+ into, − out of fruit)	+0.47	−0.72	+0.45	−0.93

[a] Estimated from increment in dry matter and net losses (day or night) of CO_2 by fruit.
[b] Assumes mass flow in phloem with carbon entering at 84 mg C/ml phloem sap (Pate *et al.*, 1984).
[c] +, into fruit.
[d] −, out of fruit.
[e] Data from Atkins *et al.* (1986).
[f] J. S. Pate, M. B. Peoples, and C. A. Atkins (unpublished observations).

fruits increases greatly as the plant matures. For example, at 10 days after anthesis, fruit transpiration accounts for 23% of whole plant water loss at night *versus* only 3.1% during the day, whereas at 20 days after anthesis, when water usage by the whole plant has been greatly reduced by abscission of leaflets, fruits during day and night are estimated to have contributed 21 and 58%, respectively of whole plant transpiration loss.

IV. STRUCTURAL FEATURES OF THE FRUIT AND THEIR SIGNIFICANCE IN TERMS OF WATER RELATIONSHIPS

Aerially produced legume fruits generally show a well-cutinized epidermis, often bearing trichomes, and display much lower stomatal frequencies than do adjacent leaves (Pate and Kuo, 1981; Pate, 1987). These features, combined with partial obstruction of stomatal openings by cuticular flanges, are undoubtedly responsible for the low rates of transpiration shown generally by legume fruits, regardless of whether such water loss is expressed in terms of surface area of fruit or, as described earlier, in terms of dry matter gain by the fruit. Furthermore, fruit water use efficiency (WUE) tends to be particularly high in fast-maturing, large-seeded, cylindrical

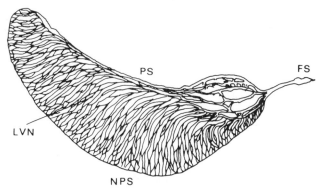

Fig. 7.4. Vascular network of wind-dispersed fruit of the mimosoid
legume *Tipuana* spp. Note the general conformation of the vasculature to the stereotype legume pattern shown for cowpea in Fig. 7.5,
despite the presence of a wing of pericarp tissue on the fruit and the
eccentric placement of the seed(s) at the proximal end of the fruit. PS,
placental suture; LVN, lateral vein network of wing of fruit; FS, fruit
stalk; NPS, nonplacental suture.

fruits with low surface area : volume relationships and fast rates of import of
assimilates from the parent plant through phloem, as exemplified, for example, by certain large-fruited domesticates of *Vigna* spp. Conversely, a much
lower WUE has been demonstrated in fruits in which the pericarp is dorsi-
ventrally flattened (e.g., *Pisum*, see Table 7.1) or would be expected of fruits
bearing wing-like photosynthetic extensions (e.g., for the samara-type,
wind-dispersed fruits of Mimosoids such as *Tipuana*) (Fig. 7.4).

Pericarp wall thickness is another highly variable feature between species, and since the bulk of the storage parenchyma of the pod wall is highly
vacuolate, tissue water reserves are likely to increase roughly commensurate
with wall thickness. This has obvious bearing on the overall water requirements of the developing fruit, especially the buffering capacity that the fruit
may possess on a regular diurnal basis or when the whole plant experiences
severe water stress.

Directly resulting from its poor ventilation, the gas space of the legume
fruit typically accumulates high levels of CO_2 (0.1–2.5% CO_2, v/v). This
carbon dioxide derives largely from the respiring seeds and is partly refixed
by the photosynthetic tissues of the pod wall. Some species possess a chlor-
oplast-containing epidermis as well as a zone of chlorenchyma in the pod
mesocarp (Pate and Kuo, 1981). The implications of recycling of this respired carbon on the total C economy of the fruits of cowpea, pea, and lupin
have been the subject of several publications (Flinn *et al.*, 1977; Atkins and

Flinn, 1978; Pate, 1984; Pate, 1987). In pea, for instance, fruit photosynthetic recycling of respired carbon effects savings equivalent to approximately one quarter of the carbon eventually laid down in the seeds (Pate, 1984).

Regardless of the overall shape of legume fruits, their size, and the number of seeds that they contain, the vasculature of legume fruits conforms to the same fundamental design (Woodcock, 1934; Fahn and Zohary, 1955). Paired left- and right-hand sets of longitudinally oriented vascular strands run the length of the placental (upper seed bearing; PS, Fig. 7.5) and nonplacental (lower; NPS, Fig. 7.5) margins of the carpel, each strand ending blindly in the distal tip of the fruit. Left and right placental strands serve seeds (S, Fig. 7.5) attached alternately to corresponding halves of this suture, and, in all examples so far investigated, an uninterrupted xylem and phloem supply enters the seed stalk and contributes directly to the vasculature of the seed coat (Pate *et al.*, 1975; Pate, 1987). An open or closed network of veins and veinlets comprises the vasculature of the lateral walls of the pod (LVN, Figs. 7.4 and 7.5), this reticulum connecting above and below with the longitudinal vasculature of the pod sutures, thus providing effective communication between all regions of each half of the pod and the seeds attached thereto. The full complexity of a fruit's whole vasculature can be appreciated only through exhaustive examination of cleared specimens in conjunction with light microscopy of sections through specific locations in the fruit. In Vita 3 cowpea, for example (Fig. 7.4), an average of 8 to 10 discrete groups of longitudinally oriented xylem elements run along each suture of the fruit. In the nonplacental (lower) suture, these files of xylem strands bifurcate at intervals along the fruit's length, with the outermost element of each branch pair eventually passing out into the lateral vein network. With such branching compensating for lateral loss of xylem strands, the total number of xylem strands is approximately the same throughout the length of the suture. By contrast, the xylem network of the upper placental suture shows successive fusions between its members, with each successively innermost member within the left- or right-hand half of the network supplying seeds (Fig. 7.5). Concurrently, strands of the lateral pod network merge progressively into the vasculature of the placental suture, thereby compensating for losses of strand members through fusions or successive losses to seeds.

In the Vita 3 cowpea fruit (Pate *et al.*, 1985) and in fruits of a number of other legumes described by Pate and Kuo (1981), phloem accompanies xylem throughout all major elements of the fruit vasculature. There are, however, examples of veinlets consisting of phloem only in the pods of certain genera (Pate and Kuo, 1981) and an unusual example of a mycelium-like network of internal phloem unaccompanied by xylem in the inner

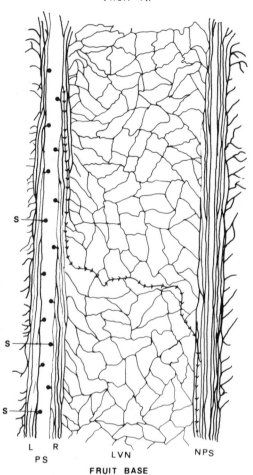

Fig. 7.5. Diagrammatic representation of the vascular network of xylem in the longitudinal half of a fruit
of cowpea (*Vigna unguiculata* cv. Vita 3). The pod illustrated contains 15 seeds (S) attached alternately to the
left (L) and right (R) halves of the upper placental
suture (PS) of the fruit. The lateral vein network (LVN)
connects between PS and the lower nonplacental suture (NPS). Note the progressive branching of the
strands of the NPS, the addition of the outermost of
these branches to LVN, and the progressive supple-
mentation of strands to the PS from the LVN as the PS
serves the seeds. The pathway marked with arrows
traces a continuous xylem connection between a seed
across the vasculature of LVN to the NPS. [Modified
from Pate *et al.* (1985).]

mesocarp of certain genotypes of *Vigna* (Kuo and Pate, 1985). The signifi-cance of these abnormalities to the functioning of the fruit has yet to be evaluated.

Where the overall shape of the fruit is unusually modified, for example, in the samara of *Tipuana* spp. (Fig. 7.4), the general vasculature is broadly similar to that described above for cowpea, but grossly distorted through the abnormal shape of the pericarp and the eccentric placement of the seeds. The same applies to subterranean fruits of genera such as *Vigna* and *Arachis* (Pate, 1987).

The overall conformation of the fruit's vasculature thus embodies the potential for free exchange of both xylem- and phloem-borne water be-tween all parts of the pod and the seeds and via the vasculature of the fruit stalk between the whole fruit and the remainder of the plant. An integrated system of this nature is clearly an essential prerequisite of the earlier-men-tioned concept of diurnally reversing xylem flow between fruit and plant. It also has relevance to the hypothesis that excess phloem water acquired by seeds returns to the pod via xylem. In this connection, the architecture of the xylem network between pod and seed (see Fig. 7.5) would suggest that excess water emanating from a specific seed might either be transpired locally after moving laterally into the adjacent vein network or, if generated in greater excess than could be accommodated by local transpiration, might join a general stream of seed-derived water traveling back to the parent plant through the fruit stalk. These possibilities are indicated by the path-way marked by arrows in Fig. 7.5.

V. TRACER STUDIES OF THE PHLOEM AND XYLEM EXCHANGES OF WATER AND SOLUTES BETWEEN FRUIT, PEDUNCLE, AND THE REMAINDER OF THE PLANT

The principal objective of an extensive series of continuing experiments on cowpea (Vita 3) has been to determine whether direct evidence can be obtained of (1) mass flow of water and assimilates into the fruit via the phloem and (2) an attendant diurnally reversing exchange of water between fruit and plant through the xylem. In keeping with other general accounts of plant transport, the terms symplast and apoplast will be employed in the ensuing discussion to denote, respectively, the membrane-bound cytoplas-mic phase and the extracellular compartment of the tissues and organs participating in solute and water exchange. Within this context, long-dis-tance symplastic transport is regarded as being accomplished by mass flow in conducting elements of the phloem, and the term apoplastic transport will be used synonymously with complementary bulk flow in xylem elements. Unless otherwise stated, details of the various experimental procedures involved in the labeling studies are as stated in Pate *et al.* (1985) or Atkins *et al.* (1986).

^{3}H-Labeled inulin and the anionic dye acid fuchsin have been used as principal markers of apoplastic flow, each being fed at various times day or night to the cut basal end of fruiting shoots via the xylem. Distribution of tracer within a whole plant and its near mature (13–16 days) fruit is then determined by radioassay of ethanolic extracts of tissues (^{3}H-labeled inulin) or by visual inspection of whole or sectioned plant organs for tracer (acid fuchsin) in xylem of vascular tissues or subsequently accumulating in the apoplast at sites of transpiration.

Feeding of ^{3}H-labeled inulin or acid fuchsin to fruiting plants at any time during the night to the early morning usually leads to a rapid intake of tracer by fruits, with all parts of the pod labeled after 1.5–2 hours. Seeds, however, always fail to acquire the dye. In marked contrast, comparable feeding during the late morning to late afternoon leads to no detectable intake of tracer into fruits. In certain instances, even the peduncle fails to absorb the tracer. These results are interpreted as fully consistent with the concept of diurnally reversing xylem flow, in that xylem intake by the pod at night is likely to coincide with a time when transpiration loss and restoration of fruit tissue water balance are not being fully met by symplastic intake of water through the phloem. Conversely, during the day, when phloem intake of water is likely to be exceeding transpiration loss of the fruit and pod, excess water will be voided back to the parent plant via the xylem (apoplast), thus effectively preventing entry of the apoplast markers into the fruit or even into upper parts of the peduncle.

The above conclusions have been further substantiated in experiments feeding $^{32}PO_4$, ^3H_2O, or NO_3 to completely intact fruiting plants through the rooting medium. Nighttime feeding of $^{32}PO_4$ results in all parts of the pod being quickly and substantially labeled, presumably via xylem, followed by a slowly increasing labeling of seeds, presumably due to xylem to phloem transfer of ^{32}P in leaf and stem and, thence, via the symplast to the seeds. When ^3H_2O is fed in the afternoon, pod walls remain unlabeled for 2.5 hours, suggesting no apoplastic transfer via xylem. Later, in a daily cycle, ^3H_2O does enter both seed and pod, presumably in conjunction with phloem import. ^3H_2O fed at night, however, travels directly in large amounts to fruit, where it accumulates intensely in pod walls but only very sparingly in seeds, if at all. Nighttime root feeding of NO_3^- to nodulated plants not previously experiencing nitrate results in induction of nitrate reductase principally in the lateral wall and lower suture of the fruit, only to a limited extent (2% of total reductase of fruit) in the upper placental suture of the fruit, and at scarcely detectable levels (less than 0.1% of activity of fruit) in seeds (Atkins *et al.*, 1986). This result is consistent with an initial apoplastic distribution of nitrate, an induction of reductase at sites adjacent to xylem distribution of the ion, and an extremely poor secondary mobility of NO_3^- in phloem (Pate *et al.*, 1984).

As a further experimental ploy, the radiosubstrates $^{32}PO_4$, ^3H_2O, and ^{14}C sucrose have been administered through a midvein leaf flap of the nurse leaf to a near mature fruit (Pate *et al.*, 1984, 1985). Initial uptake of the fed solution is assumed to be into distal regions of the leaf via the transpiration stream, whereupon some of the ^{32}P, ^3H_2O, or ^{14}C sucrose becomes loaded onto the outgoing phloem streams flanking the flap. The symplast of the fruit is thus supposed to become specifically labeled with water or fed solutes. In agreement with this interpretation, time courses of labeling of fruit parts following leaf flap feeding indicate that seeds are rapidly (1.5 hours) labeled with ^{32}P, ^{14}C, or ^3H and thereafter show consistently higher specific activities per unit tissue mass than does adjacent pod wall tissue. Moreover, cryopuncture phloem sap (Pate *et al.*, 1984) collected from the longitudinal vasculature of fruit in close proximity to the seeds is found to be intensely labeled with all three tracers, as to be expected following a predominantly symplastic transfer of label into the fruit. Moreover, the ^3H labeling of the phloem is almost entirely (99%) associated with water—a result taken as convincing evidence of direct mass flow of water into the fruit from the nurse leaf via phloem.

Possibly the most instructive class of labeling study is one in which applications of ^3H_2O are made to rooting medium, leaf flap, or the surface of the fruit. Transpired water is then collected continuously from the fruit or peduncle over a period of several days, and the water assayed for ^3H (Pate *et al.*, 1985). Root feeding of ^3H_2O is then shown to lead to much higher mean specific radioactivities in transpired water of peduncles than of fruits, consistent with greater dependence on xylem derived water by the former class of organ. As might be expected, feeding of ^3H_2O symplastically via a leaf flap produces the opposite result, namely, that fruit-transpired water is of consistently higher specific ^3H activity than is peduncle-transpired water. This result is interpreted as suggesting greater proportional reliance of the fruit than its peduncle on symplastically derived water.

In both of the above types of experiments, fluctuations in specific activity of transpired water of both the fruit and petiole have been shown to exhibit pronounced diurnal rhythms, with maxima in late afternoon and minima at or just past midnight. Daytime peaks presumably mark times of maximum import of the phloem-borne (symplast) ^3H-labeled water, and nighttime minima mark times when peduncle and fruit are active in intake of apoplastically borne (unlabeled) water from the root system.

The third class of feeding study, involving direct application of ^3H_2O to the fruit, has shown the peduncle to transpire a significant proportion of the applied water, a result consistent with backflow from fruit to plant in the xylem. Moreover, the diurnal fluctuations recorded for specific radioactivity of the transpired water of the peduncle show marked maxima in the late afternoon and minima at or near midnight. On the basis of the reverse-flow hypothesis, these maxima and minima would be assumed to correspond with alternating periods of xylem outflow and inflow of water by the fruit.

VI. GENERAL CONCLUSIONS

In summarizing the results of their anatomical and tracer studies on the Vita 3 cowpea, Pate *et al.* (1985) presented the following analysis of the diurnally reversing patterns of xylem flow for the seed-filling stages of fruit development of the species:

1. Xylem intake by pods occurs principally at night when transpiration loss of water from the wall exceeds current intake of water by mass flow in phloem.

2. Conversion by seeds of phloem-stream solutes into insoluble reserves generates a continuous excess of water, day and night. This exits via the xylem, whence it may return directly to the plant via the inner dorsal pod strands or move laterally to sites of transpiration in the pod wall.

3. Backflow of water in xylem from the whole fruit to the plant occurs mainly late in the day, when phloem intake of water is exceeding transpiration loss by the pod.

4. Fruit and peduncle utilize pools of symplastic (phloem-derived) water and recently arrived apoplastic (xylem) water for their transpiration. Fruits are generally much more dependent on phloem-derived water than are peduncles.

5. Fruit and peduncle rely more heavily on symplastic reserves of water for transpiration in the day than at night.

6. Phloem-derived water exchanges slowly with the whole symplast of the fruit and is subsequently used in fruit transpiration over a period of several days after arriving in the fruit.

7. Water flowing out of the fruit in the xylem is used for peduncle transpiration, especially in the day.

The above authors concluded from the data then available that reversible water flow in xylem would depend primarily upon the fruit exhibiting a greater diurnal amplitude in translocatory intake of water than in transpiration loss. However, as shown in the data for daily tissue water balance in

Table 7.4, we now know that nightly gains and daily losses of tissue water from the fruit also work positively in favor of reversible flow and may even allow net intake through xylem to occur at night when current phloem intake of water is not fully dissipated by fruit transpiration.

An important outcome of the experimental data supporting the above hypothesis is that xylem backflow from the fruit to the plant of cowpea is mostly, if not exclusively, associated with the fairly mature stages of fruit development, regardless of genotype (Tables 7.2 and 7.3). This is not unexpected, since during early growth of the pod and pre-embryonic stages of ovule development, the fruit is incorporating large amounts of water into an ever expanding tissue volume but converting only a small proportion of its imported assimilates into cytoplasmic food reserves. Later, when the fruit has reached full size and when embryos of seeds start to increase exponentially in their conversion of phloem assimilates to starch or protein, a situation is quickly reached in which an oversupply of phloem water is incurred, and some or all of this water accordingly returns to the parent plant in the xylem.

It remains to be seen whether reversible xylem exchange is a general physiological feature of the later stages of maturation of plant fruits. There is certainly strong evidence of similar behavior in the fruit of the legume *Phaseolus vulgaris*, judging from the studies of Mix and Marschner (1976), and in fruit of a number of other nonlegumes such as the sausage tree, *Kigelia africana* (Clements, 1940; Canny, 1973), and squash, *Cucurbita* (Ziegler, 1963).

If plant fruits are generally found to be capable of engaging in additional xylem inputs during times of low phloem intake, the phenomenon may be viewed as of adaptive advantage in supplementing the fruit's net intake of minerals mobile in xylem but not significantly in phloem (Pate, 1987). However, additional inputs effected in this manner will be of little importance to the nutrition of seeds themselves, since these organs are unlikely to acquire solutes directly from the fruit apoplast, at least during embryo fill, even during times of effective net intake of water by the rest of the fruit through xylem. This may well explain why seeds, but not pods, commonly tend to show distinct deficiency symptoms in relation to phloem-immobile nutrients — a notable case of this being the split seed disorder of *Lupinus* spp. associated with an insufficiency of the element manganese (Perry and Gartrell, 1976; Hocking *et al.*, 1977; Hannam *et al.*, 1985). The same probably applies generally to the nutrition of seeds in relation to other phloem sparingly mobile elements such as boron, calcium, or iron (Bollard, 1970; Loneragen, 1982).

Finally, there is always the possibility that return flow of water from the fruit via the xylem might carry hormonal-type factors which, when attracted to adjacent foliage, might elicit leaf senescence. This suggestion fits well with the hypothesis of fruiting-induced monocarpic senescence proposed by Noodén and his colleagues for certain cultivars of soybean (see Chapter 12 of this volume), in which it is envisaged that senescence factors produced in developing seeds engender premature senescence of their corresponding nurse leaves (Lindoo and Noodén, 1978; Noodén and Murray, 1982; Noodén, 1984). Certain cowpea genotypes, notably Vita 3, show a pattern of senescence in which the main stem leaf subtending the first-formed fruit enters senescence a week or more before its earlier- or later-formed companions (Peoples *et al.*, 1983), implying that in this cultivar, as in soybean, xylem-mobile factors emanating from the fruit might well be the causative agents of specifically targeted senescence phenomena.

REFERENCES

Atkins, C. A., and Flinn, A. M. (1978). Carbon dioxide fixation in the carbon economy of developing seeds of *Lupinus albus* (L.). *Plant Physiol.* **62**, 486–490.

Atkins, C. A., Pate, J. S., and Peoples, M. B. (1986). Water relations of cowpea fruits during development. *In* "Fundamental, Ecological and Agricultural Aspects of Nitrogen Metabolism in Higher Plants" (H. Lambers, J. J. Neeteson, and I. Stulen, eds.), pp. 235–238. Nijhoff, The Hague.

Bollard, E. G. (1970). The physiology and nutrition of developing fruits. *In* "The Biochemistry of Fruits and Their Products" (A. C. Hulme, ed.), Vol. 1, pp. 387–425. Academic Press, London.

Canny, M. J. (1973). "Phloem Translocation." Cambridge Univ. Press, London and New York.

Clements, H. F. (1940). Movement of organic solutes in the sausage tree, *Kigelia africana*. *Plant Physiol.* **15**, 689–700.

Fahn, A., and Zohary, M. (1955). On the pericarpial structure of the legumen. Its evolution and relation to dehiscence. *Phytomorphology* **5**, 99–111.

Flinn, A. M., Atkins, C. A., and Pate, J. S. (1977). The significance of photosynthetic and respiratory exchanges in the carbon economy of the developing pea fruit. *Plant Physiol.* **60**, 412–418.

Hannam, R. J., Graham, R. D., and Riggs, J. L. (1985). Diagnosis and prognosis of manganese deficiency in *Lupinus angustifolius* L. *Aust. J. Agric. Res.* **36**, 765–767.

Hocking, P. J., Pate, J. S., Wee, S. C., and McComb, A. J. (1977). Manganese nutrition of *Lupinus* spp. especially in relation to developing seeds. *Ann. Bot.* **41**, 677–688.

Kuo, J., and Pate, J. S. (1985). Unusual network of internal phloem in the pod mesocarp of cowpea (*Vigna unguiculata* (L.) Walp. (Fabaceae)). *Ann. Bot.* **55**, 635–647.

Layzell, D. B., and LaRue, T. A. (1982). Modeling C and N transport to developing soybean fruits. *Plant Physiol.* **70**, 1290–1298.

Lindoo, S. J., and Noodén, L. D. (1978). Correlation of cytokynins and abscisic acid with monocarpic senescence in soybeans. *Plant Cell Physiol.* **19**, 997–1006.

Loneragan, J. T. (1982). Mineral nutrition. III. Response of plants to trace elements. *Prog. Bot.* **44**, 92–102.

Mix, G. P., and Marschner, H. (1976). Calcium Umlagerung in Bohnen-Früchten während des Samen Wachstums (Redistribution of calcium in bean fruits during seed development). *Z. Pflanzenphysiol.* **80**, 354–366.

Noodén, L. D. (1984). Integration of soybean pod development and monocarpic senescence. *Physiol. Plant.* **62,** 273–284.

Noodén, L. D., and Murray, B. J. (1982). Transmission of the monocarpic senescence signal via the xylem in soybean. *Plant Physiol.* **69,** 754–756.

Pate, J. S. (1984). The carbon and nitrogen nutrition of fruit and seed—case studies of selected grain legumes. *In* "Seed Physiology" (D. R. Murray, ed.), Vol. 1, pp. 41–82. Academic Press, Orlando, Florida.

Pate, J. S. (1987). Legume fruits: the structure–function equation. *Biol. Leguminosae Int. Conf.,* St. Louis, Mo. (in press).

Pate, J. S., and Kuo, J. (1981). Anatomical studies of legume pods—a possible tool in taxonomic research. *In* "Advances in Legume Systematics" (R. M. Polhill and P. H. Raven, eds.), pp. 903–912. Royal Botanic Gardens, Kew, England.

Pate, J. S., Sharkey, P. J., and Lewis, O. A. M. (1975). Xylem to phloem transport of solutes in fruiting shoots of legume, studied by a phloem bleeding technique. *Planta* **122,** 11–26.

Pate, J. S., Sharkey, P. J., and Atkins, C. A. (1977). Nutrition of a developing legume fruit. Functional economy in terms of carbon, nitrogen, water. *Plant Physiol.* **59,** 506–510.

Pate, J. S., Kuo, J., and Hocking, P. J. (1978). Functioning of conducting elements of phloem and xylem in the stalk of the developing fruit of *Lupinus albus* L. *Aust. J. Plant Physiol.* **5,** 321–326.

Pate, J. S., Layzell, D. B., and Atkins, C. A. (1980). Transport exchange of carbon, nitrogen and water in the context of whole plant growth and functioning—case history of a nodulated annual legume. *Ber. Dtsch. Bot. Ges.* **93,** 243–255.

Pate, J. S., Peoples, M. B., and Atkins, C. A. (1984). Spontaneous phloem bleeding from cryopunctured fruits of a ureide-producing legume. *Plant Physiol.* **74,** 499–505.

Pate, J. S., Peoples, M. B., van Bel, A. J. E., Kuo, J., and Atkins, C. A. (1985). Diurnal water balance of the cowpea fruit. *Plant Physiol.* **77,** 148–156.

Peoples, M. B., Pate, J. S., and Atkins, C. A. (1983). Mobilization of nitrogen in fruiting plants of a cultivar of cowpea. *J. Exp. Bot.* **34,** 563–578.

Peoples, M. B., Pate, J. S., Atkins, C. A., and Murray, D. R. (1985). Economy of water, carbon and nitrogen in the developing cowpea fruit. *Plant Physiol.* **77,** 142–147.

Perry, M. W., and Gartrell, J. W. (1976). Lupin "split seed." A disorder of seed production in sweet narrow-leafed lupins. *J. Agric. West. Aust.* **17,** 20–25.

Woodcock, E. F. (1934). Carpel anatomy of the bean (*Phaseolus vulgaris* L.). *Mich. Acad. Sci. Art Lett.* **20,** 267–271.

Ziegler, H. (1963). Verwendung von ^{45}Calcium zur Analyse der Stoffversorgung wachsender Früchte. *Planta* **60,** 41–45.

Ethylene and Plant Senescence

Autar K. Mattoo
Plant Hormone Laboratory
USDA, ARS
Beltsville Agricultural Research Center
Beltsville, Maryland

Nehemia Aharoni
Department of Fruit and Vegetable Storage
Agricultural Research Organization
The Volcani Center
Bet Dagan 50-250, Israel

I. INTRODUCTION

Aging and senescence of higher plants are genetically as well as environmentally regulated processes intimately associated with hormonal interactions. Of the well-recognized plant hormones known to date, ethylene is unique in that it is a simple, gaseous hydrocarbon that is a principal feature of processes that enhance plant senescence. Ethylene is produced by most higher plants that have been studied and, in trace amounts, influences many aspects of plant growth, including aging and senescence (Lieberman, 1979). In addition, it is currently realized that production of ethylene may be a common symptom of several types of environmental stresses that a higher plant confronts. The development of a relatively simple, rapid, and highly sensitive gas chromatographic assay that does not require prior purification or special handling of biologically evolved ethylene has facilitated the determination of ethylene production by whole plants or plant organs during their normal development and senescence (Abeles, 1973). Partly because of the ease of its assay, the biology of ethylene has attracted considerable attention in recent years, which is evidenced by the voluminous literature on the subject (Burg, 1962, 1968; Hansen, 1966; Pratt and Goeschl, 1969; Abeles, 1972; Yang, 1974; Lieberman, 1979; Yang and Hoffman, 1984; Imaseki, 1986). Moreover, the elucidation of the primary ethylene biosynthetic pathway in higher plants and identification of rate-limiting steps therein (Yang and Hoffman, 1984), coupled with the recognition of relatively specific, ethylene binding protein(s) in higher plants (Sisler, 1984; Hall *et al.*, 1984) have paved the way for more definitive biochemical and molecular studies. These studies should increase our knowledge of the bioregulation of synthesis and action of this ubiquitous plant hormone. In this chapter, we wish to bring together only those particular aspects of ethylene that may impinge upon its role in promoting senescence of higher plants, with particular emphasis on regulatory controls. Aspects of ethylene chemistry and biochemistry not thoroughly dealt with in this chapter have recently been reviewed (Lieberman, 1979; Yang and Hoffman, 1984; Imaseki, 1986).

II. BIOSYNTHESIS OF ETHYLENE

A. Precursors and Pathway

Historically, the impetus for unraveling the identity of the endogenous intermediates in the biosynthesis of ethylene came from studies with chemically defined, model systems (Lieberman, 1979). Ethylene is readily generated when substrates such as linolenic acid, propanol, methional, or methionine react with free radicals or with transition metals that act as catalysts (Lieberman and Kunishi, 1968) or when methionine or its analogs are incubated in the light with flavin mononucleotide (Yang *et al.*, 1966). In the methionine–copper–ascorbate model system, ethylene was found to be derived from carbons 3 and 4 of methionine. Subsequent radiolabeling experiments with apple fruit tissue demonstrated that methionine was efficiently converted *in vivo* to ethylene and, fortuitously, as in the model system, radiolabeled ethylene originated only from ^{14}C-3,4-labeled methionine (Lieberman *et al.*, 1966). These results were reproduced with several other plant tissues (Lieberman, 1979), and methionine became established as a major precursor of ethylene in higher plants. Oxygen was found to stimulate ethylene production from methionine. It was thus assumed that the mechanism of the biosynthetic pathway was similar to that shown for the model system catalyzed by oxygen radicals (Lieberman, 1979). This notion actually hampered the identification of intermediates between methionine and ethylene, particularly in light of the inability of cell homogenates to produce ethylene. Some investigators (Burg, 1973; Murr and Yang, 1975), however, speculated that S-adenosylmethionine (SAM) was a precursor of ethylene based on the observations that: (1) uncouplers of oxidative phosphorylation inhibited formation of ethylene from methionine; (2) oxygen was necessary for this reaction; (3) 5'-methylthioadenosine (MTA) and methylthioribose (MTR) were formed in parallel during conversion of ^{14}C]methionine to ^{14}C]ethylene; and (4) aminoethoxyvinylglycine (AVG), an inhibitor of ethylene biosynthesis (Owens *et al*, 1971), also inhibited the conversion of methionine to MTA and MTR (Adams and Yang, 1977). Furthermore, in other studies, selenomethionine was found to be more effective than methionine as a substrate for ethylene (Konze *et al.*, 1978). Since selenoadenosylmethionine is more readily and efficiently formed from selenomethionine than is SAM from methionine, it was suggested that SAM is an intermediate in the methionine–ethylene pathway (Konze and Kende, 1979; Jones and Kende, 1979). Direct *in vivo* feeding experiments with SAM are difficult to accomplish because of the inability of plant cells to take up intact SAM. However, what started as speculation was shown to be true in later experiments supporting the role of SAM as an intermediate in ethylene formation from methionine. These experiments, conducted independently in two different laboratories (Adams and Yang, 1979; Lurssen *et al.*, 1979), established 1-aminocyclopropane-1-carboxylic acid (ACC) as the biological precursor of ethylene in the following metabolic reaction sequence:

$$\text{methionine} \longrightarrow \text{SAM} \longrightarrow \text{ACC} \longrightarrow \text{ethylene} \tag{1}$$

ACC is a cyclic amino acid that had been isolated and identified (Burroughs, 1957; Vahatalo and Virtanen, 1957) more than 2 decades before it was shown to be a precursor in ethylene biosynthesis. ACC is readily converted to ethylene by a variety of plant organs (Cameron *et al.*, 1979; Lurssen *et al.*, 1979). The finding of ACC as an immediate precursor in the ethylene pathway was a milestone in that its discovery helped establish the ubiquity of the biosynthetic route for ethylene in higher plants. However, under several stress conditions, for example, during chemical-induced senescence of whole plants or photodestruction of isolated membranes, copious ethylene production can occur in the absence of ACC via membrane damage with or without lipid peroxidation catalyzed by free radicals or singlet oxygen (Sandmann and Boger, 1980; Mattoo *et al.*, 1986). In these instances, selenomethionine acts as a potent inhibitor of ethylene production (Mattoo *et al.*, 1986). Selenomethionine is known to stimulate ethylene evolution in flower tissue and pea stem sections (Konze *et al.*, 1978), apple tissue slices (Lieberman, 1979), and tobacco leaf discs (Mattoo *et al.*, 1984), which produce ethylene via ACC.

B. Enzyme Systems

The confirmation of the precursorial role of ACC in the reaction sequence (1) came from elegant experiments in which a cell-free extract of tomato fruit was shown to catalyze the conversion of SAM to ACC (Boller *et al.*, 1979). This reaction was further shown to be the target site for aminoethoxyvinylglycine (AVG), an enol ether amino acid analog that was previously established as a potent inhibitor of ethylene biosynthesis (Owens *et al.*, 1971). This enzyme, now commonly called ACC synthase, was shown to require pyridoxal phosphate and involve a typical γ-elimination (1,3 elimination) reaction to produce MTA in addition to ACC from SAM (Yu *et al.*, 1979b). The enzyme was also shown to be a hydrophobic protein (Mattoo *et al.*, 1982–1983; Acaster and Kende, 1982) and is regarded as a rate-limiting enzyme in ethylene biosynthesis (Yang and Hoffman, 1984). A study on the stereochemical course of the $\text{SAM} < ^{\text{MTA}}_{\text{ACC}}$ reaction was recently completed using a partially purified ACC synthase preparation (Ramalingam *et al.*, 1985).

ACC synthase activity increases markedly during fruit ripening (Boller *et al.*, 1979), upon wounding of tissue (Boller and Kende, 1980; Yu and Yang, 1980; Mattoo and Anderson, 1984), and during carnation senescence (Mor *et al.*, 1985). The inability to recover measurable amounts of ACC synthase activity upon homogenization of several other plant tissues, particularly those rich in chlorophyll, phenolics, and other enzyme-inactivating substances, has slowed down physiological and biochemical studies of the enzyme. However, success has been achieved in purifying the enzyme by more traditional methods (Nakajima and Imaseki, 1986) and in identifying the enzyme using monoclonal antibodies to partially purified ACC synthase from tomato (Bleecker *et al.*, 1986; A. Mehta, A. K. Mattoo, and J. D. Anderson, unpublished observations). The enzyme from winter squash mesocarp is a dimer of 160,000 Da, with a subunit molecular weight of 84,000 (Nakajima and Imaseki, 1986), while the ACC synthase from wounded tomato has been shown to be either a monomer of 50,000 Da (Bleecker *et al.*, 1986) or 65,000 ± 5000 Da (Mehta *et al.*, 1987). An apparent molecular weight of 72,000 by gel filtration has been assigned to the enzyme obtained from potato tubers (Burns and Evensen, 1986). ACC synthase may exist as a monomer, a dimer, or in different charge forms depending upon the tissue. In this context, it is worth noting that wound-induced ACC synthase from tomato fruit was separated into two activity fractions with p*I*s of 7 and 9.2 on isoelectric focusing columns (Mattoo and Anderson, 1984). The possibility of limited proteolysis during isolation leading to different apparent molecular weights is an alternative explanation for the observed different molecular forms of ACC synthase. Further studies on this regulatory enzyme should reveal its role(s) in the bioregulation of plant development and senescence.

ACC synthase is inducible and developmentally regulated in higher plants, while the enzyme system that forms ethylene from ACC is generally constitutive. In preclimacteric fruits (apples) and young flower petals, however, the latter activity appears late during progressive senescence (Yang and Hoffman, 1984).

Although progress has been made in the purification and, more importantly, identification of ACC synthase, the enzyme system that catalyzes the conversion of ACC to ethylene has not been demonstrated *in vitro*. The smallest subcellular structure that upon isolation oxidizes ACC to ethylene is the vacuole (Guy and Kende, 1984). The ability to convert ACC to ethylene is lost in *Petunia* protoplasts that lack vacuoles. Upon regeneration of vacuoles in these "evacuolated" protoplasts, ethylene forming enzyme (EFE) activity was also regained (H. Erdmann, R. Griesbach, R.H. Lawson, and A. K. Mattoo, unpublished observations), confirming vacuolar location of a major portion of cellular EFE activity. Lysis of vacuoles results in total loss of EFE (Mayne and Kende, 1986), suggesting that EFE is highly structured and requires membrane integrity (Lieberman, 1979). Native EFE is dependent on oxygen (K_s = 1%, Konze *et al.*, 1980), demonstrates regioselectivity toward 2-ethyl analogs of ACC, and has an apparent K_m for ACC between 60 and 100 μM (McKeon and Yang, 1983). Inhibitors include chaotropic agents (Lieberman, 1979), cobalt (Yu and Yang, 1979), uncouplers of oxidative phosphorylation (Apelbaum *et al.*, 1981b; Mattoo and Anderson, 1984; Mayne and Kende, 1986), and free radical scavengers (Lieberman, 1979; Apelbaum *et al.*, 1981b). Several cell-free enzyme systems that cataylze conversion of ACC to ethylene *in vitro* have been reported, but none of them resemble the *in vivo* system (McKeon and Yang, 1983).

Pirrung (1983) has suggested that the conversion of ACC to ethylene involves an amine radical cation via two sequential one-electron oxidation steps, with the final production of ethylene, cyanide, and carbon dioxide. Thus, carbon 1 of ACC gives rise to cyanide, the carboxylic group to CO_2, and carbons 2 and 3 give rise to ethylene (Peiser *et al.*, 1984).

III. REGULATION OF ETHYLENE BIOSYNTHESIS

A. Methionine Recycling

With the elucidation of SAM as an intermediate in the biosynthesis of ethylene in higher plants, several interlinking pathways have become apparent (Fig. 8.1). During the metabolism of SAM to ACC, there is a stoichiometric production of MTA (Adams and Yang, 1979). MTA is also generated during aminopropyl transferase activities that utilize decarboxylated SAM in the biosynthesis of polyamines (Slocum *et al.*, 1984). MTA was shown to recycle to methionine, thereby creating an important salvage pathway that allows maximum utilization of methionine for ethylene biosynthesis, particularly in tissues where methionine is rate limiting (Yung *et al.*, 1982; Wang *et al.*, 1982; Giovanelli *et al.*, 1983). MTA is readily converted in plants to 5'-methylthioribose (MTR) by a nucleosidase (Adams and Yang, 1979; Guranowski *et al.*, 1981), thus initiating a methionine recycling pathway (Kushad *et al.*, 1983). Kushad and co-workers (1985) have further demonstrated a correlation between the MTA nucleosidase activity and ethylene production during tomato fruit ripening, suggesting a role for this enzyme (and probably MTR kinase) in regulating the synthesis of methionine and, thereby, ethylene biosynthesis. The ribose portion of MTA is incorporated into methionine and ethylene in a reaction sequence that is oxygen dependent (Wang *et al.*, 1982). The adenine moiety is salvaged into

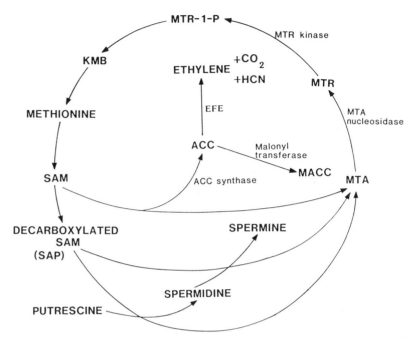

Fig. 8.1. Schematic representation of ethylene biosynthesis pathway interconnected with polyamine biosynthesis and methionine recycling.

ADP and ATP (Giovanelli *et al.*, 1983). Figure 8.1 summarizes the biochemical pathway interlinking methionine cycle with the biosynthesis pathways of ethylene and polyamines.

B. Linkage with Polyamine Biosynthesis

The antisenescence effects of naturally produced polyamines that also share SAM as a common precursor and MTA as a byproduct (Fig. 8.1) have stimulated investigations into the ability of polyamines to control SAM levels and/or influence ethylene biosynthesis. Exogenous polyamines were shown to inhibit ethylene production in petals (Suttle, 1981), leaves (Apelbaum *et al.*, 1981a), and fruit tissues (Apelbaum *et al.*, 1981a; Even-Chen *et al.*, 1982). The inhibition of ethylene biosynthesis by polyamines follows a polyvalent cationic progression, i.e., spermine, the strongest base, is the most effective, followed by spermidine and then by putrescine (Apelbaum *et al.*, 1981a). Both the formation of ACC (Even-Chen *et al.*, 1982; Fuhrer *et al.*, 1982) and its subsequent conversion to ethylene (Apelbaum *et al.*,

1981a; Suttle, 1981) were found to be inhibited by polyamines. Further-more, when ACC synthesis was blocked in the presence of polyamines or aminoethoxyvinylglycine, increased incorporation of radiolabeled methio-nine into spermidine was observed (Even-Chen *et al.*, 1982). These studies indicated that polyamines stimulated their own biosynthesis while reducing the biosynthesis of ethylene. This has been supported by the work of Rob-erts *et al.* (1984) on senescing carnation flowers. Ben-Arie *et al.* (1982) have suggested that inhibition of ethylene biosynthesis by spermine may be mediated via an interaction with cellular membranes. The mechanism of this regulation seems to be indirect, since spermine was found to inhibit the induction of ACC synthase during wounding of tomato fruit tissue. The activity of the enzyme in cell-free systems, however, was not affected (Mat-too and Anderson, 1984). These studies have indicated possible sites of regulation in the metabolism of SAM that interlink biosynthesis of ethylene with that of polyamines. Deciphering these control mechanisms should help in elucidating the nature of the balance between ethylene and polya-mine(s) levels during normal development and senescence of plants.

C. Conjugation of ACC

The availability of ACC can limit the production of ethylene. One control point was discussed above, i.e., the step of SAM conversion to ACC cata-lyzed by ACC synthase. Another control reaction is the conjugation of ACC. Amrhein *et al.* (1981) discovered 1-(malonylamino)cyclopropane-1-carbox-ylic acid (MACC) as a major metabolite of exogenous ACC fed to plant tissues. Subsequently, the natural occurrence of MACC was demonstrated (Hoffman *et al.*, 1982; Knee, 1985). Since MACC is a poor substrate for ethylene production, Yang and Hoffman (1984) have suggested that malo-nylation of ACC is a mechanism to dissipate excess ACC, thereby limiting its supply for ethylene biosynthesis. The physiological significance of MACC formation is not known. However, under several environmental stresses, the capacity of plant tissues to conjugate ACC to MACC increases markedly (Yang and Hoffman, 1984). D-amino acids block *N*-malonylation of ACC concomitant with stimulation of ACC conversion to ethylene (Satoh and Esashi, 1982; Liu *et al.*, 1983; Kionka and Amrhein, 1984). The effect of D-amino acids such as D-phenylalanine is directed at the *N*-malonyltrans-ferase enzyme that catalyzes the conjugation of ACC to MACC in the presence of malonyl-CoA (Kionka and Amrhein, 1984). From these results it would seem that conjugation of ACC can limit the availability of ACC for ethylene production. In some cases, MACC can serve also as a storage form of ACC (Jiao *et al.*, 1986). Since MACC is mostly stored in the vacuole, loss of compartmentation during senescence may enable the cell to utilize MACC for ethylene production.

There is some evidence showing competition between some D-amino acids and ACC for the N-malonyltransferase reaction (Su *et al.*, 1985), suggesting the presence of a similar or the same enzyme for N-malonylation of D-amino acids and ACC in a reaction where ACC is recognized as a D-amino acid (Liu *et al.*, 1984). Confirmation of these suggestions awaits the purification and complete characterization of the malonyl-CoA : ACC-N-malonyltransferase enzyme.

D. Membrane Association and Involvement of Membrane Function

There are two distinct mechanisms by which an effect on the membrane can regulate ethylene biosynthesis. One is a direct effect on the enzymes that associate with the membrane. The second mechanism involves the cellular membrane as a transducer whereby *de novo* synthesis of the enzymes in ethylene biosynthesis is affected. An early indication that membrane stability/function could be involved in the regulation of ethylene production was the sensitivity of ethylene production, by apple tissue, to the solute concentration of the medium. The system will withstand dehydration and continue to produce ethylene, but swelling inhibits ethylene production (Burg and Thimann, 1960; Mattoo and Lieberman, 1977). Further support for membrane involvement was provided by experiments in which ethylene production was shown to be inhibited by lipophilic membrane probes (Mattoo *et al.*, 1977; Odawara *et al.*, 1977; Anderson *et al.*, 1979; Mattoo *et al.*, 1979) and cold shock (Odawara *et al.*, 1977; Mattoo and Anderson, 1984). Discontinuity in Arrhenius plots of incubation temperature against ethylene production also suggests membrane involvement (Mattoo *et al.*, 1977; Mattoo and Anderson, 1984), possibly by affecting the EFE (Apelbaum *et al.*, 1981b; Yang and Hoffman, 1984) that is thought to be membrane associated. The stabilizing effects of calcium and magnesium ions (Lau and Yang, 1974; Anderson *et al.*, 1979; Lieberman and Wang, 1982) and of silver ions (Mattoo and Lieberman, 1982; A. K. Mattoo, R. A. Saftner, and J. D. Anderson, unpublished observations) on ethylene production seem mediated via stabilization of membrane-associated EFE (Ben-Arie *et al.*, 1982; Legge *et al.*, 1982; Burns and Evensen, 1986). Silver ions are also known to increase accumulation of ACC in leaf tissue (Philosoph-Hadas *et al.*, 1985b). Orthophosphate ions also act as reversible inhibitors of ethylene biosynthesis in higher plants (Chalutz *et al.*, 1980). This phosphate effect was subsequently shown to be directed at the EFE when internal phosphate concentrations reached 6.5 – 10 mM (Fuchs *et al.*, 1981). On the other hand, phosphate ions seem to stabilize the labile ACC synthase activity *in vitro* (Fuchs *et al.*, 1981).

Ethylene production may also be regulated by various stimuli perceived at the cellular membrane that affect the synthesis and/or activity of the enzymes involved. For example, induction of ACC synthase activity is inhibited or stimulated by agents that affect membrane potential (e.g., osmotic shock, uncouplers) (Mattoo and Anderson, 1984; Yang and Hoffman, 1984), are impermeable (e.g., lipophilic reagents, soybean trypsin inhibitor, cell wall digesting enzymes) (Anderson *et al.*, 1982; Mattoo and Anderson, 1984), or are highly charged (e.g., spermine) (Mattoo and Anderson, 1984). Calcium ions, which largely accumulate in the cell wall/cell membrane (Ferguson, 1983), also increase ACC production. Presumably, the increase in ACC is regulated by the amounts of ACC synthase or by indirect effects on its activity (Evensen, 1984; Burns and Evensen, 1986), since the isolated enzyme is not directly affected by calcium ions (Mattoo *et al.*, 1982–1983; Burns and Evensen, 1986).

The possibility that ACC synthase may directly associate with membranes is suggested by studies showing a small but significant amount of ACC synthase activity in particulate fractions from tomato fruit extracts that could be modulated by effectors such as tetrabutylammonium bromide that are known to abolish electrical gradients across membranes (Mattoo and Anderson, 1984). Certain characteristics of ACC synthase that favor its association with cellular membranes are: (1) its hydrophobic nature (Mattoo *et al.*, 1982–1983; Acaster and Kende, 1982); (2) the presence of a highly charged form with a p*I* of 9.2 (Mattoo and Anderson, 1984); and (3) the ease of its isolation from some tissues using membrane dissolving detergents (Bufler and Bangerth, 1983). Thus, membrane association of the enzyme indicates an additional means of metabolic control.

E. Feedback Controls

Ethylene biosynthesis can be positively or negatively modulated by ethylene itself. Exposure of some ripening fruits and senescing tissues to ethylene increases ethylene production (for review see Yang and Hoffman, 1984). This phenomenon, known as the *autocatalytic effect* involves stimulation of the EFE as well as the accumulation of ACC, although the initial stimulation seems directed at the EFE, causing increased conversion of ACC to ethylene by the treated tissue (Hoffman and Yang, 1982; Riov and Yang, 1982b; Chalutz *et al.*, 1984; Manning, 1985; Liu *et al.*, 1985a). This ethylene effect presumably occurs through a change in the membrane milieu around EFE (Chalutz *et al.*, 1984).

Ethylene also inhibits its own biosynthesis by a possible feedback mechanism known as *autoinhibition*. Although this type of regulation of ethylene production has been known for some time (Vendrell and McGlasson, 1971; Zeroni *et al.*, 1976; Saltviet and Dilley, 1978; Aharoni *et al.*, 1979a), the exact target site was demonstrated only after the ethylene biosynthesis pathway was elucidated. Both ethylene-treated citrus fruit tissue (Riov and Yang,

1982a) and ethylene-inhibited, indole-3-acetic acid (IAA)-treated mung bean hypocotyls (Yoshii and Imaseki, 1982) were found to have a markedly decreased activity (or amount) of ACC synthase. Furthermore, the conjugation of ACC to MACC is markedly increased when leaves (Philosoph-Hadas *et al.*, 1985b; Gupta and Anderson, 1985) and fruits (Liu *et al.*, 1985b) are exposed to ethylene. Since ethylene does not cause the above-mentioned effects in cell-free systems, the mechanisms of these ethylene effects must be indirect. In that regard, the definitions of autocatalysis and autoinhibition should be taken in a physiological rather than a biochemical sense.

F. IAA-Induced Ethylene Production

Knowledge of the regulation of ethylene biosynthesis in the course of senescence of vegetative tissues is limited. Vegetative tissues usually produce very little ethylene. Typically, the rate of ethylene synthesis is primarily regulated by auxin (Abeles and Rubinstein, 1964; Kang *et al.*, 1971; Abeles, 1973; Lau and Yang, 1973; Imaseki *et al.*, 1975). The regulation of IAA-induced ethylene biosynthesis has been studied mainly in mung bean and pea seedlings (Imaseki, 1983; Yang and Hoffman, 1984). IAA stimulates ethylene production by inducing the synthesis of ACC from SAM (Yu *et al.*, 1979a; Yang and Hoffman, 1984), as indicated by the observation of increased level of endogenous ACC that closely parallels an increase in ACC synthase activity (Jones and Kende, 1979; Yu and Yang, 1979; Yoshii and Imaseki, 1981). Based on inhibitor studies, the IAA effect requires both RNA and protein synthesis (Sakai and Imaseki, 1971). Following treatment with cycloheximide, an inhibitor of nucleocytoplasmic protein synthesis, ACC synthase activity and IAA-induced ethylene production decrease rapidly, with a half-life of about 30 minutes (Yoshii and Imaseki, 1982).

IAA-induced ethylene production in pea seedlings is stimulated by kinetin (Fuchs and Lieberman, 1968). Kinetin also stimulates ethylene production in the absence of auxin (Fuchs and Lieberman, 1968; Aharoni *et al.*, 1979a,b). The stimulatory effect of kinetin may be limited to young vegetative tissues, since kinetin was reported to suppress ethylene production in detached senescing leaves (Even-Chen *et al.*, 1978). In intact cotton leaves, cytokinins are effective stimulators of ethylene production (Suttle, 1986). This response seems species specific, since leaf tissues from bean, sunflower, and corn exhibited only a marginal response to cytokinins. Yoshii and Imaseki (1981) have demonstrated that benzyladenine (BA) stimulates ethylene production in IAA-treated mung bean hypocotyls primarily by enhancing ACC synthase activity. In this system, as well as in water-stressed wheat leaf (McKeon *et al.*, 1982), abscisic acid (ABA) inhibited ethylene production and suppressed ACC synthase activity. Although ABA suppresses ethylene production in young vegetative tissues, it shows the opposite effect in senescent tobacco leaf (Lieberman, 1979). A stimulatory effect of ABA on senescence and climacteric ethylene production has also been demonstrated in cut flowers (Mayak and Dilley, 1976). These reports suggest that tissue sensitivity to plant hormones changes as plants age. It is also possible that the ratio of "juvenile" to "senescing" hormones may regulate the aging process in plants.

1. Role of IAA Conjugates

IAA conjugates play an important role in auxin physiology and metabolism. They are thought to be involved in transport and storage of IAA, in protection of the hormone from enzymatic destruction, and in homeostatic control of IAA concentration within the plant tissue (Cohen and Bandurski, 1982). In addition to these possible roles, certain IAA conjugates also stimulate ethylene production. Applied IAA-L-alanine (IAAla) stimulates ethyl-

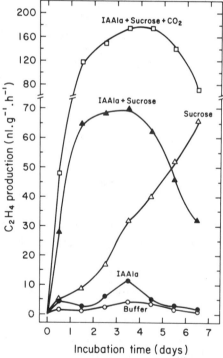

Fig. 8.2. Stimulatory effects of IAA-alanine alone or in combination with sucrose and CO_2 on ethylene production rates in tobacco leaf discs. [From Aharoni *et al.* (1984), with permission.]

ene production in pea and tomato hypocotyl segments (Hangarter and Good, 1981) and in leaf discs of tobacco, tomato, cotton, and bean (Aharoni *et al.*, 1984). The stimulatory effect of IAAla is realized only between 3 to 4 days and corresponds with the climacteric-like peak of ethylene production in control discs (Fig. 8.2). However, in the presence of 50 mM sucrose, IAAla stimulates within a few hours ethylene production that lasts for several days. During this period, acceleration of IAAla hydrolysis was observed (Meir *et al.*, 1985), presumably due to an increase in the activity of the enzyme that hydrolyzes IAAla (Meir, unpublished observations). The role of IAA conjugates in regulating ethylene production in senescing leaves is still unknown and needs to be further explored.

N. Aharoni and J. D. Cohen (unpublished observations) have isolated three different IAA esters from IAA-treated tobacco leaves, two of which were identified by gas chromatography-mass spectrometry (GCMS) as IAA-glucose and IAA-*myo*-inositol. Both these IAA conjugates were found to be more effective than free IAA in stimulating ethylene production in the presence of sucrose (Fig. 8.3). However, it is still questionable whether endogenous IAA conjugates have a role in ethylene production by the

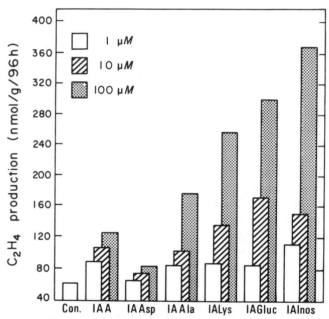

Fig. 8.3. Stimulation of ethylene production by IAA conjugates applied to tobacco leaf discs (N. Aharoni and J. D. Cohen, unpublished observations). IAA conjugates used were IAA-aspartate (IAAsp), IAA-alanine (IAAla), IAA-lysine (IALys), IAA-glucose (IAGluc), and IAA-inositol (IAInos). Con., no treatment.

senescing leaf. In detached tobacco leaf, an increase in free IAA was associated with a rise in ethylene production, both processes being suppressed by the senescence-retarding hormones, gibberellin and kinetin (Even-Chen *et al.*, 1978). A decrease in the extractable level of IAA during leaf senescence may occur by rapid turnover of free IAA in the senescent leaf (Shoji *et al.*, 1951; Sweetser and Swartzfager, 1978; Roberts and Osborne, 1981). In such a situation, IAA conjugates could serve as a source of free IAA that, in turn, may increase ethylene production (Meir *et al.*, 1985).

2. Role of Carbohydrates

Stimulation of ethylene production by different carbohydrates has been found in both petiole and lamina of excised mustard cotyledons (Moore, 1976), in mung bean hypocotyl segments (Colclasure and Yopp, 1976), in leaf discs of tobacco, tomato, bean, and cotton, as well as in attached cotton leaves (Aharoni *et al.*, 1984), and also in mature green tomato fruit (Gross, 1985). This phenomenon in vegetative tissues was ascribed to the toxic effects of galactose (Colclasure and Yopp, 1976) or mannitol (Riov and Yang, 1982c). Sucrose or glucose (5 mM) induce an increase in ethylene production lasting several days (Meir *et al.*, 1984), whereas nonmetabolized carbohydrates, 3-O-methyl glucose (Moore, 1976), and L-glucose (Meir *et al.*, 1984) are ineffective. These results indicate a metabolic rather than "toxic" syndrome for this process. The response of plant tissues to added galactose is different, being more drastic and short lived, suggestive of a toxic effect (Colclasure and Yopp, 1976; Meir *et al.*, 1984). However, this effect may be of physiological significance during senescence, as free galactose might accumulate after its release from cell wall components (Gross, 1985). Besides the stimulatory effect of various carbohydrates on the formation of ACC, which possibly is an IAA-mediated effect, sugars also enhance the formation of ethylene from ACC (Philosoph-Hadas *et al.*, 1985a). The latter effect may be related to an increase in respiratory CO_2.

It is generally accepted that the senescence-inhibitory effect of light in aging leaves is associated with retardation of carbohydrate degradation. In some systems, such as oat leaf segments, exogenous sucrose and glucose inhibit senescence (Thimann *et al.*, 1977). In the light, ethylene biosynthesis may be inhibited (Gepstein and Thimann, 1980), presumably due to a reduced level of internal CO_2 (Yang and Hoffman, 1984). In the attached leaf, there is usually only very transitory accumulation of soluble sugars, since these are transported from the leaf blade during the night. Under certain conditions in which transport and metabolism of sugars are impaired (detachment, stress and senescence), sugars can temporarily accumulate in the leaf blade and accelerate ethylene production. In this respect, free galactose could accumulate in the deteriorated leaf, especially late in senescence, and thereby accelerate ethylene production both in the senescent leaf blade and in the abscission zone cells. Sugars exhibit an opposite effect in cut flowers. Sucrose delays senescence (as in some leaves) and inhibits ethylene production (Mayak and Borochov, 1984), indicating a different mechanism of ethylene regulation by sugars in this system.

IV. ETHYLENE IN FRUIT RIPENING, SENESCENCE, AND LEAF ABSCISSION

A. Ethylene and Fruit Ripening

Studies that implicate ethylene as an enhancer of the senescence syndrome can be roughly divided into two major categories, those demonstrating the effects of exogenous ethylene and those attempting to ascertain the roles for endogenous ethylene. Useful information has emanated from both of these approaches. While it is easier to study effects of the applied hormone, investigations into the role of endogenous ethylene are physiologically more relevant. In this regard, kinetic studies seem more appropriate and critical. Plant tissues have to become physiologically "ready" or sensitive before they can produce or respond to endogenous ethylene.

The association of ethylene with fruit ripening dates back to the report of Gane (1934), who provided direct evidence that ripe apple fruit evolved ethylene. Since then, considerable evidence has accumulated implicating ethylene as a fruit-ripening hormone, coordinating many metabolic processes that are characteristic of ripening (Burg and Burg, 1962). The onset of ripening and senescence coincides, in most cases, with an increase in ethylene production. However, it should be recognized that the role of ethylene in ripening and senescence may involve interactions with other plant hormones (auxins, gibberellins, cytokinins, and abscisic acid) as well (Lieberman, 1979). Fruit ripening and senescence phenomena that are ethylene mediated are associated with: (1) changes in the rate of respiration; (2) changes in membrane permeability; (3) destruction of chlorophyll and synthesis of other pigments; (4) shifts in metabolism of carbohydrates, organic acids, and proteins; (5) induced softening; and (6) development of flavor (Sacher, 1973; Mattoo et al., 1975).

Inhibitors of ethylene biosynthesis (e.g., AVG, aminooxyacetic acid, free radical scavengers) or action (e.g., silver ions), when either sprayed or infiltrated at nontoxic concentrations into the fruit prior to harvest, delay but do not prevent fruit ripening (Wang and Mellenthin, 1977; Bangerth, 1978; Bramlage et al., 1980; Hobson et al., 1984). These studies suggest a direct role for ethylene in fruit ripening. Removal of ethylene by hypobaric storage also results in delaying ripening and senescence of fruits and flowers (Dilley, 1977).

The role of ethylene in fruit ripening is most apparent from the studies on fruit lacking ethylene sensitivity, like the single-gene ripening mutants of tomato, *rin* (ripening inhibitor), *nor* (nonripening), *Nr* (never ripe) (Tigchelaar *et al.*, 1978) and the "alcobaca" mutant (Almeida, 1961). All of these show an extended shelf life, lack the ethylene-enhanced climacteric rise in respiration, do not fully soften, and produce inferior flavor (Herner and Sink, 1973; Buescher *et al.*, 1976; Kopeliovitch *et al.*, 1980, 1982; Lobo *et al.*, 1984; Mutschler, 1984). The insensitivity of these ripening mutants to ethylene has enabled investigators to demarcate between metabolic changes that are induced or coordinated by ethylene during the ripening process and those that are not under the control of ethylene (McGlasson *et al.*, 1975; Mattoo and Vickery, 1977; Hobson, 1980; Jeffrey *et al.*, 1984).

Ethylene production precedes the expression of most ripening-related changes that cause breakdown of cell wall polymers and involve softening of the fruit tissue. By raising antibodies to purified polygalacturonase and cellulase enzymes, it has been possible to isolate specific cDNA clones to their specific messenger RNAs. These studies have demonstrated that regulation of polygalacturonase and cellulase by ethylene is directed at the transcription of their genes, causing *de novo* synthesis of these proteins during ripening (Christoffersen *et al.*, 1984; DellaPenna *et al.*, 1986). Delayed ripening, as evidenced by decreased softening of ethylene-treated avocado fruits when stored in a low oxygen environment, is associated with suppression of cellulase gene expression; both new transcription and accumulation of the protein commence upon return of these fruits to air (Kanellis *et al.*, 1986, 1987). Thus, coordinate-control of transcription and translation of several gene products occurs during fruit ripening. However, some ethylene-mediated responses are much faster than those related to the synthesis of hydrolytic enzymes in fruit, and it remains to be determined if new transcription is required also for the rapid ethylene responses.

During fruit ontogeny, ethylene production is mainly controlled by the level of ACC synthase activity and its product ACC, both being undetectable prior to the onset of ripening (Kende and Boller, 1981; Yang, 1981). Ethylene production by the preclimacteric fruit is also limited by a reduced ability to convert ACC to ethylene (Yang, 1981). McMurchie *et al.* (1972) have hypothesized that ethylene biosynthesis during fruit ripening is controlled by two systems. In system 1, ethylene production is very low and regulates the fruit maturation process, while system 2 is characterized by stimulation of ethylene production by ethylene accompanying ripening. System 1 is active in nonclimacteric fruits and is not a prerequisite for ripening. Other examples of system 1 type include *rin* and *nor* tomato ripening mutants. This concept gives more consideration to the increased tissue sensitivity to ethylene during ripening than to the actual timing of the rise in ethylene production (McGlasson, 1985). The changes in sensitivity to applied ethylene are commonly revealed by examining the response of climacteric fruits during development and senescence. Explanations of this phenomenon led to the concept of critical or threshold hormone concentration for the initiation of ripening (Biale and Young, 1981).

Applied ethylene induces respiratory bursts in fruit. In some fruit, the respiratory burst occurs only when ethylene treatment is given prior to ripening (the climacteric fruits), while in others, continuous presence of the hormone is required and the response is concentration dependent (the nonclimacteric fruits) (Rhodes, 1970). The increased respiration observed upon applying ethylene to fruit has been related to a shift of the cytochrome pathway of electron flow to the alternate cyanide-insensitive pathway (Solomos and Laties, 1974). Associated with the ethylene-mediated respiratory burst is an increase in the level of fructose-1,6-bisphosphate (Solomos and Laties, 1974), which is suggested to function as a regulator of sucrose synthesis in some higher plants (Cseke *et al.*, 1984; Kruger and Beevers, 1985). Ethylene was shown to increase the level of fructose-2,6-bisphosphate in storage tissues, carrot, and potato (Stitt *et al.*, 1986). Nichols and Laties (1985) have tested the linkage between changes in ethylene-induced mRNAs with the respiratory upsurge following exposure of carrot roots to ethylene and oxygen. These studies showed that gene expression, as seen by increases in specific mRNA levels, remains constant over a time period during which the respiration rate decreases. These authors concluded that gene expression and respiration rate are separate, uncoupled events of the ethylene response.

B. Symptoms of Leaf Senescence

Apart from studies that have considered fruit ripening as a specialized model of organ senescence, much of our current knowledge of plant senescence is also derived from studies on leaves. As a developmental process, senescence phenomena seem genetically programmed for optimal biological advantage for the survival of the species (Noodén and Leopold, 1978; Leopold, 1980; Thomas and Stoddart, 1980; Woolhouse, 1982, 1984). For instance, enhanced protein degradation during senescence provides amino acids that are exported from the senescing leaves to other plant parts, where they are reutilized or serve as reserve nutrients. Moreover, in drought conditions or during winter, abscission of leaves helps to reduce the rate of transpiration and, in deciduous trees, avoid freezing injury.

Early biochemical symptoms of leaf senescence include marked degradation of chlorophyll, protein, and RNA. These changes are associated with increases in the activity of hydrolytic enzymes such as RNase, protease, chlorophyllase, peroxidase, amylase, esterases, acid phosphatase, acid invertase, and β-1,3-glucanase (Sacher, 1973; Woolhouse, 1982). Other changes attending leaf senescence include reduction in photosynthetic capacity and a decrease in the respiratory quotient, possibly due to increased consumption of amino acids as respiratory substrates (Noodén, 1980; Thimann, 1980; Thomas and Stoddart, 1980). An increase in the permeability of plastid membranes also occurs early during leaf senescence and seems associated with a decline in membrane lipid content (Noodén and Leopold, 1978).

Symptoms of leaf senescence are induced or aggravated by some environmental conditions such as darkness, short-day photoperiod, heat stress, chilling temperatures, water stress, mineral deprivation, mechanical injuries, and invasion of pathogens. Most of these factors are known to stimulate ethylene production in some tissues (Abeles, 1973; Lieberman, 1979).

C. Exogenous Ethylene and Leaf-Blade Senescence

Ethylene can accelerate many of the physiological changes normally associated with leaf senescence. Although most of the investigations with applied ethylene have been confined to studies of the abscission zone, evidence describing the influence of ethylene on the whole leaf has also appeared. Ethylene treatment markedly enhances loss of protein (Abeles, 1973; Steffens, 1983), starch (Steffens, 1983), and chlorophyll (Burg, 1968; Aharoni and Lieberman, 1979; Gepstein and Thimann, 1981; Kao and Yang, 1983). Exogenous ethylene treatment of aging leaves has long been used commercially for the curing of tobacco and blanching of celery (Abeles, 1973). Tobacco leaves become more responsive to applied ethylene as they age. Ethrel-treated intact cotyledonary leaves of *Gosypium barbadense* senesce rapidly and accumulate a high level of amino acids (Chatterjee and Chatterjee, 1972). Chlorophyll degradation following ethylene treatment of leaves is associated with destruction of the plastid (Goldschmidt, 1980).

Ethylene treatment has been shown to result in increased activities of many hydrolytic enzymes [ATPase, acid phosphatase, α-amylase, catalase, chitinase, β-1,3-glucanase, pectinesterase, peroxidase, and cellulase (Abeles, 1972, 1973)]. Typically, flower tissues respond to ethylene treatment by reduction of RNA content and increased RNase activity and changes in membrane permeability (Abeles, 1973; Lieberman, 1979). A similar response was not found in leaf sections of *Rhoeo discolor* (Sacher and Salminen, 1969) or in bean leaf explants (Abeles, 1973). These results have raised doubts about the regulatory role of ethylene in leaf senescence (Thimann, 1980). However, it is pertinent to note here that most of these studies were conducted with excised leaf tissues. We now know that in many cases excision causes a marked increase in the rate of ethylene production. Since the dose–response curve of ethylene is asymptotic, it is possible that some of the tissues tested in earlier studies contained a saturated ethylene level, thereby rendering exogenous ethylene ineffective. An alternative possibility is that some physiological processes that are known to be ethylene-mediated may also be induced independently by excision or a related stress situation. Possible differences between flower tissue and leaves in their response to exogenous ethylene could also account for the results noted.

Although initial reports showed no effect of exogenous ethylene on the respiration rates of leaf explants and seedlings, other studies have revealed a remarkable stimulatory effect of ethylene on respiration in senescing leaves (Abeles, 1973; Sisler and Pian, 1973). In tobacco leaf discs, application of 10 ppm ethylene increased respiration rate (Aharoni and Lieberman, 1979). In this system, AVG inhibited the rise in respiration and Ag^+ blocked ethylene-stimulated respiration. Excised leaves of the evergreens *Ilex aquifolium* and *Hedera helix* can be maintained in darkness for months without undergoing senescence, but they senesce rapidly following exposure to exogenous ethylene (Woolhouse, 1982). Ethylene treatment was shown to stimulate dark-respiration in detached *Hedera helix* leaves (Solomos, 1983). These studies demonstrate the ability of exogenous ethylene to promote processes characteristic of senescence.

D. Endogenous Ethylene and Leaf-Blade Senescence

Although ethylene is a potent promoter of leaf senescence and abscission (Burg, 1968; Jackson and Osborne, 1970; Abeles, 1973; Beyer, 1975a), relatively little attention has been paid to the processes that occur in the leaf blade prior to leaf abscission. Beyer (1975a) has demonstrated that the initial effect of ethylene in abscission is actually in the leaf blade. The rate of ethylene production by the entire leaf during the course of senescence has been monitored in only a few studies. In some cases (e.g., cotton leaf), ethylene production decreases with leaf age (Hall *et al.*, 1957; Osborne, 1968). In cotton cotyledons, both ethylene production rates and internal levels increase with age, especially as the tissue becomes visibly senescent (Beyer and Morgan, 1971). McGlasson *et al.* (1975) showed that in tomato leaf segments ethylene production as well as respiratory CO_2 decreased and then increased in a pattern similar to the climacteric in fruits and flowers. These studies did not distinguish between the contribution of the petiole and leaf blade to the pattern of ethylene production observed. These studies also did not show whether ethylene production preceded or followed the onset of senescence. Aharoni *et al.* (1979b) studied ethylene production and the rate of respiration in relation to chlorophyll degradation during dark-induced senescence of pinto bean, tobacco, and sugar beet leaf discs. A surge of both ethylene production and respiratory CO_2 was found to coincide with the rapid phase of chlorophyll degradation. Similar patterns in both ethylene production and internal ethylene concentration were also found in attached tobacco and pinto bean leaves that senesced naturally on the plant (Aharoni *et al.*, 1979b). These observations may suggest that the natural rise in ethylene evolution occurs in an attached dicot leaf that is in an advanced stage of senescence. In oat (Gepstein and Thimann, 1981) and rice (Kao and Yang, 1983) leaf segments, however, the increase in ethylene production preceded chlorophyll degradation. Since the increased ethylene production in rice leaves rapidly followed excision, the investigators referred to this as an *excision-related response*. Nevertheless, these cereals, being representatives of short-lived leaves, also senesced rapidly while attached to the parent plant (Thimann, 1980). Debata and Murty (1983) have found a 10-fold increase in endogenous ethylene content during 21 days of maturation and senescence of attached rice leaves.

Although the ontogeny of ethylene production in relation to chlorophyll degradation appears to be dependent on the species (monocots versus dicots), leaf age, and probably also on the experimental system used (i.e., intact versus excised tissue), there seems little doubt that endogenous ethylene regulates a number of events during *early stages* of leaf senescence (Aharoni and Lieberman, 1979; Gepstein and Thimann, 1981; Kao and Yang, 1983). Inhibitor studies confirm the association of ethylene production with loss of chlorophyll in leaf tissues. Ag^+ and CO_2, which reportedly have anti-ethylene effects on growth, senescence, and abscission (Burg and Burg, 1967; Beyer, 1976, 1979), also retard chlorophyll loss (Fig. 8.4, Aharoni and Lieberman, 1979; Goren *et al.*, 1984). Since increasing concentrations of CO_2 and Ag^+ further delay senescence in the presence of AVG, it was concluded that a relatively low level of endogenous ethylene, which may be bound, can also accelerate senescence. During the delay in leaf senescence in the presence of both Ag^+ and CO_2, ethylene production was stimulated. This stimulation was restricted to the first phase of the senescence process (Aharoni and Lieberman, 1979). The climacteric-like rise of ethylene production at later stages of senescence was delayed in the presence of Ag^+ and CO_2. A correlation between the delay in chlorophyll loss and inhibition of ethylene binding in tobacco leaves treated with Ag^+ has also been demonstrated (Goren *et al.*, 1984). Other studies (Gepstein and Thimann, 1981; Kao and Yang, 1983) with oat and rice leaves using inhibi-

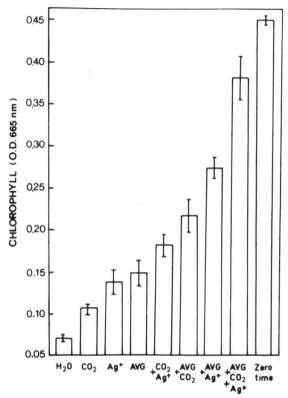

Fig. 8.4. Effect of AVG (0.1 mM), Ag^+, and CO_2 (10%) on chlorophyll retention by tobacco leaf discs allowed to senesce for 6 days in darkness. Ag^+ was applied by floating the discs for 30 minutes on a solution of $AgNO_3$ (10 mg/liter). [Adapted from Aharoni and Lieberman (1979).]

tors of ethylene biosynthesis and action are supportive of the hypothesis that ethylene is an important plant hormone involved in leaf blade senescence.

E. Interactions between Ethylene and Other Plant Hormones in Leaf-Blade Senescence

Conflicting reports on the actual time of rise in ethylene production in relation to the commencement of chlorophyll loss may be explained, in part, by changes in the sensitivity of the tissue (Trewavas, 1981). Endogenous ethylene levels in mature tobacco leaves and in other plant leaves generally range between 0.1 and 0.2 µl/liter (Aharoni, 1978; Aharoni *et al.*, 1979b), while threshold values for an ethylene effect on leaf senescence range between 0.01 and 0.1 µl/liter (Abeles, 1973). Thus, it would seem that the level of endogenous ethylene in a mature leaf is sufficient to induce senescence, provided other factors involved are not limiting. Factors other than the recognition of ethylene by its receptor *in vivo* appear to limit ethylene action because the capacity to bind ethylene exists in a developing leaf. In fact, an increase in *in situ* ethylene binding with leaf development has also been observed (Goren *et al.*, 1984).

Gibberellins and cytokinins have been shown to retard senescence of leaves of a wide range of species, whereas ABA usually accelerates senescence. Endogenous levels of IAA, gibberellins, and cytokinins decline before and with the onset of senescence symptoms (Aharoni and Richmond, 1978; Noodén and Leopold, 1978; Thimann, 1980). It seems likely, therefore, that early during leaf blade senescence, depletion of ethylene-antagonistic hormones, especially cytokinins and gibberellins, occurs. Such an event, in turn, probably releases controls on the production of ABA and ethylene and/or influences the ability of these two hormones to induce senescence. The onset of natural leaf blade senescence, in contrast to leaf abscission, does not appear to be rapid and sudden or triggered by dynamic changes in the level of any one hormone (Aharoni and Richmond, 1978). Rather, it appears to be brought about gradually by an interaction between some or all of the five known plant hormones.

F. Exogenous Ethylene and Changes in the Abscission Zone

Ethylene is a potent accelerator of abscission (Burg, 1968; Jackson and Osborne, 1970; Abeles, 1973; Morgan, 1984). A number of reviews cover most of the anatomical, biochemical, and physiological aspects of abscission (Jacobs, 1979; Sexton and Roberts, 1982; Addicott, 1982, 1983; Sexton and Woolhouse, 1984; Beyer *et al.*, 1984; Morgan, 1984; Reid, 1985). Most of the experimental data on ethylene and abscission are derived from studies with leaves or leaf explants. Several characteristics of leaf abscission, however, are common to the abscission process in other plant parts such as buds, floral structures, and fruits.

The process of abscission occurs as a result of cell wall breakdown in the separation layer formed within the abscission zone. This layer can be visually recognized due to external differences in color or shape. Prior to cell separation, target cells in the abscission zone expand (Osborne, 1979). This expansion of cells is induced by ethylene and repressed by auxin. No hormone other than ethylene seems active in inducing the enlargement of the abscission target cells (Osborne, 1982). Cell enlargement prior to abscission is associated with induction of β-1,4-glucanase (cellulase) activity. Cell wall breakdown leads to reduction of break-strength of the separation layer (Horton and Osborne, 1967). Evidence has been provided suggesting that ethylene also regulates cellulase activity in the cell wall by controlling its secretion from the cytoplasm to the cell wall (Abeles and Leather, 1971). This may explain the necessity of the continuous presence of ethylene to facilitate abscission.

Besides cellulase, another cell wall-degrading enzyme, polygalacturonase, has also been found in abscission zones (Riov, 1974; Tucker *et al.*, 1984). Polygalacturonase is selectively found in the abscission zone region of tomato flowers (Tucker *et al.*, 1984). In the pedicel separation zone of citrus fruit, polygalacturonase activity increases in response to ethylene (Greenberg *et al.*, 1975). Other cell wall-degrading enzymes also increase in response to ethylene (Abeles, 1973), but none of them was exclusively confined to the separation layer.

G. Interactions between Auxin and Ethylene in Abscission

It is the current dogma that, provided the flux of auxin from the leaf blade to the abscission zone region is maintained, the formation of a separation layer is inhibited (Burg, 1968; Abeles, 1973; Jacobs, 1979; Addicott, 1982, 1983; Beyer *et al.*, 1984; Morgan, 1984). Similar conclusions were reached in other experiments with debladed petiole explants to which auxin was applied distally to the abscission zone. Although ethylene promotes abscission, this ability is largely dependent on other factors. Among the most important factors is the hormonal sensitivity of the tissue to ethylene, which, in turn, appears to be controlled by endogenous auxin (Abeles, 1973). In this respect, it is common to divide the abscission process into two stages, as originally proposed by Rubinstein and Leopold (1963) and further elaborated by Abeles and Rubinstein (1964). In stage 1, commencing immediately after excision (or following any other stimulation within the attached leaf), auxin suppresses abscission and opposes the positive effect of ethylene. This stage becomes shorter as the leaf ages or upon ethylene treatment. With time, auxin loses its ability to retard abscission and stage 2 commences. In stage 2, applied auxin or ethylene accelerate the cell separation process.

Ethylene treatment has been found to reduce rates of auxin transport (Morgan *et al.*, 1968; Beyer and Morgan, 1971; Beyer, 1973, 1975a), enhance auxin degradation (Morgan *et al.*, 1968; Ernest and Valdovinos, 1971; Lieberman and Knegt, 1977), and decrease auxin levels (Ernest and Valdovinos, 1971). In several cases, ethylene enhances auxin conjugation (Beyer and Morgan, 1970; Ernest and Valdovinos, 1971; Jacobs, 1979; Riov and Goren, 1979), an effect that may be related to inhibition of auxin transport

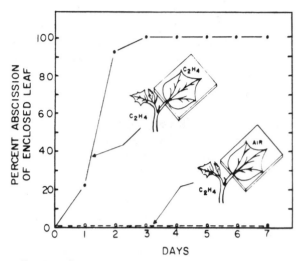

Fig. 8.5. Effect of ethylene (14 μl/liter) on abscission of the
third true leaf of cotton. [From Beyer (1975a), with permission.]

(Beyer and Morgan, 1970). Among all these effects, the inhibition of polar
auxin transport in the petiole by ethylene seems most closely related to the
abscission process. Beyer and Morgan (1971) proposed that ethylene first
reduces the auxin transport capacity of the petioles (as is naturally observed
during normal leaf aging) and then exerts a direct effect in the abscission
zone by causing induction and secretion of specific, cell wall-degrading
enzymes. As shown in Fig. 8.5, abscission occurred only after exposure of
both the blade and petiole to ethylene. Exposure to ethylene of only the leaf
blade does not result in abscission (Beyer, 1975a). Beyer's data may suggest
that the initial effect of applied ethylene is to reduce the amount of auxin
transported out of the blade, possibly by reducing auxin levels and inhibiting auxin transport in the veinal tissues (Beyer, 1975a).

H. Endogenous Ethylene in Abscission

That endogenous ethylene may regulate the induction of abscission is
based on reports that show increased ethylene production rates by pulvinar
explants (Jackson and Osborne, 1970) or by the whole senescent leaf (Beyer
and Morgan, 1971; Jackson *et al.*, 1973; Aharoni *et al.*, 1979b) prior to
abscission. Osborne (1982) reported increases in both ethylene production
and ACC content in the pulvinus tissue of intact bean leaf. This increase
preceded production of cellulase and cell enlargement. Aharoni *et al.*
(1979b) had shown a rise in ethylene production by yellow leaf blades of

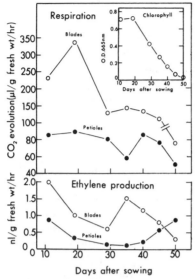

Fig. 8.6. Changes in ethylene production, respiration rate, and chlorophyll
content of leaf discs and petioles cut from
primary pinto bean leaves of various ages.
Beginning of abscission was observed 45
days after sowing. [From Aharoni *et al.*
(1979b), with permission.]

bean 10 days prior to natural abscission, whereas in the petioles the rise in
ethylene production was detected only 5 days before abscission commenced
(Fig. 8.6). Since ACC can move with the phloem (Amrhein *et al.*, 1982), it is
possible that ACC produced in the senescent leaf blade is transported to the
abscission zone, where it is converted to ethylene, thereby stimulating subsequent ethylene production. Although in some cases the climacteric peak
of ethylene production is not observed, in these instances there is enough
ethylene produced endogenously to initiate the cell separation process (Osborne and Sargent, 1976; Morgan and Durham, 1980; Roberts and Osborne,
1981).

Ethylene regulation of abscission is also suggested by experiments in
which inhibitors of either ethylene biosynthesis or action were employed.
Inhibitors of ethylene action (CO_2 and Ag^+) prevent or retard leaf and floral
abscission of many species (Baker, 1983). Likewise, 2,5-norbornadiene, a
competitive inhibitor of ethylene action, decreases the abscission-enhanc-
ing effect of ethylene in citrus leaf explants and also suppresses cellulase
and polygalaturonase activities (Sisler *et al.*, 1985). Similarly, AVG inhibits

266 Autar K. Mattoo and Nehemia Aharoni

abscission of bean explants (Kushad and Poovaiah, 1984) and citrus leaf explants (Sagee et al., 1980). Removal of endogenous ethylene by hypobaric pressure markedly delays abscission of detached *Mélia azédarach* leaflets (Morgan and Durham, 1980), and completely inhibits the decline of break-strength and cellulase activity in bean explants (Sexton and Woolhouse, 1984). Together, these data suggest that endogenous ethylene plays a principal role in regulating leaf abscission. Similar evidence exists for ethylene as a major factor also in the induction of abscission of floral structures and fruit (Section IV, A; see also Morgan, 1984).

I. Interactions between Ethylene and Other Factors in Natural Abscission

Most studies on abscission have been carried out with leaf explants. Therefore, in all such studies the preabscission phase of leaf maintenance cannot be studied (Morgan, 1984). This phase is largely dependent on the interrelationship between the leaf and other plant parts as well as on environmental conditions. The length of the leaf maintenance phase is associated with the retention of threshold levels of the "juvenile" hormones, auxin, cytokinins, and gibberellins. The role of ABA in senescence and abscission is an intriguing issue, and a number of reviews discuss this subject (Jacobs, 1979; Noodén, 1980; Thimann, 1980; Addicott, 1982, 1983; Sacher, 1983; Sexton and Woolhouse, 1984). ABA, when applied to IAA-treated *Coleus* petiole sections, reduces the IAA level and the rate of its basipetal transport, increases IAA conjugation, and accelerates abscission (Chang and Jacobs, 1973). Similar effects have been reported for other species (Addicott, 1982, 1983). Since ABA can antagonize the effects of the juvenile hormones during growth and senescence (Noodén and Leopold, 1978; Lieberman, 1979), it needs to be ascertained if ABA effects are independent or mediated via stimulation of ethylene production (Sagee et al., 1980).

V. MECHANISMS OF ETHYLENE ACTION

The discovery of ethylene as a natural product of plants was made over 30 years ago, and yet we still do not know exactly how this hormone works. Action of ethylene in plants requires oxygen, saturates at about 10 ppm ethylene, and may involve a metal ion (Burg and Burg, 1967; Lieberman, 1979), suggesting a specific receptor-like binding site(s) for the hormone. A progress report on the studies of ethylene action has been published (Sanders et al., 1986). At least two mechanisms of ethylene action have been proposed. The concept of an ethylene receptor protein in the mechanism of ethylene action gained support from studies that demonstrated direct ethylene binding by plant tissues and plant extracts (Sisler, 1984; Hall *et al.*, 1984). The ethylene binding sites were competed for by ethylene analogs, exhibited saturation kinetics, and did not metabolize ethylene. This implies that ethylene binds to its receptor site, which, in turn, switches on ethylene-specific physiological responses. However, the number of ethylene-binding sites in plant tissue seem to decline with advancing age (Thompson *et al.*, 1982; Brown *et al.*, 1986). Moreover, tissues bind ethylene at senescing as well as nonsenescing phases in a nondiscriminatory manner (Goren *et al.*, 1984). Therefore, if an ethylene-binding receptor is indeed involved in ethylene action, the ethylene-responsive tissue may possess another rate-limiting reaction system that must be present to recognize the bound ethylene–receptor complex.

An alternative proposal of Beyer (1975b) relates the action of ethylene to its actual oxidation to CO_2 and incorporation into water-soluble tissue metabolites. However, the low rate of metabolism of ethylene by plant tissue and nonsaturation of this reaction, even at 140 ppm ethylene, do not explain the physiological responses of the hormone that saturate around 10 ppm or lower. Jerie and Hall (1978) found that ethylene is metabolized in *Vicia faba*, but the product they identified was ethylene oxide. Sanders *et al.* (1986) have proposed that metabolism of ethylene provides ethylene oxide, which can then interact at an ethylene-binding site as a modulator, causing a biochemical response. The validity of such a concept needs to be tested by attempting reconstitution *in vitro* of a physiological, ethylene-metabolizing system. It is clear that the mechanism of ethylene action is an open issue, and future experimentation in this area is necessary to provide explanations for the role of ethylene binding and ethylene metabolism in the action of ethylene.

VI. CONCLUSIONS

The primary biosynthetic pathway leading to ethylene in higher plants has been fully elucidated. The key findings include the identification of ACC as an immediate precursor of ethylene and ACC synthase, the enzyme that catalyzes the formation of ACC and MTA from SAM. This enzyme appears to be developmentally regulated and acts as the pacemaker for ethylene biosynthesis. Therefore, the reaction sequence it catalyzes is a key point for metabolic regulation. The availability of ACC limits the biosynthesis of ethylene because, in most instances, the *in situ* enzyme system that oxidizes ACC to ethylene is constitutive, showing only minor fluctuations. Exceptions include some immature or over-ripe fruits and immature carnation flowers. The biochemical signal(s) that regulate the level/activity of ACC synthase and the cellular level through which the signal transduces the physiological effect are not known. Most of the cellular activity that converts ACC to ethylene seems confined to the vacuole. Attempts to demonstrate an EFE activity *in vitro* with characteristics similar to that shown for the *in vivo* system have not been successful. This enzyme system seems labile, membrane-associated, and regulated by ethylene and also, probably, by other hormones. We lack knowledge about the spatial, subcellular location of ACC synthase vis-à-vis EFE. Characterization, identification, and structure elucidation of these two enzymes and malonyl transferase and their genes is expected to unravel the intricate regulatory mechanisms that control the biosynthesis of ethylene. The preparation of monoclonal or polyclonal antibodies to these key enzymes and the isolation of the appropriate genes will undoubtedly provide the tools for engineering these genes and studying structure–function relationships of these enzymes in regulating the senescence of plants. Such probes will also help in identifying the molecular steps at which other plant hormones such as IAA and its conjugates, cytokinins, gibberellins, and ABA, and molecules like phytoalexins, carbohydrates, polyamines, and cations, interact to regulate ethylene biosynthesis.

There is no doubt that ethylene plays a dominant role in the ripening and senescence of fruit and vegetative tissues. Ethylene, as a senescence hormone, appears to interact with and influence the levels of "juvenile" hormones such as IAA as a part of its overall role in regulating metabolic processes during aging and senescence. Although such interactions between plant hormones during ripening and senescence of plants have been described or alluded to, we do not know the exact mechanisms by which ethylene brings about physiological effects, nor do we know the subcellular sites where ethylene acts. It is realized that the action of ethylene is dependent upon its recognition (sensitivity effect) by the plant tissue as well as its accumulation to a threshold level (concentration effect). Certain biochemical events, currently unknown, must take place in the tissue before it can synthesize and/or accumulate a specific threshold level of ethylene and then respond to it. Therefore, we need to develop information on the mechanisms that enable the plant to perceive physiological levels of ethylene and other plant hormones. Such information is crucial for further studies in developing technology to modify the process of hormonal perception and control ripening and senescence in plants.

Some progress has been made in demonstrating *in situ* binding of ethylene to receptor-like molecules. Also, binding of ethylene by lipophilic proteins *in vitro* points to the presence of specific receptors for this hormone. However, apart from the event of ethylene-receptor formation, the perception of such a complex for a physiological response appears to be limited by some, as yet unknown, factors in the tissue. The availability of specific single gene mutants of tomato that do not respond to ethylene and do not ripen offers a valuable tool for analysis of ethylene-specific (ripening-specific) receptors and the associated enzymes, using the tools of molecular biology. A major handicap in the elucidation of hormone-initiated processes has been the lack of a single, biological model system amenable to such studies. We need to develop isogenic mutants and select cell lines that have been genetically altered for a specific ethylene function and biochemically characterize them for missing or altered gene products in an approach towards the dissection of hormone action and regulation of ethylene biosynthesis in plants.

ACKNOWLEDGMENTS

We wish to thank and acknowledge Sonia Philosoph-Hadas and Jeffrey C. Suttle for many helpful comments on the manuscript and for making available their papers prior to publication; James D. Anderson, Jerry D. Cohen, Kenneth C. Gross, Ellen S. Lieberman, and Arkesh M. Mehta for a critical reading of the manuscript; and Ms. Roshni Mehta for composing Fig. 8.1. We thank Ms. Ruth Nash for prompt and careful typing. Some parts of our work cited herein were supported by research grants from BARD I-145-79 and I-773-84 funds.

REFERENCES

Abeles, F. B. (1972). Biosynthesis and mechanisms of action of ethylene. *Annu. Rev. Plant Physiol.* **23**, 259–292.

Abeles, F. B. (1973). "Ethylene in Plant Biology." Academic Press, New York.

Abeles, F. B., and Leather, G. R. (1971). Abscission: control of cellulase secretion by ethylene. *Planta* **97**, 87–91.

Abeles, F. B., and Rubinstein, B. (1964). Regulation of ethylene evolution and leaf abscission by auxin. *Plant Physiol.* **39**, 963–969.

Acaster, M. A., and Kende, H. (1982). Properties and partial purification of ACC synthase. *Plant Physiol.* **72**, 139–145.

Adams, D. O., and Yang, S. F. (1977). Methionine metabolism in apple tissue. *Plant Physiol.* **60**, 892–896.

Adams, D. O., and Yang, S. F. (1979). Ethylene biosynthesis: identification of 1-aminocyclopropane-1-carboxylic acid as an intermediate in the conversion of methionine to ethylene. *Proc. Natl. Acad. Sci. U.S.A.* **76**, 170–174.

Addicott, F. T. (1982). "Abscission." Univ. of California Press, Berkeley.

Addicott, F. T. (1983). Abscisic acid in abscission. *In* "Abscisic Acid" (F. T. Addicott, ed.), pp. 269–300. Praeger, New York.

Aharoni, N. (1978). Relationship between leaf water status and endogenous ethylene in detached leaves. *Plant Physiol.* **61**, 658–662.

Aharoni, N., and Lieberman, M. (1979). Ethylene as a regulator of senescence in tobacco leaf discs. *Plant Physiol.* 64, 801–804.

Aharoni, N., and Richmond, A. E. (1978). Endogenous gibberellin and abscisic acid content as related to senescence of detached lettuce leaves. *Plant Physiol.* 62, 224–228.

Aharoni, N., Anderson, J. D., and Lieberman, M. (1979a). Production and action of ethylene in senescing leaf discs: effect of indoleacetic acid, kinetin, silver ion, and carbon dioxide. *Plant Physiol.* 64, 805–809.

Aharoni, N., Lieberman, M., and Sisler, H. D. (1979b). Patterns of ethylene production in senescing leaves. *Plant Physiol.* 64, 796–800.

Aharoni, N., Philosoph-Hadas, S., and Meir, S. (1984). Control of the biosynthesis of ethylene in senescing tissues. *In* "Ethylene: Biochemical, Physiological and Applied Aspects" (Y. Fuchs and E. Chalutz, eds.), pp. 129–139. Nijoff/Junk, The Hague.

Almeida, J. L. F. (1961). Um novo aspecto de melhoramento do tomate. *Agricultura (Lisbon)* 10, 43–44.

Amrhein, N., Schneebeck, D., Skorupka, H., Tophof, S., and Stockigt, J. (1981). Identification of a major metabolite of the ethylene precursor 1-aminocyclopropane-1-carboxylic acid in higher plants. *Naturwissenschaften* 68, 619–620.

Amrhein, N., Breuing, F., Eberle, J., Skorupka, H., and Tophof, S. (1982). The metabolism of 1-aminocyclopropane-1-carboxylic acid. *In* "Plant Growth Substances" (P. F. Wareing, ed.), pp. 249–258. Academic Press, London.

Anderson, J. D., Lieberman, M., and Stewart, R. N. (1979). Ethylene production by apple protoplasts. *Plant Physiol.* 63, 931–935.

Anderson, J. D., Mattoo, A. K., and Lieberman, M. (1982). Induction of ethylene biosynthesis in tobacco leaf discs by cell wall digesting enzymes. *Biochem. Biophys. Res. Commun.* 107, 588–596.

Apelbaum, A., Burgoon, A. C., Anderson, J. D., Lieberman, M., Ben-Arie, R., and Mattoo, A. K. (1981a). Polyamines inhibit biosynthesis of ethylene in higher plant tissue and fruit protoplasts. *Plant Physiol.* 68, 453–456.

Apelbaum, A., Wang, S. Y., Burgoon, A. C., Baker, J. E., and Lieberman, M. (1981b). Inhibition of the conversion of 1-aminocyclopropane-1-carboxylic acid to ethylene by structural analogs, inhibitors of electron transfer, uncouplers of oxidative phosphorylation, and free radical scavengers. *Plant Physiol.* 67, 74–79.

Baker, J. E. (1983). Preservation of cut flowers. *In* "Plant Growth Regulating Chemicals" (L. Nickell, ed.), Vol. 2, pp. 177–191. CRC Press, Boca Raton, Florida.

Bangerth, F. (1978). The effect of substituted amino-acid on ethylene biosynthesis, respiration, ripening and preharvest drop of apple fruits. *J. Am. Soc. Hortic. Sci.* 103, 401–404.

Ben-Arie, R., Lurie, S., and Mattoo, A. K. (1982). Temperature-dependent inhibitory effects of calcium and spermine on ethylene biosynthesis in apple discs correlate with changes in microsomal membrane viscosity. *Plant Sci. Lett.* 24, 239–247.

Beyer, E. M., Jr. (1973). Abscission: support for a role of ethylene modification of auxin transport. *Plant Physiol.* 52, 1–5.

Beyer, E. M., Jr. (1975a). Abscission: the initial effect of ethylene is in the leaf blade. *Plant Physiol.* 55, 322–327.

Beyer, E. M., Jr. (1975b). $^{14}C_2H_4$: Its incorporation and metabolism by pea seedlings under aseptic conditions. *Plant Physiol.* 56, 273–278.

Beyer, E. M., Jr. (1976). A potent inhibitor of ethylene action in plants. *Plant Physiol.* 58, 268–271.

Beyer, E. M., Jr. (1979). Effect of silver ion, carbon dioxide and oxygen on ethylene action and metabolism. *Plant Physiol.* 63, 169–173.

Beyer, E. M., Jr., and Morgan, P. W. (1970). Effect of ethylene on the uptake, distribution and metabolism of indoleacetic acid-1-^{14}C and 2-^{14}C and naphthaleneacetic acid-1-^{14}C. *Plant Physiol.* 46, 157–162.

Beyer, E. M., Jr., and Morgan, P. W. (1971). Abscission: the role of ethylene modification of auxin transport. *Plant Physiol.* 48, 208–212.

Beyer, E. M., Jr., Morgan, P. W., and Yang, S. F. (1984). Ethylene. *In* "Advanced Plant Physiology" (M. B. Wilkins, ed.), pp. 111–126. Pitman, London.

Biale, J. B., and Young, R. E. (1981). Respiration and ripening in fruits—retrospect and prospect. *In* "Recent Advances in the Biochemistry of Fruit and Vegetables" (J. Friend and M. J. C. Rhodes, eds.), pp. 1–39. Academic Press, London.

Bleecker, A. B., Kenyon, W. H., Somerville, S. C., and Kende, H. (1986). Use of monoclonal antibodies in the purification and characterization of 1-aminocyclopropane-1-carboxylate synthase, an enzyme in ethylene biosynthesis. *Proc. Natl. Acad. Sci. U.S.A.* 83, 7755–7759.

Boller, T., and Kende, H. (1980). Regulation of wound ethylene synthesis in plants. *Nature (London)* 286, 259–260.

Boller, T., Herner, R. C., and Kende, H. (1979). Assay for and enzymatic formation of an ethylene precursor, 1-aminocyclopropane-1-carboxylic acid. *Planta* 145, 293–303.

Bramlage, W. J., Greene, D. W., Autio, W. R., and McLaughlin, J. M. (1980). Effects of aminoethoxyvinylglycine on internal ethylene concentrations and storage of apples. *J. Am. Soc. Hortic. Sci.* 105, 847–851.

Brown, J. H., Legge, R. L., Sisler, E. C., Baker, J. E., and Thompson, J. E. (1986). Ethylene binding to senescing carnation petals. *J. Exp. Bot.* 37, 526–534.

Buescher, R. W., Sistrunk, W. A., Tigchelaar, E. C., and Ng, T. H. (1976). Softening, pectolytic activity and storage life of *rin* and *nor* tomato hybrids. *HortScience* 11, 603–604.

Bufler, G., and Bangerth, F. (1983). Effects of propylene and oxygen on the ethylene producing system of apples. *Physiol. Plant.* 58, 486–492.

Burg, S. P. (1962). The physiology of ethylene formation. *Annu. Rev. Plant Physiol.* 13, 265–302.

Burg, S. P. (1968). Ethylene, plant senescence and abscission. *Plant Physiol.* 43, 1503–1511.

Burg, S. P. (1973). Ethylene in plant growth. *Proc. Natl. Acad. Sci. U.S.A.* 70, 591–597.

Burg, S. P., and Burg, E. A. (1962). Role of ethylene in fruit ripening. *Plant Physiol.* 37, 179–189.

Burg, S. P., and Burg, E. A. (1967). Molecular requirements for the biological activity of ethylene. *Plant Physiol.* 42, 144–152.

Burg, S. P., and Thimann, K. V. (1960). Studies on the ethylene production of apple tissue. *Plant Physiol.* 35, 24–35.

Burns, J. K., and Evensen, K. C. (1986). Ca^{2+} effects on ethylene, carbon dioxide and 1-aminocyclopropane-1-carboxylic acid synthase activity. *Physiol. Plant.* 66, 609–615.

Burroughs, L. F. (1957). 1-Aminocyclopropane-1-carboxylic acid: a new amino acid in perry pears and cider apples. *Nature (London)* 179, 360–361.

Cameron, A. C., Fenton, C. A. L., Yu, Y. B., Adams, D. O., and Yang, S. F. (1979). Increased production of ethylene by plant tissues treated with 1-aminocyclopropane-1-carboxylic acid. *HortScience* 14, 178–180.

Chalutz, E., Mattoo, A. K., Solomos, T., and Anderson, J. D. (1984). Enhancement by ethylene of Cellulysin-induced ethylene production by tobacco leaf discs. *Plant Physiol.* 74, 99–103.

Chalutz, E., Mattoo, A. K., and Fuchs, Y. (1980). Biosynthesis of ethylene: The effect of phosphate. *Plant Cell Environ.* 3, 349–356.

Chang, Y. P., and Jacobs, W. P. (1973). The regulation of abscission and IAA by senescence factor and ABA. *Am. J. Bot.* 60, 10–16.

Chatterjee, S., and Chatterjee, S. K. (1972). Ethrel effect on senescence of cotyledonary leaves of *Gosypium barbadense* L. *Sci. Cult.* 38, 32–34.

Christoffersen, R. E., Tucker, M. L., and Laties, G. G. (1984). Cellulase gene expression in ripening avocado fruit: The accumulation of cellulase mRNA and protein as demonstrated by cDNA hybridization and immuno-detection. *Plant Mol. Biol.* **3**, 385–391.

Cohen, J. D., and Bandurski, R. S. (1982). Chemistry and physiology of the bound auxins. *Annu. Rev. Plant Physiol.* **33**, 403–430.

Colclasure, G. C., and Yopp, J. H. (1976). Galactose-induced ethylene evolution in mung bean hypocotyls: a possible mechanism for galactose retardation of plant growth. *Physiol. Plant* **37**, 298–302.

Cseke, C., Balogh, A., Wong, J. H., Buchanan, B. B., Stitt, M., Herzog, B., and Heldt, H. W. (1984). Fructose-2,6-bisphosphate: a regulator of carbon processing in leaves. *Trends Biochem. Sci.* **12**, 533–535.

Debata, A., and Murty, K. S. (1983). Endogenous ethylene content in rice leaves during senescence. *Indian J. Plant Physiol.* **26**, 425–427.

DellaPenna, D., Alexander, D. C., and Bennett, A. B. (1986). Molecular cloning of tomato fruit polygalacturonase: Analysis of polygalacturonase mRNA levels during ripening. *Proc. Natl. Acad. Sci. U.S.A.* **83**, 6420–6424.

Dilley, D. R. (1977). Hybobaric storage of perishable commodities-fruits, vegetables, flowers, and seedlings. *Acta Hortic.* **62**, 61–70.

Ernest, L. C., and Valdovinos, J. G. (1971). Regulation of auxin levels in *Coleus blumei* by ethylene. *Plant Physiol.* **48**, 402–406.

Even-Chen, Z., Atsmon, D., and Itai, C. (1978). Hormonal aspects of senescence in detached tobacco leaves. *Plant Physiol.* **44**, 377–382.

Even-Chen, Z., Mattoo, A. K., and Goren, R. (1982). Inhibition of ethylene biosynthesis by aminoethoxyvinylglycine and by polyamines shunts label from 3,4-(^{14}C)methionine into spermidine in aged orange peel discs. *Plant Physiol.* **69**, 385–388.

Evensen, K. B. (1984). Calcium effects on ethylene and ethane production and 1-aminocyclopropane-1-carboxylic acid content in potato disks. *Physiol. Plant.* **60**, 125–128.

Ferguson, I. B. (1983). Calcium in plant senescence and fruit ripening. *Plant Cell Environ.* **7**, 477–489.

Fuchs, Y., and Lieberman, M. (1968). Effects of kinetin, IAA, and gibberellin on ethylene production and their interaction in growth of seedlings. *Plant Physiol.* **43**, 2029–2036.

Fuchs, Y., Mattoo, A. K., Chalutz, E., and Rot, I. (1981). Biosynthesis of ethylene in higher plants: The metabolic site of inhibition by phosphate. *Plant Cell Environ.* **4**, 291–295.

Fuhrer, J., Kaur-Sawhney, R., Shih, L. M., and Galston, A. W. (1982). Effects of exogenous 1,3-diaminopropane and spermidine on senescence of oat leaves. II. Inhibition of ethylene biosynthesis and possible mode of action. *Plant Physiol.* **70**, 1597–1600.

Gane, R. (1934). Production of ethylene by some ripening fruit. *Nature (London)* **134**, 1008.

Gepstein, S., and Thimann, K. V. (1980). The effect of light on the production of ethylene from 1-aminocyclopropane-1-carboxylic acid by leaves. *Planta* **149**, 196–199.

Gepstein, S., and Thimann, K. V. (1981). The role of ethylene in the senescence of oat leaves. *Plant Physiol.* **68**, 349–354.

Giovanelli, J., Datko, A. H., Mudd, S. H., and Thompson, G. A. (1983). *In vivo* metabolism of 5'-methylthioadenosine in *Lemna*. *Plant Physiol.* **71**, 319–326.

Goldschmidt, E. E. (1980). Pigment changes associated with fruit maturation and their control. *In* "Senescence in Plants" (K. V. Thimann, ed.), pp. 207–217. CRC Press, Boca Raton, Florida.

Goren, R., Mattoo, A. K., and Anderson, J. D. (1984). Ethylene binding during leaf development and senescence and its inhibition by silver nitrate. *J. Plant Physiol.* **117**, 243–248.

Greenberg, J., Goren, R., and Riov, J. (1975). The role of cellulase and polygalacturonase in abscission of young and mature Shamouti orange fruits. *Physiol. Plant.* **34**, 1–7.

Gross, K. C. (1985). Promotion of ethylene evolution and ripening of tomato fruit by galactose. *Plant Physiol.* 79, 306–307.

Gupta, K., and Anderson, J. D. (1985). Characteristics of ethylene stimulated ethylene biosynthesis by Cellulysin: effect of temperature. *Plant Physiol.* 77, Suppl., 158.

Guranowski, A. B., Chiang, P. K., and Cantoni, G. L. (1981). 5'-Methylthioadenosine nucleosidase. Purification and characterization of the enzyme from *Lupinus luteus* seeds. *Eur. J. Biochem.* 114, 293–299.

Guy, M., and Kende, H. (1984). Conversion of 1-aminocyclopropane-1-carboxylic acid to ethylene by isolated vacuoles of *Pisum sativum* L. *Planta* 160, 281–287.

Hall, M. A., Smith, A. R., Thomas, C. J. R., and Howorth, C. J. (1984). Binding sites for ethylene. *In* "Ethylene: Biochemical, Physiological and Applied Aspects" (Y. Fuchs and E. Chalutz, eds.), pp. 55–63. Nijhoff/Junk, The Hague.

Hall, W. C., Truchelut, G. B., Leinweber, G. L., and Herrero, F. A. (1957). Ethylene production by the cotton plant and its effect under experimental and field conditions. *Physiol. Plant.* 10, 306–317.

Hangarter, R.P., and Good, N. E. (1981). Evidence that IAA conjugates are slow-release sources of free IAA in plant tissues. *Plant Physiol.* 68, 1424–1427.

Hansen, E. (1966). Postharvest physiology of fruits. *Annu. Rev. Plant Physiol.* 17, 459–480.

Herner, R. C., and Sink, K. C. (1973). Ethylene production and respiratory behaviour of the *rin* tomato mutant. *Plant Physiol.* 52, 38–42.

Hobson, G. E. (1980). Effect of the introduction of nonripening mutant genes on the composition and enzyme content of tomato fruits. *J. Sci. Food Agric.* 31, 578–584.

Hobson, G. E., Harman, J. E., and Nichols, R. (1984). Ethylene and the control of tomato fruit ripening. *In* "Ethylene: Biochemical, Physiological, and Applied Aspects" (Y. Fuchs and E. Chalutz, eds.), pp. 281–289. Nijhoff/Junk, The Hague.

Hoffman, N. E., and Yang, S. F. (1982). Enhancement of wound-induced ethylene synthesis by ethylene in preclimacteric cantaloupe. *Plant Physiol.* 69, 317–322.

Hoffman, N. E., Yang, S. F., and McKeon, T. (1982). Identification of 1-(malonylamino)cyclopropane-1-carboxylic acid as a major conjugate of 1-aminocyclopropane-1-carboxylic acid, an ethylene precursor in higher plants. *Biochem. Biophys. Res. Commun.* 104, 765–770.

Horton, R. F., and Osborne, D. J. (1967). Senescence, abscission and cellulase activity in *Phaseolus vulgaris. Nature (London)* 214, 1086–1088.

Imaseki, H. (1983). Regulation of ethylene biosynthesis in auxin-treated plant tissues. *In* "The New Frontiers in Plant Biochemistry" (T. Akazawa, T. Asashi, and H. Imaseki, eds.), pp. 133–151. Nijhoff/Junk, The Hague.

Imaseki, H. (1986). Ethylene. *In* "Chemistry of Plant Hormones" (N. Takahashi, ed.), pp. 249–264. CRC Press, Boca Raton, Florida.

Imaseki, H., Kondo, K., and Watanabe, A. (1975). Mechanisms of cytokinin action on auxin-induced ethylene production. *Plant Cell Physiol.* 16, 777–787.

Jackson, M. B., and Osborne, D. J. (1970). Ethylene, the natural regulator of leaf abscission. *Nature (London)* 225, 1019–1022.

Jackson, M. B., Hartley, C. B., and Osborne, D. J. (1973). Timing abscission in *Phaseolus vulgaris* by controlling ethylene production and sensitivity to ethylene. *New Phytol.* 72, 1251–1260.

Jacobs, W. P. (1979). "Plant Hormones and Development." Cambridge Univ. Press, London and New York.

Jeffrey, D., Smith, C., Goodenough, P., Prosser, I., and Grierson, D. (1984). Ethylene-independent and ethylene-dependent biochemical changes in ripening tomatoes. *Plant Physiol.* 74, 32–38.

Jerie, P. H., and Hall, M. A. (1978). The identification of ethylene oxide as a major metabolite of ethylene in *Vicia faba* L. *Proc. R. Soc. London, Ser. B* 200, 87–94.

Jiao, X. Z., Philosoph-Hadas, S., Su, L.-Y., and Yang, S. F. (1986). The conversion of 1(malon-ylamino)cyclopropane-1-carboxylic acid to 1-aminocyclopropane-1-carboxylic acid in plant tissues. *Plant Physiol.* 81, 637–641.

Jones, J. F., and Kende, H. (1979). Auxin-induced ethylene biosynthesis in subapical stem sections of etiolated seedlings of *Pisum sativum* L. *Planta* 146, 649–656.

Kanellis, A. K., Solomos, T., and Mattoo, A. K. (1986). Interactions between O_2 concentrations and enzymatic activities in the course of fruit ripening. *HortScience* 21, 811.

Kanellis, A.K., Solomos,T., Mehta, A. M., and Mattoo, A. K. (1987). Decreased cellulase activity in avocado fruit subjected to 2.5% O_2 correlates with lowered cellulase transcript level. *Plant Physiol.* 83, Suppl., 126.

Kang, B. G., Newcomb, W., and Burg, S.P. (1971). Mechanisms of auxin-induced ethylene production. *Plant Physiol.* 47, 504–509.

Kao, C. H., and Yang, S. F. (1983). Role of ethylene in the senescence of detached rice leaves. *Plant Physiol.* 73, 881–885.

Kende, H., and Boller, T. (1981). Wound ethylene and 1-aminocyclopropane-1-carboxylate synthase in ripening tomato fruit. *Planta* 151, 476–481.

Kionka, C., and Amrhein, N. (1984). The enzymatic malonylation of 1-aminocyclopropane-1-carboxylic acid in homogenates of mung-bean hypocotyls. *Planta* 162, 226–235.

Knee, M. (1985). Metabolism of 1-aminocyclopropane-1-carboxylic acid during apple fruit development. *J. Exp. Bot.* 36, 670–678.

Konze, J. R., and Kende, H. (1979). Interaction of methionine and selenomethionine with methionine adenosyltransferase and ethylene-generating systems. *Plant Physiol.* 63, 507–510.

Konze, J. R., Schilling, N., and Kende, H. (1978). Enhancement of ethylene formation by selenoamino acids. *Plant Physiol.* 62, 397–401.

Konze, J. R., Jones, J. F., Boller,T., and Kende, H. (1980). Effect of 1-aminocyclopropane-1-car-boxylic acid on the production of ethylene in senescing flowers of *Ipomea tricolor* cav. *Plant Physiol.* 66, 566–571.

Kopeliovitch, E., Mizrahi, Y., Rabinowitch, H. D., and Kedar, N. (1980). Physiology of the tomato mutant *Alcobaca. Physiol. Plant.* 48, 307–311.

Kopeliovitch, E., Mizrahi, Y., Rabinowitch, H. D., and Kedar, N. (1982). Effect of the fruit ripening mutant genes *rin* and *nor* on the flavor of tomato fruit. *J. Am. Soc. Hortic. Sci.* 107, 361–364.

Kruger, N. H., and Beevers, H. (1985). Synthesis and degradation of fructose-2,6-bisphosphate in endosperm of castor bean seedlings. *Plant Physiol.* 77, 358–364.

Kushad, M. M., and Poovaiah, B. W. (1984). Deferral of senescence and abscission by chemical inhibition of ethylene synthesis and action in bean explants. *Plant Physiol.* 76, 293–296.

Kushad, M. M., Richardson, D. G., and Ferro, A. J. (1983). Intermediates in the recycling of 5-methylthioribose to methionine in fruits. *Plant Physiol.* 73, 257–261.

Kushad, M. M., Richardson, D. G., and Ferro, A. J. (1985). 5′-Methylthioadenosine nucleosidase and 5-methylthioribose kinase activities and ethylene production during tomato fruit development and ripening. *Plant Physiol.* 79, 525–529.

Lau, O. L., and Yang, S. F. (1973). Mechanisms of a synergistic effect of kinetin on auxin-induced ethylene production: suppression of auxin conjugation. *Plant Physiol.* 51, 1011–1014.

Lau, O. L., and Yang, S. F. (1974). Synergistic effect of calcium and kinetin on ethylene production by the mung bean hypocotyl. *Planta* 118, 1–6.

Legge, R. L., Thompson, J. E., Baker, J. E., and Lieberman, M. (1982). The effect of calcium on the fluidity and phase properties of microsomal membranes isolated from post-climacteric golden delicious apple. *Plant Cell Physiol.* 23, 161–169.

Leopold, A. C. (1980). Aging and senescence in plant development. *In* "Senescence in Plants" (K. V. Thimann, ed.), pp. 2–12. CRC Press, Boca Raton, Florida.

Lieberman, M. (1979). Biosynthesis and action of ethylene. *Annu. Rev. Plant Physiol.* **30**, 533–591.

Lieberman, M., and Knegt, E. (1977). Influence of ethylene on IAA concentration in etiolated pea epicotyl tissue. *Plant Physiol.* **60**, 475–477.

Lieberman, M., and Kunishi, A. T. (1968). Origins of ethylene in plants. *In* "Biochemical Regulation in Diseased Plants or Injury" (T. Hirai, Z. Hidoka, and I. Uritani, eds.), pp. 165–179. Phytopathol. Soc. Jpn., Tokyo.

Lieberman, M., and Wang, S. Y. (1982). Influence of calcium and magnesium on ethylene production by apple tissue slices. *Plant Physiol.* **69**, 1150–1155.

Lieberman, M., Kunishi, A. T., Mapson, L. W., and Wardale, D. A. (1966). Stimulation of ethylene production in apple tissue slices by methionine. *Plant Physiol.* **41**, 376–382.

Liu, Y., Hoffman, N. E., and Yang, S. F. (1983). Relationship between the malonylation of 1-aminocyclopropane-1-carboxylic acid and D-amino acids in mung bean hypocotyls. *Planta* **158**, 437–441.

Liu, Y., Su, L.-Y., and Yang, S. F. (1984). Stereoselectivity of 1-aminocyclopropane carboxylate malonyltransferase toward stereoisomers of 1-amino-2-ethylcyclopropanecarboxylic acid. *Arch. Biochem. Biophys.* **235**, 319–325.

Liu, Y., Hoffman, N. E., and Yang, S. F. (1985a). Promotion by ethylene of the capability to convert 1-aminocyclopropane-1-carboxylic acid to ethylene in preclimacteric tomato and cantaloupe fruits. *Plant Physiol.* **77**, 407–411.

Liu, Y., Hoffman, N. E., and Yang, S. F. (1985b). Ethylene-promoted malonylation of 1-amino-cyclopropane-1-carboxylic acid participates in autoinhibition of ethylene synthesis in grapefruit flavedo discs. *Planta* **164**, 565–568.

Lobo, M., Bassett, M. J., and Hannah, L. C. (1984). Inheritance and characterization of the fruit ripening mutation in "Alcobaca" tomato. *J. Am. Soc. Hortic. Sci.* **109**, 741–745.

Lurssen, K., Naumann, K., and Schroder, R. (1979). 1-Aminocyclopropane-1-carboxylic acid —an intermediate of the ethylene biosynthesis in higher plants. *Z. Pflanzenphysiol.* **92**, 285–294.

McGlasson, W. B. (1985). Ethylene and fruit ripening. *HortScience* **20**, 51–54.

McGlasson, W. B., Poovaiah, B. W., and Dostal, H. C. (1975). Ethylene production in aging leaf segments and in disks of fruit tissue of normal and mutant tomatoes. *Plant Physiol.* **56**, 547–549.

McKeon, T. A., Hoffman, N. E., and Yang, S. F. (1982). The effect of plant hormone pre-treatments on ethylene production and synthesis of 1-aminocyclopropane-1-carboxylic acid in water-stressed wheat leaves. *Planta* **155**, 437–443.

McKeon, T. A., and Yang, S. F. (1983). A comparison of the conversion of 1-amino-2-ethylcyclopropane-1-carboxylic acid stereoisomers to 1-butene by pea epicotyls and by a cell-free system. *Planta* **160**, 84–87.

McMurchie, E. J., McGlasson, W. B., and Eaks, I. L. (1972). Treatment of fruit with propylene gives information about the biogenesis of ethylene. *Nature (London)* **237**, 497–501.

Manning, K. (1985). The ethylene forming enzyme system in carnation flowers. *Proc. Easter Sch. Agric. Sci., 39th, Univ. Nottingham, (Ethylene Plant Dev.)* pp. 83–92.

Mattoo, A. K., and Anderson, J. D. (1984). Wound-induced increase in 1-aminocyclopropane-1-carboxylate synthase activity: regulatory aspects and membrane association of the enzyme. *In* "Ethylene: Bioichemical, Physiological, and Applied Aspects" (Y. Fuchs and E. Chalutz, eds.), pp. 139–147. Nijhoff/Junk, The Hague.

Mattoo, A. K., and Lieberman, M. (1977). Localization of the ethylene-synthesizing system in apple tissue. *Plant Physiol.* **60**, 794–799.

Mattoo, A. K., and Lieberman, M. (1982). Role of silver ions in controlling senescence and conversion of 1-aminocyclopropane-1-carboxylic acid to ethylene. *Plant Physiol.* **69**, Suppl., 18.

Mattoo, A. K., and Vickery, R. S. (1977). Subcellular distributions of isoenzymes in fruits of a normal cultivar of tomato and the *rin* mutant at two stages of development. *Plant Physiol.* **60**, 496–498.

Mattoo, A. K., Murata, T., Pantastico, E. B., Chachin, K., Ogata, K., and Phan, C. T. (1975). Chemical changes during ripening and senescence. In "Postharvest Physiology: Handling and Utilization of Tropical and Subtropical Fruits and Vegetables" (E. B. Pantastico, ed.), pp. 103–127. AVI, Westport, Connecticut.

Mattoo, A. K., Baker, J. E., Chalutz, E., and Lieberman, M. (1977). Effect of temperature on the ethylene-synthesizing systems in apple, tomato and *Penicillium digitatum*. *Plant Cell Physiol.* **18**, 715–719.

Mattoo, A. K., Chalutz, E., and Lieberman, M. (1979). Effect of lipophilic and water soluble membrane probes on ethylene synthesis in apple and *Penicillium digitatum*. *Plant Cell Physiol.* **20**, 1097–1106.

Mattoo, A. K., Adams, D. O., Patterson, G. W., and Lieberman, M. (1982–1983). Inhibition of 1-aminocyclopropane-1-carboxylic acid synthase by phenothiazines. *Plant Sci. Lett.* **28**, 173–179.

Mattoo, A. K., Baker, J. E., and Moline, H. E. (1984). Different mechanisms in *Spirodela* and *Nicotiana* of copper-induced ethylene production. *Plant Physiol.* **75**, Suppl., 185.

Mattoo, A. K., Baker, J. E., and Moline, H. E. (1986). Induction by copper ions of ethylene production in *Spirodela oligorrhiza*: Evidence for a pathway independent of 1-aminocyclopropane-1-carboxylic acid. *J. Plant Physiol.* **123**, 193–202.

Mayak, S., and Borochov, A. (1984). Nonosmotic inhibitions by sugars of the ethylene-forming activity associated with microsomal membranes from carnation petals. *Plant Physiol.* **76**, 191–195.

Mayak, S., and Dilley, D. R. (1976). Regulation of senescence in carnation (*Dianthus caryophyllus*). Effect of abscisic acid and carbon dioxide on ethylene production. *Plant Physiol.* **58**, 663–665.

Mayne, R. G., and Kende, H. (1986). Ethylene biosynthesis in isolated vacuoles of *Vicia faba* L.—requirement for membrane integrity. *Planta* **167**, 159–165.

Mehta, A. M., Mattoo, A. K., Jordan, R., Sloger, M., and Anderson, J. D. (1987). ACC synthase from tomato fruit: Identification, general occurrence and developmental regulation using monoclonal antibodies. *Plant Physiol.* **83**, Suppl., 114.

Meir, S., Philosoph-Hadas, S., and Aharoni, N. (1984). Role of IAA conjugates in inducing ethylene production by tobacco leaf discs. *J. Plant Growth Regul.* **3**, 169–181.

Meir, S., Philosoph-Hadas, S., Epstein, E., and Aharoni, N. (1985). Carbohydrates stimulate ethylene production in tobacco leaf discs. I. Interaction with auxin and the relation to auxin metabolism. *Plant Physiol.* **78**, 131–138.

Moore, K. G. (1976). Effects of sugars on ethylene production by excised *sinapis* cotyledons. *Ann. Bot.* **40**, 543–549.

Mor, Y., Halevy, A. H., Spiegelstein, H., and Mayak, S. (1985). The site of 1-aminocyclopropane-1-carboxylic acid synthesis in senescing carnation petals. *Physiol. Plant.* **65**, 196–202.

Morgan, P. W. (1984). Is ethylene the natural regulator of abscission. In "Ethylene: Biochemical, Physiological and Applied Aspects" (Y. Fuchs and E. Chalutz, eds.), pp. 231–240. Nijhoff/Junk, The Hague.

Morgan, P. W., and Durham, J. I. (1980). Ethylene production and leaflet abscission in *Melia azedarach* L. *Plant Physiol.* **66**, 88–92.

Morgan, P. W., Beyer, E. M., Jr., and Gausman, H. W. (1968). Ethylene effects on auxin physiology. *In* "Biochemistry and Physiology of Plant Growth Substances" (F. Wightman and G. Setterfield, eds.), pp. 1255–1273. Rung Press, Ottawa.

Murr, D. P., and Yang, S. F. (1975). Inhibition of *in vivo* conversion of methionine to ethylene by L-canaline and 2,4-dinitrophenol. *Plant Physiol.* 55, 79–82.

Mutschler, M. (1984). Ripening and storage characteristics of the "Alcobaca" ripening mutant in tomato. *J. Am. Soc. Hortic. Sci.* 109, 504–507.

Nakajima, N., and Imaseki, H. (1986). Purification and properties of 1-aminocyclopropane-1-carboxylate synthase of mesocarp of *Cucurbita maxima* Duch Fruits. *Plant Cell Physiol.* 27, 969–980.

Nichols, S. E., and Laties, G. G. (1985). Differential control of ethylene-induced gene expression and respiration in carrot roots. *Plant Physiol.* 77, 753–757.

Noodén, L. D. (1980). Senescence in the whole plant. *In* "Senescence in Plants" (K. V. Thimann, ed.), pp. 220–258. CRC Press, Boca Raton, Florida.

Noodén, L. D., and Leopold, A. C. (1978). Phytohormones and the endogenous regulation of senescence and abscission. *In* "Phytohormones and Related Compounds: A Comprehensive Treatise" (D. S. Latham, P. B. Goodwin, and T. J. V. Higgins, eds.), Vol. 2, pp. 329–369. Elsevier/North-Holland, Amsterdam.

Odawara, S., Watanabe, A., and Imaseki, H. (1977). Involvement of cellular membrane in regulation of ethylene production. *Plant Cell Physiol.* 18, 569–575.

Osborne, D. J. (1968). Ethylene as a plant hormone. *In* "Plant Growth Regulators," Monogr. No. 31, pp. 236–249. Soc. Chem. Ind., London.

Osborne, D. J. (1979). Target cells-new concepts for plant regulation in horticulture. *Sci. Hortic. (Canterbury, Engl.)* 30, 1–13.

Osborne, D. J. (1982). The ethylene regulation of cell growth in specific target tissues of plants. *In* "Plant Growth Substances" (P. F. Wareing, ed.), pp. 279–290. Academic Press, London.

Osborne, D. J., and Sargent, J. A. (1976). The positional differentiation of abscission zones during the development of leaves of *Sambucus nigra* and the response of cells to auxin and ethylene. *Planta* 132, 197–204.

Owens, L. D., Lieberman, M., and Kunishi, A. T. (1971). Inhibition of ethylene production by rhizobitoxine. *Plant Physiol.* 48, 1–4.

Peiser, G. D., Wang, T.-T., Hoffman, N. E., Yang, S. F., Liu, H.-W., and Walsh, C. T. (1984). Formation of cyanide from carbon 1 of 1-aminocyclopropane-1-carboxylic acid during its conversion to ethylene. *Proc. Natl. Acad. Sci. U.S.A.* 81, 3059–3063.

Philosoph-Hadas, S., Meir, S., and Aharoni, N. (1985a). Carbohydrates stimulate ethylene production in tobacco leaf discs: II. Sites of stimulation in the ethylene biosynthesis pathway. *Plant Physiol.* 78, 139–143.

Philosoph-Hadas, S., Meir, S., and Aharoni, N. (1985b). Autoinhibition of ethylene production in tobacco leaf discs: Enhancement of 1-aminocyclopropane-1-carboxylic acid conjugation. *Physiol. Plant.* 63, 431–437.

Pirrung, M. C. (1983). Ethylene biosynthesis. 2. Stereochemistry of ripening, stress and model reactions. *J. Am. Chem. Soc.* 105, 7207–7209.

Pratt, H. K., and Goeschl, J. D. (1969). Physiological roles of ethylene in plants. *Annu. Rev. Plant Physiol.* 20, 541–584.

Ramalingam, K., Lee, K.-M., Woodard, R. W., Bleecker, A. B., and Kende, H. (1985). Stereochemical course of the reaction catalyzed by the pyridoxal phosphate-dependent enzyme 1-aminocyclopropane-1-carboxylate synthase. *Proc. Natl. Acad. Sci. U.S.A.* 82, 7820–7824.

Reid, M. S. (1985). Ethylene and abscission. *HortScience* 20, 45–50.

Rhodes, M. J. C. (1970). The climacteric and ripening in fruits. *In* "The Biochemistry of Fruits and Their Products" (A. C. Hulme, ed.), pp. 520–533. Academic Press, London.

Riov, J. (1974). A polygalacturonase from citrus leaf explants. *Plant Physiol.* 53, 12–16.

Riov, J., and Goren, R. (1979). Effect of ethylene on auxin transport and metabolism in midrib sections in relation to leaf abscission of woody plants. *Plant Cell Environ.* **2**, 83–89.

Riov, J., and Yang, S. F. (1982a). Autoinhibition of ethylene production in citrus peel discs. Suppression of 1-aminocyclopropane-1-carboxylic acid synthesis. *Plant Physiol.* **69**, 687–690.

Riov, J., and Yang, S. F. (1982b). Effects of exogenous ethylene on ethylene production in citrus leaf tissue. *Plant Physiol.* **70**, 136–141.

Riov, J., and Yang, S. F. (1982c). Stimulation of ethylene production in citrus leaf discs by mannitol. *Plant Physiol.* **70**, 142–146.

Roberts, D. R., Walker, M. A., Thompson, J. E., and Dumbroff, E. B. (1984). The effects of inhibitors of polyamine and ethylene biosynthesis on senescence, ethylene production and polyamine levels in cut carnation flowers. *Plant Cell Physiol.* **25**, 315–322.

Roberts, J. A., and Osborne, D. J. (1981). Auxin and the control of ethylene production during the development and senescence of leaves and fruits. *J. Exp. Bot.* **32**, 875–887.

Rubinstein, B., and Leopold, A. C. (1963). Analysis of the auxin control of bean leaf abscission. *Plant Physiol.* **38**, 262–267.

Sacher, J. A. (1973). Senescence and postharvest physiology. *Annu. Rev. Plant Physiol.* **24**, 197–224.

Sacher, J. A. (1983). Abscisic acid in leaf senescence. In "Abscisic Acid" (F. T. Addicott, ed.), pp. 479–522. Praeger, New York.

Sacher, J. A., and Salminen, S.O. (1969). Comparative studies of effect of auxin and ethylene on permeability and synthesis of RNA and protein. *Plant Physiol.* **44**, 1371–1377.

Sagee, O., Goren, R., and Riov, J. (1980). Abscission of citrus leaf explants. Interrelationships of ABA, ethylene and hydrolytic enzymes. *Plant Physiol.* **66**, 750–753.

Sakai, S., and Imaseki, H. (1971). Auxin-induced ethylene production by mung bean hypocot- segments. *Plant Cell Physiol.* **12**, 349–359.

Saltviet, M. E., and Dilley, D. R. (1978). Rapidly induced wound ethylene from excised seg- ments of etiolated *Pisum sativum* L., cv. Alaska. II. Oxygen and temperature dependency. *Plant Physiol.* **61**, 675–679.

Sanders, I. O., Smith, A. R., and Hall, M. A. (1986). Ethylene metabolism and action. *Physiol. Plant.* **66**, 723–726.

Sandmann, G., and Boger, P. (1980). Copper-mediated lipid peroxidation processes in photo- synthetic membranes. *Plant Physiol.* **66**, 797–800.

Satoh, S., and Esashi, Y. (1982). Effects of α-aminoisobutyric acid and D- and L-amino acids on ethylene production and content of 1-aminocyclopropane-1-carboxylic acid in cotyledonary segments of cocklebur seeds. *Physiol. Plant.* **54**, 147–152.

Sexton, R., and Roberts, J. A. (1982). Cell biology of abscission. *Annu. Rev. Plant Physiol.* **33**, 133–162.

Sexton, R., and Woolhouse, H. W. (1984). Senescence and abscission. In "Advanced Plant Physiology" (M. B. Wilkins, ed.), pp. 469–497. Pitman, London.

Shoji, K., Addicott, F. T., and Swets, W. A. (1951). Auxin in relation to leaf blade abscission. *Plant Physiol.* **26**, 189–191.

Sisler, E. C. (1984). Distribution and properties of ethylene-binding component from plant tissue. In "Ethylene: Biochemical, Physiological and Applied Aspects" (Y. Fuchs and E. Chalutz, eds.), pp. 45–54. Nijhoff/Junk, The Hague.

Sisler, E. C., and Pian, A. (1973). Effect of ethylene and cyclic olefins on tobacco leaves. *Tob. Sci.* **17**, 68.

Sisler, E. C., Goren, R., and Huberman, M. (1985). Effect of 2,5-norbornadiene on abscission and ethylene production in citrus leaf explants. *Physiol. Plant.* **63**, 114–120.

Slocum, R. D., Kaur-Sawhney, R., and Galston, A. W. (1984). The physiology and biochemistry of polyamines in plants. *Arch. Biochem. Biophys.* **235**, 283–303.

Solomos, T. (1983). Respiration and energy metabolism in senescing plant tissues. *In* "Post-Harvest Physiology and Crop Preservation" (M. Lieberman, ed.), pp.61–98. Plenum, New York.

Solomos, T., and Laties, G. G. (1974). Similarities between the actions of ethylene and cyanide in initiating the climacteric and ripening of avocados. *Plant Physiol.* **54**, 506–511.

Steffens, G. L. (1983). Tobacco leaf yellowing and curing agents. *In* "Plant Growth Regulating Chemicals" (L. G. Nickell, ed.), Vol. 1, pp. 82–88. CRC Press, Boca Raton, Florida.

Stitt, M., Czeke, C., and Buchanan, B. (1986). Ethylene-induced increase in fructose-2,6-bisphosphate in plant storage tissues. *Plant Physiol.* **80**, 246–248.

Su, L.-Y., Liu, Y., and Yang, S. F. (1985). Relationship between 1-aminocyclopropane carboxylate malonyltransferase and D-amino acid malonyltransferase. *Phytochemistry* **24**, 1141–1145.

Suttle, J. C. (1981). Effect of polyamines on ethylene production. *Phytochemistry* **20**, 1477–1480.

Suttle, J. C. (1986). Cytokinin-induced ethylene biosynthesis in non-senescing cotton leaves. *Plant Physiol.* **82**, 930–935.

Sweetser, P. B., and Swartzfager, D. G. (1978). Indole-3-acetic acid levels of plant tissue as determined by a new high performance liquid chromatographic method. *Plant Physiol.* **61**, 254–258.

Thimann, K. V. (1980). The senescence of leaves. *In* "Senescence in Plants" (K. V. Thimann, ed.), pp. 85–115. CRC Press, Boca Raton, Florida.

Thimann, K. V., Tetley, R. M., and Krivak, B. M. (1977). Metabolism of oat leaves during senescence. V. Senescence in light. *Plant Physiol.* **59**, 448–454.

Thomas, H., and Stoddart, J. L. (1980). Leaf senescence. *Annu. Rev. Plant Physiol.* **31**, 83–111.

Thompson, J. E., Mayak, S., Shinitzky, M., and Halevy, A. H. (1982). Acceleration of membrane senescence in cut carnation flowers by treatment with ethylene. *Plant Physiol.* **69**, 859–863.

Tigchelaar, E. C., McGlasson, W. B., and Buescher, R. W. (1978). Genetic regulation of tomato fruit ripening. *HortScience* **13**, 508–518.

Trewavas, A. (1981). How do plant growth substances work. *Plant Cell Environ.* **4**, 203–228.

Tucker, G. A., Schindler, C. B., and Roberts, J. A. (1984). Flower abscission in mutant tomato plants. *Planta* **160**, 164–167.

Vahatalo, M. L., and Virtanen, A. I. (1957). A new cyclic α-aminocarboxylic acid in berries of crowberry. *Acta Chem. Scand.* **11**, 741–743.

Vendrell, M., and McGlasson, W. B. (1971). Inhibition of ethylene production in banana fruit tissue by ethylene treatment. *Aust. J. Biol. Sci.* **24**, 885–895.

Wang, C. Y., and Mellenthin, W. M. (1977). Effect of aminoethoxy analog of rhizobitoxine on ripening of pears. *Plant Physiol.* **59**, 546–549.

Wang, S. Y., Adams, D. O., and Lieberman, M. (1982). Recycling of 5'-methylthioadenosine ribose carbon into methionine in tomato tissue in relation to ethylene production. *Plant Physiol.* **70**, 117–121.

Woolhouse, H. W. (1982). Leaf senescence. *In* "The Molecular Biology of Plant Development" (H. Smith and D. Grierson, eds.), Bot. Monogr., Vol. 18, pp. 256–281. Blackwell, Oxford.

Woolhouse, H. W. (1984). The biochemistry and regulation of senescence in chloroplasts. *Can. J. Bot.* **62**, 2934–2942.

Yang, S. F. (1974). The biochemistry of ethylene biogenesis and metabolism. *Recent Adv. Phytochem.* **7**, 131–164.

Yang, S. F. (1981). Biosynthesis of ethylene and its regulation. *In* "Recent Advances in the Biochemistry of Fruit and Vegetables" (J. Friend and M. J. C. Rhodes, eds.), pp. 89–106. Academic Press, London.

Yang, S. F., and Hoffman, N. E. (1984). Ethylene biosynthesis and its regulation in higher plants. *Annu. Rev. Plant Physiol.* **35**, 155–189.

Yang, S. F., Ku, H. S., and Pratt, H. K. (1966). Photochemical production of ethylene from methionine and its analogues in the presence of flavin mononucleotide. *J. Biol. Chem.* **242**, 5274–5280.

Yoshii, H., and Imaseki, H. (1981). Biosynthesis of auxin-induced ethylene: effects of indole-3-acetic acid, benzyladenine and abscisic acid on endogenous levels of 1-aminocyclopropane-1-carboxylic acid (ACC) and ACC synthase. *Plant Cell Physiol.* **22**, 369–379.

Yoshii, H., and Imaseki, H. (1982). Regulation of auxin-induced ethylene biosynthesis. Repression of inductive formation of 1-aminocyclopropane-1-carboxylate synthase of ethylene. *Plant Cell Physiol.* **23**, 639–649.

Yu, Y. B., and Yang, S. F. (1979). Auxin-induced ethylene production and its inhibition by aminoethoxyvinylglycine and cobalt ion. *Plant Physiol.* **64**, 1074–1077.

Yu, Y. B., and Yang, S. F. (1980). Biosynthesis of wound ethylene. *Plant Physiol.* **66**, 281–285.

Yu, Y. B., Adams, D.O., and Yang, S. F. (1979a). Regulation of auxin-induced ethylene production in mung bean hypocotyls. Role of 1-aminocyclopropane-1-carboxylic acid. *Plant Physiol.* **63**, 589–590.

Yu, Y. B., Adams, D. O., and Yang, S. F. (1979b). 1-Aminocyclopropane-carboxylate synthase, a key enzyme in ethylene biosynthesis. *Arch. Biochem. Biophys.* **198**, 280–286.

Yung, K. H., Yang, S. F., and Schlenk, F. (1982). Methionine synthesis from 5-methylthioribose in apple tissue. *Biochem. Biophys. Res. Commun.* **104**, 771–777.

Zeroni, M., Galil, J., and Ben-Yehoshua, S. (1976). Autoinhibition of ethylene formation in nonripening stages of the fruit of sycamore fig (*Ficus sycomorus* L.). *Plant Physiol.* **57**, 647–650.

Cytokinins and Senescence

Johannes Van Staden and
Elizabeth L. Cook
UN/CSIR Research Unit for Plant Growth and Development
Department of Botany
University of Natal
Pietermaritzburg
Republic of South Africa

Larry D. Noodén
Biology Department
University of Michigan
Ann Arbor, Michigan

I. INTRODUCTION

Cytokinins play an important role in controlling many of the processes that contribute to plant senescence (Noodén and Leopold, 1978; Noodén, 1980; Thimann, 1980). This view originated mainly as a result of two lines of research. First, the classical experiments of Richmond and Lang (1957) showed that the application of Kn[1] to detached leaves delays their senescence. Second, rooting and root exudates were found to extend leaf longevity. Many early investigators (see Molisch, 1938; Mothes, 1960) showed that root formation greatly increased the life of excised leaves, and the studies of Kulaeva (1962) indicated that Kn-like senescence-retarding factors were produced by the roots. Today, it is accepted that cytokinins are ubiquitous plant constituents and that they participate in a wide range of plant developmental processes. In particular, these hormones have been implicated in the maintenance of chlorophyll, protein, and RNA levels (Richmond and Lang, 1957), all of which decline during senescence. This chapter briefly summarizes some important aspects of cytokinin biochemistry and then examines the observations that connect cytokinins with senescence processes in different plant organs.

II. CYTOKININ BIOCHEMISTRY AND PHYSIOLOGY

Cytokinin biochemistry and physiology have been reviewed extensively elsewhere (Letham, 1967a, 1978; Helgeson, 1968; Skoog and Armstrong, 1970; Kende, 1971; Hall, 1973; Van Staden and Davey, 1979; Letham and Palni, 1983; Koshimizu and Iwamura, 1986). Therefore, this section will not provide a detailed outline of the literature pertaining to cytokinins in general but a synopsis of the information most pertinent to senescence. Despite a great deal of research, the mode(s) of cytokinin action remains obscure, although they may promote or sustain several biochemical processes including RNA synthesis.

A. Cytokinin Structure

The structural requirements for high cytokinin activity are fairly well known (Skoog *et al.*, 1967; Leonard *et al.*, 1969; Skoog and Armstrong, 1970; Letham, 1978; Koshimizu and Iwamura, 1986). With a few exceptions, most notably the diphenyl urea derivatives, a purine or very similar ring system is required. Usually, the rings have side chains with 4 to 7 carbon atoms attached to the amino group at the 6 position. Among the

---

[1] For abbreviations used in this chapter, see Table 9.1.

TABLE 9.1

Abbreviations Used in This Chapter

A and AR: adenine and adenosine

Isopentenyl and Its Derivatives
  iP: N^6-(Δ^2-isopentenyl) adenine
  iP7G: 7-β-D-glucopyranosyl-iP
  iPR: 9-β-D-ribofuranosyl-iP
  iPMP: 5'-monophosphate of iPR

Zeatin and Its Derivatives and Its Isomers
  Z: zeatin (trans isomer)
  LA: lupinic acid, 9-alanylzeatin
  Z7G: 7-β-D-glucopyranosylzeatin
  Z9G: 9-β-D-glucopyranosylzeatin
  OGZ: O-β-D-glucopyranosylzeatin
  OGZR: 9-β-D-ribofuranosyl-OGZ
  ZR: 9-β-D-ribofuranosylzeatin
  ZMP: 5'-monophosphate of ZR
  *cis*Z: *cis*-zeatin
  *cis*ZR: 9-β-D-ribofuranosyl-*cis*Z

Dihydrozeatin and Its Derivatives
  DZ: dihydrozeatin
  DLA: dihydrolupinic acid
  DZ9G: 9-β-D-glucopyranosyldihydrozeatin
  OGDZ: O-β-D-glycopyranosyldihydrozeatin
  OGDZR: 9-β-D-ribofuranosyl-OGDZ
  DZR: 9-β-D-ribofuranosyldihydrozeatin
  DZMP: 5'-monophosphate of DZR

Benzyladenine and Its Derivatives
  BA: 6-benzyladenine
  BA3G: 3-β-D-glucopyranosyl-BA
  BA7G: 7-β-D-glucopyranosyl-BA
  BA9G: 9-β-D-glucopyranosyl-BA

Kn: kinetin

---

purine derivatives having N^6-substituents of optimal size, activity is also influenced by the spatial arrangement as well as the type of atoms present in the side chain. Matsubara (1980) has pointed out the importance of such side chain characteristics as the absence of a carboxyl group, the presence of a double bond at the 2,3-position, introduction of a second methyl group at the 3-position, hydroxylation at the 4-position, and correct stereochemistry of the substituents attached to the double bond for high cytokinin activity. For example, the natural optical isomer (-)DZ is less active than the unnatural form (+)DZ (Matsubara *et al.*, 1977; Corse *et al.*, 1983; Noodén and Letham, 1986).

Because of the prominence of cytokinin treatments in senescence studies (Sections I and III), a substantial literature is available to illustrate the effectiveness of different cytokinins on this process. Table 9.2 summarizes those involving mainly natural cytokinins. The synthetic cytokinins are covered elsewhere (Bruce *et al.*, 1965; Kulaeva *et al.*, 1965; Skoog *et al.*, 1967; Letham, 1967b, 1978; Fawcett and Wright, 1968; Matsubara *et al.*, 1978; Wilcox *et al.*, 1978; Karanov *et al.*, 1980; Matsubara, 1980; Wilcox *et al.*, 1981; Letham and Palni, 1983). In general, the structure–activity relations for cytokinin in senescence bioassays such as chlorophyll retention seem similar to those of other assays such as the standard callus growth assays with one marked exception. Synthetic cytokinins such as BA and Kn are generally much more active in the senescence assays than the natural cytokinins such as Z and ZR (Letham and Palni, 1983; Tao *et al.*, 1983). Tao *et al.* (1983) attributed this difference in activity to more rapid metabolism of the natural cytokinins (e.g., Z) as compared to the synthetic cytokinins (e.g., BA). Thus, hormone and hormone analog activity are determined not only by the structural relationship between the hormone and the receptor at the target site but also by its stability and penetration (permeability and/or transport) to the active site(s). The sum of these factors probably differs when the mode of application for the test substances differs from the natural supply pathway, for example, application of cytokinins to the leaf surface as opposed to supply through the xylem which seems to be the natural transport route (Section II, C). When cytokinins were supplied through the xylem in the transpiration stream, the activity of DZ, DZR, and ZR is equal to or above that of BA (Garrison *et al.*, 1984). Supplying the hormone through the natural pathway is likely to yield structure–activity relationships more closely related to biological function. In this regard, it is important that BA is metabolized differently when applied to intact roots as compared to a rootless shoot (through the xylem) in tomatoes (Van Staden and Mallett, 1988). Although such differential metabolism is important, practical uses often depend on surface treatments and therefore data derived from such applications have value for those purposes.

B. Sites of Cytokinin Production

The now generally accepted view that the roots are sites of cytokinin synthesis, probably the major sources, has been strengthened by seven types of experiments (Letham, 1978; Van Staden and Davey, 1979) that showed that: (1) roots, particularly the apex, contain substantial amounts of cytokinin (Weiss and Vaadia, 1965; Short and Torrey, 1972); (2) xylem sap from the roots contains cytokinins (Kulaeva, 1962; Kende, 1964; Section II,C); (3) environmental factors that affect root growth and other activities also affect the production of these hormones (Itai and Vaadia, 1965; Burrows and Carr, 1969; Davey and Van Staden, 1976; Sattelmacher and Marschner, 1978); (4) root initiation on organ explants results in increased cytokinin levels within the explants (Wheeler, 1971; Engelbrecht, 1972; Forsyth and Van Staden, 1981); (5) cytokinin-like activity occurs in the medium used to culture excised roots (Koda and Okazawa, 1978; Van Staden and Smith, 1978); (6) excised root tissues were able to convert ^{14}C-A to cytokinins (Van Staden and Forsyth, 1984; Chen *et al.*, 1985); (7) root excision and substitution experiments (Theimer *et al.*, 1976), particularly with soybean explants (Section IV,E), indicate that the roots supply the cytokinins required for normal development and delaying leaf senescence.

Roots are apparently not the only site of cytokinin synthesis. Some limited evidence suggests that shoot apices (Kannangara and Booth, 1974), leaves (Vonk, 1979; Chen *et al.*, 1985), seeds, endosperm and/or embryos (Miura and Hall, 1973; Hahn *et al.*, 1974; Thomas *et al.*, 1978; Nessling and Morris, 1979; Noodén and Letham, 1984), or other plant parts (Sheldrake, 1973; Chen and Petschow, 1978; Van Staden and Davey, 1979) may be able to synthesize their own cytokinins. Generally, this evidence should, however, be augmented by direct biochemical studies such as conversion of labeled precursors to cytokinin. There is also some evidence, albeit indirect, that mature leaves cannot synthesize cytokinins (Kannangara, 1977). Since diphenylurea appears to work by activating cytokinin synthesis (Mok *et al.*, 1979), this compound and its analogs probably also induces cytokinin synthesis in leaf tissues where they delay chlorophyll loss (Bruce *et al.*, 1965; Letham, 1978).

Unfortunately, the chemistry of cytokinin biosynthesis in higher plants is still poorly understood (Letham and Palni, 1983; Horgan, 1986). Cytokinin nucleotides, particularly iPMP, seem to be intermediates in cytokinin biosynthesis (Taya *et al.*, 1978; Palni *et al.*, 1983; Horgan, 1986).

C. Cytokinin Transport

A number of reports have indicated that applied synthetic (Mothes *et al.*, 1961; Sachs and Thimann, 1964) and natural cytokinins (Van Staden and Davey, 1981; Vonk and Davelaar, 1981; Van Staden, 1982; Hutton and Van Staden, 1985) are not readily transported from their sites of application, except when they are applied in such a way that they can enter the transpiration stream. Cytokinins introduced into the xylem are transported to and metabolized within leaves but are not readily exported from these organs (Davey and Van Staden, 1981a; Noodén and Letham, 1984). Because of the relatively low mobility of applied cytokinins, there was some question about the hormonal role of cytokinins until the discovery of cytokinins in root

TABLE 9.2

Comparison of the Activity of Various Cytokinins in Different Senescence-Related Bioassays

Assay type	Concentration ranged tested (M)	Order of activity[a]	Reference
Retardation of chlorophyll breakdown			
Chinese cabbage leaf disks	$0.05-15 \times 10^{-6}$	Kn>Z>iP	Letham (1967b)
Tobacco leaf disks	$0.05-15 \times 10^{-6}$	Kn>Z>iP	Letham (1967b)
Radish leaf disks	$0.05-15 \times 10^{-6}$	Kn=Z	Letham (1967b)
Detached leaves			
3 Monocot species	10^{-5}	Kn>BA>Z	Mishra and Misra (1973)
5 Dicot species	10^{-5}	BA>Kn>Z	Mishra and Misra (1973)
Radish cotyledons	$10^{-7}-3.2 \times 10^{-4}$	BA>Kn>iP	Hamzi and Skoog (1964)
Radish cotyledons	$10^{-6}-10^{-4}$	(+)DZ>(−)DZR>(−)DZ>(−)DZR	Matsubara et al. (1977)
Wheat leaf segments	$10^{-8}-10^{-4}$	Kn>BA>Z=ZR>>(±) DZ=(±)DZR>iP=cZ=iPR>cZR	Kuhnle et al. (1977)
Oat leaf sections	$10^{-8}-10^{-4}$	Kn>BA>>Z=iP	Varga and Bruinsma (1973)
Oat leaf sections	$10^{-11}-10^{-7}$	BA>Kn>Z>>iP	Tetley and Thimann (1974)
Oat leaf sections	$10^{-7}-10^{-3}$	BA>Kn>>ZR=Z>iPR>iP	Dumbroff and Walker (1979)
Oat leaf sections	$10^{-9}-10^{-5}$	BA>Kn>>Z>iP	Biddington and Thomas (1978)
Oat leaf sections	$10^{-7}-10^{-3}$	Kn≥BA>Z>iP	Kaminek and Lustinec (1978)

Oat leaf sections	$2 \times 10^{-7} - 5 \times 10^{-6}$	BA>>OGZ>Z=(±)DZ>>(D,L)LA	Letham et al. (1983)
Rice leaf segments	10^{-5}	BA=Kn>Z=iP	Kao (1978)
Soybean leaf disks cv. 1039	$10^{-7} - 10^{-4}$	BA>Z=(±)DZ>iP	Yu and Kao (1981)
cv. Shih-shih	$10^{-7} - 10^{-4}$	iP>BA>Z>>DZ	Yu and Kao (1981)
Soybean explants (supplied via xylem)	3×10^{-7}	DZR>BA>DZ>ZR>Z>iP>iPR	Garrison et al. (1984)
Soybean explants (supplied via xylem)	$10^{-8} - 10^{-7}$	(+)DZ>(−)DZ≥Z	Noodén and Letham (1986)
Transpiration			
Oat leaf segments (supplied through the xylem)	$10^{-9} - 10^{-5}$	BA>Kn>>Z=iP	Biddington and Thomas (1978)
Stomatal aperture Grass (Anthephora) epidermal strips	$10^{-8} - 10^{-4}$	Kn=(±)DZ=ZR=Z=(±)DZR>BA=iPR>iP	Jewer and Incoll (1980)
Stomatal resistance Soybean explants (supplied via xylem)	3×10^{-7}	ZR>Z=(±)DZ=(±)DZR=iPR>BA>iP	Garrison et al. (1984)

*This order may differ at the concentration extremes tested. The abbreviations are explained in Table 9.1.

287

xylem sap (Kulaeva, 1962; Kende, 1965). Root-produced cytokinins move predominantly via the transpiration stream, xylem (Letham, 1978; Van Staden and Davey, 1979; Letham and Palni, 1983). Compared with AR, the movement of ZR is restricted (Noodén and Letham, 1984) which suggests that the side chain greatly influences mobility.

Z and especially ZR are major cytokinin constituents of xylem sap, but the dihydro forms, DZ and DZR, are also present, frequently in a high proportion (Horgan *et al.*, 1973; Purse *et al.*, 1976; Letham, 1978; Van Staden and Davey, 1979; Heindl *et al.*, 1982). O-glucoside-like cytokinin activity also occurs in xylem sap (Davey and Van Staden, 1978a; Davey and Van Staden, 1979; Van Staden and Dimalla, 1980b). Recent studies (Palmer and Wong, 1985) indicate that cytokinin nucleotides may be more significant xylem sap components than previously realized. Estimates of the maximum concentrations of cytokinins in xylem sap from podded soybeans vary a lot ranging from 230 nM (Letham *et al.*, unpublished data) to 19 nM (Heindl *et al.*, 1982). Somewhat higher values have been reported in the past (see King, 1976).

Long-distance transport can also be achieved through the phloem (Hall and Baker, 1972; Phillips and Cleland, 1972), but the role of phloem cytokinins and phloem transport is unclear. It is even uncertain where the phloem cytokinins originate, i.e., from *de novo* synthesis coupled with export from shoot organs or lateral transfer from the xylem. Cytokinin concentrations of about 30 nM have been reported in phloem sap (Vonk, 1979; Weiler and Ziegler, 1981). Some older reports place these concentrations higher (see King, 1976). Both Z and iP derivatives occur in phloem sap (Weiler and Zeigler, 1981), and some evidence indicates that O-glucosides (Van Staden, 1976a) and nucleotides (Vonk, 1978) are present in large amounts. Ringing of the bark causes a decrease in cytokinin activity in the leaves of willow (Van Staden and Brown, 1977). This could be due to decreased transpiration (Kriedemann *et al.*, 1976) resulting in less cytokinin being transported into the leaves. The decrease in O-glucoside activity in the bark above the girdle also indicates that this important phloem sap constituent was not moving down through the phloem.

Except for one report suggesting that cytokinins were present in chloroplasts (Davey and Van Staden 1981b), nothing is known about the distribution or transport of cytokinins within cells or even among different cells within a tissue. Cytokinins are able to alter both mitochondrial and chloroplast activities (Sections IV, A, 2, a and b); however, these effects could be indirect.

D. Cytokinin Metabolism

Cytokinin biochemistry has made its greatest advances in the field of metabolism over the past decade. Many cytokinin metabolites and derivatives are now known (Letham and Palni, 1983; Koshimizu and Iwamura, 1986). There obviously are many reasons why both natural and synthetic cytokinins need to be metabolized, regulation of endogenous levels being the most important. The stability and extent to which cytokinins are metabolized in a particular organ may determine their effect on senescence (Tao *et al.*, 1983 Noodén and Letham, 1984, 1986; Zhang *et al.*, 1987). The nature of the metabolites formed may differ among tissues (Noodén and Letham, 1984, 1986; Van Staden and Mallett, 1988) or even among the same tissues in different species (Mok and Mok, 1987). Exactly why there are so many different cytokinins is still unclear. They may be active forms that react with specific receptor sites, storage forms that are reversibly sequestered, inactivation products, transport forms, or metabolic intermediates.

Largely due to availability, most attention has focused on Kn, BA, Z, ZR, iP, and DZ. Because the latter is almost always prepared by reduction of Z, it usually consists of a mixture of optical isomers [natural (−) and unnatural (+) (Matsubara *et al.*, 1977)]. A great number of metabolites can be formed, and these may be important in regulating senescence. First, ribosyl, ribosyl-5′-phosphate, glucosyl, xylosyl, or alanyl moieties may be attached to the 3-, 7- or 9-positions of the purine ring (Fox *et al.*, 1973; Parker and Letham, 1973; Letham *et al.*, 1975, 1979; MacLeod *et al.*, 1976; Laloue *et al.*, 1977; Miernyk and Blaydes, 1977; Cowley *et al.*, 1978; Duke *et al.*, 1979; Letham and Palni, 1983; Lee *et al.*, 1985; Mok and Mok, 1987). Second, the side chain may be modified, particularly the isoprenoid side chain in the natural cytokinins. The side chain modifications may take the form of side chain removal, oxidation/ reduction, and/or conjugation. Reduction of the side chain produces dihydro derivatives that are more stable and are resistant to cytokinin oxidase (Henson, 1978a,b; Whitty and Hall, 1974; Noodén and Letham, 1984, 1986; Singh *et al.*, 1988). The dihydro derivatives are apparently metabolized via another enzymic pathway. Oxidation of the side chain could result either in its complete removal yielding adenine (Parker and Letham, 1973; Gordon *et al.*, 1974; Whitty and Hall, 1974; Henson and Wheeler, 1977; Cowley *et al.*, 1978) or in the production of trihydroxy-zeatin (Van Staden *et al.*, 1982). The attachment of glucose to the oxygen on the isoprenoid side chain appears to stabilize the cytokinins (Palmer *et al.*, 1981c; Letham and Palni, 1983). This may be why the O-glucosides accumulate while other cytokinins are decreasing in senescing tissues (Table 9.3; Section III,A). The same may apply when the glucosyl group is linked to the ring (7 or 9 positions), but these modifications are less general. In addition to side chain reduction and glucosylation, alanine conjugation also seems to stabilize cytokinins (Parker *et al.*, 1978; Palmer *et al.*, 1981b,c; Letham *et al.*, 1983; Palni *et al.*, 1984; Zhang *et al.*, 1987). The glucosyl and alanyl derivatives appear to be at least temporarily inactivated. The side chain of Z and its derivatives has the trans configuration, and where the cis forms (*cis*Z and

TABLE 9.3

Changes in Levels of Cytokinins or Cytokinin-Like Activity in Relation to Senescence

Authors	Tissue	Developmental pattern	Purification	Method of measuring	Pattern of change[a]
Davey and Van Staden (1978a)	Attached leaves, white lupine	Monocarpic senescence	Ion exchange chromatography, paper chromatography	Callus growth bioassay	No significant change in activity resembling (D)Z and (D)ZR
Davey and Van Staden (1978b)	Pod wall, white lupine	Fruit ripening and desiccation	Ion exchange chromatography, paper chromatography, Sephadex LH-20 column chromatography	Callus growth bioassay	Activity resembling (D)Z and (D)ZR decreased, activity like the glucosides increased
Engelbrecht (1971b)	Attached leaves, poplar and the plane tree (*Acer platanoides*)	Autumnal senescence	Ion exchange chromatography, paper chromatography	Callus growth bioassay	(D)Z- and (D)ZR-like activity decreased quite early and activity resembling zeatin nucleotide increased
Even-Chen *et al.* (1978)	Detached tobacco leaves	Induced senescence	Ion exchange chromatography, paper chromatography	Chlorophyll formation in etiolated cucumber cotyledons	Cytokinin activity declined very rapidly after excision and again just as chlorophyll loss started
Featonby-Smith and Van Staden (1981)	Attached leaves, common bean	Progressive senescence	Ion exchange chromatography, paper chromatography	Callus growth bioassay	Activity resembling (D)Z and (D)ZR decreased, activity like the glucosides increased
Henson and Wareing (1976)	Attached leaves, cocklebur	Progressive senescence	Column chromatography on Sephadex LH-20	Callus growth bioassay	Activity resembling (D)Z and (D)ZR decreased, activity like the glucosides increased
Hewett and Wareing (1973b)	Attached leaves, poplar	Autumnal senescence	Ion exchange chromatography, paper chromatography	Callus growth bioassay	Activity similar to (D)Z and (D)ZR decreased, activity resembling the glucosides increased
Ilan and Goren (1979)	Attached leaves, lemon	Progressive senescence	Ion exchange chromatography, paper chromatography	Callus growth bioassay	A broad chromatographic spectrum of cytokinins remained at high levels
Lindoo and Noodén (1978)	Attached leaves, soybean	Monocarpic senescence	Partitioning, PVP column chromatography	*Amaranthus* betacyanin bioassay	Cytokinin activity decreased

Reference	Material	Senescence type	Methods	Assay	Results
Lorenzi et al. (1975)	Attached leaves, Sitka spruce	Seasonal senescence	Ion exchange chromatography, partitioning, Sephadex LH-20 column chromatography; some identities were confirmed with gas chromatography-mass spectroscopy	Callus growth bioassay	(D)ZR-like activity increased while a fraction resembling Z9G decreased
Mayak and Halevy (1970)	Attached petals rose cut flowers	Petal senescence	Partitioning, paper chromatography	Callus growth bioassay	A long-lasting variety contained more cytokinin activity than a short-lived variety
Mayak et al. (1972)	Attached petals rose cut flowers	Petal senescence	Partitioning, ion exchange chromatography, paper chromatography	Callus growth bioassay	A broad chromatographic band of activity resembling (D)Z and (D)ZR increased, a zone similar to glucosides also increased
Oritani and Yoshida (1971)	Attached leaves, rice	Monocarpic senescence	Partitioning, paper chromatography	Rice leaf segment chlorophyll retention	Activity of a broad chromatographic zone resembling (D)Z and (D)ZR decreased, while another zone corresponding to glucosides increased
Oritani and Yoshida (1973)	Attached leaves, rice	Monocarpic senescence	Partitioning, ion exchange chromatography, thin layer chromatography	Gas chromatography with flame ionization detection	(D)Z- and (D)ZR-like activity decreased
Oritani and Yoshida (1973)	Attached leaves, soybean	Monocarpic senescence	Partitioning, ion exchange chromatography	Callus growth bioassay	Activity of a broad spectrum of cytokinins decreased
Thomas (1977)	Detached brussels sprout buttons	Induced senescence	Partitioning, paper chromatography	Amaranthus betacyanin bioassay	Cytokinin activity decreased
Van Meeteren and Van Gelder (1980)	Attached petals, Gerbera cut flowers	Induced senescence	Partitioning, PVP column chromatography	Amaranthus betacyanin bioassay	Free and "bound" cytokinin activity decreased

TABLE 9.3 *Continued*

Authors	Tissue	Developmental pattern	Purification	Method of measuring	Pattern of change[a]
Van Staden (1973)	Attached leaves, *Streptocarpus*	Tip to base senescence within a leaf and autumnal senescence	Partitioning, paper chromatography	Callus growth bioassay	Butanol-soluble activity [(D)Z and (D)ZR] decreased, butanol-insoluble activity (possibly nucleotides) increased
Van Staden (1976b)	Attached leaves, *Ginkgo*	Autumnal senescence	Ion exchange chromatography, paper chromatography, Sephadex	Callus growth bioassay	Activity resembling (D)ZR decreased, while that similar to (D)Z increased, and the *O*-glucoside-like activity remained about the same
Van Staden (1977)	Attached leaves, willow	Autumnal senescence	Ion exchange chromatography, paper chromatography, Sephadex LH-20 chromatography	Callus growth bioassay	Activity resembling (D)Z and (D)ZR decreased, while that similar to glucosides increased
Van Staden and Dimalla (1980a)	Attached petals, carnation cut flowers	Petal senescence	Ion exchange chromatography, Sephadex LH-20 chromatography	Callus growth bioassay	Activity resembling *O*-glucosides decreased, while that similar to (D)Z and (D)ZR dropped, rose and finally fell

[a]The notations (D)Z and (D)ZR refer to unresolved mixtures of Z with DZ and ZR with DZR.

*cis*ZR) occur in higher plant tissues, they may be derived from breakdown of tRNA or from microbes (Letham, 1978; Letham and Palni, 1983). The synthetic cytokinins such as BA may be metabolized differently from Z and ZR in the same tissue (Letham and Palni, 1983; Zhang *et al.*, 1987; Forsyth and Van Staden, 1986, 1988). This metabolism may consist of side chain removal or formation of glucosyl, ribosyl, or alanyl derivatives. In soybean leaves undergoing monocarpic senescence, the metabolism of ZR and BA does not radically change in quantity or quality as senescence progresses (Noodén and Letham, 1986; Zhang *et al.*, 1987). Senescent radish cotyledons, however, convert more Z or ZR to A and AR but less to Z7G than nonsenescent cotyledons do (Letham and Gollnow, 1985). The senescent cotyledons also produce less BA3G and the ratio of BA7G/BA9G decreases. Some of the synthetic compounds that delay senescence and are not N^6-substituted adenines, for example diphenylurea and its derivatives (Bruce *et al.*, 1965; Letham, 1978), may also be more stable than their purine counterparts (Mok *et al.*, 1982). They too can be glucosylated (Burrows and Leworthy, 1976; Letham and Palni, 1983).

III EVIDENCE TO IMPLICATE CYTOKININS IN THE REGULATION OF SENESCENCE

The impetus for attributing a regulatory role in senescence to cytokinins comes mainly from the senescence-delaying effects of cytokinin treatments and from the ability of roots to produce cytokinins and to delay senescence (Section I).

Because of the potential and realized economic benefits from delaying senescence of various tissues with cytokinin treatments, a voluminous literature has grown around this subject (Weaver, 1972; McGlasson *et al.*, 1978; Wills *et al.*, 1981; Burton, 1982; Baker, 1983). The sum total of this information is that cytokinin applications given in the right dose and at the right time delay senescence in most, but not all, tissues. The senescence in the leaves of a few species is not delayed by cytokinin, while it is delayed by other hormones (Noodén and Leopold, 1978; Chapter 10). In the past, it was believed that cytokinin treatments of attached leaves were ineffective, but now it is clear that usually cytokinins are also effective in attached leaves (Section IV,A,1). Attached leaves may sometimes be less responsive owing to sufficient endogenous cytokinins (Section IV,A,1). The response to applied cytokinins also diminishes as the leaves age and senesce (Naito *et al.*, 1978). Sometimes, however, even yellow leaves regreen in response to cytokinin treatments (Mothes and Baudisch, 1959). Generally, synthetic cytokinins are more effective than natural cytokinins, mainly due to greater

stability of the synthetic cytokinins (Section II,D). These exogenous cytokinins appear to function primarily by correcting an internal deficiency of
cytokinins.

Another important line of evidence implicating cytokinins in the regulation of senescence comes from time course studies showing a decline in
cytokinin levels prior to or during senescence (Table 9.3). While these studies are extensive, they do have some significant limitations. First, most of
them are directed at leaves, and relatively few deal with flower parts or
other organs. Some studies have been done on fruits (McGlasson *et al.*,
1978), but the role of cytokinins in fruit senescence is not clear (Section
IV,D). Second, the methods used have now been improved, new procedures
developed, and the identity of the naturally occurring cytokinins is much
better known (Letham and Palni, 1983; Koshimizu and Iwamura, 1986). For
example, the dihydro derivatives, e.g., DZ and DZR, are now known to be
quantitatively important cytokinins. Unfortunately, these tend to cochro-
matograph with their unsaturated counterparts, Z and ZR, and would generally be included in the values given for Z and ZR (Table 9.3), hence the
designations (D)Z and (D)ZR to represent the mixtures. These mixtures can
now be resolved easily by reverse phase chromatography. β-Glucosidase
and alkaline phosphatase can be used to confirm tentatively the identity of
the 0-glucosides and the nucleotides, respectively. More rigorous methods
such as mass spectroscopy are now available to confirm the identity of the
compounds present, and less reliance should be placed on chromatographic
mobility as a means of identification. Most of the early analyses were therefore not aimed at single, specific compounds, thereby making correction for
losses during purification difficult, if not impossible. The use of bioassays
has well-known limitations due to possible interference by impurities. In
addition, the bioassay of cytokinin mixtures poses a particular problem,
because the relative activity of different cytokinins in the commonly used
callus growth bioassays may differ from their activity in retarding senescence. It will be of value to reexamine some of these systems using the newer
methods and improved knowledge of the natural cytokinins to obtain a
more complete qualitative picture as well as more precise quantification.
The cytokinin immunoassays which represent great advances in sensitivity
and possibly convenience (Weiler, 1984) are also subject to interference,
especially from phenolic compounds, and cannot be run on impure samples. Moreover, antibodies usually have to be prepared for each cytokinin to
be analyzed. Nonetheless, the general picture of cytokinin changes in relation to senescence as described above seems well established through a
variety of studies on many systems. The correlation between senescence
and the decline in cytokinin levels is convincing, and the parallel variations
discussed below reinforce the idea that cytokinins are very important en-

dogenous antisenescence hormones. There are, however, several exceptions such as attached lemon leaves (Ilan and Goren, 1979) and white lupine leaves (Davey and Van Staden, 1978a) where levels of (D)Z- and (D)ZR-like activity remain high during senescence. In Sitka spruce leaves, (D)ZR-like activity even increases (Lorenzi *et al.*, 1975). These may, of course, be cases where other hormones regulate senescence (Chapter 10). In support of this idea, senescence of orange leaves, which are closely related to lemon leaves, is not delayed by cytokinin treatments (Arguelles and Guardiolla, 1977).

In many respects, the experimentally induced parallel changes of senescence and endogenous cytokinin levels provide the strongest evidence for a link between senescence and cytokinins. The most extensive evidence comes from the correlation of root activity with cytokinin production and their inverse relationship to leaf senescence. For example, rooting of leaf cuttings delayed their senescence (Section I), and at the same time, it increased the cytokinin activity in the leaves (Engelbrecht, 1972; Featonby-Smith and Van Staden 1981). Conversely, a variety of treatments which decrease cytokinin production by the roots also promote leaf senescence, presumeably by reducing their cytokinin levels. These include derooting, salt stress, water logging, mineral nutrient deficiency, and a variety of other factors (Itai and Vaadia, 1965; Itai *et al.*, 1968; Wagner and Michael, 1971; McDavid *et al.*, 1973; Skene, 1975; Salama and Wareing, 1979; Van Staden and Davey, 1979; Forsyth and Van Staden, 1981; Levitt, 1980a,b; Carmi and Van Staden, 1983). Shoot tip removal or partial defoliation, procedures which delay senescence of the remaining leaves, also increase the cytokinin activity in those leaves (Wareing *et al.*, 1968; Hewett and Wareing, 1973b; Henson and Wareing, 1976; Colbert and Beever, 1981; Palmer *et al.*, 1981a). Often, light is able to delay leaf senescence, and it may do so, at least in part, by increasing the cytokinin levels in the leaves (Uheda and Kuraishi, 1977; Thimann, 1980; Biswal and Biswal, 1984). Still another line of evidence comes from studies on the islands of green tissue that persist in leaves which are otherwise losing their chlorophyll. The green islands appear to be maintained by cytokinins produced by the organisms that cause them (Engelbrecht, 1971a; Van Staden and Davey, 1978).

IV. CYTOKININS AND ORGAN OR ORGANISM SENESCENCE

In addition to the common features of cytokinin biochemistry and senescence outlined above in Sections I–III, it also seems important to examine the possible roles of cytokinins in organ and organism senescence. This organization represents a more traditional approach and reflects the existing literature. In addition, the physiology of senescence or the senescence syndrome may differ a bit among organs or even among the same organs of different species (Chapters 1 and 10). Therefore, the senescence of different organs needs to be examined separately. As indicated above, we are not implying that the cytokinins are the primary factors involved in regulating senescence in all of these organs. In a few situations such as xylem differentiation (Shininger, 1979; Aloni, 1982), abscission (Osborne and Moss, 1963; Abeles *et al.*, 1967; Van Staden, 1973) and leaf senescence (Mothes *et al.*, 1959; Leopold and Kawase, 1964), cytokinins may promote senescence.

A. Leaves

While it does seem clear that leaf senescence is regulated by cytokinin produced in the roots and transported to the leaves via the xylem (Section III), it has not been established exactly which cytokinins are active in preventing senescence, why the foliar cytokinins decline, or which cellular processes are the most important.

1. Cytokinin Physiology in Relation to Leaf Senescence

A decrease in cytokinin titer seems to play a central role in causing leaf senescence (Table 9.3, Section III). Inasmuch as the roots are the major sources of leaf cytokinins, they obviously are important in regulating leaf senescence, and this subject will be reviewed further in connection with whole plant senescence (Section IV,E). Intact and detached leaves show important differences in their responses to applied cytokinins (Noodén and Leopold, 1978; Noodén 1980). Generally, cytokinins are most effective when applied to detached plant organs (Mothes, 1960; Kulaeva, 1962; Engelbrecht, 1964; Müller and Leopold, 1966), but it can also delay the senescence of attached leaves (Fletcher, 1969; Adedipe *et al.*, 1971; Lindoo and Noodén, 1978; Noodén and Leopold, 1978). Detachment may alter the metabolism of leaves to some extent (Chapter 1), but the main effect of detachment may be to cut off the supply of cytokinin from the roots. Applied cytokinins appear to be most effective in organs that contain low levels of endogenous cytokinins (Thomas, 1968; Rybicka *et al.*, 1977), and that may be why they often exert a greater effect on detached leaves. As explained earlier (Section II,A), the effectiveness of the different cytokinins and even their relative activities depend on the mode of application.

The levels of cytokinins in the leaves may be determined to a great extent by the rate of their production in the roots (Section IV,E.). Thus, treatments and environmental factors which alter root activity and cytokinin production may exert parallel effects on foliar cytokinin levels and corresponding effects on leaf senescence.

In addition to the overall quantitative changes in foliar cytokinin levels, there are also different quantitative changes among the different cytokinins. Unfortunately, many reports on the changes in endogenous cytokinin levels in developing organs do not extend into senescence. The cytokinin content of growing leaves qualitatively resembles that of the transpiration stream; Z, ZR (and/or their dihydro derivatives) appear to be the dominant cytokinins. In deciduous trees as well as annuals (Engelbrecht, 1971b; Hewett and Wareing, 1973a,b,c; Henson and Wareing, 1976; Henson and Wheeler, 1976; Van Staden, 1976b, 1977, 1980; Hoad *et al.*, 1977; Davey and Van Staden, 1978a; Henson, 1978a; Kannangara *et al.*, 1978; Van Staden and Davey, 1978; Van Staden *et al.*, 1983) and evergreen leaves (Lorenzi *et al.*, 1975; Ilan and Goren, 1979; Hendry *et al.*, 1982) the cytokinin composition changes as the leaves develop. Generally, the youngest leaves contain more of (D)ZR-like and less of (D)Z-like compounds, while growing leaves have similar amounts of (D)ZR- and (D)Z-like compounds as well as a polar cytokinin-like derivative(s) (Hewett and Wareing, 1973b,c; Van Staden, 1976b; Palmer *et al.*, 1981b). Fully expanded and senescing leaves contain less of both the (D)ZR- and (D)Z-like compounds, while the unknown polar compound(s) increase greatly. In mature leaves, the polar compound(s) may represent 80% of the detectable cytokinin activity.

A number of polar derivatives are possible, some apparently being *O*-glucosides, as these peaks were often hydrolyzed with β-glucosidase, which breaks *O*-glycosidic bonds and releases the aglycone moiety, Z, ZR, DZ, or DZR (Palmer *et al.*, 1981a; Letham and Palni, 1983). In some species, however, 9-glucosides, which are resistant to β-glucosidase, accumulate (Lorenzi *et al.*, 1975). These polar cytokinins could be formed from cytokinin bases or ribosides imported into the leaves through the xylem (Noodén and Letham, 1984, 1986; Singh *et al.*, 1988). Exactly, what causes these changes in the cytokinin complement of maturing and senescing leaves has not been determined, but it could be due to changes in synthesis or metabolism. Thus, the proportion of the more stable forms, i.e., DZ, DZR, and the *O*-glucosides, would increase over time. Soybean leaves do not show any substantial change in their metabolism of ZR or BA as pod development and monocarpic senescence progresses (Noodén and Letham, 1986; Zhang *et al.*, 1987). In *Alnus glutinosa*, the mature leaves convert more ^{14}C-Z to *O*-glucosides, including OGDZ, than immature leaves (Henson, 1978a,b). When DZ is applied, it is predominantly glucosylated. If there is any consistent change in the pattern of cytokinin metabolism with leaf maturity and age, it is a shift towards glucosylation or at least an increase in the proportion of glucosyl derivatives. In any case, the net result is that mature and yellow senescing leaves may contain high levels of cytokinin *O*-glucosides which the leaf is apparently unable to utilize and/or export. In view of the cytokinin glucosides present in senescing leaves, their ability to retard senescence is doubtful, and it has been suggested that their formation could actually promote leaf senescence and abscission (Van Staden *et al.*, 1983). Since the activity of OGZ markedly exceeds that of Z in the oat leaf senescence assay (Letham *et al.*, 1983), it can be concluded that they in fact retard senescence. The endogenous cytokinin glucosides are probably ineffective in preventing the senescence of intact leaves, because they are compartmentalized within the leaf tissues or within its cells. On the other hand, the activity of OGZ in bioassays may be due to its hydrolysis to the aglycone Z in the test tissues (Palni *et al.*, 1984).

Light may delay senescence in a manner superficially similar to cytokinins (Hopkinson, 1966; Goldthwaite and Laetsch, 1967; Mishra and Pradhan, 1973; Letham, 1978; Thimann, 1980; Biswal and Biswal, 1984). Light may work through enhancing the activity of cytokinins (Singh and Mishra, 1965; Thimann and Satler, 1979) or elevating cytokinin levels (Hewett and Wareing, 1973d; Wareing and Thompson, 1976; Uheda and Kuraishi, 1977).

All studies conducted on green island leaf galls indicate that higher levels of cytokinin are maintained in the infected green areas (Engelbrecht, 1971a; Van Staden and Davey, 1978). Although the green islands are probably caused by cytokinins from the causal agent, wounding may also be a factor. Recently, it has been shown that wounding, which is a normal occurrence in the case of insect gall formation and maintenance (Rohfritsch and Shorthouse, 1982), considerably delays chlorophyll and protein loss of oat leaves kept in the dark (Giridhar and Thimann, 1985). Wounding has also been shown to promote cell division and to increase cell division factors (Kahl, 1982), which include cytokinins (Mitchell and Van Staden, 1983).

2. Effects on Stomata

Cytokinins promote stomatal opening in leaves of many species (Livne and Vaadia, 1965; Biddington and Thomas, 1978; Jewer and Incoll, 1980; Kurnishi *et al.*, 1981; Garrison *et al.*, 1984; Incoll and Jewer, 1987). Tests with several cytokinins show different activity profiles with respect to chlorophyll retention and stomatal opening, which suggests these may be independent effects (Garrison *et al.*, 1984).

An antagonism between abscisic acid and cytokinin can be seen at the level of the stomata, for abscisic acid causes stomatal closure (Farquhar and Sharkey, 1982; Chapter 10), while cytokinins promote stomatal opening. These hormones may, however, interact in other ways too (Chapter 10).

Not only can stomata regulate the gas exchange rate in leaves and thereby transpiration and possibly photosynthesis (Farquhar and Sharkey, 1982), but stomatal closure or opening may promote or retard leaf senescence (Thimann *et al.*, 1982). Thus, cytokinin effects on stomata may be of importance in both the senescence of the leaf per se and the whole plant; this will be discussed in Section IV,E. Since the stromata do not seem to senesce, or at least not until after the rest of the leaf (Chapter 1), these hormone effects are probably not direct effects on stomatal senescence.

3. Effects on Leaf Abscission

Leaf abscission may be retarded by cytokinins. Application of cytokinins to the surfaces of leaves attached to whole plants (Lindoo and Noodén, 1978; Noodén *et al.*, 1979) or through the xylem in soybean explants (Garrison *et al.*, 1984) delays blade abscission. These could be indirect effects. The observation (Van Staden, 1973) that cytokinins also delay abscission when applied directly to abscission layers also suggests that a more direct action is possible too. Sometimes cytokinin treatments may promote abscission (see the beginning of Section IV), and this could involve ethylene (Abeles *et al.*, 1967).

4. Effects on Cellular Components and Activities

a. **The Photosynthetic Apparatus.** The senescence of leaves and green cotyledons involves changes in their photosynthetic apparatus. Because yellowing is so conspicuous, chlorophyll breakdown has served as the major parameter for the measurement of leaf senescence. The fact that cytokinins are so effective in delaying this breakdown (Section III) indicates that these hormones are somehow involved in maintaining the photosynthetic apparatus of plant organs. Usually, cytokinin treatment stimulates photosynthesis (Meidner, 1967; Treharne *et al.*, 1970; Adedipe *et al.*, 1971; Parthier, 1979; Dong and Arteca, 1982; Vassileva and Dimitrova, 1984), but it also inhibits photosynthesis in some tissues (Erismann and Wegner, 1967). This connection between photosynthesis and cytokinin is further strengthened by experimentally induced parallel variations. Decapitation or partial defoliation treatments increase photosynthetic activity (Meidner, 1970; Hodgkinson, 1974; Carmi and Koller, 1979; Binnie and Clifford, 1980) as well as the endogenous cytokinins in the remaining leaves (Colbert and Beever, 1981; Van Staden and Carmi, 1982).

Cytokinin treatments increase chloroplast DNA, promote chloroplast protein synthesis, maintain pigment levels, and alter membrane permeability as well as promote chloroplast replication, grana formation, and influence maturation (Kursanov and Kulaeva, 1964; Shaw and Manocha, 1965; Laetsch and Stetler, 1965; Boasson *et al.*, 1972; Laetsch and Boasson, 1972;

Mlodzianowski and Kwintkiewicz, 1973; Lichtenthaler and Buschmann, 1978; Naito *et al.*, 1978, 1979; Parthier, 1979; Tsuji *et al.*, 1979; Caers *et al.*, 1985). Cytokinins may also selectively increase the levels of certain enzymes associated with the photosynthetic process (Feierabend, 1969; De Boer and Feierabend, 1974). It is not clear whether the enhanced activity is due to greater synthesis, inhibition of degradation, or activation of the enzymes. It has been suggested that cytokinins exert their effect on chloroplast metabolism indirectly through action on the nucleus or cytoplasm (Thimann *et al.*, 1977; Parthier, 1979; Legocka and Szweykowska, 1981). Cytokinins increase chlorophyll levels (Caers *et al.*, 1985), but it is not clear whether cytokinins act by stimulating chlorophyll synthesis or by inhibiting its breakdown. Cytokinins do increase the activity of α-aminolevulinic acid synthetase (Fletcher and McCullagh, 1971; Fletcher *et al.*, 1973), which could lead to an increase in chlorophyll. On the other hand, cytokinins reduce the activity of chlorophyllase, which may degrade chlorophyll (Sabater and Rodriguez, 1978; Fukuda and Toyama, 1982; Purohit, 1982). While these data suggest that cytokinins regulate photosynthetic pigment levels, a few experiments indicate that neither chlorophyll accumulation nor the formation of lamellar chlorophyll–protein complexes in greening leaves are affected by Kn and BA (Alberte and Naylor, 1975). Perhaps, the role of cytokinins in regulating development of the photosynthetic apparatus differs with developmental stage and/or species. Furthermore, as mentioned above (Section III), attached leaves may not always be very responsive to exogenous cytokinin.

With respect to leaf structure, there is a marked similarity between the effects of decapitation, which changes cytokinin distribution to the primary leaves of beans (Van Staden and Carmi, 1982), and the application of synthetic cytokinins to such leaves on intact plants (Bosselaers, 1983). In both instances, the leaves retain their chlorophyll, their surface area increases somewhat, and they become much thicker. In intact plants, both BA and Kn applied to leaves cause a significant decrease in the intercellular air space volume. The stomata of these leaves neither close fully in the darkness nor do they open as wide as those of control plants during the light period. Thus, cytokinin treatments produce not only dramatic anatomical changes but important effects on total leaf diffusion resistance to CO_2. It is therefore clear that cytokinins may effect a great number of reactions associated with the photosynthetic apparatus. Whether these responses are primary or secondary and how they relate to senescence remains to be determined.

b. Respiration. Respiration is one of the last metabolic processes to become disrupted during senescence (Chapters 1 and 4), probably because energy is required for the senescence processes and mobilization of its breakdown products. In cut asparagus shoots, BA inhibits respiration as it represses senescence (Dedolph *et al.*, 1961). Cytokinins inhibit or delay the climacteric-like rise in respiration which sometimes occurs in senescing tissues (Halevy *et al.*, 1966; Tetley and Thimann, 1974). Likewise, cytokinins may also maintain the coupling between respiration and phosphorylation (Tetley and Thimann, 1974). There are indications that glycolysis may be retarded (Tuli *et al.*, 1964), but Z and ZR do not inhibit malate respiration (Miller, 1982). Nonetheless, the synthetic cytokinins BA and Kn do affect substrate oxidation further complicating any attempts to explain the action of cytokinin on respiration.

c. Membranes. Cytokinins have been shown to alter membrane permeability, generally increasing the movement of polar solutes (Livne and Graziani, 1972; Feng, 1973; Van Steveninck, 1976). They do, however, also delay the massive increase in solute leakage from leaves along with chlorophyll loss (Wittenbach, 1977).

As the efficiency of different cytokinins varies greatly with respect to chlorophyll loss, it is to be expected that their ability to preserve membrane integrity will also vary. For example, synthetic but not natural cytokinins inhibit phosphate leakage from leaves (Sabater *et al.*, 1981). Kn reduces the levels of lipase (Sodek and Wright, 1969) and lipoxygenase (Grossman and Leshem, 1978), which have been associated with membrane breakdown. Kn and Z also inhibit the decline in the fatty acid content of leaves (Kull *et al.*, 1978), and this may reflect maintenance of the membranes. A decrease of endogenous cytokinins may thus alter both the maintenance and permeability of plant membranes.

d. Proteins and Nucleic Acids. The early observations (Richmond and Lang, 1957; Wollgiehn, 1961, 1967) that cytokinins exert parallel effects in maintaining protein or nucleic acid levels while inhibiting senescence has led to the generalization that cytokinins delay senescence by maintaining or promoting protein and nucleic acid synthesis. In view of limited space and the excellent reviews by Jacobsen and Higgins (1978a,b) and in Jacobs and Fox (1987) the literature on cytokinin effects on protein and nucleic acid synthesis is not covered here except as specifically relevant to senescence. Spencer and Wildman (1964) attributed most of the protein synthesized in cytokinin-treated leaves to that produced in the chloroplasts where the effect is mainly on ribulose-bisphosphate carboxylase (Feierabend, 1969). Kn affects neither the rate of [^{14}C]leucine incorporation into proteins nor the overall period of amino acid incorporation in isolated chloroplasts (Richmond *et al.*, 1971). Other data also suggest that the cytokinin effect ι n chloroplasts may be mediated by RNA synthesis in the nucleus (Legocka and Szweykowska, 1981) as seems to be the case for other aspects of chloroplast metabolism (Section IV,A,2,a). The triggers responsible for controlling protein synthesis, and thus chloroplast breakdown, are therefore apparently located outside the organelle (Thomas and Stoddart, 1980; Legocka and Szweykowska, 1981; Chapter 15). Cytokinin may promote RNA polymerase I preferentially with no effect on polymerase II (Schneider *et al.*, 1978). Interestingly, Z alters the change in leucyl tRNA species which accompanies senescence in pea leaves (Wright *et al.*, 1973). Cytokinin also prevents the senescence-related rise in certain RNases and proteolytic enzymes (Anderson and Rowan, 1965; Sodek and Wright, 1969; Wyen *et al.*, 1972; Legocka and Szweykowska, 1983). In leaves of *Lolium temulentum*, three phases of amino acid incorporation have been recorded (Hedley and Stoddart, 1972). The final phase, a decline, coinciding with senescence, is delayed by cytokinins. However, if the cytokinin is applied after the commencement of the final phase, it has little effect on chlorophyll retention. Thus, it appears that the disassembly process can be blocked by prolonging the second phase of protein synthesis which occurs in mature exporting leaves (Stoddart and Thomas, 1982). Such leaves usually contain relatively high levels of ZR and Z which may be necessary for prolonging the second phase, preventing the commencement of the third and final phase.

e. Nutrient Distribution.   The movement of assimilates in plants is an important feature of their development, and there is evidence that cytokinins play a regulatory role in these processes, particularly in leaves. Cytokinin influences both the redistribution, which involves salvaging previously absorbed and synthesized compounds, and the partitioning of new assimilates (Chapter 12).

The classical experiments of Mothes and Engelbrecht (1961) and Mothes *et al.* (1961) and subsequently those of Leopold and Kawase (1964) provided the first indications that cytokinins can influence nutrient redistribution in detached organs. In detached leaves, nutrients such as nitrogenous substances and sugars are not only retained at the site of Kn application, but they move from nontreated parts of the leaf to treated areas (Mothes *et al.*, 1961; Seth and Wareing, 1967; Patrick *et al.*, 1979; Penot *et al.*, 1981). The green islands induced in leaves by cytokinin-secreting organisms seem to reflect a similar phenomenon in intact plants (Engelbrecht, 1971a). This promotion of nutrient redistribution from untreated to the cytokinin-treated parts could be a factor in the acceleration of senescence in the untreated parts (Leopold and Kawase, 1964). Z supplied through the xylem of soybean explants seems to inhibit the release and redistribution of mobile minerals and nitrogenous substances from the leaves (Mauk and Noodén 1983; Neumann *et al.*, 1983; Noodén, 1985). How cytokinins work is not clear; they may prevent breakdown and release of these materials in the leaves and/or it may alter outbound movement across membranes. Certainly, it is well established that cytokinins inhibit the net breakdown of proteins, nucleic acids, chlorophyll, and other leaf constituents. A voluminous literature also indicates that cytokinins may alter solute penetration in many tissues (Section IV,A,4,c), and this probably includes phloem loading. Indeed, localized cytokinin applications seem to influence solute movement within a leaf through an effect on the phloem (Müller and Leopold, 1966). The effects of cytokinins on stomatal opening (Section IV,A,2) and how that may affect transpiration and xylem flux of minerals are discussed in connection with whole plant senescence (Section IV,E).

Looking at an opposite perspective, inorganic cations may increase the responsiveness of tissues to cytokinins (Knypl and Chylinska, 1972; Ezekiel *et al.*, 1978; Elliott, 1979; Neumann and Noodén, 1983). In particular, potassium may enhance the senescence-retarding activity of cytokinins (Green and Muir, 1978). Since potassium may have an important role in stomatal opening, it may also effect the transpiration rate and thus may influence cytokinin import into leaves. Calcium enhances the action of potassium (Green and Muir, 1978), and it has been suggested that cytokinins act on plant tissues by altering the potassium to calcium ratios (Ilan *et al.*, 1971; Göring and Mardanov, 1976). It is also possible that minerals retard cytokinin metabolism in leaves and/or promote cytokinin synthesis in roots or elsewhere.

From the evidence provided, it is clear that cytokinins influence both nutrient movement and retention within a plant or organ. Mineral redistribution does not, however, appear to be a primary cause of senescence (Chapter 12).

B. Cotyledons

Cotyledons also senesce as the seedlings bearing them develop, and cytokinins have been implicated. Much of the data on senescence of leaves above also applies to cotyledons, but there is a voluminous literature on the cotyledons themselves. In the epigeal species (cotyledons above ground in seedlings), these organs may become quite leaf-like and can fulfill many of the functions of leaves. Those of hypogeal (cotyledons below ground) species are quite different. In both epigeal and hypogeal seeds, however, the cotyledons provide nutrients for early seedling development. This development is characterized by massive mobilization of the stored nutrients within the cotyledons (Laidman, 1982; Murray, 1984). Enlargement and other developmental changes in the cotyledons are dependent on the presence of the embryonic axis. Since cytokinins, but not auxin and gibberellins (Gepstein and Ilan, 1980), can substitute for the axis in many species (Esashi and Leopold, 1969; Kursanov *et al.*, 1969; Gilad *et al.*, 1970; Lovell and Moore, 1970; Sen and Sharma, 1972; Huff and Ross, 1975; Dei, 1978; Metivier and Paulilo, 1980; Murray, 1984), it seems that the influence of the axis may be mediated by cytokinin.

Cotyledonary expansion is one of the first readily visible correlates with nutrient mobilization in these organs. Cytokinins promote not only cell expansion but also microbody development (Theimer *et al.*, 1976; Chen and Leisner, 1985), DNA synthesis (Galli, 1984), and enzyme synthesis (Howard and Witham, 1983) in cotyledons. Generally, this pattern of influences is similar to that brought about by cytokinins applied to leaves. In addition, cytokinins increase a number of enzymes which affect mobilization of storage components such as isocitrate lyase (Penner and Ashton, 1967), amylase (Gepstein and Ilan, 1979), invertase (Howard and Witham, 1983), and hydroxypyruvate reductase, which is involved in the glycolate pathway (Chen and Leisner, 1985). There is evidence (Chen and Leisner, 1985) that some of these may be induced at the level of mRNA synthesis. Some may also be regulated at the level of protein synthesis. Thus, cytokinins appear to be necessary for the increase in hydrolytic enzymes which mobilize nutrients from the cotyledons and for enzymes which process those nutrients for use in axis development.

Cytokinins appear to promote chloroplast development within epigeal cotyledons as they do in leaves (Section IV,A,2,a). Cytokinin treatments also retard changes in membrane permeability, an important senescence-related process (Gilbert *et al.*, 1980; Green, 1983; Takeuchi *et al.*, 1985). Likewise, they increase chlorophyll formation (Dei, 1982, 1984, 1985; Fletcher *et al.*, 1982).

Analysis of endogenous cytokinin levels in the cotyledons of germinating been seeds indicates two periods of high cytokinin-like activity (Hutton *et al.*, 1982). The first peak occurs during early imbibition, but this activity declines during cotyledon expansion and chloroplast development. The second peak occurs 3 days later and corresponds to the start of radicle growth. Since radicle growth often correlates with an increase in cytokinins in the cotyledons (Letham, 1971; Dei, 1978), this may reflect cytokinin synthesis in the young roots. Applied cytokinins can delay senescence in detached or attached cotyledons (Sprent, 1968; Gilbert *et al.*, 1980). Moreover, removal of sunflower seedling roots promotes senescence of the cotyledons but applied Kn retards the senescence of these cotyledons (Theimer *et al.*, 1976). Thus, attached cotyledons appear to depend on the roots for their cytokinins and their senescence may be promoted by a depletion in cytokinins as is the case in leaves.

C. Flowers

Flower senescence is often, but not always, controlled by seed development in the ovary, making it a good example of correlative controls (Chapter 1). The senescence of certain flower parts not only releases nutrients for use by the ovary but eliminates unneeded parts.

While no cytokinins have as yet been unambiguously identified from flowers, chromatographic evidence indicates that during the early stages of floral development their cytokinin complement is similar to that found in leaves. Z, ZR, and their glucosyl and dihydro derivatives plus iP seem to be the major compounds present (Featonby-Smith *et al.*, 1987; Van Staden *et al.*, 1987). As in leaves, there are some inverse correlations between endogenous cytokinin activity and senescence (Table 9.3). For example, longer lived varieties of roses contain more cytokinin than short-lived varieties (Mayak and Halevy, 1970). In both rose (Mayak *et al.*, 1972) and *Cosmos sulphureus* (Saha *et al.*, 1985) flowers, cytokinin activity in the petals increase with opening and decrease after full bloom. Concomitant with the decrease in petals, there is an increase in the cytokinin levels of developing ovaries or fruits (Davey and Van Staden, 1977; Chen, 1982), indicating that the decline in endogenous cytokinins is not uniform in all parts of the flowers. Although the overall cytokinin levels are lower in detached flowers, the pattern of changes is similar. Interestingly, the cytokinin-like activity in the ovaries of cut carnations increased when the petals were irreversibly wilting and then subsequently declined (Van Staden and Dimalla, 1980a). This rise in cytokinin content of the ovaries did not occur in flowers treated with silver thiosulphate (Van Staden and Dimalla, 1980a), a treatment which delays senescence by preventing ethylene action.

Mainly as a result of the findings of Mayak and Halevy (1970), the idea developed that cytokinin treatment should extend flower longevity. Results obtained by applying cytokinins to the holding solutions of many types of cut flowers have proven to be variable (Weaver, 1972; Halevy and Mayak, 1981; Baker, 1983). Cytokinins, particularly Kn and BA, improve the longevity of carnations (Maclean and Dedolph, 1962; Heide and Qydvin, 1969; Mayak and Dilley, 1976; Mayak and Kofranek, 1976), roses (Mayak and Halevy, 1970; 1974), and *Gerbera* (Van Meeteren, 1979). The results naturally depend on the type, concentration, and site of cytokinin application, as well as the type and state of the cut flower at the time of application (Ballantyne, 1965). In the case of cut carnations, the application of cytokinins via the cut stem frequently has little effect on their senescence (Eisinger, 1977; Kelly, 1982). Part of the problem may be related to inadequate transport to the senescing tissues but other factors also seem to be involved. When the cytokinin is applied to cut carnations together with sucrose, it is more effective in delaying senescence (Mayak and Dilley, 1976). There is currently no evidence that cytokinins in, or applied to, petals are exported along with carbohydrates, which are readily exported from senescing petals (Nichols and Ho, 1975; Cook and Van Staden, 1983).

The relationship between cytokinins and ethylene, which plays such a dominant role in flower and fruit senescence, has received much attention. Applied cytokinins seem to reduce the sensitivity of floral tissues to ethylene (Mayak and Dilley, 1976; Eisinger, 1977) and/or delay ethylene production (Eisinger, 1977; Cook et al., 1985). In carnation petals, cytokinin treatment reduced ethylene biosynthesis through a decrease in endogenous ACC levels and a diminished capacity of the tissues to convert ACC to ethylene (Mor et al., 1983; Cook et al., 1985). In the petals, decreased cytokinin and increased ethylene levels appeared to be involved in accelerating senescence.

D. Fruit and Seed Senescence

Most of the studies on fruits have been directed more toward ripening than senescence. Since these processes are different (Chapter 1) but generally are not distinguished, much of that literature will be omitted here. Similarly, the loss of seed viability is not senescence but a passive process, aging (Chapter 1). In any case, cytokinin does not seem to play a significant role in the aging process (Chapters 13 and 14). Individual seed parts such as the seed coat may senesce as the seed matures (Chapter 1), but little is known about the role of cytokinins therein. The senescence of cotyledons after seed germination is considered in Section IV,B.

The cytokinins present in fruits and seeds have been the subject of innumerable studies, largely because these structures are very rich sources of cytokinins (Letham, 1963,1973; Letham and Williams, 1969; Shindy and Smith, 1975; Davey and Van Staden, 1977; McGlasson et al., 1978; Letham and Palni, 1983). Young seeds and fruits contain the highest levels of cytokinins and these gradually decline to relatively low levels at maturity (Burrows and Carr, 1970; Sandstedt, 1974; Davey and Van Staden, 1979; Hopping et al., 1979; Jameson et al., 1982; Nagar et al., 1982). The cytokinins in the lupin pod walls undergo changes similar to those detected in leaves, a decrease in (D)Z- and (D)ZR-like activity accompanied by an increase in cytokinin glucoside-like activity (Davey and Van Staden, 1978b). The pattern of ZR metabolism in soybean pod walls, however, appears to differ from that in the leaves (Noodén and Letham, 1986). Although import into the fruits could occur via both the xylem and phloem (Davey and Van Staden, 1981a; Van Staden and Davey, 1981; Van Staden, 1983), such import, particularly that into the seeds, appears to be very limited (Noodén and Letham, 1984, 1986), and the young, developing fruits, especially the seeds, may synthesize their own cytokinins (Section II,B).

In fruits, chlorophyll loss and the conversion of chloroplasts to chromo-plasts is frequently accompanied by a decrease in cytokinin titer (Abdel-Rahman *et al.*, 1975; Monselise *et al.*, 1978; Mapelli, 1981; McGlasson *et al.*, 1978). Fruits of the nonripening *rin* tomato variety have a high cytokinin content at the full-green stage, and this persists, whereas in the normally ripening control, the cytokinins decrease as the fruits change color (Davey and Van Staden, 1978c). Thus, cytokinins could be involved in preventing the differentiation of chloroplasts to chromoplasts. These color changes in fruits are, however, more characteristic of ripening than senescence. In fruits, senescence may not always depend on a decline in endogenous cytokinins (McGlasson *et al.*, 1978). In olive fruits, cytokinin treatments altered the color changes characteristic of ripening but not the softening which may reflect senescence (Shulman and Lavee, 1973). Thus, the role of cytokinin in fruit senescence may be fairly complex with big differences among species and even tissues within a fruit. In general, the role of cyto-kinins in fruit senescence seems less striking than their role in leaf senes-cence (McGlasson *et al.*, 1978).

E. Whole Plant Senescence

Fruits and seeds play major roles in the correlative control of growth and development of other plant organs including monocarpic senescence (Chapter 12). The stimulus (senescence signal) and mechanism for this control of monocarpic senescence by fruits and seeds is unknown, but one idea holds that the developing fruits divert the cytokinins flowing up through the xylem thereby creating a deficiency in the leaves (Woolhouse, 1982). There is indirect evidence against this theory (Noodén and Lindoo, 1978), but it has been tested directly. Using soybean explants which consist of a leaf, one or more pods, and a subtending stem segment, defined solu-tions can be substituted for the roots and labeled cytokinins can be fed into the xylem through the cut base of the stem. The pods developing on these explants neither divert the flux of ^{3}H-Z or -ZR through the xylem away from the leaf nor do they withdraw the cytokinins from that leaf (Noodén and Letham, 1984, 1986). Thus, the pods do not induce leaf senescence by directing cytokinins away from the foliage, i.e., the senescence signal is not cytokinin diversion.

The evidence that root-produced cytokinins affect shoots and their senes-cence has been discussed in Sections II,B and III. Many environmental factors, including temperature (Itai *et al.*, 1973; Atkin *et al.*, 1973; Banko and Boe, 1975), pH (Banko and Boe, 1975), nutrient stress (Menary and Van Staden, 1976; Salama and Wareing, 1979), salinity (Itai *et al.*, 1968), photo-period (Van Staden and Wareing, 1972), growth regulator application

(Banko and Boe, 1975), and nematode infestation (Van Staden and Dimalla, 1977) diminish cytokinin production by the roots and thereby cytokinin flux to the shoot. This decrease in turn promotes shoot senescence. Formation of new roots increases cytokinin levels in the leaves (Engelbrecht, 1972; Forsyth and Van Staden, 1981) and delays chlorophyll loss. The connection between root cytokinin production and photosynthetic activity in the leaves is further reinforced by observations that partial defoliation or partial decapitation increases both cytokinin levels and photosynthesis in the leaves (Carmi and Koller, 1978, 1979; Carmi and Van Staden, 1983). Conversely, partial root excision in bean seedlings reduces foliar chlorophyll as well as cytokinin activity levels, and this can be compensated by the application of BA to the leaves (Carmi and Koller, 1978; Carmi and Van Staden, 1983). The most direct evidence to implicate root-produced cytokinins in sustaining the foliage and preventing monocarpic senescence comes from soybean explant studies. By substituting defined solutions of minerals and cytokinins for the roots in explants, it can be shown that the cytokinin required to sustain foliar function and pod development is produced by the roots and this production must decline in order for the pods to induce leaf senescence (Neumann et al., 1983; Noodén, 1985). From the above evidence, it can be concluded that maintenance of root function, particularly cytokinin production, is a major determinant of shoot longevity; however, the decline in cytokinin flux from the roots does not itself cause monocarpic senescence (Neumann et al., 1983; Noodén, 1985).

Root growth is severely reduced during the reproductive phase of the plant life cycle (Leonard, 1962; Noodén, 1980), and this would influence their cytokinin production (Sitton et al., 1967; Letham, 1978; Van Staden and Davey, 1979). Indeed, the cytokinin flux from the roots of soybean plants does decrease during pod development (Heindl et al., 1982). In polycarpic plants, decreases in root cytokinins seem to be a temporary phenomenon as the production of cytokinins again increases after flower senescence (Holland et al., 1981). In monocarpic plants, photosynthate diversion to the fruits at the expense of the roots may contribute to the permanent decrease in growth and cytokinin production in roots (Chapter 12).

During monocarpic senescence, cytokinin activity levels decline in the leaves of rice and soybean (Oritani and Yoshida, 1971, 1973; Lindoo and Noodén, 1978; Table 9.2) but not in the leaves of white lupine (Davey and Van Staden, 1978a; Table 9.2). Although these results need to be reexamined using the newer methods and information on the natural cytokinins (Section III), it does appear that foliar cytokinin activity does decrease during fruit development in most monocarpic plants.

The metabolism of Z and ZR carried through the xylem into the leaves of soybean explants proceeded at a very rapid rate (Noodén and Letham, 1984,

1986). This metabolism, mostly conversion to A and AR and to a lesser extent to O-glucosides, does not change markedly in quality or quantity as senescence progresses. Thus, it appears that the foliar cytokinin levels may be determined by their production in the roots.

While it may seem logical that cytokinins could promote their own flux into the leaves through stimulation of transpiration as described above, this would not change the net production of cytokinin and therefore would not alter foliar cytokinin levels. In reality, the promotive effect of cytokinins on xylem flux is relatively small, and their major effect is to prolong transpiration by extending the life of a leaf (Garrison *et al.*, 1984). It is possible, however, that changes in xylem architecture and thereby cytokinin flux within the whole plant may reinforce progressive leaf senescence (Neumann and Stein, 1984).

It is clear that roots and their ability to produce cytokinins under different environmental conditions and developmental stages of the plant constitute a major factor in both organ and whole plant senescence. However, more attention needs to be given to the significance of the various cytokinins produced in and exported from the roots.

IV. RELATIONSHIPS BETWEEN CYTOKININS AND OTHER HORMONES

Given the importance of multiple hormone action in regulating plant development including senescence (Leopold and Noodén, 1984; Wareing, 1986), it seems important at least to take note of such actions that might involve cytokinins. These interrelations have been studied in leaves, flowers, and fruit, but the overall picture is fragmentary.

Cytokinins do seem to be able to influence both senescence-promoting and -inhibiting hormones (Chapter 10; Letham, 1978). Reciprocally, other hormones are able to influence cytokinin levels and cytokinin action. Numerous examples (Chapter 10) show that exogenous cytokinins can counteract the senescence-promoting effects of abscisic acid, and there are some data to indicate that cytokinins may influence endogenous abscisic acid levels. In some tissues, cytokinins seem to antagonize abscisic acid competitively, but in others, they do not, i.e., they do not completely overcome the abscisic acid effect. In nasturtium leaf disks where both gibberellic acid and Kn were able to retard senescence, Kn caused an increase in gibberellin-like activity (Chin and Beevers, 1970). This suggests that the Kn treatment could act through an effect on gibberellin levels, but there is also evidence in other species that gibberellin and cytokinin may retard leaf senescence through different types of action (Back and Richmond, 1971). Abscisic acid treatments also reduced cytokinin levels in nasturtium leaves (Chin and Beevers, 1970), which would promote senescence. Conversely, cytokinin treatments lowered ABA levels (Aharoni and Richmond, 1978), but as indicated above, abscisic acid may also exert its effects independently of counteracting cytokinins in other species. The nature of the interrelation between cytokinins and abscisic acid seems to differ among tissues and species (Chapter 10).

Cytokinin and ethylene generally alter senescence in opposite directions; however, the relationship between these hormones is complex. Exogenous cytokinin counteracted ethylene, but most of those studies which involved senescence-related processes dealt with fruits (McGlasson *et al.*, 1978) and flowers (Halevy and Mayak, 1979; Mayak and Halevy, 1980; Baker, 1983). Consistent with the usual actions of cytokinin and ethylene on senescence, cytokinins inhibit senescence and ethylene synthesis in carnation flower petals (Eisinger, 1977; Mor *et al.*, 1983; Cook *et al.*, 1985). In other tissues, however, cytokinins, even at such low concentrations as 10^{-7} M, promote ethylene synthesis (Abeles *et al.*, 1967; Yu *et al.*, 1981; Suttle, 1986). This action could account for the rare cases where cytokinin promotes senescence (Mothes *et al.*, 1959; Leopold and Kawase, 1964; Mishra and Gaur, 1980) or abscission (Abeles *et al.*, 1967). In detached rice leaves, however, BA promotes ethylene production and delays senescence at the same time (Kao and Yang, 1983). Silver thiosulphate, an agent which inhibits ethylene production, eliminates a curious transient rise in cytokinin activity in senescing carnation ovaries (Van Staden and Dimalla, 1980a). Cytokinin treatments also seem to decrease tissue sensitivity to ethylene (Mayak and Kofranek, 1976; Eisinger, 1977; Mayak *et al.*, 1977; Kao and Yang, 1983). Cytokinin and ethylene do seem to work together in regulating senescence, but that connection may be mostly indirect.

IV. CONCLUSIONS

Several lines of evidence indicate that cytokinins are important antisenescence hormones in plants and a decline (deficiency) in endogenous cytokinins is often an important factor promoting (or allowing) senescence. The evidence consists mainly of (1) delay of senescence through cytokinin treatments, and (2) correlation of senescence with a decline in endogenous cytokinin levels. The latter usually involves correlation with changes which occur during the natural course of senescence; however, experimental manipulations, such as rooting, have also been used. The data are most extensive for leaves, but the principle seems to apply to other organs such as petals. There also appear to be some cases of noncorrelation, e.g., failure of cytokinins to decline during senescence.

What are the major problems to be worked out in relating cytokinins to senescence? While it seems likely that the past studies have yielded a good outline of the qualitative and quantitative changes of cytokinins in relation to senescence, this needs to be reinforced and made more precise using the recently developed techniques for identifying and measuring the cytokinins. The decline of endogenous cytokinins in senescing tissues may be due to metabolism, to a decrease in biosynthesis, or to diminished transport. The relative importance of each may vary among tissues and species; however, this has not yet been analyzed comprehensively for any single system. It also seems important to know the distribution of the various cytokinins among the tissues of presenescent and senscing organs or even within their constituent cells. Compartmentation may explain why some endogenous cytokinins such as the 0-glucosides seem to be inactive. At this time, however, these problems are technically very difficult to study. The existence of so many types of cytokinins, e.g., Z, DZ, ZR, and DZR, also poses yet unresolved questions about their functions. A better understanding of the mechanisms by which cytokinins work, particularly in tissues where they retard senescence, should help to elucidate the roles of these cytokinins in senescence. One aspect of this analysis of cytokinin action could be better characterization of their protein receptors and localization (e.g., immunocytochemistry) of those which mediate cytokinin action. This would reveal which tissues, cells, and even parts of cells are the targets of cytokinin action.

Looking to the future, it seems that biotechnology should yield some new ways to extend the longevity of harvested plant organs and to maintain their function. First, this could be done by maintaining cytokinin production in and export from the roots or other biosynthetic sites. Second, the inactivation of cytokinins by metabolism could be prevented. Third, it may be possible to develop cytokinins which are more resistant to inactivation and would therefore make more effective senescence-delaying treatments. It must be noted, however, that quite a lot of effort has already been expended on the production of synthetic cytokinins and nothing dramatically more effective than BA has materialized. Fourth, symbiotic or even mildly pathogenic microorganisms could be employed to supply cytokinins. The symbiotic rhizobium bacteria (Badenoch-Jones *et al.*, 1984) and numerous pathogenic microbes (Elstner, 1983) do secrete cytokinins. An interesting case is that of *Psychotria* where leaf disks with bacterial nodules have greater cytokinin levels than those without (Edwards and LaMotte, 1975). Of course, it is important, and not easy, to get the microbes to supply these cytokinins in the right amounts, at the right time and in the right place. Fifth, it should be possible to introduce new genes for cytokinin synthesis into plants or modify the regulation of the existing genes in plants. As above for the microbes, control is important. Specifically in the case of introduced genes, the right promoters and other controlling elements are essential. Indiscriminate cytokinin production would disrupt development rather than just delaying senescence.

REFERENCES

Abdel-Rahman, M., Thomas, T. H., Doss, G. J., and Howell, L. (1975). Changes in endogenous plant hormones in cherry tomato fruits during development and maturation. *Physiol. Plant.* **34**, 39–43.

Abeles, F. B., Holm, R. E., and Gahagan, H. E. (1967). Abscission: The role of aging. *Plant Physiol.* **42**, 1351–1356.

Adedipe, N. O., Hunt, L. A., and Fletcher, R. A. (1971). Effect of benzyladenine on photosynthesis, growth and senescence of bean plant. *Physiol. Plant.* **25**, 151–153.

Aharoni, N., and Richmond, A. E. (1978). Endogenous gibberellin and abscisic acid as related to senescence of detached lettuce leaves. *Plant Physiol.* **62**, 224–228.

Alberte, R. S., and Naylor, A. W. (1975). The role of cytokinins in chloroplast lamellar development. *Plant Physiol.* **55**, 1079–1081.

Aloni, R. (1982). Role of cytokinin in differentiation of secondary xylem fibres. *Plant Physiol.* **70**, 1631–1633.

Anderson, J. W., and Rowan, K. S. (1965). Activity of peptidase in tobacco leaf tissue in relation to senescence. *Biochem. J.* **97**, 741–746.

Arguelles, T., and Guardiola, J. L. (1977). Hormonal control of senescence in excised orange leaves. *J. Hortic. Sci.* **52**, 199–204.

Atkin, R. K., Barton, G. E., and Robinson, D. K. (1973). Effect of root growing temperature on growth substances in xylem exudate of *Zea mays*. *J. Exp. Bot.* **24**, 475–487.

Back, A., and Richmond, A. E. (1971). Interrelations between gibberellic acid, cytokinins and abscisic acid in retarding leaf senescence. *Physiol. Plant.* **24**, 76–79.

Badenoch-Jones, J., Rolfe, B. G., and Letham, D. S. (1984). Phytohormones, *Rhizobium* mutants and nodulation in legumes. V. Cytokinin metabolism in effective and ineffective pea root nodules. *Plant Physiol.* **74**, 239–246.

Baker, J. E. (1983). Preservation of cut flowers. In "Plant Growth Regulating Chemicals" (L. G. Nickell, ed.), pp. 177–191. CRC Press, Boca Raton, Florida.

Ballantyne, D J. (1965). Senescence of daffodil (*Narcissus pseudonarcissus*) cut flowers treated with benzyladenine and auxin. *Nature (London)* **205**, 819.

Banko, T. J., and Boe, A. A. (1975). Effects of pH, temperature, nutrition, ethephon and chlormequat on endogenous cytokinin levels of *Coleus blumei*. *J. Am. Soc. Hortic. Sci.* **100**, 168–172.

Biddington, N. L., and Thomas, T. H. (1978). Influence of different cytokinins on the transpiration and senescence of excised oat leaves. *Physiol. Plant.* **42**, 369–374.

Binnie, R. G., and Clifford, P. E. (1980). Effects of some defoliation and decapitation treatments on the productivity of French beans. *Ann. Bot.* **46**, 811–813.

Biswal, U. C., and Biswal, B. (1984). Photocontrol of leaf senescence. *Photochem. Photobiol.* **39**, 875–879.

Boasson, R., Bonner, J. J., and Laetsch, W. M. (1972). Introduction and regulation of chloroplast replication in mature tobacco leaf tissue. *Plant Physiol.* **49**, 97–101.

Bosselaers, J. P. (1983). Cytokinin effects on leaf architecture in *Phaseolus vulgaris* L. *J. Exp. Bot.* **34**, 1007–1017.

Bruce, M. I., Zwar, J. A., and Kefford, N. P. (1965). Chemical structure and plant kinin activity—the activity of urea and thiourea derivatives. *Life Sci.* **4,** 461–466.

Burrows, W. J., and Carr, D. J. (1969). Effects of flooding the root system of sunflower plants on the cytokinin content in the xylem sap. *Physiol. Plant.* **22,** 1105–1112.

Burrows, W. J., and Carr, D. J. (1970). Cytokinin content of pea seeds during their growth and development. *Physiol. Plant.* **23,** 1064–1070.

Burrows, W. J., and Leworthy, D. P. (1976). Metabolism of N,N^1-diphenylurea by cytokinin-dependent tobacco callus. *Biochem. Biophys. Res. Commun.* **70,** 1109–1114.

Burton, W. G. (1982). "Post-harvest Physiology of Food Crops." Longman, New York.

Caers, M., Rudelsheim, P., Van Onckelen, H., and Horemans, S. (1985). Effect of heat stress on photosynthetic activity and chloroplast ultrastructure in correlation with endogenous cytokinin concentration in maize seedlings. *Plant Cell Physiol.* **26,** 47–52.

Carmi, A., and Koller, D. (1978). Effects of the roots on the rate of photosynthesis in primary leaves of bean (*Phaseolus vulgaris* L.). *Photosynthetica* **12,** 178–184.

Carmi, A., and Koller, D. (1979). Regulation of photosynthetic activity in the primary leaves of bean (*Phaseolus vulgaris* L.) by materials moving in the water conducting system. *Plant Physiol.* **64,** 285–288.

Carmi, A., and Van Staden, J. (1983). Role of roots in regulating the growth rate and cytokinin content of leaves. *Plant Physiol.* **73,** 76–78.

Chen, C.-M., and Leisner, S. M. (1985). Cytokinin-modulated gene expression in excised pumpkin cotyledons. *Plant Physiol.* **77,** 99–103.

Chen, C.-M., and Petschow, B. (1978). Cytokinin biosynthesis in cultured rootless tobacco plants. *Plant Physiol.* **62,** 861–805.

Chen, C.-M., Ertl, J. R., Leisner, S. M. and Chang, C.-C. (1985). Localization of cytokinin biosynthetic sites in pea plants and carrot roots. *Plant Physiol.* **78,** 510–513.

Chen, W. (1982). Cytokinins in the developing mango fruit. *Plant Physiol.* **71,** 356–361.

Chin, T., and Beevers, L. (1970). Changes in endogenous growth regulators in nasturtium leaves during senescence. *Planta* **92,** 178–188.

Colbert, K. A., and Beever, J. E. (1981). Effect of disbudding on root cytokinin export and leaf senescence in tomato and tobacco. *J. Exp. Bot.* **32,** 121–127.

Cook, D., Rasche, M., and Eisinger, W. (1985). Regulation of ethylene biosynthesis and action in cut carnation flower senescence by cytokinins. *J. Am. Soc. Hortic. Sci.* **110,** 24–21.

Cook, E. L., and Van Staden, J. (1983). Senescence of cut carnation flowers. Ovary development and CO_2 fixation. *Plant Growth Regul.* **1,** 221–232.

Corse, J., Gaffield, W., and Lundin, R. E. (1983). Dihydrozeatin: An improved synthesis and resolution of both isomers. *J. Plant Growth Regul.* **2,** 47–57.

Cowley, D. E., Duke, C. C., Liepa, A. J., MacLeod, J. K., and Letham, D. S. (1978). The structure and synthesis of cytokinin metabolites. I. The 7- and 9-β-D-glucofuranosides and pyranosides of zeatin and 6-benzylaminopurine. *Aust. J. Chem.* **31,** 1095–1111.

Davey, J. E., and Van Staden, J. (1976). Cytokinin translocation: Changes in zeatin and zeatin-riboside levels in the root exudate of tomato plants during their development. *Planta* **130,** 69–72.

Davey, J. E., and Van Staden, J. (1977). A cytokinin complex in the developing fruits of *Lupinus albus*. *Physiol. Plant.* **39,** 221–224.

Davey, J. E., and Van Staden, J. (1978a). Cytokinin activity in *Lupinus albus*. I. Distribution in vegetative and flowering plants. *Physiol. Plant.* **43,** 77–81.

Davey, J. E., and Van Staden, J. (1978b). Cytokinin activity in *Lupinus albus*. III. Distribution in fruits. *Physiol. Plant.* **43,** 87–93.

Davey, J. E., and Van Staden, J. (1978c). Endogenous cytokinins in fruits of ripening and non-ripening tomatoes. *Plant Sci. Lett.* **11,** 359–364.

Davey, J. E., and Van Staden, J. (1979). Cytokinin activity in *Lupinus albus*. IV. Distribution in seeds. *Plant Physiol.* **51**, 45–48.

Davey, J. E., and Van Staden, J. (1981a). Cytokinin activity in *Lupinus albus*. V. Translocation and metabolism of 8(^{14}C)t-zeatin applied to the xylem of fruiting plants. *Physiol. Plant.* **51**, 45–48.

Davey, J. E., and Van Staden, J. (1981b). Cytokinins in spinach chloroplasts. *Ann. Bot.* **48**, 243–246.

DeBoer, J., and Feierabend, J. (1974). Comparison of the effects of cytokinins on enzyme development in different cell compartments of the shoot organs of rye seedlings. *Z. Pflanzenphysiol.* **71**, 261–270.

Dedolph, R. R., Wittwer, S. A., and Tuli, W. (1961). Senescence inhibition and respiration. *Science* **134**, 1075.

Dei, M. (1978). Inter-organ control of greening in etiolated cucumber cotyledons. *Physiol. Plant.* **43**, 94–98.

Dei, M. (1982). A two-fold action of benzyladenine on chlorophyll formation in etiolated cucumber cotyledons. *Physiol. Plant.* **56**, 407–414.

Dei, M. (1984). Benzyladenine-induced stimulation of two components of chlorophyll formation in etiolated cucumber cotyledons. *Physiol. Plant.* **62**, 521–526.

Dei, M. (1985). Benzyladenine-induced stimulation of 5-aminolevulinic acid accumulation under various light intensities in levulinic acid-treated cotyledons of etiolated cucumber. *Physiol. Plant.* **64**, 153–160.

Dong, C. N., and Arteca, R. N. (1982). Changes in photosynthetic rates and growth following root treatments of tomato plants with phytohormones. *Photosynth. Res.* **3**, 45–52.

Duke, C. C., Letham, D. S., Parker, C. W., MacLeod, J. K., and Summons, R. E. (1979). The complex of 0-glucosylzeatin derivatives formed in *Populus* species. *Phytochemistry* **18**, 819–824.

Dumbroff, E. B., and Walker, M. A. (1979). The oat leaf test for cytokinin reconsidered. *Ann. Bot.* **44**, 767–769.

Edwards, R. G., and La Motte, C. E. (1975). Evidence for cytokinin in bacterial leaf nodules of *Psychotria punctata* (Rubiaceaa). *Plant Physiol.* **56**, 425–428.

Eisinger, W. (1977). Role of cytokinins in carnation flower senescence. *Plant Physiol.* **59**, 707–709.

Elliott, D. C. (1979). Ionic regulation for cytokinin-dependent betacyanin synthesis in *Amaranthus* seedlings. *Plant Physiol.* **63**, 264–268.

Elstner, E. F. (1983). Hormones and metabolic regulation in disease. *In* "Biochemical Plant Pathology" (J. A. Callow, ed.). Wiley, Chichester, England.

Engelbrecht, L. (1964). Über Kinetinwirkungen bei intakten Blättern von *Nicotiana rustica*. *Flora (Jena)* **154**, 57–69.

Engelbrecht, L. (1971a). Cytokinin activity in larval infected leaves. *Biochem. Physiol. Pflanzen* **162**, 9–27.

Engelbrecht, L. (1971b). Cytokinins in the buds and leaves during growth and ageing (with a comparison of two bioassays). *Biochem. Physiol. Pflanzen* **162**, 547–558.

Engelbrecht, L. (1972). Cytokinins in leaf cuttings of *Phaseolus vulgaris* L. during their development. *Biochem. Physiol. Pflanzen* **163**, 335–343.

Erismann, K. H., and Wegner, F. (1967). Der Einfluss einer wachstumshemmenden Kinetinkonzentration auf Chlorophyllgehalt, Photosynthesrate und Stärkeproduktion von *Lemna minor* L. *Flora (Jena), Abt. A* **158**, 433–442.

Esashi, Y., and Leopold, A. C. (1969). Cotyledon expansion as a bioassy for cytokinins. *Plant Physiol.* **44**, 618–620.

Even-Chen, Z., Atsmon, D., and Itai, C. (1978). Hormonal aspects of senescence in detached tobacco leaves. *Physiol. Plant.* **44**, 377–382.

Ezekiel, R., Sastry, K. S., and Udayakumor, M. (1978). Benzyladenine and potassium induced changes in protein in excised cucumber cotyledons under normal and stress conditions. *Indian J. Exp. Biol.* **16**, 519–522.

Farquhar, G. D., and Sharkey, T. D. (1982). Stomatal conductance and photosynthesis. *Annu. Rev. Plant Physiol.* **33**, 317–345.

Fawcett, C. H., and Wright, S. T. C. (1968). Cytokinin activity in a homologous series of ω-hydroxypolymethyleneaminopurines. *Phytochemistry* **7**, 1719–1725.

Featonby-Smith, B. C., and Van Staden, J. (1981). Endogenous cytokinins and rooting of leaf cuttings of *Phaseolus vulgaris*. *Z. Pflanzenphysiol.* **102**, 329–336.

Featonby-Smith, B. C., Van Staden, J., and Hofman, P. J. (1987). Cytokinins in cut carnation flowers. I. The complex in ovaries. *Plant Growth Regul.* **5**, 15–23.

Feierabend, J. (1969). Der Einfluss von Cytokinin auf die Bildung von Photosyntheseenzyme im Roggenkeimlingen. *Planta* **84**, 11–29.

Feng, K. A. (1973). Effects of kinetin on the permeability of *Allium cepa* cells. *Plant Physiol.* **51**, 868–870.

Fletcher, R. A. (1969). Retardation of leaf senescence by benzyladenine in intact bean plants. *Planta* **89**, 1–8.

Fletcher, R. A., and McCullagh, D. (1971). Cytokinin-induced chlorophyll formation in cucumber cotyledons. *Planta* **101**, 88–90.

Fletcher, R. A., Teo, C., and Ali, A. (1973). Stimulation of chlorophyll synthesis in cucumber cotyledons by benzyladenine. *Can. J. Bot.* **51**, 937–939.

Fletcher, R. A., Kallidumbil, V., and Steele, P. (1982). An improved bioassay for cytokinins using cucumber cotyledons. *Plant Physiol.* **69**, 675–677.

Forsyth, C., and Van Staden, J. (1981). The effect of root decapitation on lateral root formation and cytokinin production in *Pisum sativum* L. *Physiol. Plant.* **51**, 375–379.

Forsyth, C., and Van Staden, J. (1986). The metabolism and cell division activity of adenine derivatives in soybean callus. *J. Plant Physiol.* **124**, 275–287.

Forsyth, C., and Van Staden, J. (1988). Cytokinin metabolism in tomato plants. II. Metabolites of kinetin and benzyladenine in decapitated roots. *Plant Growth Regul.* in press.

Fox, J. E., Cornette, J., Deleuze, G., Dyson, W., and Giersak, C. (1973). The formation, isolation and biological activity of a cytokinin 7-glucoside. *Plant Physiol.* **52**, 627–632.

Fukuda, K., and Toyama, S. (1982). Electron microscope studies on the morphogenesis of plastids. XI. Ultrastructural changes of the chloroplasts in tomato leaves treated with ethylene and kinetin. *Cytologia* **47**, 725–736.

Galli, M. G. (1984). Synthesis of DNA in excised watermelon cotyledons grown in water and benzyladenine. *Planta* **160**, 193–199.

Garrison, F. R., Brinker, A. M., and Noodén, L. D. (1984). Relative activities of xylem-supplied cytokinins in retarding soybean leaf senescence and sustaining pod development. *Plant Cell Physiol.* **25**, 213–224.

Gepstein, S., and Ilan, I. (1979). Cytokinin-induced amylolytic activity in bean cotyledons: Identification of the regulated enzyme. *Plant Cell Physiol.* **20**, 1603–1607.

Gepstein, S., and Ilan, I. (1980). Evidence for involvement of cytokinins in the regulation of proteolytic activity in cotyledons of germinating peas. *Plant Cell Physiol.* **21**, 57–63.

Gilad, T., Ilan, I., and Reinhold, L. (1970). The effect of kinetin and of the embryo axis on the level of reducing sugars in sunflower cotyledons. *Isr. J. Bot.* **19**, 429–433.

Gilbert, M. L., Thompson, J. E., and Dumbroff, E. B. (1980). Delayed cotyledon senescence following treatment with a cytokinin: an effect at the level of membranes. *Can. J. Bot.* **58**, 1797–1802.

Giridhar, G., and Thimann, K.V. (1985). Interaction between senescence and wounding in oat leaves. *Plant Physiol.* **78**, 29–33.

Göring, H., and Mardanov, A. A. (1976). Relations between the K^+/CA^{++} ratio in tissues and the effect of cytokinins in higher plants. *Biol. Rundsch.* **14,** 177–189.

Goldthwaite, J. J., and Laetsch, W. M. (1967). Regulation of senescence in bean leaf disks by light and chemical growth regulators. *Plant Physiol.* **42,** 1757–1762.

Gordon, M. E., Letham, D. S., and Parker, C. W. (1974). The metabolism and translocation of zeatin in intact radish seedlings. *Ann. Bot.* **38,** 809–825.

Green, J. (1983). The effect of potassium and calcium on cotyledon expansion and ethylene evolution induced by cytokinins. *Physiol. Plant.* **57,** 57–61.

Green J., and Muir, R. M. (1978). The effects of potassium on cotyledon expansion induced by cytokinins. *Physiol. Plant.* **43,** 213–218.

Grossman, S., and Leshem, Y. (1978). Lowering of endogenous lipoxygenase activity in *Pisum sativum* foliage by cytokinin as related to senescence. *Physiol. Plant.* **43,** 359–362.

Hahn, H., deZacks, R., and Kende, H. (1974). Cytokinin formation in pea seeds. *Naturwissenschaften* **61,** 170.

Halevy, A. H., and Mayak, S. (1979). Senescence and postharvest physiology of cut flowers, part 1. *Horti. Rev.* **1,** 204–236.

Halevy, A. H., and Mayak, S. (1981). Senescence and postharvest physiology of cut flowers, part 2. *Horti. Rev.* **3,** 59–153.

Halevy, A. H., Dilley, D. R., and Wittwer, S. H. (1966). Senescence inhibition and respiration induced by growth retardants and ^6N-benzyladenine. *Plant Physiol.* **41,** 1085–1089.

Hall, R. H. (1973). Cytokinins as a probe of developmental processes. *Annu. Rev. Plant Physiol.* **24,** 415–444.

Hall, S. M., and Baker, D. A. (1972). The chemical composition of *Ricinus* phloem exudate. *Planta* **106,** 131–140.

Hamzi, H. Q., and Skoog, F. (1964). Kinetin-like growth-promoting activity of 1-substituted adenines (1-benzyl-6-aminopurine and 1-6,6-dimethylallyl-6-aminopurine). *Proc. Natl. Acad. Sci. USA* **51,** 76–83.

Hedley, C. L., and Stoddart, J. L. (1972). Patterns of protein synthesis in *Lolium temulentum* L. I. Changes occurring during leaf development. *J. Exp. Bot.* **23,** 490–501.

Heide, O. M., and Qydvin, J. (1969). Effect of 6-benzylaminopurine on the keeping quality and respiration of glasshouse carnations. *Hortic. Res.* **9,** 26–36.

Heindl, J. C., Carlson, D. R., Brun, W. A., and Brenner, M. L. (1982). Ontogenetic variation of four cytokinins in soybean root pressure exudate. *Plant Physiol.* **70,** 1619–1625.

Helgeson, J. P. (1968). The cytokinins. *Science* **161,** 974–981.

Hendry, N. S., Van Staden, J., and Allan, P. (1982). Cytokinins in *Citrus.* I. Fluctuations in the leaves during seasonal and developmental changes. *Sci. Hortic. (Amsterdam)* **16,** 9–16.

Henson, I. E. (1978a). Types, formation and metabolism of cytokinins in leaves of *Alnus glutinosa* L. Gaertn. *J. Exp. Bot.* **29,** 935–951.

Henson, I. E. (1978b). Cytokinins and their metabolism in leaves of *Alnus glutinosa* L. Gaertn. Effects on leaf development. *Z. Pflanzenphysiol.* **86,** 363–369.

Henson, I. E., and Wareing, P. F. (1976). Cytokinins in *Xanthium strumarium* L.: The distribution in the plant and production in the root system. *J. Exp. Bot.* **27,** 1267–1278.

Henson, I. E., and Wheeler, C. T. (1976). Hormones in plants bearing nitrogen-fixing nodules: The distribution of cytokinins in *Vicia faba* L. *New Phytol.* **76,** 443–439.

Henson, I. E., and Wheeler, C. T. (1977). Hormones in plants bearing nitrogen-fixing root nodules: Metabolism of [8-^{14}C] zeatin in root nodules of *Alnus glutinosa* L. Gaertn. *J. Exp. Bot.* **28,** 1087–1098.

Hewett, E. W., and Wareing, P. F. (1973a). Cytokinins in *Populus x robusta*: Changes during chilling and bud burst. *Physiol. Plant.* **28,** 393–399.

Hewett, E. W., and Wareing, P. F. (1973b). Cytokinins in *Populus x robusta*: Qualitative changes during development. *Physiol. Plant.* **29**, 386–389.

Hewett, E. W., and Wareing, P. F. (1973c). Cytokinins in *Populus x robusta*: A complex in leaves. *Planta* **112**, 225–233.

Hewett, E. W., and Wareing, P. F. (1973d). Cytokinins in *Populus x robusta*: Light effects on endogenous levels. *Planta* **114**, 119–129.

Hoad, S. V., Loveys, B. R., and Skene, K. G. M. (1977). The effect of fruit removal on cytokinins and gibberellin-like substances in grape leaves. *Planta* **136**, 25–30.

Hodgkinson, K. C. (1974). Influence of partial defoliation on photosynthesis, photorespiration and transpiration by lucerne leaves of different ages. *Aust. J. Plant Physiol.* **1**, 561–578.

Holland, S., Kemp, T. R., and Buxton, J. W. (1981). Cytokinin activity of root tissue during chrysanthemum development. *HortScience* **16**, 93–94.

Hopkinson, J. M. (1966). Studies on the expansion of the leaf surface. VI. Senescence and the usefulness of old leaves. *J. Exp. Bot.* **17**, 762–770.

Hopping, M. E., Young, H., and Bukovac, M. J. (1979). Endogenous growth substances in developing fruit of *Prunus cerasus* L. VI. Cytokinins in relation to initial fruit development. *J. Am. Soc. Hortic. Sci.* **104**, 47–52.

Horgan, R. (1986). Cytokinin biosynthesis and metabolism. In "Plant Growth Substances 1985" (M. Bopp, ed.), pp. 92–98. Springer-Verlag, Berlin and New York.

Horgan, R., Hewett, E. W., Purse, J. G., Horgan, J. M., and Wareing, P. F. (1973). Identification of a cytokinin in sycamore sap by gas chromatography-mass spectrometry. *Plant Sci. Lett.* **1**, 321–324.

Howard, H. F., and Witham, F. H. (1983). Invertase activity and the kinetin stimulated enlargement of detached radish cotyledons. *Plant Physiol.* **73**, 304–308.

Huff, A. K., and Ross, C. W. (1975). Promotion of radish cotyledon enlargement and reducing sugar content by zeatin and red light. *Plant Physiol.* **56**, 429–433.

Hutton, M. J., and Van Staden, J. (1985). Cytokinins in the leaves of *Ginkgo biloba*. II. Metabolism and transport of $8(^{14}C)$zeatin applied to shoot explants. *Plant Growth Regul.* **3**, 87–98.

Hutton, M. J., Van Staden, J., and Davey, J. E. (1982). Cytokinins in germinating seeds of *Phaseolus vulgaris* L. I. Changes in endogenous levels within the cotyledons. *Ann. Bot.* **49**, 685–691.

Ilan, I., and Goren, R. (1979). Cytokinins and senescence of lemon leaves. *Physiol. Plant.* **45**, 93–95.

Ilan, I., Gilad, T., and Reinhold, L. (1971). Specific effects of kinetin on the uptake on monovalent cations by sunflower cotyledons. *Physiol. Plant.* **24**, 337–341.

Incoll, L. D., and Jewer, P. C. (1987). Cytokinins and stomata. In "Stomatal Function" (E. Zeiger, G. D. Farquhar, and I. R. Cowan, eds.), pp. 281–292. Stanford Univ. Press, Stanford, California.

Itai, C., and Vaadia, Y. (1965). Kinetin-like activity in root exudate of water-stressed sunflower plants. *Physiol. Plant.* **18**, 941–944.

Itai, C., Richmond, A., and Vaadia, Y. (1968). The role of cytokinins during water and salinity stress. *Isr. J. Bot.* **17**, 187–195.

Itai, C., Ben-Zioni, A., and Ordin, L. (1973). Correlative changes in endogenous hormone levels and shoot growth induced by heat treatment to the root. *Physiol. Plant.* **29**, 355–360.

Jacobs, M., and Fox, J. E., eds. (1987). "Molecular Biology of Plant Growth Control." Alan R. Liss, New York.

Jacobsen, J. V., and Higgins, T. J. V. (1978a). The influence of phytohormones on replication and transcription. In "Phytohormones and Related Compounds: A Comprehensive Treatise. Vol. 1: The Biochemistry of Phytohormones and Related Compounds" (D. S. Letham, P. B. Goodwin, and T. J. V. Higgins, eds.), pp. 515–582. Elsevier/North-Holland, Amsterdam.

Jacobsen, J. V., and Higgins, T. J. V. (1978b). Posttranscriptional, translational and posttranslational effects of plant hormones. *In* "Phytohormones and Related Compounds: A Comprehensive Treatise. Vol. 1: The Biochemistry of Phytohormones and Related Compounds" (D. S. Letham, P. B. Goodwin, and T. J. V. Higgins, eds.), pp. 583–622. Elsevier/North-Holland, Amsterdam.

Jameson, P. E., McWha, J. A., and Wright, G. J. (1982). Cytokinins and changes in their activity during the development of grains of wheat (*Triticum aestivum* L.). *Z. Pflanzenphysiol.* **106,** 27–36.

Jewer, P. C., and Incoll, L. D. (1980). Promotion of stomatal opening in the grass *Anthephora pubescens* Nees by a range of natural and synthetic cytokinins. *Planta* **150,** 218–221.

Kahl, G. (1982). Molecular biology of wound healing: The conditioning phenomenon. *In* "Molecular Biology of Plant Tumors" (G. Kahl and J. S. Schell, eds.), pp. 211–267. Academic Press, New York.

Kaminek, M., and Lustinec, J. (1978). Sensitivity of oat leaf chlorophyll retention bioassay to natural and synthetic cytokinins. *Biol. Plant.* **20,** 377–382.

Kannangara, T. (1977). The regulation of cytokinin levels in mature leaves of *Dahlia variabilis.* *Z. Pflanzenphysiol.* **83,** 85–88.

Kannangara, T., and Booth, A. (1974). Diffusible cytokinins in shoot apices of *Dahlia variabilis.* *J. Exp. Bot.* **25,** 459–467.

Kannangara, T., Durley, R. C., and Simpson, G. M. (1978). High performance chromatographic analysis of cytokinins in *Sorghum bicolor* leaves. *Physiol. Plant.* **44,** 295–299.

Kao, C. H. (1978). Senescence of rice leaves. II. Antisenescent action of cytokinins. *Proc. Natl. Sci. Counc. Repub. China* **2,** 391–398.

Kao, C. H., and Yang, S. F. (1983). Role of ethylene in the senescence of detached rice leaves. *Plant Physiol.* **73,** 881–885.

Karanov, E. N., Vunkova, R., Barth, A., and Pogoncheva, E. (1980). Chemical structure and growth regulating relationship of some piperidinoacetanilides. II. Inhibition of chlorophyll degradation in detached leaves and the influence of chlorophyllase activity. *Biochem. Physiol. Pflanzen* **175,** 140–147.

Kelly, J. (1982). Cytokinin metabolism during senescence. Ph.D. Thesis, Ohio State Univ., Columbus.

Kende, H. (1965). Kinetinlike factors in root exudate of sunflower. *Proc. Natl. Acad. Sci. USA* **53,** 1302–1307.

Kende, H. (1971). The cytokinins. *Int. Rev. Cytol.* **31,** 301–338.

King, R. W. (1976). Implication for plant growth of the transport of regulatory compounds in phloem and xylem. *In* "Transport and Transfer Processes in Plants" (I.F. Wardlaw and J. B. Passioura, eds.), pp. 415–431. Academic Press, New York.

Knypl, J. S., and Chylinska, K. M. (1972). Comparison of the stimulatory effect of potassium on growth, chlorophyll and protein synthesis in the lettuce cotyledons with the effects produced by other univalent ions. *Biochem. Physiol. Pflanzen* **163,** 52–63.

Koda, Y., and Okazawa, Y. (1978). Cytokinin production by tomato roots: Occurrence of cytokinins in staled medium of root culture. *Physiol. Plant.* **44,** 412–416.

Koshimizu, K., and Iwamura, H. (1986). Cytokinins. *In* "Chemistry of Plant Hormones" (N. Takahashi, ed.), pp. 153–199. CRC Press, Boca Raton, Florida.

Kriedemann, P. E., Loveys, B. R., Possingham, J. V., and Satoh, M. (1976). Sink effects on stomatal physiology and photosynthesis. *In* "Transport and Transfer Processes in Plants" (I. F. Wardlaw and J. B. Passioura, eds.), pp. 401–414. Academic Press, New York.

Kuhnle, J. A., Fuller, G., Corse, J., and Bruce E. M. (1977). Antisenescence activity of natural cytokinins. *Physiol. Plant.* **41,** 14–21.

Kulaeva, O. N. (1962). The effect of roots on leaf metabolism in relation to the action of kinetin on leaves. *Sov. Plant Physiol. (Engl. Transl.)* **9,** 182–189.

Kulaeva, O. N., Chernyshev, E. A., Kayutenko, L. A., Dolgaya, M. E., Vorobeva, I. P., Popova, E. A., and Klyachko, N. L. (1965). Synthesis and testing of the physiological activity of certain compounds of the kinin series. *Sov. Plant Physiol. (Engl. Transl.)* **12**, 789–794.

Kull, U., Kühn, B., Schweizer, J., and Weiser, H. (1978). Short-term effects of cytokinins on the lipid fatty acids of green leaves. *Plant Cell Physiol.* **19**, 801–810.

Kuraishi, S. (1976). Ineffectiveness in cytokinin-induced chlorophyll retention in hypostomatous leaf discs. *Plant Cell Physiol.* **17**, 875–885.

Kuraishi, S., Hashimoto, Y., Shiraishi, M. (1981). Latent periods of cytokinin-induced stomatal opening in the sunflower leaf. *Plant Cell Physiol.* **22**, 911–916.

Kursanov, S. L., and Kulaeva, O. N. (1964). Restoration of cellular structure and metabolism in yellow leaves under the action of benzylaminopurine. *Sov. Plant Physiol. (Engl. Transl.)* **11**, 838–847.

Kursanov, A. L., Kulaeva, O. N., and Mikulovich, T. P. (1969). Combined effects of 6-benzylaminopurine, gibberellic acid, and 3-indoleacetic acid on the expansion of isolated pumpkin cotyledons. *Am. J. Bot.* **56**, 767–772.

Laetsch, W. M., and Boasson, R. (1972). Effect of growth regulation on organelle development. *In* "Hormonal Regulation in Plant Growth and Development" (H. Kaldewey and A. Vardar, eds.), pp. 453–465. Verlag Chemie, Weinheim.

Laetsch, W. M., and Stetler, D. A. (1965). Chloroplast structure and function in cultured tobacco tissue. *Am. J. Bot.* **52**, 798–804.

Laidman, D. L. (1982). Control mechanisms in the mobilisation of stored nutrients in germinating cereals. *In* "The Physiology and Biochemistry of Seed Dormancy and Germination" (A. A. Khan, ed.), pp. 371–405. Elsevier, Amsterdam.

Laloue, M., Terrine, C., and Guern, J. (1977). Cytokinins: metabolism and biological activity of N^6-(Δ^2-isopentenyl) adenosine and N^6-(Δ^2-isopentenyl) adenine in tobacco cells and callus. *Plant Physiol.* **59**, 478–483.

Lee, Y., Mok, M. C., Mok, D. W. S., Griffin, D. A., and Shaw, G. (1985). Cytokinin metabolism in *Phaseolus* embryos. Genetic difference and the occurrence of novel zeatin metabolites. *Plant Physiol.* **77**, 635–641.

Legocka, J., and Szweykowska, A. (1981). The role of cytokinins in the development and metabolism of barley leaves. III. The effect on the RNA metabolism in various cell compartments during senescence. *Z. Pflanzenphysiol.* **102**, 363–374.

Legocka, J., and Szweykowska, A. (1983). The role of cytokinins in the development and metabolism of barley leaves. VI. The effect on the protein metabolism in various cell compartments during leaf senescence. *Acta Physiol. Plant.* **5**, 11–20.

Leonard, E. R. (1962). Inter-relations of vegetative and reproductive growth, with special reference to indeterminate plants. *Bot. Rev.* **28**, 353–410.

Leonard, N. J., Hecht, S. M., Skoog, F., and Schmitz, R. Y. (1969). Cytokinins: Synthesis, mass spectra and biological activity of compounds related to zeatin. *Proc. Natl. Acad. Sci. USA* **63**, 175–182.

Leopold, A. C., and Kawase, M. (1964). Benzyladenine effects on bean leaf growth and senescence. *Am. J. Bot.* **51**, 294–298.

Leopold, A. C., and Noodén, L. D. (1984). Hormonal regulatory systems in plants. *In* "Encyclopedia of Plant Physiology. N.S. Vol. 10: Hormonal Regulation of Development II" (T. K. Scott, ed.), pp. 4–22. Springer-Verlag, Berlin and New York.

Leshem, Y. Y. (1984). Interaction of cytokinins with lipid-associated oxy-free radicals during senescence: A prospective mode of cytokinin action. *Can. J. Bot.* **62**, 2943–2949.

Letham, D. S. (1963). Zeatin a factor inducing cell division from *Zea mays. Life Sci.* **2**, 569–573.

Letham, D. S. (1967a). Chemistry and physiology of kinetin-like compounds. *Annu. Rev. Plant Physiol.* **18**, 349–364.

Letham, D. S. (1967b). Regulators of cell division in plant tissues. V. A comparison of the activities of zeatin and other cytokinins in five bioassays. *Planta* 74, 228–242.

Letham, D. S. (1971). Regulators of cell division in plant tissues XII. A cytokinin bioassay using excised radish cotyledons. *Physiol. Plant.* 25, 391–396.

Letham, D. S. (1973). Cytokinins from *Zea mays. Phytochemistry* 12, 2445–2455.

Letham, D. S. (1978). Cytokinins. In "Phytohormones and Related Compounds: A Comprehensive Treatise. Vol. 1: The Biochemistry of Phytohormones and Related Compounds" (D. S. Letham, P. B. Goodwin, and T. J. V. Higgins, eds.), pp. 205–263. Elsevier/North-Holland, Amsterdam.

Letham, D. S., and Gollnow, B. I. (1985). Regulators of cell division in plant tissues XXX. Cytokinin metabolism in relation to radish cotyledon expansion and senescence. *J. Plant Growth Regul.* 4, 129–146

Letham, D. S., and Palni, L. M. S. (1983). The biosynthesis and metabolism of cytokinins. *Annu. Rev. Plant Physiol.* 34, 163–197.

Letham, D. S., and Williams, M. W. (1969). Regulators of cell division in plant tissues. VIII. The cytokinins of the apple fruit. *Physiol. Plant.* 22, 925–936.

Letham, D. S., Wilson, M. M., Parker, C. W., Jenkins, I. D., MacLeod, J. K., and Summons, R. E. (1975). The identity of an unusual metabolite of 6-benzylaminopurine. *Biochim. Biophys. Acta* 399, 61–70.

Letham, D. S., Summons, R. E., Parker, C. W., and MacLeod, J. K. (1979). Regulators of cell division in plant tissues XXVII. Identification of an amino-acid conjugate of 6-benzylaminopurine formed in *Phaseolus vulgaris* seedlings. *Planta* 146, 71–74.

Letham, D. S., Palni, L. M. S., Tao, G.-Q., Gollnow, B. I., and Bates, C. M. (1983). Regulators of cell division in plant tissues: XXIX. The activities of cytokinin glucosides and alanine conjugates in cytokinin bioassays. *J. Plant Growth Regul.* 2, 103–115.

Levitt, J. (1980a). "Responses of Plants to Environmental Stresses. Vol. 1: Chilling, Freezing, and High Temperature Stresses." Academic Press, New York.

Levitt, J. (1980b). "Responses of Plants to Environmental Stresses. Vol. 2: Water, Radiation, Salt and Other Stresses." Academic Press, New York.

Lichtenthaler, H., and Buschmann, C. (1978). Control of chloroplast development. In "Plant Biology 2. Chloroplast Development" (G. Akoyunoglou and J. H. Argyroudi-Akoyunoglou), pp. 801–816. Elsevier, Amsterdam.

Lindoo, S. J., and Noodén, L. D. (1978). Correlations of cytokinins and abscisic acid with monocarpic senescence in soybean. *Plant Cell Physiol.* 19, 997–1006.

Livne, A., and Graziani, Y. (1972). A rapid effect of kinetin on rehydration of tobacco leaf tissue. *Plant Physiol.* 49, 124–126.

Livne, A., and Vaadia, Y. (1965). Stimulation of transpiration rate in barley leaves by kinetin and gibberellic acid. *Physiol. Plant.* 18, 658–664.

Lorenzi, R., Horgan, R., and Wareing, P. F. (1975). Cytokinins in *Picea sitchensis* C.: Identification and relation to growth. *Biochem. Physiol. Pflanzen* 168, 333–339.

Lovell, P., and Moore, K. (1970). The effects of 6-benzylaminopurine on growth and ^{14}C translocation in excised mustard cotyledons. *Physiol. Plant.* 23, 179–186.

McDavid, C. R., Sagar, G. R., and Marshall, C. (1973). The effect of root pruning and 6-benzylaminopurine on the chlorophyll content, $^{14}CO_2$ fixation and the shoot/root ratio in seedlings of *Pisum sativum* L. *New Phytol.* 72, 465–470.

McGlasson, W. B., Wade, N. L., and Adato, I. (1978). Phytohormones and fruit ripening. In "Phytohormones and Related Compounds: A Comprehensive Treatise. Vol. 2: Phytohormones and the Development of Higher Plants" (D. S. Letham, P. B. Goodwin, and T. J. V. Higgens, eds.), pp. 447–493. Elsevier/North-Holland, Amsterdam

MacLean, D. C., and Dedolph, R. R. (1962). Effects of N⁶-benzylaminopurine on postharvest respiration of *Chrysanthemum morifolium* and *Dianthus caryophyllus. Bot. Gaz.* 124, 20–21.

MacLeod, J. K., Summons, R. E., and Letham, D. S. (1976). Mass spectrometry of cytokinin metabolites. Per (trimethylsilyl) and per methyl derivatives of glucosides of zeatin and 6-benzylaminopurine. *J. Org. Chem.* **41**, 3959–3967.

Mapelli, S. (1981). Changes in cytokinin in the fruits of parthenocarpic and normal tomatoes. *Plant Sci. Lett.* **22**, 227–233.

Matsubara, S. (1980). Structure-activity relationships of cytokinins. *Phytochemistry* **19**, 2239–2253.

Matsubara, S., Shiojiri, S., Fujii, T., Ogawa, N., Imamura, K., Yamagishi, K., and Koshimizu, K. (1977). Synthesis and cytokinin activity of (R)-(+)- and (S)-(-)-dihydrozeatins and their ribosides. *Phytochemistry* **16**, 933–937.

Matsubara, S., Sugiyama, T., and Hashizume, T. (1978). Cytokinin activity of benzoylamino-deazapurines, pentanoylaminodeazapurines and their corresponding purine analogs in five bioassays. *Physiol. Plant.* **42**, 114–118.

Mauk, C. S., and Noodén, L. D. (1983). Cytokinin control of mineral nutrient redistribution between the foliage and seeds in soybean explants. *Plant Physiol.* 72 Suppl., 167.

Mayak, S., and Dilley, D. R. (1976). Effect of sucrose on response of cut carnation to kinetin, ethylene and abscisic acid. *J. Am. Soc. Hortic. Sci.* **101**, 583–585.

Mayak, S., and Halevy, A. H. (1970). Cytokinin activity in rose petals and its relation to senescence. *Plant Physiol.* **46**, 497–499.

Mayak, S., and Halevy, A. H. (1974). The action of kinetin in improving the water balance and delaying senescence processes of cut rose flowers. *Physiol. Plant.* **32**, 330–336.

Mayak, S., and Halevy, A. H. (1980). Flower senescence. In "Senescence in Plants" (K. V. Thimann, ed.), pp. 131–156. CRC Press, Boca Raton, Florida.

Mayak, S., and Kofranek, A. (1976). Altering the sensitivity of carnation flowers (*Dianthus caryophyllus* L.) to ethylene. *J. Am. Soc. Hortic. Sci.* **101**, 503–506.

Mayak, S., Halevy, A. H., and Katz, M. (1972). Correlative changes in phytohormones in relation to senescence in rose petals. *Physiol. Plant.* **27**, 1–4.

Mayak, S., Vaadia, Y., and Dilley, D. R. (1977). Regulation of senescence in carnation, *Dianthus caryophyllum*, by ethylene. Mode of action. *Plant Physiol.* **59**, 591–593.

Meidner, H. (1967). The effect of kinetin on stomatal opening and the rate of intake of carbon dioxide in mature primary leaves of barley. *J. Exp. Bot.* **18**, 556–561.

Meidner, H. (1970). Effects of photoperiodic induction and debudding in *Xanthium pennsylvanieum* and of partial defoliation in *Phaseolus vulgaris* on rates of net photosynthesis and stomatal conductances. *J. Exp. Bot.* **21**, 164–169.

Menary, R. C., and Van Staden, J. (1976). Effect of phosphorus nutrition and cytokinin on flowering in the tomato *Lycopersicon esculentum* Mill. *Aust. J. Plant Physiol.* **3**, 201–205.

Metivier, J., and Paulilo, M. T. (1980). The utilization of cotyledonary reserves in *Phaseolus vulgaris* L. cv. Carioca. II. The effects of 6- benzyladenine and gibberellic acid upon embryonated and detached cotyledons. *J. Exp. Bot.* **31**, 1271–1282.

Miernyk, J. A., and Blaydes, D. F. (1977). Short-term metabolism of radioactive kinetin during lettuce seed germination. *Physiol. Plant.* **39**, 4–8.

Miller, C. O. (1982). Cytokinin modification of mitochondrial function. *Plant Physiol.* **69**, 1274–1277.

Mishra, D., and Misra, B. (1973). Retardation of induced senescence of leaves from crop plants by benzimidazole and cytokinins. *Exp. Gerontol.* **8**, 235–239.

Mishra, D., and Pradhan, P. K. (1973). Regulation of senescence in detached rice leaves by light, benzimidazole and kinetin. *Exp. Gerontol.* **8**, 153–155.

Mishra, S. D., and Gaur, B. K. (1980). Growth regulator control of senescence in discs of betel (*Piper betle* L.) leaf: Effect of rate and degree of senescence. *Indian J. Exp. Bot.* **18**, 297–298.

Mitchell, J. J., and Van Staden, J. (1983). Cytokinins and the wounding response in potato tissue. *Z. Pflanzenphysiol.* **109**, 1–5.

Miura, G. A. and Hall, R. H. (1973). *trans*-Ribosylzeatin. Its biosynthesis in *Zea mays* endosperm and the mycorrhizal fungus *Rhizopogon roseolus. Plant Physiol.* **51,** 563–569.

Mlodzianowski, F., and Kwintkiewicz, M. (1973). The inhibition of kohlrabi chloroplast degeneration by kinetin. *Protoplasma* **76,** 211–226.

Mok, D. W. S., and Mok, M. C. (1987). Metabolism of ^{14}C-zeatin in *Phaseolus* embryos. Occurrence of 0-xylosyldihydrozeatin and its ribonucleoside. *Plant Physiol.* **84,** 596–599.

Mok, M. C., Kim, S.-G., Armstrong, D. J., and Mok, D. W. S. (1979). Induction of cytokinin autonomy by N, N^1-diphenylurea in tissue cultures of *Phaseolus lunatus* L. *Proc. Natl. Acad. Sci. USA* **76,** 3880–3884.

Mok, M. C., Mok, D. W. S., Armstrong, D. J., Shudo, K., Isogai, Y., and Okamoto, T. (1982). Cytokinin activity of N-phenyl-N-1,2,3-thiadiazol-5-ylurea (Thidiazuron). *Phytochemistry* **21,** 1509–1511.

Molisch, H. (1938). "The Longevity of Plants" (H. Fulling, transl.). Science Press, Lancaster, Pennsylvania.

Monselise, S. P., Varga, A., Knegt, E., and Bruinsma, J. (1978). Course of the zeatin content in tomato fruits and seeds developing on intact or partially defoliated plants. *Z. Pflanzenphysiol.* **90,** 451–460.

Mor, Y., Spiegelstein, H., and Halevy, A. H. (1983). Inhibition of ethylene biosynthesis in carnation petals by cytokinin. *Plant Physiol.* **71,** 541–546.

Mothes, K. (1960). Über das Altern der Blätter und die Moglichkeit ihrer Wiederverjüngung. *Naturwissenschaften* **47,** 337–351.

Mothes, K., and Baudisch, W. (1958). Untersuchungen über die Reversibilität der Ausbleichung grüner Blätter. *Flora (Jena)* **146,** 521–531.

Mothes, K., and Engelbrecht, L. (1961). Kinetin-induced directed transport of substances in excised leaves in the dark. *Phytochemistry* **1,** 58–62.

Mothes, K., Engelbrecht, L., and Kulaeva, O. (1959). Über die Wirkung des Kinetins auf Stickstoffverteilung und Eiweisssynthese in isolierte Blättern. *Flora (Jena)* **147,** 445–464.

Mothes, K., Engelbrecht, L., and Schütte, H. R. (1961). Über die Akkumulation von α-Aminoisobuttersäure in Blatt gewebe unter dem Einfluss von Kinetin. *Physiol. Plant.* **14,** 72–75.

Müller, K., and Leopold, A. C. (1966). The mechanism of kinetin-induced transport in corn leaves. *Planta* **68,** 186–205.

Murray, D. R. (1984). Axis-cotyledon relationships during reserve mobilization. *In* "Seed Physiology. Vol. 2: Germination and Reserve Mobilization" (D. R. Murray, ed.), pp. 247–280. Academic Press, Orlando, Florida.

Nagar, P. K., Iyer, R. I., and Sircar, P. K. (1982). Cytokinins in developing fruits of *Moringa pteriogosperma* Gaertn. *Physiol. Plant.* **55,** 45–50.

Naito, K., Tsuji, H., and Hatakeyama, I. (1978). Effect of benzyladenine on DNA, RNA, protein and chlorophyll contents in intact bean leaves: Differential responses to benzyladenine according to leaf age. *Physiol. Plant.* **43,** 367–371.

Naito, K., Tsuji, H., Hatakeyama, I., and Ueda, K. (1979). Benzyladenine-induced increase in DNA content per cell, chloroplast size and chloroplast number per cell in intact bean leaves. *J. Exp. Bot.* **30,** 1145–1151.

Nessling, F. A., and Morris, D. A. (1979). Cytokinin levels and embryo abortion in interspecific *Phaseolus* crosses. *Z. Pflanzenphysiol.* **91,** 345–358.

Neumann, P. M., and Noodén, L. D. (1983). Interaction of mineral and cytokinin supply in control of leaf senescence and seed growth in soybean explants. *J. Plant Nutr.* **6,** 735–742.

Neumann, P. M., and Stein, Z. (1984). Relative rates of delivery of xylem solute to shoot tissues: Possible relationship to sequential leaf senescence. *Physiol. Plant.* **62,** 390–397.

Neumann, P. M., Tucker, A. T., and Noodén, L. D. (1983). Characterization of leaf senescence and pod development in soybean explants. *Plant Physiol.* **72,** 182–185.

Nichols, R., and Ho, L. C. (1975). An effect of ethylene on the distribution of ¹⁴C-sucrose from the petals to other flower parts in the senescent cut inflorescence of *Dianthus caryophyllus*. *Ann. Bot.* **39**, 433–438.

Noodén, L. D. (1980). Senescence in the whole plant. *In* "Senescence in Plants" (K. V. Thimann, ed.), pp. 219–258. CRC Press, Boca Raton, Florida.

Noodén, L. D. (1985). Regulation of soybean senescence. *In* "World Soybean Research Conference III: Proceedings" (R. Shibles, ed.), pp. 891–900. Westview Press, Boulder, Colorado.

Noodén, L. D., and Leopold, A. C. (1978). Photohormones and the endogenous regulation of senescence and abscission. *In* "Phytohormones and Related Compounds: A Comprehensive Treatise. Vol. 2: Phytohormones and the Development of Higher Plants" (D. S. Letham, P. B. Goodwin, and T. J. V. Higgins, eds.), pp. 329–369. Elsevier/North-Holland, Amsterdam.

Noodén, L. D., and Letham, D. S. (1984). Translocation of zeatin riboside and zeatin in soybean explants. *J. Plant Growth Regul.* **2**, 265–279.

Noodén, L. D., and Letham, D. S. (1986). Cytokinin control of monocarpic senescence in soybean. *In* "Plant Growth Substances 1985" (M. Bopp, ed.), pp. 324–332. Springer-Verlag, Berlin and New York.

Noodén, L. D., and Lindoo, S. J. (1978). Monocarpic senescence. *What's New Plant Physiol.* **9**, 25–28.

Noodén, L. D., Kahanak, G. M., and Okatan, Y. (1979). Prevention of monocarpic senescence in soybeans with auxin and cytokinin: An antidote for self-destruction. *Science* **206**, 841–843.

Oritani, T., and Yoshida, R. (1971). Studies on nitrogen metabolism in crop plants. XI. The changes of abscisic acid and cytokinin-like activity accompanying with growth and senescence in the crop plants. *Proc. Crop Sci. Soc. Jpn.* **40**, 325–331.

Oritani, T., and Yoshida, R. (1973). Studies on nitrogen metabolism in crop plants. XII. Cytokinins and abscisic acid-like substances levels in rice and soybean leaves during their growth and senescence. *Proc. Crop Sci. Soc. Jpn.* **42**, 280–287.

Osborne, D. J., and Moss, S. E. (1963). Effect of kinetin on senescence and abscission in explants of *Phaseolus vulgaris*. *Nature (London)* **200**, 1299–1301.

Palmer, M. V., and Wong, O. C. (1985). Identification of cytokinins from xylem exudate of *Phaseolus vulgaris* L. *Plant Physiol.* **79**, 296–298.

Palmer, M. V., Horgan, R., and Wareing, P. F. (1981a). Cytokinin metabolism in *Phaseolus vulgaris* L. I. Variations in cytokinin levels in leaves of decapitated plants in relation to lateral bud outgrowth. *J. Exp. Bot.* **32**, 1231–1241.

Palmer, M. V., Horgan, R., and Wareing, P. F. (1981b). Cytokinin metabolism in *Phaseolus vulgaris* L. III. Identification of endogenous cytokinins and metabolism of [8-¹⁴C]-dihydrozeatin in stems of decapitated plants. *Planta* **153**, 297–302.

Palmer, M. V., Scott, I. M., and Horgan, R. (1981c). Cytokinin metabolism in *Phaseolus vulgaris* L. II. Comparative metabolism of exogenous cytokinins by detached leaves. *Plant Sci. Lett.* **22**, 187–195.

Palni, L. M. S., Horgan, R., Darrall, N. M., Stuchbury, T., and Wareing, P. F. (1983). Cytokinin biosynthesis in crown-gall tissue of *Vinca rosea*: The significance of nucleotides. *Planta* **159**, 50–59.

Palni, L. M. S., Palmer, M. V., and Letham, D. S. (1984). The stability and biological activity of cytokinin metabolites in soybean (*Glycine max*) callus tissue. *Planta* **160**, 242–249.

Parker, C. W., and Letham, D. S. (1973). Metabolism of zeatin by radish cotyledons and hypocotyls. *Planta* **114**, 199–218.

Parker, C. W., Letham, D. S., Gollnow, B. I., Summons, R. E., Duke, C. C., and MacLeod, J. K. (1978). Metabolism of zeatin by lupin seedlings. *Planta* **142**, 239–251.

324   Johannes Van Staden et al.

Parthier, B. (1979). The role of phytohormones (cytokinins) in chloroplast development. *Biochem. Physiol. Pflanzen* **174**, 173–214.

Patrick, J. W., Johnstone, G. F. S., and Wareing, P. F. (1979). Mobilizing ability of gibberellic acid and kinetin applied to mature decapitated stems of *Phaseolus vulgaris* L. *Ann. Bot.* **44**, 517–519.

Penner, D., and Ashton, F. M. (1967). Hormonal control of isocitrate lyase synthesis. *Biochim. Biophys. Acta* **148**, 481–485.

Penot, M., Béraud, J., and Poder, D. (1981). Relationship between hormone-directed transport and transpiration in isolated leaves of *Pelargonium zonale* (L.) Aiton. *Physiol. Veg.* **19**, 391–399.

Phillips, D. A., and Cleland, C. F. (1972). Cytokinin activity from the phloem sap of *Xanthium strumarium* L. *Planta* **102**, 173–178.

Purohit, S. S. (1982). Prevention by kinetin of ethylene-induced chlorophyllase activity in senescing detached leaves of *Helianthus annuus*. *Biochem. Physiol. Pflanzen* **177**, 625–627.

Purse, J. G., Horgan, R., Horgan, J. M., and Wareing, P. F. (1976). Cytokinins in sycamore sap. *Planta* **132**, 1–8.

Richmond, A. E., and Lang, A. (1957). Effect of kinetin on protein content and survival of detached *Xanthium* leaves. *Science* **125**, 650–651.

Richmond, A. E., Sachs, B., and Osborne, D. J. (1971). Chloroplasts, kinetin and protein synthesis. *Physiol. Plant.* **24**, 176–180.

Rohfritsch, O., and Shorthouse, J. D. (1982). Insect galls. *In* "Molecular Biology of Plant Tumors" (G. Kahl and J. S. Schell, eds.), pp. 131–152. Academic Press, New York.

Rybicka, H., Engelbrecht, L., Mikulovich, T. P., and Kulaeva, O. N. (1977). Investigation of endogenous substances with cytokinin activity in pumpkin cotyledons in connection with characteristics of action of exogenous cytokinins on them. *Sov. Plant Physiol. (Engl. Transl.)* **24**, 292–299.

Sabater, B., and Rodriquez, M. T. (1978). Control of chlorophyll degradation in detached leaves of barley and oat through effect of kinetin on chlorophyllase levels. *Physiol. Plant.* **43**, 274–276.

Sabater, B., Rodriquez, M. T., and Zamorano, A. (1981). Effects and interactions of gibberellic acid and cytokinins on the retention of chlorophyll and phosphate in barley leaf segments. *Physiol. Plant.* **51**, 361–364.

Sachs, T., and Thimann, K. V. (1964). Release of lateral buds from apical dominance. *Nature (London)* **201**, 939–940.

Saha, S., Nagar, P. K., and Sircar, P. K. (1985). Changes in cytokinin activity during flower development in *Cosmos sulphureus* Cav. *Plant Growth Regul.* **3**, 27–35.

Salama, A. M. el D., and Wareing, P. F. (1979). Effects of mineral nutrition on endogenous cytokinin in plants of sunflower. *J. Exp. Bot.* **30**, 971–981.

Sandstedt, T. (1974). Relative activities of some cytokinin fractions of developing cotton fruit. *Physiol. Plant.* **30**, 168–171.

Sattelmacher, B., and Marschner, H. (1978). Nitrogen nutrition and cytokinin activity in *Solanum tuberosum*. *Physiol. Plant.* **42**, 185–189.

Schneider, J., Gwozdz, E., and Szweykowska, A. (1978). Role of cytokinins in the development and metabolism of barley leaves: II. The effect on the DNA-dependent RNA polymerase during leaf senescence. *Z. Pflanzenphysiol.* **86**, 31–40.

Sen, D. N., and Sharma, K. D. (1972). Role of cytokinins and certain growth regulators on excised cotyledons of *Merremia aegyptia* (L.) Urban. *Biochem. Physiol. Pflanzen* **163**, 556–561.

Seth, A. K., and Wareing, P. F. (1967). Hormone-directed transport of metabolites and its possible role in plant senescence. *J. Exp. Bot.* **18**, 65–77.

Shaw, M., and Manocha, M. S. (1965). Fine structure in detached, senescing wheat leaves. *Can. J. Bot.* **43**, 747–755.

Sheldrake, A. R. (1973). The production of hormones in higher plants. *Biol. Rev. Cambridge Philos. Soc.* **48**, 509–560.

Shindy, W. W., and Smith, O. E. (1975). Identification of plant hormones from cotton ovules. *Plant Physiol.* **55**, 550–554.

Shininger, T. L. (1979). The control of vascular development. *Annu. Rev. Plant Physiol.* **30**, 313–337.

Short, K. C., and Torrey, J. G. (1972). Cytokinins in seedling roots of pea. *Plant Physiol.* **49**, 155–160.

Shulman, Y., and Lavee, S. (1973). The effect of cytokinins and auxins on anthocyanin accumulation in green Manzanillo olives. *J. Exp. Bot.* **24**, 655–661.

Singh, N., and Mishra, D. (1965). The effect of benzimidazole and red light on the senescence of detached leaves of *Oryza sativa* cv. Ratna. *Physiol. Plant.* **34**, 67–74.

Singh, S., Letham, D. S., Jameson, P. E., Zhang, R., Parker, C. W., Badenoch-Jones, J., and Noodén, L. D. (1988). Cytokinin biochemistry in relation to leaf senescence. IV. Cytokinin metabolism in soybean explants. In preparation.

Sitton, D., Itai, C., and Kende, H. (1967). Decreased cytokinin production in the roots as a factor in shoot senescence. *Planta* **73**, 296–300.

Skene, K. G. M. (1975). Cytokinin production by roots as a factor in the control of plant growth. *In* "The Development and Function of Roots" (J. G. Torrey and D. T. Clarkson, eds.), pp. 365–396. Academic Press, London.

Skoog, F., and Armstrong, D. J. (1970). Cytokinins. *Annu. Rev. Plant Physiol.* **21**, 359–384.

Skoog, F., Hamzi, H. Q., Szweykowska, A. M., Leonard, N. J., Carraway, K. L., Fujii, T., Helgeson, J. P., and Loeppky, R. N. (1967). Cytokinins: Structure activity relationships. *Phytochemistry* **6**, 1169–1192.

Sodek, L., and Wright, S. T. C. (1969). The effect of kinetin on ribonuclease acid phosphatase, lipase and esterase levels in detached wheat leaves. *Phytochemistry* **8**, 1629–1640.

Spencer, D., and Wildman, S. G. (1964). The incorporation of amino acids into protein by cell-free extracts from tobacco leaves. *Biochemistry* **3**, 954–959.

Sprent, J. I. (1968). The effects of benzyladenine on the growth and development of peas. *Planta* **78**, 17–24.

Stoddart, J. L., and Thomas, H. (1982). Leaf senescence. *Encycl. Plant Physiol., New Ser.* **14A**, 592–636.

Suttle, J. C. (1986). Cytokinin-induced ethylene biosynthesis in nonsenescing cotton leaves. *Plant Physiol.* **82**, 930–935.

Takeuchi, Y., Saito, M., Kondo, N., and Sugahara, K. (1985). Inhibition of zeatin-induced growth of cucumber cotyledons by sulfite ions. *Plant Cell Physiol.* **26**, 123–130.

Tao, G.-Q., Letham, D. S., Palni, L. M. S., and Summons, R. E. (1983). Cytokinin biochemistry in relation to leaf senescence. I. The metabolism of 6-benzylaminopurine and zeatin in oat leaf segments. *J. Plant Growth Regul.* **2**, 89–102.

Taya, Y., Tanaka, Y., and Nishimura, S. (1978). 5^1-AMP is a direct precursor of cytokinin in *Dictyostelium discoideum*. *Nature (London)* **271**, 545–547.

Tetley, R. M., and Thimann, K. V. (1974). The metabolism of oat leaves during senescence. I. Respiration, carbohydrate metabolism, and the action of cytokinins. *Plant Physiol.* **54**, 294–303.

Theimer, R. R., Anding, G., and Matzner, P. (1976). Kinetin action on the development of microbody enzymes in sunflower cotyledons in the dark. *Planta* **128**, 41–47.

Thimann, K. V. (1980). The senescence of leaves. *In* "Senescence in Plants" (K. V. Thimann, ed.), pp. 85–115. CRC Press, Boca Raton, Florida.

Thimann, K. V., and Satler, S. O. (1979). Interrelation between leaf senescence and stomatal aperture. *Proc. Natl. Acad. Sci. USA* **76**, 2295–2298.

Thimann, K. V., Tetley, R. M., and Krivak, B. M. (1977). Metabolism of oat leaves during senescence. V. Senescence in light. *Plant Physiol.* **59**, 448–454.

Thimann, K. V., Satler, S. O., and Trippi, V. (1982). Further extension of the syndrome of leaf senescence. *In* "Plant Growth Substances 1982" (P. F. Wareing, ed.), pp. 539–548. Academic Press, London.

Thomas, H., and Stoddart, J. L. (1980). Leaf senescence. *Annu. Rev. Plant Physiol.* **31**, 83–111.

Thomas, T. H. (1968). Studies on senescence-delaying substances extracted from *Brassica oleracea gemmifera* L. *J. Hortic. Sci.* **43**, 59–68.

Thomas, T. H. (1977). Hormonal control of brussel sprout senescence. *Acta Hortic.* **62**, 295–300.

Thomas, T. H., Biddington, N. L., and O'Toole, D. F. (1978). The location of cytokinins and gibberellins in wheat seeds. *Physiol. Plant.* **42**, 61–66.

Treharne, K. J., Stoddart, J. L., Pughe, J., Paranjothy, K., and Wareing, P. F. (1970). Effects of gibberellin and cytokinins on the activity of photosynthetic enzymes and plastid ribosomal RNA synthesis in *Phaseolus vulgaris* L. *Nature (London)* **228**, 129–131.

Tsuji, H., Naito, K., Hatakeyama, I., and Ueda, K. (1979). Benzyladenine-induced increase in DNA content per cell, chloroplast size and chloroplast number per cell in intact bean leaves. *J. Exp. Bot.* **30**, 1145–1151.

Tuli, V., Dilley, D. R., and Wittwer, S. H. (1964). N^6-Benzyladenine: Inhibitor of respiratory kinases. *Science* **146**, 1477–1479.

Uheda, E., and Kuraishi, S. (1977). Increase of cytokinin activity in detached etiolated cotyledons of squash after illumination. *Plant Cell Physiol.* **18**, 481–483.

Van Meeteren, U. (1979). Water relations and keeping quality of cut *Gerbera* flowers. III. Water content, permeability and dry weight of ageing petals. *Sci. Hortic. (Amsterdam)* **10**, 261–269.

Van Meeteren, U., and Van Gelder, H. (1980). Water relations and keeping-quality of cut gerbera flowers. V. Role of endogenous cytokinins. *Sci. Hortic. (Amsterdam)* **12**, 273–281.

Van Staden, J. (1973). Changes in endogenous cytokinin levels during abscission and senescence of *Streptocarpus* leaves. *J. Exp. Bot.* **24**, 667–673.

Van Staden, J. (1976a). Occurrence of a cytokinin glucoside in the leaves and honeydew of *Salix babylonica*. *Physiol. Plant.* **36**, 225–228.

Van Staden, J. (1976b). Seasonal changes in the cytokinin content of *Ginkgo biloba* leaves. *Physiol. Plant.* **38**, 1–5.

Van Staden, J. (1977). Seasonal changes in the cytokinin content of the leaves of *Salix babylonica*. *Physiol. Plant.* **40**, 296–299.

Van Staden, J. (1980). Endogenous cytokinins in *Bougainvillea* 'San Diego Red'. II. The complex in mature leaves. *Bot. Gaz.* **141**, 245–247.

Van Staden, J. (1982). Transport of $8(^{14}C)$t-zeatin from mature rose leaves after shoot decapitation. *Bot. Gaz.* **143**, 201–205.

Van Staden, J. (1983). Seeds and cytokinins. *Physiol. Plant.* **58**, 340–346.

Van Staden, J., and Brown, N. A. C. (1977). The effect of ringing on cytokinin distribution in *Salix babylonica*. *Physiol. Plant.* **39**, 266–270.

Van Staden, J., and Carmi, A. (1982). The effects of decapitation on the distribution of cytokinins and growth of *Phaseolus vulgaris* plants. *Physiol. Plant.* **55**, 39–44.

Van Staden, J., and Davey, J. E. (1978). Endogenous cytokinins in the laminae and galls of *Erythrina latissima* leaves. *Bot. Gaz.* **139**, 36–41.

Van Staden, J., and Davey, J. E. (1979). The synthesis, transport and metabolism of endogenous cytokinins. *Plant Cell Environ.* **2**, 93–106.

Van Staden, J., and Davey, J. E. (1981). Cytokinin activity in *Lupinus albus*. VI. Translocation and metabolism of 8(^{14}C)t-zeatin applied to the leaves and fruits of fruiting plants. *Physiol. Plant.* **51**, 49–52.

Van Staden, J., and Dimalla, G. G. (1977). A comparison of the endogenous cytokinins in the roots and xylem exudate of nematode-resistant and susceptible tomato cultivars. *J. Exp. Bot.* **28**, 1351–1356.

Van Staden, J., and Dimalla, G. G. (1980a). The effect of silver thiosulphate preservative on the physiology of cut carnations. II. Influence on endogenous cytokinins. *Z. Pflanzenphysiol.* **99**, 19–26.

Van Staden, J., and Dimalla, G. G. (1980b). Endogenous cytokinins in *Bougainvillea* 'San Diego Red'. I. Occurrence of cytokinins glucosides in the root sap. *Plant Physiol.* **65**, 852–854.

Van Staden, J., and Forsyth, C. (1984). Adenine incorporation into cytokinins in aseptically cultured tomato roots. *J. Plant Physiol.* **117**, 249–255.

Van Staden, J., and Mallett, J. M. (1988). Metabolism and transport of [8-^{14}C]benzyladenine applied to rootless shoots and to the roots of intact tomato plants. *Plant Physiol. Biochem.* **26**. In press.

Van Staden, J., and Smith A. R. (1978). The synthesis of cytokinins in excised roots of maize and tomato under aseptic conditions. *Ann. Bot.* **42**, 751–753.

Van Staden, J., and Wareing, P. F. (1972). The effect of photoperiod on levels of endogenous cytokinins in *Xanthium strumarium*. *Physiol. Plant.* **27**, 331–337.

Van Staden, J., Drewes, S. E., and Hutton, M. J. (1982). Biological activity of 6-(2,3,4-trihydroxy-3-methylbutylamino)purine, an oxidation production of zeatin. *Physiol. Plant.* **55**, 143–148.

Van Staden, J., Hutton, M. J., and Drewes, S. E. (1983). Cytokinins in the leaves of *Ginkgo biloba*. I. The complex in mature leaves. *Plant Physiol.* **73**, 223–227.

Van Staden, J., Featonby-Smith, B. C., Mayak, S., Spiegelstein, H., and Halevy, A. H. (1987). Cytokinins in cut carnation flowers. II. Relationship between ethylene and endogenous levels in the petals. *Plant Growth Regul.* **5**, 75–86.

Van Steveninck, R. F. M. (1976). Effect of hormones and related substances on ion transport. *Encycl. Plant Physiol., New Ser.* **11B**, 307–342.

Varga, A., and Bruinsma, J. (1973). Effects of different cytokinins on senescence of detached oat leaves. *Planta* **111**, 91–93.

Vassileva, V. S., and Dimitrova, A. P. (1984). Influence of zeatin on certain photosynthetic indicators in young pea plants. *Biol. Physiol.* **37**, 1379–1382.

Vonk, C. R. (1978). Formation of cytokinin nucleotides in a detached inflorescence stalk and occurrence of nucleotides in phloem exudate from attached *Yucca* plants. *Physiol. Plant.* **44**, 161–166.

Vonk, C. R. (1979). Origin of cytokinins transported in the phloem. *Physiol. Plant.* **46**, 235–240.

Vonk, C. R., and Davelaar, E. (1981). 8(^{14}C)t-Zeatin metabolites and their transport from leaf to phloem exudate of *Yucca*. *Physiol. Plant.* **52**, 101–107.

Wagner, H., and Michael, G. (1971). Einfluss unterschiedlicher N-Versorgung auf die Cytokininbildung in Wurzeln von Sonnen Blumenpflanzen. *Biochem. Physiol. Pflanzen* **162**, 147–158.

Wareing, P. F. (1986). Plant cell responses and the role of growth substances. *In* "Plant Growth Substances 1985" (M. Bopp, ed.), pp. 1–9. Springer-Verlag, Berlin and New York.

Wareing, P. F., and Thompson, A. G. (1976). Rapid effects of red light on hormone levels. *In* "Light and Plant Development" (H. Smith, ed.), pp. 285–294. Butterworth, London.

Wareing, P. F., Khalifa, M. M., and Treharne, K. J. (1968). Rate-limiting processes in photosynthesis at saturating light intensities. *Nature (London)* **220**, 453–457.

Weaver, R. J. (1972). "Plant Growth Substances in Agriculture." Freeman, San Francisco, California.

328   *Johannes Van Staden et al.*

Weiler, E. W. (1984). Immunoassay of plant growth regulators. *Annu. Rev. Plant Physiol.* **35,** 85–95.

Weiler, E. W., and Ziegler, H. (1981). Determination of phytohormones in phloem exudate from tree species by radioimmunoassay. *Planta* **152,** 168–170.

Weiss, C., and Vaadia, Y. (1965). Kinetin-like activity in root apices of sunflower plants. *Life Sci.* **4,** 1323–1326.

Wheeler, A. W. (1971). Auxins and cytokinins exuded during formation of roots by detached primary leaves and stems of dwarf french bean (*Phaseolus vulgaris* L.). *Planta* **98,** 128–135.

Whitty, C. D., and Hall, R. H. (1974). A cytokinin oxidase in *Zea mays. Can. J. Biochem.* **52,** 789–799.

Wilcox, E. J., Selby, C., and Wain, R. L. (1978). Studies on plant growth regulating substances I. The cytokinin activity of some substituted benzyloxy purines. *Ann. Appl. Biol..* **88,** 439–444.

Wilcox, E. J., Selby, C., and Wain, R. L. (1981). Cytokinin activities of 6-alpha alkylbenzyloxy purines. *Ann. Appl. Biol.* **97,** 221–226.

Wills, R. H. H., Lee, T. H., Graham, D., McGlasson, W. B., and Hall, E. G. (1981). ''Postharvest.'' Avi, Westport, Connecticut.

Wittenbach, V. A. (1977). Induced senescence of intact wheat seedlings and its reversibility. *Plant Physiol.* **59,** 1039–1042.

Wollgiehn, R. (1961). Untersuchungen über den Einfluss des Kinetins auf den Nucleinsäure- und Proteinstoffwechsel isolierter Blätter. *Flora (Jena)* **151,** 411–437.

Wollgiehn, R. (1967). Nucleic acid and protein metabolism of excised leaves. *Symp. Soc. Exp. Biol.* **21,** 231–246.

Woolhouse, H. W. (1982). Hormonal control of senescence allied to reproduction in plants. *In* ''Strategies of Plant Reproduction'' (W. J. Meudt, ed.), BARC Symp., No. 6, pp. 201–233. Littlefield-Adams, Totowa, New Jersey.

Wright, R. D., Pillay, T. N., and Cherry, J. H. (1973). Changes in leucyl tRNA species of pea leaves during senescence and after zeatin treatment. *Mech. Aging Dev.* **1,** 403–412.

Wyen, N. V., Erdei, S., Udvardy, J., Bagi, G., and Farkas, G. L. (1972). Hormonal control of nuclease level in excised *Avena* leaf tissues. *J. Exp. Bot.* **23,** 37–44.

Yu, S.-M., and Kao, C.-H. (1981). A comparison of activities of various cytokinins on the senescence of soybean *Glycine max* L. leaf discs. *Bot. Bull. Acad. Sin.* **22,** 49–56.

Yu, Y., Yang, S. F., Corse, J., Kuhnle, J. A., and Hua, S. (1981). Structures of cytokinins influence synergistic production of ethylene. *Phytochemistry* **20,** 1191–1195.

Zhang, R., Letham, D. S., Wong, O. C., Noodén, L. D., and Parker, C. W. (1987). Cytokinin biochemistry in relation to leaf senescence. II. The metabolism of 6-benzylaminopurine in soybean leaves and the inhibition of its conjugation. *Plant Physiol.* **83,** 334–340.

10

Abscisic Acid, Auxin, and Other Regulators of Senescence

L. D. Noodén
Biology Department
University of Michigan
Ann Arbor, Michigan

SENESCENCE AND AGING IN PLANTS

I. INTRODUCTION

While ethylene (Chapter 8) and cytokinin (Chapter 9) play prominent roles in the regulation of senescence, there are undoubtedly other regulators. Some clear examples include abscisic acid (ABA), auxin, and gibberellin (GA), but there are also several others, some yet to be characterized. Not only are ethylene and cytokinin (CK) unable to account for all correlative controls governing senescence, but other hormones may work in conjunction with ethylene and CK, even where these seem to have prominent regulatory roles. The generalization that regulation of development may be controlled by combinations of hormones seems to apply to senescence as it does to other processes (Leopold and Noodén, 1984).

With respect to the hormones and regulators covered in this chapter, there is quite a difference among tissues and even among the same tissues in different species or in different developmental stages. The reader is therefore warned that what will emerge from this chapter is not a cohesive picture of the role of other hormones regulating senescence, but an effort to integrate the fragments of information available on these hormones. Such an integration should help lay a foundation for further analysis of the hormonal controls of senescence. As with ethylene and CK, more attention needs to be directed to analyzing the developmental rules of hormones in intact plants.

Much can be learned from studies of the effects of exogenous applications of hormones and attempts to correlate changes in endogenous levels with senescence-related processes (Chapter 1). These data are helpful in determining whether or not a particular hormone controls a designated process. This chapter does include some discussion of fruits, since certain fruit parts (Chapter 1) do undergo senescence; however, the chapter sidesteps the specialized senescence processes related to seed maturation, seed germination, and abscission, which are discussed briefly in Chapter 1 and more extensively elsewhere (Addicott, 1982; Murray, 1984; Bewley and Black, 1985). Similarly, this chapter will not attempt extensive coverage of the functional aspects of these hormones in processes other than senescence. This chapter will begin with the promoters of senescence and then examine the retardants.

Some weaknesses and complications in the available information should be noted at the outset. First, because senescence is a very important aspect of postharvest physiology, an enormous literature exists concerning the effects of hormone treatments on maintenance and survival of plant materials in storage, especially for fruits and flowers, for example, fruit ripening (Chapter 1) or flower opening. Such studies usually do not aim at senescence per se. It is not appropriate to try to cover these comprehensively here, especially where other maturation processes are involved. Summaries can be found elsewhere (see, e.g., Weaver, 1972; Sacher, 1973, 1983; McGlasson *et al.*, 1978; Halevy and Mayak, 1981; Rhodes, 1980; Wills *et al.*, 1981; Burton, 1982; Bruinsma, 1983; Nickell, 1983). Second, the endogenous levels, particularly those of ABA and β inhibitor, are often measured with bioassays not involving senescence, for example, inhibition of coleoptile growth has been a standard assay for measuring ABA-like activity. Nonetheless, these data from a variety of sources generally point in the same direction, and many are supported by newer, more rigorous procedures. Third, for fairly obvious reasons, the measures of senescence, especially in leaves, depend heavily, though not exclusively, on chlorophyll loss. While this is usually valid, other parameters should also be measured in conjunction with senescence (Chapters 1 and 15).

II. ABSCISIC ACID AND SENESCENCE PROCESSES

Second to ethylene, ABA is the most promising of the senescence promoters. Yet the information on its endogenous role is quite incomplete and even puzzling at times. Inasmuch as abscission is related to senescence (Chapter 1), the studies leading up to the discovery of ABA also implicate it in regulation (promotion) of senescence (Addicott and Carns, 1983; Sacher, 1983). The more direct linkage of ABA with senescence processes such as leaf yellowing began with El-Antably *et al.* (1967), who found that ABA promoted yellowing in discs from a wide variety of species, but not all. When applied to intact leaves, however, ABA generally had no effect on yellowing, even in species where it induced dormant bud development. This and other observations have raised substantial questions about the applicability of results with excised parts to the intact plant (Chapter 1); however, ABA has been shown to act on intact organs (see below).

The data relating ABA with senescence tend to fall into three groups: (1) influence of exogenous ABA, (2) correlation of endogenous ABA, and (3) the relationships between ABA and the other hormones. The role of ABA in whole plant senescence will be discussed in Chapter 12.

A. Influence of Exogenous Abscisic Acid

Applied ABA promotes a wide range of senescence-related processes in a variety of organs (see, e.g., Weaver, 1972; Sacher, 1973, 1983; McGlasson *et al.*, 1978; Halevy and Mayak, 1981; Rhodes, 1980; Wills *et al.*, 1981; Burton, 1982; Bruinsma, 1983; Nickell, 1983). The documentation on promotion of chlorophyll loss in both detached and attached leaves is especially extensive (Aspinall *et al.*, 1967; Osborne, 1967; Beevers, 1968; Sankhla and Sankhla, 1968; Oritani *et al.*, 1969; Sloger and Caldwell, 1970; Paranjothy and Wareing, 1971; Goldthwaite, 1972; Thomas and Stoddart, 1975; Lindoo and Noodén, 1978; Gepstein and Thimann, 1981; Grossman and Jung, 1982; Mondal and Choudhuri, 1984; Ray and Choudhuri, 1984, to cite only a few examples); however, there are several cases (Colquhoun and Hillman, 1972; Bhargavi *et al.*, 1977; Hall and McWha, 1981; Stamp, 1981) where ABA actually retards chlorophyll loss. In some of these cases, the high concentrations (10^{-4} M) used may have interfered with senescence in a nonspecific manner. Indeed, the ABA dose-response (chlorophyll loss) curve for *Rumex* leaf disks shows a reversal from promotion to inhibition at about 10^{-4} M (Manos and Goldthwaite, 1975). While ABA apparently promotes chlorophyll breakdown, it also inhibits chlorophyll synthesis (Bengtson *et al.*, 1977; Uheda and Kuraishi, 1978), and the relative contributions of these two processes are uncertain. The relative resistance of attached leaves to exogenous ABA could be related to their ability to export ABA (Walton, 1980; Chapter 12) or to high levels of senescence retardants (e.g., cytokinin). It is possible that where exogenous ABA effects on attached leaves do occur, they are indirect results of ABA translocated to other parts, e.g., roots (Chapter 12).

Several reports (Mittelheuser and Van Steveninck, 1971, 1972; Thomas and Stoddart, 1975; Gepstein and Thimann, 1980; Garaizabal and Rodriguez, 1983) show ABA produces a greater effect in darkness than in light. This may be due to light-activated breakdown of the ABA (Gepstein and Thimann, 1980) or decreased sensitivity of tissues in light.

Usually, ABA promotes net protein breakdown and inhibits total protein synthesis (Osborne, 1967; Beevers, 1968; LeLeo and Sacher, 1970; Paranjothy and Wareing, 1971; Thomas, 1975; Thomas and Stoddart, 1975; Borochov *et al.*, 1976; Grossmann and Jung, 1982), but it may promote synthesis (or at least the activity) of enzymes related to protein catabolism (Grossmann and Jung, 1982). Simple, generalized inhibition of protein synthesis does not cause senescence (Chapters 5 and 15), so ABA must operate through some more specific effects. ABA also inhibits nucleic acid synthesis, usually producing stronger decreases in RNA than in DNA (Beevers, 1968; DeLeo and Sacher, 1970; Paranjothy and Wareing, 1971; Knypl and Mazurczyk, 1972; Grossmann and Jung, 1982). ABA also increases the levels of nucleic acid-degrading enzymes, promotes net breakdown of RNA, and decreases total nucleic acid synthesis (DeLeo and Sacher, 1970; Udvardy and Farkas, 1972; Grossmann and Jung, 1982). In addition, ABA is able to promote a wide range of other degradative processes, including acid phosphatase (DeLeo and Sacher, 1970), and it may increase respiration (Goldthwaite, 1974). It also promotes petal senescence (Mayak and Halevy, 1980) and fruit ripening (McGlasson et al., 1978; Rhodes, 1980). On the other hand, while β-1,3-glucan hydrolase normally increases during senescence, ABA may inhibit this increase as it promotes senescence (Moore and Stone, 1972a,b).

Although few studies of ABA action on senescence also include measurements of its effects on photosynthesis, inhibition would be expected to follow from the decline of chlorophyll and protein contents. Indeed, ABA decreases photosynthetic activity in several tissues (Tillberg et al., 1981; Thimann et al., 1982; Cornic and Miginiac, 1983). While ABA could influence photosynthesis through control of stomatal opening (Walton, 1980; Van Steveninck and Van Steveninck, 1983), that does not seem to be the main way by which the inhibition occurs (Burschka et al., 1985; Raschke and Hedrich, 1985). There is some doubt that ABA inhibits photosynthesis by acting directly on the photosynthetic apparatus (Mawson et al., 1981; Raschke and Hedrich, 1985).

A large number of reports now indicate that ABA may alter membrane structure (Walton, 1980; Ho, 1983; Van Steveninck and Van Steveninck, 1983) and cause a decline in all cellular acyl lipids (Hancock et al., 1983). This may be an important aspect of its action on senescence (DeLeo and Sacher, 1970; Glinka and Reinhold, 1971; Thimann et al., 1982; Chapter 2). While ABA can induce a generalized leakiness, apparently as a late component of the senescence process, it can also exert some specific effects on permeability, not all of which are related to senescence. The type of effect exerted by ABA on membranes differs markedly, depending on the tissue or even the species (Ho, 1983; Van Steveninck and Van Steveninck, 1983; Thomas, 1986).

ABA (3.8×10^{-6} M) accelerates the normal ultrastructural changes in detached wheat leaves (Mittelheuser and Van Steveninck, 1971), but 10^{-4} M ABA has been reported to cause a different pattern of changes in radish leaf disks (Colquhoun et al., 1975). Thus, the changes caused by ABA do not necessarily reflect normal senescence.

B. Correlation with Endogenous Abscisic Acid

Table 10.1 shows that levels of ABA or ABA-like (β-inhibitor) activity may rise before or during senescence in a very wide range of tissues, both excised and attached. The amount of ABA in the phloem and xylem also increases during these periods, and this apparently reflects ABA in transit. ABA levels often decrease during late senescence. Sometimes both the ABA levels and senescence can be modified in parallel through experimental manipulations. For example, decapitation of bean seedlings reverses both the rise in endogenous ABA levels and senescence of the cotyledons (Van Onckelen et al., 1981). Thus, even though the reports cited employ a wide range of methods for purifying and measuring ABA and the degree of rigor varies, the general picture shows some correlation. A greater variety of patterns for changes in ABA can be seen in fruits (McGlasson et al., 1978; Rhodes, 1980); however, it should be kept in mind that (1) both ripening and senescence are taking place (Chapter 1) and (2) not only are fruits complex structurally, but these structures and the underlying physiology may differ from one species to the next.

There are some interesting noncorrelations between ABA levels and senescence (Noodén, 1980); these may ultimately tell us a lot about the control of senescence. For example, mature green leaves on a strawberry plant contain far more ABA-like activity in September than similar-looking leaves in June (Rudnicki et al., 1968). Young, growing leaves often contain much higher levels of ABA than mature, nongrowing, or even senescing leaves (Powell, 1975; Raschke and Zeevaart, 1976; Weiler, 1980). Another discrepancy occurs where ABA export from the leaves is blocked by phloem destruction or by fruit removal. Because large quantities of ABA normally travel from the leaves to the developing fruit, defruiting or phloem destruction in the petiole will lead to accumulation of ABA in the leaves (Loveys and Kriedemann, 1974; Goldbach et al., 1977; Düring, 1978; Setter et al., 1980a,b, 1981; Noodén and Obermeyer, 1981). In spite of the high ABA levels, defruiting prevents senescence in soybean and other plants (Chapter 12), which may be due to correspondingly high levels of antisenescence factors such as cytokinins.

Stress, particularly drought, elevates ABA levels (Wright, 1978; Walton, 1980), and this could account for the variability of ABA levels sometimes observed in field-grown plants (Ciha et al., 1978). There is also some reason to believe that some water stress develops normally during the later phases of senescence, and this could cause some elevation of the ABA levels (Dumbroff et al., 1977). Still, the rise in ABA levels also occurs in tissues that are bathed in water (Mayak and Halevy, 1972; Gepstein and Thimann, 1980). Furthermore, intact petals of Gerbera or rose cut flowers (Van Meeteren,

1979; Halevy and Mayak, 1981) and leaves on whole soybean plants (Zur *et al.*, 1981) may not increase their water potential until very late senescence. Thus, the increase in ABA levels in senescing tissues is not necessarily due to water stress.

The regulation of ABA levels (Walton, 1980; Milborrow, 1983) may involve synthesis, transport, and breakdown. Little is known about these regulatory mechanisms in relation to senescence; however, breakdown of ABA (Gepstein and Thimann, 1980) and conversion to conjugated ABA, apparently the glucosyl ester (Weiler, 1980), have been implicated.

C. Relationships between Abscisic Acid and Other Hormones

The hormonal controls of senescence, as with many other processes, often involve multiple hormones, and the relationships between hormones may take many forms (Leopold and Noodén, 1984; Wareing, 1986). In many cases, ABA is able to influence the endogenous levels of other hormones and vice versa. Such internal interactions are particularly striking for ABA and ethylene, each of which may produce increases in the other. Examples are found in leaves (Aharoni and Richmond, 1978), petals (Mayak *et al.*, 1972; Mayak and Halevy, 1972; Mayak and Dilley, 1976; Ronen and Mayak, 1981), and a variety of fruits (McGlasson *et al.*, 1978; Rhodes, 1980). Correspondingly, combined treatments with ethylene and ABA may promote senescence or related processes in many of these tissues. On the other hand, CEPA (an ethylene-releasing agent) decreases the ABA-like activity in attached broad bean leaves, while it promotes senescence (El-Beltagy *et al.*, 1976). Ethylene (CEPA) and ABA do not have much effect on each other in attached tobacco leaves (Even-Chen *et al.*, 1978). Finally, during the course of normal ripening/senescence changes in certain flowers (e.g., roses and carnations) or certain fruits (e.g., avocado), ethylene production may rise before endogenous ABA levels, suggesting elevated ethylene leads to increases in ABA, which, in turn, causes ripening/senescence. Then, why do ABA treatments also promote ethylene production? Perhaps, this is a toxic response in some cases. ABA has also been reported to alter the sensitivity of carnation flowers to ethylene (Mayak and Dilley, 1976; Ronen and Mayak, 1981).

While ABA acts in the same direction as ethylene, CK, GA, and auxin usually act in a direction opposite to ABA (Chapter 9 and Sections IV and V). Often ABA alters the levels of the other hormones or vice versa (Chin and Beevers, 1970; Even-Chen and Itai, 1975; Brisker *et al.*, 1976; Aharoni and Richmond, 1978; Even-Chen *et al.*, 1978; Biswas and Choudhuri, 1980; Gepstein and Thimann, 1980; Iliev *et al.*, 1982), but there appear to be substantial species differences in these responses. In *Rumex* leaf disks (Back

TABLE 10.1
Changes in Levels of Abscisic Acid or Abscisic Acid-Like Activity in Relation to Senescence

Authors	Tissue	Developmental stages	Purification	Method of measuring	Pattern of change
Aharoni and Richmond (1978)	Lettuce leaves, attached	Progressive senescence	Partitioning and TLC	Gas chromatography with electron capture detection	Decrease
	detached	Induced senescence			Increase
Alvim et al. (1976)	Willow xylem sap	Autumnal senescence	Partitioning and paper chromatography	Wheat coleoptile segment growth bioassay	Increase preceding yellowing then decrease
			Partitioning, polyvinylpyrrolidone chromatography, and TLC	Gas chromatography with electron capture detection	Same but decreases earlier
Borochov et al. (1976)	Petals of leafless cut roses	Induced senescence	Partitioning, thin layer chromatography (2X)	Gas chromatography with electron capture detection	Decrease after cutting then a rise
Bowen and Hoad (1968)	Xylem and phloem (aphid) sap from willow stems	Autumnal senescence	Partitioning and paper chromatography	Wheat coleoptile segment growth bioassay	Increase
Böttger (1970)	Diffusate from coleus leaves	Progressive senescence	Paper chromatography	Oat coleoptile segment growth bioassay	Increase
Brenner et al. (1982)	Diffusate from soybean leaves	Monocarpic senescence	HPLC	Gas chromatography with electron capture detection	No significant change
Chin and Beevers (1970)	Nasturtium leaves, excised	Induced senescence	Partitioning and TLC	Wheat coleoptile segment growth assay	Increase
Ciha et al. (1978)	Leaves of fruiting soybean, attached, with variable H$_2$O stress	Monocarpic senescence	Partitioning and HPLC	Gas chromatography with electron capture detection	Variable
Colquhoun and Hillman (1975)	Bean leaves, attached	Progressive senescence	Partitioning and TLC (2X)	Circular dichroism	Variable
Dumbroff et al. (1977)	Bean cotyledons, attached	Senescence	Partitioning and TLC	Gas chromatography with electron capture detection	No significant change on a per cotyledon basis
El-Beltagy et al. (1976)	Broad bean leaves, attached	Monocarpic senescence	Partitioning and paper chromatography	Oat coleoptile segment growth bioassay	Increase followed by a decrease
Even-Chen and Itai (1975)	Tobacco leaves, detached	Induced senescence	Partitioning and TLC (2X)	Gas chromatography with electron capture detection	Increase
Gepstein and Thimann (1980)	Oat leaf segments	Induced senescence	TLC	Gas chromatography with flame ionization detection	Increase
Halevy and Mayak (1975)	Petals of cut rose flower shoots	Senescence	Paper chromatography	Wheat coleoptile segment growth bioassay	Increase

Reference	Material	Senescence type	Purification	Detection method	Result
Hein et al. (1984a)	Intact seed coats	Seed coat senescence	HPLC (2×)	Gas chromatography with electron capture detection	No change
Hein et al. (1984b)	Leaves of a fruiting soybean, attached	Monocarpic senescence	HPLC (2×)	Gas chromatography with electron capture detection	Increase
Lindoo and Nooden (1978)	Leaves of a fruiting soybean, attached	Monocarpic senescence	Partitioning and paper chromatography	Oat coleoptile segment growth senescence	Increase followed by a decrease
Mayak and Halevy (1972)	Petals of cut rose flower shoots	Senescence	Partitioning and paper chromatography	Wheat coleoptile segment growth bioassay	Increase, but the increase is greater in a short-lived variety than in a long-lived variety
Mayak et al. (1972)	Petals of cut rose flowers	Senescence	Partitioning and paper chromatography	Wheat coleoptile segment growth bioassay	Increase
Ortiani and Yoshida (1973)	Attached leaves of rice plants with developing grain	Monocarpic senescence	Partitioning and paper chromatography	Rice seedling growth bioassay	Increase before chlorophyll loss starts, then decrease
	Attached leaves of soybean plants with developing pods	Monocarpic senescence	Partitioning and paper chromatography	Rice seedling growth bioassay	Increase
Osborne et al. (1972)	Bean leaves, attached	Progressive senescence	Partitioning and TLC	Bean explant abscission bioassay	Less in yellow leaves than in green leaves
Rudnicki et al. (1968)	Strawberry leaves, attached	Progressive senescence	Partitioning and paper chromatography	Wheat coleptile segment growth bioassay	Increase followed by a decrease
Samet and Sinclair (1980)	Leaves of fruiting soybean plants, attached	Progressive and monocarpic senescence	Partitioning, polyvinylpyrrolidone column chromatography	Gas chromatography with electron capture detection	Increase
Van Onckelen et al. (1981)	Cotyledons of bean seedlings, attached	Senescence	Partitioning, polyvinylpyrrolidone column chromatography HPLC	Gas chromatography with electron capture detection	Increase
Weiler (1980)	Hyoscyamus niger leaves, attached	Progressive senescence	None	Radioimmunoassay	No change
	Betula papyrifera leaves, attached	Autumnal senescence	None	Radioimmunoassay	Increase
	Acer pseudoplatanus leaves, attached	Autumnal senescence	None	Radioimmunoassay	Increase
Weinbaum and Powell (1975)	Diffusate from crab apple leaves	Progressive senescence	Partitioning and column chromatography	Gas chromatography with electron capture detection	Increase

et al., 1972), however, ABA decreases CK breakdown, which seems opposite to the usual senescence-promoting effect of ABA in that tissue.

Exogenous ABA counteracts the senescence-retarding actions of added cytokinin and gibberellin (Aspinall et al., 1967; El-Antably et al., 1967; Beevers, 1968; Sankhla and Sankhla, 1968; Oritani et al., 1969; Back and Richmond, 1971; Manos and Goldthwaite, 1975). In some cases (Aspinall et al., 1967; Back and Richmond, 1971), cytokinin can completely overcome the senescence-promoting actions of ABA. In other situations (Beevers, 1968; Manos and Goldthwaite, 1975), the effects of ABA could not be completely overcome. Thus, it appears that, depending on the tissue involved, cytokinin or gibberellin could exert their senescence-retarding action by counteracting ABA; however, they also seem to work in other ways as well (Section V,C).

Auxin–ABA interrelations have been studied less extensively, yet, there are some indications that they can work against each other when supplied to senescing tissues (DeLeo and Sacher, 1970). Auxin (NAA) can diminish the rise in ABA during senescence of detached tobacco leaves (Even-Chen et al., 1978). The documentation of auxin–ABA antagonistic effects is much greater in the case of abscission (Addicott, 1982).

In conclusion, a very substantial literature now implicates ABA as a promoter of senescence; however, its role in the regulation of senescence in normal intact parts needs further study. ABA may also act by more than one mechanism.

III. OTHER PROMOTERS OF SENESCENCE

A wide range of naturally occurring organic chemicals have been implicated in various ways as senescence promoters. Even though evidence for their natural involvement in senescence is limited, it seems useful to review what information we have on these potential senescence-inducing hormones.

A. Fatty Acids

Free fatty acids, especially the short chain fatty acids, and some of their esters are active in promoting senescence (Weaver, 1972; Letham, 1978). They appear to be components of the β-inhibitor complex (Section II, E). The implication of free fatty acids in senescence seems to have grown mainly out of the observation that they increase during senescence and they are physiologically active, e.g., inhibit mitochondrial oxidations (Baddeley, 1971). The breakdown of cell membranes, particularly the thylakoid membranes, in senescing tissues, releases large quantities of free fatty acids, especially linolenic acid (Draper, 1969; Baddeley, 1971; Thomas, 1982; Chapters 2 and 3). Several C_{18}-unsaturated fatty acids, including linolenic, actively promote chlorophyll loss in the detached oat leaf assay. The methyl esters are much less active than the free acids, while the saturated fatty acids (stearic and palmitic) are inactive (Ueda and Kato, 1982). Free linolenic acid inhibits photosynthesis in isolated chloroplasts (McCarty and Jagendorf, 1965; Mvé Akamba and Siegenthaler, 1979).

The fatty acid release may be a result rather than a cause of chloroplast breakdown (Percival *et al.*, 1980). Still, these fatty acids may activate protein- and chlorophyll-degrading enzymes and/or increase access of the enzymes to their substrate through detergent action (Thomas, 1982). While the free fatty acids could function as senescence promoters, so far that role seems to be intracellular, as opposed to hormonal, since these fatty acids may not be highly mobile (Weaver, 1972). Moreover, large doses, e.g., 7×10^{-4} M linolenic acid (Percival *et al.*, 1980), are required to induce senescence, suggesting a possible detergent-like effect.

B. Serine

L-Serine accelerates yellowing in oat leaf segments at concentrations above 10^{-3} M (Thimann *et al.*, 1972) or in excised bean leaves at 3×10^{-2} M (Chen, 1972). Serine is more effective in darkness than in light (Veierskov *et al.*, 1985). D-serine is inactive (Shibaoka and Thimann, 1970). L-serine also inhibits [^{14}C]leucine uptake but increases protein degradation, proteolytic activity, and free amino acid levels (Martin and Thimann, 1972; Veierskov *et al.*, 1985). In conjunction with kinetin, it decreases the cellular lipids (Hancock *et al.*, 1983). It also counteracts the chlorophyll-retaining effects of kinetin, IAA, and adenine.

The role of serine *in vivo* is unknown. It is a by-product of photosynthesis and a mobile component of photosynthate (Ziegler, 1975; Pate, 1980). In senescing tissues where the different amino acids have been analyzed, serine concentration may not increase much more than other amino acids (Bugge, 1976; Malik, 1982), or it may rise disproportionately (Leckstein and Llewellyn, 1975; Pate *et al.*, 1977; Vander Westhuizen and de Swardt, 1978).

Cysteine is active in promoting senescence but not as active as serine (Shibaoka and Thimann, 1970; Martin and Thimann, 1972). Arginine appears to compete with serine, and it is able to offset completely the serine promotion of chlorophyll and protein loss in oat leaf segments (Shibaoka and Thimann, 1970; Martin and Thimann, 1972). In excised oat leaves, arginine, lysine, and ornithine have also been reported to enhance senescence (Von Abrams, 1974).

C. Jasmonic Acid and Related Compounds

Methyl jasmonate (MJ), which occurs widely in plants, can promote chlorophyll loss in oat leaf segments (Ueda and Kato, 1980). The natural (−)-MJ appears to be more active than the (+)-MJ in promotion of chlorophyll loss (Ueda *et al.*, 1981). Jasmonic acid is much less active than its methyl ester (Ueda *et al.*, 1981), but this may be related in part to penetration. A variety of analogs have also been tested and found to be active (Ueda *et al.*, 1981). MJ also promotes amino acid release, increases respiration, and causes stomatal closure (Satler and Thimann, 1981). In unripe tomato fruits (detached), applied MJ promotes ethylene production but not visible chlorophyll loss, and it inhibits the red pigment accumulation (Saniewski and Czapski, 1983, 1985). At this time, no information is available on a hormonal role for MJ; however, it possesses physiological activities that warrant further investigation.

D. Miscellaneous Promoters

In addition to the compounds listed above, there are some natural senescence promoters that deserve mention. Both auxin and gibberellin can promote senescence in some tissues (Sections IV and V). Ascorbic acid and the bacterial toxin, coronatine, stimulate ethylene production (Cooper *et al.*, 1968; Ferguson and Mitchell, 1985) and promote chlorophyll loss. On the other hand, rhizobitoxine, produced by certain strains of *Rhizobium japonicum*, induces leaf yellowing but inhibits ethylene synthesis (Owens and Wright, 1965; Yang and Hoffman, 1984). Thus, the connection between ethylene and leaf senescence (Chapter 8) may be complex. Capillin and capillen, which are aromatic rings with aliphatic side chains, promote chlorophyll loss in oat leaf segments in light, but in darkness they cause chlorophyll retention (Ueda *et al.*, 1984). D-Glucosamine has similar effects (Mittelheuser and Van Steveninck, 1974). Rose Bengal promotes declines of chlorophyll, carotenoids, fatty acid content, photosynthetic electron transport, and net photosynthesis in senescing flax cotyledons (Percival and Dodge, 1983). Many naturally occurring inhibitors exist (Letham, 1978), and some may well turn out to be senescence promoters.

Synthetic compounds that cause senescence-like responses, particularly chlorophyll loss, are very diverse chemically, and many are used in herbicides (Audus, 1976).

E. Unidentified Promoters

Plant extracts have been shown to contain senescence-promoting substances that have not yet been identified. Special interest would apply to such extracts that come from senescing tissues.

Inhibitor β is a zone of growth-inhibiting activity in acidic ether extracts, and it runs at about R_f 0.6 on paper chromatogram developed in isopropanol, water, and NH_4OH (Bennet-Clark and Kefford, 1953; Hemberg, 1961). Inhibitor β shows significant correlation changes with several important processes, for example, with dormant bud development and autumnal leaf senescence (Phillips and Wareing, 1958; Hemberg, 1961; El-Antably *et al.*, 1967; Noodén and Weber, 1978; Addicott and Carns, 1983). Inhibitor β contains ABA and thus may be called ABA-like, as in Table 10.1, but it also includes several physiologically active compounds including azelaic acid, salicylic acid, coumarin, scopoletin, and probably others (Housley and Taylor, 1958; Hemberg, 1961; Ryugo, 1969; Holst, 1971; Noodén and Weber, 1978; Addicott and Carns, 1983). In some of the reports on changes in ABA-like (inhibitor β) activity (Table 10.1), the profiles for the actual distribution of inhibitory activity along the chromatograms are shown, and it can be seen that the inhibitory zone is broader and/or there is more activity than can be accounted for by ABA alone (see, e.g., Lenton *et al.*, 1972; Goldschmidt *et al.*, 1973; El-Beltagy and Hall, 1975; Alvim *et al.*, 1976; Dörffling *et al.*, 1978; Lindoo and Noodén, 1978). While it is possible that this wide active zone is simply due to ABA spread by cochromatographing contaminants, it is more likely that other senescence-promoting compounds occur in this chromatographic region.

Physiologically active compounds occur in other extract fractions besides the acidic ether fraction, in particular, the aqueous (nonether soluble) and the neutral ether fractions. Inhibitors, including neutral inhibitors, may increase in broad bean leaves during senescence (El-Beltagy and Hall, 1975; El-Beltagy *et al.*, 1976). Likewise, other inhibitors increase in maple leaves during senescence (Dörffling, 1963). In addition, ethylene treatments that promote chlorophyll loss and increase ABA levels in orange peel also elevate a neutral inhibitor of coleoptile growth (Goldschmidt *et al.*, 1973).

In addition to the unidentified growth-inhibiting compounds cited above, there are numerous reports concerning "senescence" factors (Osborne, 1955, 1959a; Hall *et al.*, 1961; Osborne *et al.*, 1972; Chang and Jacobs, 1973; Dörffling *et al.*, 1978) that promote abscission, but they may well be concerned with other aspects of leaf senescence as well. These factors differ from ABA and seem to be combinations of several different compounds.

During germination of seeds or the subsequent growth of the seedling, the cotyledons (at least for hypogeal species) and/or endosperm may senesce (Chapter 1), and this generally seems to be controlled by the embryo axis (Young *et al.*, 1960; Leopold, 1961; Laidman, 1982; Murray, 1984;

Bewley and Black, 1985). The nature of the substances mediating these correlative controls may differ with the species and tissues; however, GA seems to fulfill this role in the cereal seeds (Laidman, 1982; Murray, 1984; Bewley and Black, 1985). Ray cell senescence occurs during heartwood formation, and the factors involved are also unknown but may include the toxic phenolics that accululate in heartwood (Stewart, 1966; Kozlowski, 1971). In addition, a long-day-induced and relatively low mobility stimulus causes senescence in leaves of *Kleinia articulata* (Kulkarni and Schwabe, 1985).

An "organelle-damaging" factor that could play some role in senescence has been isolated from mung bean leaves (Tomomatsu and Asahi, 1981).

There are hormone-like stimuli variously termed necrohormones, lepto-hormones, or wound hormones, but these are mainly concerned with wound healing rather than cell degeneration (Kahl, 1982, 1983).

F. Hypersensitive Response

In many cases, higher plant resistance to a pathogen involves necrosis (Chapter 1) of the plant tissue near the invasion site and serves to isolate the pathogen. This reaction, which is called the hypersensitive or sometimes the hyperimmune response, is associated with the development of electrolyte leakage, disorganization of the subcellular structures, and increased synthesis of secondary compounds (Bailey and Mansfield, 1982; Sigee, 1984). Among the secondary compounds synthesized in this reaction are phytoalexins, which help to defend against the invading microbial pathogens. At higher doses, phytoalexins may themselves cause necrosis of the higher plant cells (Bell, 1981; Keen, 1981; Bailey and Mansfield, 1982). The phytoalexins, a very diverse group of chemicals, are induced by elicitors that may be host cell wall fragments released by the pathogen, pathogen wall components, or toxins from the pathogen (Bell, 1981). Thus, phytoalexins, their elicitors, or other toxins could induce degeneration, leading to death of the plant cells. Whether or not any of these substances also function in normal senescence processes independent of disease is unknown; however, this possibility should be kept in mind.

IV. AUXIN AND SENESCENCE PROCESSES

Generally, auxin functions as a retardant of senescence, but in some tissues, e.g., xylem differentiation and certain flower parts, it promotes senescence. The literature on auxin in relation to senescence is nowhere near as extensive as that concerning CK (Chapter 9); nonetheless, enough data exist to indicate that auxin is important beyond its role in delaying abscission (Addicott, 1982).

A. Influence of Exogenous Auxin

Both synthetic and natural auxins can delay senescence in a wide range of tissues (Stewart, 1949; Sacher, 1957, 1959, 1963, 1965; Osborne, 1958; Osborne and Hallaway, 1960, 1961; Engelbrecht and Conrad, 1961; Ballantyne, 1965; James *et al.*, 1965; Mishra and Misra, 1968; Thimann *et al.*, 1972; McGlasson *et al.*, 1978; Noodén *et al.*, 1979; Pech and Romani, 1979; Rhodes, 1980; Biswas and Choudhuri, 1981; Baker, 1983; Lyons and Widmer, 1984, to cite a relative few). Tissues affected include leaves, fruits, flower parts, and even embryos. Auxin alters senescence-related processes such as chlorophyll loss, RNA degradation, RNA synthesis, protein degradation, protein synthesis, wilting, membrane breakdown, and changes in the level of several enzymes (some increase, some decrease) in ways that are consistent with a senescence-delaying effect. As it delays leaf senescence, auxin does, however, tend to change the pattern of yellowing of the interveinal relative to the veinal tissues, suggesting that exogenous auxin may sometimes alter as well as delay the pattern of senescence (Osborne, 1959b). There are, however, numerous cases where auxin does not delay senescence (Richmond and Lang, 1957; Fletcher and Osborne, 1966; El-Antably *et al.*, 1967; Osborne, 1967; Mishra and Misra, 1968; Even-Chen *et al.*, 1978), and it may even promote senescence in some cases, such as flower petals and xylem differentiation but also some leaves (Wetmore and Sorokin, 1955; Arditti and Knauft, 1969; Nichols, 1971; Jacobs, 1979; Mishra and Gaur, 1980). In addition, auxins may affect the action or synthesis of other hormones, particularly promoting ethylene synthesis (Section IV,C). These varied responses can be viewed as differences between tissues or species rather than as inconsistencies. It is also possible that inhibition of senescence frequently observed with high auxin concentrations, e.g., 10^{-4} M or greater, could be due to a nonspecific interference with senescence (Lewis *et al.*, 1967; Mishra and Misra, 1968; Khan and Padhy, 1977; Misra and Biswal, 1980; Biswas and Choudhuri, 1981). The requirement for auxin to maintain the integrity of cultured cells is interesting; this seems to involve maintenance of the plasma membrane (Pech and Romani, 1979). Fruit ripening/senescence is often altered by auxin treatments (Weaver, 1972; Sacher, 1973; McGlasson *et al.*, 1978; Rhodes, 1980).

In some flowers, auxin may exert its effect at a location (petals) remote from the site of application (pistil) (Burg and Dijkman, 1967; Arditti and

Knauft, 1969; Nichols, 1977, 1982). Likewise, in bean plants, the senescence-inducing effect of the seeds on the leaves can be duplicated by replacing the seeds with auxin (Tamas et al., 1981). Conversely, low levels of auxin can substitute for the seeds in retarding the senescence of the pod walls (Sacher, 1959). These remote effects could be mediated by transmitted auxin or some other hormone or may involve some other action, e.g., a sink effect induced by auxin (Osborne and Hallaway, 1961, 1964; Seth and Wareing, 1967; Penot and Béraud, 1978).

B. Correlation with Endogenous Auxin

Generally, the level of endogenous IAA (or, more often, auxin activity in bioassays) decreases during or before (in preparation for) senescence (Table 10.2); however, in some cases, it does not change, e.g., Ecballium leaves (Roberts and Osborne, 1981) and soybean seed coats (Hein et al., 1984a). In several cases (Table 10.2), diffusible auxin (auxin in transit) from detached leaves has also been found to decrease. In two cases (Dörffling, 1963; Chua, 1976), the level of auxin activity in leaves rises just before abscission, and in several cases (Wheeler, 1968; El-Beltagy et al., 1976; Atsumi et al., 1976; Atsumi and Hayashi, 1979), auxin activity increases even earlier. It is, however, uncertain whether these rises reflect an increase in the levels of endogenous IAA or greater conversion of precursors to IAA during extraction (Atsumi and Hayashi, 1979; Roberts and Osborne, 1981). It has also been suggested that auxin is normally produced by autolyzing tissues, e.g., differentiating xylem (Sheldrake and Northcote, 1968a,b; Sheldrake, 1973). In bean and rubber tree (Hevea) leaves, the increase in free auxin is related to a decrease in bound auxin, indicating a release of free auxin from the bound form (Wheeler, 1968; Chua, 1976). Apex removal, which retards senescence of the bean leaves, also increases both free and bound auxin extractable from these leaves (Wheeler, 1968). Thus, it is not possible to formulate a general picture for the relation of auxin to senescence.

Another type of senescence involving auxin is that occurring during xylem cell differentiation (Chapter 1). It has been shown that xylem regeneration in stems is induced by auxin coming from nearby leaves (Jacobs, 1952, 1979).

C. Relationship between Auxin and Other Hormones

The interactions between auxin and other hormones includes a promotion of ethylene production in some tissues (e.g., flowers, Mayak and Halevy, 1980), but auxin generally inhibits it in fruit tissues (McGlasson et al., 1978; Rhodes, 1980). Auxin promotion of ethylene production appears to be important in postpollination changes in a number of flowers, though not necessarily all (Mayak and Halevy, 1980; Nichols, 1977, 1982). For example, Burg and Dijkman (1967) have proposed that auxin from the pollen on the stigma enters the column of a *Vanda* orchid flower and triggers a chain reaction of ethylene synthesis, which results in petal senescence. Whether auxin delays or promotes fruit ripening seems to depend on whether auxin inhibits or promotes ethylene synthesis (McGlasson *et al.*, 1978). In leaves, CEPA (an ethylene-releasing agent) decreases IAA-like activity (El-Beltagy *et al.*, 1976), and the synthetic auxin NAA promotes ethylene synthesis (Even-Chen *et al.*, 1978). The ethylene–auxin interaction relating to abscission is considered in detail by Addicott (1982).

The interrelations between auxin and ABA are discussed in Section II,C.

Little information is available on the interrelation of auxin and GA in senescing systems. The positive synergism between auxin and gibberellin in delaying cyclamen peduncle wilting and petiole senescence (Lyons and Widmer, 1983, 1984) suggests that the flower or leaf blade maintain the peduncle or petiole, respectively, by supplying auxin and gibberellin.

While auxin itself may also contribute to prevention of senescence in certain tissues, it may also act in conjunction with CK. In detached tobacco leaves, both kinetin and IAA inhibit yellowing; however, each causes a different and incomplete pattern of chlorophyll retention (Fig. 10.1; Engel-

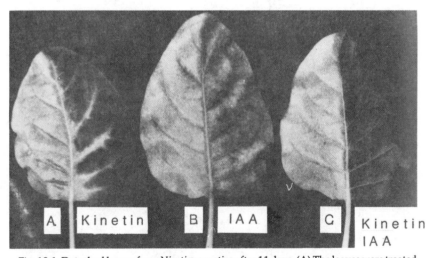

Fig. 10.1. Detached leaves from *Nicotiana rustica* after 11 days. (A) The leaves were treated with 2.32 × 10⁻⁷ M kinetin (applied to the surface on the right side); (B) 1.1 × 10⁻⁶ M IAA; and (C) kinetin and IAA combined. Note that the kinetin treatment retains green (dark) between the main veins, while the IAA treatment tends to keep the area along the main veins green. [Reprinted with permission from Engelbrecht and Conrad (1961).]

TABLE 10.2

Changes in Levels of Auxin or Auxin-Like Activity in Relation to Senescence

Authors	Tissue	Developmental stages	Purification	Method of measuring	Pattern of change
Allen and Baker (1980)	Castor bean leaves, attached	Progressive senescence	Partitioning	Gas chromatography and mass spectroscopy with selected ion monitoring	IAA level decreases as growth ceases, well before senescence
Atsumi and Hayashi (1979)	Pea and bean leaves, attached	Progressive senescence	Partitioning and paper chromatography	Oat coleoptile curvature bioassay	Auxin activity increases in senescing (yellow) leaves
Atsumi et al. (1976)	Cultured tobacco cells	Aging cultures	Partitioning and paper chromatography	Oat coleoptile curvature bioassay	Auxin activity increases in the senescent cultures
Böttger (1970)	Coleus leaves, attached	Progressive senescence	Paper chromatography	Oat coleoptile section growth bioassay	Diffusible auxin activity from the base decreases
Chua (1976)	Rubber tree leaves, attached	Seasonal senescence	Partitioning and paper chromatography	Oat mesocotyl segment growth bioassay	Auxin activity declines and then rises just before leaf fall
Conrad (1962)	Hemp leaves, attached	Monocarpic senescence	Partitioning and paper chromatography	Agrostemma hypocotyl segment elongation bioassay	Auxin activity rises during leaf yellowing
Conrad (1965)	Rape and pumpkin leaves, detached	Induced senescence	Partitioning and paper chromatography	Agrostemma hypocotyl segment elongation bioassay	Auxin activity decreases and then rises late in senescence
Dörffling (1963)	Maple tree leaves, attached	Autumnal senescence	Partitioning and paper chromatography	Oat coleoptile segment growth bioassay	Auxin activity decreases after growth ceases and then rises before leaf fall

Reference	Material	Type of senescence	Method	Assay	Observation
El-Beltagy et al. (1976)	Broad bean leaves, attached	Monocarpic senescence	Partitioning and paper chromatography	Oat coleoptile segment growth bioassay	Acidic auxin activity decreases in one variety and not in another; neutral auxin activity increases in one variety and not in another
Even-Chen et al. (1978)	Tobacco leaves, detached	Induced senescence	Partitioning	Fluorescence of the indolo-α-pyrone derivative of IAA	IAA-like activity increases sharply after chlorophyll loss has begun
Hein et al. (1984a)	Soybean seed coat	Seed coat senescence	HPLC (3×)	Fluorescence	No change in IAA
Hein et al. (1984b)	Soybean leaves, attached	Early monocarpic senescence	HPLC (3×)	Fluorescence	IAA decreased during podfill
Roberts and Osborne (1981)	Bean and Ecballium elaterium leaves, attached	Progressive senescence	Partitioning	Fluorescence of indolo-α-pyrone derivative of IAA	IAA levels decrease before leaf yellowing in bean and Prunus, but not in Ecballium
Sheldrake and Northcote (1968a)	Excised bean leaves	Induced senescence	Partitioning and paper chromatography	Oat coleoptile segment growth bioassay	Auxin activity rises
	Excised oat leaves	Induced senescence			Auxin activity rises and then falls
Shoji et al. (1951)	Bean seedling leaves, attached	Progressive senescence	Ether extraction	Oat coleoptile curvature	Auxin activity decreases
Thomas (1977)	Outer leaves of detached brussels sprout buttons	Induced senescence	Partitioning and paper chromatography	Wheat coleoptile segment elongation bioassay	Auxin activity decreases following chlorophyll
Wetmore and Jacobs (1953)	Coleus leaves, attached	Progressive senescence		Oat coleoptile curvature bioassay	Diffusible auxin activity decreases
Wheeler (1968)	Cotyledons and primary leaves of bean seedlings	Progressive senescence	Partitioning and paper chromatography	Wheat coleoptile segment elongation bioassay	Free auxin activity increases during senescence but may drop as water is lost from the cotyledons; bound auxin increases in cotyledons but decreases in leaves

347

brecht and Conrad, 1961). Together, they produce a uniform retention of chlorophyll. Auxin (NAA) and CK (BA) also exert different leaf-preserving effects in intact soybean plants (Noodén et al., 1979). The inhibition of BA metabolism by NAA (Zhang et al., 1987) probably contributes to this interaction between auxin and CK. For detached rape and pumpkin leaves, where auxin retards yellowing, kinetin sustains the levels of endogenous auxin activity (Conrad, 1965). In cocklebur leaf disks, where auxin does not delay chlorophyll loss, IAA may counteract the preserving effects of kinetin (Osborne, 1967; Biswas and Choudhuri, 1978). For leaves of a few species, auxin treatments delay senescence where cytokinin does not (Osborne and Hallaway, 1964; Osborne,1967).

Setting aside the apparent rise in auxin activity in some senescing tissues, the combined data on the effects of exogenous auxin and changes in the levels of exogenous auxin suggest a role for auxin in retardation of senescence in leaves and probably other tissues.

V. GIBBERELLIN AND SENESCENCE PROCESSES

A. Influence of Exogenous Gibberellin

A considerable literature exists concerning GA effects on senescence (Brian et al., 1959; Lockhart and Gottschall, 1961; Kelley and Schlamp, 1964; Ellis et al., 1965; Halevy and Wittwer, 1965; Humphries and French, 1965; Fletcher and Osborne, 1965, 1966; Harada, 1966; Whyte and Luckwill, 1966; Aspinall et al., 1967; Beevers and Guernsey, 1967; El-Antably et al., 1967; Beevers, 1966, 1968; Goldthwaite and Laetsch, 1968; Back and Richmond, 1969, 1971; Fletcher et al., 1969; Reynolds, 1969; Schwabe, 1970; Goldthwaite, 1972, 1974; Gupta and Chatterjee, 1974; Manos and Goldthwaite, 1975; Aharoni et al., 1975; Thomas, 1975; Karanov and Pogoncheva, 1976; Arguelles and Guardiola, 1977; Davies et al., 1977; Thomas, 1977; Aharoni and Richmond, 1978; Even-Chen et al., 1978; Garrod and Harris, 1978; Proebsting et al., 1978; Mayak and Halevy, 1980; Mishra and Gaur, 1980; Misra and Biswal, 1980; Biswas and Choudhuri, 1981; Sabater et al., 1981; Steinitz et al., 1981; Harada and Nakayuma, 1982; Baker, 1983; Lyons and Widmer, 1983, 1984; Westerman and Roddick, 1983; Mondal and Choudhuri, 1984) to mention only some of the relevant papers. Most of these studies show GA retardation of chlorophyll loss in leaves; however, a wide range of other processes and tissues have been studied. Chlorophyll loss is inhibited in a variety of tissues besides leaves; these include fruit, pea shoot apices, cotyledons, and flower stalks. GA can inhibit many other processes, such as RNA and protein breakdown, that may be associated with senescence. GA may also delay senescence in petals and petioles. In addition, there is a large literature relating to gibberellin effects on fruit ripening (Weaver, 1972; McGlasson *et al.*, 1978; Rhodes, 1980). GA also promotes the breakdown of reserves and mobilization of nutrients in the storage tissues of seeds (Murray, 1984; Bewley and Black, 1985), which may or may not be senescence processes (Chapter 1). Probably, the most striking feature of this literature is the diversity of the responses to GA. Even for a single process such as chlorophyll breakdown in leaves, some species (e.g., *Rumex*, nasturtium) respond with retardation by GA$_3$ (Section V,A), while others show promotion of chlorophyll loss (bean, peanut, *Taxodium*, and others; El-Antably *et al.*, 1967; Harada and Nakayama, 1982) or no significant effect (rye grass, tobacco, barley, radish, cowpea; Aspinall *et al.*, 1967; Mishra and Misra, 1968; Moore and Stone, 1972a,b; Thomas, 1975; Wittenbach, 1977; Even-Chen *et al.*, 1978; Lindoo and Noodén, 1978; Sabater *et al.*, 1981). As with many other GA-responding systems, the different gibberellins seem to differ markedly in their activity (see, e.g., Goldschmidt and Eilati, 1970; Davies *et al.*, 1977), but apparently not in all instances (Fletcher *et al.*, 1969). Some differences in GA response appear to depend on whether the tissue in question is excised or part of an intact system (Mishra and Misra, 1968; Misra and Biswal, 1980; Biswas and Choudhuri, 1981; Harada and Nakayama, 1982). For example, GA does not alter chlorophyll loss in detached rice leaves but does alter attached leaves, and that seems to be an indirect effect (Harada and Nakayama, 1982). Age is also an important factor; GA promotes chlorophyll loss in disks from leaves in immature Brussels sprouts but exerts the opposite effect on those from mature Brussels sprouts (Thomas, 1977). Illumination may also influence the GA response (Biswal and Biswal, 1984).

GA is also able to inhibit N redistribution from the leaves to the grain in rice (Harada and Nakayama, 1982) and to direct the movement of ions much as CK does in *Pelargonium* leaves (Penot and Béraud, 1978). In some cases, the GA treatments affect these senescence-related processes differentially, indicating they are not tightly coupled (Chapter 15).

B. Correlation with Endogenous Gibberellin

GA activity has been found to decline prior to or during senescence in a wide variety of tissues (Table 10.3). The role of gibberellin in apex senescence is discussed elsewhere (Sponsel, 1985; Davies *et al.*, 1986) in detail. For all of the tissues showing a decline in GA activity (Table 10.3), exogenous GA delays senescence, thus supporting the argument that for these tissues and these species a decline in GA plays a role in senescence. Indeed,

TABLE 10.3

Changes in Levels of Gibberellin or Gibberellin-Like Activity in Relation to Senescence

Authors	Tissue	Developmental stages	Purification	Method of measuring	Pattern of change
Aharoni and Richmond (1978)	Lettuce leaves, attached	Progressive senescence	Partitioning and paper chromatography	Barley endosperm bioassay and radioimmunoassay	GA activity decreases
Chin and Beevers (1970)	Nasturtium leaves, detached	Senescence	Partitioning and paper chromatography	Lettuce hypocotyl growth bioassay	GA activity decreases
Fletcher et al. (1969)	Dandelion leaves, attached	Progressive senescence	Partitioning and TLC	Barley endosperm and dandelion leaf disk senescence bioassays	GA activity declines
Proebsting et al. (1978)	Pea plants with pods	Monocarpic senescence	Partitioning and silica gel column chromatography	Lettuce hypocotyl bioassay	GA activity in leaves decreases in response to senescence-inducing photo-period (LD)
Thomas (1977)	Outer leaves of detached Brussels sprout buttons	Induced senescence	Partitioning and paper chromatography	Lettuce hypocotyl growth bioassay	GA activity rises after chlorophyll loss has started, then drops

exogenous GA seems to be most effective at stages when the endogenous GA is low (Fletcher *et al.*, 1969). Senescing tissues seem to metabolize GA more rapidly and to contain more bound GA (Goldschmidt and Galily, 1974; Aharoni and Richmond, 1978). By contrast, there are tissues where GA appears to exert no effect or where it promotes senescence (Section V,A).

It seems that application of GA-synthesis inhibitors should be useful in elucidating the role of gibberellin (Noodén and Leopold, 1978); however, these often alter senescence in the same direction as gibberellin (Fletcher and Osborne, 1965; Harada, 1966; Beevers and Guernsey, 1967; Beevers, 1968; Mishra and Misra, 1968; Thomas, 1968; Weaver, 1972; Misra and Biswal, 1973; Looney *et al.*, 1974; Thomas, 1977; Bhargavi *et al.*, 1977; McGlasson *et al.*, 1978; Harada and Nakayama, 1982). This and other evidence (Audus, 1972; Graebe and Ropers, 1978; McGlasson *et al.*, 1978) suggests the GA synthesis inhibitors may exert some additional effects. Furthermore, in many cases, the effects of these inhibitors may also be reversed by CK as well as gibberellin (Ruddat and Pharis, 1966; Beevers, 1968). Thus, the senescence-retarding effects of GA-synthesis inhibitors are interesting for their own sake (as well as being potentially useful) more than for what they tell about the role of GA in senescence.

C. Relationship between Gibberellin and Other Hormones

The literature that interrelates GA and other hormones that may regulate senescence processes falls into two main groups: (1) comparison of GA activities with those of other hormones and (2) alteration of GA levels or activities by other hormones or vice versa.

First, regarding the similarity or difference of GA and other hormones altering senescence, the major question here is the extent to which GA and CK resemble each other. In many leaf tissues (e.g., lettuce, radish, orange, and *Rumex*; references cited in Section V,A), GA and CK act in the same direction, i.e., retarding senescence. The same applies to citrus fruits (Coggins *et al.*, 1960a,b; Rasmussen, 1973; Goldschmidt *et al.*, 1977). Most often, though, CK-responsive tissues, particularly leaves, are not likewise affected by GA (e.g., cocklebur, Osborne, 1967; tobacco leaves, Moore and Stone, 1972b; Even-Chen *et al.*, 1978; rye grass leaves, Thomas, 1975; cowpea leaves, Mondal and Choudhuri, 1984). However, senescence is retarded by GA and not CK in a few tissues such as excised orange leaves (Arguelles and Guardiola, 1977), betel leaf disks (Mishra and Gaur, 1980), and *Kleinia articulata* leaf disks (Schwabe, 1970). Thus, it is clear that many patterns of response to the different hormones exist, even in leaf tissues, and again, species differ greatly in their responses. The interrelations between GA and ABA or auxin (Section II,C and IV,C) also show some species differences.

The second aspect, the influence of GA₃ on other hormones and vice versa, is rather sketchy, yet enough is known to say that there clearly are some important phenomena here. Both ABA (Section II,C) and auxin (Section IV,C) show some interconnection with GA, with ABA generally working in the opposite direction and auxin in the same direction as GA.

From these seemingly diverse details, we can imagine some possible hormonal regulatory mechanisms. In particular, the similarity between GA and CK may derive from elevation of GA levels by CK in orange fruits (Goldschmidt et al., 1972) and lettuce leaves (Aharoni and Richmond, 1978), where both cytokinin and GA retard senescence. On the other hand, GA₃ does not alter CK levels in tobacco leaves, though the senescence of these leaves is also not significantly altered by GA (Even-Chen et al., 1978). In *Taraxacum* leaf disks, high concentrations of GA₃ do not exert any effect above that obtained with kinetin, indicating that the two may act similarly and the system is saturated (Back and Richmond, 1969). In nasturtium leaf disks (Back and Richmond, 1969), however, GA₃ seems to act on top of saturating doses of CK, which suggests a difference. Likewise, GA₃ and CK show a positive synergistic effect on chlorophyll retention in *Rumex* leaf disks (Goldthwaite, 1972) and in soybean explants in which the hormone solutions are substituted for the roots (Noodén, 1986). In the latter case, exogenous GA exerts little or no effect on its own. Thus, CK and GA may interact in some tissues, possibly through alteration of each other's metabolism, but that interaction may differ (or even not occur) depending on the species.

GA also shows a strong interrelation with ABA in senescing tissues (Section II,C). At this point, it should be noted that, at least for low ABA doses, the antagonism between ABA and CK in *Rumex* and *Taraxacum* leaf disks showed competitive kinetics, while that between ABA and GA did not (Back and Richmond, 1971). This further indicates some difference in the way GA and CK act on senescence.

VI. OTHER RETARDANTS OF SENESCENCE

In addition to mineral nutrients and sucrose, a variety of naturally occurring compounds can delay senescence in pre- or early senescent tissues. The ability of ABA to inhibit senescence (Section II,A) may be an artifact. A mixture of amino acids (peptone) is actually more active than kinetin or GA₃ in retarding chlorophyll loss in *Rumex* leaf disks (Reynolds, 1969). Certain phenolic compounds, e.g., coumarin, quercitin, and rutin, and vanillin also inhibit senescence (Knypl, 1970; Knypl and Mazurczyk, 1971; Karanov and Pogoncheva, 1976). Other retardants include fusicoccin (Thimann and Satler, 1979), aliphatic alcohols (Satler and Thimann, 1980), ethanol (Heins and Blakely, 1980), cyclic AMP (Chaudhuri and Sen, 1980), ascorbic acid (Garg and Kapoor, 1972; Cooper *et al.*, 1968), hinesol (Ueda *et al.*, 1983), and triacontinol (Debata and Murty, 1984). Capillin and some aliphatic compounds related to capillin (Ueda *et al.*, 1984) can also retard senescence; however, at higher concentrations, most of these can also promote senescence. In addition, there are the still unknown factors that retard the ripening and senescence of attached fruit in some species (McGlasson *et al.*, 1978); Bruinsma, 1983). Even though they may not function as hormones, an extensive literature indicates that exogenous polyamines are active in retarding senescence and may well have an important natural role; this interesting group warrants further study (Cohen *et al.*, 1979; Altman, 1982; Shih *et al.*, 1982; Galston, 1983; Smith, 1985; see also Chapter 2). The function of these senescence retardants remains to be determined, but it seems unlikely that any will be as important as cytokinin.

VII. SUMMARY

A. What Hormone Is in Control?

Because of the practical importance of senescence, considerable effort has been made to alter its course in whole plants, attached organs, or, most often, detached parts, as in postharvest applications. This has produced a large quantity of data concerning hormone effects on senescence and related processes. While observations of this type can be indicative, they do not by themselves constitute proof that the hormone regulates senescence (Chapter 1). Studies on hormone effects on detached organs or tissue fragments (e.g., leaf blade disks), have been informative, especially when integrated with studies on endogenous hormone levels and the location of the hormone source. Parallel variation occurs in many systems, at least in the sense that the hormone levels change prior to or in conjunction with senescence. Combined data from exogenous applications, excision, substitution, and isolation can provide a stronger case for hormonal control (Chapter 1). Ultimately, some generalizations should be possible, even though different hormone controls function in different species. In any case, diverse data implicate senescence-retarding and -promoting hormones, in addition to CK and ethylene, but now more integrated analyses (Chapter 1) are needed.

B. Hormone Combinations

Hormones often achieve regulatory controls by acting in combinations (Leopold and Noodén, 1984; Wareing, 1986). This is clearly the case in senescence, where interrelations take many forms, both in terms of hormones combined and the mechanisms involved. Unfortunately, this further complicates the hormonal control picture, but with recognition and further study, it should become possible to make some generalizations.

It seems obvious that the interactions between senescence retardants and senescence promoters will prove to be important. Again, what seems to be needed now is more integrated studies on particular systems.

C. Integrated Hormone Systems

It would now be valuable to focus on a few systems to work out a more integrated picture of hormonal controls under identical or similar conditions.

It is in whole plant senescence (Chapter 12) that the importance of integrating separate studies into a larger picture really becomes most obvious, but other, simpler examples exist. A clear warning about the need to consider the larger picture is provided by cut rose flowers, where ABA exerts opposing effects on senescence depending on whether or not the leaves have been removed (Halevy et al., 1974).

Most of the studies reported are already directed toward a small number of systems. For a few systems, tobacco leaves, *Rumex* leaves (but several species have been used), lettuce leaves, Brussels sprouts, citrus fruits, avocado fruits, tomato fruits, grape berries, carnation flowers, rose flowers, rice plants, and soybean plants, a substantial start toward integrated studies has already been made.

D. New Hormones?

No doubt, additional hormones will be found to be involved in senescence. A variety of naturally occurring organic substances do alter senescence, and some could function as hormones, but that remains to be determined. In addition, known hormones do not sufficiently account for some of the known correlative controls of senescence (e.g., pod induction of monocarpic senescence in soybean, Chapter 12).

E. Conclusion

Senescence of a cell, a tissue, an organ, or a whole plant is often, if not always, under correlative control. It follows that hormones must play a central role in regulating senescence. ABA, auxin, GA, and other hormones are certainly involved in the regulation of senescence of various tissues, in addition to CK and ethylene. Better integration of the excision and substitution part of this literature with the correlations of endogenous hormones would greatly enhance progress.

REFERENCES

Addicott, F. T. (1982). "Abscission." Univ. of California Press, Berkeley.

Addicott, F. T., and Carns, H. R. (1983). History and introduction. *In* "Abscisic Acid" (F. Addicott, ed.), pp. 1–21. Praeger, New York.

Aharoni, N., and Richmond, A. E. (1978). Endogenous gibberellin and abscisic acid as related to senescence of detached lettuce leaves. *Plant Physiol.* **62**, 224–228.

Aharoni, N., Back, A., Benyehoshua, S., and Richmond, A. E. (1975). Exogenous gibberellic acid and the cytokinin isopentenyladenine retardants of senescence in romaine lettuce. *J. AM. Soc. Hortic. Sci.* **100**, 4–6.

Allen, J. R. F., and Baker, D. A. (1980). Free tryptophan and IAA levels in the leaves and vascular path ways of *Ricinis-communis var. gibsonii. Planta* **148**, 69–74.

Altman, A. (1982). Retardation of radish leaf senescence by polyamines. *Physiol. Plant.* **54**, 189–193.

Alvim, R., Hewett, E. W., and Saunders, P. F. (1976). Seasonal variation in the hormone content of willow. I. Changes in abscisic acid content and cytokinin activity in the xylem sap. *Plant Physiol.* **57**, 474–476.

Arditti, J., and Knauft, R. L. (1969). The effects of auxin, actinomycin D, ethionine, and puromycin on post-pollination behavior by *Cymbidium* (Orchidaceae) flowers. *Am. J. Bot.* **56**, 620–628.

Arguelles, T., and Guardiola, J. L. (1977). Hormonal control of senescence in excised orange leaves. *J. Hortic. Sci.* **52**, 199–204.

Aspinall, D., Paleg, L., and Addicott, F. (1967). Abscisin II and some hormone-regulated plant responses. *Aust. J. Biol. Sci.* **20**, 869–882.

Atsumi, S., and Hayashi, T. (1979). Examination of the pronounced increase in auxin content of senescent leaves. *Plant Cell Physiol.* **20**, 861–865.

Atsumi, S., Kuraishi, S., and Hayashi, T. (1976). An improvement of auxin extraction procedure and its application to cultured plant cells. *Planta* **129**, 245–247.

Audus, L. J. (1972). "Plant Growth Substances. Vol. 1: Chemistry and Physiology." Barnes & Noble, New York.

Audus, L. J., ed. (1976). "Herbicides: Physiology, Biochemistry, Ecology." Academic Press, London.

Back, A., and Richmond, A. (1969). An interaction between the effects of kinetin and gibberellin in retarding leaf senescence. *Physiol. Plant.* **22**, 1207–1216.

Back A., and Richmond, A. E. (1971). Interrelations between gibberellic acid, cytokinins and abscisic acid in retarding leaf senescence. *Physiol. Plant.* **24**, 76–79.

Back A., Bittner, S., and Richmond, A. E. (1972). The effect of abscisic acid on the metabolism of kinetin in detached leaves of *Rumex pulcher. J. Exp. Bot.* **23**, 744–750.

Baddeley, M. S. (1971). Biochemical aspects of senescence. *In* "Ecology of Leaf Surface Microorganisms" (T. F. Preece and G. H. Dickson, eds.), pp. 415–429. Academic Press, London.

Bailey, J. A., and Mansfield, J. W., eds. (1982). "Phytoalexins." Wiley, New York.

Baker, J. E. (1983). Preservation of cut flowers. *In* "Plant Growth Regulating Chemicals" (L. G. Nickell, ed.), Vol. 2, pp. 177–191. CRC Press, Boca Raton, Florida.

Ballantyne, D. J. (1965). Senescence of daffodil *(Narcissus pseudonarcissus)* cut flowers treated with benzyladenine and auxin. *Nature (London)* **205**, 819.

Beevers, L. (1966). Effect of gibberellic acid on the senescence of leaf disks of nasturtium *(Tropaeolum majus). Plant Physiol.* **41**, 1074–1076.

Beevers, L. (1968). Growth regulator control of senescence in leaf discs of nasturtium *(Tropaeolum majus). In* "Physiology of Plant Growth Substances" (F. Wightman and G. Setterfield, eds.), pp. 1417–1435. Runge Press, Ottawa.

Beevers, L., and Guernsey, F. S. (1967). Interaction of growth regulators in the senescence of nasturtium leaf disks. *Nature (London)* **214**, 941–942.

Bell, A. A. (1981). Biochemical mechanisms of disease resistance. *Annu. Rev. Plant Physiol.* **32**, 21–81.

Bengtson, C., Klockare, B., Larsson, S., and Sundquist, C. (1977). The effect of phytohormones on chlorophyllide protochlorophyllide and carotenoid formation in greening dark grown wheat leaves. *Physiol. Plant.* **40**, 198–204.

Bennet-Clark, T. A., and Kefford, N. P. (1953). Chromatography of the growth substances in plant extracts. *Nature (London)* **171**, 645–647.

Bewley, J. D., and Black, M. (1985). "Seeds. Physiology of Development and Germination." Plenum, New York.

Bhargavi, K., Rao Madhusadana, I., and Swamy, P. M. (1977). Promotion of rooting and delay of senescence in detached leaves of *Gomphrena globosa* by growth regulators and CA^{+2}. *Indian J. Exp. Biol.* **15**, 1069–1070.

Biswal, U. C., and Biswal, B. (1984). Photocontrol of leaf senescence. *Photochem. Photobiol.* **39**, 875–879.

Biswas, A. K., and Choudhuri, M. A. (1978). Regulatory of some hormones and nutrients on senescence development of soybean leaf disks. *Indian J. Exp. Biol.* **16**, 1313–1314.

Biswas, A. K., and Choudhuri, M. A. (1980). Mechanism of monocarpic senescence in rice. *Plant Physiol.* **65**, 340–345.

Biswas, A. K., and Choudhuri, M. A. (1981). Mobilization of metabolites as the cause of flag leaf senescence in rice (*Oryza sativa* Jaya). *Indian J. Exp. Biol.* **19**, 434–436.

Böttger, M. (1970). Die hormonal Regulation des Blattfalls bei *Coleus rehneltianus* Berger. II. Die natürliche Rolle von Abscinäure im Blattfallprozess. *Planta* **93**, 205–213.

Borochov, A., Tirosh, T., and Halevy, A. H. (1976). Abscisic acid content of senescing petals on cut rose flowers as affected by sucrose and water stress. *Plant Physiol.* **58**, 175–178.

Bowen, M. R., and Hoad, G. V. (1968). Inhibitor content of phloem and xylem sap obtained from willow (*Salix viminalis* L.) entering dormancy. *Planta* **81**, 64–70.

Brenner, M. L., Hein, M. B., Schussler, J., Daie, J., and Brun, W. A. (1982). Coordinate control: The involvement of abscisic acid, its transport and metabolism. *In* "Plant Growth Substances 1982" (P. F. Wareing, ed.), pp. 343–352. Academic Press, London.

Brian, P. W., Petty, J. H. P., and Richmond, P. T. (1959). Effects of gibberellic acid on development of autumn colour and leaf fall of deciduous woody plants. *Nature (London)* **183**, 58–59.

Brisker, H. E., Goldschmidt, E. E., and Goren, R. (1976). Ethylene-induced formation of abscisic acid in *Citrus* peel as related to chloroplast transformations. *Plant Physiol.* **58**, 377–379.

Bruinsma, J. (1983). Hormonal regulation of senescence, ageing, fading and ripening. *In* "Post-Harvest Physiology and Crop Preservation" (M. Lieberman, ed.), pp. 141–163. Plenum, New York.

Bugge, G. (1976). Zur Bildung der Stickstoffverbindungen im Laufe der Ontogenese bei *Lolium multiflorum* L. I. Menge und Zusammensetzung. *Z. Acker- Pflanzenbau* **142**, 194–205.

Burg, S. P., and Dijkman, M. J. (1967). Ethylene and auxin participation in pollen induced fading of *Vanda* orchid blossoms. *Plant Physiol.* **42**, 1648–1650.

Burschka, C., Lange, O. L., and Hartung, W. (1985). Effects of abscisic acid on stomatal conductance and photosynthesis in leaves of intact *Arbutus unedo* plants under natural conditions. *Oecologia* **67**, 593–595.

Burton, W. G. (1982). "Post-harvest Physiology of Food Crops." Longman, New York.

Chang, Y., and Jacobs, W. P. (1973). The regulation of abscission and IAA by senescence factor and abscisic acid. *Am. J. Bot.* **60**, 10–16.

Chaudhuri, C., and Sen, S. P. (1980). Effect of kinetin and cyclic adenosine monophosphate on ageing Bonavist bean leaf disks. *Plant Biochem. J.* **1,** 37–53.

Chen, Y. M. (1972). Certain aspects of light and plant hormones in control of senescence. *Taiwania* **17,** 81–91.

Chin, T., and Beevers, L. (1970). Changes in endogenous growth regulators in *Nasturtium* leaves during senescence. *Planta* **92,** 178–188.

Chua, S. E. (1976). Role of growth promoter and growth inhibitor in foliar senescence and abscission of *Hevea brasiliensis. J. Rubber Res. Inst. Malaysia* **24,** 202–214.

Ciha, A. J., Brenner, M. L., and Brun, W. A. (1978). Effect of pod removal on abscisic acid levels in soybean tissue. *Crop Sci.* **18,** 776–779.

Coggins, C. W., Jr., Hield, H. Z., and Garber, M. J. (1960a). The influence of potassium gibberellate on Valencia orange trees and fruit. *Proc. Am. Soc. Hortic. Sci.* **76,** 193–198.

Coggins, C. W., Jr., Hield, H. Z., and Boswell, S. B. (1960b). The influence of potassium gibberellate on Lisbon lemon trees and fruit. *Proc. Am. Soc. Hortic. Sci.* **76,** 199–207.

Cohen, A. S., Popovic, R. B., and Zalik, S. (1979). Effects of polyamines on chlorophyll and protein content, photochemical activity and chloroplast ultrastructure of barley, *Hordeum vulgare,* leaf discs during senescence. *Plant Physiol.* **64,** 717–720.

Colquhoun, A. J., and Hillman, J. R. (1972). The effects of abscisic acid on senescence in leaf discs of radish, *Raphanus sativus* L. *Planta* **105,** 213–224.

Colquhoun, A. J., and Hillman, J. R. (1975). Endogenous abscisic acid and the senescence of leaves *Phaseolus vulgaris* L. *Z. Pflanzenphysiol.* **76,** 326–332.

Colquhoun, A. J., Hillman, J. R., Crewe, C., and Bowes, B. G. (1975). An ultrastructural study of the effects of abscisic acid on senescence of leaves of radish (*Raphanus sativus* L.). *Protoplasma* **84,** 205–222.

Conrad, K. (1962). Über geschlechtsgebundene Unterschiede im Wüchsstoffgehalt männlicher und weiblicher Hanfpflanzen. *Flora (Jena)* **152,** 68–73.

Conrad, K. (1965). Über den Auxin- und Glucobrassin-Haushalt von kinetinbehandelten isolierten Blättern. *Flora (Jena)* **155,** 441–451.

Cooper, W. C., Rasmussen, G. K., and Smoot, J. J. (1968). Induction of degreening of tangerines by preharvest applications of ascorbic acid and other ethylene-releasing agents. *Citrus Ind.* **49,** 25–27.

Cornic, G., and Miginiac, E. (1983). Non-structural inhibition of net CO_2 uptake by (±) abscisic acid in *Pharbitis nil. Plant Physiol.* **73,** 529–533.

Davies, P. J., Proebsting, W. M., and Gianfagna, T. J. (1977). Hormonal relationships in whole plant senescence. *In* "Plant Growth Regulation" (P. E. Pilet, ed.), pp. 273–280. Springer-Verlag, Berlin and New York.

Davies, P. J., Birnberg, P. R., Maki, S. L., and Brenner, M. L. (1986). Photoperiod modification of [^{14}C] gibberellin $A_{1}2$ aldehyde metabolism in shoots of pea, line G2. *Plant Physiol.* **81,** 991–996.

Debata, A., and Murty, K. S. (1984). Effect on growth regulators and nitrogen on panicle senescence in rice. *Indian J. Plant Physiol.* **27,** 393–397.

DeLeo, P., and Sacher, J. A. (1970). Control of ribonuclease and acid phosphatase by auxin and abscisic acid during senescence of *Rheo* leaf sections. *Plant Physiol.* **46,** 806–811.

Dörffling, K. (1963). Über das Wuchsstoff-Hemstoff-system von *Acer pseudoplatanus* L. I. Der Jahresgang der Wuchs- und Hemmstoffe in Knospen, Blättern und in Kambium. *Planta* **60,** 390–412.

Dörffling, K., Böttger, M., Martin, D., Schmidt, V., and Borowski, D. (1978). Physiology and chemistry of substances accelerating abscission in senescent petioles and fruit stalks. *Physiol. Plant.* **43,** 292–296.

Draper, S. R. (1969). Lipid changes in senescing cucumber cotyledons. *Phytochemistry* **8**, 1641–1647.

Düring, H. (1978). Untersuchungen zur umweltabhängigkeit der stomatären transpiration bei reben II. Ringelungs und temperatureffekte. *Vitis* **17**, 1–9.

Dumbroff, E. B., Brown, D. C. W., and Thompson, J. E. (1977). Effect of senescence on levels of free abscisic acid and water potentials in cotyledons of bean. *Bot. Gaz.* **138**, 261–265.

El-Antably, H. M. M., Wareing, P. F., and Hillman, J. (1967). Some physiological responses to D. L abscisin (Dormin). *Planta* **73**, 74–90.

El-Beltagy, A. S., and Hall, M. A. (1975). Studies on endogenous levels of ethylene and auxin in *Vicia faba* during growth and development. *New Phytol.* **75**, 215–224.

El-Beltagy, A. S., Hewett, E. W., and Hall, M. A. (1976). Effect of Ethephon (2-choroethyl phosphonic acid) on endogenous levels of auxin, inhibitors and cytokinins in relation to senescence and abscission in *Vicia faba* L. *J. Hortic. Sci.* **51**, 451–465.

Ellis, P. E., Carlisle, D. B., and Osborne, D. J. (1965). Desert locusts: Sexual maturation delayed by feeding on senescent vegetation. *Science* **149**, 546–547.

Engelbrecht, L., and Conrad, K. (1961). Vergleichende Untersuchungen zur Wirkung von Kinetin und Auxin. *Ber. Dtsch. Bot. Ges.* **74**, 42–46.

Even-Chen, Z., and Itai, C. (1975). The role of abscisic acid in senescence of detached tobacco leaves. *Physiol. Plant.* **34**, 97–100.

Even-Chen, Z., Atsom, D., and Itai, C. (1978). Hormonal aspects of senescence in detached tobacco leaves. *Physiol. Plant.* **44**, 377–382.

Ferguson, I. B., and Mitchell, R. E. (1985). Stimulation of ethylene production in bean leaf discs by the pseudomonad phytotoxin coronatine. *Plant Physiol.* **77**, 969–973.

Fletcher, R. A., and Osborne, D. J. (1965). Regulation of protein and nucleic acid synthesis by gibberellin during leaf senescence. *Nature (London)* **207**, 1176–1177.

Fletcher, R. A., and Osborne, D. J. (1966). Gibberellin, as a growth regulator of protein and ribonucleic acid synthesis during senescence in leaf cells of *Taraxacum officinale*. *Can. J. Bot.* **44**, 739–745.

Fletcher, R. A., Oegema, T., and Horton, R. F. (1969). Endogenous gibberellin levels and senescence in *Taraxacum officinale*. *Planta* **86**, 98–102.

Galston, A. W. (1983). Polyamines as modulators of plant development. *BioScience* **33**, 382–388.

Garaizabal, M. I. E., and Rodriguez, M. T. (1983). Effects of light and growth regulators on the reversibility of senescence in attached leaves of barley. *Z. Pflanzenphysiol.* **112**, 435–442.

Garg, O. P., and Kapoor, V. (1972). Retardation of leaf senescence by ascorbic acid. *J. Exp. Bot.* **23**, 699–703.

Garrod, J. F., and Harris, G. P. (1978). Effect of gibberellic acid on senescence of isolated petals of carnation. *Ann. Appl. Biol.* **88**, 309–312.

Gepstein, S., and Thimann, K. V. (1980). Changes in the abscisic acid content of oat leaves during senescence. *Proc. Natl. Acad. Sci. USA* **77**, 2050–2053.

Gepstein, S., and Thimann, K. V. (1981). The role of ethylene in the senescence of oat leaves. *Plant Physiol.* **68**, 349–354.

Glinka, Z., and Reinhold, L. (1971). Abscisic acid raises the permeability of plant cells to water. *Plant Physiol.* **48**, 103–105.

Goldbach, H., Goldbach, E., and Michael, G. (1977). Transport of abscisic acid from leaves to grains in wheat and barley plants. *Naturwissenschaften* **64**, 488.

Goldschmidt, E. E., and Eilati, S. K. (1970). Gibberellin-treated Shamouti oranges: Effects on coloration and translocation within peel of fruits attached or detached from the tree. *Bot Gaz.* **131**, 116–122.

Goldschmidt, E. E., and Galily, D. (1974). The fate of endogenous gibberellins and applied radioactive gibberellin A₃ during natural and ethylene-induced senescence in citrus peel. *Plant Cell Physiol.* **15**, 485–491.

Goldschmidt, E. E., Eilati, S. K., and Goren, R. (1972). Increase in ABA-like growth inhibitors and decrease in gibberellin-like substances during ripening and senescence of citrus fruits. *In* "Plant Growth Substances 1970" (D. J. Carr, ed.), pp. 611–617. Springer-Verlag, Berlin and New York.

Goldschmidt, E. E., Goren, R., Even-Chen, Z., and Bittner, S. (1973). Increase in free and bound abscisic acid during natural and ethylene-induced senescence in citrus fruit peel. *Plant Physiol.* **51**, 879–882.

Goldschmidt, E. E., Aharoni, Y., Elati, S. K., Riov, J. W., and Monselise, S. P. (1977). Differential counteraction of ethylene effects by gibberellin A₃ and N6-benzyladenine in senescing citrus peel. *Plant Physiol.* **59**, 193–195.

Goldthwaite, J. J. (1972). Further studies of hormone-regulated senescence in *Rumex* leaf tissue. *In* "Plant Growth Substances 1970" (D. J. Carr, ed.), pp. 581–588. Springer-Verlag, Berlin and New York.

Goldthwaite, J. J. (1974). Energy metabolism of *Rumex* leaf tissue in the presence of senescence-regulating hormones and sucrose. *Plant Physiol.* **54**, 399–403.

Goldthwaite, J. J., and Laetsch, W. M. (1968). Control of senescence in *Rumex* leaf discs by gibberellic acid. *Plant Physiol.* **43**, 1855–1858.

Graebe, J. E., and Ropers, H. J. (1978). Gibberellins. *In* "Phytohormones and Related Compounds—A Comprehensive Treatise" (D. S. Letham, P. B. Goodwin, and T. J. V. Higgins, eds.), pp. 107–204. Elsevier/North-Holland, Amsterdam.

Grossmann, K., and Jung, J. (1982). Pflanzlicher Seneszenzvorgänge. *Z. Acker- Pflanzenbau* **151**, 149–165.

Gupta, K. K., and Chatterjee, S. K. (1974). Cotyledonary senescence of *Xanthium strumarium* Linn. *Bot. Gaz.* **135**, 275–280.

Halevy, A. H., and Mayak, S. (1975). Interrelationship of several phytohormones in the regulation of rose petal senescence. *Acta Hortic.* **41**, 103–116.

Halevy, A. H., and Mayak, S. (1981). Senescence and postharvest physiology of cut flowers—Part 2. *Hortic. Rev.* **3**, 59–143.

Halevy, A. H., and Wittwer, S. H. (1965). Chemical regulation of leaf senescence. *Mich. Agric. Exp. Stn. Q. Bull.* **48**, 30–35.

Halevy, A. H., Mayak, S., Tirosh, T., Spiegelstein, H., and Kofranek, A. M. (1974). Opposing effects of abscisic acid on senescence of rose flowers. *Plant Cell Physiol.* **15**, 813–821.

Hall, H. K., and McWha, J. A. (1981). Effects of abscisic acid on growth of wheat (*Triticum aestivum* L.). *Ann. Bot.* **47**, 427–433.

Hall, W. C., Herrero, F. A., and Katterman, F. R. H. (1961). Leaf abscission in cotton. IV. Effects of a natural promoter and amino acids on abscission in cotyledonary node explants. *Bot. Gaz.* **123**, 29–34.

Hancock, J. F., Antonio, T. M., Dalgarn, D. S., and Newman, D. W. (1983). Lipids of senescent leaf tissue induced by inhibition of synthesis and acceleration of breakdown. *Ohio J. Sci.* **83**, 50–54.

Harada, H. (1966). Retardation of the senescence of *Rumex* leaves by growth retardants. *Plant Cell Physiol.* **7**, 701–703.

Harada, J., and Nakayama, H. (1982). Effect of gibberellin applications after heading on the longevity of rice *Oryza sativa* leaves with reference to grain development. *Bull. Hokuriku Natl. Agric. Exp. Stn.* **24**, 85–102.

Hein, M. B., Brenner, M. L., and Brun, W. A. (1984a). Concentrations of abscisic acid and indole-3-acetic acid in soybean seeds during development. *Plant Physiol.* **76**, 951–954.

Hein, M. B., Brenner, M. L., and Brun, W. A. (1984b). Effects of pod removal on the transport and accumulation of abscisic acid and indole-3-acetic acid in soybean leaves. *Plant Physiol.* **76**, 955–958.

Heins, R. D., and Blakely, N. (1980). Influence of ethanol on ethylene biosynthesis and flower senescence of cut carnation. *Sci. Hortic. (Amsterdam)* **13**, 361–369.

Hemberg, T. (1961). Biogenous inhibitors. *Encycl. Plant Physiol.* **14**, 1162–1184.

Ho, T. D. (1983). Biochemical mode of action of abscisic acid. *In* "Abscisic Acid" (F. T. Addicott, ed.), pp. 147–169. Praeger, New York.

Holst, U. (1971). Some properties of inhibitor β from *Solanum tuberosum* compared to ABA. *Physiol. Plant.* **24**, 392–396.

Housley, S., and Taylor, W. C. (1958). Studies on plant growth hormones. VI. The nature of inhibitor β in potato. *J. Exp. Bot.* **9**, 458–471.

Humphries, E. C., and French, S. A. W. (1965). A growth study of sugar beet treated with gibberellic acid and (2-chloroethyl) trimethylammonium chloride (CCC). *Ann. Appl. Biol.* **55**, 159–173.

Iliev, L. K., Karonov, E. N., Boumova, I. M., and Angelova, J. M. (1982). On the content of ABA in radish cotyledons and isolated leaf disks after cytokinin effects. *Dokl. Bolg. Akad. Nauk* **35**, 229–232.

Jacobs, W. P. (1952). The role of auxin in differentiation of xylem around a wound. *Am. J. Bot.* **39**, 301–309.

Jacobs, W. P. (1979). "Plant Hormones and Plant Development." Cambridge Univ. Press, London and New York.

James, A. L., Anderson, I. C., and Greer, H. A. L. (1965). Effects of naphthaleneacetic acid on field-grown soybeans. *Crop Sci.* **5**, 472–474.

Kahl, G. (1982). Molecular biology of wound healing: the conditioning phenomenon. *In* "Molecular Biology of Plant Tumors" (G. Kahl and J. S. Schell, eds.), pp. 211–267. Academic Press, New York.

Kahl, G. (1983). Wound repair and tumor induction in higher plants. *In* "The New Frontiers in Plant Biochemistry" (T. Akazawa, T. Asahi, and H. Imaseki, eds.), pp. 193–216. Jpn. Sci. Soc., Tokyo.

Karanov, E. N., and Pogoncheva, E. M. (1976). Effect of abscisic acid and of its interaction with other growth regulators on chlorophyll destruction in detached leaves. *Fiziol. Rast. (Sofia)* **2**, 3–17.

Keen, N. T. (1981). Evaluation of the role of phytoalexins. *In* "Plant Disease Control" (R. C. Staples and G. H. Toenniessen, eds.), pp. 155–177. Wiley, New York.

Kelley, J. D., and Schlamp, A. L. (1964). Keeping quality, flower size and flowering response of three varieties of Easter lilies to gibberellic acid. *Proc. Am. Soc. Hortic. Sci.* **85**, 631–634.

Khan, P. A., and Padhy, B. (1977). Effect of growth regulators on degradation of chlorophyll, protein and carbohydrate in detached rice leaves during senescence. *Sci. Cult.* **43**, 359–360.

Knypl, J. S. (1970). Arrest of yellowing in senescing leaf disks of maize by growth retardants, coumarin and inhibitors of RNA and protein synthesis. *Biol. Plant.* **12**, 199–207.

Knypl, J. S., and Mazurczyk, W. (1971). Arrest of chlorophyll and protein breakdown in senescing leaf discs of kale by cycloheximide and vanillin. *Curr. Sci.* **40**, 294–295.

Kozlowski, T. T. (1971). "Growth and Development of Trees." Academic Press, New York.

Kulkarni, V. J., and Schwabe, W. W. (1985). Graft transmission of longday-induced leaf senescence in *Kleinia articulata. J. Exp. Bot.* **36**, 1620–1633.

Laidman, D. L. (1982). Control mechanisms in the mobilisation of stored nutrients in germinating cereals. *In* "The Physiology and Biochemistry of Seed Development, Dormancy and Germination" (A. A. Khan, ed.), pp. 371–405. Elsevier, Amsterdam.

Leckstein, P. M., and Llewellyn, M. (1975). Quantitative analysis of seasonal variation in the amino acids in phloem sap of *Salix alba* L. *Planta* **124**, 89–92.

Lenton, J. R., Perry, V. M., and Saunders, P. F. (1972). Endogenous abscisic acid in relation to photoperiodically induced bud dormancy. *Planta* **106**, 13–22.

Leopold, A. C. (1961). Senescence in plant development. *Science* **134**, 1727–1732.

Leopold, A. C., and Noodén, L. D. (1984). Hormonal regulatory systems in plants. *Encycl. Plant Physiol., New Ser.* **10**, 4–22.

Letham, D. S. (1978). Naturally-occurring plant growth regulators other than the principal hormones of higher plants. In "Phytohormones and Related Compounds: A Comprehensive Treatise" (D. S. Letham, P. B. Goodwin, and T. J. V. Higgins, eds.), Vol. 1, pp. 349–417. Elsevier/North-Holland, Amsterdam.

Lewis, L. N., Coggins, C. W., Labanauskas, C. K., Jr., and Dugger, W. M. (1967). Biochemical changes associated with natural and gibberellin A₃ delayed senescence in the navel orange rind. *Plant Cell Physiol.* **8**, 151–160.

Lindoo, S. J., and Noodén, L. D. (1978). Correlations of cytokinins and abscisic acid with monocarpic senescence in soybean. *Plant Cell Physiol.* **19**, 997–1006.

Lockhart, J. A., and Gottschall, V. (1961). Fruit-induced and apical senescence in *Pisum sativum*. *Plant Physiol.* **36**, 389–398.

Looney, N. E., McGlasson, W. B., and Coombe, B. G. (1974). Control of fruit ripening in peach, *Prunis persica:* Action of succinic acid-2,2-dimethylhydrazide and (2-chlorethyl) phosphonic acid. *Aust. J. Plant Physiol.* **1**, 77–86.

Loveys, B. R., and Kriedemann, P. E. (1974). Internal control of stomatal physiology and photosynthesis. I. Stomatal regulation and associated changes in endogenous levels of abscisic and phaseic acids. *Aust. J. Plant Physiol.* **1**, 407–415.

Lyons, R. E., and Widmer, R. E. (1983). Effects of gibberellic acid and naphthaleneacetic acid on petiole senescence and subtended peduncle growth of *Cyclamen persicum* Mill. *Ann. Bot.* **52**, 885–890.

Lyons, R. E., and Widmer, R. E. (1984). A gibberellin-auxin associated with peduncle elongation and senescence in *Cyclamen persicum* Mill. "Swan Lake". *Bot. Gaz.* **145**, 170–175.

McCarty, R. E., and Jagendorf, A. T. (1965). Chloroplast damage due to enzymatic hydrolysis of endogenous lipids. *Plant Physiol.* **40**, 725–735.

McGlasson, W. B., Wade, N. L., and Adato, I. (1978). Phytohormones and fruit ripening. In "Phytohormones and Related Compounds: A Comprehensive Treatise" (D. S. Letham, P. B. Goodwin, and T. J. V. Higgins, eds.), Vol. 2, pp. 447–493. Elsevier/North-Holland, Amsterdam.

Malik, N. S. A. (1982). Senescence in detached oat leaves. I. Changes in free amino acid levels. *Plant Cell Physiol.* **23**, 49–57.

Manos, P. J., and Goldthwaite, J. (1975). A kinetic analysis of the effects of gibberellic acid, zeatin and abscisic acid on leaf tissue senescence in *Rumex. Plant Physiol.* **55**, 192–198.

Martin, C., and Thimann, K. V. (1972). Role of protein synthesis in the senescence of leaves II. The influence of amino acids on senescence. *Plant Physiol.* **50**, 432–437.

Mawson, B. T., Colman, B., and Cummins, W. R. (1981). Abscisic acid and photosynthesis in isolated leaf mesophyll cell. *Plant Physiol.* **67**, 233–236.

Mayak, S., and Dilley, D. R. (1976). Regulation of senescence in carnation *(Dianthus caryophyllus)*. Effect of abscisic acid and carbon dioxide on ethylene production. *Plant Physiol.* **58**, 663–665.

Mayak, S., and Halevy, A. H. (1972). Interrelationships of ethylene and abscisic acid in the control of rose petal senescence. *Plant Physiol.* **50**, 341–346.

Mayak, S., and Halevy, A. H. (1980). Flower senescence. In "Senescence in Plants" (K. V. Thimann, ed.), pp. 131–156. CRC Press, Boca Raton, Florida.

Mayak, S., Halevy, A. H., and Katz, M. (1972). Correlative changes in phytohormones in relation to senescence processes in rose petals. *Physiol. Plant.* **27**, 1–4.

Milborrow, B. V. (1983). Pathways to and from abscisic acid. *In* "Abscisic Acid" (F. T. Addicott, ed.), pp. 79–111. Praeger, New York.

Mishra, D., and Misra, B. (1968). Effect of growth regulating chemicals on degradation of chlorophyll and starch on detached leaves of crop plants. *Z. Pflanzenphysiol.* **58**, 207–211.

Mishra, S. D., and Gaur, B. K. (1980). Growth regulator control of senescence in discs of betel (*Piper betle* L.) leaf. Effect of rate and degree of senescence. *Indian J. Exp. Biol.* **18**, 297–298.

Misra, A. N., and Biswal, U. C. (1980). Effect of phytohormones on chlorophyll degradation during aging of chloroplasts *in vivo* and *in vitro*. *Protoplasma* **105**, 1–8.

Misra, G., and Biswal, U. ,C. (1973). Factors concerned in leaf senescence. I. Effects of age, chemicals, petiole, and photoperiod on senescence in detached leaves of *Hibiscus rosa-sinensis* L. *Bot. Gaz.* **134**, 5–11.

Mittelheuser, C. J., and Van Steveninck, R. F. M. (1971). The ultrastructure of wheat leaves. I. Changes due to natural senescence and the effects of kinetin and ABA on detached leaves incubated in the dark. *Protoplasma* **73**, 239–252.

Mittelheuser, C. J., and Van Steveninck, R. F. M. (1972). Effects of ABA and kinetin on ultrastructure of senescing wheat leaves. *In* "Plant Growth Substances 1970" (D. J. Carr, ed.), pp. 618–623. Springer-Verlag, Berlin and New York.

Mittelheuser, C. J., and Van Steveninck, R. F. M. (1974). The effects of D-glucosamine on leaf senescence and ultrastructure. *Bull. R. Soc. N.Z.* **12**, 849–854.

Mondal, R., and Choudhuri, M. A. (1984). Interaction on phytohormones with H_2O_2 metabolism and senescence of excised leaves of some C_3 pathway and C_4 plants. *Biochem. Physiol. Pflanzen* **179**, 463–471.

Moore, A. E., and Stone, B. A. (1972a). Effect of senescence and hormone treatment on the β-1,3-glucan hydrolase in *Nicotiana glutinosa* leaves. *In* "Plant Growth Substances 1970" (D. J. Carr, ed.), pp. 598–603. Springer-Verlag, Berlin and New York.

Moore, A. E., and Stone, B. A. (1972b). Effect of senescence and hormone treatment on the activity of a β-1,3-glucan hydrolase in *Nicotiana glutinosa* leaves. *Planta* **104**, 93–109.

Murray, D. R., ed. (1984). "Seed Physiology. Vol. 2: Germination and Reserve Mobilization." Academic Press, Orlando, Florida.

Mvé Akamba, L., and Siegenthaler, P.-A. (1979). Effect of linolenate on photosynthesis by intact spinach chloroplasts II. Influence of preillumination of leaves on the inhibition of photosynthesis by linolenate. *Plant Cell Physiol.* **20**, 405–411.

Nichols, R. (1971). Induction of flower senescence and gynaecium development in the carnation (*Dianthus caryophyllus*) by ethylene and 2-chloroethyl-phosphonic acid. *J. Hortic. Sci.* **46**, 323–332.

Nichols, R. (1977). A descriptive model of the senescence of the carnation (*Dianthus caryophyllus*) inflorescence. *Acta Hortic.* **71**, 227–232.

Nichols, R. (1982). Growth regulators and flower senescence. *In* "Growth Regulators in Plant Senescence" (M. B. Jackson, B. Grout, and I. A. Mackenzie, eds.), Monogr. No. 8, pp. 113–120. Br. Plant Growth Regul. Group, Wantage, England.

Nickell, L. G., ed. (1983). "Plant Growth Regulating Chemical," Vols. 1 and 2. CRC Press, Boca Raton, Florida.

Noodén, L. D. (1980). Senescence in the whole plant. *In* "Senescence in Plants" (K. V. Thimann, ed.), pp. 219–258. CRC Press, Boca Raton, Florida.

Noodén, L. D. (1986). Synergism between gibberellins and cytokinin in delaying leaf senescence in soybean explants. *Plant Cell Physiol.* **27**, 577–579.

Noodén, L. D., and Leopold, A. C. (1978). Phytohormones and the endogenous regulation of senescence and abscission. *In* "Phytohormones and Related Compounds: A Comprehensive

Treatise" (D. S. Letham, P. B. Goodwin, and T. J. Higgins, eds.), Vol. 2, pp. 329–369. Elsevier/North-Holland, Amsterdam.

Noodén, L. D., and Obermeyer, W. R. (1981). Changes in abscisic acid translocation and during pod development and senescence in soybean. *Biochem. Physiol. Pflanzen* **176**, 859–868.

Noodén, L. D., and Weber, J. A. (1978). Environmental and hormonal control of dormancy in terminal buds of plants. *In* "Dormancy and Developmental Arrest" (M. E. Clutter, ed.), pp. 221–268. Academic Press, New York.

Noodén, L. D., Kahanak, G. M., and Okatan, Y. (1979). Prevention of monocarpic senescence in soybeans with auxin and cytokinin: An antidote for self-destruction. *Science* **206**, 841–843.

Oritani, T., and Yoshida, R. (1973). Studies on nitrogen metabolism in crop plants. XII. Cytokinins and abscisic acid-like substance levels in rice and soybean leaves during their growth and senescence. *Proc. Crop. Sci. Soc. Jpn.* **42**, 280–287.

Oritani, T., Yoshida, R., and Oritani, T. (1969). Studies on the nitrogen metabolism in crop plants VI. Interactive effects of abscisic acid and kinetin on the changes of the amount of chlorophyll and nucleic acid in the rice leaf sections during senescence. *Nippon Sakumotsu Gakkai Kiji* **38**, 587–592.

Osborne, D. J. (1955). Acceleration of abscission by a factor produced in senescent leaves. *Nature (London)* **176**, 1161–1163.

Osborne, D. J. (1958). The role of 2,4,5-T butyl ester in the control of leaf abscission in some tropical woody species. *Trop. Agric.* **35**, 145–158.

Osborne, D. J. (1959a). Identity of the abscission-accelerating substance in senescence leaves. *Nature (London)* **183**, 1593.

Osborne, D. J. (1959b). Control of leaf senescence by auxins. *Nature (London)* **183**, 1459.

Osborne, D. J. (1967). Hormonal regulation of leaf senescence. *Symp. Soc. Exp. Biol.* **21**, 179–213.

Osborne, D. J., and Hallaway, M. (1960). Auxin control of protein-levels in detached autumn leaves. *Nature (London)* **188**, 240–241.

Osborne, D. J., and Hallaway, M. (1961). The role of auxins in the control of leaf senescence. Some effects of local applications of 2,4-dichlorophenoxyacetic acid on carbon and nitrogen metabolism. *In* "Plant Growth Regulation" (R. M. Klein, ed.), pp. 329–340. Iowa State Univ. Press, Ames.

Osborne, D. J., and Hallaway, M. (1964). The auxin, 2,4-dichlorophenoxyacetic acid, as a regulator of protein synthesis and senescence in detached leaves of Prunus. *New Phytol.* **63**, 334–346.

Osborne, D. J., Jackson, M., and Milborrow, B. V. (1972). Physiological properties on abscission accelerator from senescent leaves. *Nature (London), New Biol.* **240**, 98–101.

Owens, L. D., and Wright, D. A. (1965). Rhizobial-induced chlorosis in soybeans: Isolation, production in nodules, and varietal specificity of the toxin. *Plant Physiol.* **40**, 927–930.

Paranjothy, K., and Wareing, P. F. (1971). The effects of abscisic acid, kinetin and 5-1 fluorouracil on ribonucleic acid and protein synthesis in senescing radish leaf disks. *Planta* **99**, 112–119.

Pate, J. S. (1980). Transport and partitioning of nitrogenous solutes. *Annu. Rev. Plant Physiol.* **31**, 313–340.

Pate, J. S., Sharkey, P. J., and Atkins, C. A. (1977). Nutrition of a developing legume fruit. Functional economy in terms of carbon, nitrogen, water. *Plant Physiol.* **59**, 506–510.

Pech, J. C., and Romani, R. J. (1979). Senescence of pear *Pyrus communis* fruit cells cultured in a continuously renewed auxin-deprived medium. *Plant Physiol.* **63**, 814–817.

Penot, M., and Béraud, J. (1978). Migrations orientées et phytohormones — Valeur de la feuille détachee comme matérial expérimental. *Physiol. Plant.* **42**, 14–20.

Percival, M. P., and Dodge, A. D. (1983). Photodynamic effects of Rose Bengal on senescent flax cotyledons. *J. Exp. Bot.* 34, 47–54.

Percival, M. P., Williams, W. P., Chapman, D., and Quinn, P. J. (1980). Loss of Hill activity in isolated chloroplasts is not directly related to free fatty acid release during ageing. *Plant Sci. Lett.* 19, 47–54.

Phillips, I. D. J., and Wareing, P. F. (1958). Studies of dormancy of sycamore I. Seasonal changes in the growth-substance content of the shoot. *J. Exp. Bot.* 9, 350–364.

Powell, L. E. (1975). Some abscisic acid relationships in apple. *Riv. Ortoflorofruttic. Ital.* 59, 424–432.

Proebsting, W. M., Davies, P. J., and Marx, G. A. (1978). Photoperiod-induced changes in gibberellin metabolism in relation to apical growth and senescence in genetic lines of peas (*Pisum sativum* L.). *Planta* 141, 231–238.

Raschke, K., and Hedrich, R. (1985). Simultaneous and independent effects of abscisic acid on stomata and the photosynthetic apparatus in whole leaves. *Planta* 163, 105–118.

Raschke, K., and Zeevaart, J. A. D. (1976). Abscisic acid content, transpiration, and stomatal conductance as related to leaf age in plants of *Xanthium strumarium* L. *Plant Physiol.* 58, 169–174.

Rasmussen, G. K. (1973). The effect of growth regulators on degreening and regreening of citrus fruit. *Acta Hortic.* 34, 473–478.

Ray, S., and Choudhuri, M. A. (1984). Senescence of rice leaves at the vegetative stage as affected by growth substances. *Biol. Plant.* 26, 267–274.

Reynolds, T. (1969). Senescence retardation in dock leaves by soluble peptone. *Nature (London)* 223, 505–506.

Rhodes, M. J. C. (1980). The maturation and ripening of fruits. *In* "Senescence in Plants" (K. V. Thimann, ed.), pp. 157–205. CRC Press, Boca Raton, Florida.

Richmond, A. E., and Lang, A. (1957). Effect of kinetin on protein content and survival of detached *Xanthium* leaves. *Science* 125, 650–651.

Roberts, J. A., and Osborne, D. J. (1981). Auxin and the control of ethylene production during development and senescence of leaves and fruits. *J. Exp. Bot.* 32, 875–888.

Ronen, M., and Mayak, S. (1981). Interrelationship between abscisic acid and ethylene in control of senescence processes in carnation flowers. *J. Exp. Bot.* 32, 759–766.

Ruddat, M., and Pharis, R. P. (1966). Enhancement of leaf senescence by Amo-1618, a growth retardant and its reversal by gibberellin and kinetin. *Plant Cell Physiol.* 7, 689–692.

Rudnicki, E., Pieniazek, J., and Pieniazek, N. (1968). Abscisin II in strawberry plants at two different stages of growth. *Bull. Acad. Sci. Pol. Sci.* 16, 127–130.

Ryugo, K. (1969). Abscisic acid, a component of the beta-inhibitor complex in the *Prunus* endocarp. *J. Am. Soc. Hortic. Sci.* 94, 5–8.

Sabater, B. (1984). Hormonal regulation of senescence. *In* "Hormonal Regulation of Plant Growth and Development" (S. S. Purohit, ed.), Vol. 1, pp. 169–217. Agro Botanical Publishers, Bikaner, India.

Sabater, B., Rodriguez, M. T., and Zamorano, A. (1981). Effects and interactions of gibberellic acid and cytokinins on the retention of chlorophyll and phosphate in barley leaf segments. *Physiol. Plant.* 51, 361–364.

Sacher, J. A. (1957). Relationship between auxin and membrane-integrity in tissue senescence and abscission. *Science* 125, 1199–1200.

Sacher, J. A. (1959). Studies on auxin-membrane permeability relations in fruit and leaf tissues. *Plant Physiol.* 34, 365–372.

Sacher, J. A. (1963). Senescence: hormone action and metabolism of nucleic acids and proteins in plant tissue. *Life Sci.* 2, 866–871.

Sacher, J. A. (1965). Senescence: hormonal control of RNA and protein synthesis in excised bean pod tissue. *Am. J. Bot.* **52**, 841–848.

Sacher, J. A. (1973). Senescence and postharvest physiology. *Annu. Rev. Plant Physiol.* **24**, 197–224.

Sacher, J. A. (1983). Abscisic acid in leaf senescence. *In* "Abscisic Acid" (F. T. Addicott, ed.), pp. 479–522. Praeger, New York.

Samet, J. S., and Sinclair, T. R. (1980). Leaf senescence and abscisic acid in leaves of field-grown soybean. *Plant Physiol.* **66**, 1164–1168.

Saniewski, M., and Czapski, J. (1983). The effect of methyl jasmonate on lycopene and β-carotene accumulation in ripening red tomatoes. *Experientia* **39**, 1373–1374.

Saniewski, M., and Czapski, J. (1985). Stimulatory effect of methyl jasmonate on the ethylene production in tomato fruits. *Experientia* **41**, 256–257.

Sankhla, N., and Sankhla, D. (1968). Abscisin II-kinetin interaction in leaf senescence. *Experientia* **24**, 294–295.

Satler, S. O., and Thimann, K. V. (1980). The influence of aliphatic alcohols on leaf senescence. *Plant Physiol.* **66**, 395–399.

Satler, S. O., and Thimann, K. V. (1981). Le jasmonate de methyle: noveau et puissant promoteur de la senescence des feuilles. *C. R. Seances Acad. Sci., Ser. 3* **293**, 735–740.

Schwabe, W. W. (1970). The control of leaf senescence in *Kleinia articulata* by photoperiod. *Ann. Bot.* **34**, 43–57.

Seth, A. K., and Wareing, P. F. (1967). Hormone-directed transport of metabolites and its possible role in plant senescence. *J. Exp. Bot.* **18**, 65–77.

Setter, T. L., Brun, W. A., and Brenner, M. L. (1980a). Stomatal closure and photosynthetic inhibition in soybean leaves induced by petiole girdling and pod removal. *Plant Physiol.* **65**, 884–887.

Setter, T. L., Brun, W. A., and Brenner, M. L. (1980b). Effect of obstructed translocation on leaf abscisic acid, and associated stomatal closure and photosynthesis decline. *Plant Physiol.* **65**, 1111–1115.

Setter, T. L., Brun, W. A., and Brenner, M. L. (1981). Abscisic acid translocation and metabolism in soybeans following depodding and petiole girdling treatments. *Plant Physiol.* **67**, 774–779.

Sheldrake, A. R. (1973). The production of hormones in higher plants. *Biol. Rev. Cambridge Philos. Soc.* **48**, 509–560.

Sheldrake, A. R., and Northcote, D. H. (1968a). Production of auxin by detached leaves. *Nature (London)* **217**, 195.

Sheldrake, A. R., and Northcote, D. H. (1968b). The production of auxin by autolysing tissues. *Planta* **80**, 227–230.

Shibaoka, H., and Thimann, K. V. (1970). Antagonisms between kinetin and amino acids. Experiments on the mode of action and cytokinins. *Plant Physiol.* **46**, 212–220.

Shih, L., Kaur-Sawhney, R., Fuhrer, J., Samonta, S., and Galston, A. W. (1982). Effects of exogenous 1,3-diaminopropane and spermidine on senescence of oat leaves. I. Inhibition of protease activity, ethylene production, and chlorophyll loss as related to polyamine loss. *Plant Physiol.* **70**, 1592–1596.

Shoji, K., Addicott, F. T., and Swets, W. A. (1951). Auxin in relation to leaf blade abscission. *Plant Physiol.* **26**, 189–191.

Sigee, D. C. (1984). Induction of leaf cell death by phytopathogenic bacteria. *In* "Cell Ageing and Cell Death" (I. Davies and D. C. Sigee, eds.), pp. 295–322. Cambridge Univ. Press, London and New York.

Sloger, C., and Caldwell, B. E. (1970). Response of Cultivars of soybean to synthetic abscisic acid. *Plant Physiol.* **45**, 634–635.

Smith, T. A. (1985). Polyamines. *Annu. Rev. Plant Physiol.* **36**, 117–143.

Sponsel, V. M. (1985). Gibberellins in *Pisum sativum*—their nature, distribution and involvement in growth and development of the plant. *Physiol. Plant.* **65**, 533–583.

Stamp, P. (1981). Aktivitäten photosynthetischer Enzyme und Pigmentgehalte in Blättern junger Maispflanzen bei Kühle in Abhängigkeit von Behandlung mit Phytohormonen. *Angew. Bot.* **55**, 409–417.

Steinitz, B., Cohen, A., and Leshem, B. (1981). Factors controlling the retardation of chlorophyll degradation during senescence of detached statice *Limonium sinuatum* flower stalks. *Z. Pflanzenphysiol.* **100**, 343–350.

Stewart, C. M. (1966). Excretion and heartwood formation in living trees. *Science* **153**, 1068–1074.

Stewart, W. S. (1949). Effects of 2,4-dichlorophenoxyacetic acid and 2,4,5-trichlorophenoxyacetic acid on citrus fruit storage. *Proc. Am. Soc. Hortic. Sci.* **54**, 109–117.

Tamas, I. A., Engels, C. A., Kaplan, S. L., Ozbun, J. L., and Wallace, D. H. (1981). Role of indoleacetic acid and abscisic acid in the correlative control by fruits of axillary bud development and leaf senescence. *Plant Physiol.* **68**, 476–481.

Thimann, K. V., and Satler, S. (1979). Relation between senescence and stomatal opening: Senescence in darkness. *Proc. Natl. Acad. Sci. U.S.A.* **76**, 2770–2773.

Thimann, K. V., Shibaoka, H., and Martin, C. (1972). On the nature of senescence in oat leaves. *In* "Plant Growth Substances 1970" (D. J. Carr, ed.), pp. 561–570. Springer-Verlag, Berlin and New York.

Thimann, K. V., Satler, S. O., and Trippi, V. (1982). Further extension of the syndrome of leaf senescence. *In* "Plant Growth Substances 1982" (P. F. Wareing, ed.), pp. 539–548. Academic Press, London.

Thomas, H. (1975). Regulation of alanine aminotransferase in leaves of *Lolium temulentum* during senescence. *Z. Pflanzenphysiol.* **74**, 208–218.

Thomas, H. (1982). Control of chloroplast demolition during leaf senescence. *In* "Plant Growth Substances 1982" (P. F. Wareing, ed.), pp. 559–567. Academic Press, London.

Thomas, H., and Stoddart, J. L. (1975). Separation of chlorophyll degradation from other senescence processes in leaves of a mutant genotype of meadow fescue (*Festuca pratensis* L.). *Plant Physiol.* **56**, 438–441.

Thomas, T. H. (1968). Studies on senescence-delaying substances extracted from *Brassica oleracea gemmifera* L. *J. Hortic. Sci.* **43**, 59–68.

Thomas, T. H. (1977). Hormonal control of brussels sprout senescence. *Acta Hortic.* **62**, 295–300.

Thomas, T. H. (1986). Hormonal control of assimilate movement and compartmentation. *In* "Plant Growth Substances 1985" (M. Bopp, ed.), pp. 350–359. Springer-Verlag, Berlin and New York.

Tillberg, E., Dons, C., Haugstad, M., and Nilsen, S. (1981). Effect of abscisic acid on CO_2 exchange in *Lemna gibba. Physiol. Plant.* **52**, 402–406.

Tomomatsu, A., and Asahi, T. (1981). The mode of action of organelle-damaging factor from mung bean leaves. *Plant Cell Physiol.* **22**, 91–98.

Udvardy, J., and Farkas, G. L. (1972). Abscisic acid stimulation of aging-specific nuclease in *Avena* leaves. *J. Exp. Bot.* **23**, 914–920.

Ueda, J., and Kato, J. (1980). Isolation and identification of a senescence-promoting substance from wormwood (*Artemisia absinthum* L.). *Plant Physiol.* **66**, 246–249.

Ueda, J., and Kato, J. (1982). Abscisic acid and C_{18}-unsaturated fatty acids as senescence-promoting substances from oat plants. *J. Plant Growth Regul.* **1**, 195–203.

Ueda, J., Kato, J., Yamane, Y., and Takahashi, N. (1981). Inhibitory effect of methyl jasmonate and its related compounds on kinetin-induced retardation of oat leaf senescence. *Physiol. Plant.* **52**, 305–309.

Ueda, J., Shiotanti, Y., Kojima, T., Kato, J., Yokota, T., and Takahashi, N. (1983). Identification of hinesol as a chlorophyll-preserving substance. *Plant Cell Physiol.* **24**, 873–876.

Ueda, J., Kojima, T., Nichimura, M., and Kato, J. (1984). Isolation and identification of aliphatic compounds as chlorophyll-preserving and/or degrading substances from *Artemisia capillaris* Thunb. *Z. Pflanzenphysiol.* **113**, 189–199.

Uheda, E., and Kuraishi, S. (1978). The relationship between transpiration and chlorophyll synthesis in etiolated squash cotyledons. *Plant Cell Physiol.* **19**, 825–831.

Vander Westhuizen, A. J., and de Swardt, G. M. (1978). Changes in the individual free amino acid concentrations in petals of carnations during the vase life of the flowers. *Z. Pflanzenphysiol.* **86**, 125–134.

Van Meeteren, U. (1979). Water relations and keeping-quality of cut gerbera flowers. IV. Internal water relations of aging petal tissue. *Sci. Hortic. (Amsterdam)* **11**, 83–93.

Van Onckelen, H. A., Horemans, S., and deGreef, J. A. (1981). Functional aspects of abscisic acid metabolism in cotyledons of *Phaseolus vulgaris* L. seedlings. *Plant Cell Physiol.* **22**, 507–515.

Van Stevenick, R. F. M., and Van Stevenick, M. E. (1983). Abscisic acid and membrane transport. *In* "Abscisic Acid" (F. T. Addicott, ed.), pp. 171–235. Praeger, New York.

Veierskov, B., Statler, S. O., and Thimann, K. V. (1985). Metabolism of oat leaves during senescence. *Plant Physiol.* **78**, 315–319.

Von Abrams, G. J. (1974). An effect of ornithine on degradation of chlorophyll and protein in excised leaf tissue. *Z. Pflanzenphysiol.* **72**, 410–421.

Walton, D. C. (1980). Biochemistry and physiology of abscisic acid. *Annu. Rev. Plant Physiol.* **31**, 453–489.

Wareing, P. F. (1986). Plant cell responses and the role of growth substances. *In* "Plant Growth Substances 1985" (M. Bopp, ed.), pp. 1–9. Springer-Verlag, Berlin and New York.

Weaver, R. J. (1972). "Plant Growth Substances in Agriculture." Freeman, San Francisco, California.

Weiler, E. W. (1980). Radioimmunoassays for the differential and direct analysis of free and conjugated abscisic acid in plant extracts. *Planta* **148**, 262–272.

Weinbaum, S. A., and Powell, L. E. (1975). Diffusible abscisic acid and its relationship to leaf age in tea crabapple. *J. Am. Soc. Hortic. Sci.* **100**, 583–588.

Westerman, L., and Roddick, J. G. (1983). Effects of senescence and gibberellic acid treatment on sterol levels in detached leaves of dandelion *(Taraxacum officinale)*. *Phytochemistry* **22**, 2318–2319.

Wetmore, R. H., and Jacobs, W. P. (1953). Studies on abscission: The inhibiting effect of auxin. *Am. J. Bot.* **40**, 272–276.

Wetmore, R. H., and Sorokin, S. (1955). On the differentiation of xylem. *J. Arnold Arbor., Harv. Univ.* **36**, 305–317.

Wheeler, A. W. (1968). Changes in auxin in expanding and senescent primary leaves of dwarf french beans *(Phaseolus vulgaris)*. *J. Exp. Bot.* **19**, 102–107.

Whyte, P., and Luckwill, L. C. (1966). Sensitive bioassays for gibberellins based upon retardation of leaf senescence in *Rumex obtusifolius*. *Nature (London)* **210**, 1360.

Wills, R. H. H., Lee, T. H., Graham, D., McGlasson, W. B., and Hall, E. G. (1981). "Postharvest." Avi, Westport, Connecticut.

Wittenbach, V. A. (1977). Induced senescence of intact wheat seedlings and its reversibility. *Plant Physiol.* **59**, 1039–1042.

Wright, S. T. C. (1978). Phytohormones and stress phenomena. *In* "Phytohormones and Related Compounds: A Comprehensive Treatise" (D. S. Letham, P. B. Goodwin, and T. J. V. Higgins, eds.), Vol. 2, pp. 495–536. Elsevier/North-Holland, Amsterdam.

Yang, S. F., and Hoffman, N. E. (1984). Ethylene biosynthesis and its regulation in higher plants. *Annu. Rev. Plant Physiol.* **35**, 155–189.

Young, J. L., Huang, R. C., Vanecko, S., Marks, J. D., and Varner, J. E. (1960). Conditions affecting enzyme synthesis in cotyledons of germinating seeds. *Plant Physiol.* **35**, 288–292.

Zhang, R., Letham, D. S., Wong, O. C., Noodén, L. D., and Parker, C. W. (1987). Cytokinin biochemistry in relation to leaf senescence. II. The metabolism of 6-benzylaminopurine in soybean leaves and the inhibition of its conjugation. *Plant Physiol.* **83**, 334–340.

Ziegler, H. (1975). Nature of transported substances. *Encycl. Plant Physiol., New Ser.* **1**, 59–100.

Zur, B., Boote, K. J., and Jones, J. W. (1981). Changes in internal water relations and osmotic properties of leaves in maturing soybean plants. *J. Exp. Bot.* **32**, 1181–1191.

11

Calcium and Senescence

B. W. Poovaiah
Department of Horticulture
Washington State University
Pullman, Washington

I. INTRODUCTION

A major re-evaluation is occurring in our thinking about the role of calcium ions in mediating diverse physiological processes in plants. It is clear that calcium has an important role in controlling senescence. The influence of calcium on cell wall structure and membrane integrity has been well documented for many years. Recent investigations suggest that calcium plays a central role in regulating various metabolic processes in plants (Reddy and Poovaiah, 1987).

The possible participation of calcium in senescence in plants may be inferred from the fact that calcium is widely known to play a major role in

SENESCENCE AND AGING IN PLANTS

membrane structure and function (Jones and Lunt, 1967). Its importance in the regulation of ion transport is well established (Epstein, 1961). Its effects on the maintenance of RNA and protein levels have been described by Trewavas (1970, 1972), and these components are considered to be central indices of senescence. Each of the parameters of senescence, such as chlorophyll loss, protein decrease, and increases in apparent free space and hydraulic conductivity, is affected by changes in the calcium status of the tissue (Poovaiah and Leopold, 1973a; Poovaiah, 1987).

The function of Ca^{2+} as a second messenger in animal cells has been recognized for years. Only in the last 10 years have plant scientists come to recognize the importance of Ca^{2+} in the regulation of plant metabolism. The role of calcium in signal transduction and cell function is beginning to be understood at the molecular level. The discovery of the calcium-binding protein, calmodulin (Cheung, 1980; Anderson and Cormier, 1978), and recent investigations demonstrating changes in intracellular calcium concentrations in response to primary stimuli such as light and hormones have provided the basis for suggesting that calcium serves as a second messenger in plants as well (Roux and Slocum, 1982; Marme and Dieter, 1983; Veluthambi and Poovaiah, 1984a; Poovaiah, 1985; Hepler and Wayne, 1985; Poovaiah and Reddy, 1987; Poovaiah *et al.*, 1987a).

Calcium distribution at the cellular level plays a critical role in cell function. A high level of free Ca^{2+} in the cytoplasm is injurious to the cell. At such a level, Ca^{2+} reacts with inorganic phosphate to form an insoluble precipitate. Thus, if cytosolic Ca^{2+} concentrations were allowed to reach the millimolar levels present in the extracellular space, phosphate-based energy metabolism would be seriously inhibited. At submicromolar levels of Ca^{2+}, its reaction with inorganic phosphate is negligible (Kretsinger, 1977). To maintain these submicromolar levels of intracellular calcium in the presence of millimolar levels in the extracellular space plants require the active pumping of calcium out of the cytoplasm. It is believed that deterioration of this active pumping mechanism can lead to senescence and cell death.

The major barrier to the flow of information into the cell is the plasma membrane, where transduction mechanisms translate external signals, such as hormones and light, into internal signals. A transient flux of Ca^{2+} appears to be the trigger allowing the chemical messages to be relayed to the biochemical machinery within the cell. Cells have evolved an elaborate system of proteins that interact with the calcium ion, controlling the transmission and reception of the intracellular message. Unraveling the intricacies of these interactions may lead to better control over intracellular Ca^{2+} concentration, a possibility that has broad implications for the control of plant growth and development.

II. CALCIUM AND HORMONE INTERACTIONS

Since the discovery by Richmond and Lang (1957) that cytokinins could delay leaf senescence, it has become increasingly evident that each of the five known plant hormones is capable of altering senescence. A general concept of endogenous regulation of senescence by hormones is, however, made less attractive by the difficulties of producing major alterations in senescence development through application of hormones to intact plants. Earlier investigations have shown that calcium ions can significantly alter some aspects of senescence development and abscission in leaves (Poovaiah, 1979a, 1986; Poovaiah and Leopold, 1973a,b; Poovaiah and Rasmussen, 1973a,b; Suwwan and Poovaiah, 1978). Recently, the role of calcium in mediating the cytokinin effect was studied by first depleting calcium from corn leaf discs by an EGTA pretreatment and then transferring them to a medium containing benzyladenine (BA) with or without calcium. After the EGTA-pretreatment, BA was no longer effective in delaying the loss of protein (Fig. 11.1). However, the cytokinin effect was restored by the addition of calcium. These results clearly point to a central role for calcium in hormone action as it relates to senescence.

Earlier investigations by Saunders and Hepler (1982) have shown that the calcium ionophore A 23187 could mimic the effect of cytokinin in the bud formation of *Funaria*. Furthermore, their results indicate that stimulus-response coupling involves an influx of calcium into the cytoplasm. Evidence for a calcium influx into the cytoplasm in response to a stimulus was obtained by Williamson and Ashley (1982), who demonstrated that inhibition of cytoplasmic streaming in *Chara* cells is associated with an increase in cytoplasmic Ca^{2+} concentration in response to action potentials. Recently, calcium redistribution during cell division (Keith *et al.*, 1985) and tuberization (Balamani *et al.*, 1986) have been observed.

Leakiness of membranes deprived of exogenous Ca^{2+} is observed in almost all kinds of plant tissues. The concept that membrane failure may be involved in leaf senescence was first suggested by Sacher (1957). Eilam (1965) showed that senescence of bean leaves was associated with a leakage of potassium from the leaves and an associated increase in apparent free space. The most conspicuous role for Ca^{2+} in the apoplast is the maintenance of the integrity of the plasma membrane. Poovaiah and Leopold (1973a) have shown an interaction of calcium and cytokinin in altering membrane permeability during the progression of senescence. Thimann and Satler (1979) suggest that stomatal apperture is the principal cytokinin-sensitive factor in delaying senescence. The induction of stomatal closure can be driven by abscisic acid (ABA) when water supply is suboptimal

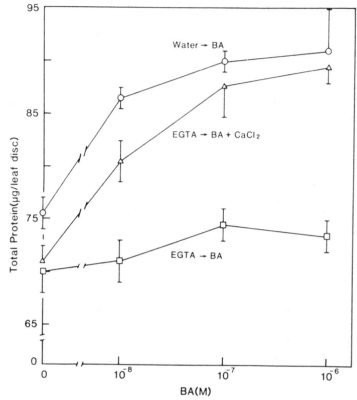

Fig. 11.1. Effect of pretreatment of 1 mM EGTA on the protein content of corn leaf discs. After pretreatment for 5 hours, leaf discs were transferred to 10^{-8}–10^{-6} M BA with or without 1 mM $CaCl_2$ and incubated in the dark for 4 days. Initial value of total protein was 120.2 ± 6.2 (J. K. Rhee and B. W. Poovaiah, unpublished observations).

(Mansfield and Davies, 1981). Recent studies show a synergistic interaction between Ca^{2+} and ABA in maintaining stomatal closure (Hetherington *et al.*, 1986). Their results are consistent with the hypothesis that ABA increases the permeability of the guard cell to Ca^{2+}. Calcium might then operate as a second messenger in the hormonal regulation of the ionic fluxes that determine guard cell turgor. Earlier studies by Poovaiah and Leopold (1974, 1976a) and Leopold *et al.* (1974) have shown that calcium could have strong modifying effects on the functions of each of the five known plant hormones, in some cases amplifying the hormonal response, and in other cases suppressing it.

III. CYTOSOLIC AND APOPLASTIC ROLES OF CALCIUM

A. Cell Walls and Membranes

Calcium is essential for structural integrity of both membranes and cell walls (Jones and Lunt, 1967; Poovaiah, 1985). In plants, the major portion of the Ca^{2+} occurs in the apoplastic compartment, primarily complexed with cell wall moieties and the plasma membrane. Rossignol *et al.* (1977) have estimated that at least 60% of the total Ca^{2+} in plants is associated with the cell wall and the remaining with the membranes and soluble fraction. The importance of Ca^{2+} in cell-to-cell adhesion is well recognized (Demarty *et al.*, 1984). The cementing effect is due primarily to the Ca–pectate of the middle lamella laid down during cytokinesis. The Ca–pectate complex is essential for the maintenance of cell wall structure, especially in fruits and other storage organs. Under conditions of calcium deficiency, membranes become leaky, cellular compartmentation is lost (Marinos, 1962), and Ca^{2+} cross-linkage with the pectin in the middle lamella is weakened. The living cell surface is able to accommodate a rather wide variation in composition and pH of the apoplastic solution only in the presence of adequate Ca^{2+} in the extracellular space. Concentrations of 1 to 5 mM Ca^{2+} are essential to protect the plasma membrane from the deleterious effects of low pH, salinity, toxic ions, and nutrient imbalance (Hanson, 1983). Without such protection, the plasma membrane fails to discriminate between ions, the active pumping mechanism fails, and senescence is accelerated.

There is evidence that calcium alters the actual architecture of membranes. Its introduction into natural (Paliyath *et al.*, 1984) or artificial membranes (Gary-Bobo, 1970) results in an enormous change in fluidity and water permeability. Earlier studies in our laboratory showed that the fluorescence polarization of membrane-embedded diphenyl hexatriene increased in membranes from rapidly senescing apples as compared to normal cold-stored apples (Paliyath *et al.*, 1984). This indicates an increase in microviscosity of apple membranes with senescence.

There is now considerable evidence that the rate of senescence in some fruits and vegetables is influenced by the calcium content of the tissue. The calcium effect can be clearly seen in fruits such as apples, where senescence is gradual and spans a period of months. In addition, vacuum infiltration of apples with calcium chloride delays senescence (Poovaiah and Moulton, 1982). It has been suggested that in apples, the bulk of the infiltrated calcium remains in the cell wall region and results in firmer fruit (Poovaiah *et al.*, 1988). To understand the process of softening in fruits, researchers have observed changes in cell wall composition and the activity of cell wall-degrading enzymes during ripening. The softening of the apple fruit appears to be due to the transfer of divalent cations, particularly calcium,

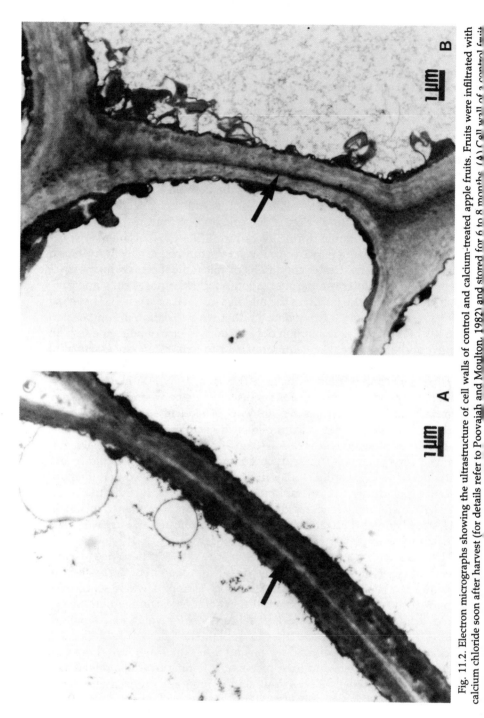

Fig. 11.2. Electron micrographs showing the ultrastructure of cell walls of control and calcium-treated apple fruits. Fruits were infiltrated with calcium chloride soon after harvest (for details refer to Poovaiah and Moulton, 1982) and stored for 6 to 8 months. (A) Cell wall of a control fruit

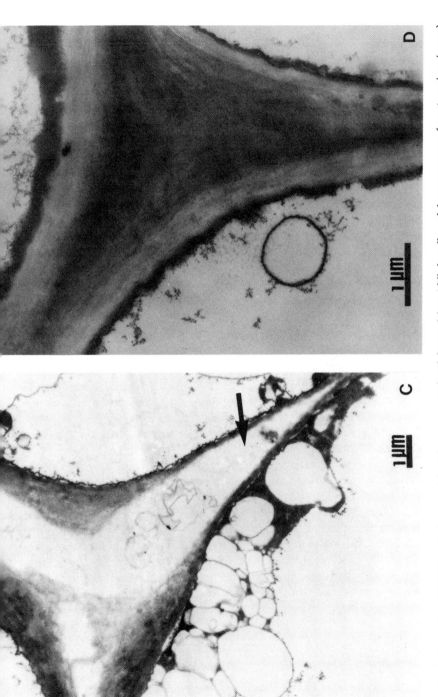

Fig. 11.2. *(continued)* (C) Cell wall of a control fruit showing severe breakdown of the middle lamella and the appearance of empty regions (arrow). (D) Cell wall of a calcium-treated fruit showing tightly packed and fibrillar middle lamella.

from the cell wall into storage compartments inside the cell. Calcium has long been thought to be important as a cross-linking component between polygalacturonide chains in plant cell walls (Knee, 1973; Demarty *et al.*, 1984). Knee (1973) also found that ripening apples tend to lose galactose residues from the cell wall fractions, and this observation has since been confirmed by other workers (Bartley, 1974; Wallner, 1978). Doesburg (1957) reported the solubilization of pectin during apple ripening and proposed that it may be caused by reduced levels of Ca^{2+} in the cell walls. Mizrahi and Kopeliovitch (1983) found the pectin solubilization in tomatoes to be positively related to softening. Buescher and Hobson (1982) reported that calcium inhibits polygalacturonate degradation in tomatoes. Degradation was accelerated when EDTA or citrate was used to chelate calcium in cell wall tissue. Conway and Sams (1984) suggested that calcium treatment of apples results in increased firmness and less soluble pectin through cooperative binding with free carboxyl groups on polygalacturonate polymers in the cell wall and middle lamella. There are some indications that calcium actually promotes the synthesis of cell wall polymers. Ray and Baker (1965) observed increased incorporation of labeled glucose into cell wall components of plant tissues treated with calcium. Research in our laboratory indicates that calcium promotes the activity of β-glucan synthase, a key enzyme involved in cell wall synthesis (Poovaiah and Veluthambi, 1986; Paliyath and Poovaiah, 1988). Cell wall synthesis and degradation may occur simultaneously during senescence. Cell wall synthesis may decline, while the net cell wall degradation leads to softening.

Postharvest calcium treatments were performed using apples in order to study their effects on changes in proteins and ultrastructure of the cell wall. Some qualitative differences in cell wall proteins were observed during prolonged storage periods, and dramatic changes in cell wall structure were noted (Fig. 11.2) (G. M. Glenn and B. W. Poovaiah, unpublished observations). During senescence, dissolution of the middle lamella of control fruits occurs, resulting in cell separation. Calcium-treated fruits, which remain much firmer during storage, have a densely stained middle lamella and greater cell cohesion. At higher magnifications, control fruits show disintegration of fibrillar material throughout the cell wall, whereas the cell wall structure is preserved in calcium-treated fruits. These results suggest that calcium has a major effect on cell wall changes during ripening and senescence.

B. Calcium and Calmodulin

In plants, the level of free calcium in the cytosol is relatively low, in the range of 0.01 to 1.0 μM. Vacuoles, mitochondria, chloroplasts, and endo-

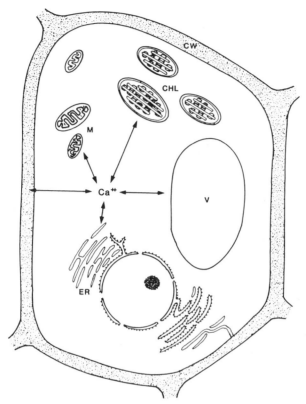

Fig. 11.3. Major calcium stores in the plant cell: endoplasmic reticulum (ER), mitochondria (M), vacuole (V), and chloroplasts (CHL). The cell wall (CW) also contains high amounts (millimolar range) of Ca^{2+}.

plasmic reticulum sequester large quantities of calcium (Fig. 11.3). Vacuolar calcium is separated from cellular metabolism in the form of chelates and precipitates of oxalate and phosphate. While intracellular free calcium levels are submicromolar, the concentration of the closely related divalent cation, Mg^{2+}, is in the millimolar range. However, despite this higher concentration of Mg^{2+}, cellular processes often display an enormous selectivity for calcium.

For a substance to act as an intracellular messenger, a target protein must be able to bind tightly with it and with high specificity. This binding changes the conformation of the target molecule, thereby altering its state of activity. A 10-fold increase in messenger concentration may be needed to change the state of the target protein. Calcium has an advantage over Mg^{2+} and other cations in acting as a second messenger because of its low intracellular concentration. The low cytosolic calcium concentration is maintained by active Ca^{2+} pumping out of the cytoplasm by Ca-transporting ATPases on the plasma membrane. Recent investigations provide convincing evidence that Ca-transporting ATPase activities of microsomal membranes are controlled by the regulator protein, calmodulin, in a Ca-dependent manner (Marme and Dieter, 1983).

Calmodulin is a calcium-modulated protein that has multiple biochemical activities, including activation of enzymes involved in the regulation of a variety of cellular processes. While calmodulin is one member of the family of calcium-modulated proteins, its ubiquitous distribution in all higher plants as well as its highly conserved structure and function suggest that it may be serving a fundamental role in cellular homeostasis. This regulator protein is present in the cytoplasm and associated with membranes and organelles.

Stimuli such as light, gravity, and hormones have been shown to alter the Ca^{2+} concentration in the cytoplasm, thus allowing calcium to act as an intracellular signal (Fig. 11.4). This change in cytoplasmic Ca^{2+} concentration alters calmodulin activity. Each calmodulin molecule can bind up to four Ca^{2+} ions. The binding of Ca^{2+} activates calmodulin by altering its conformation and thereby exposing hydrophobic regions of the molecule. The Ca^{2+}–calmodulin complex can then bind to target enzymes and activate them. The general mechanism by which calmodulin regulates these enzymes has been reviewed elsewhere (Cheung, 1980; Marme and Dieter, 1983; Poovaiah, 1985; Poovaiah and Reddy, 1987).

Calmodulin activity has been reported to be modulated in animal systems by a variety of compounds. The presence of a natural inhibitor of calmodulin action was detected in recent investigations on the role of calmodulin in the biochemical action of calcium in delaying senescence (Paliyath and Poovaiah, 1984, 1985a,b). Such an inhibitor could have a wide-ranging physiological role in developmental processes in plants. Since calmodulin regulates a multitude of processes, and many different classes of chemicals inhibit its activity, the question arises as to whether it could be possible to alter selectively calmodulin-dependent events in plants. It is conceivable that in the foreseeable future scientists might be able to regulate calcium- and calmodulin-mediated changes in order to induce or to delay senescence.

Inhibitors might block calmodulin action by a variety of mechanisms (Fig. 11.5): (1) by reducing the availability of Ca^{2+} [this is possible by inhibiting the entry of Ca^{2+} into cells, by inhibiting its release from intracellular stores (see Fig. 11.3), or by chelating it]; (2) by binding to calmodulin and altering its ability to bind Ca^{2+}; (3) by binding to the Ca^{2+}–calmodulin complex and altering its activity; (4) by binding to the calmodulin-recognition site on the calmodulin-sensitive enzyme, thereby preventing interaction of the Ca^{2+}– calmodulin complex with the enzyme; (5) by interacting with the catalytic

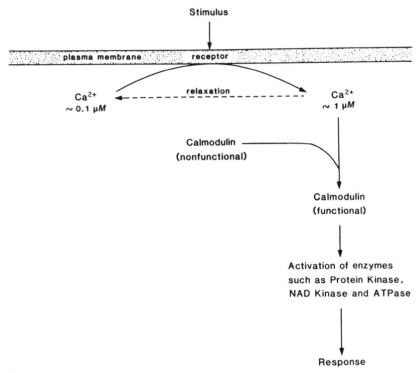

Fig. 11.4. Calcium- and calmodulin-dependent regulation in higher plant cells. In the unstimulated cell, free calcium concentration in the cytoplasm remains low, in the submicromolar range. Thus, Ca^{2+} cannot bind to calmodulin. Following stimulation, the Ca^{2+} concentration in the cytoplasm increases and calcium binds to calmodulin, making it functional. The calcium–calmodulin complex binds to the enzyme, forming the functional calmodulin–Ca–enzyme complex and induction of the response.

portion of the calmodulin-sensitive enzyme; and (6) by interacting with the ternary Ca^{2+}-calmodulin enzyme complex (Prozialeck and Weiss, 1985). The calmodulin inhibitors such as chlorpromazine, trifluoperazine, and N-(6-aminohexyl)5-chloro-1-naphthalene-sulfonamide   hydrochloride (W-7) are known to block calmodulin action and have an effect on senescence (J. K. Rhee and B. W. Poovaiah, unpublished observations). However, since many calmodulin inhibitors have nonspecific effects, caution must be exercised in interpreting results when such chemicals are used.

C. Protein Phosphorylation

The molecular mechanisms by which cells communicate with each other are of central importance to the physiology of multicellular organisms. It is

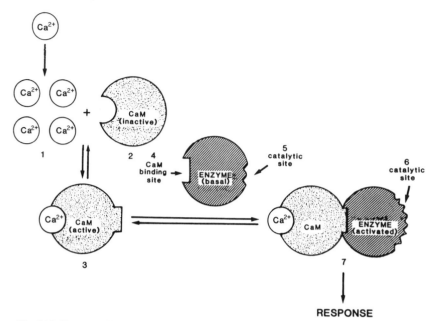

Fig. 11.5. Diagram illustrating the mechanisms by which calmodulin action is inhibited. See text for description.

now becoming clear that post-translational modification of enzymes may represent a key regulatory step in the molecular mechanism by which second messengers such as calcium respond to various external stimuli (Greengard, 1978; Cohen, 1982). Covalent modification of enzymes between active and inactive forms is a key process involved in metabolic regulation. Covalent modifications caused by reversible phosphorylation of enzymes catalyzed by protein kinases and phosphatases are well studied (Schulman et al., 1980; Trewavas, 1976). The physiological roles of protein kinases are well known in animal systems (Greengard, 1978). Calcium- and calmodulin-promoted protein phosphorylation has been reported in many plant systems (Hetherington and Trewavas, 1982; Polya and Davies, 1982; Salimath and Marme, 1983; Veluthambi and Poovaiah, 1984a,b; Poovaiah and Veluthambi, 1986). The promotion of Ca^{2+} and calmodulin-dependent protein kinases by Ca^{2+} and calmodulin provides a mechanism by which calcium can regulate diverse processes including senescence. The occurrence of Ca^{2+} and calmodulin-dependent protein kinases in membranes and soluble proteins from a wide variety of plant tissues (Fig. 11.6) suggests that such a phosphorylation system could be of general importance as a biochemical mechanism of calcium action. These observations offer a promising ap-

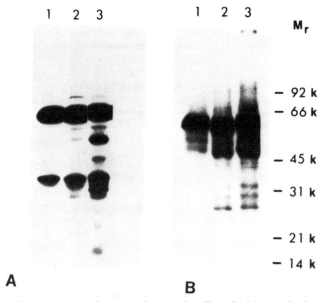

Fig. 11.6. Autoradiographs showing the effect of calcium and calmodulin on the phosphorylation of soluble polypeptides from (A) corn coleoptiles and (B) membrane polypeptides from apple fruits. Protein phosphorylation was carried out as described earlier by Veluthambi and Poovaiah (1984a,b) using [γ-³²P]ATP. *In vitro* phosphorylations were performed in the (1) absence of Ca, (2) in the presence of CaCl₂, or (3) in the presence of CaCl₂ and calmodulin. The molecular weights of representative phosphorylated polypeptides are indicated.

proach for studying the biochemical mechanism of action of calcium as a second messenger in plant systems. Moreover, phosphorylation/dephosphorylation in the regulation of chloroplast membrane function and photosynthetic electron transport is well recognized (Bennett, 1977; Horton, 1983).

Ca-dependent phosphorylation is activated by the influx of calcium into the cytoplasm in response to stimuli. An example of Ca-stimulated phosphorylation at micromolar-free Ca²⁺ concentrations is shown in Fig. 11.7. Such Ca-stimulated phosphorylation is known to decrease during senescence (Paliyath and Poovaiah, 1984, 1985a,b). It is also known to change at different stages of growth and development (Raghothama *et al.*, 1985b; Veluthambi and Poovaiah, 1986).

Physiological studies have shown the possible involvement of protein phosphorylation in ion transport across membranes. In a recent study, proton translocation across the plasma membrane, an integral part of

Free Ca (µM)   0   <1   <1   1   15   40

$M_r.10^{-3}$

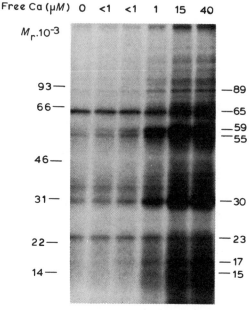

93 —   — 89
66 —   — 65
                             — 59
                             — 55

46 —

31 —   — 30

22 —   — 23
                             — 17
14 —   — 15

Fig. 11.7. Effect of micromolar concentrations of free Ca^{2+} on *in vitro* protein phosphorylation. All reaction mixtures contained 0.2 mM EGTA, and total $[Ca^{2+}]$ was varied from 0 to 0.25 mM. Free Ca^{2+} concentrations, as determined using a Ca^{2+}-sensitive electrode, are indicated on the top. Molecular weight standards and M_r values of some representative polypeptides are indicated on the sides.

auxin-induced growth, has been found to be affected by the level of phosphorylation of membrane proteins (Zocchi *et al.*, 1983). Various stresses can result in depression of this pump action; for example, wounding or cold shock of corn roots results in rapid inhibition of net H^+ efflux, presumably due to the decrease in activity of H^+–ATPase of the plasma membrane. Such treatments produce a passive influx of Ca^{2+} from the apoplast into a phase, presumably the protoplast. Hanson and Trewavas (1982) suggest that calcium and calmodulin might regulate the activity of H^+–ATPase of the plasma membrane. Active transport of calcium out of the cytoplasm or into the internal stores, such as mitochondria and endoplasmic reticulum (Williamson and Ashley, 1982), reduces the cytoplasmic calcium concentration, thus resulting in the recovery of the system to the basal state.

Recently we observed a decrease in calcium- and calmodulin-promoted protein phosphorylation in membranes from senesced apples (Paliyath and

Poovaiah, 1985b). Although equal amounts of membrane proteins were used from both normal and senesced apples, the phosphorylation of proteins promoted by Ca^{2+} and calmodulin was considerably reduced in membrane proteins from senesced apples. Similar results were observed when soluble proteins from ripening tomato fruits were used for phosphorylation (Raghothama *et al.*, 1985b). Phosphoprotein phosphatase activity in membrane preparations from normal and senesced apples did not differ much, which suggests that a relatively high phosphoprotein phosphatase activity in senesced apple membranes could not be the major factor resulting in the decrease in calcium- and calmodulin-promoted protein phosphorylation. Thus, it appears that the decrease in membrane protein phosphorylation during senescence could be due to: (1) selective degradation of protein kinases and substrates or (2) inhibition of enzyme activities by an unfavorable microenvironment. The inhibition of calcium- and calmodulin-promoted protein phosphorylation could alter the biochemical processes in the cell and could participate in the onset and progress of senescence.

IV. ROLE OF INOSITOL PHOSPHOLIPIDS IN CALCIUM MESSENGER SYSTEM

The behavior of cells from one instant to another is controlled by signaling systems that translate external information into intracellular events. Recently, much attention has been given to the turnover of inositol phospholipids in the membrane (Poovaiah *et al.*, 1987b). At present, there is no direct evidence that the turnover of inositol phospholipids is involved in senescence. However, inositol trisphosphate can release calcium from the intracellular stores and alter the free calcium status of the cell. This change in free calcium concentration could then play a major role in cellular regulation. A schematic diagram suggesting the turnover of inositol phospholipids and calcium mobilization leading to cellular response is shown in Fig. 11.8. This diagrammatic model presents an exciting area for further research. As shown in the figure, the primary stimulus, such as a hormone, interacts with the plasma membrane receptor. This results in the activation of phospho lipase C and the cleavage of the membrane lipid phosphatidylinositol 4,5-bisphosphate (PIP_2) into diacylglycerol (DG) and inositol trisphosphate (IP_3). Inositol trisphosphate stimulates the release of calcium from the endoplasmic reticulum. This released calcium can activate calmodulin-dependent enzymes, including protein kinases. Together with diacylglycerol, it can also activate protein kinase C, ultimately leading to protein phosphorylation and cellular response (Nishizuka, 1984; Berridge and Irvine, 1984). Recent evidence suggests the existence of similar pathways in trans-

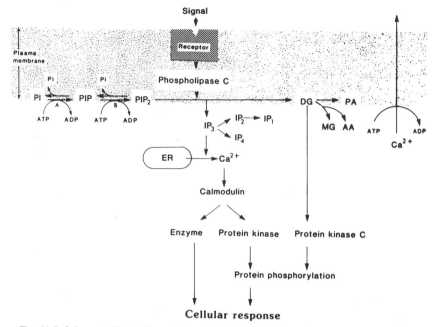

Fig. 11.8. Schematic illustration of stimulus-induced turnover of phosphatidylinositol 4,5-bisphosphate (PIP_2) and the role of turnover products in the Ca^{2+} messenger system. This pathway is shown to occur in animal cells and evidence for its existence in plants is being accumulated. Interaction of extracellular signals with a receptor on the plasma membrane activates phospholipase C leading to hydrolysis of PIP_2. Diacylglycerol (DG) and inositol 1,4,5-trisphosphate (IP_3), the hydrolysis products of PIP_2, play a key role in signal transduction. DG activates protein kinase C. IP_3 releases Ca^{2+} from endoplasmic reticulum, thereby raising cytosolic free Ca^{2+} and activating Ca^{2+}- and Ca^{2+}-calmodulin dependent enzymes. PI, phosphatidylinositol; PIP, phosphatidylinositol 4-phosphate; A, PI kinase; B, PIP kinase; ER, endoplasmic reticulum; IP_4, inositol tetrakisphosphate; IP_3 inositol trisphosphate; IP_2, inositol bisphosphate; IP_1 inositol monophosphate; MG, monoglyceride; AA, arachidonic acid; PA, phosphatidic acid. [From Poovaiah and Reddy (1987).]

ducing extracellular signals in plants (Reddy *et al.*, 1987). The presence of polyphosphoinositides has been shown in plant tissue culture cells (Boss and Massel, 1985). Inositol trisphosphate-induced calcium mobilization from microsomal fractions has been observed in our laboratory (Reddy and Poovaiah, 1987) and elsewhere (Drobak and Ferguson, 1985). We also have preliminary evidence indicating that most of the calcium released by inositol trisphosphate is from the endoplasmic reticulum. Moreover, protein kinase C-like activity has been reported in plants (Schafer *et al.*, 1985). Further investigations on this pathway are vital for a better understanding of signal transduction in plants. Additional information is needed to clarify the significance of this pathway in plant growth and development in general and senescence in particular.

V. CONCLUSION

Calcium effects on various parameters of senescence, such as loss of chlorophyll and protein, increased membrane leakage, dissolution of middle lamella, and associated changes in the cell wall, are well established. However, the mechanism of calcium action is just beginning to be unraveled at the molecular level. Investigations on calcium- and calmodulin-mediated biochemical processes as well as the turnover of inositol phospholipids are in their infancy in plants. Additional information is necessary regarding the intracellular fluctuations in calcium concentration. Accurate and direct measurements of free cytoplasmic calcium concentrations are required to further clarify the involvement of calcium in senescence. There is potential for major breakthroughs. The prospects are promising.

ACKNOWLEDGMENTS

The author is indebted to all the former and current members of this laboratory who have made this chapter possible. This work was supported in part by the National Science Foundation grant DCB-8502215.

REFERENCES

Anderson, J. M., and Cormier, M. J. (1978). Calcium-dependent regulation of NAD kinase in higher plants. *Biochem. Biophys. Res. Commun.* **84**, 595–602.

Balamani, V., Veluthambi, K., and Poovaiah, B. W. (1986). Effect of calcium on tuberization in potato (*Solanum tuberosum* L.). *Plant Physiol.* **80**, 856–858.

Bartley, I. M. (1974). β-Galactosidase activity in ripening apples. *Phytochemistry* **13**, 2107–2111.

Bennett, J. (1977). Phosphorylation of chloroplast membrane polypeptides. *Nature (London)* **269**, 344–346.

Berridge, M. J., and Irvine, R. F. (1984). Inositol trisphosphate, a novel second messenger in cellular signal transduction. *Nature (London)* **312**, 315–321.

Boss, W. F., and Massel, M. O. (1985). Polyphosphoinositides are present in plant tissue culture cells. *Biochem. Biophys. Res. Commun.* **132**, 1018–1023.

Buescher, R. W., and Hobson, G. E. (1982). Role of calcium and chelating agents in regulating the degradation of tomato fruit tissue by polygalacturonase. *J. Plant Biochem.* **6**, 147–160.

Cheung, W. Y. (1980). Calmodulin plays a pivotal role in cellular regulation. *Science* **207**, 19–27.

Cohen, P. (1982). The role of protein phosphorylation in neural and hormonal control of cellular activity. *Nature (London)* **296**, 613–619.

B. W. Poovaiah

Conway, W. S., and Sams, C. E. (1984). Possible mechanisms by which postharvest calcium treatment reduces decay in apples. *Phytopathology* **74**, 208–210.

Demarty, M., Morvan, C., and Thellier, M. (1984). Calcium and the cell wall. *Plant Cell Environ.* **7**, 441–448.

Doesburg, J. J. (1957). Relation between the solubilization of pectin and the fate of organic acids during maturation of apples. *J. Sci. Food Agric.* **8**, 206–216.

Drobak, B. K., and Ferguson, I. B. (1985). Release of Ca^{2+} from plant hypocotyl microsomes by inositol-4,5-trisphosphate. *Biochem. Biophys. Res. Commun.* **130**, 1241–1246.

Eilam, Y. (1965). Permeability changes in senescing tissue. *J. Exp. Bot.* **16**, 614–627.

Epstein, E. (1961). The essential role of calcium in selective cation transport by plant cells. *Plant Physiol.* **36**, 437–444.

Gary-Bobo, C. M. (1970). Effect of Ca^{++} on the water and non-electrolyte permeability of phospholipid membranes. *Nature (London)* **228**, 1101–1102.

Greengard, P. (1978). Phosphorylated proteins as physiological effectors. *Science* **199**, 146–152.

Hanson, J. B. (1983). The roles of calcium in plant growth. *In* "Current Topics in Plant Biochemistry and Physiology" (D. D. Randall, D. G. Blevins, and R. Larson, eds.), Vol. 1, pp. 1–24. Univ. of Missouri Press, Columbia.

Hanson, J. B., and Trewavas, A. J. (1982). Regulation of plant cell growth: The changing perspective. *New Phytol.* **90**, 1–18.

Hepler, P. K., and Wayne, R. O. (1985). Calcium and plant development. *Annu. Rev. Plant Physiol.* **36**, 397–439.

Hetherington, A. M., and Trewavas, A. (1982). Calcium-dependent protein kinase in pea shoot membranes. *FEBS Lett.* **145**, 67–71.

Hetherington, A. M., DeSilva, D. L. R., Cox, R. C., and Mansfield, T. A. (1986). Abscisic acid, calcium ions and stomatal function. *In* "Molecular and Cellular Aspects of Calcium in Plant Development" (A. J. Trewavas, ed.), pp. 387–388. Plenum, New York.

Horton, P. (1983). Control of chloroplast electron transport by phosphorylation of thylakoid proteins. *FEBS Lett.* **152**, 47–51.

Jones, R. G. W., and Lunt, O. R. (1967). The function of calcium in plants. *Bot. Rev.* **33**, 407–426.

Keith, C. H., Ratan, R., Maxfield, F. R., Bajer, A., and Shelanski, M. L. (1985). Local cytoplasmic calcium gradients in living mitotic cells. *Nature (London)* **316**, 848–850.

Knee, M. (1973). Polysaccharide changes in cell walls of ripening apples. *Phytochemistry* **12**, 1543–1549.

Kretsinger, R. H. (1977). Evolution of the informational role of calcium in eukaryotes. *In* "Calcium-Binding Proteins and Calcium Function" (R. H. Wasserman, R. A. Corradino, E. Carafoli, R. H. Kretsinger, D. H. MacLennan, and F. L. Siegel, eds.), pp. 63–72. North-Holland Publ., New York.

Leopold, A. C., Poovaiah, B. W., Dela Fuente, R. K., and Williams, R. J. (1974). Regulation of growth with inorganic solutes. *In* "Plant Growth Substances," pp. 780–788. Hirokawa Press, Tokyo.

Mansfield, T. A., and Davies, W. J. (1981). Stomata and stomatal mechanisms. *In* "The Physiology and Biochemistry of Drought Resistance in Plants" (L. G. Paleg and D. Aspinall, eds.), pp. 315–346. Academic Press, New York.

Marinos, N. G. (1962). Studies on submicroscopic aspects of mineral deficiencies. I. Calcium deficiency in the shoot apex of barley. *Am. J. Bot.* **49**, 834–841.

Marme, D., and Dieter, P. (1983). Role of Ca^{++} and calmodulin in plants. *In* "Calcium and Cell Function" (W. Y. Cheung, ed.), Vol. 4, pp. 263–311. Academic Press, New York.

Mizrahi, Y., and Kopeliovitch, E. (1983). Pectic substances: changes in soft and firm tomato cultivars and in non-ripening mutants. *J. Am. Soc. Hortic. Sci.* **85,** 111–116.

Nishizuka, Y. (1984). The role of protein kinase C in cell surface signal transduction and tumour promotion. *Nature (London)* **308,** 693–698.

Paliyath, G., and Poovaiah, B. W. (1984). Calmodulin inhibitor in senescing apples and its physiological and pharmacological significance. *Proc. Natl. Acad. Sci. U.S.A.* **81,** 2065–2069.

Paliyath, G., and Poovaiah, B. W. (1985a). Identification of naturally occurring calmodulin inhibitors in plants and their effects on calcium- and calmodulin-promoted protein phosphorylation. *Plant Cell Physiol.* **26,** 201–209.

Paliyath, G., and Poovaiah, B. W. (1985b). Calcium- and calmodulin-promoted phosphorylation of membrane proteins during senescence in apples. *Plant and Cell Physiol.* **26,** 977–986.

Paliyath, G., and Poovaiah, B. W. (1988). Promotion of β-glucan synthase activity in corn microsomal membranes by calcium and protein phosphorylation. *Plant Cell Physiol.* **29,** 67–73.

Paliyath, G., Poovaiah, B. W., Munske, G. R., and Magnuson, J. (1984). Membrane fluidity in senescing apples: Effects of temperature and calcium. *Plant Cell Physiol.* **25,** 1083–1087.

Polya, G. M., and Davies, J. R. (1982). Resolution of Ca^{++}-calmodulin activated protein kinase from wheat germ. *FEBS Lett.* **150,** 167–171.

Poovaiah, B. W. (1979a). Effects of inorganic cations on ethephon-induced increases in membrane permeability. *J. Am. Soc. Hortic. Sci.* **104,** 164–166.

Poovaiah, B. W. (1979b). Role of calcium in ripening and senescence. *Commun. Soil Sci. Plant Anal.* **10,** 83–88.

Poovaiah, B. W. (1985). Role of calcium and calmodulin in plant growth and development. *HortScience* **20,** 347–352.

Poovaiah, B. W. (1986). Role of calcium in prolonging storage life of fruits and vegetables. *Food Technol.* **40,** 86–89.

Poovaiah, B. W. (1987). The role of calcium and calmodulin in senescence. *In* "Plant Senescence: Its Biochemistry and Physiology" (W. W. Thomson, E. A. Nothnagel, and R. C. Huffaker, eds.), pp. 182–189. Am. Soc. Plant Physiol., Rockville, Maryland.

Poovaiah, B. W., and Leopold, A. C. (1973a). Deferral of leaf senescence with calcium. *Plant Physiol.* **52,** 236–239.

Poovaiah, B. W., and Leopold, A. C. (1973b). Inhibition of abscission by calcium. *Plant Physiol.* **51,** 848–851.

Poovaiah, B. W., and Leopold, A. C. (1974). Hormone-solute interactions in the lettuce hypocotyl hook. *Plant Physiol.* **54,** 289–293.

Poovaiah, B. W., and Leopold, A. C. (1976a). Effects of inorganic solutes on the binding of auxin. *Plant Physiol.* **58,** 783–785.

Poovaiah, B. W., and Leopold, A. C. (1976b). Effects of inorganic salts on tissue permeability. *Plant Physiol.* **58,** 182–185.

Poovaiah, B. W., and Moulton, G. A. (1982). Vacuum pressure infiltration process for fresh produce. U.S. Patent 4,331,691.

Poovaiah, B. W., and Rasmussen, H. P. (1973a). Effect of calcium, 2-chloroethylphosphonic acid, and ethylene on bean leaf abscission. *Planta* **113,** 207–214.

Poovaiah, B. W., and Rasmussen, H. P. (1973b). Calcium distribution in the abscission zone of bean leaves: electron microprobe X-ray analysis. *Plant Physiol.* **52,** 683–684.

Poovaiah, B. W., and Reddy, A. S. N. (1987). Calcium messenger system in plants. *CRC Crit. Rev. Plant Sci.* **6,** 47–103.

Poovaiah, B. W., and Veluthambi, K. (1986). The role of calcium and calmodulin in hormone action in plants: Importance of protein phosphorylation. *In* "Molecular and Cellular Aspects of Calcium in Plant Development" (A. J. Trewavas, ed.), pp. 83–90. Plenum, New York.

Poovaiah, B. W., McFadden, J. J., and Reddy, A. S. N. (1987a). The role of calcium in gravity signal perception and transduction. *Physiol. Plant.* **71,** 401–407.

Poovaiah, B. W., Reddy, A. S. N., and McFadden, J. J. (1987b). Calcium messenger system: Role of protein phosphorylation and inositol phospholipids. *Physiol. Plant.* **69,** 569–573.

Poovaiah, B. W., Glenn, G. M., and Reddy, A. S. N. (1988). Calcium and fruit softening: Physiology and biochemistry. *Hortic. Rev.* (in press).

Prozialeck, W. C., and Weiss, B. (1985). Mechanisms of pharmacologically altering calmodulin activity. *In* "Calcium in Biological Systems" (R. P. Rubin, G. B. Weiss, and J. W. Putney, Jr., eds.), pp. 255–264. Plenum, New York.

Raghothama, K. G., Mizrahi, Y., and Poovaiah, B. W. (1985a). Effect of calmodulin antagonists on auxin-induced elongation. *Plant Physiol.* **79,** 28–33.

Raghothama, K. G., Veluthambi, K., and Poovaiah, B. W. (1985b). Stage-specific changes in calcium-regulated protein phosphorylation in developing fruits. *Plant Cell Physiol.* **26,** 1565–1572.

Raghothama, K. G., Reddy, A. S. N., Friedmann, M., and Poovaiah, B. W. (1988). Effect of calcium on *in vivo* protein phosphorylation in corn root tips. *Plant Physiol.* (in press).

Ray, P. M., and Baker, D. B. (1965). The effect of auxin on synthesis of oat coleoptile cell wall constituents. *Plant Physiol.* **41,** 353–360.

Reddy, A. S. N., and Poovaiah, B. W. (1987). Inositol 1,4,5-triphosphate induced calcium release from corn coleoptile microsomes. *J. Biochem. (Tokyo)* **101,** 569–573.

Reddy, A. S. N., McFadden, J. J., Friedmann, M., and Poovaiah, B. W. (1987). Signal transduction in plants: Evidence for the involvement of calcium and turnover of inositol phospholipids. *Biochem. Biophys. Res. Commun.* **149,** 334–339.

Richmond, A. E., and Lang, A. (1957). Effect of kinetin on protein content and survival of detached *Xanthium* leaves. *Science* **125,** 650–651.

Rossignol, M., Lamant, D., Salsac, L., and Heller, R. (1977). Calcium fixation by the roots of calcicole and calcifuge plants: the importance of membrane systems and their lipid composition. *In* "Transmembrane Ionic Exchange in Plants" (M. Thellier, A. Monnier, M. Demarty, and J. Dainty, eds.), pp. 483–490. CNRS, Paris and Editions Univ., Rouen.

Roux, S. J., and Slocum, R. D. (1982). Role of calcium in mediating cellular functions important for growth and development in higher plants. *In* "Calcium and Cell Function" (W. Y. Cheung, ed.), Vol. 3, pp. 409–453. Academic Press, New York.

Sacher, J. A. (1957). Relationship between auxin and membrane-integrity in tissue senescence and abscission. *Science* **125,** 1199–1200.

Salimath, B. P., and Marme, D. (1983). Protein phosphorylation and its regulation by calcium and calmodulin in membrane fractions from zucchini hypocotyls. *Planta* **158,** 560–568.

Saunders, M. J., and Hepler, P. K. (1982). Calcium ionophore A23187 stimulates cytokinin-like mitosis in *Funaria. Science* **217,** 943–945.

Schafer, A., Bygrave, F., Matzenauer, S., and Marme, D. (1985). Identification of a calcium- and phospholipid-dependent protein kinase in plant tissue. *FEBS Lett.* **187,** 25–28.

Schulman, H., Wieland, B. H., and Greengard, P. (1980). Calcium-dependent protein phosphorylation in mammalian brain and other tissues. *In* "Calcium and Cell Function" (W. Y. Cheung, ed.), Vol. 1, pp. 220–248. Academic Press, New York.

Suwwan, M. A., and Poovaiah, B. W. (1978). Association between elemental content and fruit ripening in *rin* and normal tomatoes. *Plant Physiol.* **61,** 883–885.

Thimann, K. V., and Satler, S. (1979). Interrelation between leaf senescence and stomatal aperture. *Proc. Natl. Acad. Sci. U.S.A.* **76,** 2295–2298, 2770–2773.

Trewavas, A. (1970). The turnover of nucleic acids in *Lemna minor. Plant Physiol.* **45,** 742–751.

Trewavas, A. (1972). Control of protein turnover rates in *Lemna minor. Plant Physiol.* **49,** 47–51.

Trewavas, A. (1976). Post-translational modification of proteins by phosphorylation. *Annu. Rev. Plant Physiol.* **27**, 349–374.

Veluthambi, K., and Poovaiah, B. W. (1984a). Calcium-promoted protein phosphorylation in plants. *Science* **223**, 167–169.

Veluthambi, K., and Poovaiah, B. W. (1984b). Calcium- and calmodulin-regulated phosphorylation of soluble and membrane proteins from corn coleoptiles. *Plant Physiol.* **76**, 359–365.

Veluthambi, K., and Poovaiah, B. W. (1986). *In vitro* and *in vivo* protein phosphorylation in *Avena sativa* L. coleoptiles: Effects of Ca^{++}, calmodulin antagonists and auxin. *Plant Physiol.* **81**, 836–841.

Wallner, S. J. (1978). Apple fruit β-galactosidase and softening in storage. *J. Am. Soc. Hortic. Sci.* **103**, 364–366.

Williamson, R. E., and Ashley, C. C. (1982). Free Ca^{++} and cytoplasmic streaming in algae *Chara. Nature (London)* **296**, 647–651.

Zocchi, G., Rogers, S. A., and Hanson, J. B. (1983). Inhibition of proton pumping in corn roots is associated with increased phosphorylation of membrane proteins. *Plant Sci. Lett.* **81**, 215–221.

Whole Plant Senescence

L. D. Noodén
Biology Department
University of Michigan
Ann Arbor, Michigan

SENESCENCE AND AGING IN PLANTS

I. INTRODUCTION

The processes described in the preceeding chapters truly become integrated in the context of whole plant senescence. Here, it is especially important to sort out the temporal and regulatory interrelations of individual processes and the interconnections between individual organs. Efforts need to be made to integrate the data already available and thereafter new findings as they are reported (Noodén, 1984). Indeed, several whole plant modeling programs already have started this process from a different perspective (e.g., Curry *et al.*, 1980; Acock *et al.*, 1983; Meyer, 1985, for soybean; Day and Atkin, 1985, for wheat; Penning de Vries and Van Laar, 1982, for a variety of applications). These clearly demonstrate the feasibility of sophisticated quantitative descriptions of whole plant development, even if the models are not yet complete in terms of their underlying physiological regulatory mechanisms.

The subject of whole plant senescence presently can be subdivided into patterns, correlative controls, cessation of vegetative growth, declining assimilatory processes, assimilate partitioning, and hormonal controls. This organization follows a progression from a consideration of general characteristics of whole plant senescence to the physiological changes leading to death and, then, their controls. The linear thinking that is productive in purely biochemical studies is inadequate here and must be replaced with a concept of three- or even four-dimensional changes, e.g., progression with time. Complex as this seems, it is tractable if one aspect is examined at a time and if attention is given to relating these tightly focused studies to the larger picture of the whole plant.

II. PATTERNS OF WHOLE PLANT SENESCENCE

It is obvious that sooner or later all organisms die. The two principal patterns of organism death and senescence are monocarpy and polycarpy, representing, respectively, a single reproductive phase followed by death and repeated reproductive phases (Chapter 1). In polycarpic plants, the reproductive development seems unconnected with the death of the plant, whereas there is a close link in monocarpic plants. While monocarpic plants usually degenerate rapidly, polycarpic plants undergo a more gradual decline. Thus, the causes of death may not be the same in monocarpic and polycarpic plants. Consequently, this review will deal primarily with monocarpic senescence, leaving polycarpic plants to a brief section (VIII) near the end.

Since monocarpic plants degenerate following their reproductive phase whenever that occurs, anything that delays flowering likewise postpones monocarpic senescence. Thus, single gene changes that alter the photoperiod or vernalization requirements for flowering may secondarily shift monocarpic senescence, e.g., annual sugar beets can be made biennial (Whaley, 1965). Similarly, a number of annuals (e.g., *Viola tricolor*) will germinate and grow vegetatively but not flower if planted in the fall (Molisch, 1938; Crocker, 1939; Wangermann, 1965); flowering and, thence, monocarpic senescence occur early in the subsequent growing season. By contrast, spring seedlings produce plants that flower and die all in the same growing season. Likewise, soil nutritional conditions that promote or delay flowering exert similar effects on senescence (Russell, 1932; Leonard, 1962; Wangermann, 1965; see also Section IV). These observations demonstrate: first, monocarpic senescence is generally coupled with (subsequent to) flowering and/or fruiting (to be discussed further in Section III,B), and, second, these monocarpic plants may be capable of surviving substantial environmental adversity, and therefore endogenous, not environmental, factors cause them to die.

Just as species may show significant differences in their hormonal responses (Chapter 10), important physiological differences are known to occur in monocarpic senescence (Noodén and Lindoo, 1978; Noodén, 1980a). Thus, some caution needs to be applied in extrapolating results from one species to another.

III. CORRELATIVE CONTROLS

Obviously, a complex organism such as a whole plant must coordinate and integrate the activity of its parts. Different organs are able to signal each other through various means, apparently mostly hormonal (Goodwin, 1978; Goodwin *et al.*, 1978; Chapter 1). Of course, regulatory signals must also be exchanged during whole plant senescence, and some of these signals are, no doubt, the same as those involved in the earlier developmental phases.

A. Cells and Organs as Components of the Organism

Plant cells, excepting those lacking nuclei, appear to be capable of multiplying and growing indefinitely if excised and cultured as calluses (Murashige, 1974; Noodén, 1980a). In certain locations, however, these same cells may be targeted to become xylem cells that senesce during differentiation (Chapter 1). A branch on a tree will eventually die along with the tree, but if it is excised and rooted, the branch can become a new, vigorous tree (Section VIII,A). Likewise, the longevity of the leaves of many species can be greatly extended by excising and rooting them (Molisch, 1938; also many later workers). Thus, the individual cells may die because they are selectively targeted to do so as part of the normal differentiation processes in an organism or because they are components of an organ or organism that is undergoing senescence (Noodén, 1980a). This raises questions about causal mechanisms; for example, do individual cells and organs die because they are signaled to senesce or because the life-sustaining supply of nutrients and H_2O is shut off? These problems are considered in the subsequent sections and in Chapter 1. In any case, correlative controls are important in senescence.

B. Control Centers versus Targets

At least for monocarpic plants, it is possible to analyze whole plant (monocarpic) senescence in terms of control centers and target organs. Indeed, understanding which structures induce senescence (controllers) and which are the primary responders (targets) is essential for analysis of the regulatory mechanisms and even the biochemistry of the senescence process.

The sequential coupling of reproductive development and monocarpic senescence is discussed above in Section II. It has also been possible to prevent or delay monocarpic senescence by removal of certain parts, usually reproductive structures. In fact, it has been known among gardeners and horticulturists for a very long time that removal of flowers after petal fading prolongs flower production in many species, and removal of fruit before maturity not only extends fruit production, but the life of the plant as well (Reichert, 1821; Johnson, 1862; Molisch, 1938; Wangermann, 1965; also many current seed catalogs). For example, in cucumbers and snap beans, cutting off the fruit before the start of yellowing extends the life of the plant, whereas allowing the fruit to reach this stage causes rapid degeneration of the plant. Similarly, sterile hybrids derived from annual and biennial parents may become perennial (Braun, 1851; Wangermann, 1965). The prevention of rapid death of soybeans by depodding is well known (Leopold *et al.*, 1959; Lindoo and Noodén, 1977; Fig. 12.1). Likewise, male-sterile soy-

Fig. 12.1. Soybean plants (cv. Anoka) grown in the field in southeast Michigan using standard farming practices, except that they were irrigated if no rain fell within a week. The plant on the right was depodded as the pods reached full extension, the plant on the left was not. Photographed on September 14; by September 22, the podded plants were completely brown and leafless, whereas the depodded plants maintained their green, healthy appearance.

beans that set relatively few pods stay green (Burke *et al.*, 1984) and maintain their N_2-fixing capacity longer (Imsande and Ralston, 1982). Even in soybean, where depodding may prevent rapid death, it may not prevent the decline in photosynthesis and other parameters generally associated with senescence (Woodward and Rawson, 1976; Mondal *et al.*, 1978; Section V,B). For wheat, head removal retarded some, but not all, of the changes associated with the senescence syndrome (King *et al.*, 1967; Feller, 1979; Patterson and Brun, 1980). Nonetheless, the seeds are responsible for the rapid degeneration and death in the pea, red kidney bean, soybean, and sunflower (Lockhart and Gottschall, 1961; Wareing and Seth, 1967; Lindoo and Noodén, 1977; Purohit, 1982). Similarly, decapitation, which removes the reproductive structures and keeps the female hemp plants vegetative, also delays the yellowing of the leaves (Conrad, 1962). It is of particular interest that removal of the flowers on male spinach plants can also delay monocarpic senescence in that species (Leopold *et al.*, 1959). Removal of the flowers of male hemp plants does not prevent the death of the plant (Conrad, 1962). On the other hand, deflowering does not prevent senescence in cocklebur; however, the deflowered plants look different from normal plants (Krizek *et al.*, 1966). Moreover, for some species such as corn, barley, and pepper, defruiting actually seems to promote leaf senescence (Allison and Weinmann, 1970; Mandahar and Garg, 1975; Hall and Milthorpe, 1978), but the metabolic decline in defruited plants may have other explanations (Section V,B). In many cases, but not all, the reproductive structures, particularly the seeds, induce or control monocarpic senescence.

What then is the primary target of the influence exerted by the reproductive structures? Long ago, Lindemuth (1901) noted that the rootstock of a herbaceous annual *Modiola caroliniana* lived for 3 years and 5 months, long beyond its normal life, when grafted together with a scion from the perennial *Abutilon Thompsoni*. Likewise, grafting a young soybean stock on to an old root system renews N_2 fixation in the latter (Malik, 1983). Reciprocally, a young pea shoot grafted onto an older rootstock does not senesce prematurely (Malik and Berrie, 1980). These observations indicate that longevity may be determined more by the shoot than the root system.

Modifications of the soybean plant also suggest the shoot system plays a more important role than the roots (Lindoo and Noodén, 1977). Root/shoot grafting experiments (Fig. 12.2) and photoperiod manipulations of soybeans indicate that the reason the plants die during pod maturation is because the leaves senesce (Noodén, 1980b). Thus, it appears that the soybean plant dies because the leaves no longer supply needed assimilates and hormones to the roots. As a result, the roots decline, and this further contributes to the demise of the whole plant. Thus, the leaves and not the roots or even the stem appear to be the primary target of the influence (senescence signal) exerted by the fruit, though it must be noted that this particular controller–target scheme may not apply to all species (Noodén and Lindoo, 1978; Noodén, 1980a), although it does seem to hold for a good many. Given the key role of the leaves in assimilation, it is readily understandable that their loss would have a great impact on the organism as a whole.

Thus, we are in a position to answer the question of whether senescence is a system or global failure (Rosen, 1978). For soybean at least, monocarpic senescence is primarily a system (leaf) failure (Noodén, 1980a; Noodén and

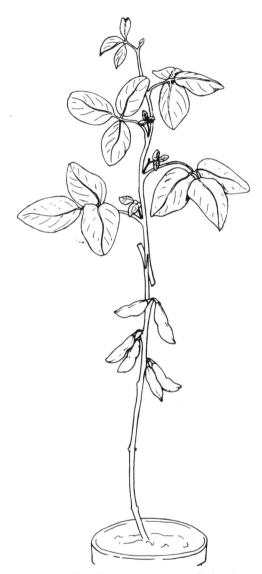

Fig. 12.2. Foliar senescence and pod development in a grafted soybean plant with Biloxi (a variety that will not flower under long days) over Anoka (a variety that flowers under long days). The graft was made while the plants were still vegetative, and the plants were kept under long days throughout. Note that the lower portion (Anoka) has produced pods and the leaves have senesced and abscised, while the upper part (Biloxi) has remained vegetative and continued to grow. The continued supply of assimilates from the active Biloxi leaves has maintained the Anoka stem and root system, thereby keeping the plant alive. [From Noodén (1980b).]

Thompson, 1985). It seems likely that this may be true for other species as well.

C. Behavior of the Senescence Signal

For convenience and without intent to prejudice thinking about the mechanism by which the reproductive structures act on the vegetative parts, particularly the leaves as described above, this influence can be called the *senescence signal* (Lindoo and Noodén, 1977). Beyond what is noted in Section III,B, little information is available on the behavior of the senescence signal in species other than soybean. The source seems to be the seeds in some, but not all, monocarpic species, e.g., monocarpic male plants (Section III,B). Further information on the behavior of the senescence signal is available for soybean, but not other species at this time. The exertion of this influence (or, at least, its final stages) seems to occur during very late podfill; depodding even quite late in podfill still prevents the rapid yellowing and quick death of the plant (Lindoo and Noodén, 1977; Noodén et al., 1978). The movement of the senescence signal is restricted, though clearly less constrained, than the nutrients that support pod development, for monocarpic senescence and pod development can be uncoupled (Noodén et al., 1978). The senescence signal is exerted mainly on the leaf closest to an individual pod or pod cluster (Noodén, 1980b). Beyond this, the senescence signal seems to travel mainly downward, but stays within the same orthostichy as the source pods (Lindoo and Noodén, 1977; Noodén, 1980b). The main influence, that on the nearest leaf, is not blocked by steam girdling of the petiole thereby indicating that it is exerted via the xylem (Noodén and Murray, 1982; Noodén, 1985; Fig. 12.3). The influence moving downward is blocked by steam girdling, which suggests that it acts via the phloem (Murray and Noodén, 1982). Unfortunately, these observations have been incorrectly reported elsewhere (Wang and Woolhouse, 1982; Sexton and Woolhouse, 1984). For soybean at least, the senescence signal seems to differ from florigen (Noodén, 1980b, 1985).

In *Kleinia articulata*, there appears to be a different transmissible senescence factor in that it originates in the leaves, where it is induced by a long-day photoperiod (Kulkarni and Schwabe, 1985). This influence is even less mobile than the senescence signal of soybean.

IV. CESSATION OF VEGETATIVE GROWTH AS A COMPONENT OF WHOLE PLANT SENESCENCE

In addition to the assimilatory functions, growth must decline and stop in senescing plants. Under normal circumstances, individual organs have fi-

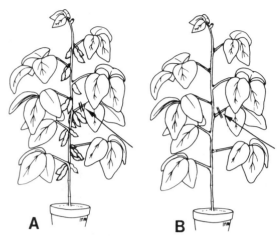

Fig. 12.3. Phloem destruction (steam) treatments (indicated by arrows) of soybean plants at early-mid podfill. (A) Phloem destruction in the petiole of a leaf in the middle of a fully podded plant. (B) Same treatment of a plant completely depodded from the start of podfill and thereafter as the pods reached a length of 1 cm. The treated leaf on a podded plant (A) senesces (yellows), while the treated leaf on a completely depodded plant (B) does not. Thus, phloem destruction does not block the influence of the pods (senescence signal), but the treatment itself does not induce senescence independently from the pods. Additional data show that the treated leaf does not senesce as an indirect result of senescence of the rest of the plant. [From Noodén and Murray (1982).]

nite functional lives after which they must be replaced (Molisch, 1938; Wangermann, 1965). Although the life and function of assimilatory organs can be extended, e.g., apex removal may temporarily rejuvenate the lower leaves (Chapter 1), assimilatory organs usually have to be renewed during the life of an organism. The relationship of growth cessation to monocarpic senescence is somewhat paradoxical in that it is important, and even necessary, but apparently not in itself a primary cause (Noodén, 1980a). That is to say, a plant obviously will not die if it keeps growing and forming new parts when the older parts senesce, as appears to be the case with clonal growth (Section VIII,B). Yet, the cessation of growth and organ production does not in itself cause the death of a plant, at least in monocarpic plants; monocarpic senescence is induced in the otherwise healthy organs.

An extensive and old literature documents what seems to be an "antagonism" between vegetative and reproductive growth in both monocarpic and polycarpic plants (Loomis, 1953; Leonard, 1962; Evans, 1972; Noodén, 1980a). In fact, treatments, such as application of mineral fertilizers, that promote vegetative growth may postpone flowering (Russell, 1932; Loomis, 1953). On the other hand, the decreased vegetative growth does not seem to be caused by a limited mineral nutrient supply; for example, tomato and soybean plants grown with an ample supply of nutrients still decrease their vegetative growth during fruiting (Murneek, 1926; Derman et al., 1978). This tradeoff between vegetative and reproductive growth serves to increase reproductive output (Evans, 1972; Denholm, 1975; Noodén, 1980a; Willson, 1983; Paltridge et al., 1984).

The decline in vegetative growth, particularly the production of new leaves, obviously prevents the renewal of these important assimilatory organs and naturally sets the stage for a decline in photosynthesis. This reduction in organ production is of course reflected in meristematic activity, not only in the apical meristem, but also in the cambium (Wilton and Roberts, 1936; Wilton, 1938; Struckmeyer and Roberts, 1939; Struckmeyer, 1941; Woolhouse, 1982). One important result of the decreased cambial activity is less active phloem tissue. Although the measurements may not be as extensive or precise, it is clear that production of new root apices and the growth of roots also decline early in the reproductive phase or even before flowers appear. However, the exact timing of cessation varies even within a species (e.g., soybean roots, Noodén, 1984) and is probably influenced by the root environment. Similarly, shoot parts excised from aging or senescent plants are less able to form roots (Bijhower, 1931; Passeker, 1941; Trippi and Brulfert, 1973b; Hartmann and Kester, 1975). The cessation of vegetative growth in general, with particular reference to shoot elongation, is often referred to as determinate growth. Often, this refers to conversion of the shoot apex to reproductive growth (Jackson, 1953), which naturally terminates vegetative growth, whereas apices not ending in reproductive structures do not terminate their growth as sharply (indeterminate). This is the sense employed in connection with soybean (Fehr and Caviness, 1977), among other plants, and that has been incorrectly criticized (Sexton and Woolhouse, 1984). In a more restricted usage, which seems preferable, determinate refers to growth of limited duration, as in floral meristems and most leaves (Little and Jones, 1980), but this would also include apex senescence, as in the pea (Chapter 1).

In some species such as soybean (Lindoo and Noodén, 1976; Noodén, 1980b, 1984), defruiting restores vegetative growth little if at all, while in others such as mignonette and Vienna wallflowers, vegetative growth is essentially fully restored (Reichert, 1821; Hildebrand, 1882; Molisch, 1938; Wangermann, 1965). In this way, mignonette, which is normally just a small herbaceous plant, can be induced to become a small tree. Likewise, prevention of flowering may allow monocarpic plants to reach a much greater size and age than normal. For example, avoiding the chilling required by cabbage and sugar beet prevents flowering, thereby allowing these plants to live more than 2 years and also to become very large (Curtis and Clark, 1950; Curth, 1959). Under a noninductive photoperiod, soybean plants can be induced to reach a height of more than 7 m and to last more than 15 months (Noodén, 1980b). The soybean case presents a particularly interesting problem, because defruiting does not reinstate the shoot elongation, although it may promote root growth somewhat (Loong and Lenz, 1974; Derman *et al.*, 1978; Sutton, 1983) or leaf and stem thickening (Lenz and Williams, 1973; Mondal *et al.*, 1978; Noodén, 1984). Thus, the flowering signal (or some concurrent) signal and not some influence from the pods inhibits vegetative growth (Noodén, 1980b, 1984). For the common pea, apex senescence may occur in the absence of flowering (Lockhart and Gottschall, 1961; Reid, 1980), and, therefore, the apex senescence factor and the flowering factor seem to be different. Since the termination of stem elongation and node production in soybean seems to be a more localized influence than florigen (Noodén, 1980b, 1984; Guiamet and Nakayama, 1984), the factors that induce flowering and terminate apex growth in soybean may differ. In addition, foliar senescence, which is central to monocarpic senescence [called fruit-induced senescence by Lockhart and Gottschall (1961) and Reid and Murfet (1984)], is not directly related to apex senescence in the pea. Thus, apex senescence and monocarpic senescence are different phenomena in the pea, and careful distinction between them will be helpful.

In soybean, a combination of genes that produce the determinate growth pattern (here early termination of shoot elongation by conversion of the shoot apex to reproductive growth) also seems to cause delayed leaf senescence (Abu-Shakra *et al.*, 1978; Pierce *et al.*, 1984; Phillips *et al.*, 1984). This interesting observation runs counter to the idea that termination of shoot vegetative growth promotes whole plant senescence; however, this does not establish a causal connection between stem termination and senescence delay, for these genes may alter vegetative growth and leaf senescence through different means (i.e., they may be pleiotropic). Indeed, apex removal does not promote monocarpic senescence in soybean (Noodén *et al.*, 1979b). On the other hand, unfavorable light–dark cycles (e.g., 6 hour/6 hour or 24 hour/24 hour) cause not only termination of growth, but premature death of tomato plants; however, these plants do not die as a consequence of apex senescence (Highkin and Hanson, 1954).

The cessation of vegetative growth is an important component of the monocarpic senescence syndrome, but it (particularly apex senescence) does not seem to be a primary cause of monocarpic senescence.

V. DECLINE IN ASSIMILATORY PROCESSES

A. Changes in Assimilation in the Roots and Leaves

Even though all parts of a plant, and thereby all processes within it, are to some degree interconnected, it is necessary and appropriate to make this section substantially less than a summary of the entire story of plant metabolism as it is known today. The most important aspects of the metabolic changes during senescence are covered extensively in other chapters of this volume. A common difficulty with integrating and relating the literature to the whole plant is the lack of cross referencing between different parts or processes within the plant (Noodén, 1984).

The reduction in leaf production and root growth early during the reproductive phase of monocarpic plants (Section IV) foreshadows the decreases in the physiological activities of these organs as described below.

Although the timing of the start of the decline and the final cessation of root growth is variable, both root growth and their assimilatory processes (mineral nutrient uptake and nitrogen fixation) do seem to begin their decline relatively early in reproductive development (Loehwing, 1951; Noodén, 1980a). In annual plants, the uptake of different minerals may decline at different times (Harper, 1971; Hocking and Pate, 1977; Pate and Hocking, 1978; Noodén and Mauk, 1987). The reduction in cytokinin production by the roots, and thereby cytokinin flux up through the xylem into the leaves, may occur later in reproductive development (Noodén, 1980a; Heindl *et al.*, 1982; Chapter 9). For leaves in general and those of soybean in particular, a reduction of mineral influx through the xylem does not seem to be a primary cause of senescence, though it may be part of a preparative process (Noodén, 1980a, 1985).

During monocarpic senescence, the leaves show decreases in a wide range of physiological functions (Noodén, 1980a; Thimann, 1980; Thomas and Stoddart, 1980). These reductions may start right after leaf blade expansion or some time later. They may involve parallel processes that are not tightly coupled rather than a single sequence of changes (Noodén, 1984). Thus, for example, there are differences in the relative timing of the declines in chlorophyll, photosynthesis, and total nitrogen in the leaves of senescing soybean plants under different conditions (Kumura and Naniwa, 1965; Woodward and Rawson, 1976; Mondal *et al.*, 1978; Wittenbach *et al.*, 1980; Okatan *et al.*, 1981; Secor *et al.*, 1983). In any case, one can readily point to the decrease in photosynthesis as an important component of monocarpic senescence. Under most conditions, photosynthesis does not seem to be regulated by stomatal aperature so much as changes within the leaves (Farquhar and Sharkey, 1982); however, there may be circumstances in which the stomata control photosynthesis. The decline in photosynthetic rate seems more closely linked to photosynthetic electron transport than to chlorophyll or photosynthetic enzymes (Sesták, 1963; Adler *et al.*, 1979; Thomas and Stoddart, 1980; Chapter 3). Further effort to pinpoint the metabolic processes responsible for foliar senescence as a component of monocarpic senescence will be greatly aided by a better understanding of the hormonal mediators of the correlative controls.

It is important to note there may be some large differences among species as to when the overall decline in photosynthesis occurs relative to reproductive development. For example, it may not start until later, during podfill in soybean (Kumura and Naniwa, 1967; Dornhoff and Shibles, 1970; Woodward and Rawson, 1976) or during grain ripening in the grass *Poa annua* (Ong and Marshall, 1975). A decrease in photosynthesis may begin at the time of flowering in flax, sugarcane, and wheat (Singh and Lal, 1935). In the cases of oilseed rape *(Brassica napus)* and turnip rape *(B. campestris)*, the leaves senesce before pod growth becomes rapid (Allen *et al.*, 1971; Krogman and Hobbs, 1975). Here, foliar photosynthate is initially stored in the stems and then redistributed to the seeds (Major *et al.*, 1978).

Root assimilation may decline ahead of photosynthesis in the leaves (Noodén, 1980a, 1984). Why? Part of the answer may lie in the changes in translocation of photosynthate, i.e., priority to the reproductive structures at the expense of the roots (Section VI,B), but hormonal controls are probably also involved (Section VII,C).

B. Metabolic Decline in Plants with Reproductive Structures Removed ("Desinked")

As indicated in Section III, B, defruiting may not prevent all of the metabolic declines normally associated with monocarpic senescence even where it prevents or at least markedly postpones death. This raises some important questions about what constitutes senescence and about the role of fruits as control centers.

Some evidence indicates that photosynthetic rate may be regulated by "sink" activity (Herold, 1980). Rapidly growing fruits consume large quantities of assimilates, and they seem to stimulate photosynthesis in a variety of species including soybean, pepper, and barley (Noodén, 1980a; Lauer and Shibles, 1987). Conversely, removal of the fruits in pepper or corn may decrease the photosynthetic rate in the leaves (Hall and Milthorpe, 1978; Christensen *et al.*, 1981). In wheat with developing grains, source-sink manipulations can readily increase or decrease the photosynthetic rate of the existing leaves (King *et al.*, 1967; Rawson *et al.*, 1976). The stimulatory effect of sink demand may also apply to uptake of some minerals by roots

(Kollman *et al.*, 1974; Derman *et al.*, 1978; Noodén and Mauk, 1987). In many monocarpic species, vegetative growth is severely constrained once the plants enter their reproductive phase and cannot be restored by removing the reproductive structures (Section IV), hence vegetative "sinks" may not replace the reproductive "sinks" when the latter are removed. Since assimilatory metabolism, especially photosynthesis, may be coupled with or regulated by consumption of ("demand" for) its products, defruiting could be expected to cause a decline in assimilatory metabolism in monocarpic plants.

Photosynthesis declines during pod development in soybean, and blocking pod development by depodding or male sterility does not prevent this (Woodward and Rawson, 1976; Mondal *et al.*, 1978; Wittenbach, 1982, 1983; Huber *et al.*, 1983; Burke *et al.*, 1984; Crafts-Brandner *et al.*, 1984b,c; Israel *et al.*, 1985; Schweitzer and Harper, 1985a,b). It is possible, however, that the decline of photosynthetic rate in depodded plants is a desinking effect rather than senescence. The effects of depodding on other parameters such as foliar chlorophyll, ribulose-bisphosphate carboxylase, and even death present a somewhat different picture from photosynthesis. Whereas photosynthetic rate represents the functioning of the photosynthetic system, chlorophyll content and the levels of photosynthetic enzymes provide a measure of photosynthetic capacity. Thus, it is possible for photosynthesis to decline without a concomitant drop in the components of capacity. In several cases, foliar chlorophyll (Derman *et al.*, 1978; Mondal *et al.*, 1978; Wittenbach, 1982) and ribulose-bisphosphate carboxylase (Mondal *et al.*, 1978; Schweitzer and Harper, 1985b) do not decline substantially in podless plants, whereas these decrease in numerous other cases (Huber *et al.*, 1983; Wittenbach, 1983; Burke *et al.*, 1984; Crafts-Brandner *et al.*, 1984b,c; Israel *et al.*, 1985). Depodding also prevents the rapid death of soybean plants as long as it is not done too late in pod development and it works even in the field if conditions are favorable (Leopold *et al.*, 1959; Lindoo and Noodén, 1977; Derman *et al.*, 1978; Noodén *et al.*, 1978; Fig. 1), but it does not do so in all the cases cited above in connection with photosynthesis.

Why is there such diversity in the changes in photosynthetic components and even the death of depodded plants? Most of these podless plants showing declines in photosynthetic components and even death are field-grown plants facing adversities at the end of the growing season plus varying degrees of drought and disease. The influence of environmental factors on mature plants is illustrated by the studies on sunflowers where deheading retards many changes in the leaves of greenhouse-grown plants but not field-grown plants (Ho *et al.*, 1987). Similarly, depodding may prevent the decline of foliar chlorophyll in chamber-grown soybean plants (Wittenbach, 1982) but not field-grown plants (Wittenbach, 1983). We (Velasco,

Murray, and Noodén, unpublished data, 1987) find that high humidity (85% RH) retards leaf yellowing in depodded soybean cuttings (explants), compared with low humidity (15% RH). The older, depodded plants appear to be more vulnerable to stress. Decreased stomatal responsiveness with age may be a factor (Raschke, 1979; Farquhar and Sharkey, 1982; Wardle and Short, 1983; Reich, 1984). Perhaps, the depodded plants lose their ability to regenerate from stress damage just as they have lost most of their vegetative growth capacity. Nonuse may be another factor in the decline of photosynthetic components, but there may be still other causes. This discussion is not intended as a critique of the use of field-grown plants, but a plea that the additional factors introduced by field conditions be recognized.

The decrease in photosynthesis and that in chlorophyll or other photosynthetic components may be different phenomena. In depodded plants, photosynthesis may decline due to sink loss, whereas in podded plants, this decrease may be caused by the loss of photosynthetic components. It does not seem right to call the decreased photosynthesis in depodded plants senescence, particularly since it doesn't cause death. In podded plants, the photosynthetic components appear to decline as part of the senescence or at least the senescence syndrome (Chapter 15). They may or may not be lost in depodded plants, but where they are lost, that process seems to be driven stress, even mild stress, rather than the pods.

Another important issue that underlies the observations on depodded plants is whether or not the fruit (specifically the seeds in soybean) control monocarpic senescence. Clearly, the death and the final stages of monocarpic senescence are prevented by depodding in soybean if grown under favorable conditions and before the pods develop too far. Significantly, depodding prevents the collapse of the permeability barrier (dye exclusion) in the leaf cells (Artis *et al.*, 1985), an important terminal event (Chapter 1). Moreover, careful inspection of the graphs (e.g., Burke *et al.*, 1984; Crafts-Brandner *et al.*, 1984b,c) where chlorophyll declines shows that it may level off and hold at a late stage. Other types of studies employing pod-bearing soybean explants also indicate a connection between pod development and leaf senescence (Neumann *et al.*, 1983; Noodén, 1985). For soybean, the best studied case, the final phase of monocarpic senescence seems to be under pod control, and this is consistent with the observation that the pods exert their irreversible influence quite late (Section III,C; see also Noodén, 1985). At the same time, questions can be raised as to whether or not all of the early metabolic decline in fruiting soybean plants is really senescence or really a preparatory phase (Noodén, 1985).

The problems discussed above are not unique to soybean, for other monocarpic plants such as wheat (King *et al.*, 1967; Feller, 1979; Patterson and Brun, 1980), pea (Malik and Berrie, 1977), corn (Crafts-Brandner *et al.*,

1984a), and sunflower (Ho *et al.*, 1987) may undergo changes that are not prevented by defruiting. Moreover, similar sorts of variability in the response to defruiting depending on conditions and genotype have been observed in corn (Crafts-Brandner *et al.*, 1984a).

A lot of confusion and controversy can be avoided if it is recognized that not all metabolic declines represent senescence (see Chapter 1) and that some of the effects of defruiting reflect adjustment to a decreased demand for assimilates. In addition, these observations do challenge the use of photosynthetic rate as a measure of senescence. It may be alright as a measure of the progression of the senescence syndrome in normal plants, but not when the sinks are altered.

VI. PARTITIONING AND REDISTRIBUTION OF ASSIMILATES IN RELATION TO SENESCENCE

A. Nutrient Diversion and Redistribution

One need only look at the drastic decrease or even cessation in vegetative growth concomitant with the rapid increase in reproductive growth to be convinced that a very large change in the distribution of newly assimilated materials (photosynthate and minerals) has occurred. This shift (nutrient diversion) away from the vegetative parts and to the developing fruits has been considered to play a causal role in monocarpic senescence (Noodén and Leopold, 1978; Noodén, 1980a). In addition, nutrients invested in one part of a plant may be redistributed to another part, particularly to the fruit. Certain aspects of partitioning, mobilization, and redistribution are discussed in Chapters 5 and 6. Rather than attempt to summarize all aspects of transport and changes in partitioning of assimilates, here we will focus on three aspects that seem most relevant to whole plant senescence: (1) a shift in the partitioning of photosynthate from the roots to the fruit; (2) competition between the leaves and fruits for mineral nutrients assimilated by the roots; and (3) controls of assimilate movement.

B. Shift in Photosynthate Partitioning during Reproductive Development

An extensive literature (Noodén, 1980a) indicates that ^{14}C-compounds derived from $^{14}C-CO_2$ through photosynthesis are distributed differently during the reproductive phase, with more going to the fruit and less to the vegetative parts. The decrease in root growth during reproductive development (Section IV) implies that the movement of photosynthate to the roots also drops. Direct observations on labeled photosynthate or sucrose show that these assimilates travel mainly to the developing fruit at the expense of the roots in soybean and common bean plants (Hume and Criswell, 1973; Wien *et al.*, 1976). In wheat, field pea, lupine, cowpea, and others; however, this shift is less dramatic (Pate, 1966, 1985; Rawson and Hofstra, 1969; Waters *et al.*, 1980; Noodén, 1980a). Not only is the supply of photosynthate to the roots reduced by a shift in allocation, but that decrease is compounded by a drop in photosynthesis (Section V,B). While a reduction of C flux to the roots may contribute to the decline in root growth and other activities (e.g., N_2 fixation), there is some evidence that these may diminish for reasons other than C deficiency, even in soybean (Sutton, 1983), probably due to hormonal controls (Section VII,C). There can be no doubt that the partitioning of photosynthate usually changes during reproductive development, but its role as a causal factor in monocarpic senescence is less clear (Section VII,F).

C. Competition between the Fruits and Leaves for Mineral Nutrients Assimilated by the Roots

A major aspect of the nutrient diversion explanation for monocarpic senescence is that developing fruits compete with the leaves (divert) for mineral nutrients (and/or essential hormones) coming up through the xylem from the roots. Considering the relative partitioning of water flowing up through the xylem into the leaves compared with the fruit (Zimmerman, 1983), this idea has a weak start. Nonetheless, given the possibility of xylem to phloem transfer (Pate, 1975), this putative competition might take the form of increased transfer of materials from the xylem to the phloem that feeds the fruit. Despite the potential importance of this mechanism, rather little has been done to test it directly. Studies utilizing soybean explants, which are essentially pod-bearing cuttings with a leaf, one or more pods, and a subtending stem segment, show that labeled phosphate and [86]Rb (a K analog) introduced into the xylem tends to partition in proportion to the transpiration stream, the vast majority going directly to the leaf blade (Neumann and Noodén, 1984; Mauk *et al.*, 1985). Both the P and ^{86}Rb are then translocated (redistributed) from the leaf blade to the pods. Another line of study involving ^{14}C-amino acids fed to cut white lupine shoots demonstrated that certain amino acids (e.g., asparagine, glutamine, serine) tend to be redistributed from the leaves or transferred from xylem to phloem, while others (e.g., aspartate, glutamate) are retained in the leaves (McNeil *et al.*, 1979). Thus, the nature of the nitrogenous materials synthesized by the roots may determine their distribution. Although the minerals usually relocate from the leaves to the fruit, the evidence tends to run against the idea that the developing fruits compete directly with the leaves for the supply of mineral nutrients flowing up from the roots through the xylem. Moreover, when isolated oat leaves senesce, the amino acids released are actively transported basipetally, but if they are attached to the plant, they travel down to the roots or perhaps to other growing regions (Thimann et al., 1974). Thus, redistribution may be due to active processes in the source more than competitive action of sinks.

D. Controls of Assimilate Movement

Although the developing fruits play a prominent role in monocarpic senescence and they are very conspicuous sinks, it is not clear that they control assimilate movement directly. The implication that sinks drain the rest of the plant simply by their greater consumption, coupled with some passive mechanism analogous to chemical mass action, is certainly a great oversimplification. Some of the most prominent sinks such as soybean, common bean, and other seeds do not even have a direct symplastic connection with the main compartments that circulate assimilate within the plant (Thorne, 1980, 1985; Patrick and McDonald, 1980). It may be that some nutrients are sent to the fruits from the leaves with some, maybe most, regulation taking place in the leaves. The indirect movement of P and Rb (K) to pods via the leaves in soybean explants is consistent with this idea (Section VI,C). In support of this idea, neither pod dose nor excision of the seeds greatly influences P movement from the leaves to the seeds in the short term (Neumann and Noodén, 1984). Likewise, the leaves of depodded soybean plants continue to export photosynthate, but the export is to the stem rather than the pods (Kollman et al., 1974; Ciha and Brun, 1978).

A wide variety of mechanisms for controlling solute movement have been proposed; we will consider only the few most relevant to monocarpic senescence. First, xylem flux in general could be regulated by stomatal aperture, which may control transpiration. In unstressed plants at least, stomatal resistance does not increase markedly until quite late, after redistribution has progressed quite far and yellowing is about to start (Kumura and Naniwa, 1965; Gee and Federer, 1972; Woodward and Rawson, 1976; Garrison et al., 1984; Noodén, 1985) and, therefore, unlikely to regulate xylem flux as a prelude to monocarpic senescence. Stomatal aperture may still provide a quick mechanism for preventing excessive water loss (Noodén, 1985). Stomatal closure may promote senescence through a more direct influence (Thimann et al., 1982); however, since stomatal closure may actually accompany delayed senescence in the intact plant (see, e.g., Thorne and Koller, 1974; Setter et al., 1980; Noodén, 1985), other factors also must be involved. A second mechanism for regulation of xylem or phloem flux could be the vascular architecture, which may change through formation of new tissues or selective blockages (Noodén, 1980a; Murray *et al.*, 1982; Zimmerman, 1983; Neumann, 1987). The decrease in functional phloem and even xylem due to nonrenewal as a result of diminished vegetative growth (Section IV) would certainly influence transport quantitatively and possibly also influence distribution patterns. Third, the physiological function and strategic placement of transfer cells suggest they could regulate solute partitioning through changes in their locations or in the activity of already differentiated transfer cells (Pate and Gunning, 1972). Fourth, the loading and unloading of the xylem and phloem through routes other than transfer cells may also be important. Hormones (Section VII), in addition to other factors such as pH, other solutes, and turgor, very likely play a key role here as well as in the transfer cells cited above (Pate, 1975; Geiger, 1979; Ho and Baker, 1982; Patrick, 1982, 1986; Thorne, 1985). Fifth, as indicated above (Section VI,C), the partitioning of N could be regulated by the nature of the amino acids formed, and the same could apply to hormones and other compounds. In fact, both cytokinin and the ureides are relatively restricted in their movement (Noodén and Letham, 1984; Thorne, 1985).

E. Nutrient Redistribution

In many, but not all, senescing tissues, limiting nutrients are reclaimed (released and translocated to other parts where they are reutilized). The role of this process in senescence will be considered in the next section; here, we will simply try to describe it and look at its regulation.

The redistribution of mineral nutrients from the leaves to developing fruits, particularly in monocarpic plants, is the most striking example of redistribution, though the redistribution from the leaves to the trunks of trees in autumn or to the underground parts of herbaceous perennials (top senescence) is also quantitatively important (Miller, 1938; Loehwing, 1951; Williams, 1955). Minerals may be recovered from other organs or tissues such as petals (Chapter 1; see also Halevy and Mayak, 1979). Some minerals, as well as photosynthate, may be stored in temporary depots such as the stem, enlarged roots, or other organs (Noodén, 1980a). The so-called mobile elements, e.g., N and P, are redistributed to a greater extent than the less mobile elements such as Ca and Fe, but even Ca may be mobilized to some extent (Miller, 1938; Hocking and Pate, 1977; Marschner, 1983).

Exactly what regulates this redistribution is uncertain. Presumably, redistribution begins with release of the minerals from the tissues where they have been invested. The regulation of the degradative enzymes and their relationship to the disassembly of the metabolic machinery needs to be clarified, particularly in the context of monocarpic senescence. Contrary to expectations, redistribution, even for mobile materials such as P or N, may be inhibited by a deficiency in these elements or promoted by an abundant supply (Noodén, 1980a). Moreover, neither applications of NPK to soybean leaf surfaces (Schreyer and Noodén, 1975; Sesay and Shibles, 1980) nor force-feeding via the xylem (Mauk and Noodén, 1983) prevented losses of these minerals from the leaves. Similarly, foliar applications of urea did not retard chlorophyll loss in corn (Below *et al.*, 1985). In addition, where the redistribution from the leaves to the fruit is blocked by defruiting, the starch (sugar) is exported to the stem instead (Ciha and Brun, 1978) and ribulose-bisphosphate carboxylase is converted to seed storage proteins within the leaves (Franceschi *et al.*, 1983). The redistribution or release of minerals from the leaves of soybean plants is controlled (inhibited) at least in part by the cytokinin flux up through the xylem of soybean plants (Mauk and Noodén, 1983). Clearly, the interplay between the sinks (developing fruits) and the sources (vegetative parts, especially leaves) is more complex than a simple withdrawal.

F. Exhaustion Death: Real or Apparent?

Given the obvious and sometimes massive loss of constituents from the leaves, and their concomitant appearance in the fruit of monocarpic plants (Doflein, 1919; Molisch, 1938), it is quite understandable that monocarpic senescence has been viewed as exhaustion death. Nonetheless, the exhaustion death hypothesis has been questioned (Mothes and Engelbrecht, 1952; Leopold *et al.*, 1959; Mothes, 1960). The fact that monocarpic plants (such as spinach and hemp) bearing only small male flowers senesce even though they do not carry a heavy load of developing seeds, and therefore are not exhausted, created doubts about the exhaustion theory. Indeed, the male plants senesce before the female plants. The observation that removal of the male flowers delayed monocarpic senescence in male spinach plants (Leopold *et al.*, 1959) really should have solidified these reservations. When we (Lindoo and Noodén, 1977; Noodén *et al.*, 1978) found that monocarpic senescence in soybean was independent of pod number (sink size) over a very wide range, it came as a surprise. Subsequently, three lines of evidence based on very different approaches have shown that the nutritional requirements of the developing soybean seeds can be satisfied without sacrificing the plant if the assimilatory capacities are maintained. First, surgical experiments that take advantage of the limited mobility of the senescence signal show that when the plants are modified so that the leaves are not contiguous to the pods, the latter can develop without killing the feeder leaves (Lindoo and Noodén, 1977; Noodén *et al.*, 1978; Noodén, 1980b). For example, these plants might be "Y"-shaped with pods on one branch only or a single axis with the pod cluster three nodes above or below a single leaf. Regardless of the criticisms by Woolhouse (see further discussion below), these experiments do separate seed development and leaf senescence. Furthermore, contrary to Wang and Woolhouse (1982), the pod reduction cited above reduced the seed dry weight and N accumulation roughly proportionally (Noodén et al., 1978). Second, a nonsenescing mutant seems to produce a normal load of pods, (at least under some conditions) without the usual breakdown of the plant's assimilatory apparatus (Abu-Shakra et al., 1978). Third, foliar spray treatments with a combination of auxin and cytokinin can override the senescence signal and prevent monocarpic senescence (Noodén et al., 1979a). From an agronomic viewpoint, this is of special interest, because it suggests that soybean seed yield may not be limited simply by redistribution of the inventory built up in the vegetative parts (Noodén, 1980b, 1984). Whether or not this applies to other species remains to be determined, but it may. Looking back, it can also be seen that the "demand" created by the rapidly growing reproductive structures may actually stimulate assimilation in several species rather than exhaust the plants (Section V,B). Moreover, seed "demand" does not correlate well with monocarpic senescence when species are compared (Sinclair and de Wit, 1975). In some monocarpic plants such as wild rice (Grava and Raisanen, 1978), there is little or no mineral redistribution. Similarly, field bean (*Vicia faba*) shows little redistribution of its foliar N to the fruit (Cooper et al., 1976). In addition, feeding mineral nutrients to the leaves via their surface or through their xylem does not prevent their senescence (Section VI,E). Thus, monocarpic senescence may occur without foliar mineral depletion. Taking advantage of the photoperiod controls of monocarpic senescence in G2 peas independent of pod development, Gianfagna and Davies (1981) have shown that nutrient demand by the seeds does not in itself cause monocarpic senescence.

Several characteristics of the soybean senescence signal (Section III,C) suggest it is not nutrient diversion or withdrawal. First, it is less mobile within the soybean plant than are the nutrients required to support pod (seed) development. Second, the senescence signal is exerted quite late in seed development after most of the dry matter accumulation is finished. In both of these cases, nutrient withdrawal or diversion is needed before pod development takes place, but this does not cause the plant to die. Third, the simplest and clearest evidence against the nutrient withdrawal mechanism comes from experiments in which the petiole phloem is destroyed, as shown in Fig. 12.1. Even though the withdrawal route (the phloem) is blocked, the pods are still able to trigger senescence (yellowing) in the nearest leaf (Noodén and Murray, 1982; see also discussion in Section III,C). The phloem destruction procedure itself does not cause this yellowing, for it does not induce yellowing in the leaves of depodded plants. Likewise, this effect of phloem destruction, combined with the pods, cannot be explained away as an induction of stomatal closure leading to reduced nutrient and cytokinin flux into the leaves (Noodén, 1985).

The interpretations of the behavior of the soybean senescence signal are questioned by Woolhouse (Wang and Woolhouse, 1982; Sexton and Woolhouse, 1984), primarily on the basis of differences in age of the leaves involved and possible modification of xylem flux by treatment effects on R_S. The assertion that age of the leaves is the primary determinant of when the leaves in fruiting soybean plants senesce ignores the well-known fact that the main leaves senesce more or less together in monocarpic senescence in soybean and several other species (Singh and Lal, 1935; Kumura and Naniwa, 1965; Lindoo and Noodén, 1977; Noodén, 1980a; Chapter 1). In fact, progressive senescence seems to come to more or less of a halt; for example, senescence of the lower leaves is retarded unless they are heavily shaded or otherwise stressed. Furthermore, the senescence of excised leaves in pod-bearing explants is determined by the development of the pods, not the age of the leaf (Noodén, 1985). Modification of xylem flux does not account for our observations relating to senescence signal behavior (Section VI,D; see also Noodén, 1985).

In summary, the nutrient deficiency mechanisms (withdrawal and diversion) do not account for monocarpic senescence in soybean, though they could be background factors (Noodén, 1985). Monocarpic senescence has not been studied as extensively in other species as in soybean, yet there are good indications that the nutrient deficiency mechanisms may not provide the full explanation in other species either.

VII. HORMONAL CONTROLS

A. Introduction

Given the highly coordinated nature of monocarpic senescence and the development of the reproductive structures in the whole plant during this period, correlative controls must be major components in the regulation (Section III) of monocarpic senescence. Yet, it is clear that neither the overall pattern of these controls nor the nature of the chemical mediators is well understood. Analysis of the correlative controls is the first step in unraveling the major components of the interactions between parts. By definition, monocarpic senescence is related to development of the reproductive structures (Section II and Chapter 1), so they must be considered in any control scheme. Moreover, since the plant's efforts are directed toward supporting the reproductive structures, it would make sense for these structures to play some role, perhaps a dominant role, in regulating the metabolism of the parts that supply them (Section III,B), but the story is incomplete, and there appear to be important differences between species. Second to understanding the correlative controls is the need to know the timing of the declines in the major metabolic processes in different parts of the plant. For soybean, an effort has been made to begin to assemble the diverse reports into an integrated picture (Noodén, 1984, 1987). Here, the major components (organs) involved are the seeds, which are the control centers, and the leaves, which are the main targets (Section III,B). The influence exerted by the seeds is termed the senescence signal (Section III,C). The root system and the stem must also be considered, even if their roles are only secondary and supporting. Although nutrient fluxes could be important in mediating the influences of these different components on each other, hormones are probably the major regulators (Goodwin *et al.*, 1978; Leopold and Noodén, 1984; Noodén, 1984), but other, still unknown, factors are possible. The subsequent discussion attempts to integrate what we know about these hormonal controls in whole plants plus the limited data relating to monocarpic senescence into a general hormonal regulatory scheme for monocarpic senescence.

B. The Senescence Signal

The senescence signal (Section III,C) has been presumed to be a nutritional phenomenon (Section VI,F). Even though we favor the possibility that the senescence signal is a hormone produced by the fruit (seeds), at least in the soybean, it should be noted that nutritional factors probably are part of the background (Lindoo and Noodén, 1977; Noodén, 1980a, 1985). Presently, the most direct and detailed information regarding the senescence signal is for soybean. Even here, it is incorrect to conclude that the evidence from surgical manipulations shows that the senescence signal is a senescence-promoting hormone (Woolhouse, 1982), only that this is the simplest and best explanation (Noodén, 1980a,b, 1984).

One difficulty with the senescence hormone theory has been the notion that nothing can come out of an active sink such as a growing fruit, but there are many precedents and even direct evidence for materials including hormones coming out of fruits and seeds (Wanner and Bachofen, 1961; Antoszewski and Lis, 1968; Grochowska, 1968a,b, 1974; Bourbouloux and Bonnemain, 1972; Nitsch, 1972; Kriedemann *et al.*, 1976; Tamas *et al.*, 1981, 1985; Gianfagna and Davies, 1983). Another problem has been the difficulty in visualizing the mechanism for outflow from the fruits, but recent work indicates that water may flow out from the fruit (Chaney, 1981;

414   *L. D. Noodén*

Oparka and Gates, 1981; Jenner, 1982; Pate *et al.*, 1985), and outward transport across the seed coat can occur in soybean (Bennett *et al.*, 1984). The studies of Pate and co-workers (Chapter 7) provides the first clear and integrated picture of how this outflow works.

How do known senescence-promoting hormones fit the picture? Ethylene is certainly an important senescence promoter in many tissues (Chapter 8). Although ethylene can promote foliar senescence in some species (Noodén and Leopold, 1978; Chapter 8), it does not seem to play an important role in monocarpic senescence of soybean. Both (1) the limited mobility of the senescence signal (too limited for a gaseous hormone spreading by diffusion) and (2) the inability of the 2% (v/v) CO_2 to delay the monocarpic senescence of soybean significantly (Schreyer and Noodén, 1975; Lindoo and Noodén, 1978) argue against ethylene as the trigger of monocarpic senescence. By contrast, 2% CO_2 dramatically delayed senescence of the soybean flower petals (Schreyer and Noodén, 1975; Lindoo and Noodén, 1978), a tissue whose senescence is generally controlled by ethylene (Mayak and Halevy, 1980; Chapter 8).

Abscisic acid (ABA) seems a much better candidate. ABA has been shown to promote senescence in a wide range of detached leaves (Beevers, 1976; Noodén and Leopold, 1978; Thimann, 1980; Chapter 10); however, like cytokinin, it is often inactive on attached leaves (Noodén and Leopold, 1978; Noodén, 1980b). Foliar ABA treatments do, however, accelerate monocarpic senescence of soybean (Lindoo and Noodén, 1978). Side-stepping the possible role of ABA in autumnal or other patterns of foliar senescence (Noodén and Leopold, 1978; Noodén and Weber, 1978), there are some limited published data that correlate foliar ABA levels with monocarpic senescence and senescence in general (Chapter 10). Using quite different methods of analysis, several groups (Oritani and Yoshida, 1973; Lindoo and Noodén, 1978; Samet and Sinclair, 1980) found that ABA-like activity in the leaves increased during the period preceding visible yellowing when the seeds induce senescence. Our preliminary studies (also using highly purified ABA and gas liquid chromatography with an electron capture detector) probed the relation between foliar ABA levels and senescence in surgically modified soybean plants (L. D. Noodén, unpublished observations). For example, reduction in pod load (50%), which does not alter foliar senescence (leaf yellowing and abscission) kinetics (Noodén *et al.*, 1978), actually produces an increase in foliar ABA. Foliar senescence in plants with only one pod cluster and one leaf (separated by three internodes) is very different, depending on whether the leaf is above the pod cluster or vice versa (Noodén *et al.*, 1978), yet the ABA levels in the leaves are not greatly different. Other inconsistencies remain (Noodén, 1980b); one is that young leaves may contain more ABA than mature, green leaves. Second, complete depodding, which prevents foliar senescence in soybean plants, increases foliar ABA levels (Setter *et al.,* 1980). A third is the failure of foliar ABA applications to induce senescence (i.e., to substitute for pods) of depodded soybeans (Lindoo and Noodén, 1978). High levels of senescence-retarding hormones (e.g., cytokinin), which counteract the ABA in the leaves of younger or depodded plants, could be a cause of these discrepancies.

When injected into the seed cavity of soybean pods, ^{14}C-ABA penetrates the seeds, but only very small amounts move from the injected pods into the target leaves; even during the phase when the seeds induce the senescence of the leaves (Noodén and Obermeyer, 1981). Thus, it appears the ABA may not be the "senescence signal" for monocarpic senescence in soybeans. Still, ABA may play some role in the senescence process, though probably in conjunction with other factors.

Since a variety of natural products, some still unidentified, have been reported to promote senescence (Chapter 10), ABA is not the only candidate for a senescence hormone. These include methyl jasmonate, serine, capillin, capillen, aliphatic alcohols, and fatty acids such as linolenic acid (Chapter 10). The relation of Osborne's (1959) senescence factor to the senescence signal of monocarpic senescence remains to be determined, but this senescence factor may be more of an abscission factor (Chapter 10).

Inasmuch as developing fruits and seeds can release solutes, including hormones, into the plant (see above), it is possible and even likely that the seeds secrete regulatory signals (hormones) into the rest of the plant (Noodén, 1984, 1987). By injecting very high specific activity [3H]acetate into pods on soybean explants, we (Noodén *et al.,* 1987) have demonstrated that ^{3}H-labeled metabolites may travel from the pods to the leaves. More ^{3}H moves from the pods to the leaves at mid and late podfill than at other stages before or after, and this corresponds to the behavior of the senescence signal. Using various labeled compounds introduced into the pea pods by different means (e.g., [14C]CO_2 fixed by the pods or several ^{14}C compounds injected into the pods), Gianfagna and Davies (1983) have observed the transport of labeled substances out of the developing pods to the shoot apices in relation to the induction of apex senescence. Some of this label has been attributed to aromatic amides, but they are not the inducers of apex senescence (Gianfagna and Davies, 1980). The labeled material was not abscisic or phaseic acid and remains unknown. Thus, solutes do move out of the fruits to the vegetative parts, where they probably play regulatory roles, including induction of senescence.

Our (J. Tsuji, M. Schneider and L. D. Noodén, unpublished observations) recent results indicate that soybean seeds excised at the stages when they are known to be exerting the senescence signal produce factors that induce senescence if supplied to excised leaves in a manner similar to the way the senescence signal would be supplied *in vivo* (i.e., through the xylem).

While ABA cannot be offered as a candidate for the senescence signal, a new, yet unknown, hormone seems possible. We now have some direct evidence, as well as indirect evidence, that the soybean senescence signal is a hormone, though one can still invoke a secondary role for nutrient withdrawal and diversion.

C. The Root/Shoot (Leaf) Interaction

The root and shoot systems obviously interact nutritionally; the shoot (leaves) provide photosynthate for the roots and the roots, in turn, supply mineral nutrients to the shoot. There is also evidence that hormones play a role in mediating root–shoot interactions.

The first effort to explain the root–shoot interaction on a hormonal basis was by Sachs (1972), who proposed a positive feedback control involving auxin flowing from the leaves to the roots and cytokinin from the roots to the leaves.

The ability of exogenous auxins to induce adventitious root development has been known for a long time (Thimann, 1935), and the widespread practical use of this knowledge has produced a huge literature (Hartmann and Kester, 1975; Batten and Goodwin, 1978; Goodwin, 1978). Auxin may also stimulate the formation of lateral roots on the main root (Wightman and Thimann, 1980). In contrast to its effect on root initiation; auxin generally inhibits, though sometimes it may promote, root elongation (Batten and Goodwin, 1978; Goodwin, 1978; Pilet and Saugy, 1985).

Where these root-promoting auxins come from in the intact plant is not certain, but since the leaves are known to produce auxin, this seems a likely source (Shoji *et al.*, 1951; Wetmore and Jacobs, 1953; Jacobs, 1979; Addicott, 1982). At least the radioactive label from IAA applied to the leaves is translocated to the roots and apparently also to the fruit (see, e.g., Eschrich, 1968; Morris *et al.*, 1969; Bourbouloux and Bonnemain, 1972, 1979; Morris and Kadir, 1972; Morris *et al.*, 1973; Morris, 1977); however, we do not know anything about the changes in partitioning patterns of IAA (e.g., translocation from the leaves to pods versus roots) during fruiting. Auxin applied to the shoots generally promotes root growth, further supporting the idea that the leaves produce auxin that travels to the roots (McDavid *et al.*, 1972; Goodwin, 1978).

Some data implicate auxin in senescence (Chapter 10), and this includes monocarpic senescence. We know that diffusible auxin activity from leaf blades decreases with age (Shoji *et al.*, 1951; Wetmore and Jacobs, 1953);

indeed, this decrease in downward flux of auxin from the blade probably controls leaf abscission (Noodén and Leopold, 1978; Addicott, 1982). The IAA levels in common bean and soybean leaves decrease as they mature and during early pod development (Roberts and Osborne, 1981; Hein *et al.*, 1984). Depodding does not inhibit this early decline of IAA in soybean leaves (Hein *et al.*, 1984); however, it could prevent further decrease later during the abscission induction period. In many (but not all) species, including soybean, auxin applied to the leaves delays leaf yellowing (Chapter 10), which supports the idea that a decrease in endogenous auxin levels does play a causal role in foliar senescence beyond its effect on abscission. By contrast, the levels of auxin activity in hemp plants appear to rise during leaf yellowing (Conrad, 1962; Chapter 10). Auxin flux in a different direction (from pods to leaves) has been implicated as a factor regulating photosynthesis in beans (Tamas *et al.*, 1981, 1985), but wheat and soybean may be different (King *et al.*, 1967; Noodén and Noodén, 1985).

The continued flux of auxin from the leaf blade is needed to suppress leaf abscission, and therefore any curtailment of this flux would favor abscission and cessation of transport of all materials out of the leaf (Noodén and Leopold, 1978; Jacobs, 1979; Addicott, 1982). A basipetal polar auxin transport system exists in the petiole that connects the leaf blade with the rest of the plant, and this polar transport through the petiole diminishes with age (McCready and Jacobs, 1963; Veen and Jacobs, 1969; Davenport *et al.*, 1980). This would compound the effect of decreased auxin synthesis in decreasing the flux of auxin from the leaf blades. In contrast, an acropetal transport has been proposed for soybean leaves (Hein *et al.*, 1984).

Despite its potential importance, there really is very little information on auxin flux in the whole plant or the influence of fruit development on auxin flux.

While auxin is certainly the best candidate for mediating the influence of the leaves on the roots, it is not the only one. In addition to the photosynthate already mentioned, both thiamine and abscisic acid are also possibilities (Noodén, 1987). In fact, it may be that root development, like many other developmental processes, is regulated by a combination of hormones, and this may provide better control (Leopold and Noodén, 1984). There is some evidence that the leaves are major sources of thiamine and abscisic acid, that these compounds can be translocated from the leaves to the roots, and that they can promote root growth (Audus, 1959; Chin *et al.*, 1969; Yamaguchi and Street, 1977; Goodwin, 1978; Walton, 1980; Watts *et al.*, 1981).

On the other side of Sachs' positive-feedback loop, the cytokinin flux from the roots to the shoots is now well established (Letham, 1978; Van Staden and Davey, 1979; Letham and Palni, 1983; Noodén and Letham, 1986; Chapter 9). The root apices appear to be the major, though probably not the only, sites of cytokinin synthesis in the whole plant. Extensive evidence reviewed in Chapter 9 indicates that cytokinin is a major antisenescence hormone and that maintenance of high cytokinin levels inhibits senescence.

It is now also possible to implicate cytokinin flux from the roots in monocarpic senescence, particularly in soybean (Noodén, 1985; Noodén and Letham, 1986). Because the young root apices are generally more active than older ones in the production of cytokinins and assimilation of mineral nutrients for supply to the foliage and pods, the cessation of root growth seems particularly important (Letham, 1978; Van Staden and Davey, 1979; Noodén, 1980a, 1985). It has, however, been difficult to analyze the role of mineral and cytokinin flux from the roots in regulating foliar senescence and pod development. In general, it does appear that mineral uptake and cytokinin production (Pate and Hocking, 1978; Noodén, 1980a; Heindl et al., 1982; Noodén and Mauk, 1987) decrease during podfill when root growth would also be declining (Shibles et al., 1975; Noodén, 1980a, 1984).

Our (Neumann et al., 1983) recently developed explant system (a cutting with a leaf, one or more pods, and a subtending stem segment) offers opportunities for more direct analysis of the root contribution to pod development and foliar maintenance by substituting defined solutions for the roots. From these experiments it appears that a decrease in the flux of mineral nutrients and cytokinins from the roots up through the xylem is an important factor in senescence of the leaves; however, this is not in itself causal (Neumann et al., 1983; Noodén, 1985). These observations indicate that the pods and not the decreased cytokinin and mineral flux are the principal cause of monocarpic senescence (Noodén, 1985). A decrease in root assimilates is nonetheless an important contributory factor in the early (preparatory) phase of whole plant senescence.

One mechanism proposed for the fruit induction of monocarpic senescence holds that the developing fruits monopolize the supply of cytokinins flowing up from the roots to the leaves, thereby creating a deficiency in the leaves and hence senescence (Noodén, 1980a). The explant system described above can be used to test this idea directly. When ^{3}H derived from [^{3}H]zeatin riboside (ZR) or [^{3}H]zeatin (Z) are supplied as a pulse (1 hour) through the base of an explant at early podfill or just before podfill, relatively little ^{3}H travels to the fruit (2.1% of the soluble ^{3}H at the end of the pulse), and most of that is in the carpels, with very little in the seeds, minute amounts in the seed coats, but no detectable quantities in the embryos. This is not the flux pattern which one would expect if the pods (or the "hungry" seeds) were competing with the leaves for cytokinin fluxing up the stem (Noodén and Letham, 1984, 1986). Furthermore, analysis of the nature of soluble ^{3}H indicates that the ^{3}H-Z and -ZR are rapidly metabolized, so little of the ^{3}H in the pods is still cytokinin. Importantly, this metabolism of Z and

ZR does not seem to change as monocarpic senescence progresses (Noodén and Letham, 1986). The basic regulatory scheme proposed by Sachs (1972) for vegetative plants seems to be applicable to monocarpic senescence; however, more study is required for cytokinin's, and especially auxin's roles. In addition, other hormones will no doubt be added. It seems probable that the roots may maintain shoot (leaf) function through production of more than just cytokinin. In particular, the roots may produce gibberellin, and leaf senescence seems to be regulated by gibberellin, at least in some species (Chapter 10). There is some evidence (Ruddat and Pharis, 1966; Noodén, 1986) that gibberellins could influence monocarpic senescence. For peas, a decline in gibberellin flux from the roots seems to be important in promoting monocarpic senescence (Proebsting *et al.*, 1978). Woolhouse (1982; Sexton and Woolhouse, 1984) has expanded on Sachs' model and attempted to adapt it to whole plant senescence, but, remarkably, almost everything added is at least inconsistent with the literature of that time. For example, the leaves rather than the roots are the main sources of abscisic acid in the whole plant (Walton, 1980), and the fruit do not compete with the leaves for cytokinin flux (Noodén and Lindoo, 1978; Noodén and Letham, 1984, 1986).

VIII. SENESCENCE IN POLYCARPIC PLANTS

A. Introduction

Generally, polycarpic plants decline much more slowly than monocarpic plants, and attrition of the individuals may be spread over a long time (Wangermann, 1965; Wareing and Seth, 1967; Harper, 1977; Touzet, 1985). Another distinction is that monocarpic senescence is generally coupled with the development of the reproductive structures (Section III,B). Polycarpic plants often invest a lesser proportion of their assimilate in their reproductive structures than monocarpic plants (Harper, 1977; Willson, 1983). In at least some polycarpic plants (Pinero *et al.*, 1982), a high reproductive load may decrease longevity. The causes of decline leading to death in polycarpic plants are not clear; nonetheless, some attempt needs to be made to summarize this literature.

The belief that polycarpic plants, especially trees, are endowed with the potential for perpetual life was disputed by Molisch (1938) some time ago. The range of maximum longevities is quite great, and longevity is in fact characteristic of a species (Kanngiesser, 1907, 1909; Molisch, 1938; Tamm, 1948; Altman and Dittmer, 1962; Wangermann, 1965; Kozlowski, 1971; Harper, 1977; Ogden, 1978; Table 12.1). This suggests genetic determination of life span, but longevity of polycarpic plants could also be determined

TABLE 12.1
Maximal Life Spans of Various Polycarpic Plants[a]

Species	Maximal age (years)
Bristlecone pine (Pinus aristata)	4,600
Giant sequoia (Sequoia gigantea)	3,200
Huon pine (Dacrydium franklinii)	2,200+
Common juniper (Juniperus communis)	2,000
Stone pine (Pinus cembra)	1,200
Queensland kauri (Agathis microstachya)	1,060
European beech (Fagus sylvatica)	600–930
Olive (Olea europaea)	700
Scots pine (Pinus silvestris)	500
Pear (Pyrus communis)	300
Black walnut (Juglans nigra)	250
European ash (Fraxinus excelsior)	250
Apple (Pyrus malus)	200
English ivy (Hedera helix)	200
Arctic willow (Salix arctica)	130
Flowering dogwood (Cornus florida)	125
European white birch (Betula verrucosa)	120
Quaking aspen (Populus tremuloides) (ramet)	100
European grape (Vitis vinifera)	80–100
European cyclamen (Cyclamen europaeum) (tuber)	60
Scotch heather (Calluna vulgaris)	42
Myrtle whortleberry (Vaccinium myrtillus)	28
Spring heath (Erica carnea)	21
European elder (Sambucus racemosus)	20
Eurasian solomon seal (Polygonatum multiflorum) (root stock)	16–17
Scandinavian thyme (Thymus chamaedrys)	14
Crossleaf heather (Erica tetralix)	10
Broadleaf solomon seal (Polygonatum latifolium) (root stock)	8
Yellow wood anemone (Anemone ranunculoides) (root stock)	7

[a]It should be noted that some of the earlier estimates of great longevity in woody species are not accurate and therefore have been omitted here. From Molisch (1938), Altman and Dittmer (1962), Wangermann (1965), and Ogden (1978). Sources are listed therein.

more by increased vulnerability than by a distinctive internally pro-grammed degeneration, as in many monocarpic plants.

While it may be true that cells excised from various parts of a plant may be capable of growing indefinitely in axenic culture (Chapter 1), the literature on longevity of vegetatively propagated parts can be misleading. Particu-larly, in the case of excised roots, one gets the impression they are capable of immortality and indefinite growth, but this is not strictly true. The original papers (Street, 1967) indicate that in tomato the subterminal apices must be excised and subcultured. In that case, individual meristems require periodic replacement in order to sustain overall growth of the organ. In any case, vegetatively propagated plants do appear to be genetically stable and usually retain their vigor over very long periods (Bijhower, 1931; Molisch, 1938; Crocker, 1939; Sax, 1962). Thus, passage through a sexual reproductive phase or sexual renewal is not necessary in most species if the plants are propagated artificially by vegetative means.

Because plants have such a great capacity for continuing their growth and renewing their parts, they may be viewed as *metapopulations* (White, 1979). Nonetheless, most eventually slip behind in this renewal process to the point where they die. Even if the individual parts are capable of indefinite growth when separated from the organism (Sax, 1962; Wangermann, 1965; Harper, 1977), under natural conditions, they die along with the organism of which they are a part (Chapter 1; see also Noodén, 1980a). Clonal growth, however, is a different matter; here, the parts establish enough independence to continue growing after the parent structures have died (Section VIII,B). The nature of the individual organism differs in naturally propagated, clonal species and in nonclonal species, yet a clear distinction is difficult. That is, the ramet rather than the genet of a clonal organism may be the best analog of a nonclonal organism.

Given the evidence that longevity is a characteristic of the species, at least for nonclonal species, and is genetically determined, it has been inferred that some sort of time-keeping mechanism limits longevity. Usually, the timekeeper can be reset and complete rejuvenation is affected by passage through a sexual cycle (Weber, 1919; Wangermann, 1965). While clonal (asexually reproducing) species may continue with undiminished vigor, this does not always occur (Lansing effect). Just as in rotifers, where the asexual progeny from older individuals display less vigor (Lansing, 1945), a few plant species (e.g., duckweed) produce less vigorous asexual offspring as the clone becomes older (Sax, 1962; Wangermann, 1965). Perhaps this reflects an incomplete resetting of a timekeeper during asexual reproduction, but it could also be due to accumulation of low-grade pathogens (see Section VIII,B). In any case, it is clear that the developmental program must run for this timekeeper to proceed. For example, seeds or other dormant structures placed in storage may greatly outlive their counterparts that were germinated right away (Molisch, 1938). These stored seeds do, however, gradually lose their viability, but this seems to be a different process (Chapters 13 and 14). While passage through a sexual cycle may be needed to rejuvenate most species, the long-lived clones described below also suggest that mitosis alone may provide enough cellular renewal to permit maintenance of the plant's vigor.

The ability of environmental adversities and nutritional deprivations to extend life raises some interesting questions. Are organisms metabolic integrators? Does the timekeeper referred to above measure the amount of metabolism over time so that the organism's lifetime metabolism is about the same even if it is prolonged, as in Pearl's (1928) rate of living hypothesis? It can be stated, however, that this type of mechanism does not operate in monocarpic organisms where interference with reproductive development may greatly extend life and even total growth of the individual, which means that total metabolism must also be increased (Section IV).

B. Clonal Growth

Some naturally propagated clones, such as that of the creosote bush (Vasek, 1980), seem to be capable of very long lives, perhaps indefinite or as long as the individual plant's environment is compatible (Table 12.2; see also Cook, 1983). While the records for clones propagated by humans do not extend as far back in time as the naturally propagated clones appear to, they seem capable of indefinite propagation, retaining both vigor and their phenotypic identity (Möbius, 1897; Sax, 1962; Harper, 1977; Willson, 1983; Noodén and Thompson, 1985). Nonetheless, some human-propagated clones, for example sugarcane and raspberry, may degenerate, but this seems to be due to disease (Bijhower, 1931; Crocker, 1939; Trippi and Montaldi, 1960; Trippi, 1980). The key to clonal growth lies in continued vegetative growth and renewal of the assimilatory organs; this is illustrated by the photoperiod conversion of indeterminate vegetative growth to monocarpic senescence with cessation of vegetative growth in the scarlet pimpernel (Trippi and Brulfert, 1973a,b).

C. Causes of Decline in Polycarpic Plants

A wide range of interesting mechanisms have been invoked as endogenous causes of degeneration in polycarpic plants (Westing, 1964; Kozlowski, 1971; Borchert, 1976; Clark, 1983; Zelawski, 1980; Touzet, 1985), but the problem is not easily resolved because of the long time covered by the processes leading to death in most polycarpic plants, especially woody plants, and, possibly, because several factors are involved.

Although exogenous factors may terminate the life of these organisms, disasters and adverse environmental conditions may not be the most important determinants of longevity. Once the seedling mortality phase is past, the survivorship patterns for the woody plants seems different from that expected for limitation by random disasters (Szabo, 1931; Leopold, 1961; Wangermann, 1965; Harper, 1977; Cook, 1979). Moreover, mild adversity or deprivation may prolong life (Noodén, 1980a). For example, bristlecone pines reach their maximum longevity under harsher conditions (Schulman, 1954; Wangermann, 1965), duckweeds live longer when their mineral nutrient supply is suboptimal (Wangermann, 1965), bonsai live a

TABLE 12.2

Long-lived Plant Clones

Species	Estimated age (years)	Size	Mode of propagation	Reference
Huckleberry (*Gaylussacia brachycerium*)	13,000+	1,980 m	Rhizome	Wherry (1972)
Creosote (*Larrea tridentata*)	11,000+	8 m	Basal branching	Vasek (1980)
Quaking aspen (*Populus tremuloides*)	10,000+	81 ha	Root buds	Kemperman and Barnes (1976)
Bracken (*Pteridium aquilinum*)	1,400	489 m	Rhizome	Oinonen (1967a)
Velvet grass (*Holcus mollis*)	1,000+	880 m	Tillering	Harberd (1967)
Sheep fescue (*Festuca ovina*)	1,000+	8 m	Tillering	Harberd (1962)
Red fescue (*Festuca rubra*)	1,000+	220 m	Tillering	Harberd (1961)
Ground pine (*Lycopodium complanatum*)	850	250 m	Rhizome	Oinonen (1967b)
Lily of the valley (*Convallaria majalis*)	670+	83 m	Rhizome	Oinonen (1969)
Reed grass (*Calamagrostis epigeios*)	400+	50 m	Rhizome	Oinonen (1969)
Black spruce (*Picea mariana*)	330+	14 m	Layering	Legere and Payette (1981)

424	L. D. Noodén

very long time, at least as long as a normal plant, in spite of root pruning and other restrictions (Young, 1985), and continuous pruning (hedging) seems to maintain vegetative vigor (Touzet, 1985). These data argue against the "wear and tear" (Abnutzung) theories on what limits longevity.

The combination of various rootstocks and shoots through grafting shows that genetic makeup of the root systems may be a more important determinant than the shoot (Molisch, 1938). For example, *Pistacia vera* has a maximum age of about 150 years, but this can be extended by grafting onto *P. terebinthus* stocks or shortened on *P. lentiscus.* Similarly, aged, declining scions can be rejuvenated by grafting onto vigorous seedling stocks (Wareing and Seth, 1967). Thus, the relative importance of the root system for determination of longevity in polycarpic plants differs from monocarpic plants (Section III,B).

Given the decrease in growth rate as polycarpic plants get older, it is not surprising that many of the early efforts to explain the decline of polycarpic plants have centered around the overall decrease in meristematic activity as polycarpic plants age (Heath, 1957; Wangermann, 1965). As suggested in Section VIII,A, a decrease in the renewal of assimilatory organs seems central to this overall decline. The gradual reduction of rooting ability of excised parts (propagation activity) is a common feature in aging and senescing plants (Bijhower, 1931; Passeker, 1941; Martin, 1952; Trippi and Brulfert, 1973b). Conversely, clones may survive because they can renew or replace their parts, in particular their assimilatory organs (Section VIII,B). Still, the precise nature of this reduction in growth is difficult to pinpoint, and there has even been some disagreement over whether or not meristems themselves age or simply are less active as a result of other changes in the whole plant (Wangermann, 1965). In any case, the decrease in vegetative growth must contribute to the decline of the plant; however, the case of root growth discussed in Section VIII,A suggests meristems may not be limitless.

The accrual of genetic lesions does not cause the decline of polycarpic organisms as it does in seeds (Chapter 14), for individual parts can be rejuvenated by excision and the phenotypic characters are fairly stable (Sections VIII,A and B). In growing plants, the cells with aberrant chromosomes are gradually eliminated (Roos, 1982).

Another group of suggestions to explain the decline of polycarpic plants centers around nutritional and transport problems. Aging trees may photosynthesize less, even if their total leaf area is not greatly reduced (Möller *et al.,* 1954; Clark, 1983). A lower net assimilation rate due to decreased assimilation and a greater mass of dependent tissue (respiratory burden) may contribute to the demise of some polycarpic plants (Kershaw, 1964). Another idea with evidence pro and con holds that the small veinlets (and presumably the active vascular tissue) decreases relative to photosynthetic tissues in the leaves of older plants (Crocker, 1939). Failure of the transport function in the sapwood also seems very important (Zimmerman, 1983). Although breakage (filling with gas) of water columns in the xylem must be very important in the failure of the xylem, gums, phenolics, and other materials are deposited in the wood and may contribute to xylem failure. If the amount of functioning xylem decreases because xylem failure exceeds xylem replacement, then, of course, transport from the roots into the stem and leaves will decrease. Ultimately, the volume of xylem transport could limit movement of water, mineral nutrients, cytokinins, and other root metabolites into the shoot (Went, 1942; Kozlowski, 1971). Another suggestion (Maggs, 1964) holds that the distances between shoot apices and roots in mature woody plants are too great to allow efficient transport between these parts and that causes a decline in growth. This general idea has also been invoked for monocarpic plants, but there is evidence against it in the soybean (Section IV); however, the distances involved are smaller. Still another suggestion envisions increased numbers of buds and branches, causing more competition for the available nutrients in mature trees (Moorby and Wareing, 1963).

An opposite variation of the nutrient deficiency ideas outlined above is that decline is caused by accumulation of minerals such as calcium salts and silicic acid (Molisch, 1938), and presumably other toxic accumulations could occur.

While all of the factors listed above could cause death by altering vulnerability to external agents, some characteristics clearly work that way. Decay of heartwood is a visibly important contributor to the demise of individual woody plants (Molisch, 1938; Wareing and Seth, 1967). Thus, effective healing mechanisms that prevent invasion of wood-rotting microbes (Shigo, 1984) could greatly increase longevity. Similarly, resistance to decay or fire could extend longevity (Westing, 1964). The changes in wood chemistry (resistance to decay) reported for bristlecone pine may contribute to longevity by protecting heartwood in that species, but changes in growth form also seem important (LaMarche, 1969; Fritts, 1976).

The causal mechanisms for the decline leading to death in polycarpic plants are simply not clear, but, hopefully, the problem will receive a more sustained and systematic analysis.

D. Do Polycarpic Plants Senesce?

Of course, the leaves and other parts of polycarpic plants senesce, but it is less certain that the degeneration leading to the death of polycarpic plants is really senescence (Chapter 1). As indicated above, the survivorship patterns for polycarpic plants do not seem to follow the expectations for longevity determined simply by random external events. Moreover, longevity seems to be genetically determined, which suggests endogenous controls, but it could just be vulnerability that is determined. Some of the explanations being applied to animals should be considered for polycarpic plants, especially antagonistic pleiotropy, which holds that senescence is due to accumulated genes that exert beneficial effects early in the life of an organism but deleterious effects later (Rose and Service, 1985).

Once an organism's vegetative growth diminishes, it begins to degenerate and lose its assimilatory capacity. The decline in height and/or total living matter may mark senescence (Borchert, 1976; Touzet, 1985). It is reasonable to expect that these declines may eventually cause death, even if they do so by increasing vulnerability to external agents. Thus, many of the characteristics of senescence are present. At this time, there simply are not enough data to say whether the apparent senescence of polycarpic plants resembles that of monocarpic plants, with the following obvious exception. Whereas monocarpic senescence is often regulated by the developing reproductive structures, this seems not to be the case in polycarpic plants. Although it is not absolutely clear that there is polycarpic senescence, it seems a useful term at least for purposes of discussing the terminal decline in polycarpic plants.

IX. CONCLUSIONS

Even in monocarpic plants where organismal senescence is generally quite obvious, many very basic questions have incomplete or even no answers. To some extent, these are questions that pertain to senescence in general, such as, "What are the central processes in senescence?" and this problem is considered in Chapter 15. However, there are also some questions that apply more to whole plants; these concern the interrelations between parts and the integration of their activities. The greatest need here is to relate studies on individual parts or processes to what is going on in the rest of the organism (Noodén, 1980a, 1984). For example, in the case of monocarpic senescence in soybean, pod development is a useful reference (Noodén, 1984). Often, changes in individual processes seem important in organismal senescence, but no data exist to make this connection. Care must also be taken that changes observed in detached organs represent events that occur in the intact organism (see Chapter 1). Probably, some studies will have to be repeated specifically in the context of the whole plant.

Rather than emphasize the differences among species, it seems more productive to try to piece together data on the unifying features of senescing whole plants while noting differences as they arise. It appears that monocarpic senescence may be viewed in terms of a preparatory and a final phase (Noodén, 1984, 1985). The former involves a decline or even cessation of vegetative growth that renews the assimilatory organs and other tissues. Decreased mineral uptake and cytokinin production by the roots may also be important components of the preparatory phase. Although some mineral redistribution and decline in the assimilatory activities such as photosynthesis may occur early in the existing organs, the massive decrease in these activities and the major redistribution of minerals invested in this metabolic machinery seems to be part of the final phase.

ACKNOWLEDGMENT

Thanks are due to Professor K. V. Thimann for helpful suggestions concerning this chapter.

REFERENCES

Abu-Shakra, S. S., Phillips, D. A., and Huffaker, R. C. (1978). Nitrogen fixation and delayed leaf senescence in soybeans. *Science* **199**, 973–975.

Acock, B., Reddy, V. R., Whisler, F. D., Baker, D. N., Mckinion, J. M., Hodges, H. F., and Boote, K. J. (1983). "The Soybean Crop Simulator Glycim. Model Documentation 1982." USDA, ARS, Crop Simul. Res. Unit, Miss. Agric. For. Exp. Stn., Mississippi State Univ., Mississippi State, Mississippi.

Addicott, F. T. (1982). "Abscission." Univ. of California Press, Berkeley.

Adler, K., Brecht, E., Meister, A., Schmidt, O., and Süss, K.-H. (1980). Die Chloroplasten-thylakoid-membran: Biogenese, pigmentorganisation, Protein-funktionsbeziehungen und Degeneration während der Seneszenz. Eine Übersicht. *Kulturpflanze* **27**, 13–48.

Allen, E. J., Morgan, D. G., and Ridgmman, W. J. (1971). A physiological analysis of the growth of oilseed rape. *J. Agric. Sci.* **77**, 339–341.

Allison, J. C. S., and Weinmann, H. (1970). Effect of the absence of the developing grain on carbohydrate content and senescence of maize leaves. *Plant Physiol.* **46**, 435–436.

Altman, P. L., and Dittmer, D. S. (1962). "Growth, Including Reproduction and Morphological Development." Fed. Am. Soc. Exp. Biol., Washington, D. C.

Antoszewski, R., and Lis, E. (1968). Translocation of some radioactive compounds from the strawberry receptacle to the mother plant. *Bull. Acad. Pol. Sci.* **16**, 443–446.

Artis, D. E., Miksche, J. P., and Dhillon, S. S. (1985). DNA, RNA, and protein comparisons between nodulated and non-nodulated male-sterile and male-fertile genotypes of soybean (*Glycine max* L.). *Am. J. Bot.* **72**, 560–567.

Audus, L. J. (1959). "Plant Growth Substances." Wiley (Interscience), New York.

Batten, D. J., and Goodwin, P. B. (1978). Phytohormones and the induction of adventitious roots. *In* "Phytohormones and Related Compounds: A Comprehensive Treatise" (D. S. Letham, P. B. Goodwin, and T. J. V. Higgins, eds.), Vol. 2, pp. 137–145. Elsevier/North-Holland, Amsterdam.

Beevers, L. (1976). Senescence. *In* "Plant Biochemistry" (J. Bonner and J. E. Varner, eds.), 3rd Ed., pp. 771–794. Academic Press, New York.

Below, F. E., Crafts-Brandner, S. J., and Hageman, R. H. (1985). Effect of foliar applications of urea on accelerated senescence of maize induced by ear removal. *Plant Physiol.* **79**, 1077–1079.

428   L. D. Noodén

Benner, J. L., and Noodén, L. D. (1984). Translocation of photosynthate from soybean leaves to the pods during senescence. *Biochem. Physiol. Pflanzen* **179**, 269–275.

Bennett, A. B., Sweger, B. L., and Spanswick, R. M. (1984). Sink to source translocation in soybean. *Plant Physiol.* **74**, 434–436.

Bijhower, A. P. C. (1931). Old and new standpoints on senile degeneration. *J. Hortic. Sci.* **2**, 122–130.

Borchert, R. (1976). The concept of juvenility in woody plants. *Acta. Hortic.* **56**, 21–36.

Bourbouloux, A., and Bonnemain, J. L. (1972). Transport de l'auxine-^{14}C en provenance de jeunes gousses de *Vicia faba* L. *Planta* **115**, 161–172.

Bourbouloux, A., and Bonnemain, J. L. (1979). The different components of the movement and the areas of retention of labelled molecules after application of [^{3}H]-indolylacetic acid to the apical bud of *Vicia faba*. *Physiol. Plant.* **47**, 260–268.

Braun, A. (1851). "Betrachtungen Über die Erscheinung der Verjüngung in der Natur." Engelmann, Leipzig.

Burke, J. J., Kalt-Torres, W., Swafford, J. R., Burton, J. W., and Wilson, R. F. (1984). Studies on genetic male-sterile soybeans. III. The initiation of monocarpic senescence. *Plant Physiol.* **75**, 1058–1063.

Chaney, W. R. (1981). Sources of water. *In* "Water Deficits and Plant Growth" (T. T. Kozlowski, ed.), Vol. 2, pp. 1–47. Academic Press, New York.

Chin, T., Meyer, M. M., Jr., and Beevers, L. (1969). Abscisic acid-stimulated rooting of stem cuttings. *Planta* **88**, 192–196.

Christensen, L. E., Below, F. E., and Hageman, R. H. (1981). The effects of ear removal on senescence and metabolism of maize. *Plant Physiol.* **68**, 1180–1185.

Ciha, A. J., and Brun, W. A. (1978). Effect of pod removal on nonstructural carbohydrate concentration in soybean tissue. *Crop Sci.* **18**, 773–776.

Clark, J. R. (1983). Age-related changes in trees. *J. Arboric.* **9**, 201–205.

Conrad, K. (1962). Über geschlechtsgebundene Unterschiede im Wüchsstoffgehalt männlicher und weiblicher Hanfpflanzen. *Flora (Jena)* **152**, 68–73.

Cook, R. E. (1979). Patterns of juvenile mortality and recruitment in plants. *In* "Topics in Plant Population Biology" (O. T. Solbrig, S. Jain, G. B. Johnson, and P. H. Raven, eds.), pp. 207–231. Columbia Univ. Press, New York.

Cook, R. E. (1983). Clonal plant populations. *Am. Sci.* **71**, 244–253.

Cooper, D. R., Hill-Cottingham, D. G., and Lloyd-Jones, C. P. (1976). Absorption and redistribution of nitrogen during growth and development of field bean, *Vicia faba*. *Physiol. Plant.* **38**, 313–318.

Crafts-Brandner, S. J., Below, F. E., Harper, J. E., and Hageman, R. H. (1984a). Differential senescence of maize hybrids following ear removal. I. Whole plant. *Plant Physiol.* **74**, 360–367.

Crafts-Brandner, S. J., Below, F. E., Harper, J. E., and Hageman, R. H. (1984b). Effects of pod removal on metabolism and senescence of nodulating and nonnodulating soybean isolines. I. Metabolic constituents. *Plant Physiol.* **75**, 311–317.

Crafts-Brandner, S. J., Below, F. E., Harper, J. E., and Hageman, R. H. (1984c). Effects of pod removal on metabolism and senescence of nodulating and nonnodulating soybean isolines. II. Enzymes and chlorophyll. *Plant Physiol.* **75**, 318–322.

Crocker, W. (1939). Ageing in plants. *In* "E. V. Cowdry, Problems of Ageing," 1st Ed., pp. 1–31. Williams & Wilkins, Baltimore, Maryland.

Curry, R. B., Meyer, G. E., Streeter, J. G., and Mederski, H. J. (1980). Simulation of the vegetative and reproductive growth of soybeans. *In* "World Soybean Research Conference II: Proceedings" (F. T. Corbin, ed.), pp. 557–569. Westview Press, Boulder, Colorado.

Curth, P. (1959). Vegetative Zuckerrüben im sechsten Vegetationsjahr. *Zuchter* **29**, 374–375.

Curtis, O. F., and Clark, D. G. (1950). "An introduction to Plant Physiology." McGraw-Hill, New York.

Davenport T. L., Morgan, P. W., and Jordan, W. R. (1980). Reduction of auxin transport capacity with age and internal water deficits in cotton petioles. Plant Physiol. 65, 1023–1025.

Day, W., and Atkin, R. K. eds. (1985). "Wheat Growth and Modelling." Plenum, New York.

Denholm, J. V. (1975). Necessary condition for maximum yield in a senescing two-phase plant. *J. Theor. Biol.* 52, 251–254.

Derman, B. D., Rupp, D. C., and Noodén, L. D. (1978). Mineral distribution in relation to fruit development and monocarpic senescence in Anoka soybeans. *Am. J. Bot.* 65, 205–213.

Doflein, F. (1919). "Das Problem des Todes und der Unsterblichkeit bei den Pflanzen und Tieren." Cited in Molisch (1938).

Dornhoff, G. M., and Shibles, R. M. (1970). Varietal differences in net photosynthesis of soybean leaves. *Crop Sci.* 10, 42–45.

Eschrich, W. (1968). Translokation radioaktiv markierter indolyl-3-essigsäure in Siebrohren von *Vicia faba*. *Planta* 78, 144–157.

Evans, G. C. (1972). "The Quantitative Analysis of Plant Growth." Blackwell, Oxford.

Farquhar, G. D., and Sharkey, T. D. (1982). Stomatal conductance and photosynthesis. *Annu. Rev. Plant Physiol.* 33, 317–345.

Fehr, W. R., and Caviness, C. E. (1977). "Stages of Soybean Development," Spec. Rep. 80. Coop Ext. Serv., Iowa State Univ., Ames.

Feller, U. (1979). Effect of changed source/sink relations on proteolytic activity and on nitrogen mobilization in field-grown wheat (*Triticum aestivum* L.). *Plant Cell Physiol.* 20, 1577–1583.

Franceschi, V. R., Wittenbach, V. A., and Giaquinta, R. T. (1983). Paraveinal mesophyll of soybean leaves in relation to assimilate transfer and compartmentation. III. Immunohistochemical localization of specific glycopeptides in the vacuole after depodding. *Plant Physiol.* 72, 586–589.

Fritts, M. C. (1976). "Tree Rings and Climate." Academic Press, New York.

Garrison, F. R., Brinker, A. M., and Noodén, L. D. (1984). Relative activities of xylem-supplied cytokinins in retarding soybean leaf senescence and sustaining pod development. *Plant Cell Physiol.* 25, 213–224.

Gee, G. W., and Federer, C. A. (1972). Stomatal resistance during senescence of hardwood leaves. *Water Resour. Res.* 8, 1456–1460.

Geiger, D. R. (1979). Control of partitioning and export of carbon in leaves of higher plants. *Bot. Gaz.* 140, 241–248.

Gianfagna, T. J., and Davies, P. J. (1980). N-benzoylaspartate and N-phenylacetylaspartate from pea seeds. *Phytochemistry* 19, 959–961.

Gianfagna, T. J., and Davies, P. J. (1981). The relationship between fruit growth and apical senescence in the G2 line of peas. *Planta* 152, 356–364.

Gianfagna, T. J., and Davies, P. J. (1983). The transport of substances out of developing fruits in relation to the induction of apical senescence in *Pisum sativum* line. *Physiol. Plant.* 59, 676–689.

Golnow, B. I., and Letham. D. S. (1978). Root–shoot interactions. *In* "Phytohormones and Related Compounds: A Comprehensive Treatise" (D. S. Letham, P. B. Goodwin, and T. J. V. Higgins, eds.), Vol. 2, pp. 218–245. Elsevier/North-Holland, Amsterdam.

Goodwin, P. B. (1978). Phytohormones and growth and development of organs of the vegetative plant. *In* "Phytohormones and Related Compounds: A Comprehensive Treatise" (D. S. Letham, P. B. Goodwin, and T. J. V. Higgins, eds.), Vol. 2, pp. 31–173. Elsevier/North-Holland, Amsterdam.

Goodwin, P. B., Gollnow, B. I., and Letham, D. S. (1978). Phytohormones and growth correlations. In "Phytohormones and Related Compounds: A Comprehensive Treatise" (D. S. Letham, P. B. Goodwin, and T. J. V. Higgins, eds.), Vol. 2, pp. 215–249. Elsevier/North-Holland, Amsterdam.

Grava, J., and Raisanen, A. K. (1978). Growth and nutrient accumulation and distribution in wild rice. *Agron. J.* **70**, 1077–1081.

Grochowska, M. J. (1968a). Translocation of indole-3-acetic acid-2-^{14}C injected into seeds of five-week old apple fruits. *Bull. Acad. Pol. Sci.* **16**, 577–580.

Grochowska, M. J. (1968b). The influence of growth regulators inserted into apple fruitlets on flower bud initiation. *Bull. Acad. Pol. Sci.* **16**, 581–586.

Grochowska, M. J. (1974). The free movement of ^{14}C-labelled organic compounds from intact apple seeds to growing fruitlets and shoots. *Biol. Plant.* **16**, 194–198.

Guiamet, J. J., and Nakayama, F. (1984). Transmission of the long-day effects upon reproductive growth and senescence in forked soybean plants. *Phyton (Buenos Aires)* **44**, 37–42.

Halevy, A. H., and Mayak, S. (1979). Senescence and postharvest physiology of cut flowers, part 1. *Hortic. Rev.* **1**, 204–236.

Hall, A. J., and Milthorpe, F. L. (1978). Assimilate source-sink relationships in *Capsicum annuum* L. III. The effects of fruit excision on photosynthesis and leaf and stem carbohydrates. *Aust. J. Plant Physiol.* **5**, 1–13.

Harberd, D. J. (1961). Observations on population structure and longevity of *Festuca rubra* L. *New Phytol.* **60**, 184–206.

Harberd, D. J. (1962). Some observations on natural clones in *Festuca ovina. New Phytol.* **61**, 85–100.

Harberd, D. J. (1967). Observations on natural clones of *Holcus mollis. New Phytol.* **66**, 401–408.

Harper, J. E. (1971). Seasonal nutrient uptake and accumulation patterns in soybeans. *Crop Sci.* **11**, 347–350.

Harper, J. L. (1977). "Population Biology of Plants." Academic Press, London.

Hartmann, H. T., and Kester, D. E. (1975). "Plant Propagation. Principles and Practices." Prentice-Hall, Engelwood Cliffs, New Jersey.

Heath, O. V. S. (1957). Ageing in higher plants. *Symp. Inst. Biol.* No. 6, 9–20.

Hein, M. B., Brenner, M. L., and Brun, W. A. (1984). Effects of pod removal on the transport and accumulation of abscisic acid and indole-3-acetic acid in soybean leaves. *Plant Physiol.* **76**, 955–958.

Heindl, J. C., Carlson, D. R., Brun, W. A., and Brenner, M. L. (1982). Onto-genetic variation of four cytokinins in soybean root pressure exudate. *Plant Physiol.* **70**, 1619–1625.

Herold, A. (1980). Regulation of photosynthesis by sink activity—the missing link. *New Phytol.* **86**, 131–144.

Highkin, H. R., and Hanson, J. B. (1954). Possible interaction between light–dark cycles and endogenous daily rhythms on the growth of tomato plants. *Plant Physiol.* **29**, 301–302.

Hildebrand, F. (1882). Die Lebensdauer and Vegetationsweise der Pflanzen, ihre Ursachen und ihre Entwicklung. *Bot. Jahrb.* **2**, 51–135.

Ho, I., Below, F. E., and Hageman, R. H. (1987). Effect of head removal on leaf senescence of sunflower. *Plant Physiol.* **83**, 844–848.

Ho, L. C., and Baker, D. A. (1982). Regulation of loading and unloading in long distance transport systems. *Physiol. Plant.* **56**, 225–230.

Hocking, P. J., and Pate, J. S. (1977). Mobilization of minerals to developing seeds of legumes. *Ann. Bot.* **41**, 1259–1278.

Huber, S. C., Wilson, R. F., and Burton, J. W. (1983). Studies on genetic male-sterile soybeans. II. Effect of nodulation on photosynthesis and carbon partitioning in leaves. *Plant Physiol.* **73**, 713–717.

Hume, D. J., and Criswell, J. G. (1973). Distribution and utilization of ¹⁴C-labelled assimilates in soybeans. *Crop Sci.* **13**, 519–542.

Imsande, J., and Ralston, E. J. (1982). Dinitrogen fixation in male sterile soybeans. *Plant Physiol.* **69**, 745–746.

Israel, D. W., Burton, J. W., and Wilson, R. F. (1985). Studies on genetic male-sterile soybeans IV. Effect on male sterility and source of nitrogen nutrition on accumulation, partitioning and transport of nitrogen. *Plant Physiol.* **78**, 762–767.

Jackson, B. D. (1953). "A Glossary of Botanic Terms," 4th Ed. Duckworth, London.

Jacobs, W. P. (1979). "Plant Hormones and Plant Development." Cambridge Univ. Press, London and New York.

Jenner, C. F. (1982). Movement of water and mass transfer into developing grains of wheat. *Aust. J. Plant Physiol.* **9**, 69–82.

Johnson, G. W. (1862). "Science and Practice of Gardening." London.

Kanngiesser, F. (1907). Über Lebensdauer der Sträucher. *Flora (Jena)* **97**, 401–420.

Kanngiesser, F. (1909). Zur Lebensdauer der Holzpflanzen. *Flora (Jena)* **99**, 414–435.

Kelly, M. O. and Davis, P. J. (1986). Genetic and photoperiodic control of the relative rates of reproductive and vegetative development in peas. *Ann. Bot.* **58**, 13–21.

Kemperman, J. A., and Barnes, B. V. (1976). Clone size in American aspens. *Can. J. Bot.* **54**, 2603–2607.

Kershaw, K. A. (1964). "Quantitative and Dynamic Ecology." Arnold, London.

King, R. W., Wardlaw, I. F., and Evans, L. T. (1967). Effect of assimilate utilization on photosynthetic rate in wheat. *Planta* **77**, 261–276.

Kollman, G. E., Streeter, J. G., Jeffers, D. L., and Curry, R.B. (1974). Accumulation and distribution of mineral nutrients, carbohydrate, and dry matter in soybean plants as influenced by reproductive sink size. *Agron. J.* **66**, 549–554.

Kozlowski, T. T. (1971). "Growth and Development of Trees," Vol. 1. Academic Press, New York.

Kriedemann, P. E., Loveys, B. R., Possingham, J. V., and Satoh, M. (1976). Sink effects on stomatal physiology and photosynthesis. *In* "Transport and Transfer Processes in Plants" (I. F. Wardlaw and J. B. Passioura, eds.), pp. 401–414. Academic Press, New York.

Krizek, D. T., McIlrath, W. J., and Vergara, B. S. (1966). Photoperiodic induction of senescence in *Xanthium* plants. *Science* **151**, 95–96.

Krogman, K. K., and Hobbs, E. H. (1975). Yield and morphological response of rapes (*Brassica campestris* cv Span) to soil fertility and irrigation. *Can. J. Plant Sci.* **55**, 903–909.

Kulkarni, V. J., and Schwabe, W. W. (1985) Graft transmission of longday-induced leaf senescence in *Kleinia articulata. J. Exp. Bot.* **36**, 1620–1633.

Kumura, A., and Naniwa, I. (1965). Studies on dry matter production of soybean plant. I. Ontogenic changes in photosynthetic and respiratory capacity of soybean plant and its parts. *Proc. Crop Sci. Soc. Jpn.* **33**, 467–471.

LaMarche, V. C. (1969). Environment in relation to age of bristlecone pines. *Ecology* **50**, 53–59.

Lansing, A. I. (1945). A non-genic factor in the longevity of rotifer. *Ann. N. Y. Acad. Sci* **57**, 455–464.

Lauer, M. J., and Shibles, R. (1987). Soybean leaf photosynthetic response to changing sink demand. *Crop Sci.* **27**, 1197–1201.

Legere, A., and Payette, S. (1981). Ecology of a black spruce (*Picea mariana*) clonal population in the hemiarctic zone, northern Quebec: Population dynamics and spatial development. *Arct. Alp. Res.* **13**, 261–276.

Lenz, F., and Williams, C. N. (1973). Effect of fruit removal on net assimilation and gaseous diffusive resistance of soybean leaves. *Angew. Bot.* **47**, 57–63.

Leonard, E. R. (1962). Inter-relations of vegetative and reproductive growth with special reference to indeterminate plants. *Bot. Rev.* **28**, 353–410.

Leopold, A. C. (1961). Senescence in plant development. *Science* **134**, 1727–1732.

Leopold, A. C., and Noodén, L. D. (1984). Hormonal regulatory systems in plants. *Encycl. Plant Physiol. New Ser.* **10**, 4–22.

Leopold, A. C., Niedergang-Kamien, E., and Janick, J. (1959). Experimental modification of plant senescence. *Plant Physiol.* **34**, 570–573.

Letham, D. S. (1978). Cytokinins. *In* "Phytohormones and Related Compounds: A Comprehensive Treatise" (D. S. Letham, P. B. Goodwin, and T. J. V. Higgins, eds.), Vol. 1, pp. 205–263. Elsevier/North-Holland, Amsterdam.

Letham, D. S., and Palni, L. M. S. (1983). The biosynthesis and metabolism of cytokinins. *Annu. Rev. Plant Physiol.* **34**, 163–197.

Lindemuth, H. (1901). Das Verhalten durch Copulation verbundener Pflanzenarten. *Ber. Dtsch. Bot. Ges.* **19**, 515–529. Cited in Molisch. (1938).

Lindoo, S. J., and Noodén, L. D. (1976). The interrelation of fruit development and leaf senescence in 'Anoka' soybeans. *Bot. Gaz.* **137**, 218–223.

Lindoo, S. J., and Noodén, L. D. (1977). Behavior of the soybean senescence signal. *Plant Physiol.* **59**, 1136–1140.

Lindoo, S. J., and Noodén, L. D. (1978). Correlations of cytokinins and abscisic acid with monocarpic senescence in soybean. *Plant Cell Physiol.* **19**, 997–1006.

Little, R. J., and Jones, C. E. (1980). "A Dictionary of Botany." Von Nostrand-Reinhold, New York.

Lockhart, J. A., and Gottschall, V. (1961). Fruit-induced and apical senescence in *Pisum sativum*. *Plant Physiol.* **36**, 389–398.

Loehwing, F. W. (1951). Mineral nutrition in relation to the ontogeny of plants. *In* "Mineral Nutrition of Plants" (E. Troug, ed.), pp. 343–358. Univ. of Wisconsin Press, Madison.

Loomis, W. E. (1953). Growth correlation. *In* "Growth and Differentiation of Plants" (W. E. Loomis, ed.), pp. 197–217. Iowa State College Press, Ames.

Loong, S. G., and Lenz, F. (1974). Effects of nitrogen level and fruit removal on growth, nodulation and water consumption of soybean *Glycine max* (L.) Merril. *Z. Acker- Pflanzenbau* **139**, 35–43.

McCready, C.C., and Jacobs, W. P. (1963). Movement of growth regulators in plants. IV. Relationships between age, growth and polar transport in petioles of *Phaseolus vulgaris*. *New Phytol.* **62**, 360–366.

McDavid, C. R., Sagar, G. R., and Marshall, C. (1972). The effect of auxin from the shoot on root development in *Pisum sativum* L. *New Phytol.* **71**, 1027–1032.

McNeil, D. L., Atkins, C. A., and Pate, J. S. (1979). Uptake and utilization of xylem-borne amino compounds by shoot organs of a legume. *Plant Physiol.* **63**, 1076–1081.

Maggs, D. H. (1964). The distance from tree base to shoot origin as a factor in shoot and tree growth. *J. Hortic. Sci.* **39**, 298–307.

Major, D. J., Bole, J. B., and Charnetski, W. A. (1978). Distribution of photosynthesis after $^{14}CO_2$ assimilation by stem, leaves and pods of rape plants. *Can. J. Plant Sci.* **58**, 783–787.

Malik, N. S. A. (1983). Grafting experiments on the nature of the decline in N_2 fixation during fruit development in soybean. *Physiol. Plant.* **57**, 561–564.

Malik, N. S. A., and Berrie, A. M. M. (1977). Changes in leaf proteins of peas *Pisum sativum* during development on deflorated plants. *Plant Physiol.* **59**, 331–334.

Malik, N. S. A., and Berrie, M. M. (1980). The role of roots in shoot senescence of peas *Pisum sativum* L. *Z. Pflanzenphysiol.* **100**, 79–83.

Mandahar, C. L., and Garg, I. D. (1975). Effect of ear removal on sugars and chlorophyll of barley leaves. *Photosynthetica* **9**, 407–409.

Marschner, H. (1983). General introduction to the mineral nutrition of plants. *Encycl. Plant Physiol., New Ser.* **15A**, 5–60.

Martin, F. (1952). La dégénérescence de la canne à sucre. *Ind. Agric. Aliment.* **69,** 15–19.

Mauk, C. S., and Noodén, L. D. (1983). Cytokinin control of mineral nutrient redistribution between the foliage and seeds in soybean explants. *Plant Physiol.* **72,** Suppl., 167.

Mauk, C. S., Pelkii, C., and Noodén, L. D. (1985). Translocation of [86]Rubidium in soybean explants during senescence and pod development. *Plant Physiol.* **77,** Suppl., 115.

Mayak, S., and Halevy, A. H. (1980). Flower senescence. *In* "Senescence in Plants" (K. V. Thimann, ed.), pp. 131–156. CRC Press, Boca Raton, Florida.

Meyer, G. E. (1985). Simulation of moisture stress effects on soybean yield components in Nebraska. *Trans. Am. Soc. Agric. Eng.* **28,** 118–128.

Miller, E. C. (1938). "Plant Physiology." McGraw-Hill, New York.

Möbius, M. (1897). "Beiträge zur Lehre von der Fortpflanzung der Gewäcshe." Fischer, Jena.

Möller, C. M., Müller, D., and Nielsen, J. (1954). Graphic representation of dry matter production of European beech. *Forstl. Forsoegsvaes. Dan.* **21,** 327–335.

Molisch, H. (1938). "The Longevity of Plants" (H. Fulling, transl.). Science Press, Lancaster, Pennsylvania.

Mondal, M. H., Brun, W. A., and Brenner, M. L. (1978). Effects of sink removal on photosynthesis and senescence in leaves of soybean (*Glycine max* L.) plants. *Plant Physiol.* **61,** 394–397.

Moorby, J., and Wareing, P. (1963). Ageing in woody plants. *Ann. Bot.* **27,** 291–308.

Morris, D. A. (1977). Transport of exogenous auxin in two-branched dwarf pea seedlings (*Pisum sativum* L.). *Planta* **136,** 91–96.

Morris, D. A., and Kadir, G. O. (1972). Pathways of auxin transport in the intact pea seedling (*Pisum sativum* L.). *Planta* **107,** 171–182.

Morris, D. A., Briant, R. E., and Thomson, P. G. (1969). The transport and metabolism of ^{14}C-labelled indoleacetic acid in intact pea seedlings. *Planta* **89,** 178–197.

Morris, D. A., Kadir, G. O., and Barry, A. J. (1973). Auxin transport in intact pea seedlings (*Pisum sativum* L.): the inhibition of transport by 2,3,5-triiodobenzoic acid. *Planta* **110,** 173–182.

Mothes, K. (1960). Über das Altern und die Möglichkeit ihrer Wiederverjüngung. *Naturwissenschaften* **15,** 337–350.

Mothes, K., and Engelbrecht, L. (1952). Über geschlechtsverschieden Stoffwechsel Zweihäusiger einjähriger Pflanzen. I. Untersuchunger über den Stickstoff-umsatz beim Hauf (*Cannabis sativa* L.). *Flora (Jena)* **139,** 1–27.

Murashige, T. (1974). Plant propagation through tissue cultures. *Annu. Rev. Plant Physiol.* **25,** 135–166.

Murneek, A. E. (1926). Effects of correlation between vegetative and reproductive functions in the tomato (*Lycopersicon esculentum* Mill.). *Plant Physiol.* **1,** 3–56.

Murray, B. J., and Noodén, L. D. (1982). Downward transmission of the senescence signal in soybean. *Plant Physiol.* **69,** Suppl., 152.

Murray, B. J., Mauk, C., and Noodén, L. D. (1982). Restricted vascular pipelines (and orthostichies) and plants. *What's New Plant Physiol.* **13,** 33–36.

Neumann, P. M. (1987). Sequential leaf senescence and correlatively controlled increases in xylem flow resistance. *Plant Physiol.* **83,** 941–944.

Neumann, P. M., and Noodén, L. D. (1984). Pathway and regulation of phosphate translocation to the pods of soybean explants. *Physiol. Plant.* **60,** 166–170.

Neumann, P. M., and Stein, Z. (1984). Relative rates of delivery of xylem solute to shoot tissues: Possible relationship to sequential leaf senescence. *Physiol. Plant.* **62,** 390–397.

Neumann, P. M., Tucker, A. T., and Noodén, L. D. (1983). Characterization of leaf senescence and pod development in soybean explants. *Plant Physiol.* **72,** 182–185.

Nitsch, J. P. (1972). Hormonal factors in growth and development. *In* "The Biochemistry of Fruits and their Products" (A. C. Hulme, ed.), pp. 427–472. Academic Press, London.

Noodén, L. D. (1980a). Senescence in the whole plant. In "Senescence in Plants" (K. V. Thimann, ed.), pp. 219–258. CRC Press, Boca Raton, Florida.

Noodén, L.D. (1980b). Regulation of senescence. In "World Soybean Research Conference II: Proceedings" (F. T. Corbin, ed.), pp. 139–152. Westview Press, Boulder, Colorado.

Noodén, L. D. (1984). Integration of soybean pod development and monocarpic senescence. A minireview. *Physiol. Plant.* 62, 273–284.

Noodén, L. D. (1985). Regulation of soybean senescence. In "Proceedings of the World Soybean Research Conference III" (R. Shibles, ed.), pp. 891–900. Westview Press, Boulder, Colorado.

Noodén. L. D. (1986). Synergism between gibberellins and cytokinin in delaying leaf senescence in soybean explants. *Plant Cell Physiol.* 27, 577–579.

Noodén, L. D. (1987). Soybean seed growth: Regulatory mechanisms in the whole plant. In "Models in Plant Physiology and Biochemistry" (D. Newman and K. Wilson, eds.), Vol. 2. CRC Press, Boca Raton, Florida. pp. 145–147.

Noodén, L. D. and Leopold, A. C. (1978). Phytohormones and the endogenous regulation of senescence and abscission. In "Phytohormones and Related Compounds: A Comprehensive Treatise" (D. S. Letham, P. B. Goodwin, and T. J. Higgins, eds.), Vol. 2, pp. 329–369. Elsevier/North-Holland, Amsterdam.

Noodén, L. D., and Letham, D. S. (1984). Translocation of zeatin riboside and zeatin in soybean explants. *J. Plant Growth Regul.* 2, 265–279.

Noodén, L. D., and Letham, D. S. (1986). Cytokinin control of monocarpic senescence in soybean. In "Plant Growth Substances" (M. Bopp, ed.), pp. 324–332. Springer-Verlag, Berlin and New York.

Noodén, L. D., and Lindoo, S. J. (1978). Monocarpic senescence. *What's New Plant Physiol.* 9, 25–28.

Noodén, L. D., and Mauk, C. S. (1987). Changes in mineral composition of soybean xylem sap during monocarpic senescence and alterations by depodding. *Physiol. Plant.* 70, 735–742.

Noodén, L. D., and Murray, B. J. (1982). Transmission of the monocarpic senescence signal via the xylem in soybean. *Plant Physiol.* 69, 754–756.

Noodén, L. D., and Noodén, S. M. (1985). Effects of morphactin and other auxin transport inhibitors on soybean senescence and pod development. *Plant Physiol.* 78, 263–266.

Noodén, L. D., and Obermeyer, W. R. (1981). Changes in abscisic acid translocation during pod development and senescence in soybeans. *Biochem. Physiol. Pflanzen* 176, 859–868.

Noodén, L. D., and Thompson, J. E. (1985). Aging and senescence in plants. In "Handbook of the Biology of Aging" (C. E. Finch and E. L. Schneider, eds.), 2nd Ed., pp. 105–127. Van Nostrand-Reinhold, New York.

Noodén, L. D., and Weber, J. A. (1978). Environment and hormonal control of dormancy in terminal buds of plants. In "Dormancy and Developmental Arrest" (M. E. Clutter, ed.), pp. 221–268. Academic Press, New York.

Noodén. L. D., Rupp, D. C., and Derman, B. D. (1978). Separation of seed development from monocarpic senescence in soybeans. *Nature (London)* 271, 354–357.

Noodén, L. D., Kahanak, G. M., and Okatan, Y. (1979a). Prevention of monocarpic senescence in soybeans with auxin and cytokinin. *Science* 206, 841–843.

Noodén, L. D., Nahigian, C. M., and Noodén, S. M. (1979b). Correlative controls of monocarpic senescence of soybean. *Plant Physiol.* 63, Suppl., 72.

Noodén, L. D., Finkelstein, D., and Wetzel, P. (1987). Transmission of ^{3}H-compounds corresponding to the senescence signal in soybean. *Plant Physiol.* 83, Suppl. 121.

Ogden, J. (1978). On the dendrochronological potential of Australian trees. *Aust. J. Ecol.* 3, 339–356.

Oinonen, E. (1967a). The correlation between the size of Finnish bracken (Pteridium aquilinum (L.) Kuhn.) clones and certain periods of site history. *Acta For. Fenn.* **83**, 1–51.

Oinonen, E. (1967b). Summary: Sporal regeneration of ground pine (*Lycopodium complanatum* L.) in southern Finland in the light of dimensions and age of its clones. *Acta For. Fenn.* **83**, 76–85.

Oinonen, E. (1969). The time table of vegetative spreading in the Lily-of-the-Valley (*Convallaria majalis* L.) and the small reed (*Calamagrostis epigeios* [L.] Roth.) in southern Finland. *Acta For. Fenn.* **97**, 1–35.

Okatan, Y., Kahanak, G. M., and Noodén, L. D. (1981). Characterization and kinetics of maturation and monocarpic senescence. *Physiol. Plant.* **52**, 330–338.

Ong, C. K., and Marshall, C. (1975). Assimilate distribution in *Poa annua* L. *Ann. Bot.* **39**, 413–421.

Oparka, K. J., and Gates, P. (1981). Transport of assimilates in the developing caryopsis of rice. Ultrastructure of rice pericarp vascular bundle and its connections with the aleurone layer. *Planta* **151**, 561–573.

Oritani, T., and Yoshida, R. (1973). Studies on nitrogen metabolism in crop plants. XII. Cytokinins and abscisic acid-like substances levels in rice and soybean leaves during their growth and senescence. *Proc. Crop Sci. Soc. Jpn.* **42**, 280–287.

Osborne, D. J. (1959). Identity of the abscission-accelerating substance in senescent leaves. *Nature (London)* **183**, 1593.

Paltridge, G. W., Denholm, J. V., and Connor, D. J. (1984). Determinism, senescence and the yield of plants. *J. Theor. Biol.* **110**, 383–398.

Passeker, F. (1941). Die Bewurzelung von Obstecklingen. *Gartenbauwissenschaft* **15**, 380–385.

Pate, J. S. (1966). Photosynthesizing leaves and nodulated roots as donors of carbon to protein of the shoot of the field pea (*Pisum arvense* L.). *Ann. Bot.* **30**, 93–109.

Pate, J. S. (1975). Exchange of solutes between phloem and xylem and circulation in the whole plant. *Encycl. Plant Physiol. New Ser.* **1**, 451–473.

Pate, J. S. (1985). Partitioning of carbon and nitrogen in N_2-fixing grain legumes. *In* "World Soybean Research Conference III: Proceedings" (R. Shibles, ed.), pp. 715–727. Westview Press, Boulder, Colorado.

Pate, J. S., and Gunning, B. E. S. (1972). Transfer cells. *Annu. Rev. Plant Physiol.* **23**, 173–176.

Pate, J. S., and Hocking, P. J. (1978). Phloem and xylem transport in the supply of minerals to a developing legume (*Lupinus albus* L.) fruit. *Ann. Bot.* **42**, 911–912.

Pate, J. S., Peoples, M. B., van Bel, A. J. E., Kuo, J., and Atkins, C. A. (1985). Diurnal water balance of the cowpea fruit. *Plant Physiol.* **77**, 148–156.

Patrick, J. W. (1982). Hormonal control of assimilate transport. *In* "Plant Growth Substances 1982" (P. F. Wareing, ed.), pp. 669–678. Academic Press, London.

Patrick, J. W. (1986). Hormonal control of assimilate partitioning. *Plant Growth Regul. Bull.* **14**, 7–11.

Patrick, J. W., and McDonald, R. (1980). Pathway of carbon transport within developing ovules of *Phaseolus vulgaris* L. *Aust. J. Plant Physiol.* **7**, 671–684.

Patterson, T. G., and Brun, W. A. (1980). Influence of sink removal in the senescence pattern of wheat. *Crop Sci.* **20**, 19–23.

Pearl, R. (1928). "The Rate of Living." Knopf, New York.

Peat, J. R., Minchin, F. R., Summerfield, R. J., and Jeffcoat, B. (1981). Young reproductive structures promote nitrogen fixation in soya bean. *Ann. Bot.* **48**, 177–182.

Penning de Vries, F. W. T., and Van Laar, H. H., eds. (1982). "Simulation of Plant Growth and Crop Production." Cent. Agric. Publ. Docum., Wageningen, Netherlands.

Phillips, D. A., Pierce, R. O., Edie, S. A., Foster, K. W., and Knowles, P. F. (1984). Delayed leaf senescence in soybean. *Crop Sci.* **24**, 518–522.

Pierce, R.O., Knowles, P. F., and Phillips, D. A. (1984). Inheritance of delayed leaf senescence in soybean. *Crop Sci.* 24, 515–517.

Pilet, P.-E., and Saugy, M. (1985). Effect of applied and endogenous indol-3-yl-acetic acid on maize root growth. *Planta* 164, 250–258.

Piñero, D., Sarukhán, J., and Alberdi, P. (1982). The costs of reproduction in a tropical palm, *Asterocaryum mexicanum. J. Ecol.* 70, 473–481.

Proebsting, W. M., Davies, P. J., and Marx, G. A. (1978). Photoperiod-induced changes in gibberellin metabolism in relation to apical growth and senescence in genetic lines of peas (*Pisum sativum* L.). *Planta* 141, 231–238.

Purohit, S. S. (1982). Monocarpic senescence in *Helianthus annuus* L. 1. Relation of fruit induced senescence, chlorophyll and chlorophyllase activity. *Photosynthetica* 16, 542–545.

Raschke, K. (1979). Movement of stomata. *Encycl. Plant Physiol. New Ser.* 7, 383–441.

Rawson, H. M., and Hofstra, G. (1969). Translocation and remobilization of ¹⁴C assimilated at different stages by each leaf of the wheat plant. *Aust. J. Biol. Sci.* 22, 321–331.

Rawson, H. M., Gifford, R. M., and Bremner, P. M. (1976). Carbon dioxide exchange in relation to sink demand in wheat. *Planta* 132, 19–23.

Reich, P. B. (1984). Loss of stomatal function in ageing hybrid poplar leaves. *Ann. Bot.* 53, 691–698.

Reichert, C. (1821). "Lund und Gartenschatz. Praktisches Handbuch für den Blumen und Zierpflanzen Gartenbau," 6 Aufl., 5 Teil. Cited in Molisch (1938).

Reid, J. B. (1980). Apical senescence in *Pisum:* A direct or indirect role for the flowering genes? *Ann. Bot.* 45, 195–201.

Reid, J. B., and Murfet, I. C. (1984). Flowering in *Pisum:* a fifth locus, Veg. *Ann. Bot.* 53, 369–382.

Roberts, J. A., and Osborne, D. J. (1981). Auxin and the control of ethylene production during development and senescence of leaves and fruits. *J. Exp. Bot.* 32, 875–888.

Roos, E. E. (1982). Induced genetic changes in seed germplasm during storage. *In* "The Physiology and Biochemistry of Seed Development, Dormancy and Germination" (A. A. Khan, ed.), pp. 409–434. Elsevier, Amsterdam.

Rose, M. R., and Service, P. M. (1985). Evolution of aging. *Rev. Biol. Res. Aging* 2, 85–98.

Rosen, R. (1978). Feedforwards and global system failure: A general mechanism for senescence. *J. Theor. Biol.* 74, 579–590.

Ruddat, M., and Pharis, R. P. (1966). Enhancement of leaf senescence by Amo-1618, a growth retardant and its reversal by gibberellin and kinetin. *Plant Cell Physiol.* 7, 689–692.

Russell, E. J. (1932). "Soil Conditions and Plant Growth," 6th Ed. Longmans, London.

Sachs, T. (1972). A possible basis for apical organization in plants. *J. Theor. Biol.* 37, 353–361.

Samet, J. S., and Sinclair, T. R. (1980). Leaf senescence and abscisic acid in leaves of field-grown soybean. *Plant Physiol.* 66, 1164–1168.

Sax, K. (1962). Aspects of aging in plants. *Annu. Rev. Plant Physiol.* 13, 489–506.

Schreyer, S. L., and Noodén, L. D. (1975). Screening nutrients and growth promoters or inhibitors for ability to mimic or antagonize the death signal in soybeans. *Plant Physiol.* 56, Suppl., 83.

Schulman, E. (1954). Longevity under adversity in conifers. *Science* 119, 396–399.

Schweitzer, L. E., and Harper, J. E. (1985a). Effect of multiple factor source-sink manipulation on nitrogen and carbon assimilation by soybean. *Plant Physiol.* 78, 57–60.

Schweitzer, L. E., and Harper, J. E. (1985b). Leaf nitrate reductase, D-ribulose-1, 5-bisphosphate carboxylase, and root nodule development of genetic male-sterile and fertile soybean isolines. *Plant Physiol.* 78, 61–65.

Secor, J., Shibles, R., and Stewart, C. R. (1983). Metabolic changes in senescing soybean leaves of similar plant ontogeny. *Crop Sci.* 23, 106–110.

Sesay, A., and Shibles, R. (1980). Mineral depletion and leaf senescence in soya bean as influenced by foliar nutrient application during seed filling. *Ann. Bot.* **45**, 47–55.

Sesták, Z. (1963). Changes in the chlorophyll content as related to photosynthetic activity and age of leaves. *Photochem. Photobiol.* **2**, 101–110.

Setter, T. L., Brun, W. A., and Brenner, M. L. (1980). Effect of obstructed translocation on leaf abscisic acid, and associated stomatal closure and photosynthesis decline. *Plant Physiol.* **65**, 1111–1115.

Sexton, R., and Woolhouse, H. W. (1984). Senescence and abscission. *In* "Advanced Plant Physiology" (M. B. Wilkins, ed.), pp. 469–497. Pitman, London.

Shibles, R., Anderson, I. C., and Gibson, A. H. (1975). Soybean. *In* "Crop Physiology, Some Case Histories," pp. 151–159. Cambridge Univ. Press, London and New York.

Shigo, A. L. (1984). Compartmentalization: A conceptual framework for understanding how trees grow and defend themselves. *Annu. Rev. Phytopathol.* **22**, 189–214.

Shoji, K., Addicott, F. T., and Swets, W. A. (1951). Auxin in relation to leaf blade abscission. *Plant Physiol.* **26**, 189–191.

Sinclair, T. R., and de Wit, C. T. (1975). Photosynthate and nitrogen requirements for seed production by various crops. *Science* **189**, 565–567.

Singh, B. N., and Lal, K. N. (1935). Investigations of the effect of age on assimilation of leaves. *Ann. Bot.* **49**, 291–307.

Street, H. E. (1967). The ageing of root meristems. *Symp. Soc. Exp. Biol.* **21**, 517–542.

Struckmeyer, B. E. (1941). Structure of stems in relation to differentiation and abortion of blossom buds. *Bot. Gaz.* **103**, 182–191.

Struckmeyer, B. E., and Roberts, R. H. (1939). Phloem development and flowering. *Bot. Gaz.* **100**, 600–606.

Sutton, W. D. (1983). Nodule development and senescence. *In* "Nitrogen Fixation. Vol. 3: Legumes" (W. J. Broughton, ed.), pp. 144–212. Oxford Univ. Press (Clarendon), London and New York.

Szabo, I. (1931). The three types of mortality curve. *Q. Rev. Biol.* **6**, 462–463.

Tamas, I. A., Engels, C. A., Kaplan, S. L., Ozbun, J. L., and Wallace, D. H. (1981). Role of indoleacetic acid and abscisic acid in the correlative control by fruits of axillary bud development and leaf senescence. *Plant Physiol.* **68**, 476–481.

Tamas, I. A., Davies, P. J., Mazur, B. K., and Campbell, L. D. (1985). Correlative effects of fruits on plant development. *In* "World Soybean Research Conference III: Proceedings" (R. Shibles, ed.), pp. 858–865. Westview Press, Boulder, Colorado.

Tamm, C. C. (1948). Observations on reproduction and survival of some perennial herbs. *Bot. Not.* pp. 305–321.

Thimann, K. V. (1935). On an analysis of activity of two growth-promoting substances on plant tissues. *Proc. K. Ned. Akad. Wet.* **38**, 896–912.

Thimann, K. V. (1980). The senescence of leaves. *In* "Senescence in Plants" (K. V. Thimann, ed.), pp. 85–115. CRC Press, Boca Raton, Florida.

Thimann, K. V., Tetley, R. M., and Thanh, T. V. (1974). The metabolism of oat leaves during senescence II. Senescence in leaves attached to the plant. *Plant Physiol.* **54**, 859–862.

Thimann, K. V., Satler, S. O., and Trippi, V. (1982). Further extension of the syndrome of leaf senescence. *In* "Plant Growth Substances 1982" (P. F. Wareing, ed.), pp. 539–548. Academic Press, London.

Thomas, H., and Stoddart, J. L. (1980). Leaf senescence. *Annu. Rev. Plant Physiol.* **31**, 83–111.

Thorne, J. H. (1980). Kinetics of ¹⁴C-photosynthate uptake by developing soybean. *Plant Physiol.* **65**, 975–979.

Thorne, J. H. (1985). Phloem unloading of C and N assimilates in developing seeds. *Annu. Rev. Plant Physiol.* **36**, 317–343.

Thorne, J. H., and Koller, H. R. (1974). Influence of assimilate demand on photosynthesis, diffusive resistances, translocation, and carbohydrate levels of soybean leaves. *Plant Physiol.* **54**, 201–207.

Touzet, G. (1985). Perennial plants. *Interdiscipl. Top. Gerontol.* **21**, 263–283.

Trippi, V. S., (1980). "Ontogenia y Senilidad en Plantas." Dir. Gen. Publ., Univ. Nacl. Cordoba, Cordoba, Argentina.

Trippi, V. S., and Brulfert, J. (1973a). Organization of the morphophysiologic unit in *Anagallis arvensis* and its relation with the perpetuation mechanism and senescence. *Am. J. Bot.* **60**, 641–647.

Trippi, V. S., and Brulfert, J. (1973b). Photoperiodic aging in *Anagallis arvenis* clones: Its relation to RNA content, rooting capacity, and flowering. *Am. J. Bot.* **60**, 951–955.

Trippi, V., and Montaldi, E. (1960). The aging of sugar cane clones. *Phyton (Buenos Aires)* **14**, 79–91.

Van Staden, J., and Davey, J. E. (1979). The synthesis, transport and metabolism of endogenous cytokinins. *Plant Cell Environ.* **2**, 93–106.

Vasek, F. C. (1980). Creosote bush: Long-lived clones in the Mojave desert. *Am. J. Bot.* **67**, 246–255.

Veen, H., and Jacobs, W. P. (1969). Transport and metabolism of indole-3-acetic acid in *Coleus* petiole segments of increasing age. *Plant Physiol.* **44**, 1157–1162.

Walton, D. C. (1980). Biochemistry and physiology of abscisic acid. *Annu. Rev. Plant Physiol.* **31**, 453–489.

Wang, T. L., and Woolhouse, H. W. (1982). Hormonal aspects of senescence in plant development. *In* "Growth Regulators in Plant Senescence" (M. B. Jackson, B. Grout, and I. A. Mackenzie, eds.), Monogr. No. 8, pp. 5–25. Br. Plant Growth Regul. Group, Wantage, England.

Wangermann, E. (1965). Longevity and ageing in plants and plant organs. *Encycl. Plant Physiol.* **15**(2), 1037.

Wanner, H., and Bachofen, R. (1961). Transport und Verteilung von markierten Assimilaten I. *Planta* **57**, 531–542.

Wardle, K., and Short, K. C. (1983). Stomatal responses and the senescence of leaves. *Ann. Bot.* **52**, 411–412.

Wareing, P. F., and Seth, A. K. (1967). Ageing and senescence in the whole plant. *Symp. Soc. Exp. Biol.* **21**, 543–558.

Waters, L., Jr., Breen, P. J., and Mack, H. J. (1980). Translocation of ^{14}C-photosynthate, carbohydrate content, and nitrogen fixation in *Phaseolus vulgaris* L. during reproductive development. *J. Am. Soc. Hortic. Sci.* **105**, 424–427.

Watts, S., Rodriguez, J. L., Evans, S. E., and Davies, W. J. (1981). Root and shoot growth of plants treated with abscisic acid. *Ann. Bot.* **47**, 595–602.

Weber, F. (1919). Der natürliche Tod der Pflanzen. *Naturwiss. Wochenschr.* **18**, 447–457.

Went, F. W. (1942). Some physiological factors in the aging of a tree. *Proc. Natl. Shade Tree Conf.* **18**, 330–334.

Westing, A. H. (1964). The longevity and aging of trees. *Gerontologist* **4**, 10–15.

Wetmore, R. H., and Jacobs, W. P. (1953). Studies on abscission: The inhibiting effect of auxin. *Am. J. Bot.* **40**, 272–276.

Whaley, W. G. (1965). The interaction of genotype and environment in plant development. *Encycl. Plant Physiol.* **15**(1), 74–89.

Wherry, E. T. (1972). Box-huckleberry as the oldest living protoplasm. *Castanea* **37**, 94–95.

White, J. (1979). The plant as a metapopulation. *Annu. Rev. Ecol. Syst.* **10**, 109–145.

Wien, H. C., Altschuler, S. L., Ozbun, J. L., and Wallace, D. H. (1976). ^{14}C assimilate distribution in *Phaseolus vulgaris* L. during the reproductive period. *J. Am. Soc. Hortic. Sci.* **101**, 510–513.

Wightman, F., and Thimann, K. V. (1980). Hormonal factors controlling the initiation and development of lateral roots II. Effects of exogenous growth factors on lateral root formation in pea roots. *Physiol. Plant.* **49**, 304–314.

Williams, R. F. (1955). Redistribution of mineral elements during development. *Annu. Rev. Plant Physiol.* **6**, 25–42.

Willson, M. F. (1983). "Plant Reproductive Ecology." Wiley, New York.

Wilton, O. C. (1938). Correlation of cambial activity with flowering and regeneration. *Bot. Gaz.* **99**, 854–864.

Wilton, O. C., and Roberts, R. H. (1936). Anatomical structure of stems in relation to the production of flowers. *Bot. Gaz.* **98**, 45–64.

Wittenbach, V. A. (1982). Effect of pod removal on leaf senescence in soybeans. *Plant Physiol.* **70**, 1544–1548.

Wittenbach, V. A. (1983). Effect of pod removal on leaf photosynthesis and soluble protein composition of field-grown soybeans. *Plant Physiol.* **73**, 121–124.

Wittenbach, V. A., Anderson, R. C., Giaguinta, R. T., and Hebert, R. R. (1980). Changes in photosynthesis, ribulose bisphosphate carboxylase, proteolytic activity, and ultrastructure of soybean leaves during senescence. *Crop Sci.* **20**, 225–231.

Wood, L. J., Murray, B. J., Okatan, Y., and Noodén, L. D. (1986). Effect of petiole phloem disruption on starch and mineral distribution in senescing soybean leaves. *Am. J. Bot.* **73**, 1377–1383.

Woodward, R. G., and Rawson, H. M. (1976). Photosynthesis and transpiration in dicotyledonous plants. II. Expanding and senescing leaves of soybean. *Aust. J. Plant Physiol.* **3**, 257–267.

Woolhouse, H. W. (1982). Hormonal control of senescence allied to reproduction in plants. *In* "Strategies of Plant Reproduction" (W. J. Meudt, ed.), BARC Symp., No. 6, pp. 201–233. Littlefield-Adams, Totowa, New Jersey.

Wright, S. T. C. (1978). Phytohormones and stress phenomena. *In* "Phytohormones and Related Compounds: A Comprehensive Treatise" (D. S. Letham, P. B. Goodwin, and T. J. V. Higgins, eds.), Vol. 2, pp. 495–536. Elsevier/North-Holland, Amsterdam.

Yamaguchi, T., and Street, H. E. (1977). Stimulation of the growth of excised cultured roots of soya bean by abscisic acid. *Ann. Bot.* **41**, 1129–1133.

Young, D. S. (1985). "Bonsai. The Art and Technique." Prentice-Hall, Englewood Cliffs, New Jersey.

Zelawski, W. (1980). Aging of the plant organism (a survey of experiments and hypotheses). *Sov. Plant Physiol. (Engl. Transl.)* **27**, 658–665.

Zimmerman, M. H. (1983). "Xylem Structure and the Ascent of Sap." Springer-Verlag, Berlin and New York.

13

Deterioration of Membranes during Aging in Plants: Evidence for Free Radical Mediation

Bryan D. McKersie, Tissa Senaratna, Mark A. Walker,
Edward J. Kendall, and P. Richard Hetherington
Department of Crop Science
University of Guelph
Guelph, Ontario, Canada

I. INTRODUCTION

Whole plants, plant tissues, and individual plant cells commonly experience aging, or the deterioration with time. In these instances, aging and death occur as a consequence of a wide variety of events, which can be independent of any developmental process, in contrast to ordered, genetically programmed senescence. For example, leaf senescence in monocarpic species occurs as a developmental step following fruit set and is clearly a genetically programmed process. The deterioration of a seed in storage is, on the other hand, not a controlled process and obviously not a normal constitutive step in plant development. In the same context, a bud or meristem frozen over the winter months or a root tip submerged in a temporarily waterlogged soil will gradually deteriorate, resulting in cellular, tissue, and even whole plant death. The mechanism of this deterioration would not necessarily parallel that observed in natural senescence. In these latter examples, normal metabolism is suspended because the cell has been dried, frozen, or deprived of oxygen. Cells in such a state of curtailed metabolism accumulate a series of mechanical and metabolic injuries that, given sufficient time, culminate in cell death. Therefore, cells that are unable to repair the numerous small injuries occurring at this time can be considered to "age" by a nonmetabolically controlled mechanism, in contrast to natural senescence, which is actively promoted by metabolism.

Two experimental systems have been used to characterize the deterioration of cellular membranes during this "aging" process — the embryogenic axis of the soybean seed and the crown of the winter wheat seedling. Both tissues are meristematic and can tolerate prolonged periods of quiescence imposed by low water content and low winter temperatures, respectively. However, the germination and vigor of the soybean seed is reduced after prolonged storage or alternate wetting/drying periods, and, in the wheat crown, low freezing temperatures or encasement in ice reduces regrowth potential and increases ion leakage, both indicative of reduced viability.

At first, these four means of "aging" plant tissue may seem too diverse to have commonalities; but we will suggest that the deterioration that occurs at the cellular level is mechanistically similar. It is the similarity in damage at the membrane level and not the obvious differences in treatment that is the focus of the following discussion.

II. EVIDENCE FOR MEMBRANE DETERIORATION DURING AGING

A. Seed Aging

The deterioration of seed quality in storage is the classic example of aging in a plant system. The mature dry seed is quiescent and capable of initiating development of a new plant upon imbibition. In this quiescent state, the seed can maintain a high degree of viability for a considerable period of time, but, even during storage under optimum conditions, viability declines following a negatively sigmoidal curve (Priestley, 1986). The rate of this decline is dependent on the storage conditions and on the plant species involved.

Seeds that have been stored for some time exhibit lower rates of germination and seedling development, resulting in reduced emergence from the soil and reduced height or leaf area of the seedlings. The obvious economic importance of these traits has stimulated both agronomic and physiological research over the years on seed storage and seed aging (Priestley, 1986).

One of the early events that occurs during the aging of seeds is a deterioration of cellular membranes. The leakage of cytoplasmic solutes during imbibition increases dramatically with seed age (Priestley, 1986), and a close correlation between germination, the ability of the seed to retain cytoplasmic solutes, and field performance has been often observed (see, e.g., McKersie and Tomes, 1981).

The increased efflux of solutes from aged seeds implies that the integrity of the plasmalemma, or perhaps the tonoplast, has been lost during the aging process. Similarly, ultrastructural studies have shown quite convincingly that there is a disruption of membrane integrity and a coalescence of lipid bodies in aged seeds (Priestley, 1986). This perturbation of cellular fine structure becomes more dramatic as imbibition proceeds. In aged seeds, the normal developmental changes associated with germination occur more slowly, and autolysis is often evident in severely aged samples (Berjak and Villiers, 1972).

There have been three general experimental approaches used to study the deterioration of seed membranes. The first has been to compare seeds stored under natural conditions for several years, either characterizing a particular seed lot annually, or comparing different seed lots harvested in different years to give a range of ages. To shorten the time required to detect deleterious changes, seeds can be exposed to artificial or accelerated aging conditions, at approximately 40°C, 95% relative humidity, for several days. A third approach, which has been used by this research group, has been to compare desiccation injury to seeds that are naturally tolerant of desiccation, i.e., a mature seed, with those that are not tolerant, i.e., after approximately 36 hours of imbibition.

B. Desiccation Tolerance

One of the unique features of a seed is its ability to withstand drying to very low moisture contents. Embryos possess desiccation tolerance only in the late stages of seed development. For example, tolerance of desiccation is developed in the seeds of *Phaseolus vulgaris* between 22 and 26 days post-anthesis (Dasgupta *et al.*, 1982), after which moisture content of the seed declines, and a quiescent state is imposed.

Imbibition of water initiates a series of metabolic steps that lead to germination, and during this sequence of events, desiccation tolerance within the seed is lost. During the early stages of germination and prior to radical emergence in most species, the seed can be dried to its original moisture content without causing injury (Hegarty, 1978). However, the same degree of drying imposed at progressively later stages of germination dramatically reduces seed vigor and, if imposed after radical elongation has commenced, usually results in seedling death.

One of the earliest symptoms of injury following desiccation is the loss of function or structure of either the plasmalemma or organelle membranes. The kinetics of solute efflux from a seed as it imbibes water follows a biphasic profile; a rapid release of solutes during the first minutes of imbibition is followed by a slower, linear rate of efflux (Simon, 1974). During episodes of drying and rewetting, considerable physical tearing of the plasmalemma may occur, particularly along the outer cell layers, which contributes to solute leakage (Powell and Matthews, 1979). The rate of the linear phase of solute efflux, which is an indicator of the integrity of the cellular membranes, is also increased in seeds with reduced vigor. Several lines of evidence suggest that desiccation stress induces a change in the organization of the cellular membranes that is reflected in altered semipermeability (Senaratna and McKersie, 1983). The efflux of cytoplasmic solutes from lethally desiccated soybean axes increases, but to differing degrees (Table 13.1). For example, the rates of sugar efflux increases 1.8-fold, whereas phosphate efflux increases 130-fold. In addition, the Arrhenius activation energy for the efflux of the solutes, listed in Table 13.1, is different and remains above that estimated for free diffusion. Finally, the efflux of potassium and sugar from the axes is differentially sensitive to extracellular pH. Increasing pH tends to increase sugar efflux from the cell and reduces potassium efflux, an observation that suggests the selective semipermeability but not the gross integrity of the plasmalemma has been altered (Senaratna and McKersie, 1983). Collectively, the data suggest that the majority of

TABLE 13.1

Steady-State Rate of Solute Leakage from
Soybean Axes during Imbibition[a]

Solute	6 hour	36 hour
Conductivity (μmho)	88	235
Potassium (μmol)	8	30
Phosphate (μmol)	0.06	7.9
Amino acids (μmol)	2.6	15.6
Sugar (mg)	6.0	10.9
Protein (mg)	1.6	4.0

[a]Soybean seeds were imbibed for 6 or 36 hours in distilled water and the axes removed. The axes were dried to 10% moisture over 24 hours. The axes from 6-hour seeds remained viable and would germinate; the axes from 36-hour seeds were not viable after desiccation. The values represent the rate of leakage of cytoplasmic solutes from the axes between 2 and 8 hours after transfer into 10 ml distilled water and are expressed in grams per hour.
Adapted from Senaratna and McKersie (1983).

cellular membranes remain physically intact following a lethal desiccation stress, but their biophysical and biochemical properties are dramatically altered.

C. Freezing

In the overwintering tissues of herbaceous plants, such as the crown of the winter wheat seedling, ice nucleation first occurs in the large xylem vessels at temperatures slightly below freezing and proceeds along the length of the vascular system. As the temperature falls, an increasing proportion of the extracellular water is frozen and the intracellular water supercools. As a result, water leaves the protoplasm along a vapor pressure gradient to the extracellular ice crystals. Thus, under most freezing conditions the protoplasm will dehydrate and intracellular freezing will not occur. On relatively rare occasions of rapid cooling, ice crystals penetrate the plasmalemma and physically tear the membrane. This is always lethal to the cell (Olien, 1967). Under natural winter conditions, when the bud or meristem remains frozen for several months, at a temperature above its LT_{50} (lethal temperature), cellular membranes undergo deteriorative physical and chemical modifications (see, e.g., Pomeroy et al., 1985) similar in many respects to those that occur in a dried seed. Cellular membranes, particularly the plasmalemma, have been implicated as the primary site in the cell that perceives this freezing stress (Steponkus, 1984).

Examining the cellular fine structure of a tissue at subzero temperatures with extensive extracellular ice formation is technically difficult, and, not surprisingly, the results are contradictory in some details. A consistent observation is that a lethal freezing stress induces the formation of strongly osmiophilic material associated with cellular membranes, possibly indicating accumulation of lipid degradation products (Singh, 1979; Pearce, 1982). On thawing, the first sign of injury is usually a loss of cell turgor and a flaccid, water-soaked appearance. The tissue readily loses electrolytes and the semipermeability of the membranes has been dramatically altered (Palta *et al.*, 1977). However, as in the case of desiccation injury to seeds, membrane semipermeability is not completely lost. Instead, there appear to be specific alterations in potassium transport across the plasmalemma (Palta and Li, 1980).

D. Ice-Encasement

Anaerobic or hypoxic stresses are imposed on plants during periods of soil waterlogging or ice-encasement during winter. Under these conditions, cellular metabolism becomes fermentative in nature, and, in situations of

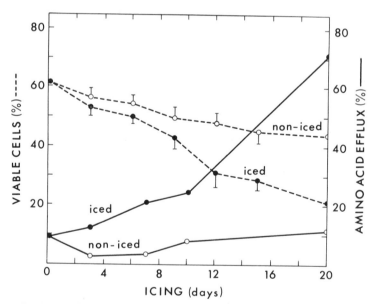

Fig. 13.1. Cell viability and amino acid efflux from isolated winter wheat cells following ice encasement at −1°C. Cells were isolated from leaves of winter wheat seedlings. Viability was estimated using fluorescence diacetate staining. [Reprinted from Pomeroy *et al.* (1983) with permission.]

complete ice-encasement, there is an accumulation of glycolytic end products such as CO_2, ethanol, and lactic acid (Andrews and Pomeroy, 1977). As a result, normal metabolism is curtailed and injuries accumulate, since repair mechanisms are absent or operating at reduced capacity. The plant cells deteriorate in an aging-like manner with time. Isolated wheat cells deteriorate when encased in ice at $-1°C$ (Fig. 13.1). This deterioration and loss of viability is accompanied by a change in membrane semipermeability, as illustrated by the increase in amino acid efflux, analogous to leakage increases noted in the whole plant (Hetherington *et al.*, 1987). [86]Rb uptake studies have shown that the earliest manifestation of injury to the plasmalemma during ice-encasement is damage to the ion transport system, particularly potassium transport, but there need not be an associated impairment of energy production or reduction of ATP supply (Pomeroy *et al.*, 1983).

In summary, at the cellular level there are similarities between the changes that occur during various types of deteriorative aging. Namely, there is a general disruption of membrane integrity, often accompanied by the formation or coalescence of osmiophilic lipid bodies, and an increase in the efflux of cytoplasmic solutes. These changes are indicative of changes in the structural and compositional properties of the cellular membranes.

III. PHYSICAL PROPERTIES OF MICROSOMAL MEMBRANES

The microsomal fraction from an homogenate of plant tissue contains a heterogenous mixture of small, vesicular membranes originating from various organelles including the plasmalemma, tonoplast, and endoplasmic reticulum and, to varying degrees, from mitochondria and plastids. This fraction has been used to examine the changes in the biophysical and biochemical properties of cellular membranes during aging for much the same reasons as it has been used in the study of changes in natural senescence (Chapter 2). Isolation of purified fractions, such as those enriched in the plasmalemma, employs separations based on buoyant density and surface charge. Both are properties that are altered during the deteriorative process (see later) and the source of the membranes at a predetermined, specific buoyant density would be expected to differ when the specific purified fraction is isolated from tissues in different stages of aging. The protein : phospholipid ratio, and therefore the buoyant density of membranes in the microsomal fraction, increases during the early stages of deterioration and, thus, membranes exhibiting symptoms of deterioration might well be excluded from a purified fraction. By sampling the entire microsomal fraction, an average estimate can be made of the physical properties and composition of cellular membranes in a tissue. Admittedly, it is not possible by this procedure to ascribe measurable changes to any specific organelle.

A. Phase Properties

A common feature of microsomal membranes isolated from aged seeds and desiccation-, freeze-, or anoxia-injured tissues is the presence of substantial portions of gel phase lipid, which is also commonly found in microsomal membranes from naturally senescing leaves or cotyledons (McKersie *et al.*, 1976). Wide-angle X-ray diffraction has been used to examine the phase properties of isolated membranes, and one can detect both liquid–crystalline and gel phases coexisting in these membranes. When phospholipids are in a liquid–crystalline phase, as in healthy biological membranes, the fatty acid side chains exhibit considerable rotational and lateral motion, and the spacing between their planes is variable, ranging from 4.4 to 4.8 Å. Each of these spacings registers in the diffraction pattern and thus gives rise to a broad X-ray diffraction band centered at an average Bragg spacing of 4.6 Å (McKersie *et al.*, 1976). When phospholipids are in the gel phase, the fatty acids are packed into a more regular hexagonal lattice, motion is restricted to rotation about the long axis of the chain, and the spacing between the planes of the acyl chains of the phospholipid molecules is more consistent. Accordingly, gel phase lipid produces a sharp X-ray diffraction band at a Bragg spacing of approximately 4.2 Å (McKersie *et al.*, 1976).

Microsomal membranes isolated from soybean axes that have been imbibed for 36 hours yield only the broad 4.6 Å band, indicative of the liquid–crystalline phase. A similar microsomal fraction, isolated from axes following 36 hours of imbibition and subsequent lethal desiccation, contains both liquid–crystalline and gel phases at room temperature, as indicated by the presence of bands at 4.6 and 4.2 Å, respectively (Senaratna *et al.*, 1984). The phase transition temperature has been measured by estimating the highest temperature at which the 4.2 Å gel phase band can be detected, and this parameter shifts from 9°C to more than 40°C following desiccation (Table 13.2).

When nonacclimated crowns of wheat seedlings are frozen to −12°C, which completely prevents regrowth and positive tetrazolium staining, there is also a formation of gel phase domains in the microsomal membrane fraction. The phase transition temperature increases by approximately 40°C following the freezing treatment (Kendall *et al.*, 1986).

The presence of gel phase domains in the cellular membranes would be expected to contribute to the loss of membrane function and the loss of cell viability. The coexistence of liquid–crystalline and gel phase domains is

TABLE 13.2

Physical Properties and Lipid Composition of
Microsomal Membranes from Soybean Axes
Following a Lethal Desiccation Treatment[a]

Measurement	Control	Desiccated
Phase transition temperature[b] (C)	9	47
Microviscosity[c] (poise)	1.30	2.30
Microsomal phospholipid recovered ($\mu mol/g$)	11	6
Phospholipid: sterol (mol: mol)	38	16
Free fatty acid: phospholipid (mol: mol)	0.034	0.343
Fatty acid unsaturation (ratio)[d]	2.5	2.2
Relative DA fluorescence[e]	100	78

[a]Soybean seeds were imbibed for 36 hours and axes removed and dried to 10% moisture. Axes were rehydrated for 2 hours and microsomal membranes isolated. Following the desiccation, the axes were unable to germinate.
[b]Measured by wide angle X-ray diffraction.
[c]Measured by fluorescence depolarization using the probe DPH.
[d]Total of $18:1 + 18:2 + 18:3$/total of $16:0 + 18:0$.
[e]Dansylaziridine.
Adapted from Senaratna et al. (1985a, 1987a).

indicative of a lateral phase separation of the phospholipids in the bilayer, which would alter the pattern of protein organization, affecting enzyme activity (Sanderman, 1978) and transport processes (Baldassare et al., 1979). A maximum in the rate of efflux of ^{22}Na from dipalmitoylphosphatidylcholine or dipalmitoylphosphatidylglycerol liposomes has been observed at the temperature where their respective liquid–crystalline to gel phase transitions occur (Papahadjopoulos et al., 1973). It has been suggested that ions diffuse through transient pores, the probability of pore formation being highest at the boundaries between liquid–crystalline and gel phases (Blok et al., 1975). The semipermeability of liposomes has been correlated with the proportion of interfacial lipid at the boundary between gel and liquid–crystalline domains (Papahadjopoulos et al., 1973; Marsh et al., 1976). Thus, the increased leakage of cytoplasmic solutes from aged, frozen, or ice-encased tissues may be the consequence of a lateral phase separation, leading to the formation of separate gel and liquid–crystalline domains, and the consequent reductions of the membrane's selective permeability.

B. Freeze Fracture Electron Microscopy

The presence of gel phase domains in membranes of frozen plants cells has also been implied from examination of membranes *in situ* using freeze fracture electron microscopy. Pearce and Willison (1985), examining laminae and leaf bases of wheat following freezing, observed the presence of intramembranous particle (IMP)-free regions in the plasmalemma. The frequency and proportion of IMP-free regions increased with freezing damage and occurred only in tissues experiencing extracellular ice formation and not low temperature per se, implying that the IMP-free regions are caused by cellular dehydration. While the authors remained skeptical and proposed several alternate mechanisms, these IMP-free domains are generally assumed to represent gel phase regions in the bilayer (Edwards *et al.*, 1984). Taken together, the freeze fracture and X-ray diffraction data support the concept that gel phase domains exist in membranes of tissues that have been lethally frozen.

C. Membrane Microviscosity

Fluorescence depolarization measures the anisotropy of fluorescence probes such as 1,6-diphenyl-1,3,5-hexatriene (DPH) and provides a measure of average membrane microviscosity. DPH partitions into both liquid–crystalline and gel phase regions of the membrane (Shinitzky and Barenholz, 1978), and, therefore, the measurements obtained are an average signal from the two domains. The probe experiences reduced mobility in gel

TABLE 13.3

Physical Properties and Lipid Composition of Microsomal
Membranes from Axes of Soybean Seeds after Natural Aging[a]

	1981 harvest		
Measurement	Control	Aged	1985 seed
Germination (%)	96	16	91
Microviscosity (poise)	ND	1.9	1.3
Free fatty acid : phospholipid (mol : mol)	0.03	0.64	0.05
Fatty acid unsaturation (ratio)	3.7	3.5	ND
DA fluorescence	ND	74	100

[a]Soybean seeds from 1981 harvest were analyzed in 1982 and stored at room temperature until 1986. Microsomal membranes were isolated from imbibed axes. A 1985 seed lot analyzed in 1986 is included for comparison. Measurements as detailed in Table 13.2. ND, not determined.
Adapted from Senaratna *et al.* (1987b).

TABLE 13.4

Physical Properties and Lipid Composition of Microsomal Membranes from Crowns of Winter Wheat Following a Lethal Freezing Stress [a]

Measurement	Control	Frozen	Frozen/thawed
Phase transition temperature (°C)	25	ND	65
Microviscosity (poise)	1.83	2.35	2.34
Microsomal phospholipid recovered (μmol/g)	0.41	0.29	0.26
Microsomal protein recovered (mg/g)	1.98	1.36	1.24
Free fatty acid : phospholipid (mol : mol)	0.23	ND	2.60
Fatty acid unsaturation (ratio)	2.7	2.8	3.5
Relative DPH fluorescence	95	ND	37
Relative DA fluorescence	100	68	63

[a] Seven-day-old winter wheat seedlings were frozen at −2°C on moistened towels and then cooled at 2°C/hour to −12°C. Samples were removed and immediately ground in homogenizing buffer. Other samples were allowed to slowly warm to 5°C for 4 hours. Microsomal membranes were isolated. The crown cells are unable to reduce tetrazolium and do not regrow following this freezing treatment. Measurements as detailed in Table 13.2.

Adapted from Borochov *et al.* (1987) and Kendall *et al.* (1986).

phase lipid, thus an increase in the proportion of gel phase domains is observed as a decreased anisotropy of the fluorescence signal.

Microsomal membranes isolated from tissues following prolonged seed storage, desiccation, freezing, and anoxia consistently have increased microviscosity (Tables 13.2–13.5). This is in agreement with the previous

TABLE 13.5

Physical Properties and Lipid Composition of Microsomal Membranes from Crowns of Winter Wheat during Encasement in Ice at −1°C[a]

	Duration of ice-encasement (days)		
Measurement	0	1	5
Regrowth (%)	100	100	0
Microviscosity (poise)	1.95	2.07	2.72
Microsomal protein recovered (mg/g)	1.08	1.15	0.57
Total lipid recovered (mg/g)	1.12	1.27	0.65
Protein : phospholipid (mg : μmol)	6.8	10.7	9.1
Fatty acid unsaturation (ratio)	2.6	2.8	2.4
Free fatty acid : phospholipid (mol : mol)	0.9	1.2	2.1

[a] Winter wheat seedlings were grown for 7 days at 20/15°C and then cold acclimated for 10 days at 2°C. The leaves were trimmed from the seedlings to allow complete ice encasement of the crown and roots for periods of 1 and 5 days. Microsomal membranes were isolated immediately from the crowns after rapidly thawing the ice. Measurements as detailed in Table 13.2

Adapted from Hetherington *et al.* (1987).

observations, suggesting *in situ* formation of gel phase domains and an elevation of the lipid phase transition temperature.

IV. LIPID AND PROTEIN COMPOSITION OF MICROSOMAL MEMBRANES

A. Membrane Lipids

As in the case of leaf and cotyledon senescence, aging processes involve a general loss of membrane constituents, notably phospholipid and protein. On a fresh or dry weight basis, there is roughly a 30–50% decline in level of phospholipid or protein recovered in the microsomal fraction following prolonged seed storage, desiccation, freezing, or ice-encasement (Tables 13.2–13.5). As with natural senescence, the degradation of the phospholipids in pregerminated soybeans appears to be random, with no selective loss of a particular phospholipid class (Table 13.6). Phospholipids (PL) are generally lost from the membrane earlier and more rapidly than the protein, and consequently there is often an increase in the protein/PL ratio (Tables 13.4 and 13.5).

Changes in fatty acid saturation have been studied extensively, primarily because of the preoccupation with the hypothesis that phospholipid degradation involves fatty acid peroxidation, especially in the case of seed aging (Wilson and McDonald, 1986). In seeds having substantial lipid reserves,

TABLE 13.6

Total Phospholipid Content of Microsomal Membranes from Soybean Axes, Imbibed for 6 Hours (Desiccation Tolerant) and 36 hours (Desiccation Intolerant) before and after Desiccation Treatment and *in Vitro* Free Radical Treatment[a]

		Phospholipid (% total)				
Tissue	Treatment	LPC	PI	PC	PE	PA
6 hours	Control	3	22	44	23	2
	Desiccated	4	20	41	21	3
36 hours	Control	3	19	48	22	3
	Desiccated	4	21	45	22	3
	Exposed to free radicals	3	20	43	20	2

[a]Free radicals were generated from xanthine oxidase. LPC: lysophosphatidylcholine; PI, phosphatidylinositol; PC, phosphatidylcholine; PE, phosphatidylethanolamine; PA, phosphatidic acid.
Adapted from Senaratna *et al.* (1987a).

the amount of phospholipid relative to total lipid is comparatively small. Most studies have focused on changes in the total seed lipids and have only inferred changes in membrane phospholipid, because of the obvious difficulties of studying membranes in a dried tissue. Not surprisingly, the evidence is somewhat contradictory, and evidence for and against a connection between changes in fatty acid saturation and seed aging has been reported (Wilson and McDonald, 1986; Priestley, 1986).

A comparison of the fatty acid composition of the microsomal membranes isolated from soybean seeds harvested in 1981 to the same seed stored at room temperature for 5 years, indicated less than a 1% change in the proportion of any fatty acid (Table 13.3), even though germination had declined from 95 to 16%. The major compositional change that could be measured in the lipid extracted from these aged membranes was an approximate 20-fold increase in the proportion of nonesterified or free fatty acids associated with the lipid bilayer (Table 13.3). Closely similar results have been reported for naturally aged soybean by Priestley *et al.* (1980).

This increase in the proportion of free fatty acids to phospholipids in the membrane bilayer is a very common observation in aged systems (Tables 13.2–13.5), including pollen that had been stored dry for several months (Fig. 13.2). Desiccation, freezing, and anoxia also promote the loss of phospholipid and the accumulation of free fatty acids, suggesting that in each case membrane phospholipids have been de-esterified, with the acyl chains remaining in the bilayer. At the same time, however, there is no accumulation of lysophosphatides (Table 13.6). Therefore, one suspects that both fatty acid chains are cleaved almost simultaneously from the phospholipid, with the result that the glycerol-head group units or their degradation products are released into the aqueous phase. These changes occur primarily while the tissue is in the dry, frozen, or anoxic state, although the changes do continue in some cases when the tissue is returned to conditions favoring active metabolism.

One major distinction between membrane deterioration in aged and in naturally senescing tissue is the accumulation of free fatty acids in aging systems. Membranes from naturally senescing tissues do not apparently accumulate free fatty acids in the membrane bilayer (Barber and Thompson, 1983), whereas those from aged tissues do. Senescing tissues are able to metabolize the free fatty acids by enzymes such as lipoxygenase (Chapter 2) and may therefore be able to mobilize the lipids into forms that could be potentially translocated to other tissues, such as the developing seed. In contrast, metabolism in these aging systems is curtailed by dehydration, temperature, or anoxia. Therefore, the immediate products of phospholipid degradation, the free fatty acids, accumulate in the membrane because their further catabolism is blocked.

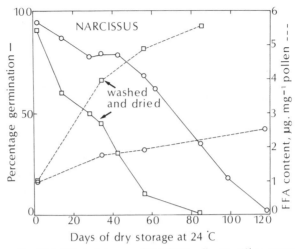

Fig. 13.2. Effect of storage of *Narcissus* pollen (5–6% moisture content) at 24°C on viability and accumulation of free fatty acids. One pollen sample was washed in germination medium for 5 minutes and immediately filtered and dried to 5–6% moisture content. [Reprinted from Hoekstra (1986), with permission of Cornell University Press.]

B. Membrane Proteins

There also appear to be qualitative, as well as the previously mentioned quantitative, changes in membrane proteins. These have not been studied extensively, but have been examined generally using the fluorescent probe, *N*-dansylaziridine (DA). The probe associates with protein thiol groups, and its fluorescence provides a quantitative estimate of the number of thiol groups present (Borochov and Shinitzky, 1976; Scouten *et al.*, 1974). The fluorescence intensity of DA per unit of membrane protein declines as cellular membranes deteriorate during storage, ice-encasement, or following desiccation or freezing (Tables 13.2–13.4; Fig. 13.3). This suggests that the number of thiol groups per unit of membrane protein has declined either through oxidative reactions or through the selective loss of thiol-rich proteins from the membrane.

V. FREE FATTY ACIDS AND LIPID PHASE PROPERTIES

The major change in the composition of the lipid bilayer of membranes from aged systems is a several-fold increase in the level of free fatty acids. The composition of this fatty acid fraction is similar to that of the total lipid

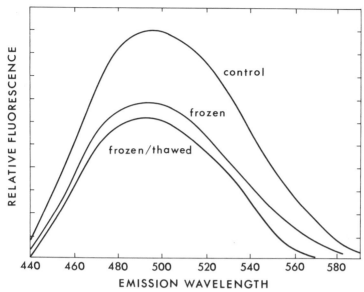

Fig. 13.3. Fluorescence emission spectra of N-dansylaziridine labeled micro-somal membranes from 7-day-old winter wheat crowns following freezing treatment. Membranes were isolated from control crowns; crowns frozen to −12°C and homogenized while frozen; and crowns frozen to −12°C and thawed for 4 hours at 5°C. Excitation was at 350 nm.

extract, approximately 25% saturated and 75% unsaturated in these in-stances. In model membranes composed of simple PL mixtures, the addition of saturated and unsaturated free fatty acids has quite complex and different effects on the physical properties of the bilayer (Jain and Wu, 1977; Mabray and Sturtevant, 1977; Verma *et al.*, 1980; Katsaras *et al.*, 1986).

Liposomes prepared from the total lipids extracted from the microsomal membrane fraction from soybean axes have a lipid phase transition temper-ature of 6°C, as determined by wide angle X-ray diffraction. Therefore, at room temperature, the bilayer is completely in the liquid–crystalline phase. Saturated free fatty acids, in amounts approximating those found in the microsomal fractions containing gel phase domains (Senaratna *et al.*, 1985a; Kendall *et al.*, 1986), were added to the lipid extract. The multilamellar liposomes prepared from these extracts had an increased phase transition temperature and increased microviscosity in a manner quantitatively simi-lar to that observed in aged membranes (Table 13.7). The addition of unsat-urated free fatty acids to the same lipid extract had a markedly different effect on the physical properties of the bilayer. The phase transition temper-ature was not changed, but the microviscosity was reduced, indicating a

TABLE 13.7

Phase Transition Temperature and Microviscosity of Liposomes Prepared from Microsomal
Membrane Lipid after Addition of Free Fatty Acids[a]

	Free fatty acid (mmol:mol phospholipid)					Phase transition temperature (°C)	Microviscos (poise)
Extract	16:0	18:0	18:1	18:2	18:3		
Control	9	2	2	15	6	6	0.82
+ Saturated FFA	109	22	2	15	6	41	1.39
+ Unsaturated FFA	9	2	22	155	66	6	0.60
+ Saturated and unsaturated FFA	109	22	22	155	66	37	1.02

[a]Lipid extracts were prepared from microsomal membranes isolated from soybean axes imbibed for 36 hours.
extracts were supplemented by the addition of free fatty acids (FFA) at the levels indicated, prior to preparation
liposomes. The phase transition temperature was recorded by X-ray diffraction. Microviscosity was calculated from
fluorescence anisotropy measurements of the lipophilic probe DPH.
Adapted from Senaratna *et al.* (1987a).

slight perturbing effect on the bilayer. The addition of both saturated and
unsaturated free fatty acids, which is the situation occurring in the membranes naturally, mimicked the response induced by the saturated free fatty
acids alone, but modulated slightly, presumably because of the counteracting perturbing effect of the unsaturated fatty acids. Consequently, the alterations in the physical properties of the membranes, namely the formation of
gel phase domains and the increased microviscosity, may be quantitatively
accounted for by the accumulation of a mixture of saturated and unsaturated free fatty acids in the bilayer.

In summary, the four experimental systems undergoing deteriorative
changes have several common features. Membrane semipermeability is
reduced and the tissues readily leak cytoplasmic solutes. The microsomal
membrane fractions contain domains of gel phase and liquid–crystalline
phase lipid. There is pronounced de-esterification of phospholipids, with
the concomitant loss of total phospholipids and the accumulation of free
fatty acids. The free saturated fatty acids contribute to the lateral phase
separation in the membrane, leading to the formation of gel phase domains.

VI. FREE RADICALS

A. Phospholipid De-esterification

There are two possible mechanisms by which phospholipids might be
de-esterified—enzymatically by phospholipase or chemically by free radicals. It is unlikely that enzymes such as phospholipase are active in dry or

frozen tissues. Not only is enzyme activity suppressed in these conditions, but the diffusion of enzymes and substrates would be greatly restricted at low water contents. Although the possibility of enzymic degradation cannot be completely discounted, it seems more likely that lipid degradation in the membranes of dry or frozen tissues is mediated chemically by a free radical mechanism. The lipid peroxidation model of free radical attack on such membranes (Wilson and McDonald, 1986) has long been postulated as the mechanism of damage in dry seeds. Since changes in fatty acid saturation are not always or even consistently observed, the theory has remained controversial. It has only been recently shown that free radicals can de-esterify phospholipids in a membrane bilayer without promoting peroxidation of the unsaturated fatty acids (San Filippo *et al.*, 1976; Niehaus, 1978; Senaratna *et al.*, 1985a).

Each of the deteriorative changes observed in the microsomal membranes *in vivo* can be simulated when isolated microsomal membranes are treated with free radicals *in vitro* from either xanthine-xanthine oxidase, paraquat, or gamma radiation in the absence of oxygen (Senaratna *et al.*, 1985a; Katsaras *et al.*, 1986; Kendall and McKersie, 1988). As illustrated in Table 13.8, membranes exposed to free radicals *in vitro*:

1. Contain gel and liquid–crystalline domains at room temperature
2. Have elevated phase transition temperatures and increased microviscosity
3. Have reduced levels of phospholipid and elevated free fatty acid content
4. Exhibit no or only slight changes in fatty acid saturation
5. Have reduced DA fluorescence, indicating a net loss of thiol groups from the membrane protein (data not shown).

TABLE 13.8

Effect of an *in Vitro* Free Radical Treatment on the Physical Properties and Composition of Microsomal Membranes from Soybean Axes[a]

Imbibition period (hours)	Free radical treatment	Phase transition temp (°C)	Phospholipid: sterol ratio (mol : mol)	FFA : phospholipid (mol : mol)	Percent fatty acid unsaturation
6	Control	7	57	0.052	77
	Treated	14	51	0.088	76
36	Control	9	52	0.043	70
	Treated	40	30	0.212	68

[a]Soybean seeds were imbibed for 6 hours (tolerant of desiccation) and 36 hours (susceptible to desiccation) and the axes removed. Microsomal membranes were isolated and treated with superoxide free radicals generated from xanthine oxidase. Measurements as detailed in Table 13.2
Adapted from Senaratna *et al.* (1985a).

In contrast, treatment of microsomal membranes from pea foliage with phospholipase A_2 activated by calcium and calmodulin may (Sridhara and Leshem, 1986) or may not (Leshem *et al.*, 1984) promote formation of gel phase domains.

B. Free Radical Scavenging Systems

The longevity of seeds in storage varies among species (Priestley *et al.*, 1985a). Plants and plant tissues may also vary in their tolerance of desiccation, freezing, and ice-encasement. Plants that are relatively more tolerant of these stresses are also relatively more tolerant of treatments that promote free radical formation. For example, wheat protoplasts isolated from cold-acclimated wheat seedlings are more tolerant of paraquat than those from nonacclimated seedlings (Kendall and McKersie, 1988). Similarly, the intact cold acclimated wheat seedling is more tolerant of the herbicide oxyfluorfen (C. Mackay, unpublished observations), which also acts by promoting free radical formation (Finckh and Kunert, 1985). The application of the triazole, S-3307, to wheat seedlings in the absence of cold acclimation increases their tolerance of freezing, ozone, and the herbicide oxyfluorfen (Mackay *et al.*, 1987, and unpublished observations).

At least one of the molecular components providing increased free radical tolerance to these plant tissues is a membrane component. Microsomal membranes isolated from plant tissues that are relatively tolerant of desiccation or freezing are themselves relatively tolerant of *in vitro* free radical treatment (Table 13.8). Treatment of the microsomal membranes isolated from 6-hour axes (i.e., desiccation tolerant) with a given dose of free radicals from xanthine-xanthine oxidase system causes less phospholipid de-esterification and smaller changes in the physical properties of the membranes than a similar treatment applied to membranes from 36-hour axes (i.e., desiccation susceptible). Soybean axes contain about 100-fold more lipid-soluble antioxidants at 6 hours of imbibition compared to 36 hours imbibition (Senaratna *et al.*, 1985b). A component of this antioxidant fraction is α-tocopherol.

α-Tocopherol (vitamin E) is associated with cellular membranes, primarily the chloroplast membranes (Lichtenhaler *et al.*, 1981), and at least one of its functions is to scavenge free radicals (Tappel, 1962). α-Tocopherol acts as the primary antioxidant in leaf tissue and is regenerated by reactions with the water soluble antioxidant, ascorbic acid (vitamin C) (Finckh and Kunert, 1985). Experiments that have attempted to correlate oxidation of tocopherol and loss of seed viability during aging are contradictory (Senaratna *et al.*, 1987b; Priestley, 1986; Priestley *et al.*, 1980; Sharma, 1977). One possible explanation may be the large lipid reserve content of the cotyledons of soybean seeds, which may have masked the quantitatively small changes occurring in the cellular membranes of the axis. In soybean seeds that had been naturally aged for 5 years, the α-tocopherol content and the total lipid soluble antioxidant content of the axis declined by approximately 30% as germination declined to 16% (Table 13.9).

C. Production of Free Radicals

A free radical is an atom or molecule with an unpaired electron such that it can accept (or donate) an electron from an adjacent molecule. Rigidly channeled free radicals play an essential role in cellular metabolism and are formed as intermediates in many metabolic reactions involving the transfer of electrons. Certain enzymes such as xanthine oxidase and lipoxygenase form free radical products. Perturbations of cellular metabolism may create "leaks" in these reactions involving electron transfer and allow the escape of free radical intermediates. For example, oxygen reduction to superoxide can occur at the flavoprotein segment of NADH dehydrogenase and at the ubiquinone–cytochrome b region of the mitochondrial electron transport chain (Rich and Bonner, 1978). If normal electron transport is disrupted, a "short circuit" in the electron transport chain may be created, leading to the production of superoxide and perhaps other oxy-free radicals. The application of KCN to isolated mitochondria from alfalfa roots increases the free fatty acid content of the mitochondria, possibly by the liberation of superoxide free radicals (Illman, 1985). Desiccation, freezing, or anoxia may

TABLE 13.9

Antioxidant Content of Naturally Aged Soybean Seeds[a]

| | 1981 harvest | | 1985 harvest |
	Control	Aged	
Germination (%)	95	16	91
Total antioxidants (% inhibition)	87	59	86
β- and γ-Tocopherol (μg/g)	ND	39.7	59.1
α-Tocopherol (μg/g)	ND	36.6	44.7

[a]Aged soybean seeds were prepared as detailed in Table 13.3. A total lipid extract was analyzed for lipid soluble antioxidants and expressed as percent inhibition of linolenic acid oxidation (Senaratna *et al.*, 1985b). Tocopherol content was analyzed by gas chromatography and expressed as (μg/g). ND, not determined.

Adapted from Senaratna *et al.* (1987b).

perturb cellular metabolism in such a way as to create "short circuits" or "leaks" in electron transport reactions and promote superoxide and hydroxyl-free radical formation.

It has been shown that microsomal membranes isolated from wheat crowns following lethal freezing produce greater quantities of free radical products than membranes from nonfrozen tissue (Fig. 13.4). Free radicals, particularly oxy-free radicals, can also be produced nonenzymatically. For example, superoxide can be formed *in situ* by photoxidative processes. Hydroxyl radicals can be formed by the reaction of peroxides and metal ions or by the radiolysis of water in the absence of oxygen (Edwards *et al.*, 1984).

The presence of organic-free radicals has been documented for soybean seeds during seed aging (Buchvarov and Grantcheff, 1984; Priestley *et al.*, 1985b), and the levels have been shown to decrease with the addition of moisture (Priestley *et al.*, 1985b). Free radicals are relatively short lived; superoxide, for example, has a half-life of nanoseconds, and it is therefore not surprising that it has not been possible to detect increases in their levels with natural aging (Priestley *et al.*, 1980).

VII. SUMMARY

These data are consistent with the following model of membrane deterioration during aging-like processes in plant cells. It differs significantly in several respects from that which occurs during natural senescence (Chapter 2) in which there is expected to be a significant contribution of cellular metabolism. In the "aging" processes, these changes occur in the absence of metabolism, when metabolism is defined as "the operation of integrated pathways of enzyme-catalyzed reactions that are regulated in rate and direction" (Lynch and Clegg, 1986). Isolated enzyme reactions can occur at low water contents (Lynch and Clegg, 1986) and also presumably in frozen tissues and certainly in anoxic tissues, and these may well contribute to the deterioration processes. In fact, these isolated enzyme reactions may be one of the sources of free radicals.

Although their method of production is not yet defined, free radicals are apparently produced and mediate the de-esterification of membrane phospholipids (Niehaus, 1978; Senaratna *et al.*, 1985b) and the reduction of protein thiol groups (Orrenius, 1985). Both of these reactions would be expected to further perturb cellular metabolism and may enhance free radical production in a cascading-type of reaction. The de-esterification of membrane phospholipids leads to a net loss of membrane material and an accumulation of free fatty acids in the bilayer. The saturated free fatty acids promote a lipid phase separation and the formation of gel phase domains.

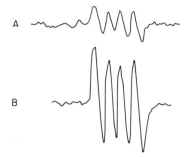

Fig. 13.4. Electron spin resonance spectra of the spin trap Tiron (5 mM) incubated with microsomal membranes (200 μg protein/ml) from 7-day-old wheat crowns. (A) Control; (b) Seedlings frozen to $-12\,^\circ$C for 16 hours. The amplitude of the ESR signal provides an estimate of the amount of quinone formed, which is proportional to the quantity of free radicals produced.

The reorganization of the lipid bilayer would also perturb the organization of membrane-bound proteins, notably transport proteins and alter their kinetics. The formation of the gel phase domains would create discontinuities in the bilayer and enhance the efflux of cytoplasmic solutes.

REFERENCES

Andrews, C. J., and Pomeroy, M. K. (1977). Mitochondrial activity and ethanol accumulation in ice-encased winter cereal seedlilngs. *Plant Physiol.* **59**, 1174–1178.

Baldassare, J., Saito, Y., and Silbert, D. (1979). Effect of sterol depletion on LM cell sterol mutants. Changes in lipid composition of the plasma membrane and their effects on 3-O-methyl-glucose transport. *J. Biol. Chem.* **254**, 1108–1113.

Barber, R. F., and Thompson, J. E. (1983). Neutral lipids rigidify unsaturated acyl chains in senescing membranes. *J. Exp. Bot.* **34**, 268–276.

Berjak, P., and Villiers, T. A. (1972). Ageing in plant embryos. II. Age-induced damage and its repairs during early germination. *New Phytol.* **71**, 135–144.

Blok, M. C., Vender Neut-kok, E. C. M., van Deenen, L. L. M., and de Gier, J. (1975). The effect of chain length and lipid phase transitions on the selective permeability properties of liposomes. *Biochim. Biophys. Acta* **406**, 187.

Borochov, A., Walker, M. A., Kendall, E. J., Pauls, K. P., and McKersie, B. D. (1987). Effect of a freeze–thaw cycle on properties of microsomal membranes from wheat. *Plant Physiol.* **84**, 131–134.

Borochov, H., and Shinitzky, M. (1976). Vertical displacement of proteins mediated by changes in microviscosity. *Proc. Natl. Acad. Sci. U.S.A.* **73**, 4526–4530.

Buchvarov, P., and Grantcheff, Ts. (1984). Influence of accelerated and natural ageing on free radical levels in soybean seeds. *Physiol. Plant.* **60,** 53–56.

Dasgupta, J., Bewley, J. D., and Yeung, E. C. (1982). Desiccation-tolerant and desiccation-intolerant stages during the development and germination of *Phaseolus vulgaris* seeds. *J. Exp. Bot.* **33,** 1045–1057.

Edwards, J. C., Chapman, D., Cramp, W. A., and Yatvin, M. B. (1984). The effects of ionizing radiation on biomembrane structure and function. *Prog. Biophys. Mol. Biol.* **43,** 77–93.

Finckh, B. F., and Kunert, K. J. (1985). Vitamin C and E. An antioxidative system against herbicide-induced lipid peroxidation in higher plants. *J. Agric. Food Chem.* **33,** 574–577.

Frankel, E. N. (1985). The chemistry of free radical and singlet oxidation of lipids. *Prog. Lipid Res.* **23,** 197–221.

Hegarty, T. W. (1978). The physiology of seed hydration and dehydration and the relation between water stress and control of germination. A review. *Plant Cell Environ.* **1,** 109–119.

Hetherington, P. R., McKersie, B. D., and Borochov, A. (1987). Ice-encasement injury to microsomal membranes from winter wheat crowns. I. Comparison of membrane properties after lethal ice-encasement and during a post-thaw period. *Plant Physiol.* **85,** 1068–1072.

Hoekstra, F. A. (1986). Water content in relation to stress in pollen. *In* "Membranes, Metabolism and Dry Organisms" (A. C. Leopold, ed.), pp. 102–122. Cornell Univ. Press, Ithaca, New York.

Illman, D. D. (1985). Isolation injury to alfalfa (*Medicago sativa* L.) mitochondrial membranes. M.S. Thesis, Univ. of Guelph, Guelph, Ontario.

Jain, M. K., and Wu, N. W. (1977). Effect of small molecules on dipalmitoyl lecithin liposomal bilayers. III. Phase transition in lipid bilayer. *J. Membr. Biol.* **34,** 157–201.

Katsaras, J., Stinson, R. H., Kendall, E. J., and McKersie, B. D. (1986). Structural simulation of free radical damage in a model membrane system: a small angle x-ray diffraction study. *Biochim. Biophys. Acta* **861,** 243–250.

Kendall, E. J., and McKersie, B. D. (1988). Free radical and freezing injury in cell membranes from *Triticum aestivum* L. *Plant Physiol.* (in press).

Kendall, E. J., McKersie, B. D., and Stinson, R. H. (1986). Phase properties of membranes following freezing injury in winter wheat. *Can. J. Bot.* **63,** 2274–2277.

Leshem, Y. Y., Sridhara, S., and Thompson, J. E. (1984). Involvement of calcium and calmodulin in membrane deterioration during senescence of pea foliage. *Plant Physiol.* **75,** 329–335.

Lichtenthaler, H. K., Prenzel, U., Douce, R., and Joyard, J. (1981). Localization of prenylquinones in the envelope of spinach chloroplasts. *Biochim. Biophys. Acta* **641,** 99–105.

Lynch, R. M., and Clegg, J. S. (1986). A study of metabolism in dry seeds of *Avena fatua* L. evaluated by incubation with ethanol-1-^{14}C. *In* "Membranes, Metabolism and Dry Organisms" (A. C. Leopold, ed.), pp. 50–58. Cornell Univ. Press, Ithaca, New York.

Mabray, S., and Sturtevant, J. M. (1977). Incorporation of saturated fatty acids into phosphatidylcholine bilayers. *Biochim. Biophys. Acta* **486,** 444–450.

Mackay, C. E., Senaratna, T., McKersie, B. D., and Fletcher, R. A. (1987). Ozone induced injury to cellular membranes in *Triticum aestivum* and protection by the triazole S-3307. *Plant Cell Physiol.* **28,** 1271–1278.

McKersie, B. D., and Tomes, D. T. (1981). A comparison of seed quality and seedling vigor in birdsfoot trefoil. *Crop Sci.* **22,** 1239–1241.

McKersie, B. D., Thompson, J. E., and Brandon, J. K. (1976). X-ray diffraction evidence for deceased lipid fluidity in senescent membranes from cotyledons. *Can. J. Bot.* **54,** 1074–1078.

Marsh, D., Watts, A., and Knowles, P. F. (1976). Evidence for phase boundary lipid: permeability of Tempo-choline into dimyristoylphosphatidylcholine vesicles at the phase transition. *Biochemistry* **15,** 3570.

Niehaus, W. J., Jr. (1978). A proposed role of superoxide anion as a biological nucleophile in the deesterification of phospholipid. *Bioorg. Chem.* **7,** 77–84.

Olien, C. R. (1967). Freezing stresses and survival. *Annu. Rev. Plant Physiol.* **18**, 387–408.

Orrenius, S. (1985). Oxidative stress studied in intact mammalian cells. *Philos. Trans. R. Soc. London, Ser. B* **311**, 673–677.

Palta, J. P., and Li, P. H. (1980). Alternatives in membrane transport properties by freezing injury in herbaceous plants: evidence against rupture theory. *Physiol. Plant.* **50**, 169–175.

Palta, J. P., Levitt, J., and Stadelman, E. J. (1977). Freezing injury in onion bulb cells. I. Evaluation of the conductivity methods and analysis of ion and sugar efflux from injured cells. *Plant Physiol.* **60**, 393–397.

Papahadjopoulos, D., Jacobsen, K., Nir, S., and Isac, T. (1973). Phase transitions in phospholipid vesicles. Fluorescent polarization and permeability measurements concerning the effect of temperature and cholesterol. *Biochim. Biophys. Acta* **311**, 330.

Pearce, R. S. (1982). Ultrastructure of tall fescue (*Festuca arundinacea* schreb cv S170) cells fixed while exposed to lethal or non-lethal extracellular freezing. *New Phytol.* **92**, 259–272.

Pearce, R. S., and Willison, J. H. M. (1985). A freeze-etch study of the effects of extracellular freezing on cellular membranes of wheat. *Planta* **163**, 304–316.

Pomeroy, M. K., Pihakaski, S. J., and Andrews, C. J. (1983). Membrane properties of isolated winter wheat cells in relation to icing stress. *Plant Physiol.* **72**, 535–539.

Pomeroy, M. K., Andrews, C. J., Stanley, K. P., and Gao, J. Y. (1985). Physiological and metabolic responses of winter wheat to prolonged freezing stress. *Plant Physiol.* **78**, 207–210.

Powell, A. A., and Matthews, S. (1979). The influence of test conditions on the imbibition and vigour of pea seeds. *J. Exp. Bot.* **30**, 193–197.

Priestley, D. A. (1986). "Seed Aging. Implications for Seed Storage and Persistence in Soil." Cornell Univ. Press, Ithaca, New York.

Priestley, D. A., McBride, M. B., and Leopold, A. C. (1980). Tocopherol and organic free radical levels in soybean seeds during natural and accelerated ageing. *Plant Physiol.* **66**, 715–719.

Priestley, D. A., Cullinan, V. I., and Wolf, J. (1985a). Differences in seed longevity at the species level. *Plant Cell Environ.* **8**, 557–562.

Priestley, D. A., Werner, B. G., Leopold, A. C., and McBride, M. B. (1985b). Organic free radical levels in seeds and pollen. The effects of hydration and ageing. *Physiol. Plant.* **64**, 88–94.

Rich, P. R., and Bonner, W. D. (1978). The sites of superoxide anion generation in higher plant mitochondria. *Arch. Biochem. Biophys.* **188**, 206–213.

Sandermann, H., Jr. (1978). Regulation of membrane enzymes by lipids. *Biochim. Biophys. Acta* **515**, 209–237.

San Filippo, J., Jr., Romano, L. J., Chern, C., and Valentine, J. S. (1976). Cleavage of esters by superoxide. *J. Org. Chem.* **41**, 586–588.

Scouten, W. H., Lubcher, R., and Baughman, W. (1974). N-dansylaziridine: a new fluorescence modification for cysteine thiols. *Biochim. Biophys. Acta* **336**, 421–426.

Senaratna, T., and McKersie, B. D. (1983). Characterization of solute efflux from dehydration injured soybean (*Glycine max* L. Merr.) seeds. *Plant Physiol.* **72**, 911–914.

Senaratna, T., McKersie, B. D., and Stinson, R. H. (1984). The association between membrane phase properties and dehydration injury in soybean axes. *Plant Physiol.* **76**, 759–762.

Senaratna, T., McKersie, B. D., and Stinson, R. H. (1985a). Simulation of dehydration injury to membranes from soybean axes by free radicals. *Plant Physiol.* **77**, 472–474.

Senaratna, T., McKersie, B. D., and Stinson, R. H. (1985b). Antioxidant levels in germinating soybean seed axes in relation to free radical and dehydration tolerance. *Plant Physiol.* **78**, 168–171.

Senaratna, T., Borochov, A., and McKersie, B. D. (1987a). Desiccation and free radical induced changes in lipid and protein of cell membranes. *J. Exp. Bot.* **38**, 2005–2014.

Senaratna, T., Gusse, J. F., and McKersie, B. D. (1987b). Age-induced changes in cellular membranes from imbibed soybean seed axes. *Physiol. Plant* (in press).

Sharma, K. D. (1977). Biochemical changes in stored oil seeds. *Indian J. Agric. Res.* **11**, 137–141.

Shinitzky, M., and Barenholz, Y. (1978). Fluidity parameters of lipid regions determined by fluorescence polarization. *Biochim. Biophys. Acta* **515**, 367–394.

Simon, E. W. (1974). Phospholipids and plant membrane permeability. *New Phytol.* **73**, 377–420.

Singh, J. (1979). Ultrastructural alterations in cells of hardened and nonhardened winter rye during hyperosmotic and extracellular freezing stresses. *Protoplasma* **98**, 329–341.

Sridhara, S., and Leshem, Y. Y. (1986). Phospholipid catabolism and senescence of pea foliage membranes: parameters of Ca^{2+}: calmodulin: phospholipase A_2 induced changes. *New Phytol.* **103**, 5–16.

Steponkus, P. L. (1984). Role of the plasma membrane in freezing injury and cold acclimation. *Annu. Rev. Plant Physiol.* **35**, 543–584.

Tappel, A. L. (1962). Vitamin E as the biological lipid antioxidant. *Vitam. Horm. (N.Y.)* **20**, 493–510.

Verma, S. P., Wallach, D. F. H., and Sakura, J. D. (1980). Raman analysis of the thermotropic behaviour of lecithin-fatty acid systems and their interaction with proteolipid apoprotein. *Biochemistry* **19**, 574–579.

Wilson, D. O., Jr., and McDonald, M. B., Jr. (1986). The lipid peroxidation model of seed ageing. *Seed Sci. Technol.* **14**, 269–300.

14

Seed Aging: The Genome and Its Expression

E. H. Roberts
Department of Agriculture
University of Reading
Reading, England

SENESCENCE AND AGING IN PLANTS

I. INTRODUCTION

The deterioration of seeds and spores under air dry conditions, which culminates in their loss of viability or death, is generally accepted unequivocally as a good example of a stochastic aging process. There is no evidence that the process is programmed, and it appears to result from the occurrence of more or less random events. This is most clearly seen in the case of single-celled bacterial spores. Their survival curves are typically linear when the logarithm of the number of survivors is plotted against time (Roberts, 1972). This means that the number of spores that die during any unit interval of time is always a constant proportion of the number of viable spores that were present at the beginning of that interval. In other words, however long a spore has lived, its chances of survival over the next unit interval of time remains the same. Because of this, some would argue that bacterial spores do not age, since one definition of aging is that the probability of death increases with time. In fact, the survival curves of spores are identical in form to the survival curves of glass tumblers in a cafeteria (Brown and Flood, 1947). The tumblers do not age, and, however long any one of them has survived, its probability of being broken during each successive period of usage remains the same.

The probability of the tumbler being the subject of an accident remains the same, of course, only if the environmental conditions (e.g., the quality of the staff or the frequency of tumbler use) remain the same. So it is with spores; the probability density of the apparently random events that cause the death of a spore can be increased by, for example, increasing the temperature of storage.

Now the survival curves of seeds are different from spores or tumblers; they are cumulative normal distributions of negative slope. This is because the distribution of lifespans among the seeds of a population is normal (Roberts, 1960, 1986; Ellis and Roberts, 1981). Consequently, the probability of death in the next unit interval of time of a seed that has survived so far does in fact increase with time — at least until the viability of the population has fallen to a very low percentage. In this sense it would appear that a seed ages. However, it has been shown by mathematical analysis (Roberts *et al.*, 1967) and by computer simulations (Roberts, 1972) that seed survival curves could be of this form (normal distributions of lifespans) even when the individual cells of the seed lose viability in the same manner as unicellular spores, i.e., the probability of the death of a cell is unaffected by how long that cell has survived. For this model to be valid it is only necessary to make two assumptions, both of which seem plausible: at least 100 or more cells have a critical role in the onset of germination, and it is necessary for a considerable proportion of these, say 80% or more, to survive for the seed to be able to germinate (Roberts, 1972).

Thus, in spite of the fact that survival curves of unicellular spores and multicellular seeds are quite different, it is not necessary to postulate any fundamental differences between these two types of propagule with respect to loss of viability. It could be argued that cells of both are subject to stochastic and potentially lethal events, and that the increasing probability of death with time observed in seeds, which is sometimes described as one of the symptoms of aging, is an inevitable consequence of the multicellular organization of cells.

Whether or not the comparison between spores and seeds is valid, it is evident that there are a number of events of different types that precede the death of a seed and are damaging but not lethal, and their accumulation leads to decreased vigor before seed death (Ellis and Roberts, 1980c). In this chapter attention will be restricted almost entirely to those events that affect the genome.

II. HISTORICAL PERSPECTIVE

A. A False Dawn: Old Seeds of *Oenothora* Contain More "Mutants" Than New Seeds (1901–1931)

I have been guilty, among others, of following Kostoff (1935) and suggesting that the history of loss of genetic integrity that is associated with seed aging started with de Vries (1901). He observed that 5-year-old seed of *Oenothera erythrosepala* gave rise to more mutant phenotypes than fresh seeds. Nilsson (1931) made similar observations that seemed to confirm this. Both scientists concluded that seed with mutant phenotypes lived longer than those with normal phenotypes; thus it was assumed that the mutants did not arise as a result of storage but were there in the beginning. Subsequent work on other species showed beyond reasonable doubt that mutations accumulate within seeds as they age; because of this some of us thought that the interpretation that de Vries and Nilsson put on their own work was somewhat perverse and probably mistaken. Accordingly, it has often been suggested that the history of induction of mutations in seeds as they age began with de Vries (see, e.g., Roberts *et al.*, 1967; Abdalla and

Roberts, 1968; Roberts, 1972, 1973b, 1978). However, Priestley (1985) has recently pointed out that *Oenothora* has unusual genetical characteristics and that the "mutants" observed by de Vries and Nilsson were not gene mutations in the modern sense; most aberrant phenotypes observed by them were the manifestations of trisomics, polyploids, or other complex genetic segregations peculiar to *Oenothera*. This, together with other evidence, makes the explanation that de Vries gave of his own work more likely. Therefore, the history of the accumulation of chromosome damage and gene mutations in seeds as they age probably did not really begin until the 1930s.

B. Chromosome Aberrations and Gene Mutations, or the Events That Give Rise to Them, Are Induced during Seed Storage (1933–1936)

In one of those remarkable coincidences not uncommon in science, several lines of enquiry all came to fruition in the early 1930s. Navashin (1933a,b) working on seeds of *Crepis tectorum*, and Peto (1933), who investigated maize seeds *(Zea mays)* appear to have been the first to have observed that high frequencies of visible chromosome aberrations occur in roots produced from old seeds. At the same time, Cartledge and Blakeslee (1933, 1934) showed that old seed of *Datura* gave increased proportions of pollen-abortion mutations. Further work by this group (Blakeslee and Avery, 1934; Avery and Blakeslee, 1936) showed that high rates of phenotypic mutations were also induced by aging in seeds; and further work on *Crepis* by Navashin and Gerassimova (1936a,b) confirmed the earlier work on the increase in chromosome aberrations that could be detected by cytological observations on young roots.

The work on accumulation of chromosomal aberrations during seed storage has subsequently been confirmed in a very wide range of species, e.g., in onion *(Allium cepa)* (Nichols, 1941; Sax and Sax, 1964), spring onion *(Allium fistulosum)* (Kato, 1951), peas *(Pisum sativum)* (D'Amato, 1951), durum wheat *(Triticum durum)*, common wheat *(T. aestivum)*, barley *(Hordeum vulgare)*, rye *(Secale cereale)*, peas *(Pisum sativum)* (Gunthardt et al., 1953), lettuce *(Lactuca sativa)* (Harrison and McLeish, 1954; Harrison, 1966), and maize *(Zea mays)* (Berjak, 1968).

C. Accumulation of Chromosome Damage Is a Function of Time, Temperature, and Moisture Content (1933–1939)

In a great deal of the early work described above, visible chromosomal damage and the results of mutations — heritable phenotypic changes in the progeny and pollen abortion — were related by the investigators to age of the seed. However, it gradually became apparent that chronological age of the seed is not the only factor involved in the induction of chromosome aberrations. Evidence that temperature and seed moisture content during storage are also important was soon to come from cytological work on *Crepis* (Navashin and Gerassimova, 1936a,b) and also from investigations on pollen abortion in *Datura* by Cartledge *et al.* (1936), who concluded, ". . . in general, the mutation rate increased with increased temperature, with increased moisture content, and with increased duration of treatment."

The importance of temperature was also suggested by the many investigators who showed that heat treatments induce chromosome breakage. Any treatment above absolute zero is, of course, in a sense, a heat treatment. What is really meant, though not always stated, is that raising the temperature increases the rate of induction of aberrations. So, for example, Peto (1933) reported that treatment of barley seeds at 95°C for 25 minutes or at 40°C at high humidity for 30 days resulted in the appearance of chromosome abnormalities. A series of papers by Navashin and Shkvarnikov (Navashin, 1933a,b; Shkvarnikov and Navashin, 1934, 1935; Shkvarnikov, 1935, 1936, 1939) on wheat and *Crepis* showed that treatment of fresh seeds with temperatures of 50–60°C for 20 days had a comparable effect on inducing chromosome aberrations with that of aging at room temperature for 6 to 7 years. They also reported that increasing the relative humidity of the air (which, of course, would have raised the seed moisture content) also raised the frequency of chromosome aberrations, particularly at high temperatures.

D. Recognition of a Simple Relation between Loss of Seed Viability and the Induction of Chromosome Damage (1967–1985)

With respect to their storage characteristics, two types of seeds are now recognized—orthodox and recalcitrant (Roberts, 1973a). Orthodox seeds can be dried without damage to very low moisture contents, usually to 5% and, in many cases, to 2% or less. Once they are below a critical moisture content, which probably varies between species, from about 15–28% (Ibrahim and Roberts, 1983; Ibrahim *et al.*, 1983; Petruzelli, 1986), the lower the moisture content, the longer the seeds survive. Longevity is also extended by decrease in temperature. All arable and forage crops and many other species produce orthodox seeds. Recalcitrant seeds cannot be dried without damage, and desiccation to moisture contents typical of the critical moisture content in orthodox species usually leads almost immediately to death. Providing they can be prevented from germinating, recalcitrant seeds survive longest when they are fully imbibed, but even then maximum longevity is typically only a few weeks or a few months or, exceptionally in a few species, a few years (King and Roberts, 1979). Almost nothing is known about possible changes in the genome and its expression with aging in recalcitrant seeds, and so nothing more will be said here about this group of seeds.

In orthodox seeds, however, even though the mechanism(s) of loss of viability remain obscure, the factors that affect longevity and their quantitative effects are now well understood. A great deal of early work had shown that the main factors affecting longevity are seed temperature and moisture content, and a number of attempts were made to quantify their effects, culminating in viability equations developed for wheat, which predicted percentage seed viability under a range of temperatures and moisture contents after any period of storage (Roberts, 1960). The same approach was then shown to apply to other species, e.g., rice (Oryza sativa) (Roberts, 1961), barley (Hordeum distichum), peas (Pisum sativum), and faba beans (Vicia faba) (Roberts and Abdalla, 1968).

These equations, however, had two faults: They were only accurate within limited ranges of temperature and moisture content, and, more important, they failed to take into account the initial quality of the seeds, which also has a considerable effect on their longevity. There is little doubt that the quality of a seed, as it affects its potential longevity, is the product of its genotype and the environment that the seed has experienced during maturation on the mother plant and during harvesting and processing, i.e., before storage is normally considered to begin. Most studies on genotypic variation in seed longevity have unconsciously confounded effects of genotype with prestorage environment or, even worse, have confounded genotypic effects with storage environment. This is because it has not been sufficiently recognized by some workers that quite minor differences in storage environment can have major effects on seed longevity. For example, a 1% difference in seed moisture content can affect seed longevity by a factor of 2 or, in some cases, even more (Roberts, 1986).

The original equations have recently been considerably modified to produce a single improved viability equation that overcomes these problems, i.e., it takes into account initial seed quality (resulting from the combined influence of genotype and prestorage environment), and it is applicable over a very wide range of storage conditions. The initial work was done on barley (Ellis and Roberts, 1980a,b), but this equation has subsequently been shown to be applicable to all species to which it has been applied, i.e., onion (Allium cepa) (Ellis and Roberts, 1981), soybean (Glycine max), chickpea (Cicer arietinum), and cowpea (Vigna unguiculata) (Ellis et al., 1982).

The viability equation, which is explained in greater detail elsewhere (see, e.g., Ellis and Roberts, 1981; Roberts and Ellis, 1982), is usually written

$$v = K_i - p/10^{K_E - C_W \log m - C_H t - C_Q t^2}$$

where v is the probit of percentage viability after time p in storage, m is moisture content (% of fresh weight basis), t is temperature in °C, K_i is the seed lot constant (a measure of seed quality determined by genotype and prestorage environment) and is the intercept value at zero storage time of the probit survival curve, the slope of which is determined by the power term in which K_E, C_W, C_H, and C_Q are constants within a species, but which differ between species. Essentially, the equation indicates that seed survival curves are cumulative normal distributions of negative slope, i.e., under any given set of constant storage conditions the lifespans of individual seeds are distributed normally. The logarithm of viability period of every seed in the population is a negative function of the logarithm of moisture content and a negative function of temperature modified by a quadratic element. This means that the relative deleterious effect of a given increment in moisture content *decreases* at higher moisture contents, whereas there is an *increase* in the relative deleterious effect of a given increment of temperature at higher storage temperatures. Thus, for example, in barley seed longevity is reduced by a factor of 2.92 when the moisture content is increased from 5 to 6%, but only by a factor of 1.75 when the moisture content is increased from 10 to 11%; whereas when the temperature is raised from 5 to 10°C, longevity is reduced by a factor of only 1.71, but by a factor of 2.08 when the temperature is raised from 25 to 30°C (Roberts, 1986).

The development of quantitative approaches to seed longevity has emphasized very strongly that seed deterioration, as measured by loss of viability, is a function of time, temperature, and moisture content. As already mentioned, there was sufficient information in the literature to indicate that it was probably also the combination of these three factors that is primarily responsible for the accumulation of chromosome damage. Some of the damage is microscopically visible and some, like point mutations, is not, but is manifest in subsequent generations as heritable phenotypic mutations. If both seed viability and chromosome damage appeared to be affected by the same factors in a similar manner, it was natural to ask the question whether the chromosome damage that is found in surviving seeds is closely correlated with loss of viability.

Systematic investigations were therefore undertaken in barley, faba beans, and peas stored over a range of temperatures (25–45°C) and moisture contents (12–18%) that examined the quantitative relations between percentage seed viability and the incidence of aberrant cells in the embryos of surviving seeds (Roberts *et al.*, 1967; Abdalla and Roberts, 1968). These investigations indicated that in most circumstances the relationship between percentage seed viability and frequency of chromosome aberration is the same, irrespective of how rapidly viability was lost or which was the more important factor, temperature or moisture content, that led to the loss of viability. The only exception to this generalization in all three species was when storage conditions were so severe as to lead to complete loss of viability in less than a week (i.e., 45°C combined with 18% moisture content). The amount of chromosome damage in the surviving seed was then less than was typical of seeds stored under all other conditions. The results for faba beans are shown in Fig. 14.1; the other two species showed similar relationships, although there were fewer aberrant cells for any given loss of viability. The general message seemed clear. Under most normal storage conditions it is not necessary to know the history of a seed lot to know how much chromosome damage it has accumulated; it is only necessary to know the percentage viability. These conclusions were supported by Murata et al. (1979, 1981), who confirmed the work on barley using a different cultivar in four different storage environments, 32 and 38°C in factorial combination with 12 and 18% moisture content. Indeed, the numerical relationship between percentage viability and number of aberrant anaphases obtained by Murata et al. (1979) was virtually identical with that obtained earlier in barley by Abdalla and Roberts (1968), as shown in a later review (Roberts and Ellis, 1984).

It is relatively easy to quantify visible chromosome aberrations and relate them to percentage seed viability. But less immediately spectacular events, such as point mutations, are more intractable. Most mutations are recessive and therefore are not manifest phenotypically in the first generation (A_1) from aged seeds. They segregate in A_2 but, because they originate in a single embryonic cell in A_1, the A_1 plant is a genetical chimera and segregation ratios in A_2 are consequently not Mendelian. Accordingly, if the genetical status of the mutation is to be confirmed, segregation ratios have to be examined in A_3. Because of these complications and especially because mutations, even when deliberately induced, are relatively infrequent events, very large numbers of plants would need to be examined to establish the quantitative form of the relationship between environmental factors and the number of point mutations induced.

Nevertheless, it was clear that point mutations were induced in barley, faba beans, and peas by various combinations of time, temperature, and moisture content that reduced viability to about 50% (Abdalla and Roberts, 1969a). More recently, it has been established in barley and peas stored under various conditions that, as would be expected, even small losses of viability of a few percent are also associated with significant increases in the frequency of point mutations (Dourado and Roberts, 1984b).

It is not, of course, possible to quantify the total amount of mutation that occurs. Most of the work in this area has concentrated on various chlorophyll-deficiency mutations since these are easy to detect. Estimates of the frequency of these in barley with those induced by X-irradiation suggest that a 50% loss of viability through aging is equivalent in terms of mutation

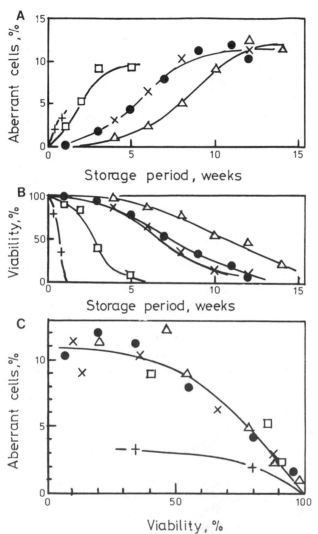

Fig. 14.1. (A) Increase in percentage of aberrant anaphase cells during early germination of seed of *Vicia faba* (cv. Claudia Super Aquadulce) after different periods of storage. (B) Seed survival curves from the same treatments. (C) Combined results of all treatments when percentage aberrant anaphase cells are plotted as a function of percentage seed viability. Storage treatments: +, 45°C, 18.0% moisture content (mc); ●, 45°C, 11.0% mc; □, 35°C, 18.0% mc; ×, 35°C, 15.3% mc; △, 25°C, 18.0% mc.

load to a dose of 10,000 rads of X rays applied to fresh seeds (Roberts, 1973b). Most mutations, however, probably go unnoticed because they have only minor effects. It is difficult to obtain incontrovertible evidence regarding minor genes, but results have been obtained (Purkar et al., 1980) suggesting that changes in polygenically inherited quantitative characters of pea are correlated with loss of seed viability.

It is almost certain that there is a relation between various types of chromosome damage that occur during seed aging so that a high incidence of chromosome aberrations will suggest that a considerable number of point mutations have also been induced. Such a relation is found when damage is caused by other agents, for example, Caldecott (1961) has shown that the frequency of chlorophyll mutations induced in barley by X-rays under anerobic conditions is linearly proportional to the frequency of chromosome aberrations.

E. The Concept of Repair during Moist Seed Storage (1974 – 1985)

It has long been known that seeds of some species in soil under natural conditions can remain viable for very long periods — for decades or even centuries (see, e.g., Kivilaan and Bandurski, 1973; Ødum, 1974). Clearly, in many environments such seeds are fully imbibed for much of the time. The viability equation if extrapolated to moist conditions would have predicted very short periods of viability and is clearly inappropriate under such conditions. The first serious investigations of this apparent paradox were by Villiers (Villiers, 1974, 1975; Villiers and Edgcumbe, 1975), who showed in lettuce seeds that at some moisture content, which was not defined but was clearly somewhere between 13% and the fully imbibed state (which in lettuce seeds is about 50% moisture content), there is a reversal of the trend of decreasing longevity with increase in moisture content. Villiers attributed this reversal to repair and turnover of faulty subcellular components, both of which, he suggested, are feasible at high moisture contents as in other tissues, but probably not in dry seeds in which normal metabolism is not possible. In an experiment which lasted for 2 years, he found no loss of viability in fully imbibed lettuce seeds maintained at 30°C, nor any increase in chromosome aberrations; in fact, there may have been a slight decrease in the number of aberrant cells as compared with those present in the seeds before storage. He concluded that moist storage of seeds might be useful when the maintenance of a high degree of genetic stability is required.

However, in the work that Villiers had described, there had been no loss of viability in the imbibed-seed storage treatments, and consequently there was not yet sufficient evidence to falsify the hypothesis that accumulation of chromosome damage in seeds is closely associated with loss of viability.

Even fully imbibed seeds do not last forever, but it was not yet known whether or not damage would occur to chromosomes in populations of imbibed seeds in which there had been some loss of viability. Furthermore, there is so far no indication of how long seeds may be maintained in the fully imbibed condition in the laboratory. No doubt these uncertainties have contributed to the fact that wet seed storage has not yet been pursued as a practical proposition. More important, though, are two major technical problems. First it is necessary to maintain seed dormancy to prevent germination in wet storage, and this is not easy in many crop species. Second, as later became evident, the presence of oxygen is an essential component of wet storage, and it would not be easy to arrange this on a large scale for thousands of accessions while, at the same time, maintaining their high moisture content. Probably the most important reason, however, why moist seed storage has not been pursued is because of the simplicity and adequacy of existing dry-storage methods, for, although chromosome damage is associated with loss of viability in dry storage, it is feasible to avoid it for very long periods by storing under conditions of low temperature and moisture content that delay both chromosome damage and seed death.

The need for full imbibition and oxygen for extended longevity in moist storage was shown later (Ibrahim and Roberts, 1983; Ibrahim *et al.*, 1983). In these investigations on lettuce seeds, it was shown that the improved viability equation applied at moisture contents at 15% or less and that in these drier conditions oxygen is somewhat deleterious to seed longevity. But above 15% moisture content, there are several changes, the most important of which is that there is now an *increase* in longevity with increasing moisture content, but *only* in the presence of oxygen; in its absence, seed longevity is but a few days at ambient temperature. The evidence suggests that there is a common moisture content at which there is a transition between oxygen being deleterious to longevity and being beneficial, at which there is a change from increasing moisture content being detrimental to longevity to it being beneficial, and at which seed survival curves change from normal to skewed distributions. The moisture content at which all these changes occur has been described as the critical moisture content (Ibrahim *et al.*, 1983). The value of the critical moisture content varies between species so that whereas in lettuce, as already mentioned, it is 15%, in onion it is about 18% (Ibrahim *et al.*, 1983; Ward and Powell, 1983); in durum wheat, Petruzelli (1986) has shown that it is in the region of 28–30%. We believe that the critical moisture content, which varies between species, may be a reflection of a more fundamental critical water potential that has a similar value in different species, probably somewhere in the region of -14.5 MPa. The main reason why seeds have different critical moisture contents is probably because of differences in oil content, because, whereas oil contributes to dry weight and therefore affects the moisture content determination, it is hydrophobic and therefore does not contribute to a reduction in water potential.

There is considerable evidence to suggest that in moisture contents below the critical value, i.e., in the range where the viability equation applies, damage to a very wide range of subcellular components, cytoplasmic as well as nuclear, accumulates at a rate dependent on temperature and moisture content (Roberts, 1972, 1979, 1983; Osborne, 1982). Villiers (1975) has suggested that in dry seeds repair or turnover is not possible, and this is why damage accumulates, ultimately to a catastrophic level, resulting in loss of viability. But when seeds are fully hydrated, repair and turnover is possible so that damage does not accumulate. We have now refined this statement to suggest that no repair is possible below the critical moisture content, but at the critical moisture content there is some repair and possibly turnover, providing oxygen is present to support normal metabolism, albeit at a very low rate. As moisture content increases above the critical moisture content, so does the rate of respiration, and also repair and turnover, so that the trend of decreasing longevity with increase in moisture content is reversed. However, it is only at full hydration that repair and turnover is fully effective, and consequently it is only then that longevity is markedly extended as compared with slightly lower moisture contents (Ibrahim et al., 1983). When seeds are stored dry, repair of some damage, including that to DNA (Osborne, 1982), is possible when seeds are hydrated during the early stages of germination.

F. The Amount of Chromosome Damage Associated with a Given Loss of Viability Is Large at Low-Moisture Contents and Is Minimal at High-Moisture Contents (1985)

It was concluded earlier that, except possibly under severe storage conditions, in those species that had been investigated quantitatively, there is a simple and common relation within a species between the number of seeds that have lost viability and the amount of chromosome damage in the surviving seeds, irrespective of storage conditions, including seed moisture content. Two considerations, however, suggested that this conclusion ought to be questioned, or at least examined, under a much wider range of moisture contents than had previously been attempted. The first was the evidence which led to the concept of a critical moisture content and the repair hypothesis associated with it. An obvious question that followed from this was: if repair is feasible when seeds are moister than the critical moisture content, would chromosome damage accumulate to the same extent for a given loss of viability as compared with seed stored below the critical moisture content? The second consideration was that when the original data on lettuce seed of Villiers (1975) were replotted as percentage of aberrant cells as a function of percentage seed viability (Roberts and Ellis, 1984), there was some indication in very dry seed (5% moisture content) that although longevity, as would be expected, was much greater than at higher moisture contents, the amount of chromosome damage for a given loss of viability was very much larger. The results were no more than indicative, however, for data were not available for viability values of less than 90% for those seeds stored at 5% moisture content.

Two investigations were therefore undertaken to question the conclusion that there is a common relationship between seed viability and chromosome aberration frequency; for while this may be true over a moderate range of seed moisture contents—typical of the range encountered in commercial storage practice—it was now questionable whether the same relationship held in either very dry or very moist seeds. The first of these investigations on onion (*Allium capa*) (S. Sirikwanchai and E. H. Roberts) have not yet been published, but some of the conclusions from this work, and from some further work on lettuce (Rao and Roberts, 1987; Rao, Roberts, and Ellis, 1987), will be summarized here.

As in most previous investigations, much of the work has concentrated on anaphase cells in radicle tip squashes taken during the first mitotic peak after germination, the purpose being to examine mainly the first cell divisions after the aging process. Some examples of the kinds of aberrations observed are shown in Fig. 14.2. Figure 14.3 shows the number of aberrant anaphase cells as a function of viability of onion seeds stored for various periods at different temperatures and moisture contents in air or nitrogen. One of the moisture contents used, 36%, was above the critical moisture content, which for onion seed is probably about 18% (Ibrahim, 1981; Ward and Powell, 1983), and the rest of the treatments were between 12.2 and 17.4% moisture content. In these latter treatments, below the critical moisture content there appears to be a common relationship between loss of viability and the accumulation of chromosome aberrations. These treatments cover a wide range in terms of rates of aging, as indicated by the range of p_{50} values (time taken for viability to fall to 50%), which varied by a factor of 7.5 (see caption to Fig. 14.3). By contrast, when seeds were stored at 36% moisture content, which is clearly well above the critical moisture content but nevertheless well below full hydration (which would be about 50%), there was no evidence of any chromosome damage in excess of that already present in the control treatment, which is a sample of the seeds taken before the deliberate aging treatments started. In fact, the results at 36% moisture content suggest that moist storage may have led to some slight reduction in chromosome aberrations, and therefore that some repair may have taken

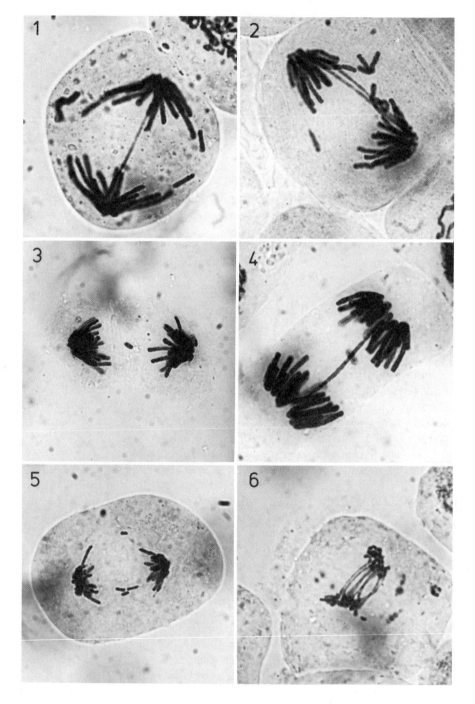

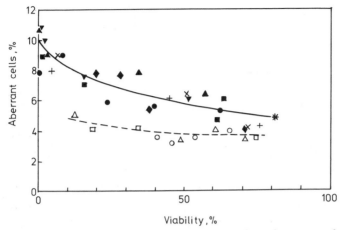

Viability,%

Fig. 14.3. Effect of seed moisture content on the relation between seed viability and accumulation of aberrant cells, examined at anaphase in early germination of seeds of *Allium cepa* (cv. White Lisbon) stored under various conditions for various periods. Moisture content was controlled either by storing seeds in sealed laminated aluminum packets or osmotically by storage on paper moistened with polyethylene glycol solution. Solid line: seeds stored below critical moisture content; dashed line: seeds stored at 36% moisture content.

Symbol	Moisture content (%)	Temperature (°C)	P_{50} (days)	Method of controlling moisture content	Gaseous environment
▼	12.2	35	23.0	Sealed packet	Air
▲	12.2	45	4.7	Sealed packet	Air
×	15.0	30	13.3	Sealed packet	Air
+	15.0	30	15.8	Sealed packet	Nitrogen
◆	17.4	25	35.4	Sealed packet	Air
■	17.4	35	7.8	Sealed packet	Air
●	17.4	45	2.3	Sealed packet	Air
○	36.0	30	15.5	Osmotic	Air
□	36.0	30	11.0	Osmotic	Nitrogen
△	36.0	30	13.0	Osmotic	Nitrogen

Fig. 14.2. Aberrant anaphase cells in early mitoses of radicle tips from aged seeds of *Vicia faba* (1, 2), *Allium cepa* (3, 4), and *Lactuca sativa* (5, 6). Chromatid-type aberrations: (1) single bridge and several unequal fragments; (3) single fragment; (4) single bridge and fragment (out-of-focus); (5) four unequal fragments. Chromosome-type aberrations: (2) double bridge and two pairs of equal fragments, and other fragments; (6) four double bridges and four pairs of equal fragments (some out-of-focus).

place. Before the experiment started, inevitably the seed had already been stored, in this case at 8.5% moisture content, for some time since harvest so that the viability had fallen to 82% before the experiment began. This accounts for the aberrant anaphase frequency in the control seeds of 5%. These results therefore suggest that when seeds are stored at a moisture content above the critical value, very few or possibly no aberrations arise during storage, even when seeds are stored long enough for there to be considerable loss of viability. It is not necessary for the seeds to be fully hydrated for this protection of the chromosomes to be achieved. This investigation, however, did not include moisture contents below the range that had already been quantitatively investigated in other species, i.e., less than 12%. The next question to be answered, therefore, was whether the relationship between loss of viability and chromosome damage is different in very dry seeds.

This question was the substance of an investigation on lettuce seeds, which, in order to confirm the results described above on onion seeds, also included treatments with a moisture content (13%), which is close to the critical moisture content in this species (15%) and other treatments more moist than this at 18.1%. The results (Fig. 14.4) show that at these higher moisture contents there was little, if any, accumulation of chromosome aberrations, even after considerable loss of viability had occurred, thus confirming the work on onion seeds. The next highest moisture content shown in Fig. 14.4 is 9.8%, which is already below the range of moisture contents (12–18%) previously investigated in barley, peas, and faba beans by Abdalla and Roberts (1968) and in barley by Murata et al. (1979, 1981). At 9.8% moisture content in lettuce, there was clearly a considerable increase in the frequency of chromosome aberrations for a given decrease in seed viability, as compared with seeds stored at higher moisture contents. The number of aberrations accumulated for a given loss of viability was even greater when lettuce seeds were stored at 8.1% moisture content, but what is particularly striking is the very considerable increase in aberrant cells when the seed moisture content was maintained at 5.5%. Paradoxically, a moisture content of 3.3% appeared marginally, but consistently, less deleterious than 5.5% in this respect (Fig. 14.4). Evidently, further cytological work is called for on seeds of this and other species at very low moisture contents, preferably supplemented by an assessment of the frequency of heritable gene mutations that are induced by storage under these conditions.

Currently the long-term seed storage conditions recommended by the International Board for Plant Genetic Resources (IBPGR) are −18°C or less in combination with 5±1% seed moisture content (Cromarty et al., 1982). In

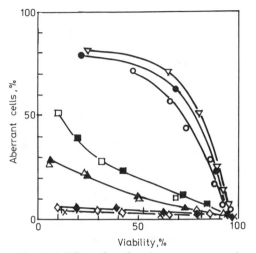

Fig. 14.4. Effect of seed moisture content on the relation between seed viability and accumulation of aberrant cells examined at anaphase in early germination of seeds of *Lactuca sativa* (cv. Trocadera improved) stored under various conditions for various periods. Moisture content was controlled by storing seeds sealed in air in laminated aluminum foil packets.

Symbol	Moisture content (%)	Temperature (°C)	P_{50} (days)
●	3.3	50	~420
○	3.3	60	72
▽	5.5	50	33
■	8.1	35	42
□	8.1	40	25
▲	9.8	35	29
△	9.8	40	4.5
+	18.1	30	7.0
×	18.1	40	2.1
*	control (see text)		

spite of the fact that in the work on lettuce considered here, the maximum frequency of chromosome aberrations for a given loss of seed viability was achieved at approximately 5% moisture content, it does not necessarily follow that the long-term seed storage conditions recommended by IBPGR should be revised; however, it might become necessary to reconsider the recommendations concerning regeneration standards. The regeneration standard is the percentage viability to which an accession in a gene bank is allowed to fall before a sample is sown to produce a fresh seed stock to replace the original accession in store. For most crops, the currently recommended standard is 85% viability (Ellis *et al.*, 1985). This is a compromise between two opposing pressures (Roberts and Ellis, 1984). First there is the need to minimize the induction of mutations and also to minimize genetic selection during storage in genetically heterogeneous accessions (since potential longevity, as already mentioned, is partly under genetic control); both of these requirements call for a relatively high regeneration standard. However, secondly, there is the need to minimize the frequency of regeneration because it is costly and carries with it dangers of genetic contamination through accidental mixture or cross-pollination, and a risk of genetic erosion unless selection pressures in the field are avoided, all of which would suggest a lower regeneration standard.

Examination of Fig. 14.4 shows that at 85% viability the percentage of cells containing chromosome aberrations was about 6% at 8.1% moisture content, but this proportion increased to about 40% aberrant cells at 5.5 moisture content, i.e., there was a 6-fold increase in aberrant cells. Another interesting comparison is that when seeds stored at 8.1% moisture content had been allowed to drop to 20% viability, the frequency of cells containing chromosome aberrations in the surviving seeds was no greater than the frequency in seed stored at 5.5% moisture content but in which the viability had only fallen to 85%.

The appropriate values of the constants for lettuce in the seed viability equation have not yet been determined, but in many ways with regard to storage the characteristics of lettuce seed are similar to onion. So it is possible to use the seed viability nomograph for onion (Ellis and Roberts, 1981) in order to estimate roughly the implications of chromosome aberrations in lettuce seeds described here. In terms of frequency of chromosome aberrations in the surviving seeds, lettuce seeds stored at 5.5% moisture content until viability has fallen to 85% are equivalent to seeds stored at 8.1% moisture content until viability has fallen to 20%; or storing seeds at 5.5% moisture content until viability has fallen to 95% is equivalent to storing seeds at 8.1% until viability has fallen to 85%. However, estimates from the viability nomographs show that for the same amount of chromosome damage, the period of storage in both cases would be more than twice as long at 5.5% moisture content than at 8.1%, in spite of the fact that far less loss of viability could be tolerated at 5.5% moisture content. Thus, it would seem that there is still a considerable advantage in using very low seed moisture contents for genetic conservation.

III. THE NATURE OF THE DAMAGE TO THE GENOME AND ITS EXPRESSION

A. The Classical and Exchange Theories of Chromosome Damage

Cytogeneticists generally explain the main types of chromosome aberrations that are observed on the basis of the particular stage in the cell cycle in which the event leading to the aberration occurred, particularly with respect to the stages before and after DNA replication during interphase. Howard and Pelc (1953) divided interphase in root-tip cells of *Vicia faba* into three stages on the basis of experiments involving incorporation of ^{32}P into chromosomal DNA. They found that incorporation occurred partway through interphase, and they designated this period S (for DNA synthesis), which is when the duplex strands of DNA are semiconservatively replicated. The first part of interphase before S was designated G_1 (the first gap in DNA synthesis), and the interval after S but before the following prophase was termed G_2 (the second gap in DNA synthesis).

Evans (1962), following this work, produced diagrams showing the types of aberration that result depending on the time of X-irradiation in relation to the mitotic cycle. These diagrams were based on what is termed the Classical Theory of breakage and reunion proposed by Sax (1938, 1940, 1941) and later developed by Lea (1946). The theory suggested that a sudden energy loss from a quantum of X-irradiation (or electromagnetic radiation of shorter wavelength) results immediately in a primary break in the chromatin (DNA duplex) thread. The broken ends have one of three fates: first, many of the breaks, it is thought, rejoin (restitution) and therefore no aberration ensues; second, if two breaks occur close together, the four ends may rejoin in a variety of ways to produce various exchange aberrations; third, some breaks do not rejoin and are manifest as single fragments.

The Classical Theory was not only applied to X-ray-induced aberrations, but it also tended to be applied to aberrations that arise "naturally" or in various other ways, including those produced by chemical mutagens. However, Revell (1959) provided a challenge to the Classical Theory based on his own work on mutagens. This is known as the Exchange Theory, and it states that the initial damage is not a break but an unstable lesion, "a primary event of damage." As the theory is now understood (Savage, 1975; Evans, 1977), a lesion may give rise to a break, but only during semiconservative replication when a break occurs in one of the two duplex DNA threads produced, i.e., in one of the resulting chromatids. Exchanges may also occur, providing two sites of potential breaks are in close proximity. Damage resulting from lesions always appears initially as chromatid-type aberrations in the first mitosis following the first replication after the lesion occurs.

E. H. Roberts

If an aberrant cell goes through a second mitosis, then what was originally a chromatid-type aberration may, of course, become a chromosome-type aberration on its second appearance because of the intervening replication. If a lesion occurs during G_2 no aberration will appear in the mitosis immediately following since no replication will have taken place; it may appear as a chromatid-type aberration in the second mitosis after the lesion first occurred, and, possibly, as a chromosome aberration in the third mitosis.

When cells are treated with X rays, the Classical Theory is still thought to apply. In support of this, Evans (1977) showed that when cells are irradiated in S or G_2, chromatid-type aberrations appear in the next mitosis, i.e., configurations appear that can be interpreted as ensuing from chromatid breaks that occurred when the cells were irradiated. When cells were exposed to X rays in G_1, the break itself is duplicated during replication so that a chromosome-type aberration is produced, i.e., the aberration that appears in the first mitosis following the irradiation is of a configuration that indicates breakage, or breakage followed by exchange, at identical loci of the two component chromatids of the chromosome. S cells exposed to nitrogen mustard also showed chromatid-type aberrations. But, in contrast to those treated with X rays, G_1 cells treated with nitrogen mustard only produced chromatid-type aberrations in the first cell division following treatment, and G_2-treated cells produced no aberrations at all during the first division but showed chromatid-type aberrations during the second mitosis after treatment. These results for nitrogen mustard are clearly compatible with the Exchange Theory, and similar results to these have been obtained with other chemical mutagens (see, e.g., Kihlman, 1966; Bender et al., 1974) and for UV radiation (Bender et al., 1973; Griggs and Bender, 1973).

B. Chromatid-Type and Chromosome-Type Aberrations in Seeds: Is the Damage Initiated during Aging or Afterward during Germination?

It is not known what causes the chromosome damage that is associated with seed aging. It would seem unlikely that chromosome aberrations are produced by direct breakages according to the Classical Theory. Such breakages appear to require high energy quanta, but it is known (Roberts et al., 1967; Roos, 1982) that the only source of these during normal storage, i.e., background radiation, has no significant effect on the frequency of chromosome aberrations found in seeds. Whatever else is the cause of the damage, then, it would be expected that chromatid-type aberrations would be prevalent during first mitoses.

In spite of these arguments, reviews of the types of chromosome aberrations associated with seed aging (see, e.g., Roos, 1982) indicate that many of the earlier workers reported that most of the damage they observed was of the chromosome type; whereas there is a tendency for more recent papers to report that most of the damage is of the chromatid type. Presumably aging seeds have not changed their habits; it seems more likely that the interpretation of chromosome configurations has changed. Change in the interpretation of aberrations produced as a result of seed aging has recently been taken one step further by Murata *et al.* (1982). They went so far as to classify the majority of aberrations they found in germinating barley seeds as subchromatid on the basis that the most common type of aberration they observed was a single bridge with no fragments, an observation (if not an interpretation) subsequently confirmed by Dourado and Roberts (1984a). However, whether the aberrations really are subchromatid is still a matter for debate, for there is some argument as to whether subchromatid aberrations exist or, at least if they do, whether they can be detected unequivocally by standard cytological observations (Kihlman and Hartley, 1967; Wolff, 1970; Savage, 1975). A single bridge with no fragments could be the result of a chromosome or two chromatid breaks followed by exchanges in which the fragment is lost, possibly because it is too small to detect or masked by other chromosomes. Alternatively, a bridge without fragments could be due to chromosome stickiness, as, indeed, Murata *et al.* (1982) suggest; but chromosome stickiness is still little understood and may not necessarily be due to subchromatid interchanges. Irrespective of the final verdict, however, the important point here is that this damage is not chromosome type.

There have been a number of publications that, while acknowledging that damage increases with aging and that chromatid-type aberrations are consistently the more common, claim that the frequency of chromosome-type aberrations increases with aging, e.g., in *Allium fistulosum* (Orlova, 1967; Orlova and Nikitina, 1968), in *Zea mays* (Sevov *et al.*, 1973), and in *Helianthus annuus* (Sizova, 1976). This conclusion depends on an assumption that the relative frequency of second mitoses to first mitoses in the samples is the same in fresh as it is in aged seeds since, as already mentioned, chromatid-type aberrations may appear as chromosome type in the following mitosis. Sampling regimes cannot properly be kept identical in all respects as between fresh and aged seeds, since the latter germinate more slowly and the time taken to germinate is more variable (Ellis and Roberts, 1981); furthermore, peak mitotic activity is less, is delayed, and occurs when the roots are longer (see, e.g., Orlova *et al.*, 1975; Murata *et al.*, 1980, 1981; Sirikwanchai, 1985). Accordingly, it is difficult to ensure that the proportion of first to second mitoses within samples taken from aged seeds remains the same as those taken from fresh seeds. Nevertheless, if it is accepted that chromosome aberrations do increase with seed aging in the species listed above, the phenomenon does not appear to be universal, since no significant changes in chromosome-type to chromatid-type aberrations were found with various seed-aging treatments in *Hordeum distichum* or *Pisum sativum* (Dourado and Roberts, 1984a) or in *Allium cepa* (Sirikwanchai, 1985). It will therefore be assumed for the purpose of the present discussion that the majority of chromosome aberrations arising as a result of seed aging and observed in first mitosis are of the chromatid type and that these are always preponderant irrespective of degree of seed aging.

The high frequency of chromatid-type aberrations in first mitoses, combined with the assumptions, often unstated, that most cells of quiescent seeds are in G_1 and that breakages occur as a result of aging according to the Classical Theory, has led several investigators to suggest that no damage is suffered by chromosomes *during* aging, but that it arises during germination *following* the aging treatment (see, e.g., Orlova and Nikitina, 1968; Corsi and Avanzi, 1969; Avanzi *et al.*, 1969; Dubinin and Dubinina, 1969; Innocenti and Avanzi, 1971; Floris and Anguillesi, 1974; Murata *et al.*, 1982). In turn, this has led to a further development of the theory, first reviewed in detail by D'Amato and Hoffman-Ostenhof (1956), that chromosome damage in seeds is due to the accumulation of automutagenic substances during aging. The new development postulates that the hypothetical mutagens only act when the seeds are rehydrated during germination after storage. However, much of the evidence for the accumulation of mutagenic substances is uncritical, equivocal, or statistically unsatisfactory, and many investigators, in spite of their best efforts, have failed to find evidence for the accumulation of mutagens in seeds (see reviews in Roberts, 1972; Roos, 1982).

Some of the better evidence for the involvement of mutagens is based on reciprocal transplants of embryos and endosperms between old and new seeds of *Triticum durum*. By this means, Nuti Ronchi and Martini (1962) obtained results suggesting the existence of chemical mutagens in old endosperms. However, Corsi and Avanzi (1969), using a similar technique, concluded that chromosome damage in the embryo induced by aging is not the result of changes in the endosperm. Studies by Floris and Anguillesi (1974) suggested that both endosperms and embryos may produce mutagenic substances, but they also concluded that age-induced aberrations in the embryo were not a consequence of endosperm aging. It is not possible to do justice here to the complex results of these and other transplant experiments. But, in spite of their ingenuity, such experiments have not yet led to a clear demonstration of the operation of mutagenic substances in intact aged seeds (Murata *et al.*, 1982).

As pointed out earlier, the argument that damage to chromosomes is initiated during germination and not during the storage that precedes it rests mainly on one fact and two assumptions. The fact, which now seems well established, is that the majority of aberrations that appear immediately after storage are of the chromatid type. The two assumptions are that cells in quiescent seeds during storage are in G_1 and that aberrations should be interpreted according to the Classical Theory. Both assumptions are now questionable. First, resting cells of pea and barley seeds are thought to contain cells in both G_1 and G_2 (Bogdanov and Jordansky, 1964; Bogdanov, 1965; Savage and Wigglesworth, 1970), and Avanzi *et al.*, (1963) have shown that cells of durum wheat seeds contain the amounts of DNA expected in G_1 or G_2 cells or amounts intermediate between the two. Second, as previously pointed out (Dourado and Roberts, 1984a) and also argued here, it seems more reasonable to adopt the Exchange Theory for application to seed aging problems. If this is done, then mosti observations on chromosome aberrations produced as a result of seed aging fall into place.

It may then be argued that lesions occur during storage at a rate dependent on temperature and moisture content, and at any level of hydration below the critical moisture content these lesions cannot be repaired. A few lesions may be repaired at the beginning of the germination process after water uptake has risen above the critical moisture content and before replication starts in G_1 cells, but, otherwise, many lesions will develop into chromatid-type aberrations during semiconservative DNA replication that are then manifest during first mitosis, and some of these aberrations will reappear as chromosome-type aberrations during second mitosis. No damage will be apparent in first mitosis of those cells which were in G_2 when lesions occurred during seed storage, but chromatid-type aberrations may appear in second mitosis. Other lesions may not result in breakages but in point mutations as a result of error-prone repair mechanisms that may operate during replication (Osborne, 1982). Lesions that have the potential for developing into chromatid breaks or point mutations probably also occur when seeds are stored at moisture contents above the critical value, but to some extent normal metabolism is possible in such seeds and the majority of lesions are repaired by prereplication, error-free mechanisms (Osborne, 1982); thus few, if any, chromosome aberrations and probably few mutations, too, are found in seeds that have been stored under moist conditions.

If this explanation is accepted, it follows that all aberrations found in the first cell divisions during the germination of aged seeds should be of the chromatid type. However, since cell divisions are not synchronous during germination, root-tip squashes timed as far as possible to coincide with the first mitotic peak will also probably include some cells in their second cycle of cell division. The proportion of chromosome-type to chromatid-type aberrations would, on the basis of this explanation, represent the number of aberrant cells in second mitosis that are derived from embryonic cells suffering lesions in G_1, expressed as a proportion of the sum total of those aberrant cells in first mitosis derived from embryonic cells suffering lesions in G_1 plus the aberrant cells in second mitosis derived from embryonic cells suffering lesions in G_2. The high proportion of chromatid-type aberrations generally observed does not mean that the primary damage occurs during germination. The initial lesions—the primary molecular faults—it is argued, actually occur during seed storage, although the breakages that are a consequence have to await seed hydration, which normally occurs during germination, for it is only then that semiconservative DNA replication can occur.

C. Speculations Concerning DNA Lesions That Result from Seed Aging

The rate of accumulation of damage to chromosomes in seeds, whether measured by frequency of chromosome aberrations or accumulation of recessive point mutations, increases with temperature and hydration up to the critical moisture content. It is a common feature of many large molecules that their structure may change, often very slowly, but at a rate dependent on temperature and the degree of hydration. Witness, for example, the denaturation of soluble proteins illustrated by the loss of activity of purified enzymes *in vitro* at a rate dependent on temperature and hydration. Similarly, the rate of depurination of DNA *in vitro* has been shown to increase with temperature and hydration by Greer and Zamenhof (1962), who considered that heat depurination is a possible cause of spontaneous mutation.

Cheah and Osborne (1978) showed that much less of the DNA extracted from dead rye seeds was spoolable as compared with that extracted from living seeds, i.e., the DNA from dead seeds was of much lower molecular weight. They interpreted this as resulting from lesions that develop in the DNA as seeds age and suggested that such lesions might subsequently lead to chromosome breakages. They also pointed out that increased chromosome breakage might be a result of impaired repair mechanisms so that not only would old seeds have more lesions, but they would be less capable of repairing them during hydration. There is some evidence, for example, that DNA polymerase in barley seeds loses activity with aging (Yamaguchi et al., 1978). Indeed, Murata et al. (1982) have suggested that loss of repair activity may be the main reason for increase in chromosome damage in aged seeds. It is difficult, however, to imagine that the decline in repair capability is the sole reason for the increase in aberrations with aging, for this would imply that fresh seeds before hydration have as many lesions as aged seeds. There is now considerably more evidence for damage to DNA at the molecular level associated with aging in seeds, and this, together with the evidence of the repair that can occur in hydrated seeds, has been comprehensively reviewed by Osborne (1982).

Seeds have been the subject for many studies in which the effects of chemical mutagens have been investigated, and there are a number of parallels with the observations that have been made on aged seeds. For example, it has been found that there is considerable repair of single-strand breaks and/or alkali-labile sites caused by alkylating agents when muta-gen-treated barley seeds are subsequently stored at 30% moisture content (Velemínský *et al.*, 1972, 1973a) but not when they are stored at 15% moisture content (Velemínský *et al.*, 1973b). This was discovered by evaluating sedimentation rates in alkaline sucrose gradients of DNA isolated from the barley embryos. Moreover, there is a decrease in chromatid aberrations of mutagen-treated seeds stored at 30% moisture content but not in drier seeds (Soyfer *et al.*, 1977; Gichner and Velemínský, 1979). As already pointed out, there is evidence that the critical moisture content for wheat seeds is about 28–30% (Petruzelli, 1986) and that for barley, because of its similar low oil content, is probably very similar. Thus, the conditions for the repair of damage caused by mutagens appear to be very similar to those necessary for the repair of aging damage. This does not necessarily imply, however, that aging damage is due to automutagens. There are a number of other possibilities, including that DNA in the chromatin is not completely stable, that repair is not possible below the critical moisture content, and that not all the damage can be repaired during the early stages of germination for one or more of the following reasons: insufficient time, there is a significant proportion of error-prone repairs, or some of the damage is too catastrophic for repair.

D. The Fate of Damage to the Genome

In assessing effects of seed aging on damage to the genome, this chapter has concentrated on chromosome aberrations that are visible during mitosis because this damage is easiest to quantify. However, most of the aberrations observed are themselves probably of little practical consequence; most of the cells containing them are removed from meristems by diplontic selection within a few cell cycles. This is because the aberrant cells may have major deletions or genetic imbalances so that they cannot function properly. Consequently, their role in the meristematic tissues is rapidly taken over by more normal cells. Thus, for example, in root tips from aged seeds the large number of aberrant cells decreases rapidly with the length of the root so that when the roots are a few centimeters long, there is generally very little sign of chromosome aberrations (Navashin, 1933b; Nichols, 1941; D'Amato, 1951; Abdalla and Roberts, 1969a). Nevertheless, some aberrations persist through many cell cycles and are visible at meiosis (Cartledge and Blakeslee,

1933, 1934, 1935; Cartledge *et al.*, 1936; Murata *et al.*, 1984; N. K. Rao and E. H. Roberts, unpublished observations). However, usually there is no evidence of transmission of these aberrations to the next generation (Harrison, 1954; Harrison and McLeish, 1966; Roos, 1982; Murata *et al.*, 1984) or, if there is, very little aberration persists (Gerassimova, 1935).

Gross chromosome abnormalities, therefore, are usually of little practical significance. However, whenever chromosome aberrations are induced there is considerable likelihood that point mutations are also induced (see, e.g., Roberts *et al.*, 1967; Abdalla and Roberts, 1969b; Dourado and Roberts, 1984b). Although a putative incomplete dominant mutation has been observed (Dourado and Roberts, 1984c), most mutations resulting from seed aging are recessive and, providing they are not lethal or very deleterious in the haploid condition, they will persist through the A_1 generation, and segregant phenotypes will appear in A_2. Most mutations are, of course, deleterious. For example, mutations that impair chlorophyll synthesis have most frequently been chosen for study, simply because they are easy to recognize when dealing with large populations, but such mutations would soon be eliminated from populations under ordinary selection pressures. This has led Murata *et al.* (1984) to point out, ". . . in all of the studies of induced genetic changes during seed aging, no evidence has been presented to show the persistence of mutations beyond the first or second seed increase." However, neither has it been thought necessary to attempt to obtain such evidence, because the general assumption is that the transmission of recessive mutations that behave in a normal Mendelian fashion is well understood. As explained earlier, in order to establish Mendelian segregation it is sufficient to examine segregation in the A_3 generation. As Murata *et al.* (1984) also point out, the history of agriculture and plant breeding (and, indeed, I would add evolution) has depended on mutations. So while it is true that very deleterious mutations cannot persist, obviously a significant proportion of other mutations must have persisted. The induction of chlorophyll mutations has simply been chosen by a number of investigators of seed aging, ionizing radiation, and chemical mutagens as a convenient model system, but other types of mutation have also been shown to result from all of these agents. Presumably most of the mutations affecting physiology and growth go undetected, since many of these have quantitative effects. The design of experiments of sufficient rigor for the unequivocal detection of minor genes, which together affect quantitative characters, is difficult. However, results of investigations by Purkar *et al.* (1980) are at least indicative that seed aging also affects minor genes that have quantitative effects on growth.

Because of the induction of heritable mutations, which is associated even with small losses of seed viability (Dourado and Roberts, 1984b), and because of selection during storage within genetically heterogeneous accessions for genotypes with greater longevity (larger K_i values), we have argued (Roberts and Ellis, 1984) that the advice of the International Board for Plant Genetic Resources to gene banks to adopt relatively high standards for regeneration of accessions (85% viability for most species) is appropriate. This view, however, has been contested by Murata *et al.* (1984), largely on the basis that recessive mutation of major genes, generally being deleterious, are unlikely to persist. No doubt the debate will continue.

E. Damage to the Cellular Systems That Express the Genome

The first steps in the expression of the genome depend on the transcription of the DNA and the translation of the mRNA transcripts into proteins. There is now considerable evidence that many components of the transcription and translation system deteriorate as a result of seed aging. The subject has recently been ably reviewed in detail by Osborne (1977, 1982), and so attention here will be drawn only to two points. First, although no significant part of the system that has been investigated appears to be totally immune to seed aging, some seem to be more stable than others. For example, of the various species of RNA, tRNA appears to be relatively stable. Although there is evidence of degradation of both mRNA and rRNA, there is also evidence that loss of integrity of associated cofactors and enzymes is also important. Second, because of the nature of the techniques used, it is difficult to know how to quantify and compare the relative deterioration of the various components *in vivo*. Accordingly, at present, it is difficult to determine which parts of the system are more critical than others in terms of the gross symptoms — loss of seed vigor and viability — to which these events may contribute.

The expression of the genome during germination and early seedling growth depends not only on the survival of the genome and its transcription and translation machinery, but also on the survival of other cell components that provide the framework for its expression; without these other components the genome cannot be expressed at all, and if they are faulty the expression will be modified. There is considerable evidence that many of the components not directly involved in the primary events of genome expression are also affected by aging, e.g., many enzyme systems — including NADPH-dependent dehydrogenases — hence the widespread use of the electron acceptor triphenyltetrazolium chloride for testing viability and vigor. However, especially important appears to be the loss of integrity of cellular membranes (see McKersie *et al.*, Chapter 13) on which the function of so many subcellular organelles depends.

No doubt it is the combined effects of most, if not all, of these changes that lead to the poor seed vigor that precedes loss of viability. Poor seed vigor is manifest in several ways, e.g., by slower and more variable germination and seedling growth, and by greater susceptibility to environmental stress of various types. It is because these symptoms precede loss of viability in each seed and because there is a normal distribution of longevity within populations that all symptoms of age-induced loss of vigor correlate well with percentage seed viability (Ellis and Roberts, 1980c, 1981; Roberts, 1986).

Providing low-vigor seedlings survive, in due course the growth rates of plants derived from them typically return to normal (Abdalla and Roberts, 1969b). However, in the conditions of intense interplant competition in which most crops are grown, the time lost in dry-matter accumulation during early growth is sometimes never retrieved and can reduce final yields (Roberts, 1986). In other words, where final yields are affected, the causes can often be traced to faults during early growth that have long since disappeared.

IV. CONCLUSIONS

It may be concluded that when those seeds that survive aging are sown, most of the damage that has accumulated disappears during seedling growth. Damage to most organelles disappears, probably partly through repair, but mainly through replacement. Some DNA lesions are repaired. Those which are not may lead to chromosome aberrations, most of which are removed by diplontic selection. Other DNA lesions may lead directly, or indirectly through error-prone repair mechanisms, to mutations. Most of these are recessive and thus are retained throughout the first generation. However, recessivity is irrelevant in the haploid condition, and some deleterious mutations expressed in the gametes may be lethal when unmasked by meiosis. These may be a factor that accounts for the increased pollen abortion that is observed in A_1 plants. Other mutations affecting the diploid plant only become detectable after segregation in the second generation. The more deleterious mutations will be removed by normal selection pressures in this and succeeding generations. Other mutations, however, particularly those of minor genes having less dramatic effects, may well be a more permanent legacy of seed aging.

ACKNOWLEDGMENTS

I am most grateful to Dr. Siriporn Sirikwanchai and Dr. N. K. Rao for allowing me to use some of their results before publication and to my wife, Dorothy, for reading the manuscript and making several useful suggestions.

REFERENCES

Abdalla, F. H., and Roberts, E. H. (1968). Effects of temperature, moisture, and oxygen on the induction of chromosome damage in seeds of barley, broad beans, and peas during storage. *Ann. Bot.* **32**, 119–136.

Abdalla, F. H., and Roberts, E. H. (1969a). The effects of temperature, and moisture on the induction of genetic changes in seeds of barley, broad beans and peas during storage. *Ann. Bot.* **33**, 153–167.

Abdalla, F. H., and Roberts, E. H. (1969b). The effects of seed storage conditions on growth and yield of barley, broad beans, and peas. *Ann. Bot.* **33**, 169–184.

Ashton, T. (1956). Genetical aspects of seed storage. In "The Storage of Seeds for Maintenance of Viability" (E. B. Owen, ed.), pp. 34–38. Commonw. Agric. Bur., Farnham Royal, England.

Avanzi, S., Brunori, A., D'Amato, F., Nuti Ronchi, V., and Scarascia Mugnozza, G. T. (1963). Occurrence of 2C(G$_1$) and 4C(G$_2$) nuclei in the radicle meristem of dry seeds in *Triticum durum* Desf. Its implications in studies on chromosome breakage and on development processes. *Caryologia* **16**, 553–558.

Avanzi, S., Innocenti, A. M., and Tagliasacchi, A. M. (1969). Spontaneous chromosome aberrations in relation to seed dormancy in *Triticum durum* Desf. *Mutat. Res.* **7**, 199–203.

Avery, A. G., and Blakeslee, A. F. (1936). Visible mutations from aged seeds. *Am. Nat.* **70**, 36–37.

Bender, M. A., Griggs, H. G., and Walker, P. L. (1973). Mechanisms of chromosomal aberration production. I. Aberration induction by ultraviolet light. *Mutat. Res.* **20**, 387–402.

Bender, M. A., Griggs, H. G., and Bedford, J. S. (1974). Mechanisms of chromosomal aberration production. III. Chemicals and ionizing radiation. *Mutat. Res.* **23**, 197–212.

Berjak, P. (1968). A study of some aspects of senescence in embryos of *Zea mays* L. Ph.D. Thesis, Univ. of Natal. Durban, South Africa.

Blakeslee, A. F., and Avery, A. G. (1934). Visible genes from aged seeds. *Am. Nat.* **68**, 466.

Bogdanov, Y. F. (1965). The relation between DNA synthesis and types of chromosome aberrations during germination of pea seeds irradiated with X-rays. *Genetika* **3**, 35–43.

Bogdanov, Y. G., and Jordansky, A. B. (1964). Autoradiographic investigation of nuclei of root meristems of germinating pea seeds with employment of H^3-thymidine. *Zh. Obshch. Biol.* **35**, 357–363.

Brown, G. W., and Flood, M. M. (1947). Tumbler mortality. *J. Am. Statist. Assoc.* **42**, 562.

Caldecott, R. S. (1961). Seedling height, oxygen availability, storage and temperature: their relation to radiation-induced genetic and seedling injury in barley. In "Effect of Ionizing Radiations in Seeds," pp. 3–24. IAEA, Vienna.

Cartledge, J. L., and Blakeslee, A. F. (1933). Mutation rate increased by aging seeds as shown by pollen abortion. *Science* **78**, 523.

Cartledge, J. L., and Blakeslee, A. F. (1934). Mutation rate increased by aging seeds as shown by pollen abortion. *Proc. Natl. Acad. Sci. U.S.A.* **20**, 103–110.

Cartledge, J. L., and Blakeslee, A. F. (1935).

Cartledge, J. L., Barton, L. V., and Blakeslee, A. F. (1936). Heat and moisture as factors in the increased mutation rate from *Datura* seeds. *Proc. Am. Philos. Soc.* **76**, 663–685.

Cheah, K. S. E., and Osborne, D. J. (1978). DNA lesions occur with loss of viability in embryos of aging rye seed. *Nature (London)* **272**, 593–599.

Corsi, G., and Avanzi, S. (1969). Embryo and endosperm response to aging in *Triticum durum* seeds as revealed by chromosomal damage in the root meristem. *Mutat. Res.* **7**, 349–355.

Cromarty, A. S., Ellis, R. H., and Roberts, E. H. (1982). "The Design of Seed Storage Facilities for Genetic Conservation." Int. Board Plant Genet. Resour., Rome.

D'Amato, F. (1951). Spontaneous chromosome aberrations in seedlings of *Pisum sativum*. *Caryologia* **3**, 285–293.

D'Amato, F., and Hoffman-Ostenhof, O. (1956). Metabolism and spontaneous mutation in plants. *Adv. Genet.* **8**, 1–28.

de Vries, H. (1901). "Die Mutationstheorie," Vol. 1. Veit, Leipzig.

Dourado, A. M., and Roberts, E. H. (1984a). Chromosome aberrations induced during storage in barley and pea seeds. *Ann. Bot.* **54**, 767–779.

Dourado, A. M., and Roberts, E. H. (1984b). Phenotypic mutations induced during storage in barley and pea seeds. *Ann. Bot.* **54**, 781–790.

Dourado, A. M., and Roberts, E. H. (1984c). The nature of the viridoalbina/striata mutant induced during storage in barley seeds. *Ann. Bot.* **54**, 791–798.

Dubinin, N. P., and Dubinina, L. G. (1969). The problem of potential changes in chromosomes during storage of dry *Crepis capillaris* seeds. *Sov. Genet.* **4**, 1139–1152.

Ellis, R. H., and Roberts, E. H. (1980a). Improved equations for the prediction of seed longevity. *Ann. Bot.* **45**, 13–30.

Ellis, R. H., and Roberts, E. H. (1980b). The influence of temperature and moisture on seed viability in barley (*Hordeum distichum* L.). *Ann. Bot.* **45**, 31–37.

Ellis, R. H., and Roberts, E. H. (1980c). Towards a rational basis for testing seed quality. *In* "Seed Production" (P. D. Hebblethwaite, ed.), pp. 605–635. Butterworth, London.

Ellis, R. H., and Roberts, E. H. (1981). The quantification of ageing and survival in orthodox seeds. *Seed Sci. Technol.* **9**, 373–409.

Ellis, R. H., Osei-Bonsu, K., and Roberts, E. H. (1982). The influence of genotype, temperature and moisture on seed longevity in chickpea, cowpea and soyabean. *Ann. Bot.* **50**, 69–82.

Ellis, R. H., Hong, T. D., and Roberts, E. H. (1985). "Handbook of Seed Technology for Genebanks," Vol. 1. Int. Board Plant Genet. Resour., Rome.

Evans, H. J. (1962). Chromosome aberrations induced by ionizing radiation. *Int. Rev. Cytol.* **13**, 221–321.

Evans, H. J. (1977). Molecular mechanisms in the induction of chromosome aberrations. *In* "Progress in Genetic Technology" (D. Scott, B. A. Bridges, and F. H. Sobels, eds.), pp. 57–74. Elsevier/North-Holland, Amsterdam.

Floris, C., and Anguillesi, M. C. (1974). Aging of isolated embryos and endosperms of durum wheat: an analysis of chromosome damage. *Mutat. Res.* **22**, 133–138.

Gerassimova, H. N. (1935). The nature and causes of mutation. II. Transmission of mutations arising in aged seeds: occurrence of homozygous dislocants among progeny of plants raised from aged seeds. *Cytologia* **6**, 431–437.

Gichner, T., and Velemínský, J. (1979). Pre-replication recovery from induced chromosomal damage. *Mutat. Res.* **66**, 135–142.

Greer, S., and Zamenhof, F. (1962). Studies on depurination of DNA by heat. *J. Mol. Biol.* **4**, 123–141.

Griggs, H. G., and Bender, M. A. (1973). Photoreactivation of ultraviolet-induced chromosomal aberrations. *Science* **179**, 86–88.

Gunthardt, H., Smith, L., Haferkamp, M. E., and Nilan, R. A. (1953). Studies on aged seeds. II. Relation of age of seeds to cytogenic effects. *Agron. J.* **45**, 438–441.

Harrison, B. J. (1966). Seed deterioration in relation to storage conditions and its influence upon germination, chromosomal damage and plant performance. *J. Natl. Inst. Agric. Bot.* **10**, 644–663.

Harrison, B. J., and McLeish, J. (1954). Abnormalities of stored seeds. *Nature (London)* **173**, 593–594.

Howard, A., and Pelc, S. R. (1953). Synthesis of desoxyribonucleic acid in normal and irradiated cells and its relation to chromosome breakage. *Heredity* **6**, Suppl., 261–273.

Ibrahim, A. E. (1981). The effect of moisture content, oxygen availability and temperature on survival of lettuce (*Lactuca sativa* L.) and onion (*Allium cepa* L.) seed. Ph.D. Thesis, Univ. of Reading, Reading, England.

Ibrahim, A. E., and Roberts, E. H. (1983). Viability of lettuce seeds. I. Survival in hermetic storage. *J. Exp. Bot.* **34**, 620–630.

Ibrahim, A., Roberts, E. H., and Murdoch, A. J. (1983). Viability of lettuce seeds. II. Survival and oxygen uptake in osmotically controlled storage. *J. Exp. Bot.* **34**, 631–640.

Innocenti, A. M., and Avanzi, S. (1971). Seed aging and chromosome breakage in *Triticum durum* Desf. *Mutat. Res.* **13**, 225–231.

Kato, Y. (1951). Spontaneous chromosome aberrations in mitosis of *Allium fistulosum* L. (a preliminary note). *Bot Mag.* **64**, 152–156.

Kihlman, B. A. (1966). "Actions of Chemicals on Dividing Cells." Prentice-Hall, Englewood Cliffs, New Jersey.

Kihlman, B. A., and Hartley, B. (1967). 'Sub-chromatid' exchanges and the 'folded fibre' model of chromosome structure. *Hereditas* **57**, 289–294.

King, M. W., and Roberts, E. H. (1979). "The Storage of Recalcitrant Seeds, Achievements and Possible Approaches." Int. Board Plant Genet. Resour., Rome.

Kivilaan, A., and Bandurski, R. S. (1973). The ninety-year period for Dr Beal's seed viability experiment. *Am. J. Bot.* **60**, 140–154.

Kostoff, D. (1935). Mutations and the aging of seeds. *Nature (London)* **135**, 107.

Lea, D. E. (1946). "Actions of Radiations on Living Cells." Cambridge Univ. Press, Cambridge, England.

Murata, M., Roos, E. E., and Tsuchiya, T. (1979). Relationship between loss of germinability and the occurrence of chromosomal aberrations in artificially aged seeds of barley. *Barley Genet. Newsl.* **9**, 65–67.

Murata, M., Roos, E. E., and Tsuchiya, T. (1980). Mitotic delay in root tips of peas induced by artificial seed aging. *Bot. Gaz.* **141**, 19–23.

Murata, M., Roos, E. E., and Tsuchiya, T. (1981). Chromosome damage induced by artificial seed aging in barley. I. Germinability and frequency of aberrant anaphases at first mitoses. *Can. J. Genet. Cytol.* **23**, 267–280.

Murata, M., Tsuchiya, T., and Roos, E. E. (1982). Chromosome damage induced by artificial seed aging in barley. II. Types of chromosomal aberrations at first mitosis. *Bot. Gaz.* **143**, 111–116.

Murata, M., Tsuchiya, T., and Roos, E. E. (1984). Chromosome damage induced by artificial seed aging in barley. *Theor. Appl. Genet.* **67**, 161–170.

Navashin, M. S. (1933a). Origin of spontaneous mutations. *Nature (London)* **131**, 436.

Navashin, M. S. (1933b). Aging of seeds is a cause of chromosome mutations. *Planta* **20**, 233–243.

Navashin, M. S., and Gerassimova, H. N. (1936a). Natur und Ursachen der Mutationen. I. Das Verhalten und die Zutologie der Pflanzen, die aus infolge Alterns mutierten Keimen Stammen. *Cytologia* **7**, 324–362.

Navashin, M. S., and Gerassimova, H. N. (1936b). Natur und Ursachen der Mutationen. III. Uber die Chromosomenmutationen, die in dem Zellen von ruhenden Pflanzenkeimen bei deren Altern aufreten. *Cytologia* **7**, 437–465.

Nichols, C. (1941). Spontaneous chromosome aberration in *Allium. Genetics* **26**, 89–100.

Nilsson, N. H. (1933). Sind die induzierten Mutationen selektive Erscheingun? *Hereditas* **15**, 320–328.

Nuti Ronchi, V., and Martini, G. (1962). Germinabilità, sviluppo delle plantule e frequenza di aberrazioni cromosomiche in rapporto all'età del seme nel frumento. *Caryologia* **15**, 293–302.

Ødum, S. (1974). Seeds in ruderal soils, their longevity and contribution to the flora of disturbed ground in Denmark. *Br. Weed Control Conf. 12th*, **3,** 1131–1144.

Orlova, N. N. (1967). Study of the mutation process in dormant Welsh onion (*Allium fistulosum* L.) seeds, stored under conditions of increased temperature and humidity. *Genetika* **11,** 15–25.

Orlova, N. N., and Nikitina, V. I. (1968). The moment of appearance of chromosome aberrations during the aging of seeds. *Sov. Genet.* **4,** 1153–1158.

Orlova, N. N., Rogatykh, N. P., and Khartina, G. A. (1975). Decrease in the mitotic potential of cells in dormant seeds of welsh onion during storage. *Sov. Plant Physiol.* **22,** 629–635.

Osborne, D. J. (1977). Nucleic acids and seed germination. *In* "The Physiology and Biochemistry of Seed Germination" (A. A. Khan, ed.), pp. 319–333. North-Holland Publ., Amsterdam.

Osborne, D. J. (1982). Deoxyribonucleic acid integrity and repair in seed germination: the importance in viability and survival. *In* "The Physiology and Biochemistry of Seed Development, Dormancy and Germination" (A. A. Khan, ed.), pp. 435–463. Elsevier, Amsterdam.

Peto, F. H. (1933). The effect of aging and heat on the chromosomal mutation rate in maize and barley. *Can. J. Res.* **9,** 261–264.

Petruzelli, L. (1986). Wheat variability at high moisture content under hemetic and aerobic storage conditions. *Ann. Bot.* **58,** 259–265.

Priestley, D. A. (1985). Hugo de Vries and the development of seed aging theory. *Ann. Bot.* **56,** 267–269.

Purkar, J. K., Banerjee, S. K., and Mehra, R. B. (1980). Seed aging induced variability in quantitative characters of pea and wheat. *ISTA Congr., Vienna* Prepr. 60.

Rao, N. K., and Roberts, E. H. (1987). Loss of variability in lettuce seeds and the accumulation of chromosome damage under different storage conditions. *Ann. Bot.* **60,** 85–96.

Rao, N. K., Roberts, E. H., and Ellis, R. H. (1987). The influence of pre- and post-storage hydration treatments on chromosomal aberrations, seedling abnormalities, and variability of lettuce seeds. *Ann. Bot.* **60,** 97–108.

Revell, S. H. (1959). The accurate estimation of chromatid breakage, and its relevance to a new interpretation of chromatid aberrations induced by ionizing radiations. *Proc. R. Soc. London, Ser. B* **150,** 563–589.

Roberts, E. H. (1960). The viability of cereal seed in relation to temperature and moisture. *Ann. Bot.* **25,** 373–380.

Roberts, E. H. (1961). The viability of rice seed in relation to temperature, moisture content, and gaseous environment. *Ann. Bot.* **25,** 381–390.

Roberts, E. H. (1972). Cytological, genetical and metabolic changes associated with loss of viability. *In* "Viability of Seeds" (E. H. Roberts, ed.), pp. 235–306. Chapman & Hall, London.

Roberts, E. H. (1973a). Predicting the viability of seeds. *Seed Sci. Technol.* **1,** 499–514.

Roberts, E. H. (1973b). Loss of seed viability: chromosomal and genetical aspects. *Seed Sci. Technol.* **1,** 515–527.

Roberts, E. H. (1978). Mutations during seed storage. *Acta Hortic.* **83,** 279–282.

Roberts, E. H. (1979). Seed deterioration and loss of viability. *Adv. Res. Technol. Seeds* **4,** 25–42.

Roberts, E. H. (1983). Loss of seed viability during storage. *Adv. Res. Technol. Seeds* **8,** 9–34.

Roberts, E. H. (1986). Quantifying seed deterioration. *In* "Physiology of Seed Deterioration" (M. B. McDonald, Jr. and C. J. Nelson, eds.), Spec. Publ. No. 11, pp. 101–122. Crop Sci. Soc. Am., Madison, Wisconsin.

Roberts, E. H., and Abdalla, F. H. (1968). The influence of temperature, moisture and oxygen on period of seed viability in barley, broad beans, and peas. *Ann. Bot.* **32,** 97–117.

Roberts, E. H., and Ellis, R. H. (1982). Physiological, ultrastructural and metbolic aspects of seed viability. *In* "The Physiology and Biochemistry of Seed Development, Dormancy and Germination" (A. A. Khan, ed.), pp. 465–485. Elsevier, Amsterdam.

Roberts, E. H., and Ellis, R. H. (1984). The implications of the deterioration of orthodox seeds during storage for genetic resources conservation. *In* "Crop Genetic Resources: Conservation and Evaluation" (J. H. W. Holden and J. T. Williams, eds.), pp. 18–37. Allen & Unwin, London.

Roberts, E. H., Abdalla, F. H., and Owen, R. J. (1967). Nuclear damage and the aging of seeds with a model for seed survival curves. *Symp. Soc. Exp. Biol.* **21,** 65–100.

Roos, E. E. (1982). Induced genetic changes in seed germplasm during storage. *In* "The Physiology and Biochemistry of Seed Development, Dormancy and Germination" (A. A. Khan, ed.), pp. 409–434. Elsevier, Amsterdam.

Savage, J. R. K. (1975). Classification and relationships of induced chromosomal structural changes. *J. Med. Genet.* **12,** 103–122.

Savage, J. R. K., and Wigglesworth, D. J. (1970). The non-uniform sensitivity of the dormant root meristem of barley seed revealed by chromosome aberrations in cells at metaphase of the first division cycle. *Radiat. Bot.* **10,** 377–390.

Sax, K. (1938). Chromosome aberrations induced by X-rays. *Genetics* **23,** 494–516.

Sax, K. (1940). An analysis of X-ray induced chromosomal aberrations in *Tradescantia. Genetics* **25,** 41–68.

Sax, K. (1941). Types and frequencies of chromosomal aberrations induced by X-rays. *Cold Spring Harbor Symp. Quant. Biol.* **9,** 93–103.

Sax, K., and Sax, H. J. (1964). Effect of X-rays on aging in seeds. *Nature (London)* **194,** 459–460.

Sevov, A., Kristov, K., and Kristova, P. (1973). Biological and cytogenetical changes in old maize seeds stored under ordinary conditions. *Genet. Sel.* **6,** 107–115.

Shkvarnikov, P. (1935). [Influence of temperature and moisture on the process of mutation in resting seeds.] *Semenovodstvo* No. 1, 46–52. Cited in Ashton (1956).

Shkvarnikov, P. (1936). Einfluss hoher Temperatur auf die Mutatiosrate bei Weizen. *Planta* **25,** 471–480.

Shkvarnikov, P. (1939). [Mutation in seeds and its significance in seed production and plant breeding.] *Bull. Acad. Sci USSR, Ser. Biol.* pp. 1009–1054. Cited in Ashton (1956).

Shkvarnikov, P., and Navashin, M. S. (1934). Über die Beschleungung des Mutationsvorganges in ruhenden Samen unter dem Einfluss von Temperatur erhöhung. *Planta* **2,** 720–736.

Shkvarnikov, P., and Navashin, M. S. (1935). [Acceleration of the mutation process in resting seeds under the influence of increased temperatures.] *Biol. Zh.* **4,** 25–38. Cited in Ashton (1956).

Sirikwanchai, S. (1985). The effects of moisture and oxygen on the accumulation of chromosome damage in relation to loss of viability in stored onion (*Allium cepa* L.) seed. Ph.D. Thesis, Reading Univ., Reading, England.

Sizova, L. I. (1976). Effect of seed aging on structural chromosome mutations induced by gamma rays in sunflower chlorophyll mutants. *Sov. Genet.* **12**(7), 24–30.

Soyfer, V. N. Krausse, G. V., Pokrovskaya, A. A., and Yakovleva, N. I. (1977). Repair of single-strand breaks and recovery of chromosomal and chromatid aberrations after treatment of plant seeds with propyl methanesulphonate *in vivo. Mutat. Res.* **42,** 51–63.

Velemínský, J., Zadražil, S., and Gichner, T. (1972). Repair of single-strand breaks in DNA and recovery of induced mutagenic effects during the storage of ethyl methanesulphonate-treated barley seeds. *Mutat. Res.* **14,** 259–261.

Velemínský, J., Zadražil, S., Pokorný, V., Gichner, T., and Švachulová, J. (1973a). Repair of single-strand breaks and fate of N-7-methylguanine in DNA during the recovery from genetical damaged induced by N-methyl-N-nitrosourea in barley seeds. *Mutat. Res.* **19**, 73–81.

Velemínský, J., Zadražil, S., Pokorný, V., Gichner, T., and Švachulová, J. (1973b). Storage effect in barley: changes in the amount of DNA lesions induced by methyl and ethyl methanesulphonates. *Mutat. Res.* **19**, 73–81.

Villiers, T. A. (1974). Seed aging: chromosome stability and extended viability of seeds stored fully imbibed. *Plant Physiol.* **53**, 875–878.

Villiers, T. A. (1975). Genetic maintenance of seeds in imbibed storage. *In* "Crop Genetic Resources for Today and Tomorrows" (O. H. Frankel and J. G. Hawkes, eds.), pp. 297–316. Cambridge Univ. Press, London and New York.

Villiers, T. A., and Edgcumbe, D. J. (1975). On the cause of seed deterioration in dry storage. *Seed Sci. Technol.* **3**, 761–764.

Ward, F. H., and Powell, A. A. (1983). Evidence for repair processes in onion seeds during storage at high seed moisture contents. *J. Exp. Bot.* **34**, 277–282.

Wolff, S. (1970). On the 'tertiary' structure of chromosomes. *Mutat. Res.* **10**, 405–414.

Wolff, S. (1981). Induced chromosome variation. *In* "Chromosomes Today" (M. D. Bennett, M. Bobrow, and G. Hewitt, eds.), Vol. 7, pp. 226–241. Allen & Unwin, London.

Yamaguchi, H., Naito, T., and Tatara, A. (1978). Decreased activity of DNA polymerase in seeds of barley during storage. *Jpn. J. Genet.* **53**, 133–135.

15

Postlude and Prospects

L. D. Noodén
Biology Department
University of Michigan
Ann Arbor, Michigan

I. SENESCENCE VERSUS EXOGENOUSLY DRIVEN DEGENERATION

In Chapter 1, we built on the efforts of others (see, e.g., Davies and Sigee, 1984) to distinguish among the various processes that cause deterioration and death of cells, organs, or organisms, with particular accommodations for plants. These processes differ primarily in being driven by endogenous factors (senescence) or by exogenous factors (necrosis and aging). At

SENESCENCE AND AGING IN PLANTS

499

present, it is much easier to make these distinctions on a conceptual basis than to define them in specific biochemical terms. Nonetheless, some clear examples seem to be available; the rapid degeneration of petals following fertilization (Chapter 1) or of leaves following fruit development in monocarpic plants (Chapter 12) are clear cases of internal programming (senescence). Chronic stress, environmental or disease, apparently can also trigger senescence. Of course, acute trauma or highly adverse conditions, which are exogenous, could also cause necrosis and death of these organs. Aging is a passive and more gradual process in which damage caused by external factors accumulates with time until the organism dies, the loss of viability in stored seeds being the best example available (Chapter 1, 13, and 14). In nature, the decline of an individual organism may often be due to a combination of these processes. At this time, it doesn't seem appropriate to attempt to define these phenomena precisely, only to recognize them as possibilities. A better understanding of the biochemistry of these processes will eventually resolve these problems.

In aging, the lesions in membranes (Chapter 13) and DNA (Chapter 14) or some combination of these seem to be the most critical. In addition, damage to other molecules, particularly proteins, could also contribute to aging. The aging process appears to be driven by factors such as ionizing radiation, active ions, and free radicals, which occur naturally in the environment (Krueger and Reed, 1976; Pryor, 1976; Fridovich, 1978; Sanders, 1983; Halliwell and Gutteridge, 1985; Taylor *et al.*, 1986). Aging is a passive process, yet organisms may differ in their susceptibility, and this would be genetically determined. For example, seeds of different species differ in their storage life (Roberts, 1972; Villiers, 1973; Osborne, 1980; Priestley *et al.*, 1985; Priestley, 1986).

Senescence does not seem to be the chaotic, breakdown of order that was once envisioned, and it is not the passive process implied by animal researchers (see, e.g., Hart and Turturro, 1985). At least in plants, and probably other organisms too, senescence is comprised of active, orderly processes, which appear to involve the synthesis of new RNAs and enzymes (Chapter 5 and 6). This orderly disassembly of the cells is evident in the ultrastructural changes (Chapter 1) and the rise of a broad array of degradative enzymes (Chapter 6) in senescing tissues. Ultimately, however, order does collapse, and the senescing cell loses its homeostatic ability. The plasma membrane and energy production are maintained until very late, but, in the end, they too succumb (Chapters 1, 2 and 4). Because the loss of homeostatic ability also appears to be the final step in the exogenously driven processes of necrosis and aging, these processes seem to share these final changes with senescence (Chapter 1).

II. WHAT IS SENESCENCE?

A. Required Processes

Because of the uncertainty over which are the central components of senescence, this term has generally been used loosely to refer to what is more accurately called the senescence syndrome (Chapter 1). Here, we will try to determine which components of metabolism are necessary for senescence.

Senescence appears to be an active, energy-requiring process. Evidence for this comes mainly from (1) the ability of anoxia and respiratory inhibitors to block development of the symptoms of senescence without killing the tissue, at least not quickly (Wood and Cruickshank, 1944; Martin and Thimann, 1972; Tetley and Thimann, 1974; Thimann, 1980; Satler and Thimann, 1983; Chapter 4) and (2) the fact that many processes that seem to be necessary components of senescence require energy. From the preceding chapters, it can be seen that many reactions involved in the senescence syndrome require energy input. Certainly, RNA and protein synthesis do, but even an initial step in protein degradation, conjugation of the protein with ubiquitin, requires ATP (Chapter 6). In addition to the senescence process itself, the continued maintenance of the cell requires energy (Penning de Vries, 1975) as does the export (phloem loading) of the solutes released by breakdown of cell constituents (Chapter 6) and the constant pumping of calcium out of the cells (Chapter 11). The persistence of the mitochondrial structure and activities until very late in senescence also speaks for their importance in the senescence process (Chapters 1 and 4). Thus, inhibition of ATP production may cause necrosis but not senescence, which is itself energy dependent.

Implicit in the idea that senescence is controlled by endogenous factors is genetic control of senescence, and presumably, therefore, messenger RNA synthesis is involved (Chapter 5). Certain RNA species increase, while others decrease; however, it is not yet known which function directly in senescence. RNA synthesis not only accompanies senescence, but it is necessary for senescence. Evidence for the necessity of RNA synthesis comes from various disruptions. All of these, particularly the selective inhibitors, may be nonspecific or produce indirect effects and need to be viewed with some caution. Nonetheless, these studies offer important insights even with this caveat and even if they do emphasize the chloroplast component of the senescence syndrome. A variety of interesting mutations that alter the senescence syndrome (chlorophyll loss, leaf abscission, fruit senescence) do exist (Bernard and Weiss, 1973; Thomas and Stoddart, 1975; Kahanak *et al.*, 1978; McGlasson *et al.*, 1978; Hardwick, 1979; Duncan *et al.*, 1981; Stoddart and Thomas, 1982; Pierce *et al.*, 1984; Thomas, 1987), although these could affect senescence indirectly (pleiotrophy). Another line of evidence for nuclear control of senescence comes from enucleation experiments (Yoshida, 1961) in *Elodea* leaf cells, where enucleation preserved the chloroplasts (determined by light microscopy and starch accumulation). In addition, treatment of the nucleated cells with RNase, then a fashionable experimental procedure, also inhibited chloroplast senescence.

Selective inhibitors of RNA synthesis, particularly actinomycin D, also confirm the nuclear role in senescence. Actinomycin D inhibited several types of senescence-related biochemical processes in a variety of tissues, including leaves and petals (De Vecchi, 1971; Matile and Winkenbach, 1971; Yoshida, 1974; Pech and Romani, 1979; Yu and Kao, 1981), whereas it was ineffective in others (Von Abrams, 1974; Thomas, 1975). Perhaps the lack of effect in certain situations is due to insufficient penetration or possibly even decomposition. Since actinomycin D is a large, polar molecule, uptake difficulties can be expected. Actinomycin can also interfere with the senescence-delaying effect of cytokinin (Wollgiehn, 1967; Takegami, 1975a). By contrast, rifampicin, which acts on microbial and organelle RNA polymerases, does not inhibit senescence (Yoshida, 1974; Yu and Kao, 1981). These interesting observations do, however, need to be supported by data showing that the rifampicin has in fact inhibited organelle RNA synthesis under these conditions. Thus, senescence appears to begin with activation of synthesis of some new mRNAs and probably inactivation of others. In addition, experiments with the inhibitor cordycepin (Takegami, 1975b) indicate the necessity of capping these nuclear RNAs with polyadenylic acid for further processing and export to the cytoplasm.

Inasmuch as the senescence-related mRNAs would be used to make proteins, it seems that selective synthesis of proteins may also be necessary for senescence. A host of studies show that cycloheximide, a selective (though not specific) inhibitor of protein synthesis on 80 S ribosomes, blocks a variety of senescence-related changes, including membrane alterations in many tissues, and it may also interfere with the senescence-retarding action of cytokinin (De Vecchi, 1971; Knypl and Mazurczyk, 1971; Chen, 1972; Martin and Thimann, 1972; Von Abrams, 1974; Dilley and Carpenter, 1975; Peterson and Huffaker, 1975; Takegami, 1975a,b; Thomas, 1975; Makovetzki and Goldschmidt, 1976; Kao, 1978; Bose and Srivastava, 1979; Thimann and Satler, 1979; Suttle and Kende, 1980; Tripathi *et al.*, 1980; Pjon, 1981; Yu and Kao, 1981). There are, however, a few reports that cycloheximide may sometimes accelerate chlorophyll loss in light or cause cell membrane leakiness (Knypl and Mazurczyk, 1971; De Luca d'Oro and Trippi, 1982), but these may differ from the normal senescence processes (Thimann *et al.*, 1982). Chloramphenicol, which acts mainly on the plastid and mitochondrial (70 S) ribosomes, generally does not retard senescence (Wollgiehn and Parthier, 1964; Knypl, 1970; Von Abrams, 1974; Peterson and Huffaker, 1975; Takegami, 1975a; Thomas, 1975; Kao, 1978), but chloramphenicol may accelerate senescence slightly in a few cases (Mothes, 1964; Makovetzki and Goldschmidt, 1976; Yu and Kao, 1981). Less extensive studies (references cited above) with other selective inhibitors of protein synthesis on 70 S and 80 S ribosomes yield a similar picture to that from cycloheximide and chloramphenicol. This points to a substantial difference in roles of proteins synthesized in the cytoplasm compared to those made in the organelles, presumably the chloroplast. Apparently, some protein synthesized on 80 S (cytoplasmic) ribosomes is important, perhaps central, to senescence, but that on 70 S (presumably plastid) ribosomes is not. How the required synthesis of proteins ends up with a loss of plasma membrane integrity and homeostasis (Section II,B below) remains to be determined.

At this time, there are not enough data to formulate a specific scheme for senescence with certainty. Instead, we will consider some general questions about the nature of the senescence process. First, what is central and what is peripheral to the senescence? Of course, senescence will eventually involve the entire metabolism of the affected cells indirectly, but only certain processes will be directly causal. Thus, the components of any scheme to describe senescence should be selected for centrality. Second, the centrality of the chloroplast in senescence needs to be reconsidered. Third, senescence may consist of parallel processes, and that possibility needs to be examined, even if only to influence future experimentation.

B. Central versus Peripheral Processes in Senescence

From the above section and Chapter 5, it can be tentatively concluded that selective activation of RNA synthesis and also the protein synthesis that follows, is not only required for the senescence process but is central to it.

Because senescence is a process of overall decline in metabolism, including RNA and protein synthesis, it is tempting to view it as a process of inhibition. However, a simple, nonspecific decline in RNA synthesis does not cause senescence. As shown above, actinomycin D does not promote senescence but generally retards it. In addition, fluorouracil, which inhibits ribosomal RNA synthesis, does not alter senescence measured as chlorophyll loss in radish leaf discs (Paranjothy and Wareing, 1971; Von Abrams, 1974). The same general picture seems to hold for protein synthesis in that protein synthesis, at least cytoplasmic protein synthesis, is required for senescence, and inhibitors of protein synthesis generally do not induce senescence. Nonetheless, cessation or reduction in the synthesis of certain RNAs may be important, even central. Thus, activation and possibly a decrease in the synthesis of certain RNAs and proteins may be central, but the overall decline of RNA and protein synthesis as well as RNA and protein levels could just follow along as peripheral changes.

In contrast to RNA and protein synthesis in the nucleus and cytoplasm, the results with both RNA- and protein-synthesis inhibitors suggest that the RNA and protein synthesis in the organelles, particularly in the chloroplasts, may not be required or play a central role in senescence, a topic that will be discussed later in connection with the role of the chloroplast.

In Chapter 1, it was argued that the loss of membrane integrity, particularly that of the plasma membrane, and homeostatic ability represent the final stage of senescence and the threshold of death. Chapter 2 documented the extensive evidence linking chemical changes in the membranes with the breakdown of selective permeability. It has been known for a long time that increased outward leakage of solutes occurs in senescing cells (Sacher, 1957; Eilam, 1965), and the cell barriers to vital dye penetration are lost in the final stages of senescence (Molisch, 1938; Gaff and Okong'o-Ogola, 1971; Chapters 1 and 2). The membranes of senescing cells show physical changes (decreased fluidity) and chemical alterations (especially less phospholipid) (Chapter 2).

A strong argument (Chapter 2) is also made that free radicals generated within the senescing cells cause the chemical changes in their membranes, apparently through reaction with the double bonds in the fatty acid component of the membrane lipids. How these membrane changes are related to the sequence involving protein synthesis as outlined above is uncertain, but there does seem to be a connection. In *Tradescantia* petals, cycloheximide arrests the development of leakiness in the cells and the decline in phospholipid levels that usually occur during senescence (Suttle and Kende, 1980). Of course, cycloheximide could act on some process other than protein synthesis, but these interesting observations still pose some important questions about the involvement of protein synthesis. It may be that the proteins which must be synthesized to cause senescence include enzymes that generate free radicals. On the other hand, these newly synthesized proteins may operate through some very different mechanisms, for example, through direct action on the phospholipids and other membrane components. In any case, the problem of how these extremely destructive free radicals would be confined to confer the selective degradation that seems to prevail until death also needs study. At this time, the question of how the changes are induced in the membranes still seems open and other enzymic mechanisms that may be more selective seem feasible.

In the past, it was considered that decreased respiration causes death in aged or senescing tissues (Nicolas, 1918; Crocker, 1939; Eilam, 1965). If the respiratory rate and/or ATP production dropped below the maintenance level, basal metabolic rate, then membrane integrity and other aspects of maintenance could not be supported (Chapter 1). As explained above in Section II,A and Chapter 4, respiration, or at least ATP production, is necessary for senescence. Thus, constraining ATP production to or near the self-maintenance level may retard senescence rather than cause it, but below this level necrosis would result.

Although the usefulness of calcium in the chemotherapy of senescence has been recognized for a long time, its more recently discovered importance as regulator of cell activities indicates a deeper importance in the senescence process even though that role is not completely understood (Chapter 11).

Especially since senescence can be viewed as a degradative process, one might suppose these newly synthesized senescence proteins are proteolytic enzymes. However, even correlating the changes in protein levels with proteolytic enzyme levels has encountered many difficulties, and invoking causality of senescence, a step beyond that, is even less certain (Noodén and Leopold, 1978; Chapter 7). In fact, even massive losses of protein need not be fatal. For example, the loss of 85% of the total protein in bean leaves is reversible (Krul, 1974). Some parallel cases exist in the storage tissues of seeds. During the early phases of seed germination, enormous amounts of stored proteins, lipids, and polysaccharides are degraded and redistributed to the growing centers of the seedling (Murray, 1984; Bewley and Black, 1985), but this degradation is not necessarily lethal to the cells involved. For some species (epigeic types), the cotyledons including the specialized storage cells are transformed into photosynthetic structures, thereby assuming a new role. In cucumber cotyledons (Butler, 1967), pine cotyledons (Sasaki and Kozlowski, 1969), and some other species (Smith, 1981), there is no indication of substantial cell death in these revamped storage tissues. Here, massive degradation, e.g., breakdown of the protein bodies, is simply a transition in the function and continuing life of a cell. The same can be said for petals that may undergo a substantial loss in their cellular proteins even as they grow, well before what is normally considered to be their senescence (Schumacher and Matthael, 1955; Halevy and Mayak, 1979). There is no doubt that proteolysis and the reclamation of nitrogenous constituents are important components of the senescence syndrome (Chapters 6 and 12), but it is not clear that these play a primary, causal role as opposed to following up on other more central changes. This is a major topic needing careful analysis in the future. Regardless, proteolysis and the other degradative processes are of great interest and warrant study for their own sake.

Although most cellular processes decline during senescence, and ultimately all of them cease, senescence is not a process of inhibition. In fact, the opposite, activation of selected metabolic systems, may be closer to the truth, for inhibition of ATP production, protein synthesis, and RNA synthesis do not cause senescence. Thus, senescence clearly does not represent a generalized, nonspecific shutdown of any of these families of processes.

Thus, the central senescence process seems to begin in the nucleus with synthesis of RNAs, which, in turn, are used to make certain proteins in the cytoplasm. Through uncertain intermediate steps, the end result is alteration of the plasma membrane and loss of homeostatic ability. These final events do not seem to be caused primarily through a reduction in ATP production, even though the loss in ATP formation does accompany these final events. In any case, attempts to outline the senescence process should be less than the totality of cell metabolism (Woolhouse, 1982, 1983) and should henceforth try to discriminate between central and peripheral processes. Although any detailed, integrated scheme formulated at this time will surely undergo great change that need has been recognized and the process started (Thimann, 1987; preface).

C. The Role of the Chloroplast in Senescence

The loss of chloroplast components, chlorophyll, and soluble protein constitute a conspicuous part of the senescence syndrome, yet these changes in the chloroplast seem to be directed mainly by genes in the nucleus instead of genes in the chloroplast. In other words, RNA synthesized in the nucleus and proteins synthesized in the cytoplasm rather than RNA and protein synthesized in the chloroplast appear to be needed for chloroplast breakdown. Another line of evidence for this idea comes from the observations of Choe and Thimann (1975), who found that isolated chloroplasts could under favorable conditions outlast their counterparts in intact cells. Similarly, the cytokinins, which are the major senescence-antagonizing hormones (Chapter 9), promote synthesis of cytoplasmic RNAs or proteins with little or no effect on the chloroplast (Legocka and Szweykowska, 1981, 1983). Thus, as suggested by Thimann in the foreword, senescence may be imposed on the chloroplast.

These observations raise the question: are the dramatic changes that occur in chloroplasts during senescence central to the senescence process? At the outset, it should be recognized that many organs, tissues, and cells grow and flourish and then senesce without ever having developed chloroplasts. Many instances are described in Chapter 1, but petals (Halevy and Mayak, 1979; Mayak and Halevy, 1980) would be a prime example. Is the loss of chloroplasts then somehow more detrimental to photosynthetic tissues than nonphotosynthetic tissues? Apparently not, as long as the cells without chloroplasts are supplied with sugar or some other energy source. For example, the famous red, yellow, or orange cacti (*Gymnocalcium* varieties) lack chlorophyll, but they flourish as long as they are grafted onto a green nurse plant (Elbert and Elbert, 1975). Moreover, many chimeral plants produce leaves which wholly or partly lack chloroplasts (Tilney-Bassett, 1986). Even the leaves of albina (white) and xantha (yellow) soybean mutants grow and eventually senesce if the shoots are grafted onto a nurse plant (Noble *et al.*, 1977; L. D. Noodén, unpublished observations). Similarly, albina tobacco shoots will grow if grafted onto a green plant (Turgeon, 1984). Obviously, the mitochondria and other ATP-generating mechanisms supply the energy needed for maintenance in these and other nongreen tissues. The upshot is that chloroplast degeneration is probably not central to leaf senescence per se, and leaf senescence descriptions (Woolhouse, 1983) that emphasize it without note seem suspect. Even in fruits, the conspicuous loss of chlorophyll may represent ripening and remodeling of the plastids more than senescence (Chapter 1; see also Goldschmidt, 1980).

At the level of the higher plant and monocarpic senescence, a paradox unfolds. For soybean plants, the leaves seem to be the primary target of the senescence-inducing influence from the seeds, and the plant appears to die as a result of the loss of photosynthate supplied by the leaves (Noodén, 1980; Chapter 12). The loss of photosynthetic capacity, obviously involving the chloroplasts, seems to be central to monocarpic senescence. Thus, whether or not chloroplast breakdown is central to senescence may depend on the context in which it occurs. In either case, however, the disassembly of the photosynthetic apparatus is an important process and is worthy of considerable attention.

D. Senescence as Parallel or Loosely Coupled Processes

Is senescence a sequential process or a set of parallel processes? Parallel processes could occur in different compartments or even within the same compartment within a cell as well as in different organs of a plant. Even if components of whole plant senescence happen in different organs, they could be coupled into a sequence through interorgan signaling and correlative controls.

In numerous cases, disjuncts or even uncouplings may be induced by environmental factors or various treatments, suggesting that some of the different components of the senescence syndrome may run in parallel, especially in whole plant senescence (Noodén, 1984). Specifically, in the case of the maturing soybean, there is a very loose coupling between such important processes as the declines in root processes, i.e., growth or mineral assimilation, and foliar characteristics including photosynthesis, nitrogen levels, chlorophyll, ribulose 1,5-bisphosphate carboxylase, etc., as well as abscission. Comparing different reports that employ different varieties and conditions, it can be seen that these changes do not always bear the same kinetic relationship to one another or even the same order of change. This is true within the leaves, where photosynthesis-related parameters and abscission may vary somewhat independently, but it also seems to apply, albeit to a lesser extent, to photosynthesis versus chlorophyll versus ribulose-1,5-bisphosphate carboxylase. To cite one example where all the comparisons were made in one study, ear removal may produce quite different effects on the changes in foliar levels of chlorophyll, total nitrogen concentration, CO_2 exchange rates, ribulose-1,5-bisphosphate carboxylase, and phospho*enol*pyruvate carboxylase in different maize lines (Crafts-Brandner and Poneleit, 1987). The coupling between these processes is loose enough to suggest that they may be parallel processes. Obviously, there may be limits to which processes within the same organ or organism can be uncoupled even if they are parallel.

Within an organ, particularly leaves, individual cells show quite a lot of heterogeneity in when they senesce (Chapter 1). This is evident in differences among parts of the leaf visible in surface view, but also in differences among tissues within the leaf, for example, tissues near the vascular bundle senesce later than those away from the vein. Similarly, studies on cell ultrastructure indicate that different parts in a cell may change at different times (Chapter 1). Whether these are parallel or sequential is difficult to ascertain at this time.

For leaves, the best known uncoupling involves mutants that prevent, or at least retard, chlorophyll loss from other components of the senescence syndrome. The nonyellowing mutant of fescue (a pasture grass) has been studied most extensively (Thomas and Stoddart, 1980; Thomas, 1987), but stay-green mutants have also been reported in soybean (Bernard and Weiss, 1973; Kahanak et al., 1978; Pierce et al., 1984), corn (Crafts-Brandner et al., 1984), and sorghum (Duncan et al., 1981). In the case of fescue leaves, numerous enzymes, even including chloroplast enzymes such as ribulose 1,5-bisphosphate carboxylase, decrease without the normal concomitant chlorophyll breakdown in the nonyellowing mutant (Thomas and Stoddart, 1980). The looseness of the coupling between chlorophyll and protein degradation is further illustrated by a variety of reports showing that chlorophyll loss may occur ahead of or even without losses in total protein (Goldthwaite and Laetsch, 1967; Lewington and Simon, 1969; Arguelles and Guardiola, 1977). Chlorophyll breakdown occurs without the normal redistribution of mineral nutrients in steam-girdled leaves on soybean plants during pod development (Wood et al., 1986), although there could be a qualitative change or turnover of these constituents.

Many examples of loose couplings, if not disconnections, among processes can be seen in the studies of hormone effects on senescing tissues. For example, cytokinin treatments that strongly retard senescence may also inhibit respiration (Person *et al.*, 1957; Dedolph *et al.*, 1961; Goldthwaite, 1974; Tetley and Thimann, 1974). In some, but clearly not all, cases, the effect of cytokinin may be more prevention of a climacteric-like rise in respiration than decrease of an established rate. Another example would be the opposing effects of different cytokinins on the senescence-related leakage of phosphate from barley leaf segments (Sabater *et al.*, 1981). While all cytokinins tested retard chlorophyll loss, kinetin and benzyladenine reduce phosphate leakage, but zeatin and isopentenyladenine promote it. Numerous disjuncts, some even paradoxical, exist in the ethylene relations to fruit ripening and senescence (McGlasson *et al.*, 1978; Rhodes, 1980), but here there is difficulty in separating effects on ripening and senescence.

Given the uncertainties about the biochemistry of senescence, these questions about parallel versus sequential processes in senescence cannot be resolved at this time, but they need to be considered.

E. Is Senescence One Process or Several?

The thrust of this volume has been to look for commonality in senescence occurring in different cells. Since it is uncertain precisely what constitutes the central processes of senescence (Section II,B), it is also not clear whether or not the central senescence processes in all senescing cells are the same. Nonetheless, it can be argued that there are some general similarities evident in ultrastructural and biochemical changes (Chapter 1) that suggest oneness. On the other hand, chloroplast degeneration (Section II,C) may be central to monocarpic senescence but not to cell senescence or even leaf senescence. Thus, it seems that senescence may sometimes differ.

F. Future Analyses of Senescence

Many aspects of cell metabolism and the changes that accompany senescence, i.e., the senescence syndrome, warrant study for their own sake, but this may not resolve the questions raised in Sections II,B – E above. In addition, it seems important to examine the interconnection of these processes and their relations to the whole organism or at least the whole organ. Along these lines, experimental perturbations could be employed to probe the interrelations of processes. These probes could be mutations, surgical treatments, hormones, or selective inhibitors, but, of course, all of these can be disruptive and can produce substantial side effects. One approach that is in fact relatively neglected, even though substantial peripheral data exist, is to work out the normal hormonal controls of senescence. Knowing these controls will greatly aid in identifying which processes are important in senescence. At present, ethylene (Chapter 8) and cytokinin (Chapter 9) are best understood, but even these are incomplete. In any case, the questions raised in Sections II,B, D, and E are considered in unraveling the senescence process.

III. WHAT HORMONE IS IN CONTROL?

Senescence of a cell, a tissue, an organ or a whole plant is often, if not always, under correlative control (Chapter 1). As mediators of these controls, it follows that hormones must play central roles in regulating senescence, but seldom have these roles been demonstrated.

Because of the economic importance of senescence, considerable effort has been made to alter its course with hormone treatments of whole plants, attached organs, or, most often, detached parts, as in postharvest applications. This has produced a large quantity of data concerning hormone effects on senescence and related processes. While observations of this type do not by themselves constitute proof that the hormone regulates senescence, they can be indicative (Chapter 1). These studies have been particularly informative about endogenous controls when they have been integrated with data on the changes in endogenous hormone levels. Parallel variation of endogenous hormone levels have been observed in many systems, at least in the sense that the hormone levels change prior to or in conjunction with senescence. Experimental manipulations that produce parallel alterations of senescence and hormone levels seem even stronger. In addition, the separation of the target tissue from the hormone source by excision of either the target or the source, combined with hormone applications to substitute for the source, can help to verify any links. In any case, all of these studies, hormone treatments, and the analyses of endogenous hormone levels need to be integrated with studies on the correlative controls, the location of the hormone source, and the hormone transport pathway. Diverse data implicate senescence-retarding and -promoting hormones (Chapter 10) in addition to cytokinin and ethylene, but more consideration of control by multiple hormones is needed for all hormone studies (Chapter 1). Even if the hormone controls in different species show some differences, some generalizations should ultimately be possible.

It is in whole plant senescence (Chapter 12) that the importance of integrating separate studies into a larger picture really becomes most obvious, but other, simpler examples exist. Studies on the time course of change in any parameter should be related to other parameters, preferably controls or some key reference (Derman et al., 1978; Noodén, 1984). Likewise, studies on excised parts can be very important, but they may have some limitations that need to be recognized. For example, results with excised parts may not always be directly extrapolated into the whole plant due to metabolic changes in the former (Chapter 1). An instructive example of some important differences caused by surgery is provided by cut rose flowers, where abscisic acid retards flower senescence if the leaves are present but promotes senescence when the leaves have been removed (Halevy *et al.*, 1974). The movement of the hormones within the whole plant, particularly movement out of strong sinks such as fruit and growing regions, has not been studied much. The recent advances (Chapter 7) in analyzing the pathways and volume of water flux within the plant will certainly contribute greatly to our understanding of the control of hormone distribution within the whole plant.

Most of the studies reported on hormonal controls are already directed toward a relatively small number of systems. For a few systems, specifically tobacco leaves, *Rumex* (but several species have been used) leaves, lettuce leaves, Brussels sprouts, citrus fruits, avocado fruits, tomato fruits, grape berries, carnation flowers, rose flowers, rice plants, lupine plants, pea plants, and soybean plants, a very substantial start toward an integrated picture of the hormone roles has already been made.

IV. LIMITS ON LIFE

Plant organisms appear to be capable of living for hundreds of years and even several millennia in some cases (Chapter 12). Clones may survive even longer. In the case of clones, however, it can be argued that the renewal of parts is so extensive that it is not even the same individual from beginning to end. The same argument can, however, be extended to nonclonal individuals at both the cell and molecular levels level. Usually, there is extensive replacement of the cells in a whole plant, so that very few (see below) persist for long. Because of the turnover of constituents, most individual molecules within a cell (excepting, of course, cell walls and DNA) are probably also replaced. Then, the question of whether or not it is the same individual from beginning to end becomes philosophical. Perhaps we should draw the line between clonal and nonclonal organisms. The former at least maintains a semblance of the same organism, and therefore one can speak of longevity in better defined terms.

Dormant or quiescent seeds are clearly able to survive under nongrowing conditions for 400 or perhaps more years (Priestley and Posthumus, 1982; Priestley, 1986), but this is more a state of suspended animation than life proceding at a normal pace. Relatively little effort has been directed at the problem of longevity of individual, active cells; however, there are reports that indicate parenchyma cells in certain cacti (MacDougal and Long, 1927) and phloem cells in an Australian grass tree (Lamont, 1980) may persist more than 100 years. In the case of the grass tree, the pith parenchyma cells may survive more than 400 years. These cells must be able to repair whatever lesions are inflicted on them and to maintain themselves over very long periods.

Although both long-lived cells and organisms may be subject to senescence, aging processes may become more important with time, and the role of aging processes may eventually become very significant. Thus, active and passive deteriorative processes may work together in some cases. The question of how long a cell can live without the renewal provided in sexual reproduction or even mitosis is a very important biological problem, as is the question of how these processes provide renewal. The answers to these questions will contribute to our understanding of what limits the life of a cell, but longevity of an organism is also determined by factors related to its multicellularity, the functional organization of its tissues, and the renewal of their cells. Even the survival capacity of dormant or quiescent cells is of theoretical and practical importance (e.g., the survival of seeds in storage or in the soil or the survival of inactive organisms on long space flights).

V. CONCLUSIONS AND CLOSING

Senescence is clearly a fundamental developmental process with many different functions in plant ontogeny. It occurs in a variety of places within a plant and serves many functions. Despite its many manifestations, senescence in different tissues seems similar at the biochemical level, but it could also be different processes achieving the same end result, death.

Like all major developmental steps, senescence appears to be complex. Certainly, it consists of many biochemical steps, and these may influence other biochemical processes secondarily. While the exact chemical nature of senescence is unknown, it does seem to be regulated by DNA transcription processes. Hormonal controls are also important, but even these remain to be defined more exactly.

Aging is not really a developmental process. It is driven by a variety of influences that are primarily exogenous, bringing about a gradual decline in physiological processes, particularly genetic and membrane functions.

Both senescence and aging lead to a loss of homeostasis which marks the death of the cell, group of cells, or organism. It seems likely that great advances will be made in elucidating the biochemical steps leading up to this demise in both the aging and the senescence process over the next decade.

REFERENCES

Arguelles, T., and Guardiola, J. L. (1977). Hormonal control of senescence in excised orange leaves. *J. Hortic. Sci.* **52,** 199–204.

Bernard, R. L., and Weiss, M. G. (1973). Qualitative genetics. In "Soybeans: Improvements, Production and Uses" (B. E. Caldwell, ed.), pp. 117–154. Am. Soc. Agron., Madison, Wisconsin.

Bewley, J. D., and Black, M. (1985). "Seeds. Physiology of Development and Germination." Plenum, New York.

Bose, B., and Srivastava, H. S. (1979). Role of nitrate in delaying senescence of detached leaves. *Indian J. Exp. Biol.* **17,** 932–934.

Butler, R. D. (1967). The fine structure of senescing cotyledons of cucumber. *J. Exp. Bot.* **18,** 535–543.

Chen, Y. M. (1972). Certain aspects of light and plant hormones in control of senescence. *Taiwania* **17,** 81–91.

Choe, H. T., and Thimann, K. V. (1975). The metabolism of oat leaves during senescence. III. The senescence of isolated chloroplasts. *Plant Physiol.* **55,** 828–834.

Crafts-Brandner, S. J., and Poneleit, C. G. (1987). Effect of ear removal on CO_2 exchange and activities of ribulose bisphosphate carboxylase/oxygenase and phosphoenolpyruvate carboxylase of maize hybrids and inbred lines. *Plant Physiol.* **84,** 261–265.

Crafts-Brandner, S. J., Below, F. E., Harper, J. E., and Hageman, R. H. (1984). Differential senescence of maize hybrids following ear removal. I. Whole plant. *Plant Physiol.* **74,** 360–367.

Crocker, W. (1939). Ageing in plants. In "Problems of Ageing" (E. V. Cowdry, ed.). 1st Ed., pp. 1–31. Williams & Wilkins, Baltimore, Maryland.

Davies, I., and Sigee, D. C. (1984). Cell ageing and cell death: perspectives. In "Cell Ageing and Cell Death" (I. Davies and D. C. Sigee, eds.), pp. 347–350. Cambridge Univ. Press, London and New York.

Dedolph, R. R., Wittwer, S. A., and Tuli, W. (1961). Senescence inhibition and respiration. *Science* **134,** 1075.

De Luca d'Oro, G. M., and Trippi, V. S. (1982). Regulación de clorofilas y proteinas solubles por cinetina y ciclohéximida, en condiciones de luz y oscuridad, durante la senescencia foliar en *Phaseolus vulgaris* L. *Phyton (Buenos Aires)* **42,** 73–82.

Derman, B. D., Rupp, D. C., and Noodén, L. D. (1978). Mineral distribution in relation to fruit development and monocarpic senescence in Anoka soybeans. *Am. J. Bot.* **65,** 205–213.

De Vecchi, L. (1971). Fine structure of detached oat leaves senescing under different experimental conditions. *Isr. J. Bot.* **20,** 169–183.

Dilley, D. R., and Carpenter, W. J. (1975). The role of chemical adjuvants and ethylene synthesis on cut flower longevity. *Acta Hortic.* **41,** 117–132.

Duncan, R. R., Bockholt, A. J., and Miller, F. R. (1981). Descriptive comparison of senescent and nonsenescent sorghum genotypes. *Agron. J.* **73,** 849–853.

Eilam, Y. (1965). Permeability changes in senescing tissue. *J. Exp. Bot.* **16,** 614–627.

Elbert, V. F., and Elbert, G. A. (1975). "Fun with Growing Odd and Curious House Plants." Crown, New York.

Engelbrecht, L., and Nogai, K. (1964). Zur Frage der Kinetinwirkung gegenüber der Stoffwechselhemmung durch Chloramphenikol. *Flora (Jena)* **154,** 267–278.

Feller, U. (1979). Effect of changed source/sink relations on proteolytic activity and on nitrogen mobilization in field-grown wheat (*Triticum aestivum* L.). *Plant Cell Physiol.* **20,** 1577–1583.

Fridovich, I. (1978). The biology of oxygen radicals. *Science* **201**, 875–880.

Gaff, D., and Okong'o-Ogola, O. (1971). The use of non-permeating pigments for testing the survival of cells. *J. Exp. Bot.* **22**, 756–758.

Goldschmidt, E. E. (1980). Pigment changes associated with fruit maturation and their control. *In* "Senescence in Plants" (K. V. Thimann, ed.), pp. 207–217. CRC Press, Boca Raton, Florida.

Goldthwaite, J. J. (1974). Energy metabolism of *Rumex* leaf tissue in the presence of senescence-regulating hormones and sucrose. *Plant Physiol.* **54**, 399–403.

Goldthwaite, J. J., and Laetsch, W. M. (1967). Regulation of senescence in bean leaf discs by light and chemical growth regulators. *Plant Physiol.* **42**, 1757–1762.

Halevy, A. H., and Mayak, S. (1979). Senescence and postharvest physiology of cut flowers, part 1. *Hortic. Rev.* **1**, 204–236.

Halevy, A. H., Mayak, S., Tirosh, T., Spiegelstein, H., and Kofranek, A. M. (1974). Opposing effects of abscisic acid on senescence of rose flowers. *Plant Cell Physiol.* **15**, 813–821.

Halliwell, B., and Gutteridge, J. M. C. (1985). "Free Radicals in Biology and Medicine." Oxford Univ. Press, London and New York.

Hardwick, R. C. (1979). Leaf abscission in varieties of *Phaseolus vulgaris* and *Glycine max*: A correlation with propensity to produce adventitious roots. *J. Exp. Bot.* **30**, 795–804.

Hart, R. W., and Turturro, A. (1985). Review of recent biological research on theories of aging. *Rev. Biol. Res. Aging* **2**, 3–12.

Kahanak, G. M., Okatan, Y., Rupp, D. C., and Noodén, L. D. (1978). Hormonal and genetic alteration of monocarpic senescence in soybeans. *Plant Physiol.* **61**, Suppl., 26.

Kao, C. M. (1978). Senescence of rice leaves. II. Antisenescent action of cytokinins. *Proc. Natl. Sci. Counc. Repub. China* **2**, 391–398.

Knypl, J. S. (1970). Arrest of yellowing in senescing leaf discs of maize by growth retardants, coumarin and inhibitors of RNA and protein synthesis. *Biol. Plant.* **12**, 199–207.

Knypl, J. S., and Mazurczyk, W. (1971). Arrest of chlorophyll and protein breakdown in senescing leaf discs of kale by cycloheximide and vanillin. *Curr. Sci.* **40**, 294–295.

Krueger, A. P., and Reed, E. J. (1976). Biological impact of small air ions. *Science* **193**, 1209–1213.

Krul, W. R. (1974). Nucleic acid and protein metabolism in senescing and regenerating soybean cotyledons. *Plant Physiol.* **54**, 36–40.

Lamont, B. B. (1980). Tissue longevity of the aborescent monocotyledon *Kingia australis* (Xanthorrhoeacene). *Am. J. Bot.* **67**, 1262–1264.

Legocka, J., and Szweykowska, A. (1981). The role of cytokinins in the development and metabolism of barley leaves III. The effect on the RNA metabolism in various cell compartments during senescence. *Z. Pflanzenphysiol.* **102**, 363–374.

Legocka, J., and Szweykowska, A. (1983). The role of cytokinins in the development and metabolism of barley leaves. VI. The effect on the protein metabolism in various cell compartments during leaf senescence. *Acta Physiol. Plant* **5**, 11–20.

Lewington, R. J., and Simon, E. W. (1969). The effect of light on the senescence of detached cucumber cotyledons. *J. Exp. Bot.* **20**, 138–144.

MacDougal, D. T., and Long, F. L. (1927). Characters of cells attaining great age. *Am. Nat.* **61**, 385–406.

McGlasson, W. B., Wade, N. L., and Adato, I. (1978). Phytohormones and fruit ripening. *In* "Phytohormones and Related Compounds: A Comprehensive Treatise" (D. S. Letham, P. B. Goodwin, and T. J. V. Higgins, eds.), Vol. 2, pp. 447–493. Elsevier/North-Holland, Amsterdam.

Makovetzki, S., and Goldschmidt, E. E. (1976). A requirement for cytoplasmic protein synthesis during chloroplast senescence in the aquatic plant *Anacharis canadensis*. *Plant Cell Physiol.* **17**, 859-862.

Martin, C., and Thimann, K. V. (1972). The role of protein synthesis in the senescence of leaves. I: The formation of protease. *Plant Physiol.* **49**, 64-71.

Matile, P., and Winkenbach, F. (1971). Function of lysosomes and lysosomal enzymes in senescing corolla of the morning glory (*Ipomoea purpurea*). *J. Exp. Bot.* **122**, 759-771.

Mayak, S., and Halevy, A. H. (1980). Flower senescence. In "Senescence in Plants" (K. V. Thimann, ed.), pp. 131-156. CRC Press, Boca Raton, Florida.

Molisch, H. (1938). "The Longevity of Plants" (H. Fulling, transl). Science Press, Lancaster, Pennsylvania.

Mothes, K. (1964). The role of kinetin in plant regulation. In "Regulateurs Naturels de la Croissance Végétale" (J. P. Nitsch, ed.), pp. 131-140. CNRS, Paris.

Murray, D. R., ed. (1984). "Seed Physiology." Academic Press, Orlando, Florida.

Nicolas, G. (1918). Contribution a l'étude des variations de la respiration des végétaux avec l'age. *Rev. Gen. Bot.* **30**, 209-225.

Noble, R. D. Czarnota, C. D., and Cappy, J. J. (1977). Morphological and physiological characteristics of an achlorophyllous mutant soybean variety sustained to maturation via grafting. *Am. J. Bot.* **64**, 1042-1045.

Noodén, L. D. (1980). Regulation of senescence. In "World Soybean Research Conference II: Proceedings" (F. T. Corbin, ed.), pp. 139-152. Westview Press, Boulder, Colorado.

Noodén, L. D. (1984). Integration of soybean pod development and monocarpic senescence. *Physiol. Plant.* **62**, 273-284.

Noodén, L. D., and Leopold, A. C. (1978). Phytohormones and the endogenous regulation of senescence and abscission. In "Phytohormones and Related Compounds: A Comprehensive Treatise" (D. S. Letham, P. B. Goodwin, and T. J. V. Higgins, eds.), Vol. 2, pp. 329-369. Elsevier/North-Holland, Amsterdam.

Osborne, D. J. (1980). Senescence in seeds. In "Senescence in Plants" (K. V. Thimann, ed.), pp. 13-37. CRC Press, Boca Raton, Florida.

Paranjothy, K., and Wareing, P. F. (1971). The effects of abscisic acid, kinetin and 5-fluorouracil on ribonucleic acid and protein synthesis in senescing radish leaf disks. *Planta* **99**, 112-119.

Pech, J. C., and Romani, R. J. (1979). Senescence of pear *Pyrus communis* fruit cells cultured in a continuously renewed auxin-deprived medium. *Plant Physiol.* **63**, 814-817.

Penning de Vries, F. W. T. (1975). The cost of maintenance processes in plant cells. *Ann. Bot.* **39**, 77-92.

Person, C., Samborski, D. J., and Forsyth, F. R. (1957). Effect of benzimidazole on detached wheat leaves. *Nature (London)* **180**, 1294-1295.

Peterson, L. W., and Huffaker, R. C. (1975). Loss of ribulose 1, 5 diphosphate carboxylase and increase in proteolytic activity during senescence of detached primary barley leaves. *Plant Physiol.* **55**, 1009-1015.

Pierce, R. O., Knowles, P. F., and Phillips, D. A. (1984). Inheritance of delayed leaf senescence in soybean. *Crop Sci.* **24**, 515-517.

Pjon, C. J. (1981). Effects of cycloheximide and light on leaf senescence in maize and hydrangea. *Plant Cell Physiol.* **22**, 847-854.

Priestley, D. A. (1986). "Seed Aging." Comstock, Ithaca, New York.

Priestley, D. A., and Posthumus, M. A. (1982). Extreme longevity of lotus seeds from Pulantien. *Nature (London)* **299**, 148-149.

Priestley, D. A., Cullinan, V. I., and Wolfe, J. (1985). Differences in seed longevity at the species level. *Plant Cell Environ.* **8**, 557-562.

Pryor, W. A., ed. (1976). "Free Radicals in Biology," Vol. 1. Academic Press, New York.

Rhodes, M. J. C. (1980). The maturation and ripening of fruits. *In* "Senescence in Plants" (K. V. Thimann, ed.), pp. 157–205. CRC Press, Boca Raton, Florida.

Roberts, E. H. (1972). "Viability of Seeds." Chapman & Hall, London.

Sabater, B., Rodriguez, M. T., and Zamorano, A. (1981). Effects and interactions of gibberellic acid and cytokinins on the retention of chlorophyll and phosphate in barley leaf segments. *Physiol. Plant* **51**, 361–364.

Sacher, J. A. (1957). Relationship between auxin and membrane-integrity in tissue senescence and abscission. *Science* **125**, 1199–1200.

Sanders, C. L. (1983). "Ionizing Radiation." Battelle, Columbus, Ohio.

Sasaki, S., and Kozlowski, T. T. (1969). Utilization of seed reserves and currently produced photosynthesis by embryonic tissues of pine seedlings. *Ann. Bot.* **33**, 473–482.

Satler, S. O., and Thimann, K. V. (1983). Metabolism of oat leaves during senescence VII. The interaction of carbon dioxide and other atmospheric gases with light in controlling chlorophyll loss and senescence. *Plant Physiol.* **71**, 67–70.

Schumacher, W., and Matthael, H. (1955). Über den Zusammenhang zwischen Streckungswachstum und Eiweiss-synthese. *Planta* **45**, 213–216.

Smith, D. L. (1981). Cotyledons of the Leguminosae. *In* "Advances in Legume Systematics," Part 2 (R. M. Polhill and P. H. Ravin, eds.), pp. 927–940. Royal Botanic Gardens, Kew, England.

Stoddart, J. L., and Thomas, H. (1982). Leaf senescence. *Encycl. Plant Physiol., New Ser.* **14A**, 592–636.

Suttle, J. C., and Kende, H. (1980). Ethylene action and loss of membrane integrity during petal senescence in *Tradescantia*. *Plant Physiol.* **65**, 1067–1072.

Takegami, T. (1975a). A study on senescence in tobacco leaf disks I. Inhibition by benzylaminopurine of decrease in protein level. *Plant Cell Physiol.* **16**, 407–416.

Takegami, T. (1975b). A study on senescence in tobacco leaf disks II. Chloroplast and cytoplasmic rRNAs. *Plant Cell Physiol.* **16**, 417–425.

Taylor, A. E., Matalon, S., and Ward, P., eds. (1986). "Physiology of Oxygen Radicals." Am. Physiol. Soc., Bethesda, Maryland.

Tetley, R. M., and Thimann, K. V. (1974). The metabolism of oat leaves during senescence I. Respiration, carbohydrate metabolism, and the action of cytokinins. *Plant Physiol.* **54**, 294–303.

Thimann, K. V. (1980). The senescence of leaves. *In* "Senescence in Plants" (K. V. Thimann, ed.), pp. 85–115. CRC Press, Boca Raton, Florida.

Thimann, K. V. (1987). Plant senescence: A proposed integration of the constituent processes. *In* "Plant Senescence: Its Biochemistry and Physiology" (W. W. Thomson, E. A. Nothnagel, and R. C. Huffaker, eds.), pp. 1–19. Am. Soc. Plant Physiol., Rockville, Maryland.

Thimann, K. V., and Satler, S. O. (1979). Relation between leaf senescence and stomatal closure: Senescence in light. *Proc. Natl. Acad. Sci. U.S.A.* **76**, 2295–2298.

Thimann, K. V., Satler, S. O., and Trippi, V. (1982). Further extension of the syndrome of leaf senescence. *In* "Plant Growth Substances 1982" (P. F. Wareing, ed.), pp. 539–548. Academic Press, London.

Thomas, H. (1975). Regulation of alanine aminotransferase in leaves of *Lolium temulentum* during senescence. *Z. Pflanzenphysiol.* **74**, 208–218.

Thomas, H. (1987). Sid: A Mendelian locus controlling thylakoid disassembly in senescing leaves of *Festuca pratensis*. *Theor. Appl. Genet.* **73**, 551–555.

Thomas, H., and Stoddart, J. L. (1975). Separation of chlorophyll degradation from other senescence processes in leaves of a mutant genotype of meadow fescue (*Festuca pratensis* L.). *Plant Physiol.* **56**, 438–441.

Thomas, H., and Stoddart, J. L. (1980). Leaf senescence. *Annu. Rev. Plant Physiol.* **31,** 83–111.

Tilney-Bassett, R.A. E. (1986). "Plant Chimeras." Arnold, London.

Tripathi, R. K., Vohra, K., and Schlosser, E. (1980). Effect of fungicides on plant physiology III. Mechanism of cytokinin-like antisenescent action of carbendazim on wheat leaves. *Z. Pflanzenkr. Pflanzenschutz* **87,** 631–639.

Turgeon, R. (1984). Termination of nutrient import and development of vein loading capacity in albino tobacco leaves. *Plant Physiol.* **76,** 45–48.

Villiers, T. A. (1973). Aging and the longevity of seeds. *In* "Seed Ecology" (W. Heydecker, ed.), pp. 265–288. Pennsylvania State Univ. Press, University Park.

Von Abrams, G. J. (1974). An effect of ornithine on degradation of chlorophyll and protein in excised leaf tissue. *Z. Pflanzenphysiol.* **72,** 410–421.

Wollgiehn, R. (1967). Nucleic acid and protein metabolism of excised leaves. *Symp. Soc. Exp. Biol.* **21,** 231–246.

Wollgiehn, R., and Parthier, B. (1964). Der Einfluss des Kinetins auf den RNS-und Protein-Stoffwechsel in abgeschnittenen mit Hemmstoffen behandelten Tabakblättern. *Phytochemistry* **3,** 241–248.

Wood, J. G., and Cruickshank. D. H. (1944). The metabolism of starving leaves. 5. Changes in amounts of some amino acids during starvation of grass leaves; and their bearing on the nature of the relationship between proteins and amino acids. *Aust. J. Exp. Biol. Med. Sci.* **22,** 111–123.

Wood, L. J., Murray, B. J., Okatan, Y., and Noodén, L. D. (1986). Effect of petiole phloem disruption on starch and mineral distribution in senescing soybean leaves. *Am. J. Bot.* **73,** 1377–1383.

Woolhouse, H. (1982). Biochemical and molecular aspects of plant senescence. *In* "Molecular Biology of Plant Development" (H. Smith and D. Grierson, eds.), pp. 256–287. Blackwell, Oxford.

Woolhouse, H. (1983). Leaf senescence. *In* "Post Harvest Physiology and Crop Preservation" (M. Lieberman, ed.), pp. 256–281. Plenum, New York.

Yoshida, Y. (1961). Nuclear control of chloroplast activity in *Elodea* leaf cells. *Protoplasma* **54,** 476–492.

Yoshida, Y. (1974). The role of the cell nucleus in relation to the senescence of chloroplasts in detached *Elodea* leaves. *Symp. Cell Biol.* **25,** 131–140.

Yu, S. M., and Kao, C. H. (1981). Retardation of leaf senescence by inhibitors of RNA and protein synthesis. *Physiol. Plant.* **52,** 207–210.

NOTE ADDED IN PROOF. These data come primarily from disruptive procedures, especially selective inhibitors. While these procedures are subject to some caveats, they, particularly the inhibitors, have been very useful in analyzing photosynthesis and other biological processes. No doubt, they will also help in studying senescence, but they must eventually be supported by other lines of evidence.

Index